## CONCISE EDITION

# ENGLISH THESAURUS

# CONCISE EDITION

# ENGLISH THESAURUS

## GEDDES &
## GROSSET

This edition published 2009 by Geddes & Grosset,
David Dale House, New Lanark ML11 9DJ, Scotland

© 2001 Geddes & Grosset

First published 2001, reprinted 2001, 2002,
2003, 2004 (four times), 2005, 2006, 2007, 2008

This book is not published by the original publishers of
Webster's Dictionary or by their successors.

ISBN 978 1 84205 611 0

Printed and bound in India

# A

**aback** *adv* back, backward, rearward, regressively.

**abaft** *prep* (*naut*) aft, astern, back of, behind.

**abandon** *vb* abdicate, abjure, desert, drop, evacuate, forsake, forswear, leave, quit, relinquish, yield; cede, forgo, give up, let go, renounce, resign, surrender, vacate, waive. * *n* careless freedom, dash, impetuosity, impulse, wildness.

**abandoned** *adj* depraved, derelict, deserted, discarded, dropped, forsaken, left, outcast, rejected, relinquished; corrupt, demoralized, depraved, dissolute, graceless, impenitent, irreclaimable, lost, obdurate, profligate, reprobate, shameless, sinful, unprincipled, vicious, wicked.

**abandonment** *n* desertion, dereliction, giving up, leaving, relinquishment, renunciation, surrender.

**abase** *vb* depress, drop, lower, reduce, sink; debase, degrade, disgrace, humble, humiliate.

**abasement** *n* abjection, debasement, degradation, disgrace, humbleness, humiliation, shame.

**abash** *vb* affront, bewilder, confound, confuse, dash, discompose, disconcert, embarrass, humiliate, humble, shame, snub.

**abashment** *n* confusion, embarrassment, humiliation, mortification, shame.

**abate** *vb* diminish, decrease, lessen, lower, moderate, reduce, relax, remove, slacken; allow, bate, deduct, mitigate, rebate, remit; allay, alleviate, appease, assuage, blunt, calm, compose, dull, mitigate, moderate, mollify, pacify, qualify, quiet, quell, soften, soothe, tranquillize.

**abatement** *n* alleviation, assuagement, decrement, decrease, extenuation, mitigation, moderation, remission; cessation, decline, diminution, ebb, fading, lowering, sinking, settlement; allowance, deduction, rebate, reduction.

**abbey** *n* convent, monastery, priory.

**abbreviate** *vb* abridge, compress, condense, contract, cut, curtail, epitomize, reduce, retrench, shorten.

**abbreviation** *n* abridgment, compression, condensation, contraction, curtailment, cutting, reduction, shortening.

**abdicate** *vb* abandon, cede, forgo, forsake, give up, quit, relinquish, renounce, resign, retire, surrender.

**abdication** *n* abandonment, abdicating, relinquishment, renunciation, resignation, surrender.

**abdomen** *n* belly, gut, paunch, stomach.

**abduct** *vb* carry off, kidnap, spirit away, take away.

**abduction** *n* carrying off, kidnapping, removal, seizure, withdrawal.

**aberrant** *adj* deviating, devious, divergent, diverging, erratic, rambling, wandering; abnormal, anomalistic, anomalous, disconnected, eccentric, erratic, exceptional, inconsequent, peculiar, irregular, preternatural, singular, strange, unnatural, unusual.

**aberration** *n* departure, deviation, divergence, rambling, wandering; abnormality, anomaly, eccentricity, irregularity, peculiarity, singularity, unconformity; delusion, disorder, hallucination, illusion, instability.

**abet** *vb* aid, assist, back, help, support, sustain, uphold; advocate, condone, countenance, encourage, favour, incite, sanction.

**abettor** *n* ally, assistant; adviser, advocate, promoter; accessory, accomplice, associate, confederate.

**abeyance** *n* anticipation, calculation, expectancy, waiting; dormancy, inactivity, intermission, quiescence, remission, reservation, suppression, suspension.

**abhor** *vb* abominate, detest, dislike intensely, execrate, hate, loathe, nauseate, view with horror.

**abhorrence** *n* abomination, antipathy, aversion, detestation, disgust, hatred, horror, loathing.

**abhorrent** *adj* abominating, detesting, hating, loathing; hateful, horrifying, horrible, loathsome, nauseating, odious, offensive, repellent, repugnant, repulsive, revolting, shocking.

**abide** *vb* lodge, rest, sojourn, stay, wait; dwell, inhabit, live, reside; bear, continue, persevere, persist, remain; endure, last, suffer, tolerate; (*with* **by**) act up to, conform to, discharge, fulfil, keep, persist in.

**abiding** *adj* changeless, constant, continuing, durable, enduring, immutable, lasting, permanent, stable, unchangeable.

**ability** *n* ableness, adroitness, aptitude, aptness, cleverness, dexterity, efficacy, efficiency, facility, might, ingenuity, knack, power, readiness, skill, strength, talent, vigour; competency, qualification; calibre, capability, capacity, expertness, faculty, gift; parts.

**abject** *adj* base, beggarly, contemptible, cringing, degraded, despicable, dirty, grovelling, ignoble, low, mean, menial, miserable, paltry, pitiful, poor, servile, sneaking, slavish, vile, worthless, wretched.

**abjectness** *n* abasement, abjection, baseness, contemptibleness, meanness, pitifulness, servility, vileness.

**abjuration** *n* abandonment, abnegation, discarding, disowning, rejection, relinquishment, renunciation, repudiation; disavowal, disclaimer, disclaiming, recall, recantation, repeal, retraction, reversal, revocation.

**abjure** *vb* abandon, discard, disclaim, disown, forgo, forswear, give up, reject, relinquish, renounce, repudiate; disavow, disclaim, recall, recant, renounce, repeal, retract, revoke, withdraw.

**able** *adj* accomplished, adroit, apt, clever, expert, ingenious, practical, proficient, qualified, quick, skilful, talented, versed; competent, effective, efficient, fitted, quick; capable, gifted, mighty, powerful, talented; athletic, brawny, muscular, robust, stalwart, strong, vigorous.

**ablution** *n* baptism, bathing, cleansing, lavation, purification, washing.

**abnegation** *n* abandonment, denial, renunciation, surrender.

**abnormal** *adj* aberrant, anomalous, divergent, eccentric, exceptional, peculiar, odd, singular, strange, uncomfortable, unnatural, unusual, weird.

**abnormality** *n* abnormity, anomaly, deformity, idiosyncrasy, irregularity, monstrosity, peculiarity, oddity, singularity, unconformity.

**aboard** *adv* inside, within, on.

**abode** *n* domicile, dwelling, habitation, home, house, lodging, quarters, residence, residency, seat.

**abolish** *vb* abrogate, annul, cancel, eliminate, invalidate, nullify, quash, repeal, rescind, revoke; annihilate, destroy, end, eradicate, extirpate, extinguish, obliterate, overthrow, suppress, terminate.

**abolition** *n* abrogation, annulling, annulment, cancellation, cancelling, nullification, repeal, rescinding, rescission, revocation; annihilation, destruction, eradication, extinction, extinguishment, extirpation, obliteration, overthrow, subversion, suppression.

**abominable** *adj* accursed, contemptible, cursed, damnable, detestable, execrable, hellish, horrid, nefarious, odious; abhorrent, detestable, disgusting, foul, hateful, loathsome, nauseous, obnoxious, shocking, revolting, repugnant, repulsive; shabby, vile, wretched.

**abominate** *vb* abhor, detest, execrate, hate, loathe, recoil from, revolt at, shrink from, shudder at.

**abomination** *n* abhorrence, antipathy, aversion, detestation, disgust, execration, hatred, loathing, nauseation; contamination, corruption, corruptness, defilement, foulness, impurity, loathsomeness, odiousness, pollution, taint, uncleanness; annoyance, curse, evil, infliction, nuisance, plague, torment.

**aboriginal** *adj* autochthonal, autochthonous, first, indigenous, native, original, primary, prime, primeval, primitive, pristine.

**abortion** *n* miscarriage, premature labour; disappointment, failure.

**abortive** *adj* immature, incomplete, rudimental, rudimentary, stunted, untimely; futile, fruitless, idle, ineffectual, inoperative, nugatory, profitless, unavailing, unsuccessful, useless, vain.

**abound** *vb* flow, flourish, increase, swarm, swell; exuberate, luxuriate, overflow, proliferate, swarm, teem.

**about** *prep* around, encircling, surrounding, round; near; concerning, referring to, regarding, relating to, relative to, respecting, touching, with regard to, with respect to; all over, over, through. * *adv* around, before; approximately, near, nearly.

**above** *adj* above-mentioned, aforementioned, aforesaid, foregoing, preceding, previous, prior. * *adv* aloft, overhead; before, previously; of a higher rank. * *prep* higher than, on top of; exceeding, greater than, more than, over; beyond, superior to.

**above-board** *adj* candid, frank, honest, open, straightforward, truthful, upright. * *adv* candidly, fairly, openly, sincerely.

**abrade** *vb* erase, erode, rub off, scrape out, wear away.

**abrasion** *n* attrition, disintegration, friction, wearing down; scrape, scratch.

**abreast** *adv* aligned, alongside.

**abridge** *vb* abbreviate, condense, compress, shorten, summarize; contract, diminish, lessen, reduce.

**abridgment** *n* compression, condensation, contraction, curtailment, diminution, epitomizing, reduction, shortening; abstract, brief, compendium, digest, epitome, outline, précis, summary, syllabus, synopsis; deprivation, limitation, restriction.

**abroad** *adv* expansively, unrestrainedly, ubiquitously, widely; forth, out of doors; overseas; extensively, publicly.

**abrogate** *vb* abolish, annul, cancel, invalidate, nullify, overrule, quash, repeal, rescind, revoke, set aside, vacate, void.

**abrogation** *n* abolition, annulling, annulment, cancellation, cancelling, repeal rescinding, rescission, revocation, voidance, voiding.

**abrupt** *adj* broken, craggy, jagged, rough, rugged; acclivous, acclivitous, precipitous, steep; hasty, ill-timed, precipitate, sudden, unanticipated, unexpected; blunt, brusque, curt, discourteous; cramped, harsh, jerky, stiff.

**abscess** *n* boil, fester, pustule, sore, ulcer.

**abscond** *vb* bolt, decamp, elope, escape, flee, fly, retreat, run off, sneak away, steal away, withdraw.

**absence** *n* nonappearance, nonattendance; abstraction, distraction, inattention, musing, preoccupation, reverie; default, defect, deficiency, lack, privation.

**absent** *adj* abroad, away, elsewhere, gone, not present, otherwhere; abstracted, dreaming, inattentive, lost, musing, napping, preoccupied.

**absolute** *adj* complete, ideal, independent, perfect, supreme, unconditional, unconditioned, unlimited, unqualified, unrestricted; arbitrary, authoritative, autocratic, despotic, dictatorial, imperious, irresponsible, tyrannical, tyrannous; actual, categorical, certain, decided, determinate, genuine, positive, real, unequivocal, unquestionable, veritable.

**absolutely** *adv* completely, definitely, unconditionally; actually, downright, indeed, indubitably, infallibly, positively, really, truly, unquestionably.

**absoluteness** *n* actuality, completeness, ideality, perfection, positiveness, reality, supremeness; absolutism, arbitrariness, despotism, tyranny.

**absolution** *n* acquittal, clearance, deliverance, discharge, forgiveness, liberation, pardon, release, remission, shrift, shriving.

**absolutism** *n* absoluteness, arbitrariness, autocracy, despotism, tyranny.

**absolve** *vb* acquit, clear, deliver, discharge, exculpate, excuse, exonerate, forgive, free, liberate, loose, pardon, release, set free, shrive.

**absorb** *vb* appropriate, assimilate, drink in, imbibe, soak up; consume, destroy, devour, engorge, engulf, exhaust, swallow up, take up; arrest, engage, engross, fix, immerse, occupy, rivet.

**absorbent** *adj* absorbing, imbibing, penetrable, porous, receptive.

**absorption** *adj* appropriation, assimilation; imbibing, osmosis, soaking up; consumption, destroying, devouring, engorgement, engulfing, exhaustion, swallowing up; concentration, engagement, engrossment, immersion, occupation, preoccupation.

**abstain** *vb* avoid, cease, deny oneself, desist, forbear, refrain, refuse, stop, withhold.

**abstemious** *adj* abstinent, frugal, moderate, self-denying, sober, temperate.

**abstinence** *n* abstemiousness, avoidance, forbearance, moderation, self-restraint, soberness, sobriety, teetotalism, temperance.

**abstinent** *adj* abstaining, fasting; abstemious, restraining, self-denying, self-restraining, sober, temperate.

**abstract** *vb* detach, disengage, disjoin, dissociate, disunite, isolate, separate; appropriate, purloin, seize, steal, take; abbreviate, abridge, epitomize. * *adj* isolated, separate, simple, unrelated; abstracted, occult, recondite, refined, subtle, vague; nonobjective, nonrepresentational. * *n* abridgment, condensation, digest, excerpt, extract, précis, selection, summary, synopsis.

**abstracted** *adj* absent, absent-minded, dreaming, inattentive, lost, musing, preoccupied; abstruse, refined, subtle.

**abstraction** *n* absence, absent-mindedness, brown study, inattention, muse, musing, preoccupation, reverie; disconnection, disjunction, isolation, separation; abduction, appropriation; pilfering, purloining, seizure, stealing, taking.

**abstruse** *adj* abstract, attenuated, dark, difficult, enigmatic, hidden, indefinite, mysterious, mystic, mystical, obscure, occult, profound, recondite, remote, subtle, transcendental, vague.

**absurd** *adj* egregious, fantastic, foolish, incongruous, ill-advised, ill-judged, irrational, ludicrous, nonsensical, nugatory, preposterous, ridiculous, self-annulling, senseless, silly, stupid, unreasonable.

**absurdity** *n* drivel, extravagance, fatuity, folly, foolery, foolishness, idiocy, nonsense.

**abundance** *n* affluence, amplitude, ampleness, copiousness, exuberance, fertility, flow, flood, largeness, luxuriance, opulence, overflow, plenitude, profusion, richness, store, wealth.

**abundant** *adj* abounding, ample, bountiful, copious,

exuberant, flowing, full, good, large, lavish, rich, liberal, much, overflowing, plentiful, plenteous, replete, teeming, thick.

**abuse** *vb* betray, cajole, deceive, desecrate, dishonour, misapply, misemploy, misuse, pervert, pollute, profane, prostitute, violate, wrong; harm, hurt, illuse, ill-treat, injure, maltreat, mishandle; asperse, berate, blacken, calumniate, defame, disparage, lampoon, lash, malign, revile, reproach, satirize, slander, traduce, upbraid, vilify. * *n* desecration, dishonour, ill-use, misuse, perversion, pollution, profanation; ill-treatment, maltreatment, outrage; malfeasance, malversation; aspersion, defamation, disparagement, insult, invective, obloquy, opprobrium, railing, rating, reviling, ribaldry, rudeness, scurrility, upbraiding, vilification, vituperation.

**abusive** *adj* calumnious, carping, condemnatory, contumelious, damnatory, denunciatory, injurious, insolent, insulting, offensive, opprobrious, reproachful, reviling, ribald, rude, scurrilous, vilificatory, vituperative.

**abut** *vb* adjoin, border, impinge, meet, project.

**abutment** *n* bank, bulwark, buttress, embankment, fortification; abutting, abuttal, adjacency, contiguity, juxtaposition.

**abuttal** *n* adjacency, boundary, contiguity, juxtaposition, nearness, next, terminus.

**abyss** *n* abysm, chasm, gorge, gulf, pit.

**academic** *adj* collegiate, lettered, scholastic. * *n* academician, classicist, doctor, fellow, pundit, savant, scholar, student, teacher.

**academy** *n* college, high school, institute, school.

**accede** *vb* accept, acquiesce, agree, assent to, comply with, concur, consent, yield.

**accelerate** *vb* dispatch, expedite, forward, hasten, hurry, precipitate, press on, quicken, speed, urge on.

**acceleration** *n* expedition, hastening, hurrying, quickening, pickup, precipitation, speeding up, stepping up.

**accent** *vb* accentuate, emphasize, stress. * *n* cadence, inflection, intonation, tone; beat, emphasis, ictus.

**accentuate** *vb* accent, emphasize, mark, point up, punctuate, stress; highlight, overemphasize, overstress, underline, underscore.

**accept** *vb* acquire, derive, get, gain, obtain, receive, take; accede to, acknowledge, acquiesce in, admit, agree to, approve, assent to, avow, embrace; estimate, construe, interpret, regard, value.

**acceptable** *adj* agreeable, gratifying, pleasant, pleasing, pleasurable, welcome.

**acceptance** *n* accepting, acknowledgment, receipt, reception, taking; approbation, approval, gratification, satisfaction.

**acceptation** *n* construction, import, interpretation, meaning, sense, significance, signification, understanding; adoption, approval, currency, vogue.

**access** *vb* broach, enter, open, open up. * *n* approach, avenue, entrance, entry, passage, way; admission, admittance, audience, interview; addition, accession, aggrandizement, enlargement, gain, increase, increment; (*med*) attack, fit, onset, recurrence.

**accession** *n* addition, augmentation, enlargement, extension, increase; succession.

**accessory** *adj* abetting, additional, additive, adjunct, aiding, ancillary, assisting, contributory, helping, subsidiary, subordinate, supplemental. * *n* abettor, accomplice, assistant, associate, confederate, helper; accompaniment, attendant, concomitant, detail, subsidiary.

**accident** *n* calamity, casualty, condition, contingency, disaster, fortuity, incident, misadventure, miscarriage, mischance, misfortune, mishap; affection, alteration, chance, contingency, mode, modification, property, quality, state.

**accidental** *adj* casual, chance, contingent, fortuitous, undesigned, unintended; adventitious, dispensable, immaterial, incidental, nonessential.

**acclamation** *n* acclaim, applause, cheer, cry, plaudit, outcry, salutation, shouting.

**acclimatization, acclimation** *n* adaptation, adjustment, conditioning, familiarization, habituation, inurement, naturalization.

**acclimatize, acclimate** *vb* accustom, adapt, adjust, condition, familiarize, habituate, inure, naturalize, season.

**acclivity** *n* ascent, height, hill, rising ground, steep, upward slope.

**accommodate** *vb* contain, furnish, hold, oblige, serve, supply; adapt, fit, suit; adjust, compose, harmonize, reconcile, settle.

**accommodation** *n* advantage, convenience, privilege; adaptation, agreement, conformity, fitness, suitableness; adjustment, harmonization, harmony, pacification, reconciliation, settlement.

**accompaniment** *n* adjunct, appendage, attachment, attendant, concomitant.

**accompany** vb attend, chaperon, convoy, escort, follow, go with.

**accomplice** n abettor, accessory, ally, assistant, associate, confederate, partner.

**accomplish** vb achieve, bring about, carry, carry through, complete, compass, consummate, do, effect, execute, perform, perfect; conclude, end, finish, terminate.

**accomplished** adj achieved, completed, done, effected, executed, finished, fulfilled, realized; able, adroit, apt, consummate, educated, experienced, expert, finished, instructed, practised, proficient, qualified, ripe, skilful, versed; elegant, fashionable, fine, polished, polite, refined.

**accomplishment** n achievement, acquirement, attainment, qualification; completion, fulfilment.

**accord** vb admit, allow, concede, deign, give, grant, vouchsafe, yield; agree, assent, concur, correspond, harmonize, quadrate, tally. * n accordance, agreement, concord, concurrence, conformity, consensus, harmony, unanimity, unison.

**accordant** adj agreeable, agreeing, congruous, consonant, harmonious, suitable, symphonious.

**accordingly** adv agreeably, conformably, consistently, suitably; consequently, hence, so, thence, therefore, thus, whence, wherefore.

**accost** vb address, confront, greet, hail, salute, speak to, stop.

**account** vb assess, appraise, estimate, evaluate, judge, rate; (with **for**) assign, attribute, explain, expound, justify, rationalize, vindicate. * n inventory, record, register, score; bill, book, charge; calculation, computation, count, reckoning, score, tale, tally; chronicle, detail, description, narration, narrative, portrayal, recital, rehearsal, relation, report, statement, tidings, word; elucidation, explanation, exposition; consideration, ground, motive, reason, regard, sake; consequence, consideration, dignity, distinction, importance, note, repute, reputation, worth.

**accountable** adj amenable, answerable, duty-bound, liable, responsible.

**accoutre** vb arm, dress, equip, fit out, furnish.

**accredit** vb authorize, depute, empower, entrust.

**accrue** vb arise, come, follow, flow, inure, issue, proceed, result.

**accumulate** vb agglomerate, aggregate, amass, bring together, collect, gather, grow, hoard, increase, pile, store.

**accumulation** n agglomeration, aggregation, collection, heap, hoard, mass, pile, store.

**accuracy** n carefulness, correctness, exactness, fidelity, precision, strictness.

**accurate** adj close, correct, exact, faithful, nice, precise, regular, strict, true, truthful.

**accusation** n arraignment, charge, incrimination, impeachment, indictment.

**accuse** vb arraign, charge, censure, impeach, indict, tax.

**accustom** vb discipline, drill, familiarize, habituate, harden, inure, train, use.

**ace** n (cards, dice) one spot, single pip, single point; atom, bit, grain, iota, jot, particle, single, unit, whit; expert, master, virtuoso. * adj best, expert, fine, outstanding, superb.

**acerbity** n acidity, acridity, acridness, astringency, bitterness, roughness, sourness, tartness; acrimony, bitterness, harshness, severity, venom.

**achieve** vb accomplish, attain, complete, do, effect, execute, finish, fulfil, perform, realize; acquire, gain, get, obtain, win.

**achievement** n accomplishment, acquirement, attainment, completion, consummation, performance, realization; deed, exploit, feat, work.

**acid** adj pungent, sharp, sour, stinging, tart, vinegary.

**acknowledge** vb recognize; accept, admit, accept, allow, concede, grant; avow, confess, own, profess.

**acme** n apex, climax, height, peak, pinnacle, summit, top, vertex, zenith.

**acquaint** vb familiarize; announce, apprise, communicate, enlighten, disclose, inform, make aware, make known, notify, tell.

**acquaintance** n companionship, familiarity, fellowship, intimacy, knowledge; associate, companion, comrade, friend.

**acquiesce** vb bow, comply, consent, give way, rest, submit, yield; agree, assent, concur, consent.

**acquire** vb achieve, attain, earn, gain, get, have, obtain, procure, realize, secure, win; learn thoroughly, master.

**acquirement** n acquiring, gaining, gathering, mastery; acquisition, accomplishment, attainment.

**acquit** vb absolve, clear, discharge, exculpate, excuse, exonerate, forgive, liberate, pardon, pay, quit, release, set free, settle.

**acquittal** n absolution, acquittance, clearance, deliverance, discharge, exoneration, liberation, release.

**acquittance** n discharge; quittance, receipt.

**acrid** adj biting, bitter, caustic, pungent, sharp.

**acrimonious** adj acrid, bitter, caustic, censorious, crabbed, harsh, malignant, petulant, sarcastic, severe, testy, virulent.

**acrimony** n causticity, causticness, corrosiveness, sharpness; abusiveness, acridity, asperity, bitterness, churlishness, harshness, rancour, severity, spite, venom.

**act** vb do, execute, function, make, operate, work; enact, feign, perform, play. * n achievement, deed, exploit, feat, performance, proceeding, turn; bill, decree, enactment, law, ordinance, statute; actuality, existence, fact, reality.

**acting** adj interim, provisional, substitute, temporary. * n enacting, impersonation, performance, portrayal, theatre; counterfeiting, dissimulation, imitation, pretence.

**action** n achievement; activity, agency, deed, exertion, exploit, feat; battle, combat, conflict, contest, encounter, engagement, operation; lawsuit, prosecution.

**active** adj effective, efficient, influential, living, operative; assiduous, bustling, busy, diligent, industrious, restless; agile, alert, brisk, energetic, lively, nimble, prompt, quick, smart, spirited, sprightly, supple; animated, ebullient, fervent, vigorous.

**actual** adj certain, decided, genuine, objective, real, substantial, tangible, true, veritable; perceptible, present, sensible, tangible; absolute, categorical, positive.

**actuate** vb impel, incite, induce, instigate, move, persuade, prompt.

**acumen** n acuteness, astuteness, discernment, ingenuity, keenness, penetration, sagacity, sharpness, shrewdness.

**acute** adj pointed, sharp; astute, bright, discerning, ingenious, intelligent, keen, quick, penetrating, piercing, sagacious, sage, sharp, shrewd, smart, subtle; distressing, fierce, intense, piercing, pungent, poignant, severe, violent; high, high-toned, sharp, shrill; (med) sudden, temporary, violent.

**adage** n aphorism, dictum, maxim, proverb, saw, saying.

**adapt** vb accommodate, adjust, conform, coordinate, fit, qualify, proportion, suit, temper.

**add** vb adjoin, affix, annex, append, attach, join, tag; sum, sum up, total.

**addict** vb accustom, apply, dedicate, devote, habituate. * n devotee, enthusiast, fan; head, junkie, user.

**addicted** adj attached, devoted, given up to, inclined, prone, wedded.

**addition** n augmentation, accession, enlargement, extension, increase, supplement; adjunct, appendage, appendix, extra.

**address** vb accost, apply to, court, direct. * n appeal, application, entreaty, invocation, memorial, petition, request, solicitation, suit; discourse, oration, lecture, sermon, speech; ability, adroitness, art, dexterity, expertness, skill; courtesy, deportment, demeanour, tact.

**adduce** vb advance, allege, assign, offer, present; cite, mention, name.

**adept** adj accomplished, experienced, practised, proficient, skilled. * n expert, master, virtuoso.

**adequate** adj able, adapted, capable, competent, equal, fit, requisite, satisfactory, sufficient, suitable.

**adhere** vb cling, cleave, cohere, hold, stick; appertain, belong, pertain.

**adherent** adj adhering, clinging, sticking. * n acolyte, dependant, disciple, follower, partisan, supporter, vassal.

**adhesion** n adherence, attachment, clinging, coherence, sticking.

**adhesive** adj clinging, sticking; glutinous, gummy, sticky, tenacious, viscous. * n binder, cement, glue, paste.

**adieu** n farewell, goodbye, parting, valediction.

**adipose** adj fat, fatty, greasy, oily, oleaginous, sebaceous.

**adjacent** adj adjoining, bordering, conterminous, contiguous, near, near to, neighbouring, touching.

**adjoin** vb abut, add, annex, append, border, combine, neighbour, unite, verge.

**adjourn** vb defer, delay, postpone, procrastinate; close, dissolve, end, interrupt, prorogue, suspend.

**adjudge** vb allot, assign, award; decide, decree, determine, settle.

**adjunct** n addition, advantage, appendage, appurtenance, attachment, attribute, auxiliary, dependency, help.

**adjure** vb beg, beseech, entreat, pray, supplicate.

**adjust** vb adapt, arrange, dispose, rectify; regulate,

set right, settle, suit; compose, harmonize, pacify, reconcile, settle; accommodate, adapt, fit, suit.

**administer** vb contribute, deal out, dispense, supply; conduct, control, direct, govern, manage, oversee, superintend; conduce, contribute.

**admirable** adj astonishing, striking, surprising, wonderful; excellent, fine, rare, superb.

**admiration** n affection, approbation, approval, astonishment, delight, esteem, pleasure, regard.

**admirer** n beau, gallant, suitor, sweetheart; fan, follower, supporter.

**admissible** adj allowable, lawful, permissible, possible.

**admission** n access, admittance, entrance, introduction; acceptance, acknowledgement, allowance, assent, avowal, concession.

**admit** vb give access to, let in, receive; agree to, accept, acknowledge, concede, confess; allow, bear, permit, suffer, tolerate.

**admonish** vb censure, rebuke, reprove; advise caution, counsel, enjoin, forewarn, warn; acquaint, apprise, inform, instruct, notify, remind.

**admonition** n censure, rebuke, remonstrance; advice, caution, chiding, counsel, instruction, monition.

**adolescence** n minority, nonage, teens, youth.

**adolescent** adj juvenile, young, youthful. * n minor, teenager, youth.

**adopt** vb appropriate, assume; accept, approve, avow, espouse, maintain, support; affiliate, father, foster.

**adore** vb worship; esteem, honour, idolize, love, revere, venerate.

**adorn** vb beautify, decorate, embellish, enrich, garnish, gild, grace, ornament.

**adroit** adj apt, dextrous, expert, handy, ingenious, ready, skilful.

**adulation** n blandishment, cajolery, fawning, flattery, flummery, praise, sycophancy.

**adult** adj grown-up, mature, ripe, ripened. * n grown-up person.

**adulterate** vb alloy, contaminate, corrupt, debase, deteriorate, vitiate.

**advance** adj beforehand, forward, leading. * vb propel, push, send forward; aggrandize, dignify, elevate, exalt, promote; benefit, forward, further, improve, promote; adduce, allege, assign, offer, propose, propound; augment, increase; proceed, progress; grow, improve, prosper, thrive. * n march, progress; advancement, enhancement, growth, promotion, rise; offer, overture, proffering, proposal, proposition, tender; appreciation, rise.

**advancement** n advance, benefit, gain, growth, improvement, profit.

**advantage** n ascendancy, precedence, pre-eminence, superiority, upper-hand; benefit, blessing, emolument, gain, profit, return; account, behalf, interest; accommodation, convenience, prerogative, privilege.

**advantageous** adj beneficial, favourable, profitable.

**advent** n accession, approach, arrival, coming, visitation.

**adventitious** adj accidental, extraneous, extrinsic, foreign, fortuitous, nonessential.

**adventure** vb dare, hazard, imperil, peril, risk, venture. * n chance, contingency, experiment, fortuity, hazard, risk, venture; crisis, contingency, event, incident, occurrence, transaction.

**adventurous** adj bold, chivalrous, courageous, daring, doughty; foolhardy, headlong, precipitate, rash, reckless; dangerous, hazardous, perilous.

**adversary** n antagonist, enemy, foe, opponent.

**adverse** adj conflicting, contrary, opposing; antagonistic, harmful, hostile, hurtful, inimical, unfavourable, unpropitious; calamitous, disastrous, unfortunate, unlucky, untoward.

**adversity** n affliction, calamity, disaster, distress, misery, misfortune, sorrow, suffering, woe.

**advertise** vb advise, announce, declare, inform, placard, proclaim, publish.

**advertisement** n announcement, information, notice, proclamation.

**advice** n admonition, caution, counsel, exhortation, persuasion, suggestion, recommendation; information, intelligence, notice, notification; care, counsel, deliberation, forethought.

**advisable** adj advantageous, desirable, expedient, prudent.

**advise** vb admonish, counsel, commend, recommend, suggest, urge; acquaint, apprise, inform, notify; confer, consult, deliberate.

**adviser** n counsellor, director, guide, instructor.

**advocate** vb countenance, defend, favour, justify, maintain, support, uphold, vindicate. * n apologist, counsellor, defender, main-tainer, patron, pleader, supporter; attorney, barrister, counsel, lawyer, solicitor.

**aegis** n defence, protection, safeguard, shelter.

**aesthetic** adj appropriate, beautiful, tasteful.

**affable** adj accessible, approachable, communicative, conversable, cordial, easy, familiar, frank, free, sociable, social; complaisant, courteous, civil, obliging, polite, urbane.

**affair** n business, circumstance, concern, matter, office, question; event, incident, occurrence, performance, proceeding, transaction; battle, combat, conflict, encounter, engagement, skirmish.

**affairs** npl administration, relations; business, estate, finances, property.

**affect** vb act upon, alter, change, influence, modify, transform; concern, interest, regard, relate; improve, melt, move, overcome, subdue, touch; aim at, aspire to, crave, yearn for; adopt, assume, feign.

**affectation** n affectedness, airs, artificiality, foppery, pretension, simulation.

**affected** adj artificial, assumed, feigned, insincere, theatrical; assuming, conceited, foppish, vain.

**affection** n bent, bias, feeling, inclination, passion, proclivity, propensity; accident, attribute, character, mark, modification, mode, note, property; attachment, endearment, fondness, goodwill, kindness, partiality, love.

**affectionate** adj attached, devoted, fond, kind, loving, sympathetic, tender.

**affiliate** vb ally, annex, associate, connect, incorporate, join, unite. * n ally, associate, confederate.

**affinity** n connection, propinquity, relationship; analogy, attraction, correspondence, likeness, relation, resemblance, similarity, sympathy.

**affirm** vb allege, assert, asseverate, aver, declare, state; approve, confirm, establish, ratify.

**affix** vb annex, attach, connect, fasten, join, subjoin, tack.

**afflict** vb agonize, distress, grieve, pain, persecute, plague, torment, trouble, try, wound.

**affliction** n adversity, calamity, disaster, misfortune, stroke, visitation; bitterness, depression, distress, grief, misery, plague, scourge, sorrow, trial, tribulation, wretchedness, woe.

**affluent** adj abounding, abundant, bounteous, plenteous; moneyed, opulent, rich, wealthy.

**afford** vb furnish, produce, supply, yield; bestow, communicate, confer, give, grant, impart, offer; bear, endure, support.

**affray** n brawl, conflict, disturbance, feud, fight, quarrel, scuffle, struggle.

**affright** vb affray, alarm, appal, confound, dismay, shock, startle. * n alarm, consternation, fear, fright, panic, terror.

**affront** vb abuse, insult, outrage; annoy, chafe, displease, fret, irritate, offend, pique, provoke, vex. * n abuse, contumely, insult, outrage, vexation, wrong.

**afraid** adj aghast, alarmed, anxious, apprehensive, frightened, scared, timid.

**after** prep later than, subsequent to; behind, following; about, according to; because of, in imitation of. * adj behind, consecutive, ensuing, following, later, succeeding, successive, subsequent; aft, back, hind, rear, rearmost, tail. * adv afterwards, later, next, since, subsequently, then, thereafter.

**again** adv afresh, anew, another time, once more; besides, further, in addition, moreover.

**against** prep adverse to, contrary to, in opposition to, resisting; abutting, close up to, facing, fronting, off, opposite to, over; in anticipation of, for, in expectation of; in compensation for, to counterbalance, to match.

**age** vb decline, grow old, mature. * n aeon, date, epoch, period, time; decline, old age, senility; antiquity, oldness.

**agency** n action, force, intervention, means, mediation, operation, procurement; charge, direction, management, superintendence, supervision.

**agent** n actor, doer, executor, operator, performer; active element, cause, force; attorney, broker, commissioner, deputy, factor, intermediary, manager, middleman.

**agglomeration** n accumulation, aggregation, conglomeration, heap, lump, pile.

**agglutinate** vb cement, fasten, glue, unite.

**aggrandize** vb advance, dignify, elevate, enrich, exalt, promote.

**aggravate** vb heighten, increase, worsen; colour, exaggerate, magnify, overstate; enrage, irritate, provoke, tease.

**aggravation** n exaggeration, heightening, irritation.

**aggregate** vb accumulate, amass, collect, heap, pile. * adj collected, total. * n amount, gross, total, whole.

**aggressive** adj assailing, assailant, assaulting, attacking, invading, offensive; pushing, self-assertive.

**aggressor** n assailant, assaulter, attacker, invader.

**aggrieve** vb afflict, grieve, pain; abuse, ill-treat, impose, injure, oppress, wrong.

**aghast** *adj* appalled, dismayed, frightened, horrified; horror-struck, panic-stricken, terrified; amazed, astonished, startled, thunderstruck.

**agile** *adj* active, alert, brisk, lively, nimble, prompt, smart, ready.

**agitate** *vb* disturb, jar, rock, shake, trouble; disquiet, excite, ferment, rouse, trouble; confuse, discontent, flurry, fluster, flutter; canvass, debate, discuss, dispute, investigate.

**agitation** *n* concussion, shake, shaking; commotion, convulsion, disturbance, ferment, jarring, storm, tumult, turmoil; discomposure, distraction, emotion, excitement, flutter, perturbation, ruffle, tremor, trepidation; controversy, debate, discussion.

**agnostic** *n* doubter, empiricist, sceptic.

**agonize** *vb* distress, excruciate, rack, torment, torture.

**agony** *n* anguish, distress, pangs.

**agree** *vb* accord, concur, harmonize, unite; accede, acquiesce, assent, comply, concur, subscribe; bargain, contract, covenant, engage, promise, undertake; compound, compromise; chime, cohere, conform, correspond, match, suit, tally.

**agreeable** *adj* charming, pleasant, pleasing.

**agreement** *n* accordance, compliance, concord, harmony, union; bargain, compact, contract, pact, treaty.

**agriculture** *n* cultivation, culture, farming, geoponics, husbandry, tillage.

**aid** *vb* assist, help, serve, support; relieve, succour; advance, facilitate, further, promote. * *n* assistance, cooperation, help, patronage; alms, subsidy, succour, relief.

**ailment** *n* disease, illness, sickness.

**aim** *vb* direct, level, point, train; design, intend, mean, purpose, seek. * *n* bearing, course, direction, tendency; design, object, view, reason.

**air** *vb* expose, display, ventilate. * *n* atmosphere, breeze; appearance, aspect, manner; melody, tune.

**aisle** *n* passage, walk.

**akin** *adj* allied, kin, related; analogous, cognate, congenial, connected.

**alacrity** *n* agility, alertness, activity, eagerness, promptitude; cheerfulness, gaiety, hilarity, liveliness, vivacity.

**alarm** *vb* daunt, frighten, scare, startle, terrify. * *n* alarm-bell, tocsin, warning; apprehension, fear, fright, terror.

**alert** *adj* awake, circumspect, vigilant, watchful, wary; active, brisk, lively, nimble, quick, prompt, ready, sprightly. * *vb* alarm, arouse, caution, forewarn, signal, warn. * *n* alarm, signal, warning.

**alertness** *n* circumspection, vigilance, watchfulness, wariness; activity, briskness, nimbleness, promptness, readiness, spryness.

**alien** *adj* foreign, not native; differing, estranged, inappropriate, remote, unallied, separated. * *n* foreigner, stranger.

**alienate** *vb* (*legal*) assign, demise, transfer; disaffect, estrange, wean, withdraw.

**alienation** *n* (*legal*) assignment, conveyance, transfer; breach, disaffection, division, estrangement, rupture; (*med*) aberration, delusion, derangement, hallucination, insanity, madness.

**alike** *adj* akin, analogous, duplicate, identical, resembling, similar. * *adv* equally.

**aliment** *n* diet, fare, meat, nutriment, provision, rations, sustenance.

**alive** *adj* animate, breathing, live; aware, responsive, sensitive, susceptible; brisk, cheerful, lively, sprightly.

**allay** *vb* appease, calm, check, compose; alleviate, assuage, lessen, moderate, solace, temper.

**allege** *vb* affirm, assert, declare, maintain, say; adduce, advance, assign, cite, plead, produce, quote.

**allegiance** *n* duty, homage, fealty, fidelity, loyalty, obligation.

**allegory** *n* apologue, fable, myth, parable, story, tale.

**alleviate** *vb* assuage, lighten, mitigate, mollify, moderate, quell, quiet, quieten, soften, soothe.

**alliance** *n* affinity, intermarriage, relation; coalition, combination, confederacy, league, treaty, union; affiliation, connection, relationship, similarity.

**allot** *vb* divide, dispense, distribute; assign, fix, prescribe, specify.

**allow** *vb* acknowledge, admit, concede, confess, grant, own; authorize, grant, let, permit; bear, endure, suffer, tolerate; grant, yield, relinquish, spare; approve, justify, sanction; abate, bate, deduct, remit.

**allude** *vb* glance, hint, mention, imply, insinuate, intimate, refer, suggest, touch.

**allure** *vb* attract, beguile, cajole, coax, entice, lure, persuade, seduce, tempt. * *n* appeal, attraction, lure, temptation.

**allusion** n hint, implication, intimation, insinuation, mention, reference, suggestion.

**ally** vb combine, connect, join, league, marry, unite. * n aider, assistant, associate, coadjutor, colleague, friend, partner.

**almighty** adj all-powerful, omnipotent.

**alms** npl benefaction, bounty, charity, dole, gift, gratuity.

**alone** adj companionless, deserted, forsaken, isolated, lonely, only, single, sole, solitary.

**along** adv lengthways, lengthwise; forward, onward; beside, together, simultaneously.

**aloud** adv audibly, loudly, sonorously, vociferously.

**alter** vb change, conform, modify, shift, turn, transform, transmit, vary.

**altercation** n bickering, contention, controversy, dispute, dissension, strife, wrangling.

**alternating** adj intermittent, interrupted.

**alternative** adj another, different, second, substitute. * n choice, option, preference.

**although** conj albeit, even if, for all that, notwithstanding, though.

**altitude** n elevation, height, loftiness.

**altogether** adv completely, entirely, totally, utterly.

**always** adv continually, eternally, ever, evermore, perpetually, unceasingly.

**amalgamate** vb blend, combine, commingle, compound, incorporate, mix.

**amass** vb accumulate, aggregate, collect, gather, heap, scrape together.

**amateur** n dilettante, nonprofessional.

**amaze** vb astonish, astound, bewilder, confound, confuse, dumbfound, perplex, stagger, stupefy.

**amazement** n astonishment, bewilderment, confusion, marvel, surprise, wonder.

**ambassador** n deputy, envoy, legate, minister, plenipotentiary.

**ambiguous** adj dubious, doubtful, enigmatic, equivocal, uncertain, indefinite, indistinct, obscure, vague.

**ambition** n aspiration, emulation, longing, yearning.

**ambitious** adj aspiring, avid, eager, intent.

**ameliorate** vb amend, benefit, better, elevate, improve, mend.

**amenability** n amenableness, responsiveness; accountability, liability, responsibility.

**amenable** adj acquiescent, agreeable, persuadable, responsive, susceptible; accountable, liable, responsible.

**amend** vb better, correct, improve, mend, redress, reform.

**amends** npl atonement, compensation, expiation, indemnification, recompense, reparation, restitution.

**amenity** n agreeableness, mildness, pleasantness, softness; affability, civility, courtesy, geniality, graciousness, urbanity.

**amiable** adj attractive, benign, charming, genial, good-natured, harmonious, kind, lovable, lovely, pleasant, pleasing, sweet, winning, winsome.

**amicable** adj amiable, cordial, friendly, harmonious, kind, kindly, peaceable.

**amiss** adj erroneous, inaccurate, incorrect, faulty, improper, wrong. * adv erroneously, inaccurately, incorrectly, wrongly.

**amnesty** n absolution, condonation, dispensation, forgiveness, oblivion.

**amorous** adj ardent, enamoured, fond, longing, loving, passionate, tender; erotic, impassioned.

**amorphous** adj formless, irregular, shapeless, unshapen; noncrystalline, structureless; chaotic, characterless, clumsy, disorganized, misshapen, unorganized, vague.

**amount** n aggregate, sum, total.

**ample** adj broad, capacious, extended, extensive, great, large, roomy, spacious; abounding, abundant, copious, generous, liberal, plentiful; diffusive, unrestricted.

**amputate** vb clip, curtail, prune, lop, remove, separate, sever.

**amuse** vb charm, cheer, divert, enliven, entertain, gladden, relax, solace; beguile, cheat, deceive, delude, mislead.

**amusement** n diversion, entertainment, frolic, fun, merriment, pleasure.

**analeptic** adj comforting, invigorating, restorative.

**analogy** n correspondence, likeness, parallelism, parity, resemblance, similarity.

**analysis** n decomposition, dissection, resolution, separation.

**anarchy** n chaos, confusion, disorder, misrule, lawlessness, riot.

**anathema** n ban, curse, denunciation, excommunication, execration, malediction, proscription.

**anatomy** n dissection; form, skeleton, structure.

**ancestor** n father, forebear, forefather, progenitor.

**ancestry** n family, house, line, lineage; descent, genealogy, parentage, pedigree, stock.

**anchor** vb fasten, fix, secure; cast anchor, take firm hold. * n (naut) ground tackle; defence, hold, security, stay.

**ancient** adj old, primitive, pristine; antiquated, antique, archaic, obsolete.

**ancillary** adj accessory, auxiliary, contributory, helpful, instrumental.

**angelic** adj adorable, celestial, cherubic, heavenly, saintly, seraphic; entrancing, enrapturing, rapturous, ravishing.

**anger** vb chafe, displease, enrage, gall, infuriate, irritate, madden. * n choler, exasperation, fury, gall, indignation, ire, passion, rage, resentment, spleen, wrath.

**angle** vb fish. * n divergence, flare, opening; bend, corner, crotch, cusp, point; fish-hook, hook.

**angry** adj chafed, exasperated, furious, galled, incensed, irritated, nettled, piqued, provoked, resentful.

**anguish** n agony, distress, grief, pang, rack, torment, torture.

**anile** adj aged, decrepit, doting, imbecile, senile.

**animadversion** n comment, notice, observation, remark; blame, censure, condemnation, reproof, stricture.

**animate** vb inform, quicken, vitalize, vivify; fortify, invigorate, revive; activate, enliven, excite, heat, impel, kindle, rouse, stimulate, stir, waken; elate, embolden, encourage, exhilarate, gladden, hearten. * adj alive, breathing, live, living, organic, quick.

**animosity** n bitterness, enmity, grudge, hatred, hostility, rancour, rankling, spleen, virulence.

**annals** npl archives, chronicles, records, registers, rolls.

**annex** vb affix, append, attach, subjoin, tag, tack; connect, join, unite.

**annihilate** vb abolish, annul, destroy, dissolve, exterminate, extinguish, kill, obliterate, raze, ruin.

**annotation** n comment, explanation, illustration, note, observation, remark.

**announce** vb advertise, communicate, declare, disclose, proclaim, promulgate, publish, report, reveal, trumpet.

**announcement** n advertisement, annunciation, bulletin, declaration, manifesto, notice, notification, proclamation.

**annoy** vb badger, chafe, disquiet, disturb, fret, hector, irk, irritate, molest, pain, pester, plague, trouble, vex, worry, wound.

**annul** vb abolish, abrogate, cancel, countermand, nullify, overrule, quash, repeal, recall, reverse, revoke.

**anoint** vb consecrate, oil, sanctify, smear.

**anonymous** adj nameless, unacknowledged, unsigned.

**answer** vb fulfil, rejoin, reply, respond, satisfy. * n rejoinder, reply, response, retort; confutation, rebuttal, refutation.

**answerable** adj accountable, amenable, correspondent, liable, responsible, suited.

**antagonism** n contradiction, discordance, disharmony, dissonant, incompatibility, opposition.

**antecedent** adj anterior, foregoing, forerunning, precedent, preceding, previous. * n forerunner, precursor.

**anterior** adj antecedent, foregoing, preceding, previous, prior; fore, front.

**anticipate** vb antedate, forestall, foretaste, prevent; count upon, expect, forecast, foresee.

**anticipation** n apprehension, contemplation, expectation, hope, prospect, trust; expectancy, forecast, foresight, foretaste, preconception, presentiment.

**antidote** n corrective, counteractive, counter-poison; cure, remedy, restorative, specific.

**antipathy** n abhorrence, aversion, disgust, detestation, hate, hatred, horror, loathing, repugnance.

**antique** adj ancient, archaic, bygone, old, old-fashioned.

**anxiety** n apprehension, care, concern, disquiet, fear, foreboding, misgiving, perplexity, trouble, uneasiness, vexation, worry.

**anxious** adj apprehensive, restless, solicitous, uneasy, unquiet, worried.

**apart** adv aloof, aside, separately; asunder.

**apathetic** adj cold, dull, impassive, inert, listless, obtuse, passionless, sluggish, torpid, unfeeling.

**ape** vb counterfeit, imitate, mimic; affect. * n simian, troglodyte; imitator, mimic; image, imitation, likeness, type.

**aperture** n chasm, cleft, eye, gap, opening, hole, orifice, passage.

**aphorism** n adage, apothegm, byword, maxim, proverb, saw, saying.

**apish** adj imitative, mimicking; affected, foppish, trifling.

**aplomb** n composure, confidence, equanimity, self-confidence.

**apocryphal** *adj* doubtful, fabulous, false, legendary, spurious, uncanonical.

**apologetic** *adj* exculpatory, excusatory; defensive, vindictive.

**apology** *n* defence, justification, vindication; acknowledgement, excuse, explanation, plea, reparation.

**apostate** *adj* backsliding, disloyal, faithless, false, perfidious, recreant, traitorous, untrue. * *n* backslider, deserter, pervert, renegade, turncoat.

**apostle** *n* angel, herald, messenger, missionary, preacher; advocate, follower, supporter.

**apothegm** *n* aphorism, byword, dictum, maxim, proverb, saw, saying.

**appal** *vb* affright, alarm, daunt, dismay, frighten, horrify, scare, shock.

**apparel** *n* attire, array, clothes, clothing, dress, garments, habit, raiment, robes, suit, trappings, vestments.

**apparent** *adj* discernible, perceptible, visible; conspicuous, evident, legible, manifest, obvious, open, patent, plain, unmistakable; external, ostensible, seeming, superficial.

**apparition** *n* appearance, appearing, epiphany, manifestation; being, form; ghost, phantom, spectre, spirit, vision.

**appeal** *vb* address, entreat, implore, invoke, refer, request, solicit. * *n* application, entreaty, invocation, solicitation, suit.

**appear** *vb* emerge, loom; break, open; arise, occur, offer; look, seem, show.

**appearance** *n* advent, arrival, apparition, coming; form, shape; colour, face, fashion, feature, guise, pretence, pretext; air, aspect, complexion, demeanour, manner, mien.

**appease** *vb* abate, allay, assuage, calm, ease, lessen, mitigate, pacify, placate, quell, soothe, temper, tranquillize.

**appellation** *n* address, cognomen, denomination, epithet, style, title.

**append** *vb* attach, fasten, hang; add, annex, subjoin, tack, tag.

**appendix** *n* addition, adjunct, appurtenance, codicil; excursus, supplement.

**appetite** *n* craving, desire, longing, lust, passion; gusto, relish, stomach, zest; hunger.

**applaud** *vb* acclaim, cheer, clap, compliment, encourage, extol, magnify.

**applause** *n* acclamation, approval, cheers, commendation, plaudit.

**applicable** *adj* adapted, appropriate, apt, befitting, fitting, germane, pertinent, proper, relevant.

**application** *n* emollient, lotion, ointment, poultice, wash; appliance, exercise, practice, use; appeal, petition, request, solicitation, suit; assiduity, constancy, diligence, effort, industry.

**apply** *vb* bestow, lay upon; appropriate, convert, employ, exercise, use; addict, address, dedicate, devote, direct, engage.

**appoint** *vb* determine, establish, fix, prescribe; bid, command, decree, direct, order, require; allot, assign, delegate, depute, detail, destine, settle; constitute, create, name, nominate; equip, furnish, supply.

**apportion** *vb* allocate, allot, allow, assign, deal, dispense, divide, share.

**apposite** *adj* apt, fit, germane, pertinent, relevant, suitable, pertinent.

**appraise** *vb* appreciate, estimate, prize, rate, value.

**appreciate** *vb* appreciate, esteem, estimate, rate, realize, value.

**apprehend** *vb* arrest, catch, detain, seize, take; conceive, imagine, regard, view; appreciate, perceive, realize, see, take in; fear, forebode; conceive, fancy, hold, imagine, presume, understand.

**apprehension** *n* arrest, capture, seizure; intellect, intelligence, mind, reason; discernment, intellect, knowledge, perception, sense; belief, fancy, idea, notion, sentiment, view; alarm, care, dread, distrust, fear, misgiving, suspicion.

**apprise** *vb* acquaint, inform, notify, tell.

**approach** *vb* advance, approximate, come close; broach; resemble. * *n* advance, advent; approximation, convergence, nearing, tendency; entrance, path, way.

**approbation** *n* approval, commendation, liking, praise; assent, concurrence, consent, endorsement, ratification, sanction.

**appropriate** *vb* adopt, arrogate, assume, set apart; allot, apportion, assign, devote; apply, convert, employ, use. * *adj* adapted, apt, befitting, fit, opportune, seemly, suitable.

**approve** *vb* appreciate, commend, like, praise, recommend, value; confirm, countenance, justify, ratify, sustain, uphold.

**approximate** *vb* approach, resemble. * *adj* approaching, proximate; almost exact, inexact, rough.

**apt** *adj* applicable, apposite, appropriate, befitting,

fit, felicitous, germane; disposed, inclined, liable, prone, subject; able, adroit, clever, dextrous, expert, handy, happy, prompt, ready, skilful.

**aptitude** n applicability, appropriateness, felicity, fitness, pertinence, suitability; inclination, tendency, turn; ability, address, adroitness, quickness, readiness, tact.

**arbitrary** adj absolute, autocratic, despotic, domineering, imperious, overbearing, unlimited; capricious, discretionary, fanciful, voluntary, whimsical.

**arcade** n colonnade, loggia.

**arch**[1] adj cunning, knowing, frolicsome, merry, mirthful, playful, roguish, shrewd, sly; consummate, chief, leading, pre-eminent, prime, primary, principal.

**arch**[2] vb span, vault; bend, curve. * n archway, span, vault.

**archaic** adj ancient, antiquated, antique, bygone, obsolete, old.

**archives** npl documents, muniments, records, registers, rolls.

**ardent** adj burning, fiery, hot; eager, earnest, fervent, impassioned, keen, passionate, warm, zealous.

**ardour** n glow, heat, warmth; eagerness, enthusiasm, fervour, heat, passion, soul, spirit, warmth, zeal.

**arduous** adj high, lofty, steep, uphill; difficult, fatiguing, hard, laborious, onerous, tiresome, toilsome, wearisome.

**area** n circle, circuit, district, domain, field, range, realm, region, tract.

**argue** vb plead, reason upon; debate, dispute; denote, evince, imply, indicate, mean, prove; contest, debate, discuss, sift.

**arid** adj barren, dry, parched, sterile, unfertile; dry, dull, jejune, pointless, uninteresting.

**aright** adv correctly, justly, rightly, truly.

**arise** vb ascend, mount, soar, tower; appear, emerge, rise, spring; begin, originate; rebel, revolt, rise; accrue, come, emanate, ensue, flow, issue, originate, proceed, result.

**aristocracy** n gentry, nobility, noblesse, peerage.

**arm**[1] n bough, branch, limb, protection; cove, creek, estuary, firth, fjord, frith, inlet.

**arm**[2] vb array, equip, furnish; clothe, cover, fortify, guard, protect, strengthen.

**arms** npl accoutrements, armour, array, harness, mail, panoply, weapons; crest, escutcheon.

**army** n battalions, force, host, legions, troops; host, multitude, throng, vast assemblage.

**around** prep about, encircling, encompassing, round, surrounding. * adv about, approximately, generally, near, nearly, practically, round, thereabouts.

**arouse** vb animate, awaken, excite, incite, kindle, provoke, rouse, stimulate, warm, whet.

**arraign** vb accuse, censure, charge, denounce, impeach, indict, prosecute, tax.

**arrange** vb array, class, classify, dispose, distribute, group, range, rank; adjust, determine, fix upon, settle; concoct, construct, devise, plan, prepare, project.

**arrant** adj bad, consummate, downright, gross, notorious, rank, utter.

**array** vb arrange, dispose, place, range, rank; accoutre, adorn, attire, decorate, dress, enrobe, embellish, equip, garnish, habit, invest. * n arrangement, collection, disposition, marshalling, order; apparel, attire, clothes, dress, garments; army, battalions, soldiery, troops.

**arrest** vb check, delay, detain, hinder, hold, interrupt, obstruct, restrain, stay, stop, withhold; apprehend, capture, catch, seize, take; catch, engage, engross, fix, occupy, secure, rivet. * n check, checking, detention, hindrance, interruption, obstruction, restraining, stay, staying, stopping; apprehension, capture, detention, seizure.

**arrive** vb attain, come, get to, reach.

**arrogance** n assumption, assurance, disdain, effrontery, haughtiness, loftiness, lordliness, presumption, pride, scornfulness, superciliousness.

**arrogate** vb assume, claim unduly, demand, usurp.

**arrow** n bolt, dart, reed, shaft.

**art** n business, craft, employment, trade; address, adroitness, aptitude, dexterity, ingenuity, knack, readiness, sagacity, skill; artfulness, artifice, astuteness, craft, deceit, duplicity, finesse, subtlety.

**artful** adj crafty, cunning, disingenuous, insincere, sly, tricky, wily.

**article** n branch, clause, division, head, item, member, paragraph, part, point, portion; essay, paper, piece; commodity, substance, thing.

**artifice** n art, chicanery, contrivance, cunning, deception, deceit, duplicity, effort, finesse, fraud; imposture, invention, stratagem, subterfuge, trick, trickery.

**artificial** adj counterfeit, sham, spurious; assumed, affected, constrained, fictitious, forced, laboured, strained.

**artless** adj ignorant, rude, unskilful, untaught; natural, plain, simple; candid, fair, frank, guileless, honest, plain, unaffected, simple, sincere, truthful, unsuspicious.

**ascend** vb arise, aspire, climb, mount, soar, tower.

**ascendancy, ascendency** n authority, control, domination, mastery, power, predominance, sovereignty, superiority, sway.

**ascertain** vb certify, define, determine, establish, fix, settle, verify; discover, find out, get at.

**ashamed** adj abashed, confused.

**ask** vb interrogate, inquire, question; adjure, beg, conjure, crave, desire, dun, entreat, implore, invite, inquire, petition, request, solicit, supplicate, seek, sue.

**aspect** n air, bearing, countenance, expression, feature, look, mien, visage; appearance, attitude, condition, light, phase, position, posture, situation, state, view; angle, direction, outlook, prospect.

**asperity** n ruggedness, roughness, unevenness; acrimony, causticity, corrosiveness, sharpness, sourness, tartness; acerbity, bitterness, churlishness, harshness, sternness, sullenness, severity, virulence.

**aspersion** n abuse, backbiting, calumny, censure, defamation, detraction, slander, vituperation, reflection, reproach.

**aspiration** n aim, ambition, craving, hankering, hope, longing.

**aspire** vb desire, hope, long, yearn; ascend, mount, rise, soar, tower.

**assail** vb assault, attack, invade, oppugn; impugn, malign, maltreat; ply, storm.

**assassinate** vb dispatch, kill, murder, slay.

**assault** vb assail, attack, charge, invade. * n aggression, attack, charge, incursion, invasion, onset, onslaught; storm.

**assemble** vb call, collect, congregate, convene, convoke, gather, levy, muster; converge, forgather.

**assembly** n company, collection, concourse, congregation, gathering, meeting, rout, throng; caucus, congress, conclave, convention, convocation, diet, legislature, meeting, parliament, synod.

**assent** vb accede, acquiesce, agree, concur, subscribe, yield. * n accord, acquiescence, allowance, approval, approbation, consent.

**assert** vb affirm, allege, aver, asseverate, declare, express, maintain, predicate, pronounce, protest; claim, defend, emphasize, maintain, press, uphold, vindicate.

**assertion** n affirmation, allegation, asseveration, averment, declaration, position, predication, remark,

statement, word; defence, emphasis, maintenance, pressing, support, vindication.

**assess** vb appraise, compute, estimate, rate, value; assign, determine, fix, impose, levy.

**asseverate** vb affirm, aver, avow, declare, maintain, protest.

**assiduous** adj active, busy, careful, constant, diligent, devoted, indefatigable, industrious, sedulous, unremitting, untiring.

**assign** vb allot, appoint, apportion, appropriate; fix, designate, determine, specify; adduce, advance, allege, give, grant, offer, present, show.

**assist** vb abet, aid, befriend, further, help, patronize, promote, second, speed, support, sustain; aid, relieve, succour; alternate with, relieve, spell.

**associate** vb affiliate, combine, conjoin, couple, join, link, relate, yoke; consort, fraternize, mingle, sort. * n chum, companion, comrade, familiar, follower, mate; ally, confederate, friend, partner, fellow.

**association** n combination, company, confederation, connection, partnership, society.

**assort** vb arrange, class, classify, distribute, group, rank, sort; agree, be adapted, consort, suit.

**assuage** vb allay, alleviate, appease, calm, ease, lessen, mitigate, moderate, mollify, pacify, quell, relieve, soothe, tranquillize.

**assume** vb take, undertake; affect, counterfeit, feign, pretend, sham; arrogate, usurp; beg, hypothesize, imply, postulate, posit, presuppose, suppose, simulate.

**assurance** n assuredness, certainty, conviction, persuasion, pledge, security, surety, warrant; engagement, pledge, promise; averment, assertion, protestation; audacity, confidence, courage, firmness, intrepidity; arrogance, brass, boldness, effrontery, face, front, impudence.

**assure** vb encourage, embolden, hearten; certify, insure, secure against loss, vouch for.

**astonish** vb amaze, astound, confound, daze, dumbfound, overwhelm, startle, stun, stupefy, surprise.

**astute** adj acute, cunning, deep, discerning, ingenious, intelligent, penetrating, perspicacious, quick, sagacious, sharp, shrewd.

**asylum** n refuge, retreat, sanctuary, shelter.

**athletic** adj brawny, lusty, muscular, powerful, robust, sinewy, stalwart, stout, strapping, strong, sturdy.

**athletics** npl aerobics, eurythmics, exercise, exercising, gymnastics, sports, track and field, workout.

**atom** n bit, molecule, monad, particle, scintilla.

**atone** vb answer, compensate, expiate, satisfy.

**atonement** n amends, expiation, propitiation, reparation, satisfaction.

**atrocity** n depravity, enormity, flagrancy, ferocity, savagery, villainy.

**attach** vb affix, annex, connect, fasten, join, hitch, tie; charm, captivate, enamour, endear, engage, win; (legal) distress, distrain, seize, take.

**attack** vb assail, assault, charge, encounter, invade, set upon, storm, tackle; censure, criticise, impugn. * n aggression, assault, charge, offence, onset, onslaught, raid, thrust.

**attain** vb accomplish, achieve, acquire, get, obtain, secure; arrive at, come to, reach.

**attempt** vb assail, assault, attack; aim, endeavour, seek, strive, try. * n effort, endeavour, enterprise, experiment, undertaking, venture; assault, attack, onset.

**attend** vb accompany, escort, follow; guard, protect, watch; minister to, serve, wait on; give heed, hear, harken, listen; be attendant, serve, tend, wait.

**attention** n care, circumspection, heed, mindfulness, observation, regard, watch, watchfulness; application, reflection, study; civility, courtesy, deference, politeness, regard, respect; addresses, courtship, devotion, suit, wooing.

**attentive** adj alive, awake, careful, civil, considerate, courteous, heedful, mindful, observant, watchful.

**attenuate** vb contract, dilute, diminish, elongate, lengthen, lessen, rarefy, reduce, slim, thin, weaken.

**attest** vb authenticate, certify, corroborate, confirm, ratify, seal, vouch; adjure, call to witness, invoke; confess, display, exhibit, manifest, prove, show, witness.

**attic** n garret, loft, upper storey.

**Attic** adj delicate, subtle, penetrating, pointed, pungent; chaste, classic, correct, elegant, polished, pure.

**attire** vb accoutre, apparel, array, clothe, dress, enrobe, equip, rig, robe. * n clothes, clothing, costume, dress, garb, gear, habiliment, outfit, toilet, trapping, vestment, vesture, wardrobe.

**attitude** n pose, position, posture; aspect, conjuncture, condition, phase, prediction, situation, standing, state.

**attract** vb draw, pull; allure, captivate, charm, decoy, enamour, endear, entice, engage, fascinate, invite, win.

**attraction** n affinity, drawing, pull; allurement, charm, enticement, fascination, magnetism, lure, seduction, witchery.

**attribute** vb ascribe, assign, impute, refer. * n characteristic, mark, note, peculiarity, predicate, property, quality.

**attrition** n abrasion, friction, rubbing.

**attune** vb accord, harmonize, modulate, tune; accommodate, adapt, adjust, attempt.

**audacity** n boldness, courage, daring, fearlessness, intrepidity; assurance, brass, effrontery, face, front, impudence, insolence, presumption, sauciness.

**audience** n assemblage, congregation; hearing, interview, reception.

**augment** vb add to, enhance, enlarge, increase, magnify, multiply, swell.

**augmentation** n accession, addition, enlargement, extension, increase.

**augury** n prediction, prognostication, prophecy, soothsaying; auspice, forerunner, harbinger, herald, omen, precursor, portent, sign.

**august** adj awe-inspiring, awful, dignified, grand, imposing, kingly, majestic, noble, princely, regal, solemn, stately, venerable.

**auspicious** adj fortunate, happy, lucky, prosperous, successful; bright, favourable, golden, opportune, promising, prosperous.

**austere** adj ascetic, difficult, formal, hard, harsh, morose, relentless, rigid, rigorous, severe, stern, stiff, strict, uncompromising, unrelenting.

**authentic** adj genuine, pure, real, true, unadulterated, uncorrupted, veritable; accurate, authoritative, reliable, true, trustworthy.

**authority** n dominion, empire, government, jurisdiction, power, sovereignty; ascendency, control, influence, rule, supremacy, sway; authorization, liberty, order, permit, precept, sanction, warranty; testimony, witness; connoisseur, expert, master.

**authorize** vb empower, enable, entitle; allow, approve, confirm, countenance, permit, ratify, sanction.

**auxiliary** adj aiding, ancillary, assisting, helpful, subsidiary. * n ally, assistant, confederate, help.

**avail** vb assist, benefit, help, profit, use, service.

**available** adj accessible, advantageous, applicable, beneficial, profitable, serviceable, useful.

**avarice** n acquisitiveness, covetousness, greediness, penuriousness, rapacity.

**avaricious** adj grasping, miserly, niggardly, parsimonious.

**avenge** vb punish, retaliate, revenge, vindicate.

**avenue** n access, entrance, entry, passage; alley, path, road, street, walk; channel, pass, route, way.

**aver** vb allege, assert, asseverate, avouch, declare, pronounce, protest, say.

**averse** adj adverse, backward, disinclined, indisposed, opposed, unwilling.

**aversion** n abhorrence, antipathy, disgust, dislike, hate, hatred, loathing, reluctance, repugnance.

**avid** adj eager, greedy, voracious.

**avocation** n business, calling, employment, occupation, trade, vocation; distraction, hindrance, interruption.

**avoid** vb dodge, elude, escape, eschew, shun; forebear, refrain from.

**avouch** vb allege, assert, declare, maintain, say.

**avow** vb admit, acknowledge, confess, own.

**awaken** vb arouse, excite, incite, kindle, provoke, spur, stimulate; wake, waken; begin, be excited.

**award** vb adjudge, allot, assign, bestow, decree, grant. * n adjudication, allotment, assignment, decision, decree, determination, gift, judgement.

**aware** adj acquainted, apprised, conscious, conversant, informed, knowing, mindful, sensible.

**away** adv absent, not present. * adj at a distance; elsewhere; out of the way.

**awe** vb cow, daunt, intimidate, overawe. * n abashment, fear, reverence; dread, fear, fearfulness, terror.

**awful** adj august, awesome, dread, grand, inspired; abashed, alarming, appalled, dire, frightful, portentous, tremendous.

**awkward** adj bungling, clumsy, inept, maladroit, unskilful; lumbering, unfit, ungainly, unmanageable; boorish; inconvenient, unsuitable.

**axiom** n adage, aphorism, apothegm, maxim, postulation, truism.

**axis** n axle, shaft, spindle.

**azure** adj blue, cerulean, sky-coloured.

# B

**babble** vb blather, chatter, gibber, jabber, prate, prattle. * n chat, gossip, palaver, prate, tattle.

**babel** n clamour, confusion, din, discord, disorder, hubbub, jargon, pother.

**baby** vb coddle, cosset, indulge, mollycoddle, pamper, spoil. * adj babyish, childish, infantile, puerile; diminutive, doll-like, miniature, pocket, pocket-sized, small-scale. * n babe, brat, child, infant, suckling, nursling; chicken, coward, milksop, namby-pamby, sad sack, weakling; miniature; innocent.

**bacchanal** n carouse, debauchery, drunkenness, revelry, roisterousness.

**back** vb abet, aid, countenance, favour, second, support, sustain; go back, move back, retreat, withdraw. * adj hindmost. *adv in return, in consideration; ago, gone, since; aside, away, behind, by; abaft, astern, backwards, hindwards, rearwards. *n end, hind part, posterior, rear.

**backbite** vb abuse, asperse, blacken, defame, libel, malign, revile, scandalize, slander, traduce, vilify.

**backbone** n chine, spine; constancy, courage, decision, firmness, nerve, pluck, resolution, steadfastness.

**backslider** n apostate, deserter, renegade.

**backward** adj disinclined, hesitating, indisposed, loath, reluctant, unwilling, wavering; dull, slow, sluggish, stolid, stupid. *adv aback, behind, rearward.

**bad** adj baleful, baneful, detrimental, evil, harmful, hurtful, injurious, noxious, pernicious, unwholesome, vicious; abandoned, corrupt, depraved, immoral, sinful, unfair, unprincipled, wicked; unfortunate, unhappy, unlucky, miserable; disappointing, discouraging, distressing, sad, unwelcoming; abominable, mean, shabby, scurvy, vile, wretched; defective, inferior, imperfect, incompetent, poor, unsuitable; hard, heavy, serious, severe.

**badge** n brand, emblem, mark, sign, symbol, token.

**badger** vb annoy, bait, bother, hector, harry, pester, persecute, tease, torment, trouble, vex, worry.

**baffle** vb balk, block, check, circumvent, defeat, foil, frustrate, mar, thwart, undermine, upset; bewilder, confound, disconcert, perplex.

**bait** vb harry, tease, worry. *n allurement, decoy, enticement, lure, temptation.

**balance** vb equilibrate, pose, (naut) trim; compare, weigh; compensate, counteract, estimate; adjust, clear, equalize, square. *n equilibrium, liberation; excess, remainder, residue, surplus.

**bald** adj bare, naked, uncovered, treeless; dull, inelegant, meagre, prosaic, tame, unadorned, vapid.

**baleful** adj baneful, deadly, calamitous, hurtful, injurious, mischievous, noxious, pernicious, ruinous.

**balk** vb baffle, defeat, disappoint, disconcert, foil, frustrate, thwart.

**ball** n drop, globe, orb, pellet, marble, sphere; bullet, missile, projectile, shot; assembly, dance.

**balmy** adj aromatic, fragrant, healing, odorous, perfumed.

**ban** vb anathematize, curse, execrate; interdict, outlaw. *n edict, proclamation; anathema, curse, denunciation, execration; interdiction, outlawry, penalty, prohibition

**band**¹ vb belt, bind, cinch, encircle, gird, girdle; ally, associate, combine, connect, join, league; bar, marble, streak, stripe, striate, vein. *n crew, gang, horde, society, troop; ensemble, group, orchestra.

**band**² n ligament, ligature, tie; bond, chain, cord, fetter, manacle, shackle, trammel; bandage, belt, binding, cincture, girth, tourniquet.

**bandit** n brigand, freebooter, footpad, gangster, highwayman, outlaw, robber.

**baneful** adj poisonous, venomous; deadly, destructive, hurtful, mischievous, noxious, pernicious.

**bang** vb beat, knock, maul, pommel, pound, strike, thrash, thump; slam; clatter, rattle, resound, ring. *n clang, clangour, whang; blow, knock, lick, thump, thwack, whack.

**banish** vb exile, expatriate, ostracize; dismiss, exclude, expel.

**bank**¹ vb incline, slope, tilt; embank. *n dike, embankment, escarpment, heap, knoll, mound; border, bound, brim, brink, margin, rim, strand; course, row, tier.

**bank**² vb deposit, keep, save. *n depository, fund, reserve, savings, stockpile.

**banner** n colours, ensign, flag, standard, pennon, standard, streamer.

**banter** vb chaff, deride, jeer, joke, mock, quiz, rally, ridicule. *n badinage, chaff, derision, jesting, joking, mockery, quizzing, raillery, ridicule.

**bar** vb exclude, hinder, obstruct, prevent, prohibit, restrain, stop. *n grating, pole, rail, rod; barricade, hindrance, impediment, obstacle, obstruction, stop; bank, sand bar, shallow, shoal, spit; (legal) barristers, counsel, court, judgement, tribunal.

**barbarian** adj brutal, cruel, ferocious, fierce, fell, inhuman, ruthless, savage, truculent, unfeeling. *n brute, ruffian, savage.

**barbaric** adj barbarous, rude, savage, uncivilized, untamed; capricious, coarse, gaudy, riotous, showy, outlandish, uncouth, untamed, wild.

**bare** vb denude, depilate, divest, strip, unsheathe; disclose, manifest, open, reveal, show. *adj denuded, exposed, naked, nude, stripped, unclothed, uncovered, undressed, unsheltered; alone, mere, sheer, simple; bald, meagre, plain, unadorned, uncovered, unfurnished; empty, destitute, indigent, poor.

**bargain** vb agree, contract, covenant, stipulate; convey, sell, transfer. *n agreement, compact, contract, covenant, convention, indenture, transaction, stipulation, treaty; proceeds, purchase, result.

**barren** adj childless, infecund, sterile; (bot) acarpous, sterile; bare, infertile, poor, sterile, unproductive; ineffectual, unfruitful, uninstructive.

**barricade** vb block up, fortify, protect, obstruct. *n barrier, obstruction, palisade, stockade.

**barrier** n bar, barricade, hindrance, impediment, obstacle, obstruction, stop.

**barter** vb bargain, exchange, sell, trade, traffic.

**base**[1] adj cheap, inferior, worthless; counterfeit, debased, false, spurious; baseborn, humble, lowly, mean, nameless, plebeian, unknown, untitled, vulgar; abject, beggarly, contemptible, degraded, despicable, low, menial, pitiful, servile, sordid, sorry, worthless.

**base**[2] vb establish, found, ground. *n foundation, fundament, substructure, underpinning; pedestal, plinth, stand; centre, headquarters, HQ, seat; starting point; basis, cause, grounds, reason, standpoint; bottom, foot, foundation, ground.

**bashful** adj coy, diffident, shy, timid.

**basis n base**, bottom, foundation, fundament, ground, groundwork.

**bastard** adj adulterated, baseborn, counterfeit, false, illegitimate, sham. *n love child.

**batch** vb assemble, bunch, bundle, collect, gather, group. *n amount, collection, crowd, lot, quantity.

**bathe** vb immerse, lave, wash; cover, enfold, enwrap, drench, flood, infold, suffuse. *n bath, shower, swim.

**batter**[1] vb beat, pelt, smite; break, bruise, demolish, destroy, shatter, shiver, smash; abrade, deface, disfigure, indent, mar; incline, recede, retreat, slope. *n batsman, striker.

**batter**[2] n dough, goo, goop, gunk, paste, pulp.

**battle** vb contend, contest, engage, fight, strive, struggle. *n action, affair, brush, combat, conflict, contest, engagement, fight, fray.

**bauble** n gewgaw, gimcrack, knick-knack, plaything, toy, trifle, trinket.

**bawdy** adj obscene, filthy, impure, indecent, lascivious, lewd, smutty, unchaste.

**bawl** vb clamour, cry, hoot, howl, roar, shout, squall, vociferate, yell.

**bay**[1] vb bark, howl, wail, yell, yelp.

**bay**[2] n alcove, compartment, niche, nook, opening, recess.

**bay**[3] n bight, cove, gulf, inlet.

**bays** npl applause, chaplet, fame, garland, glory, honour, plaudits, praise, renown.

**beach** vb ground, maroon, strand. *n coast, margin, rim, sands, seashore, seaside, shore, shoreline, strand, waterfront.

**beacon** vb brighten, flame, shine, signal; enlighten, illuminate, illumine, guide, light, signal. *n lighthouse, pharos, watchtower; sign, signal.

**beadle** n apparitor, church officer, crier, servitor, summoner.

**beak** n bill, mandible, (sl) nose; (naut) bow, prow, stem.

**beam** vb beacon, gleam, glisten, glitter, shine. *n balk, girder, joist, scantling, stud; gleam, pencil, ray, streak.

**bear** vb support, sustain, uphold; carry, convey, deport, transport, waft; abide, brook, endure, stand, suffer, tolerate, undergo; carry on, keep up, maintain; cherish, entertain, harbour; produce; cast, drop, sustain; endure, submit, suffer; act, operate, work. *n growler, grumbler, moaner, snarler; speculator.

**bearable** adj endurable, sufferable, supportable, tolerable.

**bearing** n air, behaviour, demeanour, deportment, conduct, carriage, conduct, mien, port; connection, dependency, relation; endurance, patience, suffering; aim, course, direction; bringing forth, producing; bed, receptacle, socket.

**beastly** adj abominable, brutish, ignoble, low, sensual, vile.

**beat** vb bang, baste, belabour, buffet, cane, cudgel, drub, hammer, hit, knock, maul, pound, pummel, punch, strike, thrash, thump, thwack, whack, whip; bray, bruise, pound, pulverize; batter, pelt; conquer, defeat, overcome, rout, subdue, surpass, vanquish; pulsate, throb; dash, strike. *adj baffled, bamboozled, confounded, mystified, nonplused, perplexed, puzzled, stumped; done, dog-tired, exhausted, tired out, worn out; beaten, defeated, licked, worsted. *n blow, striking, stroke; beating, pulsation, throb; accent, metre, rhythm; circuit, course, round.

**beatific** adj ecstatic, enchanting, enraptured, ravishing, rapt.

**beatitude** n blessing, ecstasy, felicity, happiness.

**beau** n coxcomb, dandy, exquisite, fop, popinjay; admirer, lover, suitor, sweetheart.

**beautiful** adj charming, comely, fair, fine, exquisite, handsome, lovely, pretty.

**beautify** vb adorn, array, bedeck, deck, decorate, embellish, emblazon, garnish, gild, grace, ornament, set.

**beauty** n elegance, grace, symmetry; attractiveness, comeliness, fairness, loveliness, seemliness; belle.

**become** vb change to, get, go, wax; adorn, befit, set off, suit.

**becoming** adj appropriate, apt, congruous, decent, decorous, due, fit, proper, right, seemly, suitable; comely, graceful, neat, pretty.

**bed** vb embed, establish, imbed, implant, infix, inset, plant; harbour, house, lodge. *n berth, bunk, cot, couch; channel, depression, hollow; base, foundation; receptacle, support, underlay; accumulation, layer, seam, stratum, vein.

**bedim** vb cloud, darken, dim, obscure.

**befall** vb betide, overtake; chance, happen, occur, supervene.

**befitting** adj appropriate, apt, becoming, decorous, fit, proper, right, suitable, seemly.

**befool** vb bamboozle, beguile, cheat, circumvent, delude, deceive, dupe, fool, hoax, hoodwink, infatuate, stupefy, trick.

**befriend** vb aid, benefit, countenance, encourage, favour, help, patronize.

**beg** vb adjure, ask, beseech, conjure, crave, entreat, implore, importune, petition, pray, request, solicit, supplicate.

**beggarly** adj destitute, needy, poor; abject, base, despicable, grovelling, low, mean, miserable, miserly, paltry, pitiful, scant, servile, shabby, sorry, stingy, vile, wretched.

**begin** vb arise, commence, enter, open; inaugurate, institute, originate, start.

**beginning** n arising, commencement, dawn, emergence, inauguration, inception, initiation, opening, outset, start, rise; origin, source.

**beguile** vb cheat, deceive, delude; amuse, cheer, divert, entertain, solace.

**behaviour** n air, bearing, carriage, comportment, conduct, demeanour, deportment, manner, manners, mien.

**behest** n bidding, charge, command, commandment, direction, hest, injunction, mandate, order, precept.

**behind** prep abaft, after, following. *adv abaft, aft, astern, rearward. *adj arrested, backward, checked, detained, retarded; after, behind. *n afterpart, rear, stern, tail; back, back side, reverse; bottom, buttocks, posterior, rump.

**behold** vb consider, contemplate, eye, observe, regard, see, survey, view.

**behoove** vb become, befit, suit; be binding, be obligatory.

**being** n actuality, existence, reality, subsistence; core, essence, heart, root.

**beleaguer** vb besiege, blockade, invest; beset, block, encumber, encompass, encounter, obstruct, surround.

**belief** n assurance, confidence, conviction, persuasion, trust; acceptance, assent, credence, credit, currency; creed, doctrine, dogma, faith, opinion, tenet.

**bellow** vb bawl, clamour, cry, howl, vociferate, yell.

**belt** n band, cincture, girdle, girth, zone; region, stretch, strip.

**bemoan** vb bewail, deplore, lament, mourn.

**bemused** adj bewildered, confused, fuddled, muddled, muzzy, stupefied, tipsy.

**bend** vb bow, crook, curve, deflect, draw; direct, incline, turn; bend, dispose, influence, mould, persuade, subdue; (naut) fasten, make fast; crook, deflect, deviate, diverge, swerve; bow, lower, stoop; condescend, deign. *n angle, arc, arcuation, crook, curvature, curve, elbow, flexure, turn.

**beneath** prep below, under, underneath; unbecoming, unbefitting, unworthy. *adv below, underneath.

**benediction** n beatitude, benefit, benison, blessing, boon, grace, favour.

**benefaction** n alms, boon, charity, contribution, donation, favour, gift, grant, gratuity, offering, present.

**beneficent** adj benevolent, bounteous, bountiful, charitable, generous, kind, liberal.

**beneficial** adj advantageous, favourable, helpful, profitable, salutary, serviceable, useful, wholesome.

**benefit** vb befriend, help, serve; advantage, avail, profit. *n favour, good turn, kindness, service; account, advantage, behalf, gain, good, interest, profit, utility.

**benevolence** n beneficence, benignity, generosity, goodwill, humanity, kindliness, kindness.

**benevolent** adj altruistic, benign, charitable, generous, humane, kind, kind-hearted, liberal, obliging, philanthropic, tender, unselfish.

**benign** adj amiable, amicable, beneficent, benevolent, complaisant, friendly, gentle, good, gracious, humane, kind, kindly, obliging.

**bent** adj angled, angular, bowed, crooked, curved, deflected, embowed, flexed, hooked, twisted; disposed, inclined, prone, minded; (with **on**) determined, fixed on, resolved, set on. *n bias, inclination, leaning, partiality, penchant, predilection, prepossession, proclivity, propensity

**bequeath** vb devise, give, grant, leave, will; impart, transmit.

**berate** vb chide, rate, reprimand, reprove, scold.

**bereave** vb afflict, deprive of, despoil, dispossess, divest, rob, spoil, strip.

**beseech** vb beg, conjure, entreat, implore, importune, petition, supplicate; ask, beg, crave, solicit.

**beset** vb besiege, encompass, enclose, environ, encircle, hem in, surround; decorate, embarrass, embellish, entangle, garnish, ornament, perplex, set.

**beside**[1] prep at the side of, by the side of, close to, near; aside from, not according to, out of the course of, out of the way of; not in possession of, out of.

**besides**[1] prep barring, distinct from, excluding, except, excepting, in addition to, other than, over and above, save.

**beside**[2], **besides**[2] adv additionally, also, further, furthermore, in addition, more, moreover, over and above, too, yet.

**besiege** vb beset, blockade, encircle, encompass, environ, invest, surround.

**besot** vb drench, intoxicate, soak, steep; befool, delude, infatuate, stultify, stupefy.

**bespatter** vb bedaub, befoul, besmirch, smear, spatter.

**bespeak** vb accost, address, declare, evince, forestall, imply, indicate, prearrange, predict, proclaim, solicit.

**best** vb better, exceed, excel, predominate, rival, surpass; beat, defeat, outdo, worst. *adj chief, first, foremost, highest, leading, utmost. *adv advantageously, excellently; extremely, greatly. *n choice, cream, flower, pick.

**bestial** adj beast-like, beastly, brutal, degraded, depraved, irrational, low, vile; sensual.

**bestow** vb deposit, dispose, put, place, store, stow; accord, give, grant, impart.

**bet** vb gamble, hazard, lay, pledge, stake, wage, wager. *n gamble, hazard, stake, wager.

**bethink** vb cogitate, consider, ponder, recall, recollect, reflect, remember.

**betide** vb befall, happen, occur, overtake.

**betimes** adv beforehand, early, forward, soon.

**betoken** vb argue, betray, denote, evince, imply, indicate, prove, represent, show, signify, typify.

**betray** vb be false to, break, violate; blab, discover, divulge, expose, reveal, show, tell; argue, betoken, display, evince, expose, exhibit, imply, indicate, manifest, reveal; beguile, delude, ensnare, lure, mislead; corrupt, ruin, seduce, undo.

**betroth** vb affiance, engage to marry, pledge in marriage, plight.

**better** vb advance, amend, correct, exceed, improve, promote, rectify, reform. *adj bigger, fitter, greater, larger, less ill, preferable. *n advantage, superiority, upper hand, victory; improvement, greater good.

**between** prep amidst, among, betwixt.

**bewail** vb bemoan, deplore, express, lament, mourn over, rue, sorrow.

**beware** vb avoid, heed, look out, mind.

**bewilder** vb confound, confuse, daze, distract, embarrass, entangle, muddle, mystify, nonplus, perplex, pose, puzzle, stagger.

**bewitch** vb captivate, charm, enchant, enrapture, entrance, fascinate, spellbind, transport.

**beyond** prep above, before, farther, over, past, remote, yonder.

**bias** vb bend, dispose, incline, influence, predispose, prejudice. *n bent, inclination, leaning, partiality, penchant, predilection, prepossession, proclivity, propensity, slant, tendency, turn.

**bicker** vb argue, dispute, jangle, quarrel, spar, spat, squabble, wrangle.

**bid** vb charge, command, direct, enjoin, order, require, summon; ask, call, invite, pray, request, solicit; offer, propose, proffer, tender. *n bidding, offer, proposal.

**big** adj bumper, bulking, bulky, great, huge, large, massive, monstrous; important, imposing; distended, inflated, full, swollen, tumid; fecund, fruitful, productive, teeming.

**bigoted** adj dogmatic, hidebound, intolerant, obstinate, narrow-minded, opinionated, prejudiced.

**bill**[1] vb charge, dun, invoice; programme, schedule; advertise, boost, plug, promote, publicize. *n account, charges, reckoning, score; advertisement, banner, hoarding, placard, poster; playbill, programme, schedule; bill of exchange, certificate, money; account, reckoning, statement.

**bill**[2] n beak, mandible, (sl) nose; billhook, brush-cutter, hedge-bill, hedging knife; caress, fondle, kiss, toy.

**billet** vb allot, apportion, assign, distribute, quarter, station. *n accommodation, lodgings, quarters.

**billow** vb surge, wave; heave, roll; bag, baloon, bulge, dilate, swell. *n roller, surge, swell, wave.

**bin** n box, bunker, crib, frame, receptacle.

**bind** vb confine, enchain, fetter, restrain, restrict; bandage, tie up, wrap; fasten, lash, pinion, secure, tie, truss; engage, hold, oblige, obligate, pledge; contract, harden, shrink, stiffen.

**birth** n ancestry, blood, descent, extraction, lineage, race; being, creation, creature, offspring, production, progeny.

**bit** n crumb, fragment, morsel, mouthful, piece, scrap; atom, grain, jot, mite, particle, tittle, whit; instant, minute, moment, second.

**bite** vb champ, chew, crunch, gnaw; burn, make smart, sting; catch, clutch, grapple, grasp, grip; bamboozle, cheat, cozen, deceive, defraud, dupe, gull, mislead, outwit, overreach, trick. *n grasp, hold; punch, relish, spice, pungency, tang, zest; lick, morsel, sip, taste; crick, nip, pain, pang, prick, sting.

**bitter** adj acrid; dire, fell, merciless, relentless, ruthless; harsh, severe, stern; afflictive, calamitous, distressing, galling, grievous, painful, poignant, sore, sorrowful.

**black** adj dark, ebony, inky, jet, sable, swarthy; dingy, dusky, lowering, murky, pitchy; calamitous, dark, depressing, disastrous, dismal, doleful, forbidding, gloomy, melancholy, mournful, sombre, sullen.

**blacken** vb darken; deface, defile, soil, stain, sully; asperse, besmirch, calumniate, defame, malign, revile, slander, traduce, vilify.

**blamable** adj blameable, blameworthy, censurable, culpable, delinquent. faulty, remiss, reprehensible.

**blame** vb accuse, censure, condemn, disapprove, reflect upon, reprehend, reproach, reprove, upbraid. *n animadversion, censure, condemnation, disapproval, dispraise, disapprobation, reprehension, reproach, reproof; defect, demerit, fault, guilt, misdeed, shortcoming, sin, wrong.

**blameless** adj faultless, guiltless, inculpable, innocent, irreproachable, unblemished, undefiled, unimpeachable, unspotted, unsullied, spotless, stainless.

**blanch** vb bleach, fade, etiolate, whiten.

**bland** adj balmy, demulcent, gentle, mild, soothing, soft; affable, amiable, complaisant, kindly, mild, suave.

**blandishment** n cajolery, coaxing, compliment, fascination, fawning, flattery, wheedling

**blank** adj bare, empty, vacuous, void; amazed, astonished, confounded, confused, dumbfounded, nonplussed; absolute, complete, entire, mere, perfect, pure, simple, unabated, unadulterated, unmitigated, unmixed, utter, perfect.

**blare** vb blazon, blow, peal, proclaim, trumpet. *n blast, clang, clangour, peal.

**blasphemy** n impiousness, sacrilege; cursing, profanity, swearing.

**blast** vb annihilate, blight, destroy, kill, ruin, shrivel, wither; burst, explode, kill. *n blow, gust, squall; blare, clang, peal; burst, discharge, explosion.

**blaze** vb blazon, proclaim, publish; burn, flame, glow. *n flame, flare, flash, glow, light.

**bleach** vb blanch, etiolate, render white, whiten.

**bleak** adj bare, exposed, unprotected, unsheltered, storm-beaten, windswept; biting, chill, cold, piercing, raw; cheerless, comfortless, desolate, dreary, uncongenial,

**blemish** vb blur, injure, mar, spot, stain, sully, taint, tarnish; asperse, calumniate, defame, malign, revile, slander, traduce, vilify. *n blot, blur, defect, disfigurement, fault, flaw, imperfection, soil, speck, spot, stain, tarnish; disgrace, dishonour, reproach, stain, taint.

**blend** vb amalgamate, coalesce, combine, commingle, fuse, mingle, mix, unite. *n amalgamation, combination, compound, fusion, mix, mixture, union.

**bless** vb beatify, delight, gladden; adore, celebrate, exalt, extol, glorify, magnify, praise.

**blessedness** n beatitude, bliss, blissfulness, felicity, happiness, joy.

**blight** vb blast, destroy, kill, ruin, shrivel, wither; annihilate, annul, crush, disappoint, frustrate. *n blast, mildew, pestilence.

**blind** vb blear, darken, deprive of sight; blindfold, hoodwink. *adj eyeless, sightless, stone-blind, unseeing; benighted, ignorant, injudicious, purblind, undiscerning, unenlightened; concealed, confused, dark, dim, hidden, intricate, involved, labyrinthine, obscure, private, remote; careless, headlong, heedless, inconsiderate, indiscriminate, thoughtless; blank, closed, shut. *n cover, curtain, screen, shade, shutter; blinker; concealment, disguise, feint, pretence, pretext, ruse, stratagem, subterfuge.

**blink** vb nictate, nictitate, wink; flicker, flutter, gleam, glitter, intermit, twinkle; avoid, disregard, evade, gloss over, ignore, overlook, pass over. *n glance, glimpse, sight, view, wink; gleam, glimmer, sheen, shimmer, twinkle.

**bliss** n beatification, beatitude, blessedness, blissfulness, ecstasy, felicity, happiness, heaven, joy, rapture, transport.

**blithe** adj airy, animated, blithesome, buoyant, cheerful, debonair, elated, happy, jocund, joyful, joyous, lively, mirthful, sprightly, vivacious.

**bloat** vb dilate, distend, inflate, swell.

**block** vb arrest, bar, blockade, check, choke, close, hinder, impede, jam, obstruct, stop; form, mould, shape; brace, stiffen. *n lump, mass; blockhead, dunce, fool, simpleton; pulley, tackle; execution, scaffold; jam, obstruction, pack, stoppage.

**blood** n children, descendants, offspring, posterity, progeny; family, house, kin, kindred, line, relations; consanguinity, descent, kinship, lineage, relationship; courage, disposition, feelings, mettle, passion, spirit, temper.

**bloom** vb blossom, blow, flower; thrive, prosper. *n blossom, blossoming, blow, efflorescence, florescence, flowering; delicacy, delicateness, flush, freshness, heyday, prime, vigour; flush, glow, rose.

**blossom** vb bloom, blow, flower. *n bloom, blow, efflorescence, flower.

**blot** vb cancel, efface, erase, expunge, obliterate, rub out; blur, deface, disfigure, obscure, spot, stain, sully; disgrace, dishonour, tarnish. *n blemish, blur, erasure, spot, obliteration, stain; disgrace, dishonour, stigma.

**blow**[1] n bang, beat, buffet, dab, impact, knock, pat, punch, rap, slam, stroke, thump, wallop, buffet, impact; affliction, calamity, disaster, misfortune, setback.

**blow**[2] vb breathe, gasp, pant, puff; flow, move, scud, stream, waft. *n blast, gale, gust, squall, storm, wind.

**blue** adj azure, cerulean, cobalt, indigo, sapphire, ultramarine; ghastly, livid, pallid; dejected, depressed, dispirited, downcast, gloomy, glum, mopey, melancholic, melancholy, sad.

**bluff**[1] adj abrupt, blunt, blustering, coarse, frank, good-natured, open, outspoken; abrupt, precipitous, sheer, steep. *n cliff, headland, height.

**bluff**[2] vb deceive, defraud, lie, mislead. *n deceit, deception, feint, fraud, lie.

**blunder** vb err, flounder, mistake; stumble. *n error, fault, howler, mistake, solecism.

**blunt** adj dull, edgeless, obtuse, pointless, unsharpened; insensible, stolid, thick-witted; abrupt, bluff, downright, plain-spoken, outspoken, unceremonious, uncourtly. *vb deaden, dull, numb, weaken.

**blur** vb bedim, darken, dim, obscure; blemish, blot, spot, stain, sully, tarnish. *n blemish, blot, soil, spot, stain, tarnish; disgrace, smear.

**blush** vb colour, flush, glow, redden. *n bloom, flush, glow, colour, reddening, suffusion.

**bluster** vb boast, brag, bully, domineer, roar, swagger, swell, vaunt. *n boisterousness, noise, tumult, turbulence; braggadocio, bravado, boasting, gasconade, swaggering.

**board** n deal, panel, plank; diet, entertainment, fare, food, meals, provision, victuals; cabinet, conclave, committee, council; directorate; panel.

**boast** vb bluster, brag, crack, flourish, crow, vaunt. *n blustering, boasting, bombast, brag, braggadocio, bravado, bombast, swaggering, vaunt.

**bode** vb augur, betoken, forebode, foreshadow, foretell, portend, predict, prefigure, presage, prophesy.

**bodily** adj carnal, corporeal, fleshly, physical. *adv altogether, completely, entirely, wholly.

**body** n carcass, corpse, remains; stem, torso, trunk; aggregate, bulk, corpus, mass; being, individual, mortal creature, person; assemblage, association, band, company, corporation, corps, coterie, force, party, society, troop; consistency, substance, thickness.

**boggle** vb demur, falter, hang fire, hesitate, shrink, vacillate, waver.

**boil**[1] vb agitate, bubble, foam, froth, rage, seethe, simmer. *n ebullience, ebullition.

**boil**[2] (med) gathering, pimple, pustule, swelling, tumour.

**boisterous** adj loud, roaring, stormy; clamouring, loud, noisy, obstreperous, tumultuous, turbulent.

**bold** adj adventurous, audacious, courageous; brave, daring, dauntless, doughty, fearless, gallant, hardy, heroic, intrepid, mettlesome, manful, manly, spirited, stouthearted, undaunted, valiant, valorous; assured, confident, self-reliant; assuming, forward, impertinent, impudent, insolent, push, rude, saucy; conspicuous, projecting, prominent, striking; abrupt, precipitous, prominent, steep.

**bolster** vb aid, assist, defend, help, maintain, prop, stay, support. *n cushion, pillow; prop, support.

**bolt** vb abscond, flee, fly. *n arrow, dart, missile, shaft; thunderbolt.

**bombast** n bluster, brag, braggadocio, fustian, gasconade, mouthing, pomposity, rant.

**bond** vb bind, connect, fuse, glue, join. *adj captive, enslaved, enthralled, subjugated. *n band, cord, fastening, ligament, ligature, link, nexus; bondage, captivity, chains, constraint, fetters, prison, shackle; attachment, attraction, connection, coupling, link, tie, union; compact, obligation, pledge, promise.

**bondage** n captivity, confinement, enslavement, enthralment, peonage, serfdom, servitude, slavery, thraldom, vassalage.

**bonny** adj beautiful, handsome, fair, fine, pretty; airy, blithe, buoyant, buxom, cheerful, jolly, joyous, merry, playful, sporty, sprightly, winsome.

**bonus** n gift, honorarium, premium, reward, subsidy.

**booby** n blockhead, dunce, fool, idiot, simpleton.

**book** vb bespeak, engage, reserve; programme, schedule; list, log, record, register. *n booklet, brochure, compendium, handbook, manual, monograph, pamphlet, textbook, tract, treatise, volume, work.

**bookish** adj erudite, learned, literary, scholarly, studious.

**boon** adj convivial, jolly, jovial, hearty; close, intimate. *n benefaction, favour, grant, gift, present; advantage, benefit, blessing, good, privilege.

**boor** n bumpkin, clodhopper, clown, lout, lubber, peasant, rustic, swain.

**boorish** adj awkward, bearish, clownish, course, gruff, ill-bred, loutish, lubberly, rude, rustic, uncivilized, uncouth, uneducated.

**bootless** adj abortive, fruitless, futile, profitless, vain, worthless, useless.

**booty** n loot, pillage, plunder, spoil.

**border** vb bound, edge, fringe, line, march, rim, skirt, verge; abut, adjoin, butt, conjoin, connect, neighbour. *n brim, brink, edge, fringe, hem, margin, rim, skirt, verge; boundary, confine, frontier, limit, march, outskirts.

**bore**[1] vb annoy, fatigue, plague, tire, trouble, vex, weary, worry. *n bother, nuisance, pest, worry.

**bore**[2] vb drill, perforate, pierce, sink, tunnel. *n calibre, hole, shaft, tunnel.

**borrow** vb take and return, use temporarily; adopt, appropriate, imitate; dissemble, feign, simulate.

**boss**[1] vb emboss, stud; *n knob, protuberance, stud.

**boss**[2] vb command, direct, employ, run. *n employer, foreman, master, overseer, superintendent.

**botch** vb blunder, bungle, cobble, mar, mend, mess, patch, spoil. *n blotch, pustule, sore; failure, miscarriage.

**bother** vb annoy, disturb, harass, molest, perplex, pester, plague, tease, trouble, vex, worry. *n annoyance, perplexity, plague, trouble, vexation.

**bottom** vb build, establish, found. *adj base, basic, ground, lowermost, lowest, nethermost, undermost. *n base, basis, foot, foundation, groundwork; dale, meadow, valley; buttocks, fundament, seat; dregs, grounds, lees, sediment.

**bounce** vb bound, jump, leap, rebound, recoil, spring. *n knock, thump; bound, jump, leap, spring, vault.

**bound**[1] adj assured, certain, decided, determined, resolute, resolved; confined, hampered, restricted, restrained; committed, contracted, engaged, pledged, promised; beholden, duty-bound, obligated, obliged.

**bound**[2] vb border, delimit, circumscribe, confine, demarcate, limit, restrict, terminate. *n boundary, confine, edge, limit, march, margin, periphery, term, verge.

**bound**[3] vb jump, leap, spring. *n bounce, jump, leap, spring, vault.

**boundary** n border, bourn, circuit, circumference, confine, limit, march, periphery, term, verge.

**boundless** adj endless, immeasurable, infinite, limitless, unbounded, unconfined, undefined, unlimited, vast.

**bountiful** adj beneficent, bounteous, generous, liberal, munificent, princely.

**bounty** n beneficence, benevolence, charity, donation, generosity, gift, kindness, premium, present, reward.

**bourn** n border, boundary, confine, limit; brook, burn, rill, rivulet, stream, torrent.

**bow**[1] n (naut) beak, prow, stem.

**bow**[2] vb arc, bend, buckle, crook, curve, droop, flex, yield; crush, depress, subdue; curtsy, genuflect, kowtow, submit. *n arc, bend, bilge, bulge, convex, curve, flexion; bob, curtsy, genuflection, greeting, homage, obeisance; coming out, debut, introduction; curtain call, encore.

**bowels** npl entrails, guts, insides, viscera; compassion, mercy, pity, sympathy, tenderness.

**box**[1] vb fight, hit, mill, spar. *n blow, buffet, fight, hit, spar.

**box**[2] vb barrel, crate, pack, parcel. *n case, chest, container, crate, portmanteau, trunk.

**boy** n lad, stripling, youth.

**brace** vb make tight, tighten; buttress, fortify, reinforce, shore, strengthen, support, truss. *n couple, pair; clamp, girder, prop, shore, stay, support, tie, truss.

**brag** vb bluster, boast, flourish, gasconade, vaunt.

**branch** vb diverge, fork, bifurcate, ramify, spread. *n bough, offset, limb, shoot, sprig, twig; arm, fork, ramification, spur; article, department, member, part, portion, section, subdivision.

**brand** vb denounce, stigmatize, mark. *n firebrand, torch; bolt, lightning flash; cachet, mark, stamp, tally; blot, reproach, stain, stigma.

**brave** vb dare, defy. *adj bold, courageous, fearless, heroic, intrepid, stalwart.

**bravery** n courage, daring, fearlessness, gallantry, valour.

**brawl** vb bicker, dispute, jangle, quarrel, squabble. *n broil, dispute, feud, fracas, fray, jangle, quarrel, row, scuffle, squabble, uproar, wrangle.

**brawny** adj athletic, lusty, muscular, powerful, robust, sinewy, stalwart, strapping, strong, sturdy.

**bray** vb clamour, hoot, roar, trumpet, vociferate. *n blare, crash, roar, shout.

**breach** n break, chasm, crack, disruption, fissure, flaw, fracture, opening, rent, rift, rupture; alienation, difference, disaffection, disagreement, split.

**bread** n aliment, diet, fare, food, nourishment, nutriment, provisions, regimen, victuals.

**break** vb crack, disrupt, fracture, part, rend, rive, sever; batter, burst, crush, shatter, smash, splinter; cashier, degrade, discard, discharge, dismiss; disobey, infringe, transgress, violate; intermit, interrupt, stop; disclose, open, unfold. *n aperture, breach, chasm, fissure, gap, rent, rip, rupture; break-up, crash, debacle.

**breast** vb face, oppose, resist, stem, withstand. *n bosom, chest, thorax; affections, conscience, heart; mammary gland, mammary organ, pap, udder.

**breath** n exhaling, inhaling, pant, sigh, respiration, whiff; animation, existence, life; pause, respite, rest; breathing space, instant, moment.

**breathe** vb live, exist; emit, exhale, give out; diffuse, express, indicate, manifest, show.

**breed** vb bear, beget, engender, hatch, produce; bring up, foster, nourish, nurture, raise, rear; discipline, educate, instruct, nurture, rear, school, teach, train; generate, originate. *n extraction, family, lineage, pedigree, progeny, race, strain.

**brevity** n briefness, compression, conciseness, curtness, pithiness, shortness, terseness, transiency.

**brew** vb concoct, contrive, devise, excite, foment, instigate, plot. *n beverage, concoction, drink, liquor, mixture, potation.

**bribe** vb buy, corrupt, influence, pay off, suborn. *n allurement, corruption, enticement, graft, pay-off, subornation.

**bridle** vb check, curb, control, govern, restrain. *n check, control, curb.

**brief** vb direct, give directions, instruct; capsulate, summarize, delineate, describe, draft, outline, sketch; (law) retain. *adj concise, curt, inconsiderable, laconic, pithy, short, succinct, terse; fleeting, momentary, short, temporary, transient. *n abstract, breviary, briefing, epitome, compendium, summary, syllabus; (law) precept, writ.

**brigand** n bandit, footpad, freebooter, gangster, highwayman, marauder, outlaw, robber, thug.

**bright** adj blazing, brilliant, dazzling, gleaming, glowing, light, luminous, radiant, shining, sparkling, sunny; clear, cloudless, lambent, lucid, transparent; famous, glorious, illustrious; acute, discerning, ingenious, intelligent, keen; auspicious, cheering, encouraging, exhilarating, favourable, inspiring, promising, propitious; cheerful, genial, happy, lively, merry, pleasant, smiling, vivacious.

**brilliant** adj beaming, bright, effulgent, gleaming, glistening, glittering, lustrous, radiant, resplendent, shining, sparkling splendid; admirable, celebrated, distinguished, famous, glorious, illustrious, re-nowned; dazzling, decided, prominent, signal, striking, unusual.

**brim** n border, brink, edge, rim, margin, skirt, verge; bank, border, coast, shore.

**bring** vb bear, convey, fetch; accompany, attend, conduct, convey, convoy, guide, lead; gain, get, obtain, procure, produce.

**brisk** adj active, alert, agile, lively, nimble, perky, quick, smart, spirited, spry.

**brittle** adj brash, breakable, crisp, crumbling, fragile, frangible, frail, shivery.

**broach** vb open, pierce, set; approach, break, hint, suggest; proclaim, publish, utter.

**broad** adj ample, expansive, extensive, large, spa-cious, sweeping, vast, wide; enlarged, hospitable, liberal, tolerant; diffused, open, spread; coarse, gross, indecent, indelicate, unrefined, vulgar.

**broaden** vb augment, enlarge, expand, extend, increase, spread, stretch, widen.

**broken** adj fractured, rent, ruptured, separated, severed, shattered, shivered, torn; exhausted, feeble, impaired, shaken, shattered, spent, wasted; defective, halting, hesitating, imperfect, stammering, stumbling; contrite, humble, lowly, penitent; abrupt, craggy, precipitous, rough.

**broker** n agent, factor, go-between, middleman.

**brood** vb incubate, sit. *n issue, offspring, progeny; breed, kind, line, lineage, sort, strain.

**brook** vb abide, bear, endure, suffer, tolerate. *n burn, beck, creek, rill, rivulet, run, streamlet.

**brotherhood** n association, clan, clique, coterie, fraternity, junta, society.

**brotherly** adj affectionate, amicable, cordial, friendly, kind.

**browbeat** vb bully, intimidate, overawe, overbear.

**bruise** vb contuse, crunch, squeeze; batter, break, maul, pound, pulverize; batter, deface, indent. *n blemish, contusion, swelling.

**brush**[1] n brushwood, bush, scrub, scrubwood, shrubs, thicket, wilderness.

**brush**[2] vb buff, clean, polish, swab, sweep, wipe; curry, groom, rub down; caress, flick, glance, graze, scrape, skim, touch. *n besom, broom; action, affair, collision, contest, conflict, encounter, engagement, fight, skirmish.

**brutal** adj barbaric, barbarous, brutish, cruel, fero-cious, inhuman, ruthless, savage; bearish, brusque, churlish, gruff, impolite, harsh, rude, rough, truculent, uncivil.

**brute** n barbarian, beast, monster, ogre, savage; animal, beast, creature. *adj carnal, mindless, physical; bestial, coarse, gross.

**bubble** vb boil, effervesce, foam. *n bead, blob, fluid, globule; bagatelle, trifle; cheat, delusion, hoax.

**buccaneer** n corsair, freebooter, pirate.

**buck** vb jump, leap. *n beau, blade, blood, dandy, fop, gallant, spark; male.

**bud** vb burgeon, germinate, push, shoot, sprout, vegetate. *n burgeon, gem, germ, gemmule, shoot, sprout.

**budget** vb allocate, cost, estimate. *n account, estimate, financial statement; assets, finances, funds, means, resources; bag, bundle, pack, packet, parcel, roll; assortment, batch, collection, lot, set, store.

**buffet**[1] vb beat, box, cuff, slap, smite, strike; resist, struggle against, *n blow, box, cuff, slap, strike;

**buffet**[2] n cupboard, sideboard; refreshment counter.

**buffoon** n antic, clown, droll, fool, harlequin, jester, mountebank.

**build** vb construct, erect, establish, fabricate, fashion, model, raise, rear. *n body, figure, form, frame, physique; construction, shape, structure.

**building** n construction, erection, fabrication; edifice, fabric, house, pile, substructure, structure,

**bulk** n dimension, magnitude, mass, size, volume; amplitude, bulkiness, massiveness; body, major-ity, mass.

**bully** vb browbeat, bulldoze, domineer, haze, hector, intimidate, overbear. *n blusterer, browbeater, bulldozer, hector, swaggerer, roisterer, tyrant.

**bulwark** n barrier, fortification, parapet, rampart, wall; palladium, safeguard, security.

**bump** vb collide, knock, strike, thump. *n blow, jar, jolt, knock, shock, thump; lump, protuberance, swelling.

**bunch** vb assemble, collect, crowd, group, herd, pack. *n bulge, bump, bundle, hump, knob, lump, protuberance; cluster, hand, fascicle; assortment, batch, collection, group, lot, parcel, set; knot, tuft.

**bundle** vb bale, pack, package, parcel, truss, wrap. *n bale, batch, bunch, collection, heap, pack, package, packet, parcel, pile, roll, truss.

**bungler** n botcher, duffer, fumbler, lout, lubber, mismanager, muddler.

**burden** vb encumber, grieve, load, oppress, overlay, overload, saddle, surcharge, try. *n capacity, cargo, freight, lading, load, tonnage, weight; affliction, charge, clog, encumbrance, impediment, grievance, sorrow, trial, trouble; drift, point, substance, tenor, surcharge.

**bureau** n chest of drawers, dresser; counting room, office.

**burial** n burying, entombment, inhumation, interment, sepulture.

**burlesque** vb ape, imitate, lampoon, mock, ridicule, satirize. *n caricature, extravaganza, parody, send-up, take-off, travesty.

**burn**[1] n beck, brook, gill, rill, rivulet, runnel, runlet, stream. water

**burn**[2] vb blaze, conflagrate, enflame, fire, flame, ignite, kindle, light, smoulder; cremate, incinerate; scald, scorch, singe; boil, broil, cook, roast, seethe, simmer, stew, swelter, toast; bronze, brown, sunburn, suntan, tan; bake, desiccate, dry, parch, sear, shrivel, wither; glow, incandesce, tingle, warm. *n scald, scorch, singe; sunburn.

**burning** adj aflame, fiery, hot, scorching; ardent, earnest, fervent, fervid, impassioned, intense.

**burnish** vb brighten, buff, furbish, polish, shine. *n glaze, gloss, patina, polish, shine.

**burst** vb break open, be rent, explode, shatter, split open. *adj broken, kaput, punctured, ruptured, shattered, split. *n break, breakage, breach, fracture, rupture; blast, blowout, blowup, discharge, detonation, explosion; spurt; blaze, flare, flash; cloudburst, downpour; bang, crack, crash, report, sound; fusillade, salvo, spray, volley, outburst, outbreak flare-up, blaze, eruption.

**bury** vb entomb, inearth, inhume, inter; conceal, hide, secrete, shroud.

**business** n calling, employment, occupation, profession, pursuit, vocation; commerce, dealing, trade, traffic; affair, concern, engagement, matter, transaction, undertaking; duty, function, office, task, work.

**bustle** vb fuss, hurry, scurry. *n ado, commotion, flurry, fuss, hurry, hustle, pother, stir, tumult.

**busy** vb devote, employ, engage, occupy, spend, work. *adj employed, engaged, occupied; active, assiduous, diligent, engrossed, industrious, sedulous, working; agile, brisk, nimble, spry, stirring; meddling, officious.

**but** conj except, excepting, further, howbeit, moreover, still, unless, yet. *adv all the same, even, notwithstanding, still, yet.

**butchery** n massacre, murder, slaughter.

**butt**[1] vb bunt, push, shove, shunt, strike; encroach, impose, interfere, intrude, invade, obtrude. *n buck, bunt, push, shove, shunt, thrust.

**butt**[2] n barrel, cask.

**butt**[3] n aim, goal, mark, object, point, target; dupe, gull, victim.

**butt**[4] vb abut, adjoin, conjoin, connect, neighbour. *n end, piece, remainder, stub, stump; buttocks, posterior, rump.

**buttonhole** vb bore, catch, detain in conversation, importune.

**buttress** vb brace, prop, shore, stay, support. *n brace, bulwark, prop, stay, support.

**buxom** adj comely, fresh, healthy, hearty, plump, rosy, ruddy, vigorous.

**byword** n adage, aphorism, apothegm, dictum, maxim, proverb, saying, saw.

# C

**cabal** vb conspire, intrigue, machinate, plot. * n clique, combination, confederacy, coterie, faction, gang, junta, league, party, set; conspiracy, intrigue, machination, plot.

**cabbalistic, cabalistic** adj dark, fanciful, mysterious, mystic, occult, secret.

**cabaret** n tavern, inn, public house, wine shop.

**cabin** n berth, bunk, cot, cottage, crib, dwelling, hovel, hut, shack, shanty, shed.

**cabinet** n apartment, boudoir, chamber, closet; case, davenport, desk, escritoire; council, ministry.

**cachinnation** n guffaw, laugh, laughter.

**cackle** vb giggle, laugh, snicker, titter; babble, chatter, gabble, palaver, prate, prattle, titter. * n babble, chatter, giggle, prate, prattle, snigger, titter.

**cacophonous** adj discordant, grating, harsh, inharmonious, jarring, raucous.

**cadaverous** adj bloodless, deathlike, ghastly, pale, pallid, wan.

**cage** vb confine, immure, imprison, incarcerate. * n coop, pen, pound.

**caitiff** adj base, craven, pusillanimous, rascally, recreant. *n coward, knave, miscreant, rascal, rogue, scoundrel; sneak, traitor, vagabond, villain, wretch.

**cajole** vb blandish, coax, flatter, jolly, wheedle; beguile, deceive, delude, entrap, inveigle, tempt.

**calamity** n adversity, affliction, blow, casualty, cataclysm, catastrophe, disaster, distress, downfall, evil, hardship, mischance, misery, misfortune, mishap, reverse, ruin, stroke, trial, visitation.

**calculate** vb cast, compute, count, estimate, figure, rate, reckon, weigh; tell.

**calculating** adj crafty, designing, scheming, selfish; careful, cautious, circumspect, far-sighted, politic, sagacious, wary.

**calefaction** n heating, warming; hotness, incandescence, warmth.

**calendar** n almanac, ephemeris, register; catalogue, list, schedule.

**calibre** n bore, capacity, diameter, gauge; ability, capacity, endowment, faculty, gifts, parts, scope, talent.

**call** vb christen, denominate, designate, dub, entitle, name, phrase, style, term; bid, invite, summons; assemble, convene, convoke, muster; cry, exclaim; arouse, awaken, proclaim, rouse, shout, waken; appoint, elect, ordain. *n cry, outcry, voice; appeal, invitation, summons; claim, demand, summons; appointment, election, invitation.

**calling** n business, craft, employment, occupation, profession, pursuit, trade.

**callous** adj hard, hardened, indurated; apathetic, dull, indifferent, insensible, inured, obdurate, obtuse, sluggish, torpid, unfeeling, unsusceptible.

**callow** adj naked, unfeathered, unfledged; green, immature, inexperienced, sappy, silly, soft, unfledged, unsophisticated.

**calm** vb allay, becalm, compose, hush, lull, smooth, still, tranquillize; alleviate, appease, assuage, moderate, mollify, pacify, quiet, soften, soothe, tranquillize. *adj halcyon, mild, peaceful, placid, quiet, reposeful, serene, smooth, still, tranquil, unruffled; collected, cool, composed, controlled, impassive, imperturbable, sedate, self-possessed, undisturbed, unperturbed, unruffled, untroubled. *n lull; equanimity, peace, placidity, quiet, repose, serenity, stillness, tranquillity.

**calorific** adj heat, heat-producing.

**calumniate** vb abuse, asperse, backbite, blacken, blemish, defame, discredit, disparage, lampoon, libel, malign, revile, slander, traduce, vilify.

**calumny** n abuses, aspersion, backbiting, defamation, detraction, evil-speaking, insult, libel, lying, obloquy, slander, vilification, vituperation.

**camarilla** n cabal, clique, junta, ring.

**camber** vb arch, bend, curve. *n arch, arching, convexity.

**camp**[1] vb bivouac, encamp, lodge, pitch, tent. *n bivouac, cantonment, encampment, laager; cabal, circle, clique, coterie, faction, group, junta, party, ring, set.

**camp**[2] adj affected, artificial, effeminate, exaggerated, mannered, theatrical.

**canaille** n mob, populace, proletariat, rabble, ragbag, riffraff, scum.

**canal** n channel, duct, pipe, tube.

**cancel** vb blot, efface, erase, expunge, obliterate; abrogate, annul, countermand, nullify, quash, repeal, rescind, revoke.

**candelabrum** n candlestick, chandelier, lustre.

**candid** adj fair, impartial, just, unbiased, unprejudiced; artless, frank, free, guileless, honest, honourable, ingenuous, naive, open, plain, sincere, straightforward.

**candidate** n applicant, aspirant, claimant, competitor, probationer.

**candour** n fairness, impartiality, justice; artlessness, frankness, guilelessness, honesty, ingenuousness, openness, simplicity, sincerity, straightforwardness, truthfulness.

**canker** vb corrode, erode, rot, rust, waste; blight, consume, corrupt, embitter, envenom, infect, poison, sour. *n gangrene, rot; bale, bane, blight, corruption, infection, irritation.

**canon** n catalogue, criterion, formula, formulary, law, regulation, rule, standard, statute.

**canorous** adj musical, tuneful.

**cant**[1] vb whine. *adj current, partisan, popular, rote, routine, set; argotic, slangy. *n hypocrisy; argot, jargon, lingo, slang.

**cant**[2] vb bevel, incline, list, slant, tilt, turn. *n bevel, inclination, leaning, list, pitch, slant, tilt, turn.

**cantankerous** adj contumacious, crabbed, cross-grained, dogged, headstrong, heady, intractable, obdurate, obstinate, perverse, refractory, stiff, stubborn, wilful, unyielding.

**canting** adj affected, pious, sanctimonious, whining.

**canvas** n burlap, scrim, tarpaulin.

**canvass** vb discuss, dispute; analyze, consider, examine, investigate, review, scrutinize, sift, study; campaign, electioneer, solicit votes. *n debate, discussion, dispute; examination, scrutiny, sifting.

**canyon** n gorge, gulch, ravine.

**cap** vb cover, surmount; complete, crown, finish; exceed, overtop, surpass, transcend; match, parallel, pattern. *n beret, head-cover, head-dress; acme, chief, crown, head, peak, perfection, pitch, summit, top.

**capability** n ability, brains, calibre, capableness, capacity, competency, efficiency, faculty, force, power, scope, skill.

**capable** adj adapted, fitted, qualified, suited; able, accomplished, clever, competent, efficient, gifted, ingenious, intelligent, sagacious, skilful.

**capacious** adj ample, broad, comprehensive, expanded, extensive, large, roomy, spacious, wide.

**capacitate** vb enable, qualify.

**capacity** n amplitude, dimensions, magnitude, volume; aptitude, aptness, brains, calibre, discernment, faculty, forte, genius, gift, parts, power, talent, turn, wit; ability, capability, calibre, cleverness, competency, efficiency, skill; character, charge, function, office, position, post, province, service, sphere.

**caparison** vb accoutre, costume, equip, outfit, rig out. *n accoutrements, armour, get-up, harness, housing, livery, outfit, panoply, tack, tackle, trappings, turnout.

**caper** vb bound, caracole, frisk, gambol, hop, leap, prank, romp, skip, spring. *n bound, dance, gambol, frisk, hop, jump, leap, prance, romp, skip.

**capillary** adj delicate, fine, minute, slender.

**capital** adj cardinal, chief, essential, important, leading, main, major, pre-eminent, principal, prominent; fatal; excellent, first-class, first-rate, good, prime, splendid. *n chief city, metropolis, seat; money, estate, investments, shares, stock.

**caprice** n crotchet, fancy, fickleness, freak, humour, inconstancy, maggot, phantasy, quirk, vagary, whim, whimsy.

**capricious** adj changeable, crotchety, fanciful, fantastical, fickle, fitful, freakish, humoursome, odd, puckish, queer, uncertain, variable, wayward, whimsical.

**capsize** vb overturn, upset.

**capsule** n case, covering, envelope, sheath, shell, wrapper; pericarp, pod, seed-vessel.

**captain** vb command, direct, head, lead, manage, officer, preside. *n chief, chieftain, commander, leader, master, officer, soldier, warrior.

**captious** adj carping, caviling, censorious, critical, fault-finding, hypercritical; acrimonious, cantankerous, contentious, crabbed, cross, snappish, snarling, splenetic, testy, touchy, waspish; ensnaring, insidious.

**captivate** vb allure, attract, bewitch, catch, capture, charm, enamour, enchant, enthral, fascinate, gain, hypnotize, infatuate, win.

**captivity** n confinement, durance, duress, imprisonment; bondage, enthralment, servitude, slavery, subjection, thraldom, vassalage.

**capture** vb apprehend, arrest, catch, seize. *n apprehension, arrest, catch, catching, imprisonment; seizure; bag, prize.

**carcass** n body, cadaver, corpse, corse, remains.

**cardinal** adj capital, central, chief, essential, first, important, leading, main, pre-eminent, primary, principal, vital.

**care** n anxiety, concern, perplexity, trouble, solicitude, worry; attention, carefulness, caution, circumspection, heed, regard, vigilance, wariness, watchfulness; charge, custody, guardianship, keep, oversight, superintendence, ward; burden, charge, concern, responsibility.

**careful** adj anxious, solicitous, concerned, troubled, uneasy; attentive, heedful, mindful, regardful, thoughtful; cautious, canny, circumspect, discreet, leery, vigilant, watchful.

**careless** adj carefree, nonchalant, unapprehensive, undisturbed, unperplexed, unsolicitous, untroubled; disregardful, heedless, inattentive, incautious, inconsiderate, neglectful, negligent, regardless, remiss, thoughtless, unobservant, unconcerned, unconsidered, unmindful, unthinking.

**carelessness** n heedlessness, inadvertence, inattention, inconsiderateness, neglect, negligence, remissness, slackness, thoughtlessness, unconcern.

**caress** vb coddle, cuddle, cosset, embrace, fondle, hug, kiss, pet. *n cuddle, embrace, fondling, hug, kiss.

**caressing** n blandishment, dalliance, endearment, fondling.

**cargo** n freight, lading. load.

**caricature** vb burlesque, parody, send-up, take-off, travesty. *n burlesque, farce, ludicrous, parody, representation, take-off, travesty.

**carious** adj decayed, mortified, putrid, rotten, ulcerated.

**cark** vb annoy, fret, grieve, harass, perplex, worry.

**carnage** n bloodshed, butchery, havoc, massacre, murder, slaughter.

**carnal** adj animal, concupiscent, fleshly, lascivious, lecherous, lewd, libidinous, lubricous, lustful, salacious, sensual, voluptuous; bodily, earthy, mundane. natural, secular, temporal, unregenerate, unspiritual.

**carol** vb chant, hum, sing, warble. *n canticle, chorus, ditty, hymn, lay, song, warble.

**carousal** n banquet, entertainment, feast, festival, merry-making, regale; bacchanal, carouse, debauch, jamboree, jollification, orgy, revel, revelling, revelry, saturnalia, spree, wassail.

**carp** vb cavil, censure, criticize, fault.

**carping** adj captious, cavilling, censorious, hypercritical. *n cavil, censure, fault-finding, hypercriticism.

**carriage** n conveyance, vehicle; air, bearing, behaviour, conduct, demeanour, deportment, front, mien, port.

**carry** vb bear, convey, transfer, transmit, transport; impel, push forward, urge; accomplish, compass, effect, gain, secure; bear up, support, sustain; infer, involve, imply, import, signify.

**cart** n conveyance, tumbril, van, vehicle, wagon.

**carte-blanche** n authority, power.

**carve** vb chisel, cut, divide, engrave, grave, hack, hew, indent, incise, sculpt, sculpture; fashion, form, mould, shape.

**cascade** vb cataract, descend, drop, engulf, fall, inundate, overflow, plunge, tumble. *n cataract, fall, falls, force, linn, waterfall.

**case**[1] vb cover, encase, enclose, envelop, protect, wrap; box, pack. *n capsule, covering, sheathe; box, cabinet, container, holder, receptacle.

**case**[2] n condition, plight, predicament, situation, state; example, instance, occurrence; circumstance, condition, contingency, event; action, argument, cause, lawsuit, process, suit, trial.

**case-hardened** adj hardened, indurated, steeled; brazen, brazen-faced, obdurate, reprobate.

**cash** n banknotes, bullion, coin, currency, money, payment, specie.

**cashier** vb break, discard, discharge, dismiss.

**cast** vb fling, hurl, pitch, send, shy, sling, throw, toss; drive, force, impel, thrust; lay aside, put off, shed; calculate, compute, reckon; communicate, diffuse, impart, shed, throw. *n fling, throw, toss; shade, tinge, tint, touch; air, character, look, manner, mien, style, tone, turn; form, mould.

**castaway** adj abandoned, cast-off, discarded, rejected. *n derelict, outcast, reprobate, vagabond.

**caste** n class, grade, lineage, order, race, rank, species, status.

**castigate** vb beat, chastise, flog, lambaste, lash, thrash, whip; chaste, correct, discipline, punish; criticize, flagellate, upbraid.

**castle** n citadel, fortress, stronghold.

**castrate** vb caponize, emasculate, geld; mortify, subdue, suppress, weaken.

**casual** adj accidental, contingent, fortuitous, incidental, irregular, occasional, random, uncertain, unforeseen, unintentional, unpremeditated; informal, relaxed.

**casualty** n chance, contingency, fortuity, mishap; accident, catastrophe, disaster, mischance, misfortune.

**cat** n grimalkin, kitten, puss, tabby, tomcat.

**cataclysm** n deluge, flood, inundation; disaster, upheaval.

**catacomb** n crypt, tomb, vault.

**catalogue** vb alphabetize, categorize, chronicle, class, classify, codify, file, index, list, record, tabulate. *n enumeration, index, inventory, invoice, list, record, register, roll, schedule.

**cataract** n cascade, fall, waterfall.

**catastrophe** n conclusion, consummation, denouement, end, finale, issue, termination, upshot; adversity, blow, calamity, cataclysm, debacle, disaster, ill, misfortune, mischance, mishap, trial, trouble.

**catch** vb clutch, grasp, gripe, nab, seize, snatch; apprehend, arrest, capture; overtake; enmesh, ensnare, entangle, entrap, lime, net; bewitch, captivate, charm, enchant, fascinate, win; surprise, take unawares. *n arrest, capture, seizure; bag, find, haul, plum, prize; drawback, fault, hitch, obstacle, rub, snag; captive, conquest.

**catching** adj communicable, contagious, infectious, pestiferous, pestilential; attractive, captivating, charming, enchanting, fascinating, taking, winning, winsome.

**catechize** adj examine, interrogate, question, quiz.

**catechumen** n convert, disciple, learner, neophyte, novice, proselyte, pupil, tyro.

**categorical** adj absolute, direct, downright, emphatic, explicit, express, positive, unconditional, unqualified, unreserved, utter.

**category** n class, division, head, heading, list, order, rank, sort.

**catenation** n conjunction, connection, union.

**cater** vb feed, provide, purvey.

**cathartic** adj abstergent, aperient, cleansing, evacuant, laxative, purgative. *n aperient, laxative, physic, purgative, purge.

**catholic** adj general, universal, world-wide; charitable, liberal, tolerant, unbigoted, unexclusive, unsectarian.

**cause** vb breed, create, originate, produce; effect, effectuate, occasion, produce. *n agent, creator, mainspring, origin, original, producer, source, spring; account, agency, consideration, ground, incentive, incitement, inducement, motive, reason; aim, end, object, purpose; action, case, suit, trial.

**caustic** adj acrid, cathartic, consuming, corroding, corrosive, eating, erosive, mordant, virulent; biting, bitter, burning, cutting, sarcastic, satirical, scalding, scathing, severe, sharp, stinging.

**caution** vb admonish, forewarn, warn. *n care, carefulness, circumspection, discretion, forethought, heed, heedfulness, providence, prudence, wariness, vigilance, watchfulness; admonition, advice, counsel, injunction, warning.

**cautious** adj careful, chary, circumspect, discreet, heedful, prudent, wary, vigilant, wary, watchful.

**cavalier** adj arrogant, curt, disdainful, haughty, insolent, scornful, supercilious; debonair, gallant, gay. *n chevalier, equestrian, horseman, horse-soldier, knight.

**cave** n cavern, cavity, den, grot, grotto.

**cavil** vb carp, censure, hypercriticize, object.

**cavilling** adj captious, carping, censorious, critical, hypercritical.

**cavity** n hollow, pocket, vacuole, void.

**cease** vb desist, intermit, pause, refrain, stay, stop; fail; discontinue, end, quit, terminate.

**ceaseless** adj continual, continuous, incessant, unceasing, unintermitting, uninterrupted, unremitting; endless, eternal, everlasting, perpetual.

**cede** vb abandon, abdicate, relinquish, resign, surrender, transfer, yield; convey, grant.

**celebrate** vb applaud, bless, commend, emblazon, extol, glorify, laud, magnify, praise, trumpet; commemorate, honour, keep, observe; solemnize.

**celebrated** adj distinguished, eminent, famed, famous, glorious, illustrious, notable, renowned.

**celebrity** n credit, distinction, eminence, fame, glory, honour, renown, reputation, repute; lion, notable, star.

**celerity** n fleetness, haste, quickness, rapidity, speed, swiftness, velocity.

**celestial** adj empyreal, empyrean; angelic, divine, god-like, heavenly, seraphic, supernal, supernatural.

**celibate** adj single, unmarried. *n bachelor, single, virgin.

**cellular** adj alveolate, honeycombed.

**cement** vb attach, bind, join, combine, connect, solder, unite, weld; cohere, stick. *n glue, paste, mortar, solder.

**cemetery** n burial-ground, burying-ground, churchyard, god's acre, graveyard, necropolis.

**censor** vb blue-pencil, bowdlerize, cut, edit, expurgate; classify, kill, quash, squash, suppress. *n caviller, censurer, faultfinder.

**censorious** adj captious, carping, caviling, condemnatory, faultfinding, hypercritical, severe.

**censure** vb abuse, blame, chide, condemn, rebuke, reprehend, reprimand, reproach, reprobate, reprove, scold, upbraid. *n animadversion, blame, condemnation, criticism, disapprobation, disapproval, rebuke, remonstrance, reprehension, reproach, reproof, stricture.

**ceremonious** adj civil, courtly, lofty, stately; formal, studied; exact, formal, punctilious, precise, starched, stiff.

**ceremony** n ceremonial, etiquette, form, formality, observance, solemnity, rite; parade, pomp, show, stateliness.

**certain** adj absolute, incontestable, incontrovertible, indisputable, indubitable, positive, undeniable, undisputed, unquestionable, unquestioned; assured, confident, sure, undoubting; infallible, never-failing, unfailing; actual, existing, real; constant, determinate, fixed, settled, stated.

**certainty** n indubitability, indubitableness, inevitableness, inevitability, surety, unquestionability, unquestionableness; assurance, assuredness, certitude, confidence, conviction, surety.

**certify** vb attest, notify, testify, vouch; ascertain, determine, verify, show.

**cerulean** adj azure, blue, sky-blue.

**cessation** n ceasing, discontinuance, intermission, pause, remission, respite, rest, stop, stoppage, suspension.

**cession** n abandonment, capitulation, ceding, concession, conveyance, grant, relinquishement, renunciation, surrender, yielding.

**chafe** vb rub; anger, annoy, chagrin, enrage, exasperate, fret, gall, incense, irritate, nettle, offend, provoke, ruffle, tease, vex; fret, fume, rage.

**chaff** vb banter, deride, jeer, mock, rally, ridicule, scoff. *n glumes, hulls, husks; refuse, rubbish, trash, waste.

**chaffer** n bargain, haggle, higgle, negotiate.

**chagrin** vb annoy, chafe, displease, irritate, mortify, provoke, vex. *n annoyance, displeasure, disquiet, dissatisfaction, fretfulness, humiliation, ill-humour, irritation, mortification, spleen, vexation.

**chain** vb bind, confine, fetter, manacle, restrain, shackle, trammel; enslave. *n bond, fetter, manacle, shackle, union.

**chalice** n bowl, cup, goblet.

**challenge** vb brave, call out, dare, defy, dispute; demand, require. *n defiance, interrogation, question; exception, objection.

**chamber** n apartment, hall, room; cavity, hollow.

**champion** vb advocate, defend, uphold. *n defender, promoter, protector, vindicator; belt-holder, hero, victor, warrior, winner.

**chance** vb befall, betide, happen, occur. *adj accidental, adventitious, casual, fortuitous, incidental, unexpected, unforeseen. *n accident, cast, fortuity, fortune, hap, luck; contingency, possibility; occasion, opening, opportunity; contingency, fortuity, gamble, peradventure, uncertainty; hazard, jeopardy, peril, risk.

**change** vb alter, fluctuate, modify, vary; displace, remove, replace, shift, substitute; barter, commute, exchange. *n alteration, mutation, revolution, transition, transmutation, turning, variance, variation, innovation, novelty, variety, vicissitude.

**changeable** adj alterable, inconstant, modifiable, mutable, uncertain, unsettled, unstable, unsteadfast, unsteady, variable, variant; capricious, fickle, fitful, flighty, giddy, mercurial, vacillating, volatile, wavering.

**changeless** adj abiding, consistent, constant, fixed, immutable, permanent, regular, reliable, resolute, settled, stationary, unalterable, unchanging.

**channel** vb chamfer, cut, flute, groove. *n canal, conduit, duct, passage; aqueduct, canal, chute, drain, flume, furrow; chamfer, groove, fluting, furrow, gutter.

**chant** vb carol, sing, warble; intone, recite; canticle, song.

**chaos** n anarchy, confusion, disorder.

**chapfallen** adj blue, crest-fallen, dejected, depressed, despondent, discouraged, disheartened, dispirited, downcast, downhearted, low-spirited, melancholy, sad.

**chaplet** n coronal, garland, wreath.

**char** vb burn, scorch.

**character** n emblem, figure, hieroglyph, ideograph, letter, mark, sign, symbol; bent, constitution, cast, disposition, nature, quality; individual, original, person, personage; reputation, repute; nature, traits; eccentric, trait.

**characteristic** adj distinctive, peculiar, singular, special, specific, typical. *n attribute, feature, idiosyncrasy, lineament, mark, peculiarity, quality, trait.

**charge** vb burden, encumber, freight, lade, load; entrust; ascribe, impute, lay; accuse, arraign, blame, criminate, impeach, inculpate, indict, involve; bid, command, exhort, enjoin, order, require, tax; assault, attack bear down. *n burden, cargo, freight, lading, load; care, custody, keeping, management, ward; commission, duty, employment, office, trust; responsibility, trust; command, direction, injunction, mandate, order, precept; exhortation, instruction; cost, debit, expense, expenditure, outlay; price, sum; assault, attack, encounter, onset, onslaught.

**charger** n dish, platter; mount, steed, war-horse.

**charily** adv carefully, cautiously, distrustfully, prudently, sparingly, suspiciously, warily.

**charitable** adj beneficial, beneficent, benignant, bountiful, generous, kind, liberal, open-handed; candid, considerate, lenient, mild.

**charity** n benevolence, benignity, fellow-feeling, good-nature, goodwill, kind-heartedness, kindness, tenderheartedness; beneficence, bounty, generosity, humanity, philanthropy. liberality.

**charlatan** n cheat, empiric, impostor, mountebank, pretender, quack.

**charm** vb allure, attract, becharm, bewitch, captivate, catch, delight, enamour, enchain, enchant, enrapture, enravish, fascinate, transport, win. *n enchantment, incantation, magic, necromancy, sorcery, spell, witchery; amulet, talisman; allurement, attraction, attractiveness, fascination.

**charming** adj bewitching, captivating, delightful, enchanting, enrapturing, fascinating, lovely.

**charter** vb incorporate; hire, let. *n franchise, immunity, liberty, prerogation, privilege, right; bond, deed, indenture, instrument, prerogative.

**chary** adj careful, cautious, circumspect, shy, wary; abstemious, careful, choice, economical, frugal, provident, saving, sparing, temperate, thrifty, unwasteful.

**chase** vb follow, hunt, pursue, track; emboss. *n course, field-sport, hunt, hunting.

**chasm** n cavity, cleft, fissure, gap, hollow, hiatus, opening.

**chaste** adj clean, continent, innocent, modest, pure, pure-minded, undefiled, virtuous; chastened, pure, simple, unaffected, uncorrupt.

**chasten** vb correct, humble; purify, refine, render, subdue.

**chastening** n chastisement, correction, discipline, humbling.

**chastise** vb castigate, correct, flog, lash, punish, whip; chasten, correct, discipline, humble, punish, subdue.

**chastity** n abstinence, celibacy, continence, innocence, modesty, pure-mindedness, purity, virtue; cleanness, decency; chasteness, refinement, restrainedness, simplicity, sobriety, unaffectedness.

**chat** vb babble, chatter, confabulate, gossip, prate, prattle. *n chit-chat, confabulation, conversation, gossip, prattle.

**chatter** vb babble, chat, confabulate, gossip, prate, prattle. *n babble, chat, gabble, jabber, patter, prattle.

**cheap** adj inexpensive, low-priced; common, indifferent, inferior, mean, meretricious, paltry, poor.

**cheapen** vb belittle, depreciate.

**cheat** vb cozen, deceive, dissemble, juggle, shuffle; bamboozle, befool, beguile, cajole, circumvent, deceive, defraud, chouse, delude, dupe, ensnare, entrap, fool, gammon, gull, hoax, hoodwink, inveigle, jockey, mislead, outwit, overreach, trick. *n artifice, beguilement, blind, catch, chouse, deceit, deception, fraud, imposition, imposture, juggle, pitfall, snare, stratagem, swindle, trap, trick, wile; counterfeit, deception, delusion, illusion, mockery, paste, sham, tinsel; beguiler, charlatan, cheater, cozener, impostor, jockey, knave, mountebank, trickster, rogue, render, sharper, seizer, shuffler, swindler, taker, tearer.

**check** vb block, bridle, control, counteract, curb, hinder, obstruct, repress, restrain; chide, rebuke, reprimand, reprove. *n bar, barrier, block, brake, bridle, clog, control, curb, damper, hindrance, impediment, interference, obstacle, obstruction, rebuff, repression, restraint, stop, stopper.

**cheep** vb chirp, creak, peep, pipe, squeak.

**cheer** vb animate, encourage, enliven, exhilarate, gladden, incite, inspirit; comfort, console, solace; applaud, clap. *n cheerfulness, gaiety, gladness, glee, hilarity, jollity, joy, merriment, mirth; entertainment, food, provision, repast, viands, victuals; acclamation, hurrah, huzza.

**cheerful** adj animated, airy, blithe, buoyant, cheery, gay, glad, gleeful, happy, joyful, jocund, jolly, joyous, light-hearted, lightsome, lively, merry, mirthful, sprightly, sunny; animating, cheering, cheery, encouraging, enlivening, glad, gladdening, gladsome, grateful, inspiriting, jocund, pleasant.

**cheerless** adj dark, dejected, desolate, despondent, disconsolate, discouraged, dismal, doleful, dreary, forlorn, gloomy, joyless, low-spirited, lugubrious, melancholy, mournful, rueful, sad, sombre, spiritless, woe-begone.

**cherish** vb comfort, foster, nourish, nurse, nurture, support, sustain; treasure; encourage, entertain, indulge, harbour.

**chest** n box, case, coffer; breast, thorax, trunk.

**chew** vb crunch, manducate, masticate, munch; bite, champ, gnaw; meditate, ruminate.

**chicanery** n chicane, deception, duplicity, intrigue, intriguing, sophistication, sophistry, stratagems, tergiversation, trickery, wiles, wire-pulling.

**chide** vb admonish, blame, censure, rebuke, reprimand, reprove, scold, upbraid; chafe, clamour, fret, fume, scold.

**chief** adj first, foremost, headmost, leading, master, supereminent, supreme, top; capital, cardinal, especial, essential, grand, great, main, master, paramount, prime, principal, supreme, vital. *n chieftain, commander; head, leader.

**chiffonier** n cabinet, sideboard.

**child** n babe, baby, bairn, bantling, brat, chit, infant, nursling, suckling, wean; issue, offspring, progeny.

**childbirth** n child-bearing, delivery, labour, parturition, travail.

**childish** adj infantile, juvenile, puerile, tender, young; foolish, frivolous, silly, trifling, weak.

**childlike** adj docile, dutiful, gentle, meek, obedient, submissive; confiding, guileless, ingenuous, innocent, simple, trustful, uncrafty.

**chill** vb dampen, depress, deject, discourage, dishearten. *adj bleak, chilly, cold, frigid, gelid. *n chilliness, cold, coldness, frigidity; ague, rigour, shiver; damp, depression.

**chime** vb accord, harmonize. *n accord, consonance.

**chimera** n crochet, delusion, dream, fantasy, hallucination, illusion, phantom.

**chimerical** adj delusive, fanciful, fantastic, illusory, imaginary, quixotic, shadowy, unfounded, visionary, wild.

**chink**[1] vb cleave, crack, fissure, crevasse, incise, split,

slit. *n aperture, cleft, crack, cranny, crevice, fissure, gap, opening, slit.

**chink**[2] vb, n jingle, clink, ring, ting, tink, tinkle.

**chip** vb flake, fragment, hew, pare, scrape. *n flake, fragment, paring, scrap.

**chirp** vb cheep, chirrup, peep, twitter.

**chirrup** vb animate, cheer, encourage, inspirit.

**chisel** vb carve, cut, gouge, sculpt, sculpture.

**chivalrous** adj adventurous, bold, brave, chivalric, gallant, knightly, valiant, warlike; gallant, generous, high-minded, magnanimous.

**chivalry** n knighthood, knight-errantry; courtesy, gallantry, politeness; courage, valour.

**choice** adj excellent, exquisite, precious, rare, select, superior, uncommon, unusual, valuable; careful, chary, frugal, sparing. *n alternative, election, option, selection; favourite, pick, preference.

**choke** vb gag, smother, stifle, strangle, suffocate, throttle; overcome, overpower, smother, suppress; bar, block, close, obstruct, stop.

**choleric** adj angry, fiery, hasty, hot, fiery, irascible, irritable, passionate, petulant, testy, touchy, waspish.

**choose** vb adopt, co-opt, cull, designate, elect, pick, predestine, prefer, select.

**chop** vb cut, hack, hew; mince; shift, veer. *n slice; brand, quality; chap, jaw.

**chouse** vb bamboozle, beguile, cheat, circumvent, cozen, deceive, defraud, delude, dupe, gull, hoodwink, overreach, swindle, trick, victimize. *n cully, dupe, gull, simpleton, tool; artifice, cheat, circumvention, deceit, deception, delusion, double-dealing, fraud, imposition, imposture, ruse, stratagem, trick, wile.

**christen** vb baptize; call, dub, denominate, designate, entitle, name, style, term, title.

**chronic** adj confirmed, continuing, deep-seated, inveterate, rooted.

**chronicle** vb narrate, record, register. *n diary, journal, register; account, annals, history, narration, recital, record.

**chuckle** vb crow, exult, giggle, laugh, snigger, titter. *n giggle, laughter, snigger, titter.

**chum** n buddy, companion, comrade, crony, friend, mate, pal.

**churl** n boor, bumpkin, clodhopper, clown, countryman, lout, peasant, ploughman, rustic; curmudgeon, hunks, miser, niggard, scrimp, skinflint.

**churlish** adj brusque, brutish, cynical, harsh, impolite, rough, rude, snappish, snarling, surly, uncivil, waspish; crabbed, ill-tempered, morose, sullen; close, close-fisted, illiberal, mean, miserly, niggardly, penurious, stingy.

**churn** vb agitate, jostle.

**cicatrice** n cicatrix, mark, scar, seam.

**cicesbeo** n beau, escort, gallant, gigolo.

**cincture** n band, belt, cestos, cestus, girdle.

**cipher** n naught, nothing, zero; character, device, monogram, symbol; nobody, nonentity.

**circle** vb compass, encircle, encompass, gird, girdle, ring; gyrate, revolve, rotate, round, turn. *n circlet, corona, gyre, hoop, ring, rondure; circumference, cordon, periphery; ball, globe, orb, sphere; compass, enclosure; class, clique, company, coterie, fraternity, set, society; bounds, circuit, compass, field, province, range, region, sphere.

**circuit** n ambit, circumambience, circumambiency, cycle, revolution, turn; bounds, district, field, province, range, region, space, sphere, tract; boundary, compass; course, detour, perambulation, round, tour.

**circuitous** adj ambiguous, devious, indirect, roundabout, tortuous, turning, winding.

**circulate** vb diffuse, disseminate, promulgate, propagate, publish, spread.

**circumference** n bound, boundary, circuit, girth, outline, perimeter, periphery.

**circumlocution** n circuitousness, obliqueness, periphrase, periphrasis, verbosity, wordiness.

**circumscribe** vb bound, define, encircle, enclose, encompass, limit, surround; confine, restrict.

**circumspect** adj attentive, careful, cautious, considerate, discreet, heedful, judicious, observant, prudent, vigilant, wary, watchful.

**circumstance** n accident, incident; condition, detail, event, fact, happening, occurrence, position, situation.

**circumstantial** adj detailed, particular; indirect, inferential, presumptive.

**circumvent** vb check, checkmate, outgeneral, thwart; bamboozle, beguile, cheat, chouse, cozen, deceive, defraud, delude, dupe, gull, hoodwink, inveigle, mislead, outwit, overreach, trick.

**circumvention** n cheat, cheating, chicanery, deceit, deception, duplicity, fraud, guile, imposition, imposture, indirection, trickery, wiles.

**cistern** n basin, pond, reservoir, tank.

**citation** n excerpt, extract, quotation; enumeration, mention, quotation, quoting.

**cite** vb adduce, enumerate, extract, mention, name, quote; call, summon.

**citizen** n burgess, burgher, denizen, dweller, freeman, inhabitant, resident, subject, townsman.

**civil** adj civic, municipal, political; domestic; accommodating, affable, civilized, complaisant, courteous, courtly, debonair, easy, gracious, obliging, polished, polite, refined, suave, urbane, well-bred, well-mannered.

**civility** n affability, amiability, complaisance, courteousness, courtesy, good-breeding, politeness, suavity, urbanity.

**civilize** vb cultivate, educate, enlighten, humanize, improve, polish, refine.

**claim** vb ask, assert, challenge, demand, exact, require. *n call, demand, lien, requisition; pretension, privilege, right, title.

**clammy** adj adhesive, dauby, glutinous, gummy, ropy, smeary, sticky, viscid, viscous; close, damp, dank, moist, sticky, sweaty.

**clamour** vb shout, vociferate. *n blare, din, exclamation, hullabaloo, noise, outcry, uproar, vociferation.

**clan** n family, phratry, race, sect, tribe; band, brotherhood, clique, coterie, fraternity, gang, set, society, sodality.

**clandestine** adj concealed, covert, fraudulent, furtive, hidden, private, secret, sly, stealthy, surreptitious, underhand.

**clap** vb pat, slap, strike; force, slam; applaud, cheer. *n blow, knock, slap; bang, burst, explosion, peal, slam.

**clarify** vb cleanse, clear, depurate, purify, strain.

**clash** vb collide, crash, strike; clang, clank, clatter, crash, rattle; contend, disagree, interfere. *n collision; clang, clangour, clank, clashing, clatter, crash, rattle; contradiction, disagreement, interference, jar, jarring, opposition.

**clasp** vb clutch, entwine, grasp, grapple, grip, seize; embrace, enfold, fold, hug. *n buckle, catch, hasp, hook; embrace, hug.

**class** vb arrange, classify, dispose, distribute, range, rank. *n form, grade, order, rank, status; group, seminar; breed, kind, sort; category, collection, denomination, division, group, head.

**classical** adj first-rate, master, masterly, model, standard; Greek, Latin, Roman; Attic, chaste, elegant, polished, pure, refined.

**classify** vb arrange, assort, categorize, class, dispose, distribute, group, pigeonhole, rank, systematize, tabulate.

**clatter** vb clash, rattle; babble, clack, gabble, jabber, prate, prattle. *n clattering, clutter, rattling.

**clause** n article, condition, provision, stipulation.

**claw** vb lacerate, scratch, tear. *n talon, ungula.

**clean** vb cleanse, clear, purge, purify, rinse, scour, scrub, wash, wipe. *adj immaculate, spotless, unsmirched, unsoiled, unspotted, unstained, unsullied, white; clarified, pure, purified, unadulterated, unmixed; adroit, delicate, dextrous, graceful, light, neat, shapely; complete, entire, flawless, faultless, perfect, unabated, unblemished, unimpaired, whole; chaste, innocent, moral, pure, undefiled. *adv altogether, completely, entirely, perfectly, quite, thoroughly, wholly.

**cleanse** vb clean, clear, elutriate, purge, purify, rinse, scour, scrub, wash, wipe.

**clear** vb clarify, cleanse, purify, refine; emancipate, disenthral, free, liberate, loose; absolve, acquit, discharge, exonerate, justify, vindicate; disembarrass, disengage, disentangle, extricate, loosen, rid; clean up, scour, sweep; balance; emancipate, free, liberate. *adj bright, crystalline, light, limpid, luminous, pellucid, transparent; pure, unadulterated, unmixed; free, open, unencumbered, unobstructed; cloudless, fair, serene, sunny, unclouded, undimmed, unobscured; net; distinct, intelligible, lucid, luminous, perspicuous; apparent, conspicuous, distinct, evident, indisputable, manifest, obvious, palpable, unambiguous, undeniable, unequivocal, unmistakable, unquestionable, visible; clean, guiltless, immaculate, innocent, irreproachable, sinless, spotless, unblemished, undefiled, unspotted, unsullied; unhampered, unimpeded, unobstructed; euphonious, fluty, liquid, mellifluous, musical, silvery, sonorous.

**cleave**¹ vb crack, divide, open, part, rend, rive, sever, split, sunder.

**cleave**² vb adhere, cling, cohere, hold, stick.

**cleft** adj bifurcated, cloven, forked. *n breach, break, chasm, chink, cranny, crevice, fissure, fracture, gap, interstice, opening, rent, rift.

**clemency** n mildness, softness; compassion, fellow-feeling, forgivingness, gentleness, kindness, lenience, leniency, lenity, mercifulness, mercy, mildness, tenderness.

**clement** adj compassionate, forgiving, gentle,

humane, indulgent, kind, kind-hearted, lenient, merciful, mild, tender, tender-hearted.

**clench** vb close tightly, grip; fasten, fix, rivet, secure.

**clergy** n clergymen, the cloth, ministers.

**clever** adj able, apt, gifted, talented; adroit, capable, dextrous, discerning, expert, handy, ingenious, knowing, quick, ready, skilful, smart, talented.

**click** vb beat, clack, clink, tick. *n beat, clack, clink, tick; catch, detent, pawl, ratchet.

**cliff** n crag, palisade, precipice, scar, steep.

**climate** n clime, temperature, weather; country, region.

**climax** vb consummate, crown, culminate, peak. *n acme, consummation, crown, culmination, head, peak, summit, top, zenith.

**clinch** vb clasp, clench, clutch, grapple, grasp, grip; fasten, secure; confirm, establish, fix. *n catch, clutch, grasp, grip; clincher, clamp, cramp, holdfast.

**cling** vb adhere, clear, stick; clasp, embrace, entwine.

**clink** vb, n chink, jingle, ring, tinkle; chime, rhyme.

**clip** vb cut, shear, snip; curtail, cut, dock, pare, prune, trim. *n cutting, shearing; blow, knock, lick, rap, thump, thwack, thump.

**clique** n association, brotherhood, cabal, camarilla, clan, club, coterie, gang, junta, party, ring, set, sodality.

**cloak** vb conceal, cover, dissemble, hide, mask, veil. *n mantle, surcoat; blind, cover, mask, pretext, veil.

**clock** vb mark time, measure, stopwatch; clock up, record, register. *n chronometer, horologue, timekeeper, timepiece, timer, watch.

**clog** vb fetter, hamper, shackle, trammel; choke, obstruct; burden, cumber, embarrass, encumber, hamper, hinder, impede, load, restrain, trammel. *n dead-weight, drag-weight, fetter, shackle, trammel; check, drawback, encumbrance, hindrance, impediment, obstacle, obstruction.

**cloister** n abbey, convent, monastery, nunnery, priory; arcade, colonnade, piazza.

**close**¹ adj closed, confined, snug, tight; hidden, private, secret; incommunicative, reserved, reticent, secretive, taciturn; concealed, retired, secluded, withdrawn; confined, motionless, stagnant; airless, oppressive, stale, stifling, stuffy, sultry; compact, compressed, dense, form, solid, thick; adjacent, adjoining, approaching, immediately, near, nearly, neighbouring; attached, dear, confidential, devoted, intimate; assiduous, earnest, fixed, intense, intent, unremitting; accurate, exact, faithful, nice, precise, strict; churlish, close-fisted, curmudgeonly, mean, illiberal, miserly, niggardly, parsimonious, penurious, stingy, ungenerous. *n courtyard, enclosure, grounds, precinct, yard.

**close**[2] vb occlude, seal, shut; choke, clog, estop, obstruct, stop; cease, complete, concede, end, finish, terminate; coalesce, unite; cease, conclude, finish, terminate; clinch, grapple; agree. *n cessation, conclusion, end, finish, termination.

**closet** n cabinet, retiring-room; press, store-room.

**clot** vb coagulate, concrete. *n coagulation, concretion, lump.

**clothe** vb array, attire, deck, dress, rig; cover, endow, envelop, enwrap, invest with, swathe.

**clothes** n apparel, array, attire, clothing, costume, dress, garb, garments, gear, habiliments, habits, raiment, rig, vestments, vesture.

**cloud** vb becloud, obnubilate, overcast, overspread; befog, darken, dim, obscure, shade, shadow. *n cirrus, cumulus, fog, haze, mist, nebulosity, scud, stratus, vapour; army, crowd, horde, host, multitude, swarm, throng; darkness, eclipse, gloom, obscuration, obscurity.

**cloudy** adj clouded, filmy, foggy, hazy, lowering, lurid, murky, overcast; confused, dark, dim, obscure; depressing, dismal, gloomy, sullen; clouded, mottled; blurred, dimmed, lustreless, muddy.

**clown** n churl, clod-breaker, clodhopper, hind, husbandman, lubber; boor, bumpkin, churl, fellow, lout; blockhead, dolt, clodpoll, dunce, dunderhead, numbskull, simpleton, thickhead; buffoon, droll, farceur, fool, harlequin, jack-a-dandy, jack-pudding, jester, merry-andrew, mime, pantaloon, pickle-herring, punch, scaramouch, zany.

**clownish** adj awkward, boorish, clumsy, coarse, loutish, ungainly, rough, rustic; churlish, ill-bred, ill-mannered, impolite, rude, uncivil.

**cloy** vb glut, pall, sate, satiate, surfeit.

**club** vb combine, unite; beat, bludgeon, cudgel. *n bat, bludgeon; cosh, cudgel, hickory, shillelagh, stick, truncheon; association, company, coterie, fraternity, set, society, sodality.

**clump** vb assemble, batch, bunch, cluster, group, lump; lumber, stamp, stomp, stump, trudge. *n assemblage, bunch, cluster, collection, group, patch, tuft.

**clumsy** adj botched, cumbrous, heavy, ill-made, ill-shaped, lumbering, ponderous, unwieldy; awkward, blundering, bungling, elephantine, heavy-handed, inapt, mal adroit, unhandy, unskilled.

**cluster** vb assemble, batch, bunch, clump, collect, gather, group, lump, throng. *n agglomeration, assemblage, batch, bunch, clump, collection, gathering, group, throng.

**clutch**[1] vb catch, clasp, clench, clinch, grab, grapple, grasp, grip, hold, seize, snatch, squeeze. *n clasp, clench, clinch, grasp, grip, hold, seizure, squeeze.

**clutch**[2] n aerie, brood, hatching, nest.

**clutches** npl claws, paws, talons; hands, power.

**clutter** vb confuse, disarrange, disarray, disorder, jumble, litter, mess, muss; clatter. *n bustle, clatter, clattering, racket; confusion, disarray, disorder, jumble, litter, mess, muss.

**coadjutor** n abettor, accomplice, aider, ally, assistant, associate, auxiliary, collaborator, colleague, cooperator, fellow-helper, helper, helpmate, partner.

**coagulate** vb clot, congeal, concrete, curdle, thicken.

**coalesce** vb amalgamate, blend, cohere, combine, commix, incorporate, mix, unite; concur, fraternize.

**coalition** n alliance, association, combination, compact, confederacy, confederation, conjunction, conspiracy, co-partnership, federation, league, union.

**coarse** adj crude, impure, rough, unpurified; broad, gross, indecent, indelicate, ribald, vulgar; bearish, bluff, boorish, brutish, churlish, clownish, gruff, impolite, loutish, rude, unpolished; crass, inelegant.

**coast** vb flow, glide, roll, skim, sail, slide, sweep. *n littoral, seaboard, sea-coast, seaside, shore, strand; border.

**coat** vb cover, spread. *n cut-away, frock, jacket; coating, cover, covering; layer.

**coax** vb allure, beguile, cajole, cog, entice, flatter, persuade, soothe, wheedle.

**cobble** vb botch, bungle; mend, patch, repair, tinker.

**cobweb** adj flimsy, gauzy, slight, thin, worthless. *n entanglement, meshes, snare, toils.

**cochleate** adj cochlear, cochleary, cochleous, cochleated, spiral, spiry.

**cockle** vb corrugate, pucker, wrinkle.

**coddle** vb caress, cocker, fondle, humour, indulge, nurse, pamper, pet.

**codger** n churl, curmudgeon, hunks, lick-penny, miser, niggard, screw, scrimp, skinflint.

**codify** vb condense, digest, summarize, systematize, tabulate.

**coerce** vb check, curb, repress, restrain, subdue; compel, constrain, drive, force, urge.

**coercion** n check, curb, repression, restraint; compulsion, constraint, force.

**coeval** adj coetaneous, coexistent, contemporaneous, contemporary, synchronous.

**coexistent** adj coetaneous, coeval, simultaneous, synchronous.

**coffer** n box, casket, chest, trunk; money-chest, safe, strongbox; caisson.

**cogent** adj compelling, conclusive, convincing, effective, forcible, influential, irresistible, persuasive, potent, powerful, resistless, strong, trenchant, urgent.

**cogitate** vb consider, deliberate, meditate, ponder, reflect, ruminate, muse, think, weigh.

**cognate** adj affiliated, affined, akin, allied, alike, analogous, connected, kindred, related, similar.

**cognizance** n cognition, knowing, knowledge, notice, observation.

**cohere** vb agree, coincide, conform, fit, square, suit.

**coherence** n coalition, cohesion, connection, dependence, union; agreement, congruity, consistency, correspondence, harmony, intelligibility, intelligible, meaning, rationality, unity.

**coherent** adj adherent, connected, united; congruous, consistent, intelligible, logical.

**cohort** n band, battalion, line, squadron.

**coil** vb curl, twine, twirl, twist, wind. *n convolution, curlicue, helix, knot, roll, spiral, tendril, twirl, volute, whorl; bustle, care, clamour, confusion, entanglements, perplexities, tumult, turmoil, uproar.

**coin** vb counterfeit, create, devise, fabricate, forge, form, invent, mint, originate, mould, stamp. *n coign, corner, quoin; key, plug, prop, wedge; cash, money, specie.

**coincide** vb cohere, correspond, square, tally; acquiesce, agree, harmonize, concur.

**coincidence** n corresponding, squaring, tallying; agreeing, concurrent, concurring.

**cold** adj arctic, biting, bleak, boreal, chill, chilly, cutting, frosty, gelid, glacial, icy, nipping, polar, raw, wintry; frost-bitten, shivering; apathetic, cold-blooded, dead, freezing, frigid, indifferent, lukewarm, passionless, phlegmatic, sluggish, stoical, stony, torpid, unconcerned, unfeeling,

unimpressible, unresponsive, unsusceptible, unsympathetic; dead, dull, spiritless, unaffecting, uninspiring, uninteresting. *n chill, chilliness, coldness.

**collapse** vb break down, fail, fall. *n depression, exhaustion, failure, faint, prostration, sinking, subsidence.

**collar** vb apprehend, arrest, capture, grab, nab, seize. *n collarette, gorget, neckband, ruff, torque; band, belt, fillet, guard, ring, yoke.

**collate** vb adduce, collect, compare, compose.

**collateral** adj contingent, indirect, secondary, subordinate; concurrent, parallel; confirmatory, corroborative; accessory, accompanying, additional, ancillary, auxiliary, concomitant, contributory, simultaneous, supernumerary; consanguineous, related. *n guarantee, guaranty, security, surety, warranty; accessory, extra, nonessential, unessential; consanguinean, relative.

**collation** n luncheon, repast, meal.

**colleague** n aider, ally, assistant, associate, auxiliary, coadjutor, collaborator, companion, confederate, confrere, cooperator, helper, partner.

**collect** vb assemble, compile, gather, muster; accumulate, aggregate, amass, garner.

**collected** adj calm, composed, cool, placid, self-possessed, serene, unperturbed.

**collection** n aggregation, assemblage, cluster, crowd, drove, gathering, group, pack; accumulation, congeries, conglomeration, heap, hoard, lot, mass, pile, store; alms, contribution, offering, offertory.

**colligate** vb bind, combine, fasten, unite.

**collision** n clash, concussion, crash, encounter, impact, impingement, shock; conflict, crashing, interference, opposition.

**collocate** vb arrange, dispose, place, set.

**colloquy** n conference, conversation, dialogue, discourse, talk.

**collude** vb concert, connive, conspire.

**collusion** n connivance, conspiracy, coven, craft, deceit.

**collusive** adj conniving, conspiratorial, , dishonest, deceitful, deceptive, fraudulent.

**colossal** adj Cyclopean, enormous, gigantic, Herculean, huge, immense, monstrous, prodigious, vast.

**colour** vb discolour, dye, paint, stain, tinge, tint; disguise, varnish; disguise, distort, garble, misrepresent, pervert; blush, flush, redden, show. *n hue, shade, tinge, tint, tone; paint, pigment, stain; redness, rosiness, ruddiness; complexion; appearance, disguise, excuse, guise, plea, pretence, pretext, semblance.

**colourless** adj achromatic, uncoloured, untinged; blanched, hueless, livid, pale, pallid; blank, characterless, dull, expressionless, inexpressive, monotonous.

**colours** n banner, ensign, flag, standard.

**column** n pillar, pilaster; file, line, row.

**coma** n drowsiness, lethargy, somnolence, stupor, torpor; bunch, clump, cluster, tuft.

**comatose** adj drowsy, lethargic, sleepy, somnolent, stupefied.

**comb** vb card, curry, dress, groom, rake, unknot, untangle; rake, ransack, rummage, scour, search. *n card, hatchel, ripple; harrow, rake.

**combat** vb contend, contest, fight, struggle, war; battle, oppose, resist, struggle, withstand. *n action, affair, battle, brush, conflict, contest, encounter, fight, skirmish.

**combative** adj belligerent, contentious, militant, pugnacious, quarrelsome.

**combination** n association, conjunction, connection, union; alliance, cartel, coalition, confederacy, consolidation, league, merger, syndicate; cabal, clique, conspiracy, faction, junta, ring; amalgamation, compound, mixture.

**combine** vb cooperate, merge, pool, unite; amalgamate, blend, incorporate, mix.

**combustible** adj consumable, inflammable.

**come** vb advance, approach; arise, ensue, flow, follow, issue, originate, proceed, result; befall, betide, happen, occur.

**comely** adj becoming, decent, decorous, fitting, seemly, suitable; beautiful, fair, graceful, handsome, personable, pretty, symmetrical.

**comfort** vb alleviate, animate, cheer, console, encourage, enliven, gladden, inspirit, invigorate, refresh, revive, solace, soothe, strengthen. *n aid, assistance, countenance, help, support, succour; consolation, solace, encouragement, relief; ease, enjoyment, peace, satisfaction.

**comfortable** adj acceptable, agreeable, delightful, enjoyable, grateful, gratifying, happy, pleasant, pleasurable, welcome; commodious, convenient, easeful, snug; painless.

**comfortless** adj bleak, cheerless, desolate, drear, dreary, forlorn, miserable, wretched; broken-hearted, desolate, disconsolate, forlorn, heart-broken, inconsolable, miserable, woe-begone, wretched.

**comical** adj amusing, burlesque, comic, diverting, droll, farcical, funny, humorous, laughable, ludicrous, sportive, whimsical.

**coming** adj approaching, arising, arriving, ensuing, eventual, expected, forthcoming, future, imminent, issuing, looming, nearing, prospective, ultimate; emergent, emerging, successful; due, owed, owing. *n advent, approach, arrival; imminence, imminency, nearness; apparition, appearance, disclosure, emergence, manifestation, materialization, occurrence, presentation, revelation, rising.

**comity** n affability, amenity, civility, courtesy, politeness, suavity, urbanity.

**command** vb bid, charge, direct, enjoin, order, require; control, dominate, govern, lead, rule, sway; claim, challenge, compel, demand, exact. *n behest, bidding, charge, commandment, direction, hest, injunction, mandate, order, requirement, requisition; ascendency, authority, dominion, control, government, power, rule, sway, supremacy.

**commander** n captain, chief, chieftain, commandment, head, leader.

**commemorate** vb celebrate, keep, observe, solemnize.

**commence** vb begin, inaugurate, initiate, institute, open, originate, start.

**commend** vb assign, bespeak, confide, recommend, remit; commit, entrust, yield; applaud, approve, eulogize, extol, laud, praise.

**commendation** n approbation, approval, good opinion, recommendation; praise, encomium, eulogy, panegyric.

**commensurate** adj commeasurable, commensurable; co-extensive, conterminous, equal; adequate, appropriate, corresponding, due, proportionate, proportioned, sufficient.

**comment** vb animadvert, annotate, criticize, explain, interpret, note, remark. *n annotation, elucidation, explanation, exposition, illustration, commentary, note, gloss; animadversion, observation, remark.

**commentator** n annotator, commentator, critic, expositor, expounder, interpreter.

**commerce** n business, exchange, dealing, trade, traffic; communication, communion, intercourse.

**commercial** adj mercantile, trading.

**commination** n denunciation, menace, threat, threatening.

**commingle** vb amalgamate, blend, combine, commix, intermingle, intermix, join, mingle, mix, unite.

**comminute** vb bray, bruise, grind, levigate, powder, pulverize, triturate.

**commiserate** vb compassionate, condole, pity, sympathize.

**commiseration** n compassion, pitying; condolence, pity, sympathy.

**commission** vb authorize, empower; delegate, depute. *n doing, perpetration; care, charge, duty, employment, errand, office, task, trust; allowance, compensation, fee, rake-off.

**commissioner** n agent, delegate, deputy.

**commit** vb confide, consign, delegate, entrust, remand; consign, deposit, lay, place, put, relegate, resign; do, enact, perform, perpetrate; imprison; engage, implicate, pledge.

**commix** vb amalgamate, blend, combine, commingle, compound, intermingle, mingle, mix, unite.

**commodious** adj advantageous, ample, comfortable, convenient, fit, proper, roomy, spacious, suitable, useful.

**commodity** n goods, merchandise, produce, wares.

**common** adj collective, public; general, useful; common-place, customary, everyday, familiar, frequent, habitual, usual; banal, hackneyed, stale, threadbare, trite; indifferent, inferior, low, ordinary, plebeian, popular, undistinguished, vulgar.

**commonplace** adj common, hackneyed, ordinary, stale, threadbare, trite. *n banality, cliché, platitude; jotting, memoir, memorandum, note, reminder.

**common-sense, common-sensical** adj practical, sagacious, sensible, sober.

**commotion** n agitation, disturbance, ferment, perturbation, welter; ado, bustle, disorder, disturbance, hurly-burly, pother, tumult, turbulence, turmoil.

**communicate** vb bestow, confer, convey, give, impart, transmit; acquaint, announce, declare, disclose, divulge, publish, reveal, unfold; commune, converse, correspond.

**communication** n conveyance, disclosure, giving, imparting, transmittal; commence, conference, conversation, converse, correspondence, intercourse; announcement, dispatch, information, message, news.

**communicative** adj affable, chatty, conversable, free, open, sociable, unreserved.

**communion** n converse, fellowship, intercourse;

participation; Eucharist, holy communion, Lord's Supper, sacrament.

**community** n commonwealth, people, public, society; association, brotherhood, college, society; likeness, participancy, sameness, similarity.

**compact**[1] n agreement, arrangement, bargain, concordant, contract, covenant, convention, pact, stipulation, treaty.

**compact**[2] vb compress, condense, pack, press; bind, consolidate, unite. *adj close, compressed, condensed, dense, firm, solid; brief, compendious, concise, laconic, pithy, pointed, sententious, short, succinct, terse.

**companion** n accomplice, ally, associate, comrade, compeer, confederate, consort, crony, friend, fellow, mate; partaker, participant, participator, partner, sharer.

**companionable** adj affable, conversable, familiar, friendly, genial, neighbourly, sociable.

**companionship** n association, fellowship, friendship, intercourse, society.

**company** n assemblage, assembly, band, bevy, body, circle, collection, communication, concourse, congregation, coterie, crew, crowd, flock, gang, gathering, group, herd, rout, set, syndicate, troop; party; companionship, fellowship, guests, society, visitor, visitors; association, copartnership, corporation, firm, house, partnership.

**compare** vb assimilate, balance, collate, parallel; liken, resemble.

**comparison** n collation, compare, estimate; simile, similitude.

**compartment** n bay, cell, division, pigeonhole, section.

**compass** vb embrace, encompass, enclose, encircle, environ, surround; beleaguer, beset, besiege, block, blockade, invest; accomplish, achieve, attain, carry, consummate, effect, obtain, perform, procure, realize; contrive, devise, intend, meditate, plot, purpose. *n bound, boundary, extent, gamut, limit, range, reach, register, scope, stretch; circuit, round.

**compassion** n clemency, commiseration, condolence, fellow-feeling, heart, humanity, kind-heartedness, kindness, kindliness, mercy, pity, rue, ruth, sorrow, sympathy, tenderheartedness, tenderness.

**compassionate** adj benignant, clement, commiserative, gracious, kind, merciful, pitying, ruthful, sympathetic, tender.

**compatible** adj accordant, agreeable to, congruous, consistent, consonant, reconcilable, suitable.

**compeer** n associate, comrade, companion, equal, fellow, mate, peer.

**compel** vb constrain, force, coerce, drive, necessitate, oblige; bend, bow, subdue, subject.

**compend** n abbreviation, abridgement, abstract, breviary, brief, compendium, conspectus, digest, epitome, précis, summary, syllabus, synopsis.

**compendious** adj abbreviated, abridged, brief, comprehensive, concise, short, succinct, summary.

**compensate** vb counterbalance, counterpoise, countervail; guerdon, recompense, reimburse, remunerate, reward; indemnify, reimburse, repay, requite; atone.

**compensation** n pay, payment, recompense, remuneration, reward, salary; amends, atonement, indemnification, indemnity, reparation, requital, satisfaction; balance, counterpoise, equalization, offset.

**compete** vb contend, contest, cope, emulate, rival, strive, struggle, vie.

**competence** n ability, capability, capacity, fitness, qualification, suitableness; adequacy, adequateness, enough, sufficiency.

**competent** adj able, capable, clever, equal, endowed, qualified; adapted, adequate, convenient, fit, sufficient, suitable.

**competition** n contest, emulation, rivalry, rivals.

**competitor** n adversary, antagonist, contestant, emulator, opponent.

**compile** vb compose, prepare, write; arrange, collect, select.

**complacency** n content, contentment, gratification, pleasure, satisfaction; affability, civility, complaisance, courtesy, politeness.

**complacent** adj contented, gratified, pleased, satisfied; affable, civil, complaisant, courteous, easy, gracious, grateful, obliging, polite, urbane.

**complain** vb bemoan, bewail, deplore, grieve, groan, grouch, grumble, lament, moan, murmur, repine, whine.

**complainant** n accuser, plaintiff.

**complaining** adj fault-finding, murmuring, querulous.

**complaint** n grievance, gripe, grumble, lament, lamentation, plaint, murmur, wail; ail, ailment, annoyance, disease, disorder, illness, indisposition, malady, sickness; accusation, charge, information.

**complete** vb accomplish, achieve, conclude, consummate, do, effect, effectuate, end, execute, finish, fulfil, perfect, perform, realize, terminate. *adj clean, consummate, faultless, full, perfect, perform, thorough; all, entire, integral, total, unbroken, undiminished, undivided, unimpaired, whole; accomplished, achieved, completed, concluded, consummated, ended, finished.

**completion** n accomplishing, accomplishment, achieving, conclusion, consummation, effecting, effectuation, ending, execution, finishing, perfecting, performance, termination.

**complex** adj composite, compound, compounded, manifold, mingled, mixed; complicate, complicated, entangled, intricate, involved, knotty, mazy, tangled. *n complexus, complication, involute, skein, tangle; entirety, integration, network, totality, whole; compulsion, fixation, obsession, preoccupation, prepossession; prejudice.

**complexion** n colour, hue, tint.

**complexity** n complication, entanglement, intricacy, involution.

**compliance** n concession, obedience, submission; acquiescence, agreement, assent, concurrence, consent; compliancy, yieldingness.

**complicate** vb confuse, entangle, interweave, involve.

**complication** n complexity, confusion, entanglement, intricacy; combination, complexus, mixture.

**compliment** vb commend, congratulate, eulogize, extol, flatter, laud, praise. *n admiration, commendation, courtesy, encomium, eulogy, favour, flattery, honour, laudation, praise, tribute.

**complimentary** adj commendatory, congratulatory, encomiastic, eulogistic, flattering, laudatory, panegyrical.

**comply** vb adhere to, complete, discharge, fulfil, meet, observe, perform, satisfy; accede, accord, acquiesce, agree to, assent, consent to, yield.

**component** adj composing, constituent, constituting. *n constituent, element, ingredient, part.

**comport** vb accord, agree, coincide, correspond, fit, harmonize, square, suit, tally.

**compose** vb build, compact, compound, constitute, form, make, synthesize; contrive, create, frame, imagine, indite, invent, write; adjust, arrange, regulate, settle; appease, assuage, calm, pacify, quell, quiet, soothe, still, tranquillize.

**composed** adj calm, collected, cool, imperturbable, placid, quiet, sedate, self-possessed, tranquil, undisturbed, unmoved, unruffled.

**composite** adj amalgamated, combined, complex, compounded, mixed; integrated, unitary. *n admixture, amalgam, blend, combination, composition, compound, mixture, unification.

**composition** n constitution, construction, formation, framing, making; compound, mixture; arrangement, combination, conjunction, make-up, synthesize, union; invention, opus, piece, production, writing; agreement, arrangement, compromise.

**compost** n fertilizer, fertilizing, manure, mixture.

**composure** n calmness, coolness, equanimity, placidity, sedateness, quiet, self-possession, serenity, tranquillity.

**compotation** n conviviality, frolicking, jollification, revelling, revelry, rousing, wassailing; bacchanal, carousal, carouse, debauch, orgy, revel, saturnalia, wassail.

**compound**[1] vb amalgamate, blend, combine, intermingle, intermix, mingle, mix, unite; adjust, arrange, compose, compromise, settle. *adj complex, composite. *n combination, composition, mixture; farrago, hodgepodge, jumble, medley, mess, olio.

**compound**[2] n enclosure, garden, yard.

**comprehend** vb comprise, contain, embrace, embody, enclose, include, involve; apprehend, conceive, discern, grasp, know, imagine, master, perceive, see, understand.

**comprehension** n comprising, embracing, inclusion; compass, domain, embrace, field, limits, province, range, reach, scope, sphere, sweep; connotation, depth, force, intention; conception, grasp, intelligence, understanding; intellect, intelligence, mind, reason, understanding.

**comprehensive** adj all-embracing, ample, broad, capacious, compendious, extensive, full, inclusive, large, sweeping, wide.

**compress** vb abbreviate, condense, constrict, contract, crowd, press, shorten, squeeze, summarize.

**compression** n condensation, confining, pinching, pressing, squeezing; brevity, pithiness, succinctness, terseness.

**comprise** vb comprehend, contain, embody, embrace, enclose, include, involve.

**compromise** vb adjust, arbitrate, arrange, compose, compound, settle; imperil, jeopardize, prejudice; commit, engage, implicate, pledge; agree, compound. *n adjustment, agreement, composition, settlement.

**compulsion** n coercion, constraint, force, forcing, pressure, urgency.

**compulsory** adj coercive, compelling, constraining; binding, enforced, imperative, necessary, obligatory, unavoidable.

**compunction** n contrition, misgiving, penitence, qualm, regret, reluctance, remorse, repentance, sorrow.

**computable** adj calculable, numerable, reckonable.

**computation** n account, calculation, estimate, reckoning, score, tally.

**compute** vb calculate, count, enumerate, estimate, figure, measure, number, rate, reckon, sum.

**comrade** n accomplice, ally, associate, chum, companion, compatriot, compeer, crony, fellow, mate, pal.

**concatenate** vb connect, join, link, unite.

**concatenation** n connection; chain, congeries, linking, series, sequence, succession.

**concave** adj depressed, excavated, hollow, hollowed, scooped.

**conceal** vb bury, cover, screen, secrete; disguise, dissemble, mask.

**concede** vb grant, surrender, yield; acknowledge, admit, allow, confess, grant.

**conceit** n belief, conception, fancy, idea, image, imagination, notion, thought; caprice, illusion, vagary, whim; estimate, estimation, impression, judgement, opinion; conceitedness, egoism, self-complacency, priggishness, priggery, self-conceit, self-esteem, self-sufficiency, vanity; crotchet, point, quip, quirk.

**conceited** adj egotistical, opinionated, opinionative, overweening, self-conceited, vain.

**conceivable** adj imaginable, picturable; cogitable, comprehensible, intelligible, rational, thinkable.

**conceive** vb create, contrive, devise, form, plan, purpose; fancy, imagine; comprehend, fathom, think, understand; assume, imagine, suppose; bear, become pregnant.

**concern** vb affect, belong to, interest, pertain to, regard, relate to, touch; disquiet, disturb, trouble. *n affair, business, matter, transaction; concernment, consequence, importance, interest, moment, weight; anxiety, care, carefulness, solicitude, worry; business, company, establishment, firm, house.

**concert** vb combine, concoct, contrive, design, devise, invent, plan, plot, project. *n agreement, concord, concordance, cooperation, harmony, union, unison.

**concession** n acquiescence, assent, cessation, compliance, surrender, yielding; acknowledgement, allowance, boon, confession, grant, privilege.

**conciliate** vb appease, pacify, placate, propitiate, reconcile; engage, gain, secure, win, win over.

**concise** adj brief, compact, compendious, comprehensive, compressed, condensed, crisp, laconic, pithy, pointed, pregnant, sententious, short, succinct, summary, terse.

**conclave** n assembly, cabinet, council.

**conclude** vb close, end, finish, terminate; deduce, gather, infer, judge; decide, determine, judge; arrange, complete, settle; bar, hinder, restrain, stop; decide, determine, resolve.

**conclusion** n deduction, inference; decision, determination, judgement; close, completion, end, event, finale, issue, termination, upshot; arrangement, closing, effecting, establishing, settlement.

**conclusive** adj clinching, convincing, decisive, irrefutable, unanswerable; final, ultimate.

**concoct** vb brew, contrive, design, devise, frame, hatch, invent, mature, plan, plot, prepare, project.

**concomitant** adj accessory, accompanying, attendant, attending, coincident, concurrent, conjoined. *n accessory, accompaniment, attendant.

**concord** n agreement, amity, friendship, harmony, peace, unanimity, union, unison, unity; accord, adaptation, concordance, consonance, harmony.

**concordant** adj accordant, agreeable, agreeing, harmonious.

**concordat** n agreement, bargain, compact, convention, covenant, stipulation, treaty.

**concourse** n confluence, conflux, congress; assemblage, assembly, collection, crowd, gathering, meeting, multitude, throng.

**concrete** vb cake, congeal, coagulate, harden, solidify, thicken. *adj compact, consolidated, firm, solid, solidified; agglomerated, complex, conglomerated, compound, concreted; completely, entire, individualized, total. *n compound, concretion, mixture; cement.

**concubine** n hetaera, hetaira, mistress, paramour.

**concupiscence** n lasciviousness, lechery, lewdness, lust, pruriency.

**concupiscent** adj carnal, lascivious, lecherous, lewd,

libidinous, lustful, prurient, rampant, salacious, sensual.

**concur** vb accede, acquiesce, agree, approve, assent, coincide, consent, harmonize; combine, conspire, cooperate, help.

**concurrent** adj agreeing, coincident, harmonizing, meeting, uniting; associate, associated, attendant, concomitant, conjoined, united.

**concussion** n agitation, shaking; clash, crash, shock.

**condemn** vb adjudge, convict, doom, sentence; disapprove, proscribe, reprobate; blame, censure, damn, deprecate, disapprove, reprehend, reprove, upbraid.

**condemnation** n conviction, doom, judgement, penalty, sentence; banning, disapproval, proscription; guilt, sin, wrong; blame, censure, disapprobation, disapproval, reprobation, reproof.

**condemnatory** adj blaming, censuring, damnatory, deprecatory, disapproving, reproachful.

**condense** vb compress, concentrate, consolidate, densify, thicken; abbreviate, abridge, contract, curtail, diminish, epitomize, reduce, shorten, summarize; liquefy.

**condescend** vb deign, vouchsafe; descend, stoop, submit.

**condescension** n affability, civility, courtesy, deference, favour, graciousness, obeisance.

**condign** adj adequate, deserved, just, merited, suitable.

**condiment** n appetizer, relish, sauce, seasoning.

**condition** vb postulate, specify, stipulate; groom, prepare, qualify, ready, train; acclimatize, accustom, adapt, adjust, familiarize, habituate, naturalize; attune, commission, fix, overhaul, prepare, recondition, repair, service, tune. *n case, circumstances, plight, predicament, situation, state; class, estate, grade, rank, station; arrangement, consideration, provision, proviso, stipulation; attendant, necessity, postulate, precondition, prerequisite.

**condole** vb commiserate, compassionate, console, sympathize.

**condonation** n forgiveness, overlooking, pardon.

**condone** vb excuse, forgive, pardon.

**conduce** vb contribute, lead, tend; advance, aid.

**conducive** adj conducting, contributing, instrumental, promotive, subservient, subsidiary.

**conduct** vb convoy, direct, escort, lead; administer, command, govern, lead, preside, superintend;

manage, operate, regulate; direct, lead. *n administration, direction, guidance, leadership, management; convoy, escort, guard; actions, bearing, behaviour, career, carriage, demeanour, deportment, manners.

**conductor** n guide, lead; director, leader, manager; propagator, transmitter.

**conduit** n canal, channel, duct, passage, pipe, tube.

**confederacy** n alliance, coalition, compact, confederation, covenant, federation, league, union.

**confer** vb advise, consult, converse, deliberate, discourse, parley, talk; bestow, give, grant, vouchsafe.

**confess** vb acknowledge, admit, avow, own; admit, concede, grant, recognize; attest, exhibit, manifest, prove, show; shrive.

**confession** n acknowledgement, admission, avowal.

**confide** vb commit, consign, entrust, trust.

**confidence** n belief, certitude, dependence, faith, reliance, trust; aplomb, assurance, boldness, cocksureness, courage, firmness, intrepidity, self-reliance; secrecy.

**confident** adj assured, certain, cocksure, positive, sure: bold, presumptuous. sanguine, undaunted.

**confidential** adj intimate, private, secret; faithful, trustworthy.

**configuration** n conformation, contour, figure, form, gestalt, outline, shape.

**confine** vb restrain, shut in, shut up; immure, imprison, incarcerate, impound, jail, mew; bound, circumscribe, limit, restrict. *n border, boundary, frontier, limit.

**confinement** n restraint; captivity, duress, durance, immurement, imprisonment, incarceration; childbed, childbirth, delivery, lying-in, parturition.

**confines** npl borders, boundaries, edges, frontiers, limits, marches, precincts.

**confirm** vb assure, establish, fix, settle; strengthen; authenticate, avouch, corroborate, countersign, endorse, substantiate, verify; bind, ratify, sanction.

**confirmation** n establishment, settlement; corroboration, proof, substantiation, verification.

**confiscate** vb appropriate, forfeit, seize.

**conflict** vb clash, combat, contend, contest, disagree, fight, interfere, strive, struggle. *n battle, collision, combat, contention, contest, encounter, fight, struggle; antagonism, clashing, disagreement, discord, disharmony, inconsistency, interference, opposition.

**confluence** n conflux, junction, meeting, union; army, assemblage, assembly, concourse, crowd, collection, horde, host, multitude, swarm.

**confluent** adj blending, concurring, flowing, joining, meeting, merging, uniting.

**conform** vb accommodate, adapt, adjust; agree, comport, correspond, harmonize, square, tally.

**conformation** n accordance, agreement, compliance, conformity; configuration, figure, form, manner, shape, structure.

**confound** vb confuse; baffle, bewilder, embarrass, flurry, mystify, nonplus, perplex, pose; amaze, astonish, astound, bewilder, dumfound, paralyse, petrify, startle, stun, stupefy, surprise; annihilate, demolish, destroy, overthrow, overwhelm, ruin; abash, confuse, discompose, disconcert, mortify, shame.

**confront** vb face; challenge, contrapose, encounter, oppose, threaten.

**confuse** vb blend, confound, intermingle, mingle, mix; derange, disarrange, disorder, jumble, mess, muddle; darken, obscure, perplex; befuddle, bewilder, embarrass, flabbergast, flurry, fluster, mystify, nonplus, pose; abash, confound, discompose, disconcert, mortify, shame.

**confusion** n anarchy, chaos, clutter, confusedness, derangement, disarrangement, disarray, disorder, jumble, muddle; agitation, commotion, ferment, stir, tumult, turmoil; astonishment, bewilderment, distraction, embarrassment, fluster, fuddle, perplexity; abashment, discomfiture, mortification, shame; annihilation, defeat, demolition, destruction, overthrow, ruin.

**confute** vb disprove, oppugn, overthrow, refute, silence.

**congeal** vb benumb, condense, curdle, freeze, stiffen, thicken.

**congenial** adj kindred, similar, sympathetic; adapted, agreeable, natural, suitable, suited; agreeable, favourable, genial.

**congenital** adj connate, connatural, inborn.

**congeries** n accumulation, agglomeration, aggregate, aggregation, collection, conglomeration, crowd, cluster, heap, mass.

**congratulate** vb compliment, felicitate, gratulate, greet, hail, salute.

**congregate** vb assemble, collect, convene, convoke, gather, muster; gather, meet, swarm, throng.

**congregation** n assemblage, assembly, collection, gathering, meeting.

**congress** n assembly, conclave, conference, convention, convocation, council, diet, meeting.

**congruity** n agreement, conformity, consistency, fitness, suitableness.

**congruous** adj accordant, agreeing, compatible, consistent, consonant, suitable; appropriate, befitting, fit, meet, proper, seemly.

**conjecture** vb assume, guess, hypothesize, imagine, suppose. surmise, suspect; dare say, fancy, presume. *n assumption, guess, hypothesis, supposition, surmise, theory.

**conjoin** vb associate, combine, connect, join, unite.

**conjugal** adj bridal, connubial, hymeneal, matrimonial, nuptial.

**conjuncture** n combination, concurrence, connection; crisis, emergency, exigency, juncture.

**conjure** vb adjure, beg, beseech, crave, entreat, implore, invoke, pray, supplicate; bewitch, charm, enchant, fascinate; juggle.

**connect** vb associate, conjoin, combine, couple, hyphenate, interlink, join, link, unite; cohere, interlock.

**connected** adj associated, coupled, joined, united; akin, allied, related; communicating.

**connection** n alliance, association, dependence, junction, union; commerce, communication, intercourse; affinity, relationship; kindred, kinsman, relation, relative.

**connive** vb collude, conspire, plot, scheme.

**connoisseur** n critic, expert, virtuoso.

**connotation** n comprehension, depth, force, intent, intention, meaning.

**connubial** adj bridal, conjugal, hymeneal, matrimonial, nuptial.

**conquer** vb beat, checkmate, crush, defeat, discomfit, humble, master, overcome, overpower, overthrow, prevail, quell, reduce, rout, subdue, subjugate, vanquish; overcome, surmount.

**conqueror** n humbler, subduer, subjugator, vanquisher; superior, victor, winner.

**conquest** n defeat, discomfiture, mastery, overthrow, reduction, subjection, subjugation; triumph, victor; winning.

**consanguinity** n affinity, kinship, blood-relationship, kin, kindred, relationship.

**conscientious** adj careful, exact, fair, faithful, high-principled, honest, honourable, incorruptible, just, scrupulous, straightforward, uncorrupt, upright.

**conscious** adj intelligent, knowing, percipient, sentient; intellectual, rational, reasoning, reflecting, self-conscious, thinking; apprised, awake, aware, cognizant, percipient, sensible; self-admitted, self-accusing.

**consecrate** vb dedicate, devote, ordain; hallow, sanctify, venerate.

**consecutive** adj following, succeeding.

**consent** vb agree, allow, assent, concur, permit, yield; accede, acquiesce, comply. *n approval, assent, concurrence, permission; accord, agreement, consensus, concord, cooperation, harmony, unison; acquiescence, compliance.

**consequence** n effect, end, event, issue, result; conclusion, deduction, inference; concatenation, connection, consecution; concern, distinction, importance, influence, interest, moment, standing, weight.

**consequential** adj consequent, following, resulting, sequential; arrogant, conceited, inflated, pompous, pretentious, self-important, self-sufficient, vainglorious.

**conservation** n guardianship, maintenance, preservation, protection.

**conservative** adj conservatory, moderate, moderationist; preservative; reactionary, unprogressive. *n die-hard, reactionary, redneck, rightist, right-winger; moderate; preservative.

**conserve** vb keep, maintain, preserve, protect, save, sustain, uphold. *n confit, confection, jam, preserve, sweetmeat.

**consider** vb attend, brood, contemplate, examine, heed, mark, mind, ponder, reflect, revolve, study, weigh; care for, consult, envisage, regard, respect; cogitate, deliberate, mediate, muse, ponder, reflect, ruminate, think; account, believe, deem, hold, judge, opine.

**considerate** adj circumspect, deliberate, discrete, judicious, provident, prudent, serious, sober, staid, thoughtful; charitable, forbearing, patient.

**consideration** n attention, cogitation, contemplation, deliberation, notice, heed, meditation, pondering, reflection, regard; consequence, importance, important, moment, significant, weight; account, cause, ground, motive, reason, sake, score.

**consign** vb deliver, hand over, remand, resign, transfer, transmit; commit, entrust; ship.

**consignor** n sender, shipper, transmitter.

**consistency** n compactness, consistence, density, thickness; agreement, compatibility, conformableness, congruity, consonance, correspondence, harmony.

**consistent** adj accordant, agreeing, comfortable, compatible, congruous, consonant, correspondent, harmonious, logical.

**consolation** n alleviation, comfort, condolence, encouragement, relief, solace.

**console** vb assuage, calm, cheer, comfort, encourage, solace, relieve, soothe.

**consolidate** vb cement, compact, compress, condense, conduce, harden, solidify, thicken; combine, conjoin, fuse, unite.

**consolidation** n solidification; combination, union.

**consonance** n accord, concord, conformity, harmony; accord, accordance, agreement, congruence, congruity, consistency, unison.

**consonant** adj accordant, according, harmonious; compatible, congruous, consistent. *n articulation, letter-sound.

**consort** vb associate, fraternize. *n associate, companion, fellow, husband, spouse, partner.

**conspectus** n abstract, brief, breviary, compend, compendium, digest, epitome, outline, precis, summary, syllabus, synopsis.

**conspicuous** adj apparent, clear, discernible, glaring, manifest, noticeable, perceptible, plain, striking, visible; celebrated, distinguished, eminent, famed, famous, illustrious, marked, noted, outstanding, pre-eminent, prominent, remarkable, signal.

**conspiracy** n cabal, collusion, confederation, intrigue, league, machination, plot, scheme.

**conspire** vb concur, conduce, cooperate; combine, compass, contrive, devise, project; confederate, contrive, hatch, plot, scheme.

**constancy** n immutability, permanence, stability, unchangeableness; regularity, unchangeableness; decision, determination, firmness, inflexibility, resolution, steadfastness, steadiness; devotion, faithfulness, fidelity, loyalty, trustiness, truth.

**constant** adj abiding, enduring, fixed, immutable, invariable, invariant, permanent, perpetual, stable, unalterable, unchanging, unvaried; certain, regular, stated, uniform; determined, firm, resolute, stanch, steadfast, steady, unanswering, undeviating, unmoved, unshaken, unwavering; assiduous, diligent, persevering, sedulous, tenacious, unremitting; continual, continuous, incessant, perpetual, sustained,

unbroken, uninterrupted; devoted, faithful, loyal, true, trusty.

**consternation** n alarm, amazement, awe, bewilderment, dread, fear, fright, horror, panic, terror.

**constituent** adj component, composing, constituting, forming; appointing, electoral. *n component, element, ingredient, principal; elector, voter.

**constitute** vb compose, form, make; appoint, delegate, depute, empower; enact, establish, fix, set up.

**constitution** n establishment, formation, make-up, organization, structure; character, characteristic, disposition, form, habit, humour, peculiarity, physique, quality, spirit, temper, temperament.

**constitutional** adj congenital, connate, inborn, inbred, inherent, innate, natural, organic; lawful, legal, legitimate. *n airing, exercise, promenade, stretch, walk.

**constrain** vb coerce, compel, drive, force; chain, confine, curb, enthral, hold, restrain; draw, impel, urge.

**constriction** n compression, constraint, contraction.

**construct** vb build, fabricate, erect, raise, set up; arrange, establish, form, found, frame, institute, invent, make, organize, originate.

**construction** n building, erection, fabrication; configuration, conformation, figure, form, formation, made, shape, structure; explanation, interpretation, rendering, version.

**construe** vb analyse, explain, expound, interpret, parse, render, translate.

**consult** vb advise, ask, confer, counsel, deliberate, interrogate, question; consider, regard.

**consume** vb absorb, decay, destroy, devour, dissipate, exhaust, expend, lavish, lessen, spend, squander, vanish, waste.

**consummate**[1] vb accomplish, achieve, compass, complete, conclude, crown, effect, effectuate, end, execute, finish, perfect, perform.

**consummate**[2] adj complete, done, effected, finished, fulfilled, perfect, supreme.

**consumption** n decay, decline, decrease, destruction, diminution, expenditure, use, waste; atrophy, emaciation.

**contact** vb hit, impinge, touch; approach, be heard, communicate with, reach. *n approximation, contiguity, junction, juxtaposition, taction, tangency, touch.

**contagion** n infection; contamination, corruption, infection, taint.

**contagious** adj catching, epidemic, infectious; deadly, pestiferous, pestilential, poisonous.

**contain** vb accommodate, comprehend, comprise, embody, embrace, enclose, include; check, restrain.

**contaminate** vb corrupt, defile, deprave, infect, poison, pollute, soil, stain, sully, taint, tarnish, vitiate.

**contamination** n contaminating, defilement, defiling, polluting, pollution; abomination, defilement, impurity, foulness, infection, pollution, stain, taint, uncleanness.

**contemn** vb despise, disdain, disregard, neglect, scorn, scout, slight, spurn.

**contemplate** vb behold, gaze upon, observe, survey; consider, dwell on, meditate on, muse on, ponder, reflect upon, study, survey, think about; design, intend, mean, plan, purpose.

**contemplation** n cogitation, deliberation, meditation, pondering, reflection, speculation, study, thought; prospect, prospective, view; expectation.

**contemporaneous** adj coetaneous, coeval, coexistent, coexisting, coincident, concomitant, contemporary, simultaneous, synchronous.

**contemporary** adj coetaneous, coeval, coexistent, coexisting, coincident, concomitant, concurrent, contemporaneous, current, present, simultaneous, synchronous; advanced, modern, modernistic, progressive, up-to-date. *n coeval, coexistent, compeer, fellow.

**contempt** n contumely, derision, despite, disdain, disregard, misprision, mockery, scorn, slight.

**contemptible** adj abject, base, despicable, haughty, insolent, insulting, low, mean, paltry, pitiful, scurvy, sorry, supercilious, vile, worthless.

**contemptuous** adj arrogant, contumelious, disdainful, haughty, insolent, insulting, scornful, sneering, supercilious.

**contend** vb battle, combat, compete, contest, fight, strive, struggle, vie; argue, debate, dispute, litigate; affirm, assert, contest, maintain.

**content**[1] n essence, gist, meaning, meat, stuff, substance; capacity, measure, space, volume.

**content**[2] vb appease, delight, gladden, gratify, humour, indulge, please, satisfy, suffice. *adj agreeable, contented, happy, pleased, satisfied. *n contentment, ease, peace, satisfaction.

**contention** n discord, dissension, feud, squabble, strife, quarrel, rapture, wrangle, wrangling; altercation, bickering, contest, controversy, debate, dispute, litigation, logomachy.

**contentious** adj belligerent, cross, litigious, peevish, perverse, petulant, pugnacious, quarrelsome, wrangling; captious, caviling, disputatious.

**conterminous** adj adjacent, adjoining, contiguous; co-extensive, coincident, commensurate.

**contest** vb argue, contend, controvert, debate, dispute, litigate, question; strive, struggle; compete, cope, fight, vie. *n altercation, contention, controversy, difference, dispute, debate, quarrel; affray, battle, bout, combat, conflict, encounter, fight, match, scrimmage, struggle, tussle; competition, contention, rivalry.

**contexture** n composition, constitution, framework, structure, texture.

**contiguous** adj abutting, adjacent, adjoining, beside, bordering, conterminous, meeting, near, neighbouring, touching.

**continent**[1] n mainland, mass, tract.

**continent**[2] adj abstemious, abstinent, chaste, restrained, self-commanding, self-controlled, moderate, sober, temperate.

**contingency** n accidentalness, chance, fortuity, uncertainty; accident, casualty, event, incident, occurrence.

**contingent** adj accidental, adventitious, casual, fortuitous, incidental; conditional, dependent, uncertain. *n proportion, quota, share.

**continual** adj constant, constant, perpetual, unceasing, uninterrupted, unremitting; endless, eternal, everlasting, interminable, perennial, permanent, perpetual, unending; constant, oft-repeated.

**continuance** n abiding, continuation, duration, endurance, lasting, persistence, stay; continuation, extension, perpetuation, prolongation, protraction; concatenation, connection, sequence, succession; constancy, endurance, perseverance, persistence.

**continue** vb endure, last, remain; abide, linger, remain, stay, tarry; endure, persevere, persist, stick; extend, prolong, perpetuate, protract.

**continuous** adj connected, continued, extended, prolonged, unbroken, unintermitted, uninterrupted.

**contour** n outline, profile.

**contraband** adj banned, forbidden, illegal, illicit, interdicted, prohibited, smuggled, unlawful.

**contract** vb abbreviate, abridge, condense, confine, curtail, diminish, epitomize, lessen, narrow, reduce, shorten; absorb, catch, incur, get, make, take; constrict, shrink, shrivel, wrinkle; agree, bargain, covenant, engage, pledge, stipulate. *n agreement, arrangement, bargain, bond, compact, concordat, covenant, convention, engagement, pact, stipulation, treaty.

**contradict** vb assail, challenge, controvert, deny, dispute, gainsay, impugn, traverse; abrogate, annul, belie, counter, disallow, negative, contravene, counteract, oppose, thwart.

**contradiction** n controversion, denial, gainsaying; antinomy, clashing, contrariety, incongruity, opposition.

**contradictory** adj antagonistic, contrary, incompatible, inconsistent, negating, opposed, opposite, repugnant.

**contrariety** n antagonism, clashing, contradiction, contrast, opposition, repugnance.

**contrary** adj adverse, counter, discordant, opposed, opposing, opposite; antagonistic, conflicting, contradictory, repugnant, retroactive; forward, headstrong, obstinate, refractory, stubborn, unruly, wayward, perverse. *n antithesis, converse, obverse, opposite, reverse.

**contrast** vb compare, differentiate, distinguish, oppose. *n contrariety, difference, opposition; comparison, distinction.

**contravene** vb abrogate, annul, contradict, counteract, countervail, cross, go against, hinder, interfere, nullify, oppose, set aside, thwart.

**contravention** n abrogation, contradiction, interference, opposition, transgression, traversal, violation.

**contretemps** n accident, mischance, mishap.

**contribute** vb bestow, donate, give, grant, subscribe; afford, aid, furnish, supply; concur, conduce, conspire, cooperate, minister, serve, tend.

**contribution** n bestowal, bestowment, grant; donation, gift, offering, subscription.

**contrite** adj humble, penitent, repentant, sorrowful.

**contrition** n compunction, humiliation, penitence, regret, remorse, repentance, self-condemnation, self-reproach, sorrow.

**contrivance** n design, inventive, inventiveness; contraption, device, gadget, invention, machine; artifice, device, fabrication, machination, plan, plot, scheme, shift, stratagem.

**contrive** vb arrange, brew, concoct, design, devise, effect, form, frame, hatch, invent, plan, project; consider, plan, plot, scheme; manage, make out.

**control** vb command, direct, dominate, govern, manage, oversee, sway, regulate, rule, superintend; bridle, check, counteract, curb, check, hinder, repress, restrain. *n ascendency, command, direction, disposition, dominion, government, guidance, mastery, oversight, regiment, regulation, rule, superintendence, supremacy, sway.

**controversy** n altercation, argument, contention, debate, discussion, disputation, dispute, logomachy, polemics, quarrel, strife; lawsuit.

**contumacious** adj disobedient, cross-grained, disrespectful, haughty, headstrong, intractable, obdurate, obstinate, pertinacious, perverse, rebellious, refractory, stiff-necked, stubborn.

**contumacy** n doggedness, haughtiness, headiness, obduracy, obstinacy, pertinacity, perverseness, stubbornness; contempt, disobedience, disrespect, insolence, insubordination, rebelliousness.

**contumelious** adj abusive, arrogant, calumnious, contemptuous, disdainful, insolent, insulting, opprobrious, overbearing, rude, scornful, supercilious.

**contumely** n abuse, affront, arrogance, contempt, contemptuousness, disdain, indignity, insolence, insult, obloquy, opprobrium, reproach, rudeness, scorn, superciliousness.

**contuse** vb bruise, crush, injure, knock, squeeze, wound.

**contusion** n bruise, crush, injury, knock, squeeze, wound.

**convalescence** n recovery, recuperation.

**convene** vb assemble, congregate, gather, meet, muster; assemble, call, collect, convoke, muster, summon.

**convenience** n fitness, propriety, suitableness; accessibility, accommodation, comfort, commodiousness, ease, handiness, satisfaction, serviceability, serviceableness.

**convenient** adj adapted, appropriate, fit, fitted, proper, suitable, suited; advantageous, beneficial, comfortable, commodious, favourable, handy, helpful, serviceable, timely, useful.

**convent** n abbey, cloister, monastery, priory.

**convention** n assembly, congress, convocation, meeting; agreement, bargain, compact, contract, pact, stipulation, treaty; custom, formality, usage.

**conventional** adj agreed on, bargained for, stipulated; accustomed, approved, common, customary, everyday, habitual, ordinary, orthodox, regular, standard, traditional, usual, wonted.

**conversable** *adj* affable, communicative, free, open, sociable, social, unreversed.

**conversation** *n* chat, colloquy, communion, confabulation, conference, converse, dialogue, discourse, intercourse, interlocution, parley, talk.

**converse**[1] *vb* commune; chat, confabulate, discourse, gossip, parley, talk. \*n commerce, communication, intercourse; colloquy, conversation, talk.

**converse**[2] *adj* adverse, contradictory, contrary, counter, opposed, opposing, opposite; *n* antithesis, contrary, opposite, reverse.

**conversion** *n* change, reduction, resolution, transformation, transmutation; interchange, reversal, transposition.

**convert** *vb* alter, change, transform, transmute; interchange, reverse, transpose; apply, appropriate, convince. \*n catechumen, disciple, neophyte, proselyte.

**convey** *vb* bear, bring, carry, fetch, transmit, transport, waft; abalienate, alienate, cede, consign, deliver, demise, devise, devolve, grant, sell, transfer.

**conveyance** *n* alienation, cession, transfer, transference, transmission; carriage, carrying, conveying, transfer, transmission.

**convict** *vb* condemn, confute, convince, imprison, sentence. \*n criminal, culprit, felon, malefactor, prisoner.

**convivial** *adj* festal, festive, gay, jolly, jovial, merry, mirthful, social.

**convocation** *n* assembling, convening, convoking, gathering, summoning; assembly, congress, convention, council, diet, meeting, synod.

**convoke** *vb* assemble, convene, muster, summon.

**convoy** *vb* accompany, attend, escort, guard, protect. \*n attendance, attendant, escort, guard, protection.

**convulse** *vb* agitate, derange, disorder, disturb, shake, shatter.

**convulsion** *n* cramp, fit, spasm; agitation, commotion, disturbance, shaking, tumult.

**cook** *vb* bake, boil, broil, fry, grill, microwave, roast, spit-roast, steam, stir-fry; falsify, garble.

**cool** *vb* chill, ice, refrigerate; abate, allay, calm, damp, moderate, quiet, temper. \*adj calm, collected, composed, dispassionate, placid, sedate, self-possessed, quiet, staid, unexcited, unimpassioned, undisturbed, unruffled; cold-blooded, indifferent, lukewarm, unconcerned; apathetic, chilling, freezing, frigid, repellent; bold, impertinent, impudent, self-possessed, shameless. \*n chill, chilliness, coolness; calmness, composure, coolheadedness, countenance, equanimity, poise, self-possession, self-restraint.

**coop** *vb* cage, confine, encage, immure, imprison. \*n barrel, box, cage, pen.

**cooperate** *vb* abet, aid, assist, co-act, collaborate, combine, concur, conduce, conspire, contribute, help, unite.

**cooperation** *n* aid, assistance, co-action, concert, concurrence, collaboration, synergy.

**coordinate** *vb* accord, agree, arrange, equalize, harmonize, integrate, methodize, organize, regulate, synchronize, systematize. \*adj coequal, equal, equivalent, tantamount; coincident, synchronous. \*n complement, counterpart, like, pendant; companion, fellow, match, mate.

**copartnership** *n* association, fraternity, partnership; company, concern, establishment, firm, house.

**cope** *vb* combat, compete, contend, encounter, engage, strive, struggle, vie.

**copious** *adj* abundant, ample, exuberant, full, overflowing, plenteous, plentiful, profuse, rich.

**copiousness** *n* abundance, exuberance, fullness, plenty, profusion, richness.

**copse** *n* coppice, grove, thicket.

**copulation** *n* coition, congress, coupling.

**copy** *vb* duplicate, reproduce, trace, transcribe; follow, imitate, pattern. \*n counterscript, duplicate, facsimile, off-print, replica, reproduction, transcript; archetype, model, original, pattern; manuscript, typescript.

**cord** *n* braid, gimp, line, string.

**cordate** *adj* cordiform, heart-shaped.

**cordial** *adj* affectionate, ardent, earnest, heartfelt, hearty, sincere, warm, warm-hearted; grateful, invigorating, restorative, pleasant, refreshing. \*n balm, balsam, elixir, tisane, tonic; liqueur.

**core** *n* centre, essence, heart, kernel.

**corner** *vb* confound, confuse, nonplus, perplex, pose, puzzle. \*n angle, bend, crutch, cusp, elbow, joint, knee; niche, nook, recess, retreat.

**corollary** *n* conclusion, consequence, deduction, induction, inference.

**coronal** *n* bays, chaplet, crown, garland, laurel, wreath.

**corporal** *adj* bodily; corporeal, material, physical.

**corporeal** *adj* bodily, fleshly, substantial; corporal, material, nonspiritual, physical.

**corps** *n* band, body, company, contingent, division, platoon, regiment, squad, squadron, troop.

**corpse** *n* body, carcass, corse, remains; ashes, dust.

**corpulent** *adj* big, burly, fat, fleshy, large, lusty, obese, plump, portly, pursy, rotund, stout.

**corpuscle** *n* atom, bit, grain, iota, jot, mite, molecule, monad, particle, scintilla, scrap, whit.

**correct** *vb* adjust, amend, cure, improve, mend, reclaim, rectify, redress, reform, regulate, remedy; chasten, discipline, punish. *adj* accurate, equitable, exact, faultless, just, precise, proper, regular, right, true, upright.

**correction** *n* amendment, improvement, redress; chastening, discipline, punishment.

**corrective** *adj* alternative, correctory, counteractive, emendatory, improving, modifying, rectifying, reformative, reformatory.

**correctness** *n* accuracy, exactness, faultlessness, nicety, precision, propriety, rectitude, regularity, rightness, truth.

**correlate** *n* complement, correlative, counterpart.

**correspond** *vb* accord, agree, answer, comport, conform, fit, harmonize, match, square, suit, tally; answer, belong, correlate; communicate.

**correspondence** *n* accord, agreement, coincidence, concurrence, conformity, congruity, fitness, harmony, match; correlation, counterposition; communication, letters, writing.

**corroborate** *vb* confirm, establish, ratify, substantiate, support, sustain, strengthen.

**corrode** *vb* canker, erode, gnaw; consume, deteriorate, rust, waste; blight, embitter, envenom, poison.

**corrosive** *adj* acrid, biting, consuming, cathartic, caustic, corroding, eroding, erosive, violent; consuming, corroding, gnawing, mordant, wasting, wearing; blighting, cankerous, carking, embittering, envenoming, poisoning.

**corrugate** *vb* cockle, crease, furrow, groove, pucker, rumple, wrinkle.

**corrupt** *vb* putrefy, putrid, render; contaminate, defile, infect, pollute, spoil, taint, vitiate; degrade, demoralize, deprave, pervert; adulterate, debase, falsify, sophisticate; bribe, entice. *adj* contaminated, corrupted, impure, infected, putrid, rotten, spoiled, tainted, unsound; abandoned, debauched, depraved, dissolute, profligate, reprobate, vicious, wicked; bribable, buyable.

**corruption** *n* putrefaction, putrescence, rottenness; adulteration, contamination, debasement, defilement, infection, perversion, pollution, vitiation; demoralization, depravation, depravity, immorality, laxity, sinfulness, wickedness; bribery, dishonesty.

**corsair** *n* buccaneer, picaroon, pirate, rover, sea-robber, sea-rover.

**corset** *n* bodice, girdle, stays.

**cosmonaut** *n* astronaut, spaceman.

**cosmos** *n* creation, macrocosm, universe, world; harmony, order, structure.

**cost** *vb* absorb, consume, require. *n* amount, charge, expenditure, expense, outlay, price; costliness, preciousness, richness, splendour, sumptuousness; damage, detriment, loss, pain, sacrifice, suffering.

**costly** *adj* dear, expensive, high-priced; gorgeous, luxurious, precious, rich, splendid, sumptuous, valuable.

**costume** *n* apparel, attire, dress, robes, uniform.

**cosy, cozy** *adj* comfortable, easy, snug; chatty, conversable, social, talkative.

**coterie** *n* association, brotherhood, circle, club, set, society, sodality.

**cottage** *n* cabin, chalet, cot, hut, lodge, shack, shanty.

**couch** *vb* lie, recline; crouch, squat; bend down, stoop; conceal, cover up, hide; lay, level. *n* bed, davenport, divan, lounge, seat, settee, settle, sofa.

**council** *n* advisers, cabinet, ministry; assembly, congress, conclave, convention, convocation, diet, husting, meeting, parliament, synod.

**counsel** *vb* admonish, advise, caution, recommend, warm. *n* admonition, advice, caution, instruction, opinion, recommendation, suggestion; deliberation, forethought; advocate, barrister, counsellor, lawyer.

**count** *vb* enumerate, number, score; calculate, cast, compute, estimate, reckon; account, consider, deem, esteem, hold, judge, regard, think; tell. *n* reckoning, tally.

**countenance** *vb* abet, aid, approve, assist, befriend, encourage, favour, patronize, sanction, support. *n* aspect, look, men; aid, approbation, approval, assistance, encouragement, favour, patronage, sanction, support.

**counter**[1] n abacus, calculator, computer, meter, reckoner, tabulator, totalizator; bar, buffet, shopboard, table; (naut) end, poop, stern, tail; chip, token.

**counter**[2] vb contradict, contravene, counteract, oppose, retaliate. *adj adverse, against, contrary, opposed, opposite. *adv contrariwise, contrary. *n antithesis, contrary, converse, opposite, reverse; counterblast, counterblow, retaliation.

**counteract** vb check, contrapose, contravene, cross, counter, counterpose, defeat, foil, frustrate, hinder, oppose, resist, thwart, traverse; annul, countervail, counterbalance, destroy, neutralize, offset.

**counteractive** adj antidote, corrective, counteragent, medicine, remedy, restorative.

**counterbalance** vb balance, counterpoise; compensate, countervail.

**counterfeit** vb forge, imitate; fake, feign, pretend, sham, simulate; copy, imitate. *adj fake, forged, fraudulent, spurious, supposititious; false, feigned, hypocritical, mock, sham, simulated, spurious; copied, imitated, resembling. *n copy, fake, forgery, sham.

**countermand** vb abrogate, annul, cancel, recall, repeal, rescind, revoke.

**counterpane** n coverlet, duvet, quilt.

**counterpart** n copy, duplicate; complement, correlate, correlative, reverse, supplement; fellow, mate, match, tally, twin.

**counterpoise** vb balance, counteract, countervail, counterbalance, equilibrate, offset. *n balance, counterweight.

**countersign** n password, watchword.

**countervail** vb balance, compensate, counterbalance.

**country** n land, region; countryside; fatherland, home, kingdom, state, territory; nation, people, population. *adj rural, rustic; countrified, rough, rude, uncultivated, unpolished, unrefined.

**countryman** n compatriot, fellow-citizen; boor, clown, farmer, hind, husbandman, peasant, rustic, swain.

**couple** vb pair, unite; copulate, embrace; buckle, clasp, conjoin, connect, join, link, pair, yoke. *n brace, pair, twain, two; bond, coupling, lea, link, tie.

**courage** n audaciousness, audacity, boldness, bravery, daring, derring-do, dauntlessness, fearlessness, firmness, fortitude, gallantry, hardihood, heroism, intrepidity, manhood, mettle, nerve, pluck, prowess, resolution, spirit, spunk, valorousness, valour.

**courageous** adj audacious, brave, bold, chivalrous, daring, dauntless, fearless, gallant, hardy, heroic, intrepid, lion-hearted, mettlesome, plucky, resolute, reliant, staunch, stout, undismayed, valiant, valorous.

**course** vb chase, follow, hunt, pursue, race, run. *n career, circuit, race, run; road, route, track, way; bearing, direction, path, tremor, track; ambit, beat, orbit, round; process, progress, sequence; order, regularity, succession, turn; behaviour, conduct, deportment; arrangement, series, system.

**court** vb coddle, fawn, flatter, ingratiate; address, woo; seek; invite, solicit. *n area, courtyard, patio, quadrangle; addresses, civilities, homage, respects, solicitations; retinue, palace, tribunal.

**courteous** adj affable, attentive, ceremonious, civil, complaisant, courtly, debonair, elegant, gracious, obliging, polished, polite, refined, respected, urbane, well-bred, well-mannered.

**courtesan** n harlot, prostitute, strumpet, vamp, wanton, wench, whore.

**courtesy** n affability, civility, complaisance, courteousness, elegance, good-breeding, graciousness, polish, politeness, refine, urbanity.

**courtly** adj affable, ceremonious, civil, elegant, flattering, lordly, obliging, polished, polite, refined, urbane.

**courtyard** n area, court, patio, quadrangle, yard.

**cove**[1] n anchorage, bay, bight, creek, firth, fjord, inlet.

**cove**[2] n bloke, chap, character, customer, fellow, type.

**covenant** vb agree, bargain, contract, stipulate. *n bond, deed; arrangement, bargain, compact, concordat, contract, convention, pact, stipulation, treaty.

**cover** vb overlay, overspread; cloak, conceal, curtain, disguise, hide, mask, screen, secrete, shroud, veil; defend, guard, protect, shelter, shield; case, clothe, envelop, invest, jacket, sheathe; comprehend, comprise, contain, embody, embrace, include. *n capsule, case, covering, integument, tegument, top; cloak, disguise, screen, veil; guard, defence, protection, safeguard, shelter, shield; shrubbery, thicket, underbrush, undergrowth, underwood, woods.

**covert** adj clandestine, concealed, disguised, hidden, insidious, private, secret, sly, stealthy, underhand.

*n coppice, shade, shrubbery, thicket, underwood; asylum; defence, harbour, hiding-place, refuge, retreat, sanctuary, shelter.

**covet** vb aim after, desire, long for, yearn for; hanker after, lust after.

**covetous** adj acquisitive, avaricious, close-fisted, grasping, greedy, miserly, niggardly, parsimonious, penurious, rapacious.

**cow**[1] n bovine, heifer.

**cow**[2] vb abash, break, daunt, discourage, dishearten, frighten, intimidate, overawe, subdue.

**coward** adj cowardly, timid. *n caitiff, craven, dastard, milksop, poltroon, recreant, skulker, sneak, wheyface.

**cowardly** adj base, chicken-hearted, coward, craven, dastardly, faint-hearted, fearful, lily-livered, mean, pusillanimous, timid, timorous, white-livered, yellow.

**cower** vb bend, cringe, crouch, fawn, shrink, squat, stoop.

**coxcomb** n beau, dandy, dude, exquisite, fop, jackanapes, popinjay, prig.

**coy** adj backward, bashful, demure, diffident, distant, modest, reserved, retiring, self-effacing, shrinking, shy, timid.

**coyness** n affectation, archness, backwardness, bashfulness, coquettishness, demureness, diffidence, evasiveness, modesty, primness, reserve, shrinking, shyness, timidity.

**cozen** vb beguile, cheat, chouse, circumvent, deceive, defraud, diddle, dupe, gull, overreach, swindle, trick, victimize.

**cozy** see **cosy**.

**crabbed** adj acrid, rough, sore, tart; acrimonious, cantankerous, captious, caustic, censorious, churlish, cross, growling, harsh, ill-tempered, morose, peevish, petulant, snappish, snarling, splenetic, surly, testy, touchy, waspish; difficult, intractable, perplexing, tough, trying, unmanageable.

**crabbedness** n acridity, acridness, roughness, sourness, tartness; acerbity, acrimonious, asperity, churlishness, harshness, ill-tempered, moodiness, moroseness, sullenness; difficulty, intractability, perplexity.

**crack** vb break; chop, cleave, split; snap; craze, madden; boast, brag, bluster, crow, gasconade, vapour, vaunt. *adj capital, excellent, first-class, first-rate, tip-top. *n breach, break, chink, cleft, cranny, crevice, fissure, fracture, opening, rent, rift, split; burst, clap, explosion, pop, report; snap.

**cracked** adj broken, crackled, split; crack-brained, crazed, crazy, demented, deranged, flighty, insane.

**crackle** vb crepitate, decrepitate, snap.

**craft** n ability, aptitude, cleverness, dexterity, expertness, power, readiness, skill, tact, talent; artifice, artfulness, cunning, craftiness, deceitfulness, deception, guile, shrewdness, subtlety; art, avocation, business, calling, employment, handicraft, trade, vocation; vessel.

**crafty** adj arch, artful, astute, cunning, crooked, deceitful, designing, fraudulent, guileful, insidious, intriguing, scheming, shrewd, sly, subtle, tricky, wily.

**crag** n rock; neck, throat.

**craggy** adj broken, cragged, jagged, rough, rugged, scraggy, uneven.

**cram** vb fill, glut, gorge, satiate, stuff; compress, crowd, overcrowd, press, squeeze; coach, grind.

**cramp** vb convulse; check, clog, confine, hamper, hinder, impede, obstruct, restrain, restrict. *n convulsion, crick, spasm; check, restraint, restriction, obstruction.

**crank** vb bend, crankle, crinkle, turn, twist, wind. *n bend, quirk, turn, twist, winding.

**cranny** n breach, break, chink, cleft, crack, crevice, fissure, gap, hole, interstice, nook, opening, rift.

**crapulous** adj crapulent, drunk, drunken, inebriated, intoxicated, tipsy.

**crash** vb break, shatter, shiver, smash, splinter. *adj emergency, fast, intensive, rushed, speeded-up. *n clang, clash, collision concussion, jar.

**crass** adj coarse, gross, raw, thick, unabated, unrefined.

**cravat** n neckcloth, neckerchief, necktie.

**crave** vb ask, beg, beseech, entreat, implore, petition, solicit, supplicate; desire, hanker after, long for, need, want, yearn for.

**craven** n coward, dastard, milk-sop, poltroon, recreant. *adj cowardly, chicken-hearted, lily-livered, pusillanimous, yellow.

**craving** n hankering, hungering, longing, yearning.

**craw** n crop, gullet, stomach, throat.

**craze** vb bewilder, confuse, dement, derange, madden; disorder, impair, weaken. *n fashion, mania, mode, novelty.

**crazy** adj broken, crank, rickety, shaky, shattered, tottering; crack-brained, delirious, demented, deranged, distracted, idiotic, insane, lunatic, mad, silly.

**create** vb originate, procreate; cause, design,

fashion, form, invent, occasion, produce; appoint, constitute, make.

**creation** n formation, invention, origination, production; cosmos, universe; appointment, constitution, establishment, nomination.

**creator** n author, designer, inventor, fashioner, maker, originator; god.

**creature** n animal, beast, being, body, brute, man, person; dependant, hanger-on, minion, parasite, retainer, vassal; miscreant, wretch.

**credence** n acceptance, belief, confidence, credit, faith, reliance, trust.

**credentials** npl certificate, diploma, missive, passport, recommendation, testament, testimonial, title, voucher, warrant.

**credibility** n believability, plausibility, tenability, , trustworthiness.

**credit** vb accept, believe, trust; loan, trust. *n belief, confidence, credence, faith, reliance, trust; esteem, regard, reputableness, reputation; influence, power; honour, merit; loan, trust.

**creditable** adj estimable, honourable, meritorious, praiseworthy, reputable, respectable.

**credulity** n credulousness, gullibility, silliness, simplicity, stupidity.

**credulous** adj dupable, green, gullible, naive, over-trusting, trustful, uncritical, unsuspecting, unsuspicious.

**creed** n belief, confession, doctrine, dogma, opinion, profession, tenet.

**creek** n bay, bight, cove, fjord, inlet; rivulet, streamlet.

**creep** vb crawl; steal upon; cringe, fawn, grovel, insinuate. *n crawl, scrabble, scramble; fawner, groveller, sycophant, toady.

**crenate** adj indented, notched, scalloped.

**crepitate** vb crack, crackle, decrepitate, snap.

**crest** n comb, plume, topknot, tuft; apex, crown, head, ridge, summit, top; arms, badge, bearings.

**crestfallen** adj chap-fallen, dejected, depressed, despondent, discouraged, disheartened, dispirited, downcast, down-hearted, low-spirited, melancholy, sad.

**crevice** n chink, cleft, crack, cranny, fissure, fracture, gap, hole, interstice, opening, rent, rift.

**crew** n company, complement, hands; company, corps, gang, horde, mob, party, posse, set, squad, team, throng.

**crib** vb cage, confine, encage, enclose, imprison; pilfer, purloin. *n manger, rack; bin, bunker; plagiarism, plunder, theft.

**crick** vb jar, rick; wrench, wrick. *n convulsion, cramp, jarring, spasm, rick, wrench, wrick.

**crime** n felony, misdeed, misdemeanour, offence, violation; delinquency, fault, guilt, iniquity, sin, transgression, unrighteousness, wickedness, wrong.

**criminal** adj culpable, felonious, flagitious, guilty, illegal, immoral, iniquitous, nefarious, unlawful, vicious, wicked, wrong. *n convict, culprit, delinquent, felon, malefactor, offender, sinner, transgressor.

**criminate** vb accuse, arraign, charge, convict, impeach, indict; implicate, involve.

**crimp** vb crisp, curl.

**cringe** vb bend, bow, cower, crouch, fawn, grovel, kneel, sneak, stoop, truckle.

**cripple** vb cramp, destroy, disable, enfeeble, impair, lame, maim, mutilate, paralyse, ruin, weaken.

**crisis** n acme, climax, height; conjuncture, emergency, exigency, juncture, pass, pinch, push, rub, strait, urgency.

**crisp** adj brittle, curled, friable, frizzled.

**criterion** n canon, gauge, measure, principle, proof, rule, standard, test, touchstone.

**critic** n arbiter, caviller, censor, connoisseur, judge, nit-picker, reviewer.

**critical** adj accurate, exact, nice; captious, carping, caviling, censorious, exacting; crucial, decisive, determining, important, turning: dangerous, dubious, exigent, hazardous, imminent, momentous, precarious, ticklish.

**criticism** n analysis, animadversion, appreciation, comment, critique, evaluation, judgement, review, strictures.

**criticize** vb appraise, evaluate, examine, judge.

**croak** vb complain, groan, grumble, moan, mumble, repine; die.

**crone** n hag, witch.

**crony** n ally, associate, chum, friend, mate, mucker, pal.

**crook** vb bend, bow, curve, incurvate, turn, wind. *n bend, curvature, flexion, turn; artifice, machination, trick; criminal, thief, villain

**crooked** adj angular, bent, bowed, curved, winding, zigzag; askew, aslant, awry, deformed, disfigured, distorted, twisted, wry; crafty, deceitful, devious, dishonest, dishonourable, fraudulent, insidious, intriguing, knavish, tricky, underhanded, unfair, unscrupulous.

**crop** vb gather, mow, pick, pluck, reap; browse, nibble; clip, curtail, lop, reduce, shorten. *n harvest, produce, yield.

**cross** vb intersect, pass over, traverse; hinder, interfere, obstruct, thwart; interbred, intermix. *adj transverse; cantankerous, captious, crabbed, churlish, crusty, cynical, fractious, fretful, grouchy, ill-natured, ill-tempered, irascible, irritable, morose, peevish, pettish, petulant, snappish, snarling, sour, spleeny, splenetic, sulky, sullen, surly, testy, touchy, waspish. *n crucifix, gibbet, rood; affliction, misfortune, trial, trouble, vexation; cross-breeding, hybrid, intermixture.

**cross-grained** adj cantankerous, headstrong, obdurate, peevish, perverse, refractory, stubborn, untractable, wayward.

**crossing** n intersection, overpass, traversing, under-pass.

**crossways, crosswise** adv across, over, transversely.

**crotchet** n caprice, fad, fancy, freak, quirk, vagary, whim, whimsy.

**crouch** vb cower, cringe, fawn, truckle; crouch, kneel, stoop, squat; bow, curtsy, genuflect.

**croup** n buttocks, crupper, rump.

**crow** vb bluster, boast, brag, chuckle, exult, flourish, gasconade, swagger, triumph, vapour, vaunt.

**crowd** vb compress, cram, jam, pack, press; collect, congregate, flock, herd, huddle, swarm. *n assembly, company, concourse, flock, herd, horde, host, jam, multitude, press, throng; mob, pack, populace, rabble, rout.

**crown** vb adorn, dignify, honour; recompense, requite, reward; cap, complete, consummate, finish, perfect. *n bays, chaplet, coronal, coronet, garland, diadem, laurel, wreath; monarchy, royalty, sovereignty; diadem; dignity, honour, recompense, reward; apex, crest, summit, top.

**crowning** adj completing, consummating, dignifying, finishing, perfecting.

**crucial** adj intersecting, transverse; critical, decisive, searching, severe, testing, trying.

**crude** adj raw, uncooked, undressed, unworked; harsh, immature, rough, unripe; crass, coarse, unrefined; awkward, immature, indigestible, rude, uncouth, unpolished, unpremeditated.

**cruel** adj barbarous, blood-thirsty, dire, fell, ferocious, inexorable, hard-hearted, inhuman, merciless, pitiless, relentless, ruthless, sanguinary, savage, truculent, uncompassionate, unfeeling, unmerciful, unrelenting; bitter, cold, hard, severe, sharp, unfeeling.

**crumble** vb bruise, crush, decay, disintegrate, perish, pound, pulverize, triturate.

**crumple** vb rumple, wrinkle.

**crush** vb bruise, compress, contuse, squash, squeeze; bray, comminute, crumble, disintegrate, mash; demolish, raze, shatter; conquer, overcome, overpower, overwhelm, quell, subdue.

**crust** n coat, coating, incrustation, outside, shell, surface.

**crusty** adj churlish, crabbed, cross, cynical, fretful, forward, morose, peevish, pettish, petulant, snappish, snarling, surly, testy, touchy, waspish; friable, hard, short.

**cry** vb call, clamour, exclaim; blubber, snivel, sob, wail, weep, whimper; bawl, bellow, hoot, roar, shout, vociferate, scream, screech, squawk, squall, squeal, yell; announce, blazon, proclaim, publish. *n acclamation, clamour, ejaculation, exclamation, outcry; crying, lament, lamentation, plaint, weeping; bawl, bellow, howl, roar, scream, screech, shriek, yell; announcement, proclamation, publication.

**crypt** n catacomb, tomb, vault.

**cuddle** vb cosset, nestle, snuggle, squat; caress, embrace, fondle, hug, pet. *n caress, embrace, hug.

**cudgel** vb bang, baste, batter, beat, cane, drub, thrash, thump. *n bastinado, baton, bludgeon, club, shillelagh, stick, truncheon.

**cue** vb intimate, prompt, remind, sign, signal. *n catchword, hint, intimation, nod, prompting, sign, signal, suggestion.

**cuff** vb beat, box, buffet, knock, pummel, punch, slap, smack, strike, thump. *n blow, box, punch, slap, smack, strike, thump.

**cul-de-sac** n alley, dead end, impasse, pocket.

**cull** vb choose, elect, pick, select; collect, gather, glean, pluck.

**culmination** n acme, apex, climax, completion, consummation, crown, summit, top, zenith.

**culpability** n blame, blameworthiness, criminality, culpableness, guilt, remissness, sinfulness.

**culpable** adj blameable, blameworthy, censurable, faulty, guilty, reprehensible, sinful, transgressive, wrong.

**culprit** n delinquent, criminal, evil-doer, felon, malefactor, offender.

**cultivate** vb farm, fertilize, till, work; civilize, develop, discipline, elevate, improve, meliorate, refine, train; investigate, prosecute, pursue, search, study; cherish, foster, nourish, patronize, promote.

**culture** n agriculture, cultivation, farming, husbandry, tillage; cultivation, elevation, improvement, refinement.

**cumber** vb burden, clog, encumber, hamper, impede, obstruct, oppress, overload; annoy, distract, embarrass, harass, perplex, plague, torment, trouble, worry.

**cumbersome** adj burdensome, clumsy, cumbrous, embarrassing, heavy, inconvenient, oppressive, troublesome, unmanageable, unwieldy, vexatious.

**cuneiform** adj cuneate, wedge-shaped.

**cunning** adj artful, astute, crafty, crooked, deceitful, designing, diplomatic, foxy, guileful, intriguing, machiavellian, sharp, shrewd, sly, subtle, tricky, wily; curious, ingenious. *n art, artfulness, artifice, astuteness, craft, shrewdness, subtlety; craftiness, chicane, chicanery, deceit, deception, intrigue, slyness.

**cup** n beaker, bowl, chalice, goblet, mug; cupful, draught, potion.

**cupboard** n buffet, cabinet, closet.

**cupidity** n avidity, greed, hankering, longing, lust; acquisitiveness, avarice, covetousness, greediness, stinginess.

**curative** adj healing, medicinal, remedial, restorative.

**curator** n custodian, guardian, keeper, superintendent.

**curb** vb bridle, check, control, hinder, moderate, repress, restrain. *n bridle, check, control, hindrance, rein, restraint.

**cure** vb alleviate, correct, heal, mend, remedy, restore; kipper, pickle, preserve. *n antidote, corrective, help, remedy, reparative, restorative, specific; alleviation, healing, restorative.

**curiosity** n interest, inquiringness, inquisitiveness; celebrity, curio, marvel, novelty, oddity, phenomenon, rarity, sight, spectacle, wonder.

**curious** adj interested, inquiring, inquisitive, meddling, peering, prying, scrutinizing; extraordinary, marvellous, novel, queer, rare, singular, strange, unique, unusual; cunning, elegant, fine, finished, neat, skilful, well-wrought.

**curl** vb coil, twist, wind, writhe; bend, buckle, ripple, wave. *n curlicue, lovelock, ringlet; flexure, sinuosity, undulation, wave, waving, winding.

**curmudgeon** n churl, lick-penny, miser, niggard, screw, scrimp, skinflint.

**currency** n publicity; acceptance, circulation, transmission; bills, coins, money, notes.

**current** adj common, general, popular, rife; circulating, passing; existing, instant, present, prevalent, widespread. *n course, progression, river, stream, tide, undertow. *adv commonly, generally, popularly, publicly.

**curry** vb comb, dress; beat, cudgel, drub, thrash.

**curse** vb anathematize, damn, denounce, execrate, imprecate, invoke, maledict; blast, blight, destroy, doom; afflict, annoy, harass, injure, plague, scourge, torment, vex; blaspheme, swear. *n anathema, ban, denunciation, execration, fulmination, imprecation, malediction, malison; affliction, annoyance, plague, scourge, torment, trouble, vexation; ban, condemnation, penalty, sentence.

**cursed** adj accursed, banned, blighted, curse-laden, unholy; abominable, detestable, execrable, hateful, villainous; annoying, confounded, plaguing, scourging, tormenting, troublesome, vexatious.

**cursory** adj brief, careless, desultory, hasty, passing, rapid, slight, summary, superficial, transient, transitory.

**curt** adj brief, concise, laconic, short, terse; crusty, rude, snappish, tart.

**curtail** vb abridge, dock, lop, retrench, shorten; abbreviate, contract, decrease, diminish, lessen.

**curtain** vb cloak, cover, drape, mantle, screen, shade, shield, veil. *n arras, drape, drop, portière, screen, shade.

**curvature** n arcuation, bend, bending, camber, crook, curve, flexure, incurvation.

**curve** vb bend, crook, inflect, turn, twist, wind. *n arcuation, bend, bending, camber, crook, flexure, incurvation.

**curvet** vb bound, leap, vault; caper, frisk.

**cushion** vb absorb, damp, dampen, deaden, dull, muffle, mute, soften, subdue, suppress; cradle, pillow, support. *n bolster, hassock, pad, pillow, woolsack.

**cusp** n angle, horn, point.

**custodian** n curator, guardian, keeper, sacristan, superintendent, warden.

**custody** n care, charge, guardianship, keeping, safe-keeping, protection, watch, ward; confinement, durance, duress, imprisonment, prison.

**custom** n consuetude, convention, fashion, habit, manner, mode, practice, rule, usage, use, way; form, formality, observation; patronage; duty, impost, tax, toll, tribute.

**customary** adj accustomed, common, consue-tudinary, conventional, familiar, fashionable, general, habitual, gnomic, prescriptive, regular, usual, wonted.

**cut** vb chop, cleave, divide, gash, incise, lance, sever, slice, slit, wound; carve, chisel, sculpture; hurt, move, pierce, touch; ignore, slight; abbreviate, abridge, curtail, shorten. *n gash, groove, incision, nick, slash, slice, slit; channel, passage; piece, slice; fling, sarcasm, taunt; fashion, form, mode, shape, style.

**cutthroat** adj barbarous, cruel, ferocious, murderous; competitive, exacting, exorbitant, extortionate, rivalling, ruthless, usurious, vying.*n assassin, murderer, ruffian.

**cutting** adj keen, sharp; acid, biting, bitter, caustic, piercing, sarcastic, sardonic, satirical, severe, trenchant, wounding.

**cycle** n age, circle, era, period, revolution, round.

**Cyclopean** adj colossal, enormous, gigantic, Herculean, immense, vast.

**cynical** adj captious, carping, censorious, churlish, crabbed, cross, crusty, fretful, ill-natured, ill-tempered, morose, peevish, pettish, petulant, sarcastic, satirical, snappish, snarling, surly, testy, touchy, waspish; contemptuous, derisive, misanthropic, pessimistic, scornful.

**cynosure** n attraction, centre.

**cyst** n pouch, sac.

# D

**dab** vb box, rap, slap, strike, tap touch; coat, daub, smear. * adj adept, expert, proficient; pat. * n lump, mass, pat.

**dabble** vb dip, moisten, soak, spatter, splash, sprinkle, wet; meddle, tamper, trifle.

**daft** adj absurd, delirious, foolish, giddy, idiotic, insane, silly, simple, stupid, witless; frolicsome, merry, mirthful, playful, sportive.

**dagger** n bayonet, dirk, poniard, stiletto.

**dainty** adj delicate, delicious, luscious, nice, palatable, savoury, tender, toothsome; beautiful, charming, choice, delicate, elegant, exquisite, fine, neat; fastidious, finical, finicky, over-nice, particular, scrupulous, squeamish. * n delicacy, titbit, treat.

**dale** n bottom, dell, dingle, glen, vale, valley.

**dalliance** n caressing, endearments, flirtation, fondling.

**dally** vb dawdle, fritter, idle, trifle, waste time; flirt, fondle, toy.

**damage** vb harm, hurt, impair, injure, mar. * n detriment, harm, hurt, injury, loss, mischief.

**damages** npl compensation, fine, forfeiture, indemnity, reparation, satisfaction.

**dame** n babe, baby, broad, doll, girl; lady, madam, matron, mistress.

**damn** vb condemn, doom, kill, ruin. * n bean, curse, fig, hoot, rap, sou, straw, whit.

**damnable** adj abominable, accursed, atrocious, cursed, detestable, hateful, execrable, odious, outrageous.

**damp** vb dampen, moisten; allay, abate, check, discourage, moderate, repress, restrain; chill, cool, deaden, deject, depress, dispirit. * adj dank, humid, moist, wet. * n dampness, dank, fog, mist, moisture, vapour; chill, dejection, depression.

**damper** n check, hindrance, impediment, obstacle; damp, depression, discouragement, wet blanket.

**dandle** vb amuse, caress, fondle, pet, toss; dance.

**danger** n jeopardy, insecurity, hazard, peril, risk, venture.

**dangerous** adj critical, hazardous, insecure, perilous, risky, ticklish, unsafe.

**dangle** vb drape, hang, pend, sway, swing; fawn.

**dank** adj damp, humid, moist, wet.

**dapper** adj active, agile, alert, brisk, lively, nimble, quick, ready, smart, spry; neat, nice, pretty, spruce, trim.

**dapple** vb diversify, spot, variegate. * adj dappled, spotted, variegated.

**dare** vb challenge, defy, endanger, hazard, provoke, risk. * n challenge, defiance, gage.

**daring** adj adventurous, bold, brave, chivalrous, courageous, dauntless, doughty, fearless, gallant, heroic, intrepid, valiant, valorous. * n adventurousness, boldness, bravery, courage, dauntlessness, doughtiness, fearlessness, intrepidity, undauntedness, valour.

**dark** adj black, cloudy, darksome, dusky, ebon, inky, lightless, lurid, moonless, murky, opaque, overcast, pitchy, rayless, shady, shadowy, starless, sunless, swart, tenebrous, umbrageous, unenlightened, unilluminated; abstruse, cabbalistic, enigmatical, incomprehensible, mysterious, mystic, mystical, obscure, occult, opaque, recondite, transcendental, unillumined, unintelligible; cheerless, discouraging, dismal, disheartening, funereal, gloomy; benighted, darkened, ignorant, rude, unlettered, untaught; atrocious, damnable, infamous, flagitious, foul, horrible, infernal, nefarious, vile, wicked. * n darkness, dusk, murkiness, obscurity; concealment, privacy, secrecy; blindness, ignorance.

**darken** vb cloud, dim, eclipse, obscure, shade, shadow; chill, damp, depress, gloom, sadden; benight, stultify, stupefy; obscure, perplex; defile, dim, dull, stain, sully.

**darkness** n blackness, dimness, gloom, obscurity; blindness, ignorance; cheerlessness, despondency, gloom, joylessness; privacy, secrecy.

**darling** adj beloved, cherished, dear, loved, precious, treasured. * n dear, favourite, idol, love, sweetheart.

**dart** vb ejaculate, hurl, launch, propel, sling, throw; emit, shoot; dash, rush, scoot, spring.

**dash** vb break, destroy, disappoint, frustrate, ruin, shatter, spoil, thwart; abash, confound, disappoint, surprise; bolt, dart, fly, run, speed, rush. * n blow, stroke; advance, onset, rush; infusion, smack, spice, sprinkling, tincture, tinge, touch; flourish, show.

**dashing** adj headlong, impetuous, precipitate, rushing; brilliant, gay, showy, spirited.

**dastardly** adj base, cowardly, coward, cowering, craven, pusillanimous, recreant. * n coward, craven, milksop, poltroon, recreant.

**data** npl conditions, facts, information, premises.

**date** n age, cycle, day, generation, time; epoch, era, period; appointment, arrangement, assignation, engagement, interview, rendezvous, tryst; catch, steady, sweetheart.

**daub** vb bedaub, begrime, besmear, blur, cover, deface, defile, grime, plaster, smear, smudge, soil, sully. * n smear, smirch, smudge.

**daunt** vb alarm, appal, check, cow, deter, discourage, frighten, intimate, scare, subdue, tame, terrify, thwart.

**dauntless** adj bold, brave, chivalrous, courageous, daring, doughty, gallant, heroic, indomitable, intrepid, unaffrighted, unconquerable, undaunted, undismayed, valiant, valorous.

**dawdle** vb dally, delay, fiddle, idle, lag, loiter, potter, trifle.

**dawn** vb appear, begin, break, gleam, glimmer, open, rise. * n daybreak, dawning, cockcrow, sunrise, sun-up.

**day** n daylight, sunlight, sunshine; age, epoch, generation, lifetime, time.

**daze** vb blind, dazzle; bewilder, confound, confuse, perplex, stun, stupefy. * n bewilderment, confusion, discomposure, perturbation, pother; coma, stupor, swoon, trance.

**dazzle** vb blind, daze; astonish, confound, overpower, surprise. * n brightness, brilliance, splendour.

**dead** adj breathless, deceased, defunct, departed, gone, inanimate, lifeless; apathetic, callous, cold, dull, frigid, indifferent, inert, lukewarm, numb, obtuse, spiritless, torpid, unfeeling; flat, insipid, stagnant, tasteless, vapid; barren, inactive, sterile, unemployed, unprofitable, useless. * adv absolutely, completely, downright, fundamentally, quite; direct, directly, due, exactly, just, right, squarely, straight. * n depth, midst; hush, peace, quietude, silence, stillness.

**deaden** vb abate, damp, dampen, dull, impair, muffle, mute, restrain, retard, smother, weaken; benumb, blunt, hebetate, obtund, paralyse.

**deadly** adj deleterious, destructive, fatal, lethal, malignant, mortal, murderous, noxious, pernicious, poisonous, venomous; implacable, mortal, rancorous, sanguinary.

**deal** vb allot, apportion, assign, bestow, dispense, distribute, divide, give, reward, share; bargain, trade, traffic, treat with. * n amount, degree, distribution, extent, lot, portion, quantity, share; bargain, transaction.

**dear** adj costly, expensive, high-priced; beloved, cherished, darling, esteemed, precious, treasured. * n beloved, darling, deary, honey, love, precious, sweet, sweetie, sweetheart.

**dearth** n deficiency, insufficiency, scarcity; famine, lack, need, shortage, want.

**death** n cessation, decease, demise, departure, destruction, dissolution, dying, end, exit, mortality, passing.

**deathless** adj eternal, everlasting, immortal, imperishable, undying; boring, dull, turgid.

**debacle** n breakdown, cataclysm, collapse; rout, stampede.

**debar** vb blackball, deny, exclude, hinder, prevent, prohibit, restrain, shut out, stop, withhold.

**debase** vb adulterate, alloy, depress, deteriorate, impair, injure, lower, pervert, reduce, vitiate; abase, degrade, disgrace, dishonour, humble, humiliate, mortify, shame; befoul, contaminate, corrupt, defile, foul, pollute, soil, taint.

**debate** vb argue, canvass, contest, discuss, dispute; contend, deliberate, wrangle. * n controversy, discussion, disputation; altercation, contention, contest, dispute, logomachy.

**debauch** vb corrupt, deprave, pollute, vitiate; deflower, ravish, seduce, violate. * n carousal, orgy, revel, saturnalia.

**debauchery** n dissipation, dissoluteness, excesses, intemperance; debauch, excess, intemperance, lewdness, licentiousness, lust; bacchanal, carousal, compotation, indulgence, orgies, potation, revelry, revels, saturnalia, spree.

**debilitate** vb enervate, enfeeble, exhaust, prostrate, relax, weaken.

**debility** n enervation, exhaustion, faintness, feebleness, frailty, imbecility, infirmity, languor, prostration, weakness.

**debonair** adj affable, civil, complaisant, courteous, easy, gracious, kind, obliging, polite, refined, urbane, well-bred.

**debris** n detritus, fragments, remains, rubbish, rubble, ruins, wreck, wreckage.

**debt** n arrears, debit, due, liability, obligation; fault, misdoing, offence, shortcoming, sin, transgression, trespass.

**decadence** n caducity, decay, declension, decline, degeneracy, degeneration, deterioration, fall, retrogression.

**decamp** vb abscond, bolt, escape, flee, fly.

**decapitate** vb behead, decollate, guillotine.

**decay** vb decline, deteriorate, disintegrate, fail, perish, wane, waste, wither; decompose, putrefy, rot. * n caducity, decadence, declension, decline, decomposition, decrepitude, degeneracy, degeneration, deterioration, dilapidation, disintegration, fading, failing, perishing, putrefaction, ruin, wasting, withering.

**deceased** adj dead, defunct, departed, gone, late, lost.

**deceit** n artifice, cheating, chicanery, cozenage, craftiness, deceitfulness, deception, double-dealing, duplicity, finesse, fraud, guile, hypocrisy, imposition, imposture, pretence, sham, treachery, tricky, underhandedness, wile.

**deceitful** adj counterfeit, deceptive, delusive, fallacious, hollow, illusive, illusory, insidious, misleading; circumventive, cunning, designing, dissembling, dodgy, double-dealing, evasive, false, fraudulent, guileful, hypocritical, insincere, tricky, underhanded, wily.

**deceive** vb befool, beguile, betray, cheat, chouse, circumvent, cozen, defraud, delude, disappoint, double-cross, dupe, ensnare, entrap, fool, gull, hoax, hoodwink, humbug, mislead, outwit, overreach, trick.

**deceiver** n charlatan, cheat, humbug, hypocrite, knave, impostor, pretender, rogue, sharper, trickster.

**decent** adj appropriate, becoming, befitting, comely, seemly, decorous, fit, proper, seemly; chaste, delicate, modest, pure; moderate, passable, respectable, tolerable.

**deception** n artifice, cheating, chicanery, cozenage, craftiness, deceitfulness, deception, double-dealing, duplicity, finesse, fraud, guile, hoax, hypocrisy, imposition, imposture, pretence, sham, treachery, trick, underhandedness, wile; cheat, chouse, ruse, stratagem, wile.

**deceptive** adj deceitful, deceiving, delusive, disingenuous, fallacious, false, illusive, illusory, misleading.

**decide** vb close, conclude, determine, end, settle, terminate; resolve; adjudge, adjudicate, award.

**decided** adj determined, firm, resolute, unhesitating, unwavering; absolute, categorical, positive, unequivocal; certain, clear, indisputable, undeniable, unmistakable, unquestionable.

**deciduous** adj caducous, nonperennial, temporary.

**decipher** vb explain, expound, interpret, reveal, solve, unfold, unravel; read.

**decision** n conclusion, determination, judgement, settlement; adjudication, award, decree, pronouncement, sentence; firmness, resolution.

**decisive** adj conclusive, determinative, final.

**deck** vb adorn, array, beautify, decorate, embellish, grace, ornament; apparel, attire, bedeck, clothe, dress, robe.

**declaim** vb harangue, mouth, rant, speak, spout.

**declamation** n declaiming, haranguing, mouthing, ranting, spouting.

**declamatory** adj bombastic, discursive, fustian, grandiloquent, high-flown, high-sounding, incoherent, inflated, pompous, pretentious, rhetorical, swelling, turgid.

**declaration** n affirmation, assertion, asseveration, averment, avowal, protestation, statement; announcement, proclamation, publication.

**declaratory** adj affirmative, annunciatory, assertive, declarative, definite, enunciative, enunciatory, expressive; explanatory, expository.

**declare** vb advertise, affirm, announce, assert, asseverate, aver, blazon, bruit, proclaim, promulgate, pronounce, publish, state, utter.

**declension** n decadence, decay, decline, degeneracy, deterioration, diminution; inflection, variation; declination, nonacceptance, refusal.

**declination** n bending, descent, inclination; decadence, decay, decline, degeneracy, degeneration, degradation, deterioration, diminution; aberration, departure, deviation, digression, divagation, divergence; declinature, nonacceptance, refusal.

**decline** vb incline, lean, slope; decay, droop, fail, flag, languish, pine, sink; degenerate, depreciate, deteriorate; decrease, diminish, dwindle, fade, ebb, lapse, lessen, wane; avoid, refuse, reject; inflect, vary. * n decadence, decay, declension, declination, degeneracy, deterioration, diminution, wane; atrophy, consumption, marasmus, phthisis; declivity, hill, incline, slope.

**declivity** n declination, descent, incline, slope.

**decompose** vb analyse, disintegrate, dissolve, distil, resolve, separate; corrupt, decay, putrefy, rot.

**decomposition** n analysis, break-up, disintegration, resolution; caries, corruption, crumbling, decay, disintegration, dissolution, putrescence, rotting.

**decorate** vb adorn, beautify, bedeck, deck, embellish, enrich, garnish, grace, ornament.

**decoration** n adorning, beautifying, bedecking, decking, enriching, garnishing, ornamentation, ornamenting; adornment, enrichment, embellishment, ornament.

**decorous** adj appropriate, becoming, befitting, comely, decent, fit, suitable, proper, sedate, seemly, staid.

**decorum** n appropriate behaviour, courtliness, decency, deportment, dignity, gravity, politeness, propriety, sedateness, seemliness.

**decoy** vb allure, deceive, ensnare, entice, entrap, inveigle, lure, seduce, tempt. * n allurement, lure, enticement.

**decrease** vb abate, contract, decline, diminish, dwindle, ebb, lessen, subside, wane; curtail, diminish, lessen, lower, reduce, retrench. * n abatement, contraction, declension, decline, decrement, diminishing, diminution, ebb, ebbing, lessening, reduction, subsidence, waning.

**decree** vb adjudge, appoint, command, decide, determine, enact, enjoin, order, ordain. * n act, command, edict, enactment, fiat, law, mandate, order, ordinance, precept, regulation, statute.

**decrement** n decrease, diminution, lessening, loss, waste.

**decrepit** adj feeble, effete, shattered, wasted, weak; aged, crippled, superannuated.

**decry** vb abuse, belittle, blame, condemn, denounce, depreciate, detract, discredit, disparage, run down, traduce, underrate, undervalue.

**dedicate** vb consecrate, devote, hallow, sanctify; address, inscribe.

**deduce** vb conclude, derive, draw, gather, infer.

**deducible** adj derivable, inferable.

**deduct** vb remove, subtract, withdraw; abate, detract.

**deduction** n removal, subtraction, withdrawal; abatement, allowance, defalcation, discount, rebate, reduction, reprise; conclusion, consequence, corollary, inference.

**deed** n achievement, act, action, derring-do, exploit, feat, performance; fact, truth, reality; charter, contract, document, indenture, instrument, transfer.

**deem** vb account, believe, conceive, consider, count, estimate, hold, imagine, judge, regard, suppose, think; fancy, opine.

**deep** adj abysmal, extensive, great, profound; abstruse, difficult, hard, intricate, knotty, mysterious, recondite, unfathomable; astute, cunning, designing, discerning, intelligent, insidious, penetrating, sagacious, shrewd; absorbed, engrossed; bass, grave, low; entire, great, heartfelt, thorough. * n main, ocean, water, sea; abyss, depth, profundity; enigma, mystery, riddle; silence, stillness.

**deeply** adv profoundly; completely, entirely, extensively, greatly, thoroughly; affectingly, distressingly, feelingly, mournfully, sadly.

**deface** vb blotch, deform, disfigure, injure, mar, mutilate, obliterate, soil, spoil, sully, tarnish.

**de facto** adj actual, real. * adv actually, in effect, in fact, really, truly.

**defalcate** vb abate, curtail, retrench, lop.

**defalcation** n abatement, deduction, diminution, discount, reduction; default, deficiency, deficit, shortage, shortcoming; embezzlement, fraud.

**defamation** n abuse, aspersion, back-biting, calumny, detraction, disparagement, libel, obloquy, opprobrium, scandal, slander.

**defamatory** adj abusive, calumnious, libellous, slanderous.

**defame** vb abuse, asperse, blacken, belie, besmirch, blemish, calumniate, detract, disgrace, dishonour, libel, malign, revile, slander, smirch, traduce, vilify.

**default** vb defalcate, dishonour, fail, repudiate, welsh. * n defalcation, failure, lapse, neglect, offence, omission, oversight, shortcoming; defect, deficiency, deficit, delinquency, destitution, fault, lack, want.

**defaulter** n delinquent, embezzler, offender, peculator.

**defeat** vb beat, checkmate, conquer, discomfit, overcome, overpower, overthrow, repulse, rout, ruin, vanquish; baffle, balk, block, disappoint, disconcert, foil, frustrate, thwart. * n discomfiture, downfall, overthrow, repulse, rout, vanquishment; bafflement, checkmate, frustration.

**defect** vb abandon, desert, rebel, revolt. * n default, deficiency, destitution, lack, shortcoming, spot, taint, want; blemish, blotch, error, flaw, imperfection, mistake; failing, fault, foible.

**defection** n abandonment, desertion, rebellion, revolt; apostasy, backsliding, dereliction.

**defective** adj deficient, inadequate, incomplete, insufficient, scant, short; faulty, imperfect, marred.

**defence** n defending, guarding, holding, maintaining, maintenance, protection; buckler, bulwark, fortification, guard, protection, rampart, resistance, shield; apology, excuse, justification, plea, vindication.

**defenceless** adj exposed, helpless, unarmed, unprotected, unguarded, unshielded, weak.

**defend** vb cover, fortify, guard, preserve, protect, safeguard, screen, secure, shelter, shield; assert, espouse, justify, maintain, plead, uphold, vindicate.

**defender** n asserter, maintainer, pleader, upholder; champion, protector, vindicator.

**defer**[1] vb adjourn, delay, pigeonhole, procrastinate, postpone, prorogue, protract, shelve, table.

**defer**[2] vb abide by, acknowledge, bow to, give way, submit, yield; admire, esteem, honour, regard, respect.

**deference** n esteem, homage, honour, obeisance, regard, respect, reverence, veneration; complaisance, consideration; obedience, submission.

**deferential** adj respectful, reverential.

**defiance** n challenge, daring; contempt, despite, disobedience, disregard, opposition, spite.

**defiant** adj contumacious, recalcitrant, resistant; bold, courageous, resistant.

**deficiency** n dearth, default, deficit, insufficiency, lack, meagreness, scantiness, scarcity, shortage, shortness, want; defect, error, failing, falling, fault, foible, frailty, imperfection, infirmity, weakness.

**deficient** adj defective, faulty, imperfect, inadequate, incomplete, insufficient, lacking, scant, scanty, scarce, short, unsatisfactory, wanting.

**deficit** n deficiency, lack, scarcity, shortage, shortness.

**defile**[1] vb dirty, foul, soil, stain, tarnish; contaminate, debase, poison, pollute, sully, taint, vitiate; corrupt, debauch, deflower, ravish, seduce, violate.

**defile**[2] vb file, march, parade, promenade. * n col, gorge, pass, passage, ravine, strait.

**define** vb bound, circumscribe, designate, delimit, demarcate, determine, explain, limit, specify.

**definite** adj defined, determinate, determined, fixed, restricted; assured, certain, clear, exact, explicit, positive, precise, specific, unequivocal.

**definitive** adj categorical, determinate, explicit, express, positive, unconditional; conclusive, decisive, final.

**deflect** vb bend, deviate, diverge, swerve, turn, twist, waver, wind.

**deflower** vb corrupt, debauch, defile, seduce.

**deform** vb deface, disfigure, distort, injure, mar, misshape, ruin, spoil.

**deformity** n abnormality, crookedness, defect, disfigurement, distortion, inelegance, irregularity, malformation, misproportion, misshapenness, monstrosity, ugliness.

**defraud** vb beguile, cheat, chouse, circumvent, cozen, deceive, delude, diddle, dupe, embezzle, gull, overreach, outwit, pilfer, rob, swindle, trick.

**defray** vb bear, discharge, liquidate, meet, pay, settle.

**deft** adj adroit, apt, clever, dab, dextrous, expert, handy, ready, skilful.

**defunct** adj dead, deceased, departed, extinct, gone; abrogated, annulled, cancelled, inoperative.

**defy** vb challenge, dare; brave, contemn, despise, disregard, face, flout, provoke, scorn, slight, spurn.

**degeneracy** n abasement, caducity, corruption, debasement, decadence, decay, declension, decline, decrease, degenerateness, degeneration, degradation, depravation, deterioration; inferiority, meanness, poorness.

**degenerate** vb decay, decline, decrease, deteriorate, retrograde, sink. * adj base, corrupt, decayed, degenerated, deteriorated, fallen, inferior, low, mean, perverted.

**degeneration** n debasement, decline, degeneracy, deterioration.

**degradation** n deposition, disgrace, dishonour, humiliation, ignominy; abasement, caducity, corruption, debasement, decadence, decline, degeneracy, degeneration, deterioration, perversion, vitiation.

**degrade** vb abase, alloy, break, cashier, corrupt, debase, demote, discredit, disgrace, dishonour, disparage, downgrade, humiliate, humble, lower, pervert, vitiate; deteriorate, impair, lower, sink.

**degree** n stage, step; class, grade, order, quality, rank, standing, station; extent, measure; division, interval, space.

**deify** vb apotheosize, idolize, glorify, revere; elevate, ennoble, exalt.

**deign** vb accord, condescend, grant, vouchsafe.

**deject** vb depress, discourage, dishearten, dispirit, sadden.

**dejected** adj blue, chapfallen, crestfallen, depressed, despondent, disheartened, dispirited, doleful, downcast, down-hearted, gloomy, low-spirited, miserable, sad, wretched.

**delay** vb defer, postpone, procrastinate; arrest, detain, check, hinder, impede, retard, stay, stop; prolong, protract; dawdle, linger, loiter, tarry. * n deferment, postponement, procrastination; check, detention, hindrance, impediment, retardation, stoppage; prolonging, protraction; dallying, dawdling, lingering, tarrying, stay, stop.

**delectable** adj agreeable, charming, delightful, enjoyable, gratifying, pleasant, pleasing.

**delectation** n delight, ecstasy, gladness, joy, rapture, ravishment, transport.

**delegate** vb appoint, authorize, mission, depute, deputize, transfer; commit, entrust. * n ambassador, commissioner, delegate, deputy, envoy, representative.

**delete** vb cancel, efface, erase, expunge, obliterate, remove.

**deleterious** adj deadly, destructive, lethal, noxious, poisonous; harmful, hurtful, injurious, pernicious, unwholesome.

**deliberate** vb cogitate, consider, consult, meditate, muse, ponder, reflect, ruminate, think, weigh. * adj careful, cautious, circumspect, considerate, heedful, purposeful, methodical, thoughtful, wary; well-advised, well-considered; aforethought, intentional, premeditated, purposed, studied.

**deliberation** n caution, circumspection, cogitation, consideration, coolness, meditation, prudence, reflection, thought, thoughtfulness, wariness; purpose.

**delicacy** n agreeableness, daintiness, deliciousness, pleasantness, relish, savouriness; bonne bouche, dainty, tidbit; elegance, fitness, lightness, niceness, nicety, smoothness, softness, tenderness; fragility, frailty, slenderness, slightness, tenderness, weakness; carefulness, discrimination, fastidiousness, finesse, nicety, scrupulousness, sensitivity, subtlety, tact; purity, refinement, sensibility.

**delicate** adj agreeable, delicious, pleasant, pleasing, palatable, savoury; elegant, exquisite, fine, nice; careful, dainty, discriminating, fastidious, scrupulous; fragile, frail, slender, slight, tender, delicate; pure, refined.

**delicious** adj dainty, delicate, luscious, nice, palatable, savory; agreeable, charming, choice, delightful, exquisite, grateful, pleasant.

**delight** vb charm, enchant, enrapture, gratify, please, ravish, rejoice, satisfy, transport. * n charm, delectation, ecstasy, enjoyment, gladness, gratification, happiness, joy, pleasure, rapture, ravishment, satisfaction, transport.

**delightful** adj agreeable, captivating, charming, delectable, enchanting, enjoyable, enrapturing, rapturous, ravishing, transporting.

**delineate** vb design, draw, figure, paint, sketch, trace; depict, describe, picture, portray.

**delineation** n design, draught, drawing, figure, outline, sketch; account, description, picture, portrayal.

**delinquency** n crime, fault, misdeed, misdemeanour, offence, wrong-doing.

**delinquent** adj negligent, offending. * n criminal, culprit, defaulter, malefactor, miscreant, misdoer, offender, transgressor, wrong-doer.

**delirious** adj crazy, demented, deranged, frantic, frenzied, light-headed, mad, insane, raving, wandering.

**delirium** n aberration, derangement, frenzy, hallucination, incoherence, insanity, lunacy, madness, raving, wandering.

**deliver** vb emancipate, free, liberate, release; extricate, redeem, rescue, save; commit, give, impart, transfer; cede, grant, relinquish, resign, yield; declare, emit, promulgate, pronounce, speak, utter; deal, discharge.

**deliverance** n emancipation, escape, liberation, redemption, release.

**delivery** n conveyance, surrender; commitment, giving, rendering, transference, transferral, transmission; elocution, enunciation, pronunciation; speech, utterance; childbirth, confinement, labour, parturition, travail.

**dell** n dale, dingle, glen, valley, ravine.

**delude** vb beguile, cheat, chouse, circumvent, cozen, deceive, dupe, gull, misguide, mislead, overreach, trick.

**deluge** vb drown, inundate, overflow, overwhelm, submerge. * n cataclysm, downpour, flood, inundation, overflow, rush.

**delusion** n artifice, cheat, clap-trap, deceit, dodge, fetch, fraud, imposition, imposture, ruse, snare, trick, wile; deception, error, fallacy, fancy, hallucination, illusion, mistake, mockery, phantasm.

**delusive** adj deceitful, deceiving, deceptive, fallacious, illusional, illusionary, illusive.

**demand** vb challenge, exact, require; claim, necessitate, require; ask, inquire. * n claim, draft, exaction, requirement, requisition; call, want; inquiry, interrogation, question.

**demarcation** n bound, boundary, confine, distinction, division, enclosure, limit, separation.

**demeanour** n air, bearing, behaviour, carriage, deportment, manner, mien.

**demented** adj crack-brained, crazed, crazy, daft, deranged, dotty, foolish, idiotic, infatuated, insane, lunatic.

**dementia** n idiocy, insanity, lunacy.

**demerit** n delinquency, fault, ill-desert.

**demise** vb alienate, consign, convey, devolve, grant, transfer; bequeath, devise, leave, will. * n alienation, conveyance, transfer, transference, transmission; death, decease.

**demolish** vb annihilate, destroy, dismantle, level, over-throw, overturn, pulverize, raze, ruin.

**demon** n devil, fiend, kelpie, goblin, troll.

**demoniac, demoniacal** adj demonic, demonical, devilish, diabolic, diabolical, fiendish, hellish, infernal, Mephistophelean, Mephistophelian, satanic; delirious, distracted, frantic, frenzied, feverish, hysterical, mad, overwrought, rabid.

**demonstrate** vb establish, exhibit, illustrate, indicate, manifest, prove, show.

**demonstration** n display, exhibition, manifestation, show.

**demonstrative** adj affectionate, communicative, effusive, emotional, expansive, expressive, extroverted, open, outgoing, passionate, sentimental, suggestive, talkative, unreserved; absolute, apodictic, certain, conclusive, probative; exemplificative, illustrative.

**demoralize** vb corrupt, debase, debauch, deprave, vitiate; depress, discourage, dishearten, weaken.

**demulcent** adj emollient, lenitive, mild, mollifying, sedative, soothing.

**demur** vb halt, hesitate, pause, stop, waver; doubt, object, scruple. * n demurral, hesitance, hesitancy, hesitation, objection, pause, qualm, scruple.

**demure** adj prudish; coy, decorous, grave, modest, priggish, prudish, sedate, sober, staid.

**den** n cavern, cave; haunt, lair, resort, retreat.

**denial** n contradiction, controverting, negation; abjuration, disavowal, disclaimer, disowning; disallowance, refusal, rejection.

**denizen** n citizen, dweller, inhabitant, resident.

**denominate** vb call, christen, designate, dub, entitle, name, phrase, style, term.

**denomination** n appellation, designation, name, style, term, title; class, kind, sort; body, persuasion, school, sect.

**denote** vb betoken, connote, designate, imply, indicate, mark, mean, note, show, signify, typify.

**dénouement** n catastrophe, unravelling; consummation, issue, finale, upshot, conclusion, termination.

**denounce** vb menace, threaten; arraign, attack, brand, censure, condemn, proscribe, stigmatize, upbraid; accuse, inform, denunciate.

**dense** adj close, compact, compressed, condensed, thick; dull, slow, stupid.

**dent** vb depress, dint, indent, pit. * n depression, dint, indentation, nick, notch.

**dentate** adj notched, serrate, toothed.

**denude** vb bare, divest, strip.

**denunciation** n menace, threat; arraignment, censure, fulmination, invective; exposure.

**deny** vb contradict, gainsay, oppose, refute, traverse; abjure, abnegate, disavow, disclaim, disown, renounce; disallow, refuse, reject, withhold.

**depart** vb absent, disappear, vanish; abandon, decamp, go, leave, migrate, quit, remove, withdraw; decease, die; deviate, diverge, vary.

**department** n district, division, part, portion, province; bureau, function, office, province, sphere, station; branch, division, subdivision.

**departure** n exit, leaving, parting, removal, recession, removal, retirement, withdrawal; abandonment, forsaking; death, decease, demise, deviation, exit.

**depend** vb hang, hinge, turn.

**dependant** n client, hanger-on, henchman, minion, retainer, subordinate, vassal; attendant, circumstance, concomitant, consequence, corollary.

**dependence** n concatenation, connection, interdependence; confidence, reliance, trust; buttress, prop, staff, stay, support, supporter; contingency, need, subjection, subordination.

**dependency** n adjunct, appurtenance; colony, province.

**dependent** adj hanging, pendant; conditioned, contingent, relying, subject, subordinate.

**depict** vb delineate, limn, outline, paint, pencil, portray, sketch; describe, render, represent.

**deplete** vb drain, empty, evacuate, exhaust, reduce.

**deplorable** adj calamitous, distressful, distressing, grievous, lamentable, melancholy, miserable, mournful, pitiable, regrettable, sad, wretched.

**deplore** vb bemoan, bewail, grieve for, lament, mourn, regret.

**deploy** vb display, expand, extend, open, unfold.

**deportment** n air, bearing, behaviour, breeding, carriage, comportment, conduct, demeanour, manner, mien, port.

**depose** vb break, cashier, degrade, dethrone, dismiss, displace, oust, reduce; avouch, declare, depone, testify.

**deposit** vb drop, dump, precipitate; lay, put; bank, hoard, lodge, put, save, store; commit, entrust. * n diluvium, dregs, lees, precipitate, precipitation, sediment, settlement, settlings, silt; money, pawn, pledge, security, stake.

**depositary** n fiduciary, guardian, trustee.

**deposition** n affidavit, evidence, testimony; deposit, precipitation, settlement; dethroning, displacement, removal.

**depository** n deposit, depot, storehouse, warehouse.

**depot** n depository, magazine, storehouse, warehouse.

**depravation** n abasement, corruption, deterioration, impairing, injury, vitiation; debasement, degeneracy, degeneration, depravity, impairment.

**depraved** adj abandoned, corrupt, corrupted, debased, debauched, degenerate, dissolute, evil, graceless, hardened, immoral, lascivious, lewd, licentious, lost, perverted, profligate, reprobate, shameless, sinful, vicious, wicked.

**depravity** n corruption, degeneracy, depravedness; baseness, contamination, corruption, corruptness, criminality, demoralization, immorality, iniquity, license, perversion, vice, viciousness, wickedness.

**depreciate** vb underestimate, undervalue, underrate; belittle, censure, decry, degrade, disparage, malign, traduce.

**depreciation** n belittling, censure, derogation, detraction, disparagement, maligning, traducing.

**depredation** n despoiling, devastation, pilfering, pillage, plunder, rapine, robbery, spoliation, theft.

**depress** vb bow, detrude, drop, lower, reduce, sink; abase, abash, degrade, debase, disgrace, humble, humiliate; chill, damp, dampen, deject, discourage, dishearten, dispirit, sadden; deaden, lower.

**depression** n cavity, concavity, dent, dimple, dint, excavation, hollow, hollowness, indentation, pit; blues, cheerlessness, dejection, dejectedness, despondency, disconsolateness, disheartenment, dispiritedness, dole, dolefulness, downheartedness, dumps, gloom, gloominess, hypochondria, melancholy, sadness, vapours; inactivity, lowness, stagnation; abasement, debasement, degradation, humiliation.

**deprivation** n bereavement, dispossession, loss, privation, spoliation, stripping.

**deprive** vb bereave, denude, despoil, dispossess, divest, rob, strip.

**depth** n abyss, deepness, drop, profundity; extent, measure; middle, midst, stillness; astuteness, discernment, penetration, perspicacity, profoundness, profundity, sagacity, shrewdness.

**deputation** n commission, delegation; commissioners, deputies, delegates, delegation, embassies, envoys, legation.

**depute** vb accredit, appoint, authorize, charge, commission, delegate, empower, entrust.

**deputy** adj acting, assistant, vice, subordinate. * n agent, commissioner, delegate, envoy, factor, legate, lieutenant, proxy, representative, substitute, viceregent.

**derange** vb confound, confuse, disarrange, disconcert, disorder, displace, madden, perturb, unsettle; discompose, disconcert, disturb, perturb, ruffle, upset; craze, madden, unbalance, unhinge.

**derangement** n confusion, disarrangement, disorder, irregularity; discomposure, disturbance, perturbation; aberration, alienation, delirium, dementia, hallucination, insanity, lunacy, madness, mania.

**derelict** adj abandoned, forsaken, left, relinquished; delinquent, faithless, guilty, neglectful, negligent, unfaithful. * n castaway, castoff, outcast, tramp, vagrant, wreck, wretch.

**dereliction** n abandonment, desertion, relinquishement, renunciation; delinquency, failure, faithlessness, fault, neglect, negligence.

**deride** vb chaff, flout, gibe, insult, jeer, lampoon, mock, ridicule, satirize, scoff, scorn, sneer, taunt.

**derision** n contempt, disrespect, insult, laughter, mockery, ridicule, scorn.

**derisive** adj contemptuous, contumelious, mocking, ridiculing, scoffing, scornful.

**derivation** n descent, extraction, genealogy; etymology; deducing, deriving, drawing, getting, obtaining; beginning, foundation, origination, source.

**derive** vb draw, get, obtain, receive; deduce, follow, infer, trace.

**derogate** vb compromise, depreciate, detract, diminish, disparage, lessen.

**derogatory** adj belittling, depreciative, deprecatory, detracting, dishonouring, disparaging, injurious.

**descant** vb amplify, animadvert, dilate, discourse, discuss, enlarge, expatiate. * n melody, soprano, treble; animadversion, commentary, remarks; discourse, discussion.

**descend** vb drop, fall, pitch, plunge, sink, swoop; alight, dismount; go, pass, proceed, devolve; derive, issue, originate.

**descendants** npl offspring, issue, posterity, progeny.

**descent** n downrush, drop, fall; descending; decline, declivity, dip, pitch, slope; ancestry, derivation, extraction, genealogy, lineage, parentage, pedigree; assault, attack, foray, incursion, invasion, raid.

**describe** vb define, delineate, draw, illustrate, limn, sketch, specify, trace; detail; depict, explain, narrate, portray, recount, relate, represent; characterize.

**description** n delineation, tracing; account, depiction, explanation, narration, narrative, portrayal, recital, relation, report, representation; class, kind, sort, species.

**descry** vb behold, discover, discern, distinguish, espy, observe, perceive, see; detect, recognize.

**desecrate** vb abuse, pervert, defile, pollute, profane, violate.

**desert**[1] n due, excellence, merit, worth; punishment, reward.

**desert**[2] vb abandon, abscond, forsake, leave, quit, relinquish, renounce, resign, quit, vacate.

**desert**[3] adj barren, desolate, forsaken, lonely, solitary, uncultivated, uninhabited, unproductive, untilled, waste, wild.

**deserted** adj abandoned, forsaken, relinquished.

**deserter** n abandoner, forsaker, quitter, runaway; apostate, backslider, fugitive, recreant, renegade, revolter, traitor, turncoat.

**desertion** n abandonment, dereliction, recreancy, relinquishment.

**deserve** vb earn, gain, merit, procure, win.

**desiderate** vb desire, lack, miss, need, want.

**design** vb brew, concoct, contrive, devise, intend, invent, mean, plan, project, scheme; intend, mean, purpose; delineate, describe, draw, outline, sketch, trace. * n aim, device, drift, intent, intention, mark, meaning, object, plan, proposal, project, purport, purpose, scheme, scope; delineation, draught, drawing, outline, plan, sketch; adaptation, artifice, contrivance, invention, inventiveness.

**designate** vb denote, distinguish, indicate, particularize, select, show, specify, stipulate; characterize, define, describe; call, christen, denominate, dub, entitle, name, style; allot, appoint, christen.

**designation** n indication, particularization, selection, specification; class, description, kind; appellation, denomination, name, style, title.

**designing** adj artful, astute, crafty, crooked, cunning, deceitful, insidious, intriguing, Machiavellian, scheming, sly, subtle, treacherous, trickish, tricky, unscrupulous, wily.

**desirable** adj agreeable, beneficial, covetable, eligible, enviable, good, pleasing, preferable.

**desire** vb covet, crave, desiderate, fancy, hanker after, long for, lust after, want, wish, yearn for; ask, entreat, request, solicit. * n eroticism, lasciviousness, libidinousness, libido, lust, lustfulness, passion; eagerness, fancy, hope, inclination, mind, partiality, penchant, pleasure, volition, want, wish.

**desirous** adj avid, eager, desiring, longing, solicitous, wishful.

**desist** vb cease, discontinue, forbear, pause, stay, stop.

**desolate** vb depopulate, despoil, destroy, devastate, pillage, plunder, ravage, ruin, sack. * adj bare, barren, bleak, desert, forsaken, lonely, solitary, unfrequented, uninhabited, waste, wild; companionable, lonely, lonesome, solitary; desolated, destroyed, devastated, ravaged, ruined; cheerless, comfortless, companionless, disconsolate, dreary, forlorn, forsaken, miserable, wretched.

**desolation** n destruction, devastation, havoc, ravage, ruin; barrenness, bleakness, desolateness, dreariness, loneliness, solitariness, solitude, wildness; gloom, gloominess, misery, sadness, unhappiness, wretchedness.

**despair** vb despond, give up, lose hope. * n dejection, desperation, despondency, disheartenment, hopelessness.

**despatch** see **dispatch**.

**desperado** n daredevil, gangster, marauder, ruffian, thug, tough.

**desperate** adj despairing, despondent, desponding, hopeless; forlorn, irretrievable; extreme; audacious, daring, foolhardy, frantic, furious, headstrong, precipitate, rash, reckless, violent, wild, wretched; extreme, great, monstrous, prodigious, supreme.

**desperation** n despair, hopelessness; fury, rage.

**despicable** adj abject, base, contemptible, degrading, low, mean, paltry, pitiful, shameful, sordid, vile, worthless.

**despise** vb contemn, disdain, disregard, neglect, scorn, slight, spurn, undervalue.

**despite** n malevolence, malice, malignity, spite; contempt, contumacy, defiance. * prep notwithstanding.

**despoil** vb bereave, denude, deprive, dispossess, divest, strip; devastate, fleece, pillage, plunder, ravage, rifle, rob.

**despond** vb despair, give up, lose hope, mourn, sorrow.

**despondency** n blues, dejection, depression, discouragement, gloom, hopelessness, melancholy, sadness.

**despondent** adj dejected, depressed, discouraged, disheartened, dispirited, low-spirited, melancholy.

**despot** n autocrat, dictator; oppressor, tyrant.

**despotic** adj absolute, arrogant, autocratic, dictatorial, imperious; arbitrary, oppressive, tyrannical, tyrannous.

**despotism** n absolutism, autocracy, dictatorship; oppression, tyranny.

**destination** n appointment, decree, destiny, doom, fate, foreordainment, foreordination, fortune, lot, ordination, star; aim, design, drift, end, intention, object, purpose, scope; bourne, goal, harbour, haven, journey's end, resting-place, terminus.

**destine** vb allot, appoint, assign, consecrate, devote, ordain; design, intend, predetermine; decree, doom, foreordain, predestine.

**destitute** adj distressed, indigent, moneyless, necessitous, needy, penniless, penurious, pinched, poor, reduced, wanting.

**destitution** n indigence, need, penury, poverty, privation, want.

**destroy** vb demolish, overthrow, overturn, subvert, raze, ruin; annihilate, dissolve, efface, quench; desolate, devastate, devour, ravage, waste; eradicate, extinguish, extirpate, kill, uproot, slay.

**destruction** n demolition, havoc, overthrow, ruin, subversion; desolation, devastation, holocaust, ravage; annihilation, eradication, extinction, extirpation; death, massacre, murder, slaughter.

**destructive** adj baleful, baneful, deadly, deleterious, detrimental, fatal, hurtful, injurious, lethal, mischievous, noxious, pernicious, ruinous; annihilatory, eradicative, exterminative, extirpative.

**desultory** adj capricious, cursory, discursive, erratic, fitful, inconstant, inexact, irregular, loose, rambling, roving, slight, spasmodic, unconnected, unmethodical, unsettled, unsystematic, vague, wandering.

**detach** vb disengage, disconnect, disjoin, dissever, disunite, divide, part, separate, sever, unfix; appoint, detail, send.

**detail** vb delineate, depict, describe, enumerate, narrate, particularize, portray, recount, rehearse, relate, specify; appoint, detach, send. * n account, narration, narrative, recital, relation; appointment, detachment; item, part.

**details** npl facts, minutiae, particulars, parts.

**detain** vb arrest, check, delay, hinder, hold, keep, restrain, retain, stay, stop; confine.

**detect** vb ascertain, catch, descry, disclose, discover, expose, reveal, unmask.

**detention** n confinement, delay, hindrance, restraint, withholding.

**deter** vb debar, discourage, frighten, hinder, prevent, restrain, stop, withhold.

**deteriorate** vb corrupt, debase, degrade, deprave, disgrace, impair, spoil, vitiate; decline, degenerate, depreciate, worsen.

**deterioration** n corruption, debasement, degradation, depravation, vitiation, perversion; caducity, decadence, decay, decline, degeneracy, degeneration, impairment.

**determinate** adj absolute, certain, definite, determined, established, explicit, express, fixed, limited, positive, settled; conclusive, decided, decisive, definitive.

**determination** n ascertainment, decision, deciding, determining, fixing, settlement, settling; conclusion, judgment, purpose, resolution, resolve, result; direction, leaning, tendency; firmness, constancy, effort, endeavour, exertion, grit, persistence, stamina, resoluteness; definition, limitation, qualification.

**determine** vb adjust, conclude, decide, end, establish, fix, resolve, settle; ascertain, certify, check, verify; impel, incline, induce, influence, lead, turn; decide, resolve; condition, define, limit; compel, necessitate.

**detest** vb abhor, abominate, despise, execrate, hate, loathe, nauseate, recoil from.

**detestable** adj abhorred, abominable, accursed, cursed, damnable, execrable, hateful, odious; disgusting, loathsome, nauseating, offensive, repulsive, sickening, vile.

**dethrone** vb depose, uncrown.

**detract** vb abuse, asperse, belittle, calumniate, debase, decry, defame, depreciate, derogate, disparage, slander, traduce, vilify; deprecate, deteriorate, diminish, lessen.

**detraction** n abuse, aspersion, calumny, censure, defamation, depreciation, derogation, disparagement, slander.

**detriment** n cost, damage, disadvantage, evil, harm, hurt, injury, loss, mischief, prejudice.

**detrimental** adj baleful, deleterious, destructive, harmful, hurtful, injurious, mischievous, pernicious, prejudicial.

**devastate** vb desolate, despoil, destroy, lay waste, harry, pillage, plunder, ravage, sack, spoil, strip, waste.

**devastation** n despoiling, destroying, harrying, pillaging, plundering, ravaging, sacking, spoiling, stripping, wasting; desolation, destruction, havoc, pillage, rapine, ravage, ruin, waste.

**develop** vb disentangle, disclose, evolve, exhibit, explicate, uncover, unfold, unravel; cultivate, grow, mature, open, progress.

**development** n disclosure, disentanglement, exhibition, unfolding, unravelling; growth, increase, maturation, maturing; evolution, growth, progression; elaboration, expansion, explication.

**deviate** vb alter, deflect, digress, diverge, sheer off, slew, tack, turn aside, wheel, wheel about; err, go astray, stray, swerve, wander; differ, vary.

**deviation** n aberration, departure, depression, divarication, divergence, turning; alteration, change, difference, variance, variation.

**device** n contraption, contrivance, gadget, invention; design, expedient, plan, project, resort, resource, scheme, shift; artifice, evasion, fraud, manoeuvre,

ruse, stratagem, trick, wile; blazon, emblazonment, emblem, sign, symbol, type.

**devil** n archfiend, demon, fiend, goblin; Apollyon, Belial, Deuce, Evil One, Lucifer, Old Harry, Old Nick, Old Serpent, Prince of Darkness, Satan.

**devilish** adj demon, demonic, demonical, demoniac, demoniacal, diabolic, diabolical, fiendish, hellish, infernal, Mephistophelean, Mephistophelian, satanic; atrocious, barbarous, cruel, malevolent, malicious, malign, malignant, wicked.

**devilry** n devilment, diablerie, mischief; devilishness, fiendishness, wickedness.

**devious** adj deviating, erratic, roundabout, wandering; circuitous, confusing, crooked, labyrinthine, mazy, obscure; crooked, disingenuous, misleading, treacherous.

**devise** vb brew, compass, concert, concoct, contrive, dream up, excogitate, imagine, invent, plan, project, scheme; bequeath, demise, leave, will.

**devoid** adj bare, destitute, empty, vacant, void.

**devolve** vb alienate, consign, convey, deliver over, demise, fall, hand over, make over, pass, transfer.

**devote** vb appropriate, consecrate, dedicate, destine; set apart; addict, apply, give up, resign; consign, doom, give over.

**devoted** adj affectionate, attached, loving; ardent, assiduous, earnest, zealous.

**devotee** n bigot, enthusiast, fan, fanatic, zealot.

**devotion** n consecration, dedication, duty; devotedness, devoutness, fidelity, godliness, holiness, piety, religion, religiousness, saintliness, sanctity; adoration, prayer, worship; affection, attachment, love; ardour, devotedness, eagerness, earnestness, fervour, passion, spirit, zeal.

**devotional** adj devout, godly, pious, religious, saintly.

**devour** vb engorge, gorge, gulp down, raven, swallow eagerly, wolf; annihilate, consume, destroy, expend, spend, swallow up, waste.

**devout** adj devotional, godly, holy, pious, religious, saint-like, saintly; earnest, grave, serious, sincere, solemn.

**dexterity** n ability, address, adroitness, aptitude, aptness, art, cleverness, expertness, facility, knack, quickness, readiness, skilfulness, skill, tact.

**dexterous, dextrous** adj able, adept, adroit, apt, deft, clever, expert, facile, handy, nimble-fingered, quick, ready, skilful.

**diabolic, diabolical** adj atrocious, barbarous, cruel, devilish, fiendish, hellish, impious, infernal, malevolent, malign, malignant, satanic, wicked.

**diagram** n chart, delineation, figure, graph, map, outline, plan, sketch.

**dialect** n idiom, localism, provincialism; jargon, lingo, patois, patter; language, parlance, phraseology, speech, tongue.

**dialectal** adj idiomatic, local, provincial.

**dialectic, dialectical** adj analytical, critical, logical, rational, rationalistic.

**dialogue** n colloquy, communication, conference, conversation, converse, intercourse, interlocution; playbook, script, speech, text, words.

**diaphanous** adj clear, filmy, gossamer, pellucid, sheer, translucent, transparent.

**diarrhoea** n (med) flux, looseness, purging, relaxation.

**diary** n chronicle, daybook, journal, register.

**diatribe** n disputation, disquisition, dissertation; abuse, harangue, invective, philippic, reviling, tirade.

**dictate** vb bid, direct, command, decree, enjoin, ordain, order, prescribe, require. * n bidding, command, decree, injunction, order; maxim, precept, rule.

**dictation** n direction, order, prescription.

**dictator** n autocrat, despot, tyrant.

**dictatorial** adj absolute, unlimited, unrestricted; authoritative, despotic, dictatory, domineering, imperious, overbearing, peremptory, tyrannical.

**dictatorship** n absolutism, authoritarianism, autocracy, despotism, iron rule, totalitarianism, tyranny.

**diction** n expression, language, phraseology, style, vocabulary, wording.

**dictionary** n glossary, lexicon, thesaurus, vocabulary, wordbook; cyclopedia, encyclopedia.

**dictum** n affirmation, assertion, saying; (law) award, arbitrament, decision, opinion.

**didactic, didactical** adj educational, instructive, pedagogic, preceptive.

**die** vb decease, demise, depart, expire, pass on; decay, decline, fade, fade out, perish, wither; cease, disappear, vanish; faint, fall, sink.

**diet**[1] vb eat, feed, nourish; abstain, fast, regulate, slim. * n aliment, fare, food, nourishment, nutriment, provision, rations, regimen, subsistence, viands, victuals.

**diet**[2] n assembly, congress, convention, convocation, council, parliament.

**differ** vb deviate, diverge, vary; disagree, dissent; bicker, contend, dispute, quarrel, wrangle.

**difference** n contrariety, contrast, departure, deviation, disagreement, disparity, dissimilarity, dissimilitude, divergence, diversity, heterogeneity, inconformity, nuance, opposition, unlikeness, variation; alienation, altercation, bickering, breach, contention, contest, controversy, debate, disaccord, disagreement, disharmony, dispute, dissension, embroilment, falling out, irreconcilability, jarring, misunderstanding, quarrel, rupture, schism, strife, variance, wrangle; discrimination, distinction.

**different** adj distinct, nonidentical, separate, unlike; contradistinct, contrary, contrasted, deviating, disagreeing, discrepant, dissimilar, divergent, diverse, incompatible, incongruous, unlike, variant, various; divers, heterogeneous, manifold, many, sundry.

**difficult** adj arduous, exacting, hard, Herculean, stiff, tough, uphill; abstruse, complex, intricate, knotty, obscure, perplexing; austere, rigid, unaccommodating, uncompliant, unyielding; dainty, fastidious, squeamish.

**difficulty** n arduousness, laboriousness; bar, barrier, crux, deadlock, dilemma, embarrassment, emergency, exigency, fix, hindrance, impediment, knot, obstacle, obstruction, perplexity, pickle, pinch, predicament, stand, standstill, thwart, trial, trouble; cavil, objection; complication, controversy, difference, embarrassment, embroilment, imbroglio, misunderstanding.

**diffidence** n distrust, doubt, hesitance, hesitancy, hesitation, reluctance; bashfulness, modesty, sheepishness, shyness, timidity.

**diffident** adj distrustful, doubtful, hesitant, hesitating, reluctant; bashful, modest, over-modest, sheepish, shy, timid.

**diffuse**[1] vb circulate, disperse, disseminate, distribute, intermingle, propagate, scatter, spread, strew.

**diffuse**[2] adj broadcast, dispersed, scattered, sparse, sporadic, widespread; broad, extensive, liberal, profuse, wide; copious, loose, prolix, rambling, verbose, wordy.

**diffusion** n circulation, dispersion, dissemination, distribution, extension, propagation, spread, strewing.

**diffusive** adj expansive, permeating, wide-reaching; spreading, dispersive, disseminative, distributive, distributory.

**dig** vb channel, delve, excavate, grub, hollow out, quarry, scoop, tunnel. * n poke, punch, thrust.

**digest**[1] vb arrange, classify, codify, dispose, methodize, systemize, tabulate; concoct; assimilate, consider, contemplate, meditate, ponder, reflect upon, study; master; macerate, soak, steep.

**digest**[2] n code, system; abridgement, abstract, brief, breviary, compend, compendium, conspectus, epitome, summary, synopsis.

**dignified** adj august, courtly, decorous, grave, imposing, majestic, noble, stately.

**dignify** vb advance, aggrandize, elevate, ennoble, exalt, promote; adorn, grace, honour.

**dignity** n elevation, eminence, exaltation, excellence, glory, greatness, honour, place, rank, respectability, standing, station; decorum, grandeur, majesty, nobleness, stateliness; preferment; dignitary, magistrate; elevation, height.

**digress** vb depart, deviate, diverge, expatiate, wander.

**digression** n departure, deviation, divergence; episode, excursus.

**dilapidate** vb demolish, destroy, disintegrate, ruin, waste.

**dilapidated** adj decayed, ruined, run down, wasted.

**dilapidation** n decay, demolition, destruction, disintegration, disrepair, dissolution, downfall, ruin, waste.

**dilate** vb distend, enlarge, expand, extend, inflate, swell, tend, widen; amplify, descant, dwell, enlarge, expatiate.

**dilation** n amplification, bloating, distension, enlargement, expanding, expansion, spreading, swelling.

**dilatory** adj backward, behind-hand, delaying, laggard, lagging, lingering, loitering, off-putting, procrastinating, slack, slow, sluggish, tardy.

**dilemma** n difficulty, fix, plight, predicament, problem, quandary, strait.

**diligence** n activity, application, assiduity, assiduousness, attention, care, constancy, earnestness, heedfulness, industry, laboriousness, perseverance, sedulousness.

**diligent** adj active, assiduous, attentive, busy, careful, constant, earnest, hard-working, indefatigable, industrious, laborious, notable, painstaking, persevering, persistent, sedulous, tireless.

**dilly-dally** vb dally, dawdle, delay, lag, linger, loiter, saunter, trifle.

**dilute** vb attenuate, reduce, thin, weaken. * adj attenuated, diluted, thin, weak, wishy-washy.

**dim** vb blur, cloud, darken, dull, obscure, sully, tarnish. * adj cloudy, dark, dusky, faint, ill-defined, indefinite, indistinct, mysterious, obscure, shadowy; dull, obtuse; clouded, confused, darkened, faint, obscured; blurred, dulled, sullied, tarnished.

**dimension** n extension, extent, measure.

**dimensions** npl amplitude, bigness, bulk, capacity, greatness, largeness, magnitude, mass, massiveness, size, volume; measurements.

**diminish** vb abate, belittle, contract, decrease, lessen, reduce; curtail, cut, dwindle, melt, narrow, shrink, shrivel, subside, taper off, weaken.

**diminution** n abatement, abridgement, attenuation, contraction, curtailment, decrescendo, cut, decay, decrease, deduction, lessening, reduction, retrenchment, weakening.

**diminutive** adj contracted, dwarfish, little, minute, puny, pygmy, small, tiny.

**din** vb beat, boom, clamour, drum, hammer, pound, repeat, ring, thunder. * n bruit, clamour, clash, clatter, crash, crashing, hubbub, hullabaloo, hurly-burly, noise, outcry, racket, row, shout, uproar.

**dingle** n dale, dell, glen, vale, valley.

**dingy** adj brown, dun, dusky; bedimmed, colourless, dimmed, dulled, faded, obscure, smirched, soiled, sullied.

**dint** n blow, stroke; dent, indentation, nick, notch; force, power.

**diocese** n bishopric, charge, episcopate, jurisdiction, see.

**dip** vb douse, duck, immerse, plunge, souse; bail, ladle; dive, pitch; bend, incline, slope. * n decline, declivity, descent, drop, fall; concavity, depression, hole, hollow, pit, sink; bathe, dipping, ducking, sousing, swim.

**diplomat** n diplomatist, envoy, legate, minister, negotiator.

**dire** adj alarming, awful, calamitous, cruel, destructive, disastrous, dismal, dreadful, fearful, gloomy, horrible, horrid, implacable, inexorable, portentous, shocking, terrible, terrific, tremendous, woeful.

**direct** vb aim. cast, level, point, turn; advise, conduct, control, dispose, guide, govern, manage, regulate, rule; command, bid, enjoin, instruct, order; lead, show; address, superscribe. * adj immediate, straight, undeviating; absolute, categorical, express, plain, unambiguous; downright, earnest, frank, ingenuous, open, outspoken, sincere, straightforward, unequivocal.

**direction** n aim; tendency; bearing, course; administration, conduct, control, government, management, oversight, superintendence; guidance, lead; command, order, prescription; address, superscription.

**directly** adv absolutely, expressly, openly, unambiguously; forthwith, immediately, instantly, quickly, presently, promptly, soon, speedily.

**director** n boss, manager, superintendent; adviser, counsellor, guide, instructor, mentor, monitor.

**direful** adj awful, calamitous, dire, dreadful, fearful, gloomy, horrible, shocking, terrible, terrific, tremendous.

**dirge** n coronach, elegy, lament, monody, requiem, threnody.

**dirty** vb befoul, defile, draggle, foul, pollute, soil, sully. * adj begrimed. defiled, filthy, foul, mucky, nasty, soiled, unclean; clouded, cloudy, dark, dull, muddy, sullied; base, beggarly, contemptible, despicable, grovelling, low, mean, paltry, pitiful, scurvy, shabby, sneaking, squalid; disagreeable, rainy, sloppy, uncomfortable.

**disability** n disablement, disqualification, impotence, impotency, inability, incapacity, incompetence, incompetency, unfitness, weakness.

**disable** vb cripple, enfeeble, hamstring, impair, paralyse, unman, weaken; disenable, disqualify, incapacitate, unfit.

**disabuse** vb correct, undeceive.

**disadvantage** n disadvantageousness, inconvenience, unfavourableness; damage, detriment, disservice, drawback, harm, hindrance, hurt, injury, loss, prejudice.

**disadvantageous** adj inconvenient, inexpedient, unfavourable; deleterious, detrimental, harmful, hurtful, injurious, prejudicial.

**disaffect** vb alienate, disdain, dislike, disorder, estrange.

**disaffected** adj alienated, disloyal, dissatisfied, estranged.

**disaffection** n alienation, breach, disagreement, dislike, disloyalty, dissatisfaction, estrangement, repugnance, ill will, unfriendliness.

**disagree** vb deviate, differ, diverge, vary; dissent; argue, bicker, clash, debate, dispute, quarrel, wrangle.

**disagreeable** adj contrary, displeasing, distasteful, nasty, offensive, unpleasant, unpleasing, unsuitable.

**disagreement** n deviation, difference, discrepancy, dissimilarity, dissimilitude, divergence, diversity, incongruity, unlikeness; disaccord, dissent; argument, bickering, clashing, conflict, contention, dispute, dissension, disunion, disunity, jarring, misunderstanding, quarrel, strife, variance, wrangle.

**disallow** vb forbid, prohibit; disapprove, reject; deny, disavow, disclaim, dismiss, disown, repudiate.

**disappear** vb depart, fade, vanish; cease, dissolve.

**disappoint** vb baffle, balk, deceive, defeat, delude, disconcert, foil, frustrate, mortify, tantalize, thwart, vex.

**disappointment** n baffling, balk, failure, foiling, frustration, miscarriage, mortification, unfulfilment.

**disapprobation** n blame, censure, condemnation, disapproval, dislike, displeasure, reproof.

**disapprove** vb blame, censure, condemn, deprecate, dislike; disallow, reject.

**disarrange** vb agitate, confuse, derange, disallow, dishevel, dislike, dislocate, disorder, disorganize, disturb, jumble, reject, rumple, tumble, unsettle.

**disarray** n confusion, disorder; dishabille.

**disaster** n accident, adversity, blow, calamity, casualty, catastrophe, misadventure, mischance, misfortune, mishap, reverse, ruin, stroke.

**disastrous** adj adverse, calamitous, catastrophic, destructive, hapless, ill-fated, ill-starred, ruinous, unfortunate, unlucky, unpropitious, unprosperous, untoward.

**disavow** vb deny, disallow, disclaim, disown.

**disband** vb break up, disperse, scatter, separate.

**disbelief** n agnosticism, doubt, nonconviction, rejection, unbelief.

**disburden** vb alleviate, diminish, disburden, discharge, disencumber, ease, free, relieve, rid.

**disbursement** n expenditure, spending.

**discard** vb abandon, cast off, lay aside, reject; banish, break, cashier, discharge, dismiss, remove, repudiate.

**discern** vb differentiate, discriminate, distinguish, judge; behold, descry, discover, espy, notice, observe, perceive, recognize, see.

**discernible** adj detectable, discoverable, perceptible.

**discerning** adj acute, astute, clear-sighted, discriminating, discriminative, eagle-eyed, ingenious, intelligent, judicious, knowing, perspicacious, piercing, sagacious, sharp, shrewd.

**discernment** n acumen, acuteness, astuteness, brightness, cleverness, discrimination, ingenuity, insight, intelligence, judgement, penetration, perspicacity, sagacity, sharpness, shrewdness; beholding, descrying, discerning, discovery, espial, notice, perception.

**discharge** vb disburden, unburden, unload; eject, emit, excrete, expel, void; cash, liquidate, pay; absolve, acquit, clear, exonerate, free, release, relieve; cashier, discard, dismiss, sack; destroy, remove; execute, perform, fulfil, observe; annul, cancel, invalidate, nullify, rescind. * n disburdening, unloading; acquittal, dismissal, displacement, ejection, emission, evacuation, excretion, expulsion, vent, voiding; blast, burst, detonation, explosion, firing; execution, fulfilment, observance; annulment, clearance, liquidation, payment, satisfaction, settlement; exemption, liberation, release; flow, flux, execration.

**disciple** n catechumen, learner, pupil, scholar, student; adherent, follower, partisan, supporter.

**discipline** vb breed, drill, educate, exercise, form, instruct, teach, train; control, govern, regulate, school; chasten, chastise, punish. * n culture, drill, drilling, education, exercise, instruction, training; control, government, regulation, subjection; chastisement, correction, punishment.

**disclaim** vb abandon, disallow, disown, disavow; reject, renounce, repudiate.

**disclose** vb discover, exhibit, expose, manifest, uncover; bare, betray, blab, communicate, divulge, impart, publish, reveal, show, tell, unfold, unveil, utter.

**disclosure** n betrayal, discovery, exposé, exposure, revelation, uncovering. discolour vb stain, tarnish, tinge.

**discomfit** vb beat, checkmate, conquer, defeat, overcome, overpower, overthrow, rout, subdue, vanquish, worst; abash, baffle, balk, confound, disconcert, foil, frustrate, perplex, upset.

**discomfiture** n confusion, defeat, frustration, overthrow, rout, vexation.

**discomfort** n annoyance, disquiet, distress, inquietude, malaise, trouble, uneasiness, unpleasantness, vexation.

**discommode** vb annoy, disquiet, disturb, harass, incommode, inconvenience, molest, trouble.

**discompose** vb confuse, derange, disarrange, disorder, disturb, embroil, jumble, unsettle; agitate, annoy, chafe, displease, disquiet, fret, harass, irritate, nettle, plague, provoke, ruffle, trouble, upset, vex, worry; abash, bewilder, disconcert, embarrass, fluster, perplex.

**disconcert** vb baffle, balk, contravene, defeat, disarrange, frustrate, interrupt, thwart, undo, upset; abash, agitate, bewilder, confuse, demoralize, discompose, disturb, embarrass, faze, perplex, perturb, unbalance, worry.

**disconnect** vb detach, disengage, disjoin, dissociate, disunite, separate, sever, uncouple, unlink.

**disconsolate** adj broken-hearted, cheerless, comfortless, dejected, desolate, forlorn, gloomy, heartbroken, inconsolable, melancholy, miserable, sad, sorrowful, unhappy, woeful, wretched.

**discontent** n discontentment, displeasure, dissatisfaction, inquietude, restlessness, uneasiness.

**discontinuance** n cessation, discontinuation, disjunction, disruption, intermission, interruption, separation, stop, stoppage, stopping, suspension.

**discontinue** vb cease, intermit, interrupt, quit, stop.

**discord** n contention, difference, disagreement, dissension, opposition, quarrelling, rupture, strife, variance, wrangling; cacophony, discordance, dissonance, harshness, jangle, jarring.

**discordance** n conflict, disagreement, incongruity, inconsistency, opposition, repugnance; discord, dissonance.

**discordant** adj contradictory, contrary, disagreeing, incongruous, inconsistent, opposite, repugnant; cacophonous, dissonant, harsh, inharmonious, jangling, jarring.

**discount** vb allow-for, deduct, lower, rebate, reduce, subtract; disregard, ignore, overlook. * n abatement, drawback; allowance, deduction, rebate, reduction.

**discourage** vb abase, awe, damp, daunt, deject, depress, deject, dismay, dishearten, dispirit, frighten, intimidate; deter, dissuade, hinder; disfavour, discountenance.

**discouragement** n disheartening; dissuasion; damper, deterrent, embarrassment, hindrance, impediment, obstacle, wet blanket.

**discourse** vb expiate, hold forth, lucubrate, sermonize, speak; advise, confer, converse, parley, talk; emit, utter. * n address, disquisition, dissertation, homily, lecture, preachment, sermon, speech, treatise; colloquy, conversation, converse, talk.

**discourteous** adj abrupt, brusque, curt, disrespectful, ill-bred, ill-mannered, impolite, inurbane, rude, uncivil, uncourtly, ungentlemanly, unmannerly.

**discourtesy** n abruptness, brusqueness, ill-breeding, impoliteness, incivility, rudeness.

**discover** vb communicate, disclose, exhibit, impart, manifest, show, reveal, tell; ascertain, behold, discern, espy, see; descry, detect, determine, discern; contrive, invent, originate.

**discredit** vb disbelieve, doubt, question; depreciate, disgrace, dishonour, disparage, reproach. * n disbelief, distrust; disgrace, dishonour, disrepute, ignominy, notoriety, obloquy, odium, opprobrium, reproach, scandal.

**discreditable** adj derogatory, disgraceful, disreputable, dishonourable, ignominious, infamous, inglorious, scandalous, unworthy.

**discreet** adj careful, cautious, circumspect, considerate, discerning, heedful, judicious, prudent, sagacious, wary, wise.

**discrepancy** n contrariety, difference, disagreement, discordance, dissonance, divergence, incongruity, inconsistency, variance, variation.

**discrete** adj discontinuous, disjunct, distinct, separate; disjunctive.

**discretion** n care, carefulness, caution, circumspection, considerateness, consideration, heedfulness, judgement, judicious, prudence, wariness; discrimination, maturity, responsibility; choice, option, pleasure, will.

**discrimination** n difference, distinction; acumen, acuteness, discernment, in-sight, judgement, penetration, sagacity.

**discriminatory** adj characteristic, characterizing, discriminating, discriminative, distinctive, distinguishing.

**discursive** adj argumentative, reasoning; casual, cursory, desultory, digressive, erratic, excursive, loose, rambling, roving, wandering, wave.

**discus** n disk, quoit.

**discuss** vb agitate, argue, canvass, consider, debate, deliberate, examine, sift, ventilate.

**disdain** vb contemn, deride, despise, disregard, reject, scorn, slight, scout, spurn. * n arrogance, contempt, contumely, haughtiness, hauteur, scorn, sneer, superciliousness.

**disdainful** adj cavalier, contemptuous, contumelious, haughty, scornful, supercilious.

**disease** n affection, affliction, ail, ailment, complaint, disorder, distemper, illness, indisposition, infirmity, malady, sickness.

**disembarrass** vb clear, disburden, disencumber, disengage, disentangle, extricate, ease, free, release, rid.

**disembodied** adj bodiless, disincarnate, immaterial, incorporeal, spiritual, unbodied.

**disembowel** vb degut, embowel, eviscerate.

**disengage** vb clear, deliver, discharge, disembarrass, disembroil, disencumber, disentangle, extricate, liberate, release; detach, disjoin, dissociate, disunite, divide, separate; wean, withdraw.

**disentangle** vb loosen, separate, unfold, unravel, untwist; clear, detach, disconnect, disembroil, disengage, extricate, liberate, loose, unloose.

**disfavour** n disapproval, disesteem, dislike, disrespect; discredit, disregard, disrepute, unacceptableness; disservice, unkindness. *vb disapprove, dislike, object, oppose.

**disfigure** vb blemish, deface, deform, injure, mar, spoil.

**disfigurement** n blemishing, defacement, deforming, disfiguration, injury, marring, spoiling; blemish, defect, deformity, scar, spot, stain.

**disgorge** vb belch, cast up, spew, throw up, vomit; discharge, eject; give up, relinquish, surrender, yield.

**disgrace** vb degrade, humble, humiliate; abase, debase, defame, discredit, disfavour, dishonour, disparage, reproach, stain, sully, taint, tarnish. * n abomination, disrepute, humiliation, ignominy, infamy, mortification, shame, scandal.

**disgraceful** adj discreditable, dishonourable, disreputable, ignominious, infamous, opprobrious, scandalous, shameful.

**disguise** vb cloak, conceal, cover, dissemble, hide, mask, muffle, screen, secrete, shroud, veil. * n concealment, cover, mask, veil; blind, cloak, masquerade, pretence, pretext, veneer.

**disguised** adj cloaked, masked, veiled.

**disgust** vb nauseate, sicken; abominate, detest, displease, offend, repel, repulse, revolt. * n disrelish, distaste, loathing, nausea; abhorrence, abomination, antipathy, aversion, detestation, dislike, repugnance, revulsion.

**dish** vb deal out, give, ladle, serve; blight, dash, frustrate, mar, ruin, spoil. * n bowl, plate, saucer, vessel.

**dishearten** vb cast down, damp, dampen, daunt, deject, depress, deter, discourage, dispirit.

**dished** adj baffled, balked, disappointed, disconcerted, foiled, frustrated, upset.

**dishevelled** adj disarranged, disordered, messed, tousled, tumbled, unkempt, untidy, untrimmed.

**dishonest** adj cheating, corrupt, crafty, crooked, deceitful, deceiving, deceptive, designing, faithless, false, falsehearted, fraudulent, guileful, knavish, perfidious, slippery, treacherous, unfair, unscrupulous.

**dishonesty** n deceitfulness, faithlessness, falsehood, fraud, fraudulence, fraudulency, improbity, knavery, perfidious, treachery, trickery.

**dishonour** vb abase, defame, degrade, discredit, disfavour, dishonour, disgrace, disparage, reproach, shame, taint. * n abasement, basement, contempt, degradation, discredit, disesteem, disfavour, disgrace, dishonour, disparagement, disrepute, ignominy, infamy, obloquy, odium, opprobrium, reproach, scandal, shame.

**dishonourable** adj discreditable, disgraceful, disreputable, ignominious, infamous, scandalous, shameful; base, false, falsehearted, shameless.

**disinclination** n alienation, antipathy, aversion, dislike, indisposition, reluctance, repugnance, unwillingness.

**disinfect** vb cleanse, deodorize, fumigate, purify, sterilize.

**disingenuous** adj artful, deceitful, dishonest, hollow, insidious, insincere, uncandid, unfair, wily.

**disintegrate** vb crumble, decompose, dissolve, disunite, pulverize, separate.

**disinter** vb dig up, disentomb, disinhume, exhume, unbury.

**disinterested** adj candid, fair, high-minded, impartial, indifferent, unbiased, unselfish, unprejudiced; generous, liberal, magnanimous.

**disjoin** vb detach, disconnect, dissever, dissociate, disunite, divide, part, separate, sever, sunder.

**disjointed** adj desultory, disconnected, incoherent, loose.

**disjunction** n disassociation, disconnection, disunion, isolation, parting, separation, severance.

**dislike** vb abominate, detest, disapprove, disrelish, hate, loathe. * n antagonism, antipathy, aversion, disapproval, disfavour, disgust, disinclination, displeasure, disrelish, distaste, loathing, repugnance.

**dislocate** vb disarrange, displace, disturb; disarticulate, disjoint, luxate, slip.

**dislodge** vb dismount, dispel, displace, eject, expel, oust, remove.

**disloyal** adj disaffected, faithless, false, perfidious, traitorous, treacherous, treasonable, undutiful, unfaithful, unpatriotic, untrue.

**disloyalty** n faithlessness, perfidy, treachery, treason, undutifulness, unfaithfulness.

**dismal** adj cheerless, dark, dreary, dull, gloomy, lonesome; blue, calamitous, doleful, dolorous, funereal, lugubrious, melancholy, mournful, sad, sombre, sorrowful.

**dismantle** vb divest, strip, unrig.

**dismay** vb affright, alarm, appal, daunt, discourage, dishearten, frighten, horrify, intimidate, paralyse, scare, terrify. * n affright, alarm, consternation, fear, fright, horror, terror.

**dismember** vb disjoint, dislimb, dislocate, mutilate; divide, separate, rend, sever.

**dismiss** vb banish, cashier, discard, discharge, disperse, reject, release, remove.

**dismount** vb alight, descend, dismantle, unhorse; dislodge, displace.

**disobedient** adj froward, noncompliant, noncomplying, obstinate, rebellious, refractory, uncomplying, undutiful, unruly, unsubmissive.

**disobey** vb infringe, transgress, violate.

**disobliging** adj ill-natured, unaccommodating, unamiable, unfriendly, unkind.

**disorder** vb confound, confuse, derange, disarrange, discompose, disorganize, disturb, unsettle, upset. * n confusion, derangement, disarrangement, disarray, disorganization, irregularity, jumble, litter, mess, topsy-turvy; brawl, commotion, disturbance, fight, quarrel, riot, tumult; riotousness, tumultuousness, turbulence; ail, ailment, complaint, distemper, illness, indisposition, malady, sickness.

**disorderly** adj chaotic, confused, intemperate, irregular, unmethodical, unsystematic, untidy;

lawless, rebellious, riotous, tumultuous, turbulent, ungovernable, unmanageable, unruly.

**disorganization** n chaos, confusion, demoralization, derangement, disorder.

**disorganize** vb confuse, demoralize, derange, disarrange, discompose, disorder, disturb, unsettle, upset.

**disown** vb disavow, disclaim, reject, renounce, repudiate; abnegate, deny, disallow.

**disparage** vb belittle, decry, depreciate, derogate from, detract from, doubt, question, run down, underestimate, underpraise, underrate, undervalue; asperse, defame, inveigh against, reflect on, reproach, slur, speak ill of, traduce, vilify.

**disparagement** n belittlement, depreciation, derogation, detraction, underrating, undervaluing; derogation, detraction, diminution, harm, impairment, injury, lessening, prejudice, worsening; aspersion, calumny, defamation, reflection, reproach, traduction, vilification; blackening, disgrace, dispraise, indignity, reproach.

**disparity** n difference, disproportion, inequality; dissimilarity, dissimilitude, unlikeness.

**dispassionate** adj calm, collected, composed, cool, imperturbable, inexcitable, moderate, quiet, serene, sober, staid, temperate, undisturbed, unexcitable, unexcited, unimpassioned, unruffled; candid, disinterested, fair, impartial, neutral, unbiased.

**dispatch, despatch** vb assassinate, kill, murder, slaughter, slay; accelerate, conclude, dismiss, expedite, finish, forward, hasten, hurry, quicken, speed. * n dispatching, sending; diligence, expedition, haste, rapidity, speed; completion, conduct, doing, transaction; communication, document, instruction, letter, message, missive, report.

**dispel** vb banish, disperse, dissipate, scatter.

**dispensation** n allotment, apportioning, apportionment, dispensing, distributing, distribution; administration, stewardship; economy, plan, scheme, system; exemption, immunity, indulgence, licence, privilege.

**dispense** vb allot, apportion, assign, distribute; administer, apply, execute; absolve, excuse, exempt, exonerate, release, relieve.

**disperse** vb dispel, dissipate, dissolve, scatter, separate; diffuse, disseminate, spread; disappear, vanish.

**dispirit** vb damp, dampen, depress, deject, discourage, dishearten.

**dispirited** adj chapfallen, dejected, depressed, discouraged, disheartened, down-cast, down-hearted.

**displace** vb dislocate, mislay, misplace, move; dislodge, remove; cashier, depose, discard, discharge, dismiss, oust, replace, unseat.

**display** vb expand, extend, open, spread, unfold; exhibit, show; flaunt, parade. * n exhibition, manifestation, show; flourish, ostentation, pageant, parade, pomp.

**displease** vb disgruntle, disgust, disoblige, dissatisfy, offend; affront, aggravate, anger, annoy, chafe, chagrin, fret, irritate, nettle, pique, provoke, vex.

**displeasure** n disaffection, disapprobation, disapproval, dislike, dissatisfaction, distaste; anger, annoyance, indignation, irritation, pique, resentment, vexation, wrath; injury, offence.

**disport** vb caper, frisk, frolic, gambol, play, sport, wanton; amuse, beguile, cheer, divert, entertain, relax, solace.

**disposal** n arrangement, disposition; conduct, control, direction, disposure, government, management, ordering, regulation; bestowment, dispensation, distribution.

**dispose** vb arrange, distribute, marshal, group, place, range, rank, set; adjust, determine, regulate, settle; bias, incline, induce, lead, move, predispose; control, decide, regulate, rule, settle; arrange, bargain, compound; alienate, convey, demise, sell, transfer.

**disposed** adj apt, inclined, prone, ready, tending.

**disposition** n arrangement, arranging, classification, disposing, grouping, location, placing; adjustment, control, direction, disposure, disposal, management, ordering, regulation; aptitude, bent, bias, inclination, nature, predisposition, proclivity, proneness, propensity, tendency; character, constitution, humour, native, nature, temper, temperament, turn; inclination, willingness; bestowal, bestowment, dispensation, distribution.

**dispossess** vb deprive, divest, expropriate, strip; dislodge, eject, oust; disseise, disseize, evict, oust.

**dispraise** n blame, censure; discredit, disgrace, dishonour, disparagement, opprobrium, reproach, shame.

**disproof** n confutation, rebuttal, refutation.

**disproportion** n disparity, inadequacy, inequality, insufficiency, unsuitableness; incommensurateness.

**disprove** vb confute, rebel, rebut.

**disputable** *adj* controvertible, debatable, doubtful, questionable.

**disputation** *n* argumentation, controversy, debate, dispute.

**disputatious** *adj* argumentative, bickering, captious, caviling, contentious, dissentious, litigious, polemical, pugnacious, quarrelsome.

**dispute** *vb* altercate, argue, debate, litigate, question; bicker, brawl, jangle, quarrel, spar, spat, squabble, tiff, wrangle; agitate, argue, debate, ventilate; challenge, contradict, controvert, deny, impugn; contest, struggle for. * *n* controversy, debate, discussion, disputation; altercation, argument, bickering, brawl, disagreement, dissension, spat, squabble, tiff, wrangle.

**disqualification** *n* disability, incapitation.

**disqualify** *vb* disable, incapacitate, unfit; disenable, preclude, prohibit.

**disquiet** *vb* agitate, annoy, bother, discompose, disturb, excite, fret, harass, incommode, molest, plague, pester, trouble, vex, worry. * *n* anxiety, discomposure, disquietude, disturbance, restlessness, solicitude, trouble, uneasiness, unrest, vexation, worry.

**disquisition** *n* dissertation, discourse, essay, paper, thesis, treatise.

**disregard** *vb* contemn, despise, disdain, disobey, disparage, ignore, neglect, overlook, slight. * *n* contempt, ignoring, inattention, neglect, pretermit, oversight, slight; disesteem, disfavour, indifference.

**disrelish** *vb* dislike, loathe. * *n* dislike, distaste; flatness, insipidity, insipidness, nauseousness; antipathy, aversion, repugnance.

**disreputable** *adj* derogatory, discreditable, dishonourable, disgraceful, infamous, opprobrious, scandalous, shameful; base, contemptible, low, mean, vicious, vile, vulgar.

**disrepute** *n* abasement, degradation, derogation, discredit, disgrace, dishonour, ill-repute, odium.

**disrespect** *n* disesteem, disregard, irreverence, neglect, slight.

**disrespectful** *adj* discourteous, impertinent, impolite, rude, uncivil, uncourteous.

**dissatisfaction** *n* discontent, disquiet, inquietude, uneasiness; disapprobation, disapproval, dislike, displeasure.

**dissect** *vb* analyze, examine, explore, investigate, scrutinize, sift; cut apart.

**dissemble** *vb* cloak, conceal, cover, disguise, hide; counterfeit, dissimulate, feign, pretend.

**dissembler** *n* dissimulator, feigner, hypocrite, pretender, sham.

**disseminate** *vb* circulate, diffuse, disperse, proclaim, promulgate, propagate, publish, scatter, spread.

**dissension** *n* contention, difference, disagreement, discord, quarrel, strife, variance.

**dissent** *vb* decline, differ, disagree, refuse. * *n* difference, disagreement, nonconformity, opposition, recusancy, refusal.

**dissentient** *adj* disagreeing, dissenting, dissident, factious.

**dissertation** *n* discourse, disquisition, essay, thesis, treatise.

**disservice** *n* disadvantage, disfavour, harm, hurt, ill-turn, injury, mischief.

**dissidence** *n* disagreement, dissent, nonconformity, sectarianism.

**dissimilar** *adj* different, divergent, diverse, heterogeneous, unlike, various.

**dissimilarity** *n* dissimilitude, disparity, divergent, diversity, unlikeness, variation.

**dissimulation** *n* concealment, deceit, dissembling, double-dealing, duplicity, feigning, hypocrisy, pretence.

**dissipate** *vb* dispel, disperse, scatter; consume, expend, lavish, spend, squander, waste; disappear, vanish.

**dissipation** *n* dispersion, dissemination, scattering, vanishing; squandering, waste; crapulence, debauchery, dissoluteness, drunkenness, excess, profligacy.

**dissociate** *vb* disjoin, dissever, disunite, divide, separate, sever, sunder.

**dissolute** *adj* abandoned, corrupt, debauched, depraved, disorderly, dissipated, graceless, lax, lewd, licentious, loose, profligate, rakish, reprobate, shameless, vicious, wanton, wild.

**dissolution** *n* liquefaction, melting, solution; decomposition, putrefaction; death, disease; destruction, overthrow, ruin; termination.

**dissolve** *vb* liquefy, melt; disorganize, disunite, divide, loose, separate, sever; destroy, ruin; disappear, fade, scatter, vanish; crumble, decompose, disintegrate, perish.

**dissonance** *n* cacophony, discord, discordance, harshness, jarring; disagreement, discrepancy, incongruity, inconsistency.

**dissonant** adj discordant, grating, harsh, jangling, jarring, unharmonious; contradictory, disagreeing, discrepant, incongruous, inconsistent.

**distance** vb excel, outdo, outstrip, surpass. * n farness, remoteness; aloofness, coldness, frigidity, reserve, stiffness, offishness; absence, separation, space.

**distant** adj far, far-away, remote; aloof, ceremonious, cold, cool, frigid, haughty, reserved, stiff, uncordial; faint, indirect, obscure, slight.

**distaste** n disgust, disrelish; antipathy, aversion, disinclination, dislike, displeasure, dissatisfaction, repugnance.

**distasteful** adj disgusting, loathsome, nauseating, nauseous, unpalatable, unsavoury; disagreeable, displeasing, offensive, repugnant, repulsive, unpleasant.

**distemper** n ail, ailment, complaint, disease, disorder, illness, indisposition, malady, sickness.

**distempered** adj diseased, disordered; immoderate, inordinate, intemperate, unregulated.

**distend** vb bloat, dilate, enlarge, expand, increase, inflate, puff, stretch, swell, widen.

**distil** vb dribble, drip, drop; extract, separate.

**distinct** adj definite, different, discrete, disjunct, individual, separate, unconnected; clear, defined, manifest, obvious, plain, unconfused, unmistakable, well-defined.

**distinction** n discernment, discrimination, distinguishing; difference; account, celebrity, credit, eminence, fame, name, note, rank, renown, reputation, repute, respectability, superiority.

**distinctive** adj characteristic, differentiating, discriminating, distinguishing.

**distinctness** n difference, separateness; clearness, explicitness, lucidity, lucidness, perspicuity, precision.

**distinguish** vb characterize, mark; differentiate, discern, discriminate, perceive, recognize, see, single out, tell; demarcate, divide, separate; celebrate, honour, signalize.

**distinguished** adj celebrated, eminent, famous, illustrious, noted; conspicuous, extraordinary, laureate, marked, shining, superior, transcendent.

**distort** vb contort, deform, gnarl, screw, twist, warp, wrest; falsify, misrepresent, pervert.

**distortion** n contortion, deformation, deformity, twist,

wryness; falsification, misrepresentation, perversion, wresting.

**distract** vb divert, draw away; bewilder, confound, confuse, derange, discompose, disconcert, disturb, embarrass, harass, madden, mystify, perplex, puzzle.

**distracted** adj crazed, crazy, deranged, frantic, furious, insane, mad, raving, wild.

**distraction** n abstraction, bewilderment, confusion, mystification, embarrassment, perplexity; agitation, commotion, discord, disorder, disturbance, division, perturbation, tumult, turmoil; aberration, alienation, delirium, derangement, frenzy, hallucination, incoherence, insanity, lunacy, madness, mania, raving, wandering.

**distress** vb afflict, annoy, grieve, harry, pain, perplex, rack, trouble; distrain, seize, take. * n affliction, calamity, disaster, misery, misfortune, adversity, hardship, perplexity, trial, tribulation; agony, anguish, dolour, grief, sorrow, suffering; gnawing, gripe, griping, pain, torment, torture; destitution, indigence, poverty, privation, straits, want.

**distribute** vb allocate, allot, apportion, assign, deal, dispense, divide, dole out, give, mete, partition, prorate, share; administer, arrange, assort, class, classify, dispose.

**distribution** n allocation, allotment, apportionment, assignment, assortment, dispensation, dispensing; arrangement, disposal, disposition, classification, division, dole, grouping, partition, sharing.

**district** n circuit, department, neighbourhood, province, quarter, region, section, territory, tract, ward.

**distrust** vb disbelieve, discredit, doubt, misbelieve, mistrust, question, suspect. * n doubt, misgiving, mistrust, question, suspicion.

**distrustful** adj doubting, dubious, suspicious.

**disturb** vb agitate, shake, stir; confuse, derange, disarrange, disorder, unsettle, upset; annoy, discompose, disconcert, disquiet, distract, fuss, incommode, molest, perturb, plague, trouble, ruffle, vex, worry; impede, interrupt, hinder.

**disturbance** n agitation, commotion, confusion, convulsion, derangement, disorder, perturbation, unsettlement; annoyance, discomposure, distraction, excitement, fuss; hindrance, interruption, molestation; brawl, commotion, disorder, excitement, fracas, hubbub, riot, rising, tumult, turmoil, uproar.

**disunion** n disconnection, disjunction, division, separation, severance; breach, feud, rupture, schism.

**disunite** vb detach, disconnect, disjoin, dissever, dissociate, divide, part, rend, separate, segregate, sever, sunder; alienate, estrange.

**disuse** n desuetude, discontinuance, disusage, neglect, nonobservance.

**ditch** vb canalize, dig, excavate, furrow, gouge, trench; abandon, discard, dump, jettison, scrap. * n channel, drain, fosse, moat, trench.

**divagation** n deviation, digression, rambling, roaming, straying, wandering.

**divan** n bed, chesterfield, couch, settee, sofa.

**divaricate** vb diverge, fork, part.

**dive** vb explore, fathom, penetrate, plunge, sound. * n drop, fall, header, plunge; bar, den, dump, joint, saloon.

**diverge** vb divide, radiate, separate; divaricate, separate; deviate, differ, disagree, vary.

**divers** adj different, manifold, many, numerous, several, sundry, various.

**diverse** adj different, differing, disagreeing, dissimilar, divergent, heterogeneous, multifarious, multiform, separate, unlike, variant, various, varying.

**diversion** n deflection, diverting; amusement, delight, distraction, enjoyment, entertainment, game, gratification, pastime, play, pleasure, recreation, sport; detour, digression.

**diversity** n difference, dissimilarity, dissimilitude, divergence, unlikeness, variation; heterogeneity, manifoldness, multifariousness, multiformity, variety.

**divert** vb deflect, distract, disturb; amuse, beguile, delight, entertain, exhilarate, give pleasure, gratify, recreate, refresh, solace.

**divest** vb denude, disrobe, strip, unclothe, undress; deprive, dispossess, strip.

**divide** vb bisect, cleave, cut, dismember, dissever, disunite, open, part, rend, segregate, separate, sever, shear, split, sunder; allocate, allot, apportion, assign, dispense, distribute, dole, mete, portion, share; compartmentalize, demarcate, partition; alienate, disunite, estrange.

**divination** n augury, divining, foretelling, incantation, magic, sooth-saying, sorcery; prediction, presage, prophecy.

**divine** vb foretell, predict, presage, prognosticate, vaticinate, prophesy; believe, conjecture, fancy, guess, suppose, surmise, suspect, think. * adj deiform, godlike, superhuman, supernatural; angelic,

celestial, heavenly, holy, sacred, seraphic, spiritual; exalted, exalting, rapturous, supreme, transcendent. * n churchman, clergyman, ecclesiastic, minister, parson, pastor, priest.

**division** n compartmentalization, disconnection, disjunction, dismemberment, segmentation, separation, severance; category, class, compartment, head, parcel, portion, section, segment; demarcation, partition; alienation, allotment, apportionment, distribution; breach, difference, disagreement, discord, disunion, estrangement, feud, rupture, variance.

**divorce** vb disconnect, dissolve, disunite, part, put away, separate, sever, split up, sunder, unmarry. * n disjunction, dissolution, disunion, division, divorcement, parting, separation, severance.

**divulge** vb communicate, declare, disclose, discover, exhibit, expose, impart, proclaim, promulgate, publish, reveal, tell, uncover.

**dizzy** adj giddy, vertiginous; careless, heedless, thoughtless.

**do** vb accomplish, achieve, act, commit, effect, execute, perform; complete, conclude, end, finish, settle, terminate; conduct, transact; observe, perform, practice; translate, render; cook, prepare; cheat, chouse, cozen, hoax, swindle; serve, suffice. * n act, action, adventure, deed, doing, exploit, feat, thing; banquet, event, feast, function, party.

**docile** adj amenable, obedient, pliant, teachable, tractable, yielding.

**dock**[1] vb clip, curtail, cut, deduct, truncate; lessen, shorten.

**dock**[2] .vb anchor, moor; join, meet. * n anchorage, basin, berth, dockage, dockyard, dry dock, harbour, haven, marina, pier, shipyard, wharf.

**doctor** vb adulterate, alter, cook, falsify, manipulate, tamper with; attend, minister to, cure, heal, remedy, treat; fix, mend, overhaul, repair, service. * n general practitioner, GP, healer, leech, medic, physician; adept, savant.

**doctrinaire** adj impractical, theoretical. * n ideologist, theorist, thinker.

**doctrine** n article, belief, creed, dogma, opinion, precept, principle, teaching, tenet.

**dodge** vb equivocate, evade, prevaricate, quibble, shuffle. * n artifice, cavil, evasion, quibble, subterfuge, trick.

**dogged** adj cantankerous, headstrong, inflexible, intractable, mulish, obstinate, pertinacious, perverse, resolute, stubborn, tenacious, unyielding, wilful; churlish, morose, sour, sullen, surly.

**dogma** n article, belief, creed, doctrine, opinion, precept, principle, tenet.

**dogmatic** adj authoritative, categorical, formal, settled; arrogant, confident, dictatorial, imperious, magisterial, opinionated, oracular, overbearing, peremptory, positive; doctrinal.

**dole** vb allocate, allot, apportion, assign, deal, distribute, divide, share. * n allocation, allotment, apportionment, distribution; part, portion, share; alms, donation, gift, gratuity, pittance; affliction, distress, grief, sorrow, woe.

**doleful** adj lugubrious, melancholy, piteous, rueful, sad, sombre, sorrowful, woebegone, woeful; cheerless, dark, dismal, dolorous, dreary, gloomy.

**dolorous** adj cheerless, dark, dismal, gloomy; doleful, lugubrious, mournful, piteous, rueful, sad, sorrowful, woeful.

**dolt** n blockhead, booby, dullard, dunce, fool, ignoramus, simpleton.

**domain** n authority, dominion, jurisdiction, province, sway; empire, realm, territory; lands, estate; branch, department, region.

**domestic** n charwoman, help, home help, maid, servant. * adj domiciliary, family, home, household, private; domesticated; internal, intestine.

**domesticate** vb tame; adopt, assimilate, familiarize, naturalize.

**domicile** vb domiciliate, dwell, inhabit, live, remain, reside. * n abode, dwelling, habitation, harbour, home, house, residence.

**dominant** adj ascendant, ascending, chief, controlling, governing, influential, outstanding, paramount, predominant, pre-eminent, preponderant, presiding, prevailing, ruling.

**dominate** vb control, rule, sway; command, overlook, overtop, surmount.

**domineer** vb rule, tyrannize; bluster, bully, hector, menace, swagger, swell, threaten.

**dominion** n ascendancy, authority, command, control, domain, domination, government, jurisdiction, mastery, rule, sovereign, sovereignty, supremacy, sway; country, kingdom, realm, region, territory.

**donation** n alms, benefaction, boon, contribution, dole, donative, gift, grant, gratuity, largesse, offering, present, subscription.

**done** adj accomplished, achieved, effected, ex-
ecuted, performed; completed, concluded, ended, finished, terminated; carried on, transacted, rendered, translated; cooked, prepared; cheated, cozened, hoaxed, swindled; (with **for**) damned, dished, hors de combat, ruined, shelved, spoiled, wound up.

**donkey** n ass, mule; dunce, fool, simpleton.

**donor** n benefactor, bestower, giver; donator.

**double** vb fold, plait; duplicate, geminate, increase, multiply, repeat; return. * adj binary, coupled, geminate, paired; dual, twice, twofold; deceitful, dishonest, double-dealing, false, hollow, insincere, knavish, perfidious, treacherous, two-faced. * adv doubly, twice, twofold. * n doubling, fold, plait; artifice, manoeuvre, ruse, shift, stratagem, trick, wile; copy, counterpart, twin.

**doublet** n jacket, jerkin.

**doubt** vb demur, fluctuate, hesitate, vacillate, waver; distrust, mistrust, query, question, suspect. * n dubiety, dubiousness, dubitation, hesitance, hesitancy, hesitation, incertitude, indecision, irresolution, question, suspense, uncertainty, vacillation; distrust, misgiving, mistrust, scepticism, suspicion.

**doubtful** adj dubious, hesitating, sceptical, undecided, undetermined, wavering; ambiguous, dubious, enigmatical, equivocal, hazardous, obscure, problematical, unsure; indeterminate, questionable, undecided, unquestioned.

**doubtless** adv certainly, unquestionably; clearly, indisputably, precisely.

**doughty** adj adventurous, bold, brave, chivalrous, courageous, daring, dauntless, fearless, gallant, heroic, intrepid, redoubtable, valiant, valorous.

**douse** see **dowse**.

**dowdy** adj awkward, dingy, ill-dressed, shabby, slatternly, slovenly; old-fashioned, unfashionable.

**dowel** n peg, pin, pinion, tenon.

**dower** n endowment, gift; dowry; portion, share.

**downcast** adj chapfallen, crestfallen, dejected, depressed, despondent, discouraged, disheartened, dispirited, downhearted, low-spirited, sad, unhappy.

**downfall** n descent, destruction, fall, ruin.

**downhearted** adj chapfallen, crestfallen, dejected, depressed, despondent, discouraged, disheartened, dispirited, downcast, low-spirited, sad, unhappy.

**downright** adj absolute, categorical, clear, explicit, plain, positive, sheer, simple, undisguised, unequivocal, utter; above-board, artless, blunt, direct, frank, honest, ingenuous, open, sincere, straightforward, unceremonious.

**downy** adj lanate, lanated, lanose.

**dowse, douse** vb dip, immerse, plunge, souse, submerge.

**doxy** n mistress, paramour; courtesan, drab, harlot, prostitute, strumpet, streetwalker, whore.

**doze** vb drowse, nap, sleep, slumber. * n drowse, forty-winks, nap.

**dozy** adj drowsy, heavy, sleepy, sluggish.

**draft** vb detach, select; commandeer, conscript, impress; delineate, draw, outline, sketch. * n conscription, drawing, selection; delineation, outline, sketch; bill, cheque, order.

**drag** vb draw, haul, pull, tow, tug; trail; linger, loiter. * n favour, influence, pull; brake, check, curb, lag, resistance, retardation, scotch, skid, slackening, slack-off, slowing.

**draggle** vb befoul, bemire, besmirch, dangle, drabble, trail.

**dragoon** vb compel, drive, force, harass, harry, persecute. * n cavalier, equestrian, horse-soldier.

**drain** vb milk, sluice, tap; empty, evacuate, exhaust; dry. * n channel, culvert, ditch, sewer, sluice, trench, watercourse; exhaustion, withdrawal.

**draught** n current, drawing, pulling, traction; cup, dose, drench, drink, potion; delineation, design, draft, outline, sketch.

**draw** vb drag, haul, tow, tug, pull; attract; drain, suck, syphon; extract, extort; breathe in, inhale, inspire; allure, engage, entice, induce, influence, lead, move, persuade; extend, protract, stretch; delineate, depict, sketch; deduce, derive, infer; compose, draft, formulate, frame, prepare; blister, vesicate, write.

**drawback** n defect, deficiency, detriment, disadvantage, fault, flaw, imperfection, injury; abatement, allowance, deduction, discount, rebate, reduction.

**drawing** n attracting, draining, inhaling, pulling, traction; delineation, draught, outline, picture, plan, sketch.

**dread** vb apprehend, fear. * adj dreadful, frightful, horrible, terrible; awful, venerable. * n affright, alarm, apprehension, fear, terror; awe, veneration.

**dreadful** adj alarming, appalling, awesome, dire, direful, fearful, formidable, frightful, horrible, horrid, terrible, terrific, tremendous; awful, venerable.

**dream** vb fancy, imagine, think. * n conceit, daydream, delusion, fancy, fantasy, hallucination, illusion, imagination, reverie, vagary, vision.

**dreamer** n enthusiast, visionary.

**dreamy** adj absent, abstracted, fanciful, ideal, misty, shadowy, speculative, unreal, visionary.

**dreary** adj cheerless, chilling, comfortless, dark, depressing, dismal, drear, gloomy, lonely, lonesome, sad, solitary, sorrowful; boring, dull, monotonous, tedious, tiresome, uninteresting, wearisome.

**dregs** npl feculence, grounds, lees, off-scourings, residuum, scourings, sediment, waste; draff, dross, refuse, scum, trash.

**drench** vb dowse, drown, imbrue, saturate, soak, souse, steep, wet; physic, purge.

**dress** vb align, straighten; adjust, arrange, dispose; fit, prepare; accoutre, apparel, array, attire, clothe, robe, rig; adorn, bedeck, deck, decorate, drape, embellish, trim. * n apparel, attire, clothes, clothing, costume, garb, guise, garments, habiliment, habit, raiment, suit, toilet, vesture; bedizenment, bravery; frock, gown, rob.

**dressing** n compost, fertilizer, manure; forcemeat, stuffing.

**dressy** adj flashy, gaudy, showy.

**driblet** n bit, drop, fragment, morsel, piece, scrap.

**drift** vb accumulate, drive, float, wander. * n bearing, course, direction; aim, design, intent, intention, mark, object, proposal, purpose, scope, tendency; detritus, deposit, diluvium; gallery, passage, tunnel; current, rush, sweep; heap, pile.

**drill**[1] vb bore, perforate, pierce; discipline, exercise, instruct, teach, train. * n borer; discipline, exercise, training.

**drill**[2] n channel, furrow, trench.

**drink** vb imbibe, sip, swill; carouse, indulge, revel, tipple, tope; swallow, quaff; absorb. * n beverage, draught, liquid, potation, potion; dram, nip, sip, snifter, refreshment.

**drip** vb dribble, drop, leak, trickle; distil, filter, percolate; ooze, reek, seep, weep. * n dribble, drippings, drop, leak, leakage, leaking, trickle, tricklet; bore, nuisance, wet blanket.

**drive** vb hurl, impel, propel, send, shoot, thrust; actuate, incite, press, urge; coerce, compel, constrain, force, harass, oblige, overburden, press, rush; go, guide, ride, travel; aim, intend. * n effort, energy, pressure; airing, ride; road.

**drivel** *vb* babble, blether, dote, drool, slaver, slobber. * *n* balderdash, drivelling, fatuity, nonsense, prating, rubbish, slaver, stuff, twaddle.

**drizzle** *vb* mizzle, rain, shower, sprinkle. * *n* haar, mist, mizzle, rain, sprinkling.

**droll** *adj* comic, comical, farcical, funny, jocular, ludicrous, laughable, ridiculous; amusing, diverting, facetious, odd, quaint, queer, waggish. * *n* buffoon, clown, comedian, fool, harlequin, jester, punch, Punchinello, scaramouch, wag, zany.

**drollery** *n* archness, buffoonery, fun, humour, jocularity, pleasantry, waggishness, whimsicality.

**drone** *vb* dawdle, drawl, idle, loaf, lounge; hum. * *n* idler, loafer, lounger, sluggard.

**drool** *vb* drivel, slaver.

**droop** *vb* fade, wilt, wither; decline, fail, faint, flag, languish, sink, weaken; bend, hang.

**drop** *vb* distil, drip, shed; decline, depress, descend, dump, lower, sink; abandon, desert, forsake, forswear, leave, omit, relinquish, quit; cease, discontinue, intermit, remit; fall, precipitate. * *n* bead, droplet, globule; earring, pendant.

**dross** *n* cinder, lees, recrement, scoria, scum, slag; refuse, waste.

**drought** *n* aridity, drouth, dryness, thirstiness.

**drove** *n* flock, herd; collection, company, crowd.

**drown** *vb* deluge, engulf, flood, immerse, inundate, overflow, sink, submerge, swamp; overcome, overpower, overwhelm.

**drowse** *vb* doze, nap, sleep, slumber, snooze. * *n* doze, forty winks, nap, siesta, sleep, snooze.

**drowsy** *adj* dozy, sleepy; comatose, lethargic, stupid; lulling, soporific.

**drub** *vb* bang, beat, cane, cudgel, flog, hit, knock, pommel, pound, strike, thrash, thump, whack.

**drubbing** *n* beating, caning, cudgelling, flagellation, flogging, pommelling, pounding, thrashing, thumping, whacking.

**drudge** *vb* grub, grind, plod, slave, toil, work. * *n* grind, hack, hard worker, menial, plodder, scullion, servant, slave, toiler, worker.

**drug** *vb* dose, medicate; disgust, surfeit. * *n* medicine, physic, remedy; poison.

**drunk** *adj* boozed, drunken, inebriated, intoxicated, maudlin, soaked, tipsy; ablaze, aflame, delirious, fervent, suffused. * *n* alcoholic, boozer, dipsomaniac, drunkard, inebriate, lush, soak; bacchanal, bender, binge.

**drunkard** *n* alcoholic, boozer, carouser, dipsomaniac, drinker, drunk, inebriate, reveller, sot, tippler, toper.

**dry** *vb* dehydrate, desiccate, drain, exsiccate, parch. * *adj* desiccated, dried, juiceless, sapless, unmoistened; arid, droughty, parched; drouthy, thirsty; barren, dull, insipid, jejune, plain, pointless, tame, tedious, tiresome, unembellished, uninteresting, vapid; cutting, keen, sarcastic, severe, sharp, sly.

**dub** *vb* call, christen, denominate, designate, entitle, name, style, term.

**dubious** *adj* doubtful, fluctuating, hesitant, irresolute, skeptical, uncertain, undecided, unsettled, wavering; ambiguous, doubtful, equivocal, improbable, questionable, uncertain.

**duck** *vb* dip, dive, immerse, plunge, submerge, souse; bend, bow, dodge, stoop.

**duct** *n* canal, channel, conduit, pipe, tube; blood-vessel.

**ductile** *adj* compliant, docile, facile, tractable, yielding; flexible, malleable, pliant; extensible, tensile.

**dudgeon** *n* anger, indignation, ill will, ire, malice, resentment, umbrage, wrath.

**due** *adj* owed, owing; appropriate, becoming, befitting, bounden, fit, proper, suitable, right. * *adv* dead, direct, directly, exactly, just, right, squarely, straight. * *n* claim, debt, desert, right.

**dulcet** *adj* delicious, honeyed, luscious, sweet; harmonious, melodious; agreeable, charming, delightful, pleasant, pleasing.

**dull** *vb* blunt; benumb, besot, deaden, hebetate, obtund, paralyse, stupefy; dampen, deject, depress, discourage, dishearten, dispirit; allay, alleviate, assuage, mitigate, moderate, quiet, soften; deaden, dim, sully, tarnish. * *adj* blockish, brutish, doltish, obtuse, stolid, stupid, unintelligent; apathetic, callous, dead, insensible, passionless, phlegmatic, unfeeling, unimpassioned, unresponsive; heavy, inactive, inanimate, inert, languish, lifeless, slow, sluggish, torpid; blunt, dulled, hebetate, obtuse; cheerless, dismal, dreary, gloomy, sad, sombre; dim, lack-lustre, lustreless, matt, obscure, opaque, tarnished; dry, flat, insipid, irksome, jejune, prosy, tedious, tiresome, uninteresting, wearisome.

**duly** *adv* befittingly, decorously, fitly, properly, rightly; regularly.

**dumb** *adj* inarticulate, mute, silent, soundless, speechless, voiceless.

**dumbfound, dumfound** vb amaze, astonish, astound, bewilder, confound, confuse, nonplus, pose.

**dumps** npl blues, dejection, depression, despondency, gloom, gloominess, melancholy, sadness.

**dun**[1] adj greyish-brown, brown, drab.

**dun**[2] vb beset, importune, press, urge.

**dunce** n ass, block, blockhead, clodpole, dolt, donkey, dullard, dunderhead, fool, goose, halfwit, ignoramus, jackass, lackwit, loon, nincompoop, numskull, oaf, simpleton, thickhead, witling.

**dupe** vb beguile, cheat, chouse, circumvent, cozen, deceive, delude, gull, hoodwink, outwit, overreach, swindle, trick. * n gull, simpleton.

**duplicate** vb copy, double, repeat, replicate, reproduce. * adj doubled, twofold. * n copy, counterpart, facsimile, replica, transcript.

**duplicity** n artifice, chicanery, circumvention, deceit, deception, dishonesty, dissimulation, double-dealing, falseness, fraud, guile, hypocrisy, perfidy.

**durable** adj abiding, constant, continuing, enduring, firm, lasting, permanent, persistent, stable.

**duration** n continuance, continuation, permanency, perpetuation, prolongation; period, time.

**duress** n captivity, confinement, constraint, durance, hardship, imprisonment, restraint; compulsion.

**dusky** adj cloudy, darkish, dim, murky, obscure, overcast, shady, shadowy; dark, swarthy, tawny.

**dutiful** adj duteous, obedient, submissive; deferential, respectful, reverential.

**duty** n allegiance, devoirs, obligation, responsibility, reverence; business, engagement, function, office, service; custom, excise, impost, tariff, tax, toll.

**dwarf** vb lower, stunt. * n bantam, homunculus, manikin, midget, pygmy.

**dwarfish** adj diminutive, dwarfed, little, low, pygmy, small, stunted, tiny, undersized.

**dwell** vb abide, inhabit, live, lodge, remain, reside, rest, sojourn, stay, stop, tarry, tenant.

**dwelling** n abode, cot, domicile, dugout, establishment, habitation, home, house, hutch, lodging, mansion, quarters, residence.

**dwindle** vb decrease, diminish, lessen, shrink; decay, decline, deteriorate, pine, sink, waste away.

**dye** vb colour, stain, tinge. * n cast, colour, hue, shade, stain, tinge, tint.

**dying** adj expiring; mortal, perishable. * n death, decease, demise, departure, dissolution, exit.

**dynasty** n dominion, empire, government, rule, sovereignty.

**dyspepsia** n indigestion.

# E

**eager** adj agog, avid, anxious, desirous, fain, greedy, impatient, keen, longing, yearning; animated, ardent, earnest, enthusiastic, fervent, fervid, forward, glowing, hot, impetuous, sanguine, vehement, zealous.

**eagerness** n ardour, avidity, earnestness, enthusiasm, fervour, greediness, heartiness, hunger, impatience, impetuosity, intentness, keenness, longing, thirst, vehemence, yearning, zeal.

**eagle-eyed** adj discerning, hawk-eyed, sharp-sighted.

**ear**[1] n attention, hearing, heed, regard.

**ear**[2] n head, spike.

**early** adj opportune, seasonable, timely; forward, premature; dawning, matutinal. * adv anon, beforehand, betimes, ere, seasonably, shortly, soon.

**earn** vb acquire, gain, get, obtain, procure, realize, reap, win; deserve, merit.

**earnest** adj animated, ardent, eager, cordial, fervent, fervid, glowing, hearty, impassioned, importune, warm, zealous; fixed, intent, steady; sincere, true, truthful; important, momentous, serious, weighty. * n reality, seriousness, truth; foretaste, pledge, promise; handsel, payment.

**earnings** npl allowance, emoluments, gains, income, pay, proceeds, profits, remuneration, reward, salary, stipend.

**earth** n globe, orb, planet, world; clay, clod, dirt, glebe, ground, humus, land, loam, sod, soil, turf; mankind, world.

**earthborn** adj abject, base, earthly, grovelling, low, mean, unspiritual.

**earthly** adj terrestrial; base, carnal, earthborn, low, gross, grovelling, sensual, sordid, unspiritual, worldly; bodily, material, mundane, natural, secular, temporal.

**earthy** adj clayey, earth-like, terrene; earthly, terrestrial; coarse, gross, material, unrefined.

**ease** vb disburden, disencumber, pacify, quiet, relieve, still; abate, allay, alleviate, appease, assuage, diminish, mitigate, soothe; loosen, release; facilitate, favour. * n leisure, quiescence, repose, rest; calmness, content, contentment, enjoyment, happiness, peace, quiet, quietness, quietude, relief, repose, satisfaction, serenity, tranquillity; easiness, facility, readiness; flexibility, freedom, liberty, lightness, naturalness, unconcern, unconstraint; comfort, elbowroom.

**easy** adj light; careless, comfortable, contented, effortless, painless, quiet, satisfied, tranquil, untroubled; accommodating, complaisant, compliant, complying, facile, indolent, manageable, pliant, submissive, tractable, yielding; graceful, informal, natural, unconstrained; flowing, ready, smooth, unaffected; gentle, lenient, mild, moderate; affluent, loose, unconcerned, unembarrassed.

**eat** vb chew, consume, devour, engorge, ingest, ravage, swallow; corrode, demolish, erode; breakfast, dine, feed, lunch, sup.

**eatable** adj edible, esculent, harmless, wholesome.

**ebb** vb abate, recede, retire, subside; decay, decline, decrease, degenerate, deteriorate, sink, wane. * n refluence, reflux, regress, regression, retrocedence, retrocession, retrogression, return; caducity, decay, decline, degeneration, deterioration, wane, waning; abatement, decrease, decrement, diminution.

**ebullience** n ebullition, effervescence; burst, bursting, overenthusiasm, overflow, rush, vigour.

**ebullition** n boiling, bubbling; effervescence, fermentation; burst, fit, outbreak, outburst, paroxysm.

**eccentric** adj decentred, parabolic; aberrant, abnormal, anomalous, cranky, erratic, fantastic, irregular, odd, outlandish, peculiar, singular, strange, uncommon, unnatural, wayward, whimsical. * n crank, curiosity, original.

**eccentricity** n ellipticity, flattening, flatness, oblateness; aberration, irregularity, oddity, oddness, peculiarity, singularity, strangeness, waywardness.

**ecclesiastic**[1], **ecclesiastical** adj churchish, churchly, clerical, ministerial, nonsecular, pastoral, priestly, religious, sacerdotal.

**ecclesiastic**[2] n chaplain, churchman, clergyman, cleric, clerk, divine, minister, parson, pastor, priest, reverend, shepherd.

**echo** vb reply, resound, reverberate, ring; re-echo, repeat. * n answer, repetition, reverberation; imitation.

**éclat** n acclamation, applause, brilliancy, effect, glory, lustre, pomp, renown, show, splendour.

**eclipse** vb cloud, darken, dim, obscure, overshadow, veil; annihilate, annul, blot out, extinguish. * n clouding, concealment, darkening, dimming, disappearance, hiding, obscuration, occultation, shrouding, vanishing, veiling; annihilation, blotting out, destruction, extinction, extinguishment, obliteration.

**eclogue** n bucolic, idyl, pastoral.

**economize** vb husband, manage, save; retrench.

**economy** n frugality, husbandry, parsimony, providence, retrenchment, saving, skimping, stinginess, thrift, thriftiness; administration, arrangement, management, method, order, plan, regulation, system; dispensation.

**ecstasy** n frenzy, madness, paroxysm, trance; delight, gladness, joy, rhapsody, rapture, ravishment, transport.

**eddy** vb gurgle, surge, spin, swirl, whirl. * n countercurrent; swirl, vortex, whirlpool.

**edge** vb sharpen; border, fringe, rim. * n border, brim, brink, bound, crest, fringe, hem, lip, margin, rim, verge; animation, intensity, interest, keenness, sharpness, zest; acrimony, bitterness, gall, sharpness, sting.

**edging** n border, frill, fringe, trimming.

**edible** adj eatable, esculent, harmless, wholesome.

**edict** n act, command, constitution, decision, decree, law, mandate, manifesto, notice, order, ordinance, proclamation, regulation, rescript, statute.

**edifice** n building, fabric, habitation, house, structure.

**edify** vb educate, elevate, enlightenment, improve, inform, instruct, nurture, teach, upbuild.

**edition** n impression, issue, number.

**educate** vb breed, cultivate, develop, discipline, drill, edify, exercise, indoctrinate, inform, instruct, mature, nurture, rear, school, teach, train.

**educated** adj cultured, lettered, literate.

**education** n breeding, cultivation, culture, development, discipline, drilling, indoctrination, instruction, nurture, pedagogics, schooling, teaching, training, tuition.

**educe** vb bring out, draw out, elicit, evolve, extract.

**eerie** adj awesome, fearful, frightening, strange, uncanny, weird.

**efface** vb blot, blot out, cancel, delete, destroy, erase, expunge, obliterate, remove, sponge.

**effect** vb cause, create, effectuate, produce; accomplish, achieve, carry, compass, complete, conclude, consummate, contrive, do, execute, force, negotiate, perform, realize, work. * n consequence, event, fruit, issue, outcome, result; efficiency, fact, force, power, reality; validity, weight; drift, import, intent, meaning, purport, significance, tenor.

**effective** adj able, active, adequate, competent, convincing, effectual, sufficient; cogent, efficacious, energetic, forcible, potent, powerful.

**effects** npl chattels, furniture, goods, movables, property.

**effectual** adj operative, successful; active, effective, efficacious, efficient.

**effectuate** vb accomplish, achieve, complete, do, effect, execute, fulfil, perform, secure.

**effeminate** adj delicate, feminine, soft, tender, timorous, unmanly, womanish, womanlike, womanly; camp.

**effervesce** vb bubble, ferment, foam, froth.

**effete** adj addle, barren, fruitless, sterile, unfruitful, unproductive, unprolific; decayed, exhausted, spent, wasted.

**efficacious** adj active, adequate, competent, effective, effectual, efficient, energetic, operative, powerful.

**efficacy** n ability, competency, effectiveness, efficiency, energy, force, potency, power, strength, vigour, virtue.

**efficient** adj active, capable, competent, effective, effectual, efficacious, operative, potent; able, energetic, ready, skilful.

**effigy** n figure, image, likeness, portrait, representation, statue.

**effloresce** vb bloom, flower.

**efflorescence** n blooming, blossoming, flowering.

**effluence** n discharge, efflux, effluvium, emanation, emission, flow, outflow, outpouring.

**effort** n application, attempt, endeavour, essay, exertion, pains, spurt, strain, strife, stretch, struggle, trial, trouble.

**effrontery** n assurance, audacity, boldness, brass, disrespect, hardihood, impudence, incivility, insolence, presumption, rudeness, sauciness, shamelessness.

**effulgent** adj burning, beaming, blazing, bright, brilliant, dazzling, flaming, glowing, lustrous, radiant, refulgent, resplendent, shining, splendid.

**effusion** n discharge, efflux, emission, gush, outpouring; shedding, spilling, waste; address, speech, talk, utterance.

**egg** vb (with **on**) encourage, incite, instigate, push, stimulate, urge; harass, harry, provoke.

**ego** *n* id, self, me, subject, superego.

**egotism** *n* self-admiration, self-assertion, self-commendation, self-conceit, self-esteem, self-importance, self-praise; egoism, selfishness.

**egotistic, egotistical** *adj* bumptious, conceited, egoistical, opinionated, self-asserting, self-admiring, self-centred, self-conceited, self-important, self-loving, vain.

**egregious** *adj* conspicuous, enormous, extraordinary, flagrant, great, gross, huge, monstrous, outrageous, prodigious, remarkable, tremendous.

**egress** *n* departure, emergence, exit, outlet, way out.

**eject** *vb* belch, discharge, disgorge, emit, evacuate, puke, spew, spit, spout, spurt, void, vomit; bounce, cashier, discharge, dismiss, disposes, eliminate, evict, expel, fire, oust; banish, reject, throw out.

**elaborate** *vb* develop, improve, mature, produce, refine, ripen. * *adj* complicated, decorated, detailed, dressy, laboured, laborious, ornate, perfected, studied.

**elapse** *vb* go, lapse, pass.

**elastic** *adj* rebounding, recoiling, resilient, springy; buoyant, recuperative.

**elated** *adj* animated, cheered, elate, elevated, excited, exhilarated, exultant, flushed, puffed up, roused.

**elbow** *vb* crowd, force, hustle, jostle, nudge, push, shoulder. * *n* angle, bend, corner, flexure, joining, turn.

**elder** *adj* older, senior; ranking; ancient, earlier, older. * *n* ancestor, senior; presbyter, prior, senator.

**elect** *vb* appoint, choose, cull, designate, pick, prefer, select. * *adj* choice, chosen, picked, selected; appointed, elected; predestinated, redeemed.

**election** *n* appointment, choice, preference; selection; alternative, freedom, freewill, liberty; predestination.

**elector** *n* chooser, constituent, selector, voter.

**electrify** *vb* charge, galvanize; astonish, enchant, excite, rouse, startle, stir, thrill.

**elegance, elegancy** *n* beauty, grace, propriety, symmetry; courtliness, daintiness, gentility, nicety, polish, politeness, refinement, taste.

**elegant** *adj* beautiful, chaste, classical, dainty, graceful, fine, handsome, neat, symmetrical, tasteful, trim, well-made, well-proportioned; accomplished, courtly, cultivated, fashionable, genteel, polished, polite, refined.

**elegiac** *adj* dirgeful, mournful, plaintive, sorrowful.

**elegy** *n* dirge, epicedium, lament, ode, threnody.

**element** *n* basis, component, constituent, factor, germ, ingredient, part, principle, rudiment, unit; environment, milieu, sphere.

**elementary** *adj* primordial, simple, uncombined, uncomplicated, uncompounded; basic, component, fundamental, initial, primary, rudimental, rudimentary.

**elevate** *vb* erect, hoist, lift, raise; advance, aggrandize, exalt, promote; dignify, ennoble, exalt, greaten, improve, refine; animate, cheer, elate, excite, exhilarate, rouse.

**elfin** *adj* elflike, elvish, mischievous, weird.

**elicit** *vb* draw out, educe, evoke, extort, fetch, obtain, pump, wrest, wring; deduce, educe.

**eligible** *adj* desirable, preferable; qualified, suitable, worthy.

**eliminate** *vb* disengage, eradicate, exclude, expel, remove, separate; ignore, omit, reject.

**ellipsis** *n* gap, hiatus, lacuna, omission.

**elliptical** *adj* oval; defective, incomplete.

**elocution** *n* declamation, delivery, oratory, rhetoric, speech, utterance.

**elongate** *vb* draw, draw out, extend, lengthen, protract, stretch.

**elope** *vb* abscond, bolt, decamp, disappear, leave.

**eloquence** *n* fluency, oratory, rhetoric.

**else** *adv* besides, differently, otherwise.

**elucidate** *vb* clarify, demonstrate, explain, expound, illuminate, illustrate, interpret, unfold.

**elucidation** *n* annotation, clarification, comment, commentary, elucidating, explaining, explanation, exposition, gloss, scholium.

**elude** *vb* avoid, escape, evade, shun, slip; baffle, balk, disappoint, disconcert, escape, foil, frustrate, thwart.

**elusive** *adj* deceptive, deceitful, delusive, evasive, fallacious, fraudulent, illusory; equivocatory, equivocating, shuffling.

**Elysian** *adj* blissful, celestial, delightful, enchanting, heavenly, ravishing, seraphic.

**emaciation** *n* attenuation, lankness, leanness, meagreness, tabes, tabescence, thinness.

**emanate** *vb* arise, come, emerge, flow, issue, originate, proceed, spring.

**emancipate** *vb* deliver, discharge, disenthral, enfranchise, free, liberate, manumit, release, unchain, unfetter, unshackle.

**emancipation** n deliverance, enfranchisement, deliverance, freedom, liberation, manumission, release.

**emasculate** vb castrate, geld; debilitate, effeminize, enervate, unman, weaken.

**embalm** vb cherish, consecrate, conserve, enshrine, preserve, store, treasure; perfume, scent.

**embargo** vb ban, bar, blockade, debar, exclude, prohibit, proscribe, restrict, stop, withhold. * n ban, bar, blockade, exclusion, hindrance, impediment, prohibition, prohibitory, proscription, restraint, restriction, stoppage.

**embark** vb engage, enlist.

**embarrass** vb beset, entangle, perplex; annoy, clog, bother, distress, hamper, harass, involve, plague, trouble, vex; abash, confound, confuse, discomfit, disconcert, dumbfound, mortify, nonplus, pose, shame.

**embellish** vb adorn, beautify, bedeck, deck, decorate, emblazon, enhance, enrich, garnish, grace, ornament.

**embellishment** n adornment, decoration, enrichment, ornament, ornamentation.

**embezzle** vb appropriate, defalcate, filch, misappropriate, peculate, pilfer, purloin, steal.

**embitter** vb aggravate, envenom, exacerbate; anger, enrage, exasperate, madden.

**emblem** n badge, cognizance, device, mark, representation, sign, symbol, token, type.

**embody** vb combine, compact, concentrate, incorporate; comprehend, comprise, contain, embrace, include; codify, methodize, systematize.

**embolden** vb animate, cheer, elate, encourage, gladden, hearten, inspirit, nerve, reassure.

**embosom** vb bury, cherish, clasp, conceal, enfold, envelop, enwrap, foster, hide, nurse, surround.

**embrace** vb clasp; accept, seize, welcome; comprehend, comprise, contain, cover, embody, encircle, enclose, encompass, enfold, hold, include. * n clasp, fold, hug.

**embroil** vb commingle, encumber, ensnarl, entangle, implicate, involve; confuse, discompose, disorder, distract, disturb, perplex, trouble.

**embryo** n beginning, germ, nucleus, root, rudiment.

**embryonic** adj incipient, rudimentary, undeveloped.

**emendation** n amendment, correction, improvement, rectification.

**emerge** vb rise; emanate, escape, issue; appear, arise, outcrop.

**emergency** n crisis, difficulty, dilemma, exigency, extremity, necessity, pass, pinch, push, strait, urgency; conjuncture, crisis, juncture, pass.

**emigration** n departure, exodus, migration, removal.

**eminence** n elevation, hill, projection, prominence, protuberance; celebrity, conspicuousness, distinction, exaltation, fame, loftiness, note, preferment, reputation, repute, renown.

**eminent** adj elevated, high, lofty; celebrated, conspicuous, distinguished, exalted, famous, illustrious, notable, prominent, remarkable, renowned.

**emissary** n messenger, scout, secret agent, spy.

**emit** vb breathe out, dart, discharge, eject, emanate, exhale, gust, hurl, jet, outpour, shed, shoot, spurt, squirt.

**emollient** adj relaxing, softening. soothing. * n softener.

**emolument** n compensation, gain, hire, income, lucre, pay, pecuniary, profits, salary, stipend, wages; advantage, benefit, profit, perquisites.

**emotion** n agitation, excitement, feeling, passion, perturbation, sentiment, sympathy, trepidation.

**emphasis** n accent, stress; force, importance, impressiveness, moment, significance, weight.

**emphatic** adj decided, distinct, earnest, energetic, expressive, forcible, impressive, intensive, positive, significant, strong, unequivocal.

**empire** n domain, dominion, sovereignty, supremacy; authority, command, control, government, rule, sway.

**empirical, empiric** adj experimental, experiential; hypothetical, provisional, tentative; charlatanic, quackish.

**employ** vb busy, devote, engage, engross, enlist, exercise, occupy, retain; apply, commission, use. * n employment, service.

**employee** n agent, clerk, employee, hand, servant, workman.

**employment** n avocation, business, calling, craft, employ, engagement, occupation, profession, pursuit, trade, vocation, work.

**emporium** n market, mart, shop, store.

**empower** vb authorize, commission, permit, qualify, sanction, warrant; enable.

**empty** vb deplete, drain, evacuate, exhaust; discharge, disembogue; flow, embogue. * adj blank, hollow, unoccupied, vacant, vacuous, void; deplete, destitute, devoid, hungry; unfilled, unfurnished, unsupplied; unsatisfactory, unsatisfying, unsubstantial, useless, vain; clear, deserted, desolate, exhausted, free, unburdened, unloaded, waste; foolish, frivolous, inane, senseless, silly, stupid, trivial, weak.

**empyrean, empyreal** adj aerial, airy, ethereal, heavenly, refined, sublimated, sublimed.

**emulation** n competition, rivalry, strife, vying; contention, envy, jealousy.

**enable** vb authorize, capacitate, commission, empower, fit, permit, prepare, qualify, sanction, warrant.

**enact** vb authorize, command, decree, establish, legislate, ordain, order, sanction; act, perform, personate, play, represent.

**enactment** n act, decree, law, edict, ordinance.

**enamour** vb bewitch, captivate, charm, enchant, endear, fascinate.

**enchain** vb bind, confine, enslave, fetter, hold, manacle, restrain, shackle.

**enchant** vb beguile, bewitch, charm, delude, fascinate; captivate, catch, enamour, win; beatify, delight, enrapture, rapture, ravish, transport.

**enchanting** adj bewitching, blissful, captivating, charming, delightful, enrapturing, fascinating, rapturous, ravishing.

**enchantment** n charm, conjuration, incantation, magic, necromancy, sorcery, spell, witchery; bliss, delight, fascination, rapture, ravishment, transport.

**encase** vb encircle, enclose, incase, infix, set; chase, emboss, engrave, inlay, ornament.

**encage** vb confine, coop up, impound, imprison, shut up.

**encircle** vb belt, circumscribe, encompass, enclose, engird, enring, environ, gird, ring, span, surround; twine; clasp, embrace, enfold, fold.

**enclose, inclose** vb circumscribe, corral, coop, embosom, encircle, encompass, environ, fence in, hedge, include, pen, shut in, surround; box, cover, encase, envelop, wrap.

**encomium** n applause, commendation, eulogy, laudation, panegyric, praise.

**encompass** vb belt, compass, encircle, enclose, engird, environ, gird, surround; beset, besiege, hem in, include, invest, surround.

**encounter** vb confront, face, meet; attack, combat, contend, engage, strive, struggle. * n assault, attack, clash, collision, meeting, onset; action, affair,

battle, brush, combat, conflict, contest, dispute, engagement, skirmish.

**encourage** vb animate, assure, cheer, comfort, console, embolden, enhearten, fortify, hearten, incite, inspirit, instigate, reassure, stimulate, strengthen; abet, aid, advance, approve, countenance, favour, foster, further, help, patronize, promote, support.

**encroach** vb infringe, invade, intrude, tench, trespass, usurp.

**encumber** vb burden, clog, hamper, hinder, impede, load, obstruct, overload, oppress, retard; complicate, embarrass, entangle, involve, perplex.

**encumbrance** n burden, clog, deadweight, drag, embarrassment, hampering, hindrance, impediment, incubus, load; claim, debt, liability, lien.

**end** vb abolish, close, conclude, discontinue, dissolve, drop, finish, stop, terminate; annihilate, destroy, kill; cease, terminate. * n extremity, tip; cessation, close, denouement, ending, expiration, finale, finis, finish, last, period, stoppage, wind-up; completion, conclusion, consummation; annihilation, catastrophe, destruction, dissolution; bound, limit, termination, terminus; consequence, event, issue, result, settlement, sequel, upshot; fragment, remnant, scrap, stub, tag, tail; aim, design, goal, intent, intention, object, objective, purpose.

**endanger** vb compromise, hazard, imperil, jeopardize, peril, risk.

**endear** vb attach, bind, captivate, charm, win.

**endearment** n attachment, fondness, love, tenderness; caress, blandishment, fondling.

**endeavour** vb aim, attempt, essay, labour, seek, strive, struggle, study, try. * n aim, attempt, conatus, effort, essay, exertion, trial, struggle, trial.

**endless** adj boundless, illimitable, immeasurable, indeterminable, infinite, interminable, limitless, unlimited; dateless, eternal, everlasting, never-ending, perpetual, unending; deathless, ever-enduring, ever-living, immortal, imperishable, undying.

**endorse, indorse** vb approve, back, confirm, guarantee, ratify, sanction, superscribe, support, visé, vouch for, warrant; superscribe.

**endow** vb bequeath, clothe, confer, dower, endue, enrich, gift, indue, invest, supply.

**endowment** n bequest, boon, bounty, gift, grant, largesse, present; foundation, fund, property, revenue; ability, aptitude, capability, capacity, faculty, genius, gift, parts, power, qualification, quality, talent.

**endurance** n abiding, bearing, sufferance, suffering, tolerance, toleration; backbone, bottom, forbearance, fortitude, guts, patience, resignation.

**endure** vb bear, support, sustain; experience, suffer, undergo, weather; abide, brook, permit, pocket, swallow, tolerate, stomach, submit, withstand; continue, last, persist, remain, wear.

**enemy** n adversary, foe; antagonist, foeman, opponent, rival.

**energetic** adj active, effective, efficacious, emphatic, enterprising, forceful, forcible, hearty, mettlesome, potent, powerful, strenuous, strong, vigorous.

**energy** n activity, dash, drive, efficacy, efficiency, force, go, impetus, intensity, mettle, might, potency, power, strength, verve, vim; animation, life, manliness, spirit, spiritedness, stamina, vigour, zeal.

**enervate** vb break, debilitate, devitalize, emasculate, enfeeble, exhaust, paralyse, relax, soften, unhinge, unnerve, weaken.

**enfeeble** vb debilitate, devitalize, enervate, exhaust, relax, unhinge, unnerve, weaken.

**enfold, infold** vb enclose, envelop, fold, enwrap, wrap; clasp, embrace.

**enforce** vb compel, constrain, exact, force, oblige, require, urge.

**enfranchise** vb emancipate, free, liberate, manumit, release.

**engage** vb bind, commit, obligate, pledge, promise; affiance, betroth, plight; book, brief, employ, enlist, hire, retain; arrest, allure, attach, draw, entertain, fix, gain, win; busy, commission, contract, engross, occupy; attack, encounter; combat, contend, contest, fight, interlock, struggle; embark, enlist; agree, promise, stipulate, undertake, warrant.

**engagement** n appointment, assurance, contract, obligation, pledge, promise, stipulation; affiancing, betrothment, betrothal, plighting; avocation, business, calling, employment, enterprise, occupation; action, battle, combat, encounter, fight.

**engender** vb bear, beget, breed, create, generate, procreate, propagate; cause, excite, incite, occasion, produce.

**engine** n invention, machine; agency, agent, device, implement, instrument, means, method, tool, weapon.

**engorge** vb bolt, devour, eat, gobble, gorge, gulp, swallow; glut, obstruct, stuff.

**engrave** vb carve, chisel, cut, etch, grave, hatch, incise, sculpt; grave, impress, imprint, infix.

**engross** vb absorb, engage, occupy, take up; buy up, forestall, monopolize.

**engrossment** n absorption, forestalling, monopoly.

**engulf, ingulf** vb absorb, overwhelm, plunge, swallow up.

**enhance** vb advance, aggravate, augment, elevate, heighten, increase, intensify, raise, swell.

**enhearten** vb animate, assure, cheer, comfort, console, embolden, encourage, hearten, incite, inspirit, reassure, stimulate.

**enigma** n conundrum, mystery, problem, puzzle, riddle.

**enigmatic, enigmatical** adj ambiguous, dark, doubtful, equivocal, hidden, incomprehensible, mysterious, mystic, obscure, occult, perplexing, puzzling, recondite, uncertain, unintelligible.

**enjoin** vb admonish, advise, urge; bid, command, direct, order, prescribe, require; prohibit, restrain.

**enjoy** vb like, possess, relish.

**enjoyment** n delight, delectation, gratification, happiness, indulgence, pleasure, satisfaction; possession.

**enkindle** vb inflame, ignite, kindle; excite, incite, instigate, provoke, rouse, stimulate.

**enlarge** vb amplify, augment, broaden, develop, dilate, distend, expand, extend, grow, increase, magnify, widen; aggrandize, engreaten, ennoble, expand, exaggerate, greaten; swell.

**enlighten** vb illume, illuminate, illumine; counsel, educate, civilize, inform, instruct, teach.

**enlist** vb enrol, levy, recruit, register; enrol, list; embark, engage.

**enliven** vb animate, invigorate, quicken, reanimate, rouse, wake; exhilarate, cheer, brighten, delight, elate, gladden, inspite, inspirit, rouse.

**enmity** n animosity, aversion, bitterness, hate, hatred, hostility, ill-will, malevolence, malignity, rancour.

**ennoble** vb aggrandize, dignify, elevate, engreaten, enlarge, exalt, glorify, greaten, raise.

**ennui** n boredom, irksomeness, languor, lassitude, listlessness, tedium, tiresomeness, weariness.

**enormity** n atrociousness, atrocity, depravity, flagitiousness, heinousness, nefariousness, outrageousness, villainy, wickedness.

**enormous** adj abnormal, exceptional, inordinate, irregular; colossal, Cyclopean, elephantine, Herculean, huge, immense, monstrous, vast, gigantic, prodigious, titanic, tremendous.

**enough** adj abundant, adequate, ample, plenty, sufficient. * adv satisfactorily, sufficiently. * n abundance, plenty, sufficiency.

**enquire** see **inquire**.

**enrage** vb anger, chafe, exasperate, incense, inflame, infuriate, irritate, madden, provoke.

**enrapture** vb beatify, bewitch, delight, enchant, enravish, entrance, surpassingly, transport.

**enrich** vb endow; adorn, deck, decorate, embellish, grace, ornament.

**enrobe** vb clothe, dress, apparel, array, attire, invest, robe.

**enrol** vb catalogue, engage, engross, enlist, list, register; chronicle, record.

**ensconce** vb conceal, cover, harbour, hide, protect, screen, secure, settle, shelter, shield, snugly.

**enshrine** vb embalm, enclose, entomb; cherish, treasure.

**ensign** n banner, colours, eagle, flag, gonfalcon, pennon, standard, streamer; sign, signal, symbol; badge, hatchment.

**enslave** vb captivate, dominate, master, overmaster, overpower, subjugate.

**ensnare** vb catch, entrap; allure, inveigle, seduce; bewilder, confound, embarrass, encumber, entangle, perplex.

**ensue** vb follow, succeed; arise, come, flow, issue, proceed, result, spring.

**entangle** vb catch, ensnare, entrap; confuse, enmesh, intertwine, intertwist, interweave, knot, mat, ravel, tangle; bewilder, embarrass, encumber, ensnare, involve, nonplus, perplex, puzzle.

**enterprise** n adventure, attempt, cause, effort, endeavour, essay, project, undertaking, scheme, venture; activity, adventurousness, daring, dash, energy, initiative, readiness, push.

**enterprising** adj adventurous, audacious, bold, daring, dashing, venturesome, venturous; active, adventurous, alert, efficient, energetic, prompt, resourceful, smart, spirited, stirring, strenuous, zealous.

**entertain** vb fete, receive, regale, treat; cherish, foster, harbour, hold, lodge, shelter; admit, consider; amuse, cheer, divert, please, recreate.

**entertainment** n hospitality; banquet, collation, feast, festival, reception, treat; amusement, diversion, pastime, recreation, sport.

**enthusiasm** n ecstasy, exaltation, fanaticism; ardour, earnestness, devotion, eagerness, fervour, passion, warmth, zeal.

**enthusiast** n bigot, devotee, fan, fanatic, freak, zealot; castle-builder, dreamer, visionary.

**entice** vb allure, attract, bait, cajole, coax, decoy, inveigle, lure, persuade, prevail on, seduce, tempt, wheedle, wile.

**enticement** n allurement, attraction, bait, blandishment, inducement, inveiglement, lure, persuasion, seduction.

**entire** adj complete, integrated, perfect, unbroken, undiminished, undivided, unimpaired, whole; complete, full, plenary, thorough; mere, pure, sheer, unalloyed, unmingled, unmitigated, unmixed.

**entitle** vb call, characterize, christen, denominate, designate, dub, name, style; empower, enable, fit for, qualify for.

**entomb** vb bury, inhume, inter.

**entrails** npl bowels, guts, intestines, inwards, offal, viscera.

**entrance**[1] n access, approach, avenue, incoming, ingress; adit, avenue, aperture, door, doorway, entry, gate, hallway, inlet, lobby, mouth, passage, portal, stile, vestibule; beginning, commencement, debut, initiation, introduction; admission, entrée.

**entrance**[2] vb bewitch, captivate, charm, delight, enchant, enrapture, fascinate, ravish, transport.

**entrap** vb catch, ensnare; allure, entice, inveigle, seduce; embarrass, entangle, involve, nonplus, perplex, pose, stagger.

**entreat** vb adjure, beg, beseech, crave, enjoin, implore, importune, petition, pray, solicit, supplicate.

**entreaty** n adjuration, appeal, importunity, petition, prayer, request, solicitation, suit, supplication.

**entrée** n access, admission, admittance.

**entrench, intrench** vb furrow; circumvallate, fortify; encroach, infringe, invade, trench, trespass.

**entrenchment, intrenchment** n entrenching; earthwork, fortification; defence, protection, shelter; encroachment, inroad, invasion.

**entrust** vb commit, confide, consign.

**entwine** vb entwist, interlace, intertwine, interweave, inweave, twine, twist, weave; embrace, encircle, encumber, interlace, surround.

**enumerate** vb calculate, cite, compute, count, detail, mention, number, numerate, reckon, recount, specify, tell.

**enunciate** vb articulate, declare, proclaim, promulgate, pronounce, propound, publish, say, speak, utter.

**envelop** vb encase, enfold, enwrap, fold, pack, wrap; cover, encircle, encompass, enshroud, hide, involve, surround.

**envelope** n capsule, case, covering, integument, shroud, skin, wrapper, veil, vesture, wrap.

**envenom** vb poison, taint; embitter, malign; aggravate, enrage, exasperate, incense, inflame, irritate, madden, provoke.

**environ** n begird, belt, embrace, encircle, encompass, enclose, engrid, envelop, gird, hedge, hem, surround; beset, besiege, encompass, invest.

**environs** npl neighbourhood, vicinage, vicinity.

**envoy** n ambassador, legate, minister, plenipotentiary; courier, messenger.

**envy** vb hate; begrudge, grudge; covet, emulate, desire. * n enviousness, hate, hatred, ill-will, jealousy, malice, spite; grudge, grudging.

**enwrap** vb absorb, cover, encase, engross, envelop, infold, involve, wrap, wrap up.

**ephemeral** adj brief, diurnal, evanescent, fleeting, flitting, fugacious, fugitive, momentary, occasional, short-lived, transient, transitory.

**epic** adj Homeric, heroic, narrative.

**epicure** n gastronome, glutton, gourmand, gourmet; epicurean, sensualist, Sybarite, voluptuary.

**epidemic** adj general, pandemic, prevailing, prevalent. * n outbreak, pandemia, pestilence, plague, spread, wave.

**epidermis** n cuticle, scarf-skin.

**epigrammatic** adj antithetic, concise, laconic, piquant, poignant, pointed, pungent, sharp, terse.

**episcopal** adj Episcopalian, pontifical, prelatic.

**epistle** n communication, letter, missive, note.

**epithet** n appellation, description, designation, name, predicate, title.

**epitome** n abbreviation, abridgement, abstract, breviary, brief, comment, compendium, condensation, conspectus, digest, summary, syllabus, synopsis.

**epitomize** vb abbreviate, abridge, abstract, condense, contract, curtail, cut, reduce, shorten, summarize.

**epoch** n age, date, era, period, time.

**equable** adj calm, equal, even, even-tempered, regular, steady, uniform, serene, tranquil, unruffled.

**equal** vb equalize, even, match. * adj alike, coordinate, equivalent, like, tantamount; even, level, equable, regular, uniform; equitable, even-handed, fair, impartial, just, unbiased; co-extensive, commensurate, corresponding, parallel, proportionate; adequate, competent, fit, sufficient. * n compeer, fellow, match, peer; rival.

**equanimity** n calmness, composure, coolness, peace, regularity, self-possession, serenity, steadiness.

**equestrian** adj equine, horse-like, horsy. * n horseman, rider; cavalier, cavalryman, chevalier, horse soldier, knight.

**equilibrist** n acrobat, balancer, funambulist, rope-walker.

**equip** vb appoint, arm, furnish, provide, rig, supply; accoutre, array, dress.

**equipage** n accoutrements, apparatus, baggage, effects, equipment, furniture; carriage, turnout, vehicle; attendance, procession, retinue, suite, train.

**equipment** n accoutrement, apparatus, baggage, equipage, furniture, gear, outfit, rigging.

**equipoise** n balance, equilibrium.

**equitable** adj even-handed, candid, honest, impartial, just, unbiased, unprejudiced, upright; adequate, fair, proper, reasonable, right.

**equity** n just, right; fair play, fairness, impartiality, justice, rectitude, reasonableness, righteousness, uprightness.

**equivalent** adj commensurate, equal, equipollent, tantamount; interchangeable, synonymous. * n complement, coordinate, counterpart, double, equal, fellow, like, match, parallel, pendant, quid pro quo.

**equivocal** adj ambiguous; doubtful, dubious, enigmatic, indeterminate, problematical, puzzling, uncertain.

**equivocate** vb dodge, evade, fence, palter, prevaricate, shuffle, quibble.

**equivocation** n evasion, paltering, prevarication, quibbling, shuffling; double entendre, double meaning, quibble.

**era** n age, date, epoch, period, time.

**eradicate** vb extirpate, root, uproot; abolish, annihilate, destroy, obliterate.

**erase** vb blot, cancel, delete, efface, expunge, obliterate, scrape out.

**erasure** n cancellation, cancelling, effacing, expunging, obliteration.

**erect** vb build, construct, raise, rear; create, establish, form, found, institute, plant. * adj standing, unrecumbent, uplifted, upright; elevated, vertical, perpendicular, straight; bold, firm, undaunted, undismayed, unshaken, unterrified.

**erelong** *adv* early, quickly, shortly, soon, speedily.

**eremite** *n* anchoret, anchorite, hermit, recluse, solitary.

**ergo** *adv* consequently, hence, therefore.

**erode** *vb* canker, consume, corrode, destroy, eat away, fret, rub.

**erosive** *adj* acrid, cathartic, caustic, corroding, corrosive, eating, virulent.

**erotic** *adj* amorous, amatory, arousing, seductive, stimulating, titillating.

**err** *vb* deviate, ramble, rove, stray, wander; blunder, misjudge, mistake; fall, lapse, nod, offend, sin, stumble, trespass, trip.

**errand** *n* charge, commission, mandate, message, mission, purpose.

**errant** *adj* adventurous, rambling, roving, stray, wandering.

**erratic** *adj* nomadic, rambling, roving, wandering; moving, planetary; abnormal, capricious, deviating, eccentric, irregular, odd, queer, strange.

**erratum** *n* correction, corrigendum, error, misprint, mistake.

**erroneous** *adj* false, incorrect, inaccurate, inexact, mistaken untrue, wrong.

**error** *n* blunder, fallacy, inaccuracy, misapprehension, mistake, oversight; delinquency, fault, iniquity, misdeed, misdoing, misstep, obliquity, offence, shortcoming, sin, transgression, trespass, wrongdoing.

**erudition** *n* knowledge, learning, lore, scholarship.

**eruption** *n* explosion, outbreak, outburst; sally; rash.

**escape** *vb* avoid, elude, evade, flee from, shun; abscond, bolt, decamp, flee, fly; slip. * *n* flight; release; passage, passing; leakage.

**eschew** *vb* abstain, avoid, elude, flee from, shun.

**escort** *vb* convey, guard, protect; accompany, attend, conduct. * *n* attendant, bodyguard, cavalier, companion, convoy, gallant, guard, squire; protection, safe conduct, safeguard; attendance, company.

**esculent** *adj* eatable, edible, wholesome.

**esoteric** *adj* hidden, inmost, inner, mysterious, private, recondite, secret.

**especial** *adj* absolute, chief, distinct, distinguished, marked, particular, peculiar, principal, singular,

special, specific, uncommon, unusual; detailed, minute, noteworthy.

**espousal** *n* affiancing, betrothing, espousing, plighting; adoption, defence, maintenance, support.

**espouse** *vb* betroth, plight, promise; marry, wed; adopt, champion, defend, embrace, maintain, support.

**espy** *vb* descry, detect, discern, discover, observe, perceive, spy, watch.

**esquire** *n* armiger, attendant, escort, gentleman, squire.

**essay**[1] *vb* attempt, endeavour, try. * *n* aim, attempt, effort, endeavour, exertion, struggle, trial.

**essay**[2] *n* article, composition, disquisition, dissertation, paper, thesis.

**essence** *n* nature, quintessence, substance; extract, part; odour, perfume, scent; being, entity, existence, nature.

**essential** *adj* fundamental, indispensable, important, inward, intrinsic, necessary, requisite, vital; diffusible, pure, rectified, volatile.

**establish** *vb* fix, secure, set, settle; decree, enact, ordain; build, constitute, erect, form, found, institute, organize, originate, pitch, plant, raise; ensconce, ground, install, place, plant, root, secure; approve, confirm, ratify, sanction; prove, substantiate, verify.

**estate** *n* condition, state; position, rank, standing; division, order; effects, fortune, possessions, property; interest.

**esteem** *vb* appreciate, estimate, rate, reckon, value; admire, honour, like, prize, respect, revere, reverence, value, venerate, worship; account, believe, consider, deem, fancy, hold, imagine, suppose, regard, think. * *n* account, appreciation, consideration, estimate, estimation, judgement, opinion, reckoning, valuation; credit, honour, regard, respect, reverence.

**estimable** *adj* appreciable, calculable, computable; admirable, credible, deserving, excellent, good, meritorious, precious, respectful, valuable, worthy.

**estimate** *vb* appraise, appreciate, esteem, prise, rate, value; assess, calculate, compute, count, gauge, judge, reckon. * *n* estimation, judgement, valuation; calculation, computation.

**estimation** *n* appreciation, estimate, valuation; esteem, estimate, judgement, opinion; honour, reckoning, regard, respect, reverence.

**estop** *vb* bar, impede, preclude, stop.

**estrange** vb withdraw, withhold; alienate, divert; disaffect, destroy.

**estuary** n creek, inlet, fiord, firth, frith, mouth.

**etch** vb corrode, engrave.

**eternal** adj absolute, inevitable, necessary, self-active, self-existent, self-originated; abiding, ceaseless, endless, ever-enduring, everlasting, incessant, interminable, never-ending, perennial, permanent, perpetual, sempiternal, unceasing, unending; deathless, immortal, imperishable, incorruptible, indestructible, never-dying, undying; immutable, unchangeable; constant, continual; continuous, incessant, persistent, unbroken, uninterrupted.

**ethereal** adj aerial, airy, celestial, empyreal, heavenly, unworldly; attenuated, light, subtle, tenuous, volatile; delicate, fairy, flimsy, fragile, rare, refined, subtle.

**eulogize** vb applaud, commend, extol, laud, magnify, praise.

**eulogy** n discourse, eulogium, panegyric, speech; applause, encomium, commendation, laudation, praise.

**euphonious** adj clear, euphonic, harmonious, mellifluous, mellow, melodious, musical, silvery, smooth, sweet-toned.

**evacuant** adj abstergent, cathartic, cleansing, emetic, purgative. * n cathartic, purgative.

**evacuate** vb empty; discharge, clean out, clear out, eject, excrete, expel, purge, void; abandon, desert, forsake, leave, quit, relinquish, withdraw.

**evade** vb elude, escape; avoid, decline, dodge, funk, shun; baffle, elude, foil; dodge, equivocate, fence, palter, prevaricate, quibble, shuffle.

**evanescence** n disappearance, evanishing, evanishment, vanishing; transience, transientness, transitoriness.

**evanescent** adj ephemeral, fleeting, flitting, fugitive, passing, short-lived, transient, transitory, vanishing.

**evaporate** vb distil, volatilize; dehydrate, dry, vaporize; disperse, dissolve, fade, vanish.

**evaporation** n distillation, volatilization; dehydration, drying, vaporization; disappearance, dispersal, dissolution.

**evasion** n artifice, avoidance, bluffing, deceit, dodge, equivocation, escape, excuse, funking, prevarication, quibble, shift, subterfuge, shuffling, sophistical, tergiversation.

**evasive** adj elusive, elusory, equivocating, prevaricating, shuffling, slippery, sophistical.

**even** vb balance, equalize, harmonize, symmetrize; align, flatten, flush, level, smooth, square. * adj flat, horizontal, level, plane, smooth; calm, composed, equable, equal, peaceful, placid, regular, steady, uniform, unruffled; direct, equitable, fair, impartial, just, straightforward. * adv exactly, just, verily; likewise. * n eve, evening, eventide, vesper.

**evening** n dusk, eve, even, eventide, nightfall, sunset, twilight.

**event** n circumstance, episode, fact, happening, incident, occurrence; conclusion, consequence, end, issue, outcome, result, sequel, termination; adventure, affair.

**eventful** adj critical, important, memorable, momentous, remarkable, signal, stirring.

**eventual** adj final, last, ultimate; conditional, contingent, possible. * adv always, aye, constantly, continually, eternally, ever evermore, forever, incessantly, perpetually, unceasingly.

**everlasting** adj ceaseless, constant, continual, endless, eternal, ever-during, incessant, interminable, never-ceasing, never-ending, perpetual, unceasing, unending, unintermitting, uninterrupted; deathless, ever-living, immortal, imperishable, never-dying, undying.

**evermore** adv always, constantly, continually, eternally, ever, forever, perpetually.

**everyday** adj accustomed, common, commonplace, customary, habitual, routine, usual, wonted.

**evict** vb dispossess, eject, thrust out.

**evidence** vb evince, make clear, manifest, prove, show, testify, vouch. * n affirmation, attestation, averment, confirmation, corroboration, deposition, grounds, indication, proof, testimony, token, trace, voucher, witness.

**evident** adj apparent, bold, clear, conspicuous, distinct, downright, incontestable, indisputable, manifest, obvious, open, overt, palpable, patent, plain, unmistakable.

**evil** adj bad, ill; base, corrupt, malicious, malevolent, malign, nefarious, perverse, sinful, vicious, vile, wicked, wrong; bad, deleterious, baleful, baneful, destructive, harmful, hurtful, injurious, mischievous, noxious, pernicious, profane; adverse, calamitous, diabolic, disastrous, unfortunate, unhappy, unpropitious, woeful. * n calamity, disaster, ill, misery, misfortune, pain, reverse, sorrow, suffering, woe; badness, baseness, corruption, depravity, malignity, sin, viciousness, wickedness; bale, bane, blast, canker, curse, harm, injury, mischief, wrong.

**evince** vb establish, evidence, manifest, prove, show; disclose, display, exhibit, indicate, reveal.

**eviscerate** vb disembowel, embowel, gut.

**evoke** vb arouse, elicit, excite, provoke, rouse.

**evolve** vb develop, educe, exhibit, expand, open, unfold, unroll.

**exacerbate** vb aggravate, embitter, enrage, exasperate, excite, inflame, infuriate, irritate, provoke, vex.

**exact** vb elicit, extort, mulch, require, squeeze; ask, claim, compel, demand, enforce, requisition, take. * adj rigid, rigorous, scrupulous, severe, strict; diametric, express, faultless, precise, true; accurate, close, correct, definite, faithful, literal, undeviating; accurate, critical, delicate, fine, nice, sensitive; careful, methodical, punctilious, orderly, punctual, regular.

**exacting** adj critical, difficult, exactive, rigid, extortionary.

**exaction** n contribution, extortion, oppression, rapacity, tribute.

**exactness** n accuracy, correctness, exactitude, faithfulness, faultlessness, fidelity, nicety, precision, rigour; carefulness, method, precision, regularity, rigidness, scrupulosity, scrupulousness, strictness.

**exaggerate** vb enlarge, magnify, overcharge, overcolour, overstate, romance, strain, stretch.

**exalt** vb elevate, erect, heighten, lift up, raise; aggrandize, dignify, elevate, ennoble; bless, extol, glorify, magnify, praise.

**exalted** adj elated, elevated, high, highflown, lofty, lordly, magnificent.

**examination** n inspection, observation; exploration, inquiry, inquisition, investigation, perusal, research, search, scrutiny, survey; catechism, probation, review, test, trial.

**examine** vb inspect, observe; canvass, consider, explore, inquire, investigate, scrutinize, study, test; catechize, interrogate.

**example** n archetype, copy, model, pattern, piece, prototype, representative, sample, sampler, specimen, standard; exemplification, illustration, instance, precedent, warning.

**exanimate** adj dead, defunct, inanimate, lifeless, inanimate, inert, sluggish, spiritless, torpid.

**exasperate** vb affront, anger, chafe, enrage, incense, irritate, nettle, offend, provoke, vex; aggravate, exacerbate, inflame, rouse.

**exasperation** n annoyance, exacerbation, irritation, pro- vocation; anger, fury, ire, passion, rage, wrath; aggravation, heightening, increase, worsening.

**excavate** vb burrow, cut, delve, dig, hollow, hollow out, scoop, trench.

**exceed** vb cap, overstep, surpass, transcend; excel, outdo, outstrip, outvie, pass.

**excel** vb beat, eclipse, outdo, outrival, outstrip, outvie, surpass; cap, exceed, transcend.

**excellence** n distinction, eminence, pre-eminence, superiority, transcendence; fineness, fitness, goodness, perfection, purity, quality, superiority; advantage, goodness, probity, uprightness, virtue, worth.

**excellent** adj admirable, choice, crack, eminent, first-rate, prime, sterling, superior, tiptop, transcendent; deserving, estimable, praiseworthy, virtuous, worthy.

**except** vb exclude, leave out, omit, reject. * conj unless. * prep bar, but, excepting, excluding, save.

**exceptional** adj aberrant, abnormal, anomalous, exceptive, irregular, peculiar, rare, special, strange, superior, uncommon, unnatural, unusual.

**excerpt** vb cite, cull, extract, quote, select, take. * n citation, extract, quotation, selection.

**excess** adj excessive, unnecessary, redundant, spare, superfluous, surplus. * n disproportion, fulsomeness, glut, oversupply, plethora, redundance, redundancy, surfeit, superabundance, superfluity; overplus, remainder, surplus; debauchery, dissipation, dissoluteness, intemperance, immoderation, overindulgence, unrestraint; extravagance, immoderation, overdoing.

**excessive** adj disproportionate, exuberant, superabundant, superfluous, undue; extravagant, enormous, inordinate, outrageous, unreasonable; extreme, immoderate, intemperate; vehement, violent.

**exchange** vb barter, change, commute, shuffle, substitute, swap, trade, truck; bandy, interchange. * n barter, change, commutation, dealing, shuffle, substitution, trade, traffic; interchange, reciprocity; bazaar, bourse, fair, market.

**excise**[1] n capitation, customs, dues, duty, tariff, tax, taxes, toll.

**excise**[2] vb cancel, cut, delete, edit, efface, eradicate, erase, expunge, extirpate, remove, strike out.

**excision** n destruction, eradication, extermination, extirpation.

**excitable** adj impressible, nervous, sensitive, susceptible; choleric, hasty, hot-headed, hot-tempered, irascible, irritable, passionate, quick-tempered.

**excite** vb animate, arouse, awaken, brew, evoke, impel, incite, inflame, instigate, kindle, move, prompt, provoke, rouse, spur, stimulate; create, elicit, evoke, raise; agitate, discompose, disturb, irritate.

**excitement** n excitation, exciting; incitement, motive, stimulus; activity, agitation, bustle, commotion, disturbance, ferment, flutter, perturbation, sensation, stir, tension; choler, heat, irritation, passion, violence, warmth.

**exclaim** vb call, cry, declare, ejaculate, shout, utter, vociferate.

**exclude** vb ban, bar, blackball, debar, ostracize, preclude, reject; hinder, prevent, prohibit, restrain, withhold; except, omit; eject, eliminate, expel, extrude.

**exclusive** adj debarring, excluding; illiberal, narrow, narrow-minded, selfish, uncharitable; aristocratic, choice, clannish, cliquish, fastidious, fashionable, select, snobbish; only, sole, special.

**excommunicate** vb anathematize, ban, curse, denounce, dismiss, eject, exclude, expel, exscind, proscribe, unchurch.

**excoriate** vb abrade, flay, gall, scar, scarify, score, skin, strip.

**excrement** n dejections, dung, faeces, excreta, excretion, ordure, stool.

**excrescence** n fungus, growth, knob, lump, outgrowth, protuberance, tumour, wart.

**excrete** vb discharge, eject, eliminate, separate.

**excruciate** vb agonize, rack, torment, torture.

**exculpate** vb absolve, acquit, clear, discharge, exonerate, free, justify, release, set right, vindicate.

**excursion** n drive, expedition, jaunt, journey, ramble, ride, sally, tour, trip, voyage, walk; digression, episode.

**excursive** adj devious, diffuse, digressive, discursive, erratic, rambling, roaming, roving, wandering.

**excusable** adj allowable, defensible, forgivable, justifiable, pardonable, venial, warrantable.

**excursus** n discussion, disquisition, dissertation.

**excuse** vb absolve, acquit, exculpate, exonerate, forgive, pardon, remit; extenuate, justify; exempt, free, release; overlook. * n absolution, apology,

defence, extenuation, justification, plea; colour, disguise, evasion, guise, pretence, pretext, makeshift, semblance, subterfuge.

**execrable** adj abhorrent, abominable, accursed, cursed, damnable, detestable, hateful, odious; disgusting, loathsome, nauseating, nauseous, obnoxious, offensive, repulsive, revolting, sickening, vile.

**execrate** vb curse, damn, imprecate; abhor, abominate, detest, hate, loathe.

**execute** vb accomplish, achieve, carry out, complete, consummate, do, effect, effectuate, finish, perform, perpetrate; administer, enforce, seal, sign; behead, electrocute, guillotine, hang.

**execution** n accomplishment, achievement, completion, consummation, operation, performance; warrant, writ; beheading, electrocution, hanging.

**executive** adj administrative, commanding, controlling, directing, managing, ministerial, officiating, presiding, ruling. * n administrator, director, manager.

**exegetic, exegetical** adj explanatory, explicative, explicatory, expository, hermeneutic, interpretative.

**exemplary** adj assiduous, close, exact, faithful, punctual, punctilious, rigid, rigorous, scrupulous; commendable, correct, good, estimable, excellent, praiseworthy, virtuous; admonitory, condign, monitory, warning.

**exemplify** vb evidence, exhibit, illustrate, manifest, show.

**exempt** vb absolve, except, excuse, exonerate, free, release, relieve. * adj absolved, excepted, excused, exempted, free, immune, liberated, privileged, released.

**exemption** n absolution, dispensation, exception, immunity, privilege, release.

**exercise** vb apply, busy, employ, exert, praxis, use; effect, exert, produce, wield; break in, discipline, drill, habituate, school, train; practise, prosecute, pursue; task, test, try; afflict, agitate, annoy, burden, pain, trouble. * n appliance, application, custom, employment, operation, performance, play, plying, practice, usage, use, working; action, activity, effort, exertion, labour, toil, work; discipline, drill, drilling, schooling, training; lesson, praxis, study, task, test, theme.

**exert** vb employ, endeavour, exercise, labour, strain, strive, struggle, toil, use, work.

**exertion** n action, exercise, exerting, use; attempt, effort, endeavour, labour, strain, stretch, struggle, toil, trial.

**exhalation** n emission, evaporation; damp, effluvium, fog, fume, mist, reek, smoke, steam, vapour.

**exhale** vb breathe, discharge, elect, emanate, emit, evaporate, reek; blow, expire, puff.

**exhaust** vb drain, draw, empty; consume, destroy, dissipate, expend, impoverish, lavish, spend, squander, waste; cripple, debilitate, deplete, disable, enfeeble, enervate, overtire, prostrate, weaken.

**exhaustion** n debilitation, enervation, fatigue, lassitude, weariness.

**exhibit** vb demonstrate, disclose, display, evince, expose, express, indicate, manifest, offer, present, reveal, show; offer, present, propose.

**exhibition** n demonstration, display, exposition, manifestation, representation, spectacle, show; allowance, benefaction, grant, pension, scholarship.

**exhilarate** vb animate, cheer, elate, enliven, gladden, inspire, inspirit, rejoice, stimulate.

**exhilaration** n animating, cheering, elating, enlivening, gladdening, rejoicing, stimulating; animation, cheer, cheerfulness, gaiety, gladness, glee, good spirits, hilarity, joyousness.

**exhort** vb advise, caution, encourage, incite, persuade, stimulate, urge, warm; preach.

**exhume** vb disentomb, disinhume, disinter, unbury, unearth.

**exigency, exigence** n demand, necessity, need, requirement, urgency, want; conjuncture, crisis, difficulty, distress, emergency, extremity, juncture, nonplus, quandary, pass, pinch, pressure, strait.

**exiguous** adj attenuated, diminutive, fine, small, scanty, slender, tiny.

**exile** vb banish, expatriate, expel, ostracize, proscribe. * n banishment, expatriation, expulsion, ostracism, proscription, separation; outcast, refugee.

**exist** vb be, breathe, live; abide, continue, endure, last, remain.

**existence** n being, subsisting, subsistence; being, creature, entity, essence, thing; animation, continuation, life, living, vitality, vivacity.

**exit** vb depart, egress, go, leave. * n departure, withdrawal; death, decrease, demise, end; egress, outlet.

**exonerate** vb absolve, acquit, clear, exculpate, justify, vindicate; absolve, discharge, except, exempt, free, release.

**exorbitant** adj enormous, excessive, extravagant, inordinate, unreasonable.

**exorcise** vb cast out, drive away, expel; deliver, purify; address, conjure.

**exordium** n introduction, opening, preamble, preface, prelude, proem, prologue.

**exotic** adj extraneous, foreign; extravagant.

**expand** vb develop, open, spread, unfold, unfurl; diffuse, enlarge, extend, increase, stretch; dilate, distend, enlarge.

**expanse** n area, expansion, extent, field, stretch.

**expansion** n expansion, opening, spreading; diastole, dilation, distension, swelling; development, diffusion, enlargement, increase; expanse, extent, stretch.

**ex parte** adj biased, one-sided, partisan.

**expatiate** vb amplify, decant, dilate, enlarge, range, rove.

**expatriate** vb banish, exile, expel, ostracize, proscribe. * adj banished, exiled, refugee. * n displaced person, emigrant, exile.

**expect** vb anticipate, await, calculate, contemplate, forecast, foresee, hope, reckon, rely.

**expectancy** n expectance, expectation; abeyance, prospect.

**expectation** n anticipation, expectance, expectancy, hope, prospect; assurance, confidence, presumption, reliance, trust.

**expedient** adj advisable, appropriate, convenient, desirable, fit, proper, politic, suitable; advantageous, profitable, useful. * n contrivance, device, means, method, resort, resource, scheme, shift, stopgap, substitute.

**expedite** vb accelerate, advance, dispatch, facilitate, forward, hasten, hurry, precipitate, press, quicken, urge.

**expedition** n alacrity, alertness, celerity, dispatch, haste, promptness, quickness, speed; enterprise, undertaking; campaign, excursion, journey, march, quest, voyage.

**expeditious** adj quick, speedy, swift, rapid; active, alert, diligent, nimble, prompt, punctual, swift.

**expel** vb dislodge, egest, eject, eliminate, excrete; discharge, eject, evacuate, void; bounce, discharge, exclude, exscind, fire, oust, relegate, remove; banish, disown, excommunicate, exile, expatriate, ostracize, proscribe, unchurch.

**expend** vb disburse, spend; consume, employ, exert, use; dissipate, exhaust, scatter, waste.

**expenditure** n disbursement, outlay, outlaying, spending; charge, cost, expenditure, outlay.

**expensive** adj costly, dear, high-priced; extravagant, lavish, wasteful.

**experience** vb endure, suffer; feel, know; encounter, suffer, undergo. * n endurance, practice, trial; evidence, knowledge, proof, test, testimony.

**experienced** adj able, accomplished, expert, instructed, knowing, old, practised, qualified, skilful, trained, thoroughbred, versed, veteran, wise.

**experiment** vb examine, investigate, test, try. * n assay, examination, investigation, ordeal, practice, proof, test, testimony, touchstone, trial.

**expert** adj able, adroit, apt, clever, dextrous, proficient, prompt, quick, ready, skilful. * n adept, authority, connoisseur, crack, master, specialist.

**expertise** n adroitness, aptness, dexterity, facility, promptness, skilfulness, skill.

**expiate** vb atone, redeem, satisfy.

**expiration** n death, decease, demise, departure, exit; cessation, close, conclusion, end, termination.

**expire** vb cease, close, conclude, end, stop, terminate; emit, exhale; decease, depart, die, perish.

**explain** vb demonstrate, elucidate, expound, illustrate, interpret, resolve, solve, unfold, unravel; account for, justify, warrant.

**explanation** n clarification, description, elucidation, exegesis, explication, exposition, illustration, interpretation; account, answer, deduction, justification, key, meaning, secret, solution, warrant.

**explicit** adj absolute, categorical, clear, definite, determinate, exact, express, plain, positive, precise, unambiguous, unequivocal, unreserved.

**explode** vb burst, detonate, discharge, displode, shatter, shiver; contemn, discard, repudiate, scorn, scout.

**exploit** vb befool, milk, use, utilize. * n achievement, act, deed, feat.

**explore** vb examine, fathom, inquire, inspect, investigate, prospect, scrutinize, seek.

**explosion** n blast, burst, bursting, clap, crack, detonation, discharge, displosion, fulmination, pop.

**exponent** n example, illustration, index, indication, specimen, symbol, type; commentator, demonstrator, elucidator, expounder, illustrator, interpreter.

**expose** vb bare, display, uncover; descry, detect, disclose, unearth; denounce, mask; subject; endanger, jeopardize, risk, venture.

**exposé** n exhibit, exposition, manifesto; denouncement, divulgement, exposure, revelation.

**exposition** n disclosure, interpretation; commentary, critique, elucidation, exegesis, explanation, explication, interpretation; display, show.

**expound** vb develop, present, rehearse, reproduce, unfold; clear, elucidate, explain, interpret.

**express** vb air, assert, asseverate, declare, emit, enunciate, manifest, utter, vent, signify, speak, state, voice; betoken, denote, equal, exhibit, indicate, intimate, present, represent, show, symbolize. * adj categorical, clear, definite, determinate, explicit, outspoken, plain, positive, unambiguous; accurate, close, exact, faithful, precise, true; particular, special; fast, nonstop, quick, rapid, speedy, swift. * n dispatch, message.

**expression** n assertion, asseveration, communication, declaration, emission, statement, utterance, voicing; language, locution, phrase, remark, saying, term, word; air, aspect, look, mien.

**expressive** adj indicative, meaningful, significant; demonstrative, eloquent, emphatic, energetic, forcible, lively, strong, vivid; appropriate, sympathetic, well-modulated.

**expulsion** n discharge, eviction, expelling, ousting; elimination, evacuation, excretion; ejection, excision, excommunication, extrusion, ostracism, separation.

**expunge** vb annihilate, annul, cancel, delete, destroy, efface, erase, obliterate, wipe out.

**expurgate** vb clean, cleanse, purge, purify; bowdlerize, emasculate.

**exquisite** adj accurate, delicate, discriminating, exact, fastidious, nice, refined; choice, elect, excellent, precious, rare, valuable; complete, consummate, matchless, perfect; acute, keen, intense, poignant. * n beau, coxcomb, dandy, fop, popinjay.

**extant** adj existent, existing, present, surviving, undestroyed, visible.

**extempore** adj extemporaneous, extemporary, impromptu, improvised. * adv offhand, suddenly, unpremeditatedly, unpreparedly.

**extend** vb reach, stretch; continue, elongate, lengthen, prolong, protract, widen; augment, broaden, dilate, distend, enlarge, expand, increase; diffuse, spread; give, impart, offer, yield; lie, range.

**extensible** adj ductile, elastic, extendible, extensile, protractible, protractile.

**extension** n augmentation, continuation, delay, dilatation, dilation, distension, enlargement, expansion, increase, prolongation, protraction.

**extensive** adj broad, capacious, comprehensive, expanded, extended, far-reaching, large, wide, widespread.

**extent** n amplitude, expanse, expansion; amount, bulk, content, degree, magnitude, size, volume; compass, measure, length, proportions, reach, stretch; area, field, latitude, range, scope; breadth, depth, height, width.

**extenuate** vb diminish, lessen, reduce, soften, weaken; excuse, mitigate, palliate, qualify.

**exterior** adj external, outer, outlying, outside, outward, superficial, surface; extrinsic, foreign. * n outside, surface; appearance.

**exterminate** vb abolish, annihilate, destroy, eliminate, eradicate, extirpate, uproot.

**external** adj exterior, outer, outside, outward, superficial; extrinsic, foreign; apparent, visible.

**extinct** adj extinguished, quenched; closed, dead, ended, lapsed, terminated, vanished.

**extinction** n death, extinguishment; abolishment, abolition, annihilation, destruction, excision, extermination, extirpation.

**extinguish** vb choke, douse, put out, quell, smother, stifle, suffocate, suppress; destroy, nullify, subdue; eclipse, obscure.

**extirpate** vb abolish, annihilate, deracinate, destroy, eradicate, exterminate, uproot, weed.

**extol** vb celebrate, exalt, glorify, laud, magnify, praise; applaud, commend, eulogize, panegyrize.

**extort** vb elicit, exact, extract, force, squeeze, wrench, wrest, wring.

**extortion** n blackmail, compulsion, demand, exaction, oppression, overcharge, rapacity, tribute; exorbitance.

**extortionate** adj bloodsucking, exacting, hard, harsh, oppressive, rapacious, rigorous, severe; exorbitant, unreasonable.

**extra** adj accessory, additional, auxiliary, collateral; another, farther, fresh, further, more, new, other, plus, ulterior; side, spare, supernumerary, supplemental, supplementary, surplus; extraordinary, extreme, unusual. * adv additionally, also, beyond, farthermore, furthermore, more, moreover, plus. * n accessory, appendage, collateral, nonessential, special, supernumerary, supplement; bonus,

premium; balance, leftover, remainder, spare, surplus.

**extract** vb extort, pull out, remove, withdraw; derive, distil, draw, express, squeeze; cite, determine, derive, quote, select. * n citation, excerpt, passage, quotation, selection; decoction, distillation, essence, infusion, juice.

**extraction** n drawing out, derivation, distillation, elicitation, essence, pulling out; birth, descent, genealogy, lineage, origin, parentage.

**extraneous** adj external, extrinsic, foreign; additional, adventitious, external, superfluous, supplementary, unessential.

**extraordinary** adj abnormal, amazing, distinguished, egregious, exceptional, marvellous, monstrous, particular, peculiar, phenomenal, prodigious, rare, remarkable, signal, singular, special, strange, uncommon, unprecedented, unusual, unwonted, wonderful.

**extravagance** n excess, enormity, exorbitance, preposterousness, unreasonableness; absurdity, excess, folly, irregularity, wildness; lavishness, prodigality, profuseness, profusion, superabundance; waste.

**extravagant** adj excessive, exorbitant, inordinate, preposterous, unreasonable; absurd, foolish, irregular, wild; lavish, prodigal, profuse, spendthrift.

**extreme** adj farthest, outermost, remotest, utmost, uttermost; greatest, highest; final, last, ultimate; drastic, egregious, excessive, extravagant, immoderate, intense, outrageous, radical, unreasonable. * n end, extremity, limit; acme, climax, degree, height, pink; danger, distress.

**extremity** n border, edge, end, extreme, limb, termination, verge.

**extricate** vb clear, deliver, disembarrass, disengage, disentangle, liberate, release, relieve.

**extrinsic** adj external, extraneous, foreign, outside, outward, superabundance, superfluity.

**exuberance** n abundance, copiousness, flood, luxuriance, plenitude; excess, lavishness, overabundance, overflow, overgrowth, over-luxuriance, profusion, rankness, redundancy, superabundance, superfluity.

**exuberant** adj abounding, abundant, copious, fertile, flowing, luxuriant, prolific, rich; excessive, lavish, overabundant, overflowing, over-luxuriant, profuse, rank, redundant, superabounding, superabundant, wanton.

**exude** vb discharge, excrete, secrete, sweat; infiltrate, ooze, percolate.

**exult** vb gloat, glory, jubilate, rejoice, transport, triumph, taunt, vault.

**exultation** n delight, elation, joy, jubilation, transport, triumph.

**eye** vb contemplate, inspect, ogle, scrutinize, survey, view, watch. * n estimate, judgement, look, sight, vision, view; inspection, notice, observation, scrutiny, sight, vigilance, watch; aperture, eyelet, peephole, perforation; bud, shoot.

# F

**fable** n allegory, legend, myth, parable, story, tale; fabrication, falsehood, fiction, figment, forgery, untruth.

**fabric** n building, edifice, pile, structure; conformation, make, texture, workmanship; cloth, material, stuff, textile, tissue, web.

**fabricate** vb build, construct, erect, frame; compose, devise, fashion, make, manufacture; coin, fake, feign, forge, invent.

**fabrication** n building, construction, erection; manufacture; fable, fake, falsehood, fiction, figment, forgery, invention, lie.

**fabulous** adj amazing, apocryphal, coined, fabricated, feigned, fictitious, forged, imaginary, invented, legendary, marvellous, mythical, romancing, unbelievable, unreal.

**façade** n elevation, face, front.

**face** vb confront; beard, buck, brave, dare, defy, front, oppose; dress, level, polish, smooth; cover, incrust, veneer. * n cover, facet, surface; breast, escarpment, front; countenance, features, grimace, physiognomy, visage; appearance, expression, look, semblance; assurance, audacity, boldness, brass, confidence, effrontery, impudence.

**facet** n cut, face, lozenge, surface.

**facetious** adj amusing, comical, droll, funny, humorous, jocose, jocular, pleasant, waggish, witty; entertaining, gay, lively, merry, sportive, sprightly.

**facile** adj easy; affable, approachable, complaisant, conversable, courteous, mild; compliant, ductile, flexible, fluent, manageable, pliable, pliant, tractable, yielding; dextrous, ready, skilful.

**facilitate** vb expedite, help.

**facility** n ease, easiness; ability, dexterity, expertness, knack, quickness, readiness; ductility, flexibility, pliancy; advantage, appliance, convenience, means, resource; affability, civility, complaisance, politeness.

**facsimile** n copy, duplicate, fax, reproduction.

**fact** n act, circumstance, deed, event, incident, occurrence, performance; actuality, certainty, existence, reality, truth.

**faction** n cabal, clique, combination, division, junta, party, side; disagreement, discord, disorder, dissension, recalcitrance, recalcitrancy, refractoriness, sedition, seditiousness, tumult, turbulence, turbulency.

**factious** adj litigious, malcontent, rebellious, recalcitrant, refractory, seditious. turbulent.

**factitious** adj artful, artificial, conventional, false, unnatural, unreal.

**factor** n agent, bailiff, broker, consignee, go-between, steward, component, element, ingredient; influence, reason.

**factory** n manufactory, mill, work, workshop.

**faculty** n ability, capability, capacity, endowment, power, property, quality; ableness, address, adroitness, aptitude, aptness, clearness, competency, dexterity, efficiency, expertness, facility, forte, ingenuity, knack, qualification, quickness, readiness, skill, skilfulness, talent, turn; body, department, profession; authority, prerogative, license, privilege, right.

**fade** vb disappear, die, evanesce, fall, faint, perish, vanish; decay, decline, droop, fall, languish, wither; bleach, blanch, pale; disperse, dissolve.

**faeces** npl dregs, lees, sediment, settlings; dung, excrement, ordure, settlings.

**fag** vb droop, flag, sink; drudge, toil; fatigue, jade, tire, weary. * n drudgery, fatigue, work; drudge, grub, hack; cigarette, smoke.

**fail** vb break, collapse, decay, decline, fade, sicken, sink, wane; cease, disappear; fall, miscarry, miss; neglect, omit; bankrupt, break.

**failing** adj deficient, lacking, needing, wanting; declining, deteriorating, fading, flagging, languishing, sinking, waning, wilting; unsuccessful. * prep lacking, needing, wanting. * n decay, decline; failure, miscarriage; defect, deficiency, fault, foible, frailty, imperfection, infirmity, shortcoming, vice, weakness; error, lapse, slip; bankruptcy, insolvency.

**failure** n defectiveness, deficiency, delinquency, shortcoming; fail, miscarriage, negligence, neglect, nonobservance, nonperformance, omission, slip; abortion, botch, breakdown, collapse, fiasco, fizzle; bankruptcy, crash, downfall, insolvency, ruin; decay, declension, decline, loss.

**fain** adj anxious, glad, inclined, pleased, rejoiced,

well-pleased. * adv cheerfully, eagerly, gladly, joyfully, willingly.

**faint** vb swoon; decline, fade, fail, languish, weaken. * adj swooning; drooping, exhausted, feeble, languid, listless, sickly, weak; gentle, inconsiderable, little, slight, small, soft, thin; dim, dull, indistinct, perceptible, scarce, slight; cowardly, dastardly, faint-hearted, fearful, timid, timorous; dejected, depressed, discouraged, disheartened, dispirited. * n blackout, swoon.

**faint-hearted** adj cowardly, dastardly, faint, fearful, timid, timorous.

**fair**[1] adj spotless, unblemished, unspotted, unstained, untarnished; blond, light, white; beautiful, comely, handsome, shapely; clear, cloudless, pleasant, unclouded; favourable, prosperous; hopeful, promising, propitious; clear, distinct, open, plain, unencumbered, unobstructed; candid, frank, honest, honourable, impartial, ingenuous, just, unbiased, upright; equitable, proper; average, decent, indifferent, mediocre, moderate, ordinary, passable, reasonable, respectful, tolerable.

**fair**[2] n bazaar, carnival, exposition, festival, fete, funfair, gala, kermess.

**fairy** n brownie, elf, demon, fay, sprite.

**faith** n assurance, belief, confidence, credence, credit, dependence, reliance, trust; creed, doctrine, dogma, persuasion, religion, tenet; constancy, faithfulness, fidelity, loyalty, truth, truthfulness.

**faithful** adj constant, devoted, loyal, staunch, steadfast, true; honest, upright, reliable, trustworthy, trusty; reliable, truthful; accurate, close, conscientiousness, exact, nice, strict.

**faithless** adj unbelieving; dishonest, disloyal, false, fickle, fluctuating, inconstant, mercurial, mutable, perfidious, shifting, treacherous, truthless, unsteady, untruthful, vacillating, variable, wavering.

**fall** vb collapse, depend, descend, drop, sink, topple, tumble; abate, decline, decrease, depreciate, ebb, subside; err, lapse, sin, stumble, transgress, trespass, trip; die, perish; befall, chance, come, happen, occur, pass; become, get; come, pass. * n collapse, comedown, descent, downcome, dropping, falling, flop, plop, tumble; cascade, cataract, waterfall; death, destruction, downfall, overthrow, ruin, surrender; comeuppance, degradation; apostasy, declension, failure, lapse, slip; decline, decrease, depreciation, diminution, ebb, sinking, subsidence; cadence, close, declivity, inclination, slope.

**fallacious** adj absurd, deceptive, deceiving, delusive, disappointing, erroneous, false, illusive, illusory, misleading; paralogistic, sophistical, worthless.

**fallacy** n aberration, deceit, deception, delusion, error, falsehood, illusion, misapprehension, misconception, mistake, untruth; non sequitur, paralogism, sophism, sophistry.

**fallibility** n frailty, imperfection, uncertainty.

**fallible** adj erring, frail, ignorant, imperfect, uncertain, weak.

**fallow** adj left, neglected, uncultivated, unsowed, untilled; dormant, inactive, inert.

**false** adj lying, mendacious, truthless, untrue, unveracious; dishonest, dishonourable, disingenuous, disloyal, double-faced, double-tongued, faithless, false-hearted, perfidious, treacherous, unfaithful; fictitious, forged, made-up, unreliable, untrustworthy; artificial, bastard, bogus, counterfeit, factitious, feigned, forged, hollow, hypocritical, make-believe, pretended, pseudo, sham, spurious, supposititious; erroneous, improper, incorrect, unfounded, wrong; deceitful, deceiving, deceptive, disappointing, fallacious, misleading.

**false-hearted** adj dishonourable, disloyal, double, double-tongued, faithless, false, perfidious, treacherous.

**falsehood** n falsity; fabrication, fib, fiction, lie, untruth; cheat, counterfeit, imposture, mendacity, treachery.

**falsify** vb alter, adulterate, belie, cook, counterfeit, doctor, fake, falsely, garble, misrepresent, misstate, represent; disprove; violate.

**falsity** n falsehood, untruth, untruthfulness.

**falter** vb halt, hesitate, lisp, quaver, stammer, stutter; fail, stagger, stumble, totter, tremble, waver; dodder.

**fame** n bruit, hearsay, report, rumour; celebrity, credit, eminence, glory, greatness, honour, illustriousness, kudos, lustre, notoriety, renown, reputation, repute.

**familiar** adj acquainted, aware, conversant, well-versed; amicable, close, cordial, domestic, fraternal, friendly, homely, intimate, near; affable, accessible, companionable, conversable, courteous, civil, friendly, kindly, sociable, social; easy, free and easy, unceremonious, unconstrained; common, frequent, well-known. * n acquaintance, associate, companion, friend, intimate.

**familiarity** n acquaintance, knowledge, understanding; fellowship, friendship, intimacy; closeness, friendliness, sociability; freedom, informality, liberty; disrespect, overfreedom, presumption; intercourse.

**familiarize** vb accustom, habituate, inure, train, use.

**family** n brood, household, people; ancestors, blood, breed, clan, dynasty, kindred, house, lineage, race, stock, strain, tribe; class, genus, group, kind, subdivision.

**famine** n dearth, destitution, hunger, scarcity, starvation.

**famish** vb distress, exhaust, pinch, starve.

**famous** adj celebrated, conspicuous, distinguished, eminent, excellent, fabled, famed, far-famed, great, glorious, heroic, honoured, illustrious, immortal, notable, noted, notorious, remarkable, renowned, signal.

**fan**[1] vb agitate, beat, move, winnow; blow, cool, refresh, ventilate; excite, fire, increase, rouse, stimulate. * n blower, cooler, punkah, ventilator.

**fan**[2] n admirer, buff, devotee, enthusiast, fancier, follower, pursuer, supporter.

**fanatic** n bigot, devotee, enthusiast, visionary, zealot.

**fanatical** adj bigoted, enthusiastic, frenzied, mad, rabid, visionary, wild, zealous.

**fanciful** adj capricious, crotchety, imaginary, visionary, whimsical; chimerical, fantastical, ideal, imaginary, wild.

**fancy** vb apprehend, believe, conjecture, imagine, suppose, think; conceive, imagine. * adj elegant, fine, nice, ornamented; extravagant, fanciful, whimsical. * n imagination; apprehension, conceit, conception, impression, idea, image, notion, thought; approval, fondness, inclination, judgement, liking, penchant, taste; caprice, crotchet, fantasy, freak, humour, maggot, quirk, vagary, whim, whimsy; apparition, chimera, daydream, delusion, hallucination, megrim, phantasm, reverie, vision.

**fanfaron** n blatherskite, blusterer, braggadocio, bully, hector, swaggerer, vapourer.

**fang** n claw, nail, talon, tooth; tusk.

**fantastic** adj chimerical, fanciful, imaginary, romantic, unreal, visionary; bizarre, capricious, grotesque, odd, quaint, queer, strange, whimsical, wild.

**far** adj distant, long, protracted, remote; farther, remoter; alienated, estranged, hostile. * adv considerably, extremely, greatly, very much; afar, distantly, far away, remotely.

**farce** n burlesque, caricature, parody, travesty; forcemeat, stuffing.

**farcical** adj absurd, comic, droll, funny, laughable, ludicrous, ridiculous.

**fardel** n bundle, burden, load, pack; annoyance, burden, ill, trouble.

**fare** vb go, journey, pass, travel; happen, prosper, prove; feed, live, manage, subsist. * n charge, price, ticket money; passenger, traveller; board, commons, food, table, victuals, provisions; condition, experience, fortune, luck, outcome.

**farewell** n adieu, leave-taking, valediction; departure, leave, parting, valedictory.

**far-fetched** adj abstruse, catachrestic, forced, recondite, strained.

**farrago** n gallimaufry, hodgepodge, hotchpotch, jumble, medley, miscellany, mixture, potpourri, salmagundi.

**farther** adj additional; further, remoter, ulterior. * adv beyond, further; besides, furthermore, moreover.

**farthingale** n crinoline, hoop, hoop skirt.

**fascinate** vb affect, bewitch, overpower, spellbind, stupefy, transfix; absorb, captivate, catch, charm, delight, enamour, enchant, enrapture, entrance.

**fascination** n absorption, charm, enchantment, magic, sorcery, spell, witchcraft, witchery.

**fash** vb harass, perplex, plague, torment, trouble, vex, worry. * n anxiety, care, trouble, vexation.

**fashion** vb contrive, create, design, forge, form, make, mould, pattern, shape; accommodate, adapt, adjust, fit, suit. * n appearance, cast, configuration, conformation, cut, figure, form, make, model, mould, pattern, shape, stamp; manner, method, sort, wake; conventionalism, conventionality, custom, fad, mode, style, usage, vogue; breeding, gentility; quality.

**fashionable** adj modish, stylish; current, modern, prevailing, up-to-date; customary, usual; genteel, well-bred.

**fast**[1] adj close, fastened, firm, fixed, immovable, tenacious, tight; constant, faithful, permanent, resolute, staunch, steadfast, unswerving, unwavering; fortified, impregnable, strong; deep, profound, sound; fleet, quick, rapid, swift; dissipated, dissolute, extravagant, giddy, reckless, thoughtless, thriftless, wild. * adv firmly, immovably, tightly; quickly, rapidly, swiftly; extravagantly, prodigally, reckless, wildly.

**fast**[2] vb abstain, go hungry, starve. * n abstention, abstinence, diet, fasting, starvation.

**fasten** vb attach, bind, bolt, catch, chain, cleat, fix, gird, lace, lock, pin, secure, strap, tether, tie; belay, bend; connect, hold, join, unite.

**fastidious** adj critical, dainty, delicate, difficult, exquisite, finical, hypercritical, meticulous, overdelicate, overnice, particular, precise, precious, punctilious, queasy, squeamish.

**fat** adj adipose, fatty, greasy, oily, oleaginous, unctuous; corpulent, fleshy, gross, obese, paunchy, portly, plump, pudgy, pursy; coarse, dull, heavy, sluggish, stupid; lucrative, profitable, rich; fertile, fruitful, productive, rich. * n adipose tissue, ester, grease, oil; best part, cream, flower; corpulence, fatness, fleshiness, obesity, plumpness, stoutness.

**fatal** adj deadly, lethal, mortal; baleful, baneful, calamitous, catastrophic, destructive, mischievous, pernicious, ruinous; destined, doomed, foreordained, inevitable, predestined.

**fatality** n destiny, fate; mortality; calamity, disaster.

**fate** n destination, destiny, fate; cup, die, doom, experience, lot, fortune, portion, weird; death, destruction, ruin.

**fated** adj appointed, destined, doomed, foredoomed, predetermined, predestinated, predestined, preordained.

**fatherly** adj benign, kind, paternal, protecting, tender.

**fathom** vb comprehend, divine, penetrate, reach, understand; estimate, gauge, measure, plumb, probe, sound.

**fathomless** adj abysmal, bottomless, deep, immeasurable, profound; impenetrable, incomprehensible, obscure.

**fatigue** vb exhaust, fag, jade, tire, weaken, weary. * n exhaustion, lassitude, tiredness, weariness; hardship, labour, toil.

**fatuity** n foolishness, idiocy, imbecility, stupidity; absurdity, folly, inanity, infatuation, madness.

**fatuous** adj dense, drivelling, dull, foolish, idiotic, stupid, witless; infatuated, mad, senseless, silly, weak.

**fault** n blemish, defect, flaw, foible, frailty, imperfection, infirmity, negligence, obliquity, offence, shortcoming, spot, weakness; delinquency, error, indiscretion, lapse, misdeed, misdemeanour, offence, peccadillo, slip, transgression, trespass, vice, wrong; blame, culpability.

**faultless** adj blameless, guiltless, immaculate, innocent, sinless, spotless, stainless; accurate, correct, perfect, unblemished.

**faulty** adj bad, defective, imperfect, incorrect; blameable, blameworthy, censurable, culpable, reprehensible.

**faux pas** n blunder, indiscretion, mistake.

**favour** vb befriend, countenance, encourage, patronize; approve; ease, facilitate; aid, assist, help, oblige, support; extenuate, humour, indulge, palliate, spare. * n approval, benignity, countenance, esteem, friendless, goodwill, grace, kindness; benefaction, benefit, boon, dispensation, kindness; championship, patronage, popularity, support; gift, present, token; badge, decoration, knot, rosette; leave, pardon, permission; advantage, cover, indulgence, protection; bias, partiality, prejudice.

**favourable** adj auspicious, friendly, kind, propitious, well-disposed, willing; conductive, contributing, propitious; adapted, advantage, beneficial, benign, convenient, fair, fit, good, helpful, suitable.

**favourite** adj beloved, darling, dear; choice, fancied, esteemed, pet, preferred.

**fawn** vb bootlick, bow, creep, cringe, crouch, dangle, kneel, stoop, toady, truckle.

**fealty** n allegiance, homage, loyalty, obeisance, submission; devotion, faithfulness, fidelity, honour, loyalty.

**fear** vb apprehend, dread; revere, reverence, venerate. * n affright, alarm, apprehension, consternation, dismay, dread, fright, horror, panic, phobia, scare, terror; disquietude, flutter, perturbation, palpitation, quaking, quivering, trembling, tremor, trepidation; anxiety, apprehension, concern, misdoubt, misgiving, qualm, solicitude; awe, dread, reverence, veneration.

**fearful** adj afraid, apprehensive, haunted; chicken-hearted, chicken-livered, cowardly, faint-hearted, lily-livered, nervous, pusillanimous, timid, timorous; dire, direful, dreadful, frightful, ghastly, horrible, shocking, terrible.

**fearless** adj bold, brave, courageous, daring, dauntless, doughty, gallant, heroic, intrepid, unterrified, valiant, valorous.

**feasible** adj achievable, attainable, possible, practicable, suitable.

**feast** vb delight, gladden, gratify, rejoice. * n banquet, carousal, entertainment, regale, repast, revels, symposium, treat; celebration, festival, fete, holiday; delight, enjoyment, pleasure.

**feat** n accomplishment, achievement, act, deed, exploit, performance, stunt, trick.

**feather** n plume; kind, nature, species.

**featly** adv adroitly, dextrously, nimbly, skilfully.

**feature** vb envisage, envision, picture, visualize; imagine; specialize; appear in, headline, star. * n appearance, aspect, component; conformation, fashion, make; characteristic, item, mark, particularity, peculiarity, property, point, trait; leader, lead item, special; favour, expression, lineament; article, film, motion picture, movie, story; highlight, high spot.

**fecund** adj fruitful, impregnated, productive, prolific, rich.

**fecundity** n fertility, fruitfulness, productiveness.

**federation** n alliance, allying, confederation, federating, federation, leaguing, union, uniting; affiliation, coalition, combination, compact, confederacy, entente, federacy, league, copartnership.

**fee** vb pay, recompense, reward. * n account, bill, charge, compensation, honorarium, remuneration, reward, tip; benefice, fief, feud.

**feeble** adj anaemic, debilitated, declining, drooping, enervated, exhausted, frail, infirm, languid, languishing, sickly; dim, faint, imperfect, indistinct.

**feed** vb contribute, provide, supply; cherish, eat, nourish, subsist, sustain. * n fodder, food, foodstuff, forage, provender.

**feel** vb apprehend, intuit, perceive, sense; examine, handle, probe, touch; enjoy, experience, suffer; prove, sound, test, try; appear, look, seem; believe, conceive, deem, fancy, infer, opine, suppose, think. * n atmosphere, feeling, quality; finish, surface, texture.

**feeling** n consciousness, impression, notion, perception, sensation; atmosphere, sense, sentience, touch; affecting, emotion, heartstrings, impression, passion, soul, sympathy; sensibility, sentiment, susceptibility, tenderness; attitude, impression, opinion.

**feign** vb devise, fabricate, forge, imagine, invent; affect, assume, counterfeit, imitate, pretend, sham, simulate.

**feint** n artifice, blind, expedient, make-believe, pretence, stratagem, trick.

**felicitate** vb complicate, congratulate; beatify, bless, delight.

**felicitous** adj appropriate, apt, fit, happy, ingenious,

inspired, opportune, pertinent, seasonable, skilful, well-timed; auspicious, fortunate, prosperous, propitious, successful.

**felicity** n blessedness, bliss, blissfulness, gladness, happiness, joy; appropriateness, aptitude, aptness, felicitousness, fitness, grace, propriety, readiness, suitableness; fortune, luck, success.

**fell**[1] vb beat, knock down, level, prostrate; cut, demolish, hew.

**fell**[2] adj barbarous, bloodthirsty, bloody, cruel, ferocious, fierce, implacable, inhuman, malicious, malign, malignant, pitiless, relentless, ruthless, sanguinary, savage, unrelenting, vandalistic; deadly, destructive.

**fellow** adj affiliated, associated, joint, like, mutual, similar, twin. * n associate, companion, comrade; compeer, equal, peer; counterpart, mate, match, partner; member; boy, character, individual, man, person.

**fellowship** n brotherhood, companionship, comradeship, familiarity, intimacy; participation; partnership; communion, converse, intercourse; affability, kindliness, sociability, sociableness.

**felon** n convict, criminal, culprit, delinquent, malefactor, outlaw; inflammation, whitlow.

**felonious** adj atrocious, cruel, felon, heinous, infamous, malicious, malign, malignant, nefarious, perfidious, vicious, villainous.

**female** adj delicate, gentle, ladylike, soft; fertile, pistil-bearing, pistillate.

**feminine** adj affectionate, delicate, gentle, graceful, modest; soft, tender; female, ladylike, maidenly, womanish, womanly; effeminateness, effeminacy, softness, unmanliness, weakness, womanliness.

**fen** n bog, marsh, moor, morass, quagmire, slough, swamp.

**fence** vb defend, enclose, fortify, guard, protect, surround; circumscribe, evade, equivocate, hedge, prevaricate; guard, parry. * n barrier, hedge, hoarding, palings, palisade, stockade, wall; defence, protection, guard, security, shield; fencing, swordplay, swordsmanship; receiver.

**fenny** adj boggy, fennish, swampy, marshy.

**feral, ferine** adj ferocious, fierce, rapacious, ravenous, savage, untamed, wild.

**ferment** vb agitate, excite, heat; boil, brew, bubble, concoct, heat, seethe. * n barm, leaven, yeast; agitation, commotion, fever, glow, heat, tumult.

**ferocious** adj feral, fierce, rapacious, ravenous, savage, untamed, wild; barbarous, bloody, bloodthirsty, brutal, cruel, fell, inhuman, merciless, murderous, pitiless, remorseless, ruthless, sanguinary, truculent, vandalistic, violent.

**ferocity** n ferociousness, ferocity, fierceness, rapacity, savageness, wildness; barbarity, cruelty, inhumanity.

**fertile** adj bearing, breeding, fecund, prolific; exuberant, fruitful, luxuriant, plenteous, productive, rich, teeming; female, fruit-bearing, pistillate.

**fertility** n fertileness, fertility; abundance, exuberant, fruitfulness, luxuriance, plenteousness, productiveness, richness.

**fervent** adj burning, hot, glowing, melting, seething; animated, ardent, earnest, enthusiastic, fervid, fierce, fiery, glowing, impassioned, intense, passionate, vehement, warm, zealous.

**fervour** n heat, warmth; animation, ardour, eagerness, earnestness, excitement, fervency, intensity, vehemence, zeal.

**fester** vb corrupt, rankle, suppurate, ulcerate; putrefy, rot. * n abscess, canker, gathering, pustule, sore, suppination; festering, rankling.

**festival** n anniversary, carnival, feast, fete, gala, holiday, jubilee; banquet, carousal, celebration, entertainment, treat.

**festive** adj carnival, convivial, festal, festival, gay, jolly, jovial, joyful, merry, mirthful, uproarious.

**festivity** n conviviality, festival, gaiety, jollity, joviality, joyfulness, joyousness, merrymaking, mirth.

**festoon** vb adorn, decorate, embellish, garland, hoop, ornament. * n decoration, embellishment, garland, hoop, ornament, ornamentation.

**fetch** vb bring, elicit, get; accomplish, achieve, effect, perform; attain, reach. * n artifice, dodge, ruse, stratagem, trick.

**fetid** adj foul, malodorous, mephitic, noisome, offensive, rancid, rank, rank-smelling, stinking, strong-smelling.

**fetish** n charm, medicine, talisman.

**fetter** vb clog, hamper, shackle, trammel; bind, chain, confine, encumber, hamper, restrain, tie, trammel. * n bond, chain, clog, hamper, shackle.

**feud** vb argue, bicker, clash, contend, dispute, quarrel. * n affray, argument, bickering, broil, clashing, contention, contest, discord, dissension, enmity, fray, grudge, hostility, jarring, quarrel, rupture, strife, vendetta.

**fever** n agitation, excitement, ferment, fire, flush, heat, passion.

**fey** adj clairvoyant, ethereal, strange, unusual, whimsical; death-smitten, doomed.

**fiasco** n failure, fizzle.

**fiat** n command, decree, order, ordinance.

**fibre** n filament, pile, staple, strand, texture, thread; stamina, strength, toughness.

**fickle** adj capricious, changeable, faithless, fitful, inconstant, irresolute, mercurial, mutable, shifting, unsettled, unstable, unsteady, vacillating, variable, veering, violate, volatile, wavering.

**fiction** n fancy, fantasy, imagination, invention; novel, romance; fable, fabrication, falsehood, figment, forgery, invention, lie.

**fictitious** adj assumed, fabulous, fanciful, feigned, imaginary, invented, mythical, unreal; artificial, counterfeit, dummy, false, spurious, supposititious.

**fiddle** vb dawdle, fidget, interfere, tinker, trifle; cheat, swindle, tamper. * n fraud, swindle; fiddler, violin, violinist.

**fiddle-de-dee** interj fudge, moonshine, nonsense, stuff.

**fiddle-faddle** n frivolity, gabble, gibberish, nonsense, prate, stuff, trifling, trivia, twaddle.

**fidelity** n constancy, devotedness, devotion, dutifulness, faithfulness, fealty, loyalty, true-heartedness, truth; accuracy, closeness, exactness, faithfulness, precision.

**fidget** vb chafe, fret, hitch, twitch, worry. * n fidgetiness, impatience, restlessness, uneasiness.

**fiduciary** adj confident, fiducial, firm, steadfast, trustful, undoubting, unwavering; reliable, trustworthy. * n depositary, trustee.

**field** n clearing, glebe, meadow; expanse, extent, opportunity, range, room, scope, surface; department, domain, province, realm, region.

**fiendish** adj atrocious, cruel, demoniac, devilish, diabolical, hellish, implacable, infernal, malevolent, malicious, malign, malignant.

**fierce** adj barbarous, brutal, cruel, fell, ferocious, furious, infuriate, ravenous, savage; fiery, impetuous, murderous, passionate, tearing, tigerish, truculent, turbulent, uncurbed, untamed, vehement, violent.

**fiery** adj fervent, fervid, flaming, heated, hot, glowing, lurid; ardent, fierce, impassioned, impetuous, inflamed, passionate, vehement.

**fight** vb battle, combat, war; contend, contest, dispute, feud, oppose, strive, struggle, wrestle; encounter, engage; handle, manage, manoeuvre. * n affair, affray, action, battle, brush, combat, conflict, confrontation, contest, duel, encounter, engagement, melée, quarrel, struggle, war; brawl, broil, riot, row, skirmish; fighting, pluck, pugnacity, resistance, spirit, temper.

**figment** n fable, fabrication, falsehood, fiction, invention.

**figurative** adj emblematical, representative, symbolic, representative, typical; metaphorical, tropical; florid, flowery, ornate, poetical.

**figure** vb adorn, diversify, ornament, variegate; delineate, depict, represent, signify, symbolize, typify; conceive, image, imagine, picture; calculate, cipher, compute; act, appear, perform. * n configuration, conformation, form, outline, shape; effigy, image, likeness, representative; design, diagram, drawing, pattern; image, metaphor, trope; emblem, symbol, type; character, digit, number, numeral.

**filament** n cirrus, fibre, fibril, gossamer, hair, strand, tendril, thread.

**filch** vb crib, nick, pilfer, purloin, rob, snitch, seal, thieve.

**file**[1] vb order, pigeonhole, record, tidy. * n data, dossier, folder, portfolio; column, line, list, range, rank, row, series, tier.

**file**[2] vb burnish, furbish, polish, rasp, refine, smooth.

**filibuster** vb delay, frustrate, obstruct, play for time, stall, temporize. * n frustrater, obstructionist, thwarter; adventurer, buccaneer, corsair, freebooter, pirate.

**fill** vb occupy, pervade; dilate, distend, expand, stretch, trim; furnish, replenish, stock, store, supply; cloy, congest, content, cram, glut, gorge, line, pack, pall, sate, satiate, satisfy, saturate, stuff, suffuse, swell; engage, fulfil, hold, occupy, officiate, perform.

**film** vb becloud, cloud, coat, cover, darken, fog, mist, obfuscate, obscure, veil; photograph, shoot, take. * n cloud, coating, gauze, membrane, nebula, pellicle, scum, skin, veil; thread.

**filter** vb filtrate, strain; exude, ooze, percolate, transude. * n diffuser, colander, riddle, sieve, sifter, strainer.

**filth** n dirt, nastiness, ordure; corruption, defilement, foulness, grossness, impurity, obscenity, pollution, squalor, uncleanness, vileness.

**filthy** adj defiled, dirty, foul, licentious, nasty, obscene, pornographic, squalid, unclean; corrupt, gross, impure, unclean; miry, mucky, muddy.

**final** adj eventual, extreme, last, latest, terminal, ultimate; conclusive, decisive, definitive, irrevocable.

**finale** n conclusion, end, termination.

**finances** npl funds, resources, revenues, treasury; income, property.

**find** vb discover, fall upon; gain, get, obtain, procure; ascertain, notice, observe, perceive, remark; catch, detect; contribute, furnish, provide, supply. * n acquisition, catch, discovery, finding, plum, prize, strike.

**fine**[1] vb filter, purify, refine. * adj comminuted, little, minute, small; capillary, delicate, small; choice, light; exact, keen, sharp; attenuated, subtle, tenuous, thin; exquisite, fastidious, nice, refined, sensitive, subtle; dandy, excellent, superb, superior; beautiful, elegant, handsome, magnificent, splendid; clean, pure, unadulterated.

**fine**[2] vb amerce, mulct, penalize, punish. * n amercement, forfeit, forfeiture, mulct, penalty, punishment.

**finery** n decorations, frippery, gewgaws, ornaments, splendour, showiness, trappings, trimmings, trinkets.

**finesse** vb manipulate, manoeuvre. * n artifice, contrivance, cunning, craft, manipulation, manoeuvre, manoeuvring, ruses, stratagems, strategy, wiles.

**finger** vb handle, manipulate, play, purloin.

**finical** adj critical, dainty, dapper, fastidious, foppish, jaunty, overnice, overparticular, scrupulous, spruce, squeamish, trim.

**finish** vb accomplish, achieve, complete, consummate, execute, fulfil, perform; elaborate, perfect, polish; close, conclude, end, terminate. * n elaboration, elegance, perfection, polish; close, end, death, termination, wind-up.

**finite** adj bounded, circumscribed, conditioned, contracted, definable, limited, restricted, terminable.

**fire** vb ignite, kindle, light; animate, enliven, excite, inflame, inspirit, invigorate, rouse, stir up; discharge, eject, expel, hurl. * n combustion; blaze, conflagration; discharge, firing; animation, ardour, enthusiasm, fervour, fervency, fever, force, heat, impetuosity, inflammation, intensity, passion, spirit, vigour, violence; light, lustre, radiance, splendour; imagination, imaginativeness, inspiration, vivacity; affliction, persecution, torture, trouble.

**firm**[1] adj established, coherent, confirmed, consistent, fast, fixed, immovable, inflexible, rooted, secure, settled, stable; compact, compressed, dense, hard, solid; constant, determined, resolute, staunch, steadfast, steady, unshaken; loyal, robust, sinewy, stanch, stout, sturdy, strong.

**firm**[2] n association, business, company, concern, corporation, house, partnership.

**firmament** n heavens, sky, vault, welkin.

**firmness** n compactness, fixedness, hardness, solidity; stability, strength; constancy, soundness, steadfastness, steadiness.

**first** adj capital, chief, foremost, highest, leading, prime, principal; earliest, eldest, original; maiden; elementary, primary, rudimentary; aboriginal, primal, primeval, primitive, pristine. * adv chiefly, firstly, initially, mainly, primarily, principally; before, foremost, headmost; before, rather, rather than, sooner, sooner than. * n alpha, initial, prime.

**first-rate** adj excellent, prime, superior.

**fissure** n breach, break, chasm, chink, cleft, crack, cranny, crevice, fracture, gap, hole, interstice, opening, rent, rift.

**fit**[1] vb adapt, adjust, suit; become, conform; accommodate, equip, prepare, provide, qualify. * adj capacitated, competent, fitted; adequate, appropriate, apt, becoming, befitting, consonant, convenient, fitting, good, meet, pertinent, proper, seemly, suitable.

**fit**[2] n convulsion, fit, paroxysm, qualm, seizure, spasm, spell; fancy, humour, whim; mood, pet, tantrum; interval, period, spell, turn.

**fitful** adj capricious, changeable, convulsive, fanciful, fantastic, fickle, humoursome, impulsive, intermittent, irregular, odd, spasmodic, unstable, variable, whimsical; checkered, eventful.

**fitness** n adaptation, appropriateness, aptitude, aptness, pertinence, propriety, suitableness; preparation, qualification.

**fix** vb establish, fasten, place, plant, set; adjust, correct, mend, repair; attach, bind, clinch, connect, fasten, lock, rivet, stay, tie; appoint, decide, define, determine, limit, seal, settle; consolidate, harden, solidify; abide, remain, rest; congeal, stiffen. * n difficulty, dilemma, quandary, pickle, plight, predicament.

**flabbergast** vb abash, amaze, astonish, astound, confound, confuse, disconcert, dumbfound, nonplus.

**flabby** adj feeble, flaccid, inelastic, limp, soft, week, yielding.

**flaccid** adj baggy, drooping, flabby, inelastic, lax, limber, limp, loose, pendulous, relaxed, soft, weak, yielding.

**flag**[1] vb droop, hang, loose; decline, droop, fail, faint, lag, languish, pine, sink, succumb, weaken, weary; stale, pall.

**flag**[2] vb indicate, mark, semaphore, sign, signal. * n banner, colours, ensign, gonfalon, pennant, pennon, standard, streamer.

**flagellate** vb beat, castigate, chastise, cudgel, drub, flog, scourge, thrash, whip.

**flagitious** adj abandoned, atrocious, corrupt, flagrant, heinous, infamous, monstrous, nefarious, profligate, scandalous, villainous, wicked.

**flagrant** adj burning, flaming, glowing, raging; crying, enormous, flagitious, glaring, monstrous, nefarious, notorious, outrageous, shameful, wanton, wicked.

**flake** vb desquamate, scale. * n lamina, layer, scale.

**flamboyant** adj bright, gorgeous, ornate, rococo.

**flame** vb blaze, shine; burn, flash, glow, warm. * n blaze, brightness, fire, flare, vapour; affection, ardour, enthusiasm, fervency, fervour, keenness, warmth.

**flaming** adj blazing; burning, bursting, exciting, glowing, intense, lambent, vehement, violent.

**flap** vb beat, flutter, shake, vibrate, wave. * n apron, fly, lap, lappet, tab; beating, flapping, flop, flutter, slap, shaking, swinging, waving.

**flare** vb blaze, flicker, flutter, waver; dazzle, flame, glare; splay, spread, widen. * n blaze, dazzle, flame, glare.

**flash** vb blaze, glance, glare, glisten, light, shimmer, scintillate, sparkle, twinkle. * n instant, moment, twinkling.

**flashy** adj flaunting, gaudy, gay, loud, ostentatious, pretentious, showy, tawdry, tinsel.

**flat** adj champaign, horizontal, level; even, plane, smooth, unbroken; low, prostrate, overthrow; dull, frigid, jejune, lifeless, monotonous, pointless, prosaic, spiritless, tame, unanimated, uniform, uninteresting; dead, flashy, insipid, mawkish, stale, tasteless, vapid; absolute, clear, direct, downright, peremptory, positive. * adv flatly, flush, horizontally, level. * n bar, sandbank, shallow, shoal, strand; champaign, lowland, plain; apartment, floor, lodging, storey.

**flatter** vb compliment, gratify, praise; blandish, blarney, butter up, cajole, coax, coddle, court, entice, fawn, humour, inveigle, wheedle.

**flattery** n adulation, blandishment, blarney, cajolery, fawning, obsequiousness, servility, sycophancy, toadyism.

**flaunt** vb boast, display, disport, flourish, parade, sport, vaunt; brandish.

**flaunting** adj flashy, garish, gaudy, ostentatious, showy, tawdry.

**flavour** n gust, gusto, relish, savour, seasoning, smack, taste, zest; admixture, lacing, seasoning; aroma, essence, soul, spirit.

**flaw** n break, breach, cleft, crack, fissure, fracture, gap, rent, rift; blemish, defect, fault, fleck, imperfection, speck, spot.

**flay** vb excoriate, flay; criticize.

**fleck** vb dapple, mottle, speckle, spot, streak, variegate. * n speckle, spot, streak.

**flecked** adj dappled, mottled, piebald, spotted, straked, striped, variegated.

**flee** vb abscond, avoid, decamp, depart, escape, fly, leave, run, skedaddle.

**fleece** vb clip, shear; cheat, despoil, pluck, plunder, rifle, rob, steal, strip.

**fleer** vb mock, jeer, gibe, scoff, sneer.

**fleet**[1] n armada, escadrille, flotilla, navy, squadron; company, group.

**fleet**[2] adj fast, nimble, quick, rapid, speedy, swift.

**fleeting** adj brief, caducous, ephemeral, evanescent, flitting, flying, fugitive, passing, short-lived, temporary, transient, transitory.

**fleetness** n celerity, nimbleness, quickness, rapidity, speed, swiftness, velocity.

**flesh** n food, meat; carnality, desires; kindred, race, stock; man, mankind, world.

**fleshly** adj animal, bodily, carnal, lascivious, lustful, lecherous, sensual.

**fleshy** adj corpulent, fat, obese, plump, stout.

**flexibility** n flexibleness, limbersome, lithesome, pliability, pliancy, suppleness; affability, complaisance, compliance, disposition, ductility, pliancy, tractableness, tractability, yielding.

**flexible** adj flexible, limber, lithe, pliable, pliant, supple, willowy; affable, complaisant, ductile, docile, gentle, tractable, tractile, yielding.

**flexose, flexuous** adj bending, crooked, serpentine, sinuate, sinuous, tortuous, waxy, winding.

**flibbertigibbet** n demon, imp, sprite.

**flight**[1] n flying, mounting, soaring, volition; shower, flight; steps, stairs.

**flight**[2] n departure, fleeing, flying, retreat, rout, stampede; exodus, hegira.

**flighty** adj capricious, deranged, fickle, frivolous, giddy, light-headed, mercurial, urbalanced, volatile, wild, whimsical.

**flimsy** adj slight, thin, unsubstantial; feeble, foolish, frivolous, light, puerile, shallow, superficial, trashy, trifling, trivial, weak; insubstantial, sleazy.

**flinch** vb blench, flee, recoil, retreat, shirk, shrink, swerve, wince, withdraw.

**fling** vb cast, chuck, dart, emit, heave, hurl, pitch, shy, throw, toss; flounce, wince. * n cast, throw, toss.

**flippancy** n volubility; assuredness, glibness, pertness.

**flippant** adj fluent, glib, talkative, voluble; bold, forward, frivolous, glib, impertinent, inconsiderate, irreverent, malapert, pert, saucy, trifling.

**flirt** vb chuck, fling, hurl, pitch, shy, throw, toss; flutter, twirl, whirl, whisk; coquet, dally, philander. * n coquette, jilt, philanderer; jerk.

**flirtation** n coquetry, dalliance, philandering.

**flit** vb flicker, flutter, hover; depart, hasten, pass.

**flitting** adj brief, ephemeral, evanescent, fleeting, fugitive, passing, short, transient, transitory.

**float** vb drift, glide, hang, ride, sail, soar, swim, waft; launch, support.

**flock** vb collect, congregate, gather, group, herd, swarm, throng. * n collection, group, multitude; bevy, company, convoy, drove, flight, gaggle, herd, pack, swarm, team, troupe; congregation.

**flog** vb beat, castigate, chastise, drub, flagellate, lash, scourge, thrash, whip.

**flood** vb deluge, inundate, overflow, submerge, swamp. * n deluge, freshet, inundation, overflow, tide; bore, downpour, eagre, flow, outburst, spate, rush; abundance, excess.

**floor** vb deck, pave; beat, confound, conquer, overthrow, prevail, prostrate, puzzle; disconcert, nonplus. * n storey; bottom, deck, flooring, pavement, stage.

**florid** adj bright-coloured, flushed, red-faced, rubicund; embellished, figurative, luxuriant, ornate, rhetorical, rococo.

**flounce**[1] vb fling, jerk, spring, throw, toss, wince. * n jerk, spring.

**flounce**[2] n frill, furbelow, ruffle.

**flounder** vb blunder, flop, flounce, plunge, struggle, toss, tumble, wallow.

**flourish** vb grow, thrive; boast, bluster, brag, gasconade, show off, vaunt, vapour; brandish, flaunt, swing, wave. * n dash, display, ostentation, parade, show; bombast, fustian, grandiloquence; brandishing, shake, waving; blast, fanfare, tantivy.

**flout** vb chaff, deride, fleer, gibe, insult, jeer, mock, ridicule, scoff, sneer, taunt. * n gibe, fling, insult, jeer, mock, mockery, mocking, scoff, scoffing, taunt.

**flow** vb pour, run, stream; deliquesce, liquefy, melt; arise, come, emanate, follow, grow, issue, proceed, result, spring; glide; float, undulate, wave, waver; abound, run. * n current, discharge, flood, flux, gush, rush, stream, trickle; abundance, copiousness.

**flower** vb bloom, blossom, effloresce; develop. * n bloom, blossom; best, cream, elite, essence, pick; freshness, prime, vigour.

**flowery** adj bloomy, florid; embellished, figurative, florid, ornate, overwrought.

**flowing** adj abundant, copious, fluent, smooth.

**fluctuate** vb oscillate, swing, undulate, vibrate, wave; change, vary; vacillate, waver.

**flue** n chimney, duct; flew, fluff, nap, floss, fur.

**fluency** n liquidness, smoothness; affluence, copiousness; ease, facility, readiness.

**fluent** adj current, flowing, gliding, liquid; smooth; affluent, copious, easy, facile, glib, ready, talkative, voluble.

**fluff** vb blunder, bungle, forget, fumble, mess up, miscue, misremember, muddle, muff. * n down, flew, floss, flue, fur, lint, nap; cobweb, feather, gossamer, thistledown; blunder, bungle, fumble, muff.

**flume** n channel, chute, mill race, race.

**flummery** n chaff, frivolity, froth, moonshine, nonsense, trash, trifling; adulation, blandishment, blarney, flattery; brose, porridge, sowens.

**flunky, flunkey** n footman, lackey, livery servant, manservant, valet; snob, toady.

**flurry** vb agitate, confuse, disconcert, disturb, excite, fluster, hurry, perturb. * n gust, flaw, squall; agitation, bustle, commotion, confusion, disturbance, excitement, flutter, haste, hurry, hurry-scurry, perturbation, ruffle, scurry.

**flush**[1] vb flow, rush, start; glow, mantle, redden; animate, elate, elevate, erect, excite; cleanse, drench.

* adj bright, fresh, glowing, vigorous; abundant, affluent, exuberant, fecund, fertile, generous, lavish, liberal, prodigal, prolific, rich, wealthy, well-supplied; even, flat, level, plane. * adv evenly, flat, level; full, point-blank, right, square, squarely, straight. * n bloom, blush, glow, redness, rosiness, ruddiness; impulse, shock, thrill.

**flush**[2] vb disturb, rouse, start, uncover.

**fluster** vb excite, flush, heat; agitate, disturb, flurry, hurry, perturb, ruffle; confound, confuse, discompose, disconcert. * n glow, heat; agitation, flurry, flutter, hurry, hurry-scurry, perturbation, ruffle.

**fluted** adj channelled, corrugated, grooved.

**flutter** vb flap, hover; flirt, flit; beat, palpitate, quiver, tremble; fluctuate, oscillate, vacillate, waver. * n agitation, tremor; hurry, commotion, confusion, excitement, flurry, fluster, hurry-scurry, perturbation, quivering, tremble, tumult, twitter.

**flux** n flow, flowing; change, mutation, shifting, transition; diarrhoea, dysentery, looseness; fusing, melting, menstruum, solvent.

**fly**[1] vb aviate, hover, mount, soar; flap, float, flutter, play, sail, soar, undulate, vibrate, wave; burst, explode; abscond, decamp, depart, flee, vanish; elapse, flit, glide, pass, slip.

**fly**[2] adj alert, bright, sharp, smart, wide-awake; astute, cunning, knowing, sly; agile, fleet, nimble, quick, spry.

**foal** n colt, filly.

**foam** vb cream, froth, lather, spume; boil, churn, ferment, fume, seethe, simmer, stew. * n bubbles, cream, froth, scum, spray, spume, suds.

**fodder** n feed, food, forage, provender, rations.

**foe** n adversary, antagonist, enemy, foeman, opponent.

**fog** vb bedim, bemist, blear, blur, cloud, dim, enmist, mist; addle, befuddle, confuse, fuddle, muddle. * n blear, blur, dimness, film, fogginess, haze, haziness, mist, smog, vapour; befuddlement, confusion, fuddle, maze, muddle.

**foggy** adj blurred, cloudy, dim, dimmed, hazy, indistinct, misty, obscure; befuddled, bewildered, confused, dazed, muddled, muddy, stupid.

**foible** n defect, failing, fault, frailty, imperfection, infirmity, penchant, weakness.

**foil**[1] vb baffle, balk, check, checkmate, circumvent, defeat, disappoint, frustrate, thwart.

**foil**[2] n film, flake, lamina; background, contrast.

**foist** vb impose, insert, interpolate, introduce, palm off, thrust.

**fold**[1] vb bend, cover, double, envelop, wrap; clasp, embrace, enfold, enwrap, gather, infold, interlace; collapse, fail. * n double, doubling, gather, plait, plicature.

**fold**[2] n cot, enclosure, pen.

**foliaceous** adj foliate, leafy; flaky, foliated, lamellar, lamellate, lamellated, laminated, scaly, schistose.

**folk** n kindred, nation, people.

**follow** vb ensue, succeed; chase, dog, hound, pursue, run after, trail; accompany, attend; conform, heed, obey, observe; cherish, cultivate, seek; practise, pursue; adopt, copy, imitate; arise, come, flow, issue, proceed, result, spring.

**follower** n acolyte, attendant, associate, companion, dependant, retainer, supporter; adherent, admirer, disciple, partisan, pupil; copier, imitator.

**folly** n doltishness, dullness, imbecility, levity, shallowness; absurdity, extravagance, fatuity, foolishness, imprudence, inanity, indiscretion, ineptitude, nonsense, senselessness; blunder, faux pas, indiscretion, unwisdom.

**foment** vb bathe, embrocate, stupe; abet, brew, encourage, excite, foster, instigate, promote, stimulate.

**fond** adj absurd, baseless, empty, foolish, senseless, silly, vain, weak; affectionate, amorous, doting, loving, overaffectionate, tender.

**fondle** vb blandish, caress, coddle, cosset, dandle, pet.

**fondness** n absurdity, delusion, folly, silliness, weakness; liking, partiality, predilection, preference, propensity; appetite, relish, taste.

**food** n aliment, board, bread, cheer, commons, diet, fare, meat, nourishment, nutriment, nutrition, pabulum, provisions, rations, regimen, subsistence, sustenance, viands, victuals; feed, fodder, forage, provender.

**fool** vb jest, play, toy, trifle; beguile, cheat, circumvent, cozen, deceive, delude, dupe, gull, hoodwink, overreach, trick. * n blockhead, dolt, driveller, idiot, imbecile, nincompoop, ninny, nitwit, simpleton; antic, buffoon, clown, droll, harlequin, jester, merryandrew, punch, scaramouch, zany; butt, dupe.

**foolery** n absurdity, folly, foolishness, nonsense; buffoonery, mummery, tomfoolery.

**foolhardy** adj adventurous, bold, desperate, harebrained, headlong, hot-headed, incautious, precipitate, rash, reckless, venturesome, venturous.

**foolish** adj brainless, daft, fatuous, idiotic, inane, inept, insensate, irrational, senseless, shallow, silly, simple, thick-skulled, vain, weak, witless; absurd, ill-judged, imprudent, indiscreet, nonsensical, preposterous, ridiculous, unreasonable, unwise; childish, contemptible, idle, puerile, trifling, trivial, vain.

**foolishness** n doltishness, dullness, fatuity, folly, imbecility, shallowness, silliness, stupidity; absurdity, extravagance, imprudence, indiscretion, nonsense; childishness, puerility, triviality.

**footing** n foothold, purchase; basis, foundation, groundwork, installation; condition, grade, rank, standing, state, status; settlement, establishment.

**footman** n footboy, menial, lackey, runner, servant.

**footpad** n bandit, brigand, freebooter, highwayman, robber.

**footpath** n footway, path, trail.

**footprint** n footfall, footmark, footstep, trace, track.

**footstep** n footmark, footprint, trace, track; footfall, step, tread; mark, sign, token, trace, vestige.

**fop** n beau, coxcomb, dandy, dude, exquisite, macaroni, popinjay, prig, swell.

**foppish** adj coxcombical, dandified, dandyish, dressy, finical, spruce, vain.

**forage** vb feed, graze, provender, provision, victual; hunt for, range, rummage, search, seek; maraud, plunder, raid. * n feed, fodder, food, pasturage, provender; hunt, rummage, search.

**foray** n descent, incursion, invasion, inroad, irruption, raid.

**forbear** vb cease, desist, hold, pause, stop, stay; abstain, refrain; endure, tolerate; avoid, decline, shun; abstain, omit, withhold.

**forbearance** n abstinence, avoidance, forbearing, selfrestraint, shunning, refraining; indulgence, leniency, long-suffering, mildness, moderation, patience.

**forbid** vb ban, debar, disallow, embargo, enjoin, hinder, inhibit, interdict, prohibit, proscribe, taboo, veto.

**forbidding** adj abhorrent, disagreeable, displeasing, odious, offensive, repellant, repulsive, threatening, unpleasant.

**force** vb coerce, compel, constrain, necessitate, oblige; drive, impel, overcome, press, urge; ravish, violate. * n emphasis, energy, head, might, pith, power, strength, stress, vigour, vim; agency, efficacy, efficiency, cogency,

**potency**, validity, virtue; coercion, compulsion, constraint, enforcement, vehemence, violence; army, array, battalion, host, legion, phalanx, posse, soldiery, squadron, troop.

**forcible** adj all-powerful, cogent, impressive, irresistible, mighty, potent, powerful, strong, weighty; impetuous, vehement, violent, unrestrained; coerced, coercive, compulsory; convincing, energetic, effective, efficacious, telling, vigorous.

**forcibly** adv mightily, powerfully; coercively, compulsorily, perforce, violently; effectively; energetically, vigorously.

**ford** n current, flood, stream; crossing, wading place.

**fore** adj anterior, antecedent, first, foregoing, former, forward, preceding, previous, prior; advanced, foremost, head, leading.

**forebode** vb augur, betoken, foreshow, foretell, indicate, portend, predict, prefigure, presage, prognosticate, promise, signify.

**foreboding** n augury, omen, prediction, premonition, presage, presentiment, prognostication.

**forecast** vb anticipate, foresee, predict; calculate, contrive, devise, plan, project, scheme. * n anticipation, foresight, forethought, planning, prevision, prophecy, provident.

**foreclose** vb debar, hinder, preclude, prevent, stop.

**foredoom** vb foreordain, predestine, preordain.

**forego** see **forgo**.

**foregoing** adj antecedent, anterior, fore, former, preceding, previous, prior.

**foregone** adj bygone, former, past, previous.

**foreign** adj alien, distant, exotic, exterior, external, outward, outlandish, remote, strange, unnative; adventitious, exterior, extraneous, extrinsic, inappropriate, irrelevant, outside, unnatural, unrelated.

**foreknowledge** n foresight, prescience, prognostication.

**foremost** adj first, front, highest, leading, main, principal.

**foreordain** vb appoint, foredoom, predestinate, predetermine, preordain.

**forerunner** n avant-courier, foregoer, harbinger, herald, precursor, predecessor; omen, precursor, prelude, premonition, prognosticate, sign.

**foresee** vb anticipate, forebode, forecast, foreknow, foretell, prognosticate, prophesy.

**foreshadow** vb forebode, predict, prefigure, presage, presignify, prognosticate, prophesy.

**foresight** n foreknowledge, prescience, prevision; anticipation, care, caution, forecast, forethought, precaution, providence, prudence.

**forest** n wood, woods, woodland.

**forestall** vb hinder, frustrate, intercept, preclude, prevent, thwart; antedate, anticipate, foretaste; engross, monopolize, regrate.

**foretaste** n anticipation, forestalling, prelibation.

**foretell** vb predict, prophesy; augur, betoken, forebode, forecast, foreshadow, foreshow, portend, presage, presignify, prognosticate, prophesy.

**forethought** n anticipation, forecast, foresight, precaution, providence, prudence.

**forever** adv always, constantly, continually, endlessly, eternally, ever, evermore, everlastingly, perpetually, unceasingly.

**forewarn** vb admonish, advise, caution, dissuade.

**forfeit** vb alienate, lose. * n amercement, damages, fine, forfeiture, mulct, penalty.

**forfend** vb avert, forbid, hinder, prevent, protect.

**forge** vb beat, fabricate, form, frame, hammer; coin, devise, frame, invent; counterfeit, falsify, feign. * n furnace, ironworks, smithy.

**forgery** n counterfeit, fake, falsification, imitation.

**forgetful** adj careless, heedless, inattentive, mindless, neglectful, negligent, oblivious, unmindful.

**forgive** vb absolve, acquit, condone, excuse, exonerate, pardon, remit.

**forgiveness** n absolution, acquittal, amnesty, condoning. exoneration, pardon, remission, reprieve.

**forgiving** adj absolutory, absolvatory, acquitting, clearing, excusing, pardoning, placable, releasing.

**forgo** vb abandon, cede, relinquish, renounce, resign, surrender, yield.

**fork** vb bifurcate, branch, divaricate, divide. * n bifurcation, branch, branching, crotch, divarication, division.

**forked** adj bifurcated, branching, divaricated, furcate, furcated.

**forlorn** adj abandoned, deserted, forsaken, friendless, helpless, lost, solitary; abject, comfortless, dejected, desolate, destitute, disconsolate, helpless, hopeless, lamentable, pitiable, miserable, woebegone, wretched.

**form** vb fashion model, mould, shape; build, conceive, construct, create, fabricate, make, produce; contrive, devise, frame, invent; compose, constitute, develop, organize; discipline, educate, teach, train. * n body, build, cast, configuration, conformation, contour, cut, fashion, figure, format, mould, outline, pattern, shape; formula, formulary, method, mode, practice, ritual; class, kind, manner, model, order, sort, system, type; arrangement, order, regularity, shapeliness; ceremonial, ceremony, conventionality, etiquette, formality, observance, ordinance, punctilio, rite, ritual; bench, seat; class, rank; arrangement, combination, organization.

**formal** adj explicit, express, official, positive, strict; fixed, methodical, regular, rigid, set, stiff; affected, ceremonious, exact, precise, prim, punctilious, starchy, starched; constitutive, essential; external, outward, perfunctory; formative, innate, organic, primordial.

**formality** n ceremonial, ceremony, conventionality, etiquette, punctilio, rite, ritual.

**formation** n creation, genesis, production; composition, constitution; arrangement, combination, disposal, disposition.

**formative** adj creative, determinative, plastic, shaping; derivative, inflectional, nonradical.

**former** adj antecedent, anterior, earlier, foregoing, preceding, previous, prior; late, old-time, quondam; by, bygone, foregone, gone, past.

**formidable** adj appalling, dangerous, difficult, dreadful, fearful, frightful, horrible, menacing, redoubtable, shocking, terrible, terrific, threatening, tremendous.

**forsake** vb abandon, desert, leave, quit; drop, forgo, forswear, relinquish, renounce, surrender, yield.

**forsooth** adv certainly, indeed, really, surely, truly.

**forswear** vb abandon, desert, drop, forsake, leave, quit, reject, renounce; abjure, deny, eschew, perjure, recant, repudiate, retract.

**fort** n bulwark, castle, citadel, defence, fastness, fortification, fortress, stronghold.

**forthwith** adv directly, immediately, instantly, quickly, straightaway.

**fortification** n breastwork, bulwark, castle, citadel, defence, earthwork, fastness, fort, keep, rampart, redoubt, stronghold, tower.

**fortify** vb brace, encourage, entrench, garrison, protect, reinforce, stiffen, strengthen; confirm, corroborate.

**fortitude** n braveness, bravery, courage, determination, endurance, firmness, hardiness, patience, pluck, resolution, strength, valour.

**fortuitous** adj accidental, casual, chance, contingent, incidental.

**fortunate** adj favoured, happy, lucky, prosperous, providential, successful; advantageous, auspicious, favourable, happy, lucky, propitious, timely.

**fortune** n accident, casualty, chance, contingency, fortuity, hap, luck; estate, possessions, property, substance; affluence, felicity, opulence, prosperity, riches, wealth; destination, destiny, doom, fate, lot, star; event, issue, result; favour, success.

**forward** vb advance, aid, encourage, favour, foster, further, help, promote, support; accelerate, dispatch, expedite, hasten, hurry, quicken, speed; dispatch, post, send, ship, transmit. * adj ahead, advanced, onward; anterior, front, fore, head; prompt, eager, earnest, hasty, impulsive, quick, ready, willing, zealous; assuming, bold, brazen, brazen-faced, confident, flippant, impertinent, pert, presumptuous, presuming; advanced, early, premature. * adv ahead, onward.

**foster** vb cosset, feed, nurse, nourish, support, sustain; advance, aid, breed, cherish, cultivate, encourage, favour, foment, forward, further, harbour, patronize, promote, rear, stimulate.

**foul** vb besmirch, defile, dirty, pollute, soil, stain, sully; clog, collide, entangle, jam. * adj dirty, fetid, filthy, impure, nasty, polluted, putrid, soiled, stained, squalid, sullied, rank, tarnished, unclean; disgusting, hateful, loathsome, noisome, odious, offensive; dishonourable, underhand, unfair, sinister; abominable, base, dark, detestable, disgraceful, infamous, scandalous, scurvy, shameful, wile, wicked; coarse, low, obscene, vulgar; abusive, foul-mouthed, foul-spoken, insulting, scurrilous; cloudy, rainy, rough, stormy, wet; feculent, muddy, thick, turbid; entangled, tangled.

**foul-mouthed** adj abusive, blackguardly, blasphemous, filthy, foul, indecent, insolent, insulting, obscene, scurrilous.

**found** vb base, fix, ground, place, rest, set; build, construct, erect, raise; colonize, establish, institute, originate, plant; cast, mould.

**foundation** n base, basis, bed, bottom, footing, ground, groundwork, substructure, support; endowment, establishment, settlement.

**founder**[1] n author, builder, establisher, father, institutor, originator, organizer, planter.

**founder**[2] n caster, moulder.

**founder**[3] vb sink, swamp, welter; collapse, fail, miscarry; fall, stumble, trip.

**fountain** n fount, reservoir, spring, well; jet, upswelling; cause, fountainhead, origin, original, source.

**foxy** adj artful, crafty, cunning, sly, subtle, wily.

**fracas** n affray, brawl, disturbance, outbreak, quarrel, riot, row, uproar, tumult,

**fractious** adj captious, cross, fretful, irritable, peevish, pettish, perverse, petulant, querulous, snappish, splenetic, touchy, testy, waspish.

**fracture** vb break, crack, split. * n breaking, rupture; breach, break, cleft, crack, fissure, flaw, opening, rift, rent.

**fragile** adj breakable, brittle, delicate, frangible; feeble, frail, infirm, weak.

**fragility** n breakability, breakableness, brittleness, frangibility, frangibleness; feebleness, frailty, infirmity, weakness.

**fragment** vb atomize, break, fracture, pulverize, splinter. * n bit, chip, fraction, fracture, morsel, part, piece, remnant, scrap.

**fragrance** n aroma, balminess, bouquet, odour, perfume, redolence, scent, smell.

**fragrant** adj ambrosial, aromatic, balmy, odoriferous, odorous, perfumed, redolent, spicy, sweet, sweet-scented, sweet-smelling.

**frail** adj breakable, brittle, delicate, fragile, frangible, slight; feeble, infirm, weak.

**frailty** n feebleness, frailness, infirmity, weakness; blemish, defect, failing, fault, foible, imperfection, peccability, shortcoming.

**frame** vb build, compose, constitute, construct, erect, form, make, mould, plan, shape; contrive, devise, fabricate, fashion, forge, invest, plan. * n body, carcass, framework, framing, shell, skeleton; constitution, fabric, form, structure, scheme, system; condition, humour, mood, state, temper.

**franchise** n privilege, right; suffrage, vote; exemption, immunity.

**frangible** adj breakable, brittle, fragile.

**frank** adj artless, candid, direct, downright, frank-hearted, free, genuine, guileless, ingenuous, naive, open, outspoken, outright, plain, plain-spoken, point-blank, sincere, straightforward, truthful, unequivocal, unreserved, unrestricted.

**frankness** n candour, ingenuousness, openness, outspokenness, plain speaking, truth, straightforwardness.

**frantic** adj crazy, distracted, distraught, frenzied, furious, infuriate, mad. outrageous, phrenetic, rabid, raging, raving, transported, wild.

**fraternity** n association, brotherhood, circle, clan, club, company, fellowship, league, set, society, sodality; brotherliness.

**fraternize** vb associate, coalesce, concur, consort, cooperate, harmonize, sympathize, unite.

**fraud** n artifice, cheat, craft, deception, deceit, duplicity, guile, hoax, humbug, imposition, imposture, sham, stratagem, treachery, trick, trickery, wile.

**fraudulent** adj crafty, deceitful, deceptive, dishonest, false, knavish, treacherous, trickish, tricky, wily.

**fraught** adj abounding, big, burdened, charged, filled, freighted, laden, pregnant, stored, weighted.

**fray**[1] n affray, battle, brawl, broil, combat, fight, quarrel, riot.

**fray**[2] vb chafe, fret, rub, wear; ravel, shred.

**freak** adj bizarre, freakish, grotesque, monstrous, odd, unexpected, unforeseen. * n caprice, crotchet, fancy, humour, maggot, quirk, vagary, whim, whimsey; antic, caper, gambol; abnormality, abortion, monstrosity.

**freakish** adj capricious, changeable, eccentric, erratic, fanciful, humoursome, odd, queer, whimsical.

**free** vb deliver, discharge, disenthral, emancipate, enfranchise, enlarge, liberate, manumit, ransom, release, redeem, rescue, save; clear, disencumber, disengage, extricate, rid, unbind, unchain, unfetter, unlock; exempt, immunize, privilege. * adj bondless, independent, loose, unattached, unconfined, unentangled, unimpeded, unrestrained, untrammelled; autonomous, delivered, emancipated, freeborn, liberated, manumitted, ransomed, released, self-governing; clear, exempt, immune, privileged; allowed, permitted; devoid, empty, open, unimpeded, unobstructed, unrestricted; affable, artless, candid, frank, ingenuous, sincere, unreserved; bountiful, charitable, free-hearted, generous, hospitable, liberal, munificent, openhanded; immoderate, lavish, prodigal; eager, prompt, ready, willing; available, gratuitous, spontaneous; careless, lax, loose; bold, easy, familiar, informal, overfamiliar, unconstrained. * adv openly, outright, unreservedly, unrestrainedly, unstintingly; freely, gratis, gratuitously.

**freebooter** n bandit, brigand, despoiler, footpad, gangster, highwayman, marauder, pillager, plunderer, robber; buccaneer, pirate, rover.

**freedom** n emancipation, independence, liberation, liberty, release; elbowroom, margin, play, range, scope, swing; franchise, immunity, privilege; familiarity, laxity, license, looseness.

**freethinker** n agnostic, deist, doubter, infidel, sceptic, unbeliever.

**freeze** vb congeal, glaciate, harden, stiffen; benumb, chill.

**freight** vb burden, charge, lade, load. * n burden, cargo, lading, load.

**frenzy** n aberration, delirium, derangement, distraction, fury, insanity, lunacy, madness, mania, paroxysm, rage, raving, transport.

**frequent** vb attend, haunt, resort, visit. * adj iterating, oft-repeated; common, customary, everyday, familiar, habitual, persistent, usual; constant, continual, incessant.

**fresh** adj new, novel, recent; renewed, revived; blooming, flourishing, green, undecayed, unimpaired, unfaded, unobliterated, unwilted, unwithered, well-preserved; sweet; delicate, fair, fresh-coloured, ruddy, rosy; florid, hardy, healthy, vigorous, strong; active, energetic, unexhausted, unfatigued, unwearied, vigorous; keen, lively, unabated, undecayed, unimpaired, vivid; additional, further; uncured, undried, unsalted, unsmoked; bracing, health-giving, invigorating, refreshing, sweet; brink, stiff, strong; inexperienced, raw, uncultivated, unpracticed, unskilled, untrained, unused.

**freshen** vb quicken, receive, refresh, revive.

**fret**[1] vb abrade, chafe, fray, gall, rub, wear; affront, agitate, annoy, gall, harass, irritate, nettle, provoke, ruffle, tease, vex, wear, worry; ripple, roughen; corrode; fume, peeve, rage, stew. * n agitation, fretfulness, fretting, irritation, peevishness, vexation.

**fret**[2] vb diversify, interlace, ornament, variegate. * n fretwork, interlacing, ornament; ridge, wale, whelk.

**fretful** adj captious, cross, fractious, ill-humoured, ill-tempered, irritable, peevish, pettish, petulant, querulous, short-tempered, snappish, spleeny, splenetic, testy, touchy, uneasy, waspish.

**friable** adj brittle, crisp, crumbling, powdery, pulverable.

**friction** n abrasion, attrition, grating, rubbing; bickering, disagreement, dissension, wrangling.

**friend** adj benefactor, chum, companion, comrade, crony, confidant, intimate; adherent, ally, associate, confrere, partisan; advocate, defender, encourager, favourer, patron, supporter, well-wisher.

**friendly** adj affectionate, amiable, benevolent, favourable, kind, kind-hearted, kindly, well-disposed; amicable, cordial, fraternal, neighbourly; conciliatory, peaceable, unhostile.

**friendship** n affection, attachment, benevolence, fondness, goodness, love, regard; fellowship, intimacy; amicability, amicableness, amity, cordiality, familiarity, fraternization, friendliness, harmony.

**fright** n affright, alarm, consternation, dismay, funk, horror, panic, scare, terror.

**frighten** vb affright, alarm, appal, daunt, dismay, intimidate, scare, stampede, terrify.

**frightful** adj alarming, awful, dire, direful, dread, dreadful, fearful, horrible, horrid, shocking, terrible, terrific; ghastly, grim, grisly, gruesome, hideous.

**frigid** adj cold, cool, gelid; dull, lifeless, spiritless, tame, unanimated, uninterested, uninteresting; chilling, distant, forbidding, formal, freezing, prim, repellent, repelling, repulsive, rigid, stiff.

**frill** n edging, frilling, furbelow, gathering, ruche, ruching, ruffle; affectation, mannerism.

**fringe** vb border, bound, edge, hem, march, rim, skirt, verge. * n border, edge, edging, tassel, trimming. * adj edging, extra, unofficial.

**frisk** vb caper, dance, frolic, gambol, hop, jump, play, leap, romp, skip, sport, wanton.

**frisky** adj frolicsome, coltish, gay, lively, playful, sportive.

**frivolity** n flummery, folly, fribbling, frippery, frivolousness, levity, puerility, trifling, triviality.

**frivolous** adj childish, empty, flighty, flimsy, flippant, foolish, giddy, idle, light, paltry. petty, puerile, silly, trashy, trifling, trivial, unimportant, vain, worthless.

**frolic** vb caper, frisk, gambol, lark, play, romp, sport. * n escapade, gambol, lark, romp, skylark, spree, trick; drollery, fun, play, pleasantry, sport.

**frolicsome** adj coltish, fresh, frolic, gamesome, gay, lively, playful, sportive.

**front** vb confront, encounter, face, oppose. * adj anterior, forward; foremost, frontal, headmost. * n brow, face, forehead; assurance, boldness, brass, effrontery, impudence; breast, head, van, vanguard; anterior, face, forepart, obverse; facade, frontage.

**frontier** n border, boundary, coast, confine, limits, marches.

**frosty** adj chill, chilly, cold, icy, stinging, wintry; cold, cold-hearted, frigid, indifferent, unaffectionate, uncordial, unimpassioned, unloving; dull-hearted, lifeless, spiritless, unanimated; frosted, grey-hearted, hoary, white.

**froth** vb bubble, cream, foam, lather, spume. * n bubbles, foam, lather, spume; balderdash, flummery, nonsense, trash, triviality.

**frothy** adj foamy, spumy; empty, frivolous, light, trifling, trivial, unsubstantial, vain.

**froward** adj captious, contrary, contumacious, cross, defiant, disobedient, fractious, impudent, intractable, obstinate, peevish, perverse, petulant, refractory, stubborn, ungovernable, untoward, unyielding, wayward, wilful.

**frown** vb glower, lower, scowl.

**frowzy, frowsy** adj fetid, musty, noisome, rancid, rank, stale; disordered, disorderly, dowdy, slatternly, slovenly.

**frugal** adj abstemious, careful, chary, choice, economical, provident, saving, sparing, temperate, thrifty, unwasteful.

**fruit** n crop, harvest, produce, production; advantage, consequence, effect, good, outcome, product, profit, result; issue, offspring, young.

**fruitful** adj abounding, productive; fecund, fertile, prolific; abundant, exuberant, plenteous, plentiful, rich, teeming.

**fruition** n completion, fulfilment, perfection; enjoyment.

**fruitless** adj acarpous, barren, sterile, infecund, unfertile, unfruitful, unproductive, unprolific; abortive, bootless, futile, idle, ineffectual, profitless, unavailing, unprofitable, useless, vain.

**frumpish, frumpy** adj cross, cross-grained, cross-tempered, dowdy, grumpy, irritable, shabby, slatternly, snappish.

**frustrate** vb baffle, balk, check, circumvent, defeat, disappoint, disconcert, foil, thwart; cross, hinder, outwit.

**frustrated** adj balked, blighted, dashed, defeated, foiled, thwarted; ineffectual, null, useless, vain.

**fuddled** adj befuddled, boozy, corned, crapulous, drunk, groggy, high, inebriated, intoxicated, muddled, slewed, tight, tipsy.

**fugacious** adj evanescent, fleeting, fugitive, transient, transitory.

**fugitive** adj escaping, fleeing, flying; brief, ephemeral, evanescent, fleeting, flitting, fugacious, momentary, short, short-lived, temporal, temporary, transient, transitory, uncertain, unstable, volatile. * n émigré, escapee, evacuee, fleer, outlaw, refugee, runaway.

**fulfil** vb accomplish, complete, consummate, effect, effectuate, execute, realize; adhere, discharge, do, keep, obey, observe, perform; answer, fill, meet, satisfy.

**full** adj brimful, filled, flush, replete; abounding, replete, well-stocked; bagging, flowing, loose, voluminous; chock-full, cloyed, crammed, glutted, gorged, overflowing, packed, sated, satiated, saturated, soaked, stuffed, swollen; adequate, complete, entire, mature, perfect; abundant, ample, copious, plenteous, plentiful, sufficient; clear, deep, distinct, loud, rounded, strong; broad, large, capacious, comprehensive, extensive, plump; circumstantial, detailed, exhaustive. * adv completely, fully; directly, exactly, precisely.

**fullness** n abundance, affluence, copiousness, plenitude, plenty, profusion; glut, satiety, sating, repletion; completeness, completion, entireness, perfection; clearness, loudness, resonance, strength; dilation, distension, enlargement, plumpness, rotundity, roundness, swelling.

**fully** adv abundantly, amply, completely, copiously, entirely, largely, plentifully, sufficiently.

**fulminate** vb detonate, explode; curse, denounce, hurl, menace, threaten, thunder.

**fulsome** adj excessive, extravagant, fawning; disgusting, nauseous, nauseating, offensive, repulsive; coarse, gross, lustful, questionable.

**fumble** vb bungle, grope, mismanage, stumble; mumble, stammer, stutter.

**fume** vb reek, smoke, vaporize. * n effluvium exhalation, reek, smell, smoke, steam, vapour; agitation, fret, fry, fury, passion, pet, rage, storm.

**fun** adj amusing, diverting, droll, entertaining. * n amusement, diversion, drollery, frolic, gaiety, humour, jesting, jocularity, jollity, joy, merriment, mirth, play, pranks, sport, pleasantry, waggishness.

**function** vb act, discharge, go, operate, officiate, perform, run, serve, work. * n discharge, execution, exercise, operation, performance, purpose, use; activity, business, capacity, duty, employment, occupation, office, part, province, role; ceremony, rite; dependant, derivative.

**fund** vb afford, endow, finance, invest, provide, subsidise, support; garner, hoard, stock, store. * n accumulation, capital, endowment, reserve, stock; store, supply; foundation.

**fundament** n bottom, buttocks, seat.

**fundamental** adj basal, basic, bottom, cardinal, constitutional, elementary, essential, indispensable, organic, principal, primary, radical. * n essential, principal, rule.

**funeral** n burial, cremation, exequies, internment, obsequies.

**funereal** adj dark, dismal, gloomy, lugubrious, melancholy, mournful, sad, sepulchral, sombre, woeful.

**funk** vb blanch, shrink, quail. * n stench, stink; fear, fright, panic.

**funny** adj amusing, comic, comical, diverting, droll, facetious, farcical, humorous, jocose, jocular, laughable, ludicrous, sportive, witty; curious, odd, queer, strange. * n jest, joke; cartoon, comic.

**furbish** vb burnish, brighten, polish, renew, renovate, rub, shine.

**furious** adj angry, fierce, frantic, frenzied, fuming, infuriated, mad, raging, violent, wild; boisterous, fierce, impetuous, stormy, tempestuous, tumultuous, turbulent, vehement.

**furnish** vb appoint, endow, provide, supply; decorate, equip, fit; afford, bestow, contribute, give, offer, present, produce, yield.

**furniture** n chattels, effects, household goods, movables; apparatus, appendages, appliances, equipment, fittings, furnishings; decorations, embellishments, ornaments.

**furore** n commotion, craze, enthusiasm, excitement, fad, fury, madness, mania, rage, vogue.

**furrow** vb chamfer, channel, cleave, corrugate, cut, flute, groove, hollow; pucker, seam, wrinkle. * n chamfer, channel, cut, depression, fluting, groove, hollow, line, seam, track, trench, rot, wrinkle.

**further** vb advance, aid, assist, encourage, help, forward, promote, succour, strengthen. * adj additional. * adv also, besides, farther, furthermore, moreover.

**furtive** adj clandestine, hidden, secret, sly, skulking, sneaking, sneaky, stealthy, stolen, surreptitious.

**fury** n anger, frenzy, fit, furore, ire, madness, passion, rage; fierceness, impetuosity, turbulence, turbulency, vehemence; bacchant, bacchante, bedlam, hag, shrew, termagant, virago, vixen.

**fuse** vb dissolve, melt, liquefy, smelt; amalgamate, blend, coalesce, combine, commingle, intermingle, intermix, merge, unite. * n match.

**fusion** n liquefaction, melting; amalgamation, blending, commingling, commixture, intermingling, intermixture, union; coalition, merging.

**fuss** vb bustle, fidget; fret, fume, worry. * n ado, agitation, bother, bustle, commotion, disturbance, excitement, fidget, flurry, fluster, fret, hurry, pother, stir, worry.

**fustian** n bombast, claptrap, rant, rodomontade; balderdash, inanity, nonsense, stuff, trash; twaddle.

**fusty** adj ill-smelling, malodorous, mildewed, mouldy, musty, rank.

**futile** adj frivolous, trifling, trivial; bootless, fruitless, idle, ineffectual, profitless, unavailing, unprofitable, useless, vain, valueless, worthless.

**futility** n frivolousness, triviality; bootlessness, fruitlessness, uselessness, vanity, worthlessness.

**future** adj coming, eventual, forthcoming, hereafter, prospective, subsequent. * n hereafter, outlook, prospect.

# G

**gabble** vb babble, chatter, clack, gibber, gossip, prate, prattle. * n babble, chatter, clack, gap, gossip, jabber, palaver, prate, prattle, twaddle.

**gadabout** n idler, loafer, rambler, rover, vagrant; gossip, talebearer, vagrant.

**gaffer** n boss, foreman, overseer, supervisor.

**gag**[1] n jape, jest, joke, stunt, wisecrack.

**gag**[2] vb muffle, muzzle, shackle, silence, stifle, throttle; regurgitate, retch, throw up, vomit; choke, gasp, pant. * n muzzle.

**gage** n pawn, pledge, security, surety; challenge, defiance, gauntlet, glove.

**gaiety** n animation, blithesomeness, cheerfulness, glee, hilarity, jollity, joviality, merriment, mirth, vivacity.

**gain** vb achieve, acquire, earn, get, obtain, procure, reap, secure; conciliate, enlist, persuade, prevail, win; arrive, attain, reach; clear, net, profit. * n accretion, addition, gainings, profits, winnings; acquisition, earnings, emolument, lucre; advantage, benefit, blessing, good, profit.

**gainful** adj advantageous, beneficial, profitable; lucrative, paying, productive, remunerative.

**gainsay** vb contradict, controvert, deny, dispute, forbid.

**gait** n carriage, pace, step, stride, walk.

**galaxy** n assemblage, assembly, cluster, collection, constellation, group.

**gale** n blast, hurricane, squall, storm, tempest, tornado, typhoon.

**gall**[1] n effrontery, impudence; bile; acerbity, bitterness, malice, maliciousness, malignity, rancour, spite.

**gall**[2] vb chafe, excoriate, fret, hurt; affront, annoy, exasperate, harass, incense, irritate, plague, provoke, sting, tease, vex.

**gallant** adj fine, magnificent, showy, splendid, well-dressed; bold, brave, chivalrous, courageous, daring, fearless, heroic, high-spirited, intrepid, valiant, valorous; chivalrous, fine, honourable, high-minded, lofty, magnanimous, noble. * n beau, blade, spark; lover, suitor, wooer.

**gallantry** n boldness, bravery, chivalry, courage, courageousness, fearlessness, heroism, intrepidity, prowess, valour; courtesy, courteousness, elegance, politeness.

**galling** adj chafing, irritating, vexing.

**gallop** vb fly, hurry, run, rush, scamper, speed.

**gamble** vb bet, dice, game, hazard, plunge, speculate, wager. * n chance, risk, speculation; bet, punt, wager.

**gambol** vb caper, cut, frisk, frolic, hop, jump, leap, romp, skip. * n frolic, hop, jump, skip.

**game**[1] vb gamble, sport, stake. * n amusement, contest, diversion, pastime, play, sport; adventure, enterprise, measure, plan, project, scheme, stratagem, undertaking; prey, quarry, victim.

**game**[2] adj brave, courageous, dauntless, fearless, gallant, heroic, intrepid, plucky, unflinching, valorous; enduring, persevering, resolute, undaunted; ready, eager, willing.

**game**[3] adj crippled, disabled, halt, injured, lame.

**gameness** n bravery, courage, grit, heart, mettle, nerve, pith, pluck, pluckiness, spirit, stamina.

**gamesome** adj frisky, frolicsome, lively, merry, playful, sportive, sprightly, vivacious.

**gammon** vb bamboozle, beguile, cheat, circumvent, deceive, delude, dupe, gull, hoax, humbug, inveigle, mislead, overreach, outwit. * n bosh, hoax, humbug, imposition, nonsense.

**gang** n band, cabal, clique, company, coterie, crew, horde, party, set, troop.

**gaol** see **jail**.

**gap** n breach, break, cavity, chasm, chink, cleft, crack, cranny, crevice, hiatus, hollow, interval, interstice, lacuna, opening, pass, ravine, rift, space, vacancy.

**gape** vb burst open, dehisce, open, stare, yawn.

**garb** vb attire, clothe, dress. * n apparel, attire, clothes, costume, dress, garments, habiliment, habit, raiment, robes, uniform, vestment.

**garbage** n filth, offal, refuse, remains, rubbish, trash, waste.

**garble** vb corrupt, distort, falsify, misquote, misrepresent, mutilate, pervert.

**gargantuan** adj big, Brobdingnagian, colossal, enormous, gigantic, huge, prodigious, tremendous.

**garish** adj bright, dazzling, flashy, flaunting, gaudy, glaring, loud, showy, staring, tawdry.

**garland** vb adorn, festoon, wreathe. * n chaplet, coronal, crown, festoon, wreath.

**garment** n clothes, clothing, dress, habit, vestment.

**garner** vb accumulate, collect, deposit, gather, hoard, husband, reserve, save, store, treasure.

**garnish** vb adorn, beautify, bedeck, decorate, deck, embellish, grace, ornament, prank, trim. * n decoration, enhancement, ornament, trimming.

**garrulous** adj babbling, loquacious, prating, prattling, talkative.

**gasconade** n bluster, boast, brag, bravado, swagger, vaunt, vapouring.

**gasp** vb blow, choke, pant, puff. * n blow, exclamation, gulp, puff.

**gather** vb assemble, cluster, collect, convene, group, muster, rally; accumulate, amass, garner, hoard, huddle, lump; bunch, crop, cull, glean, pick, pluck, rake, reap, shock, stack; acquire, gain, get, win; conclude, deduce, derive, infer; fold, plait, pucker, shirr, tuck; condense, grow, increase, thicken.

**gathering** n acquisition, collecting, earning, gain, heap, pile, procuring; assemblage, assembly, collection, company, concourse, congregation, meeting, muster; abscess, boil, fester, pimple, pustule, sore, suppuration, tumour, ulcer.

**gauche** adj awkward, blundering, bungling, clumsy, inept, tactless, uncouth.

**gaudy** adj bespangled, brilliant, brummagem, cheap, flashy, flaunting, garish, gimcrack, glittering, loud, ostentatious, overdecorated, sham, showy, spurious, tawdry, tinsel.

**gauge** vb calculate, check, determine, weigh; assess, estimate, guess, reckon. * n criterion, example, indicator, measure, meter, touchstone, yardstick; bore, depth, height, magnitude, size, thickness, width.

**gaunt** adj angular, attenuated, emaciated, haggard, lank, lean, meagre, scraggy, skinny, slender, spare, thin.

**gawky** adj awkward, boorish, clownish, clumsy, green, loutish, raw, rustic, uncouth, ungainly.

**gay** adj bright, brilliant, dashing, fine, showy; flashy, flaunting, garish, gaudy, glittering, loud, tawdry, tinsel; airy, blithe, blithesome, cheerful, festive, frivolous, frolicsome, gladsome, gleeful, hilarious, jaunty, jolly, jovial, light-hearted, lively, merry, mirthful, sportive, sprightly, vivacious.

**gear** vb adapt, equip, fit, suit, tailor. * n apparel, array, clothes, clothing, dress, garb; accoutrements, appliances, appointments, appurtenances, array, harness, goods, movables, subsidiaries; harness, rigging, tackle, trappings; apparatus, machinery, mechanics.

**gelid** adj chill, chilly, cold, freezing, frigid, icy.

**gem** n jewel, stone, treasure.

**genealogy** n ancestry, descent, lineage, pedigree, stock.

**general** adj broad, collective, generic, popular, universal, widespread; catholic, ecumenical; common, current, ordinary, usual; inaccurate, indefinite, inexact, vague.

**generally** adv commonly, extensively, universally, usually.

**generate** vb beget, breed, engender, procreate, propagate, reproduce, spawn; cause, form, make, produce.

**generation** n creation, engendering, formation, procreation, production; age, epoch, era, period, time; breed, children, family, kind, offspring, progeny, race, stock.

**generosity** n disinterestedness, high-mindedness, magnanimity, nobleness; bounteousness, bountifulness, bounty, charity, liberality, openhandedness.

**generous** adj high-minded, honourable, magnanimous, noble; beneficent, bountiful, charitable, free, hospitable, liberal, munificent, open-handed; abundant, ample, copious, plentiful, rich.

**genial** adj cheering, encouraging, enlivening, fostering, inspiring, mild, warm; agreeable, cheerful, cordial, friendly, hearty, jovial, kindly, merry, mirthful, pleasant.

**genius** n aptitude, aptness, bent, capacity, endowment, faculty, flair, gift, talent, turn; brains, creative power, ingenuity, inspiration, intellect, invention, parts, sagacity, wit; adeptness, master, master hand, proficiency; character, disposition, naturalness, nature; deity, demon, spirit.

**genteel** adj aristocratic, courteous, gentlemanly, ladylike, polished, polite, refined, well-bred; elegant, fashionable, graceful, stylish.

**gentility** n civility, courtesy, good breeding, politeness, refinement, urbanity.

**gentle** adj amiable, bland, clement, compassionate, humane, indulgent, kind, kindly, lenient, meek, merciful, mild, moderate, soft, tender, tender-hearted;

docile, pacific, peaceable, placid, quiet, tame, temperate, tractable; bland, easy, gradual, light, slight; soft; high-born, noble, well-born; chivalrous, courteous, cultivated, knightly, polished, refined, well-bred.

**gentlemanly** adj civil, complaisant, courteous, cultivated, delicate, genteel, honourable, polite, refined, urbane, well-bred.

**genuine** adj authentic, honest, proper, pure, real, right, true, unadulterated, unalloyed, uncorrupted, veritable; frank, native, sincere, unaffected.

**genus** n class, group, kind, order, race, sort, type.

**germ** n embryo, nucleus, ovule, ovum, seed, seed-bud; bacterium, microbe, microorganism; beginning, cause, origin, rudiment, source.

**germane** adj akin, allied, cognate, related; apposite, appropriate, fitting, pertinent, relevant, suitable.

**germinate** vb bud, burgeon, develop, generate, grow, pollinate, push, shoot, sprout, vegetate.

**gesture** vb indicate, motion, signal, wave. * n action, attitude, gesticulation, gesturing, posture, sign, signal.

**get** vb achieve, acquire, attain, earn, gain, obtain, procure, receive, relieve, secure, win; finish, master, prepare; beget, breed, engender, generate, procreate.

**gewgaw** n bauble, gimcrack, gaud, kickshaw, knick-knack, plaything, trifle, toy, trinket.

**ghastly** adj cadaverous, corpse-like, death-like, deathly, ghostly, lurid, pale, pallid, wan; dismal, dreadful, fearful, frightful, grim, grisly, gruesome, hideous, horrible, shocking, terrible.

**ghost** n soul, spirit; apparition, phantom, revenant, shade, spectre, spook, sprite, wraith.

**giant** adj colossal, enormous, Herculean, huge, large, monstrous, prodigious, vast. * n colossus, cyclops, Hercules, monster.

**gibberish** n babble, balderdash, drivel, gabble, gobbledygook, jabber, nonsense, prate, prating.

**gibe, jibe** vb deride, fleer, flout, jeer, mock, ridicule, scoff, sneer, taunt. * n ridicule, sneer, taunt.

**giddiness** n dizziness, head-spinning, vertigo.

**giddy** adj dizzy, head-spinning, vertiginous; careless, changeable, fickle, flighty, frivolous, hare-brained, headlong, heedless, inconstant, irresolute, light-headed, thoughtless, unsteady, vacillating, wild.

**gift** n alms, allowance, benefaction, bequest, bonus, boon, bounty, contribution, donation, dowry, endowment, favour, grant, gratuity, honorarium, largesse, legacy, offering, premium, present, prize, subscription, subsidy, tip; faculty, talent.

**gifted** adj able, capable, clever, ingenious, intelligent, inventive, sagacious, talented.

**gigantic** adj colossal, Cyclopean, enormous, giant, herculean, huge, immense, prodigious, titanic, tremendous, vast.

**giggle** vb, n cackle, grin, laugh, snigger, snicker, titter.

**gild** vb adorn, beautify, bedeck, brighten, decorate, embellish, grace, illuminate.

**gimcrack** adj flimsy, frail, puny; base, cheap, paltry, poor. * n bauble, knick-knack, toy, trifle.

**gird** vb belt, girdle; begird, encircle, enclose, encompass, engird, environ, surround; brace, support. * n band, belt, cincture, girdle, girth, sash, waistband.

**gist** n basis, core, essence, force, ground, marrow, meaning, pith, point, substance.

**give** vb accord, bequeath, bestow, confer, devise, entrust, present; afford, contribute, donate, furnish, grant, proffer, spare, supply; communicate, impart; deliver, exchange, pay, requite; allow, permit, vouchsafe; emit, pronounce, render, utter; produce, yield; cause, occasion; apply, devote, surrender; bend, sink, recede, retire, retreat, yield.

**glad** adj delighted, gratified, happy, pleased, rejoicing, well-contented; animated, blithe, cheerful, cheery, elated, gladsome, jocund, joyful, joyous, light, light-hearted, merry, playful, radiant; animating, bright, cheering, exhilarating, gladdening, gratifying, pleasing.

**gladden** vb bless, cheer, delight, elate, enliven, exhilarate, gratify, please, rejoice.

**gladiator** n prize-fighter, sword-player, swordsman.

**gladness** n animation, cheerfulness, delight, gratification, happiness, joy, joyfulness, joyousness, pleasure.

**gladsome** adj airy, blithe, blithesome, cheerful, delighted, frolicsome, glad, gleeful, jocund, jolly, jovial, joyful, joyous, light-hearted, lively, merry, pleased, sportive, sprightly, vivacious.

**glamour** n bewitchment, charm, enchantment, fascination, spell, witchery.

**glance** vb coruscate, gleam, glisten, glister, glitter,

scintillate, shine; dart, flit; gaze, glimpse, look, view. * n gleam, glitter; gleam, look, view.

**glare** vb dazzle, flame, flare, gleam, glisten, glitter, sparkle; frown, gaze, glower. * n flare, glitter.

**glaring** adj dazzling, gleaming, glistening, glittering; barefaced, conspicuous, extreme, manifest, notorious, open.

**glassy** adj brilliant, crystal, crystalline, gleaming, lucent, shining, transparent.

**glaze** vb burnish, calender, furbish, gloss, polish. * n coat, enamel, finish, glazing, polish, varnish.

**gleam** vb beam, coruscate, flash, glance, glimmer, glitter, shine, sparkle. * n beam, flash, glance, glimmer, glimmering, glow, ray; brightness, coruscation, flashing, gleaming, glitter, glittering, lustre, splendour.

**glean** vb collect, cull, gather, get, harvest, pick, select.

**glee** n exhilaration, fun, gaiety, hilarity, jocularity, jollity, joviality, joy, liveliness, merriment, mirth, sportiveness, verve.

**glib** adj slippery, smooth; artful, facile, flippant, fluent, ready, talkative, voluble.

**glide** vb float, glissade, roll on, skate, skim, slide, slip; flow, lapse, run, roll. * n gliding, lapse, sliding, slip.

**glimmer** vb flash, flicker, gleam, glitter, shine, twinkle. * n beam, gleam, glimmering, ray; glance, glimpse.

**glimpse** vb espy, look, spot, view. * n flash, glance, glimmering, glint, look, sight.

**glitter** vb coruscate, flare, flash, glance, glare, gleam, glisten, glister, scintillate, shine, sparkle. * n beam, beaming, brightness, brilliancy, coruscation, gleam, glister, lustre, radiance, scintillation, shine, sparkle, splendour.

**gloaming** n dusk, eventide, nightfall, twilight.

**gloat** vb exult, gaze, rejoice, stare, triumph.

**globe** n ball, earth, orb, sphere.

**globular** adj globate, globated, globe-shaped, globose, globous, round, spheral, spheric, spherical.

**globule** n bead, drop, particle, spherule.

**gloom** n cloud, darkness, dimness, gloominess, obscurity, shade, shadow; cheerlessness, dejection, depression, despondency, downheartedness, dullness, melancholy, sadness.

**gloomy** adj dark, dim, dusky, obscure; cheerless, dismal, lowering, lurid; crestfallen, dejected, depressed, despondent, disheartened, dispirited, downcast, downhearted, glum, melancholy, morose, sad, sullen; depressing, disheartening, dispiriting, heavy, saddening.

**glorify** vb adore, bless, celebrate, exalt, extol, honour, laud, magnify, worship; adorn, brighten, elevate, ennoble, make bright.

**glorious** adj celebrated, conspicuous, distinguished, eminent, excellent, famed, famous, illustrious, pre-eminent, renowned; brilliant, bright, grand, magnificent, radiant, resplendent, splendid; consummate, exalted, high, lofty, noble, supreme.

**glory** vb boast, exult, vaunt. * n celebrity, distinction, eminence, fame, honour, illustriousness, praise, renown; brightness, brilliancy, effulgence, lustre, pride, resplendence, splendour; exaltation, exceeding, gloriousness, greatness, grandeur, nobleness; bliss, happiness.

**gloss**[1] vb coat, colour, disguise, extenuate, glaze, palliate, varnish, veneer, veil. * n coating, lustre, polish, sheen, varnish, veneer; pretence, pretext.

**gloss**[2] vb annotate, comment, elucidate, explain, interpret. * n annotation, comment, commentary, elucidation, explanation, interpretation, note.

**glove** n gantlet, gauntlet, handwear, mitt, mitten; challenge.

**glow** vb incandesce, radiate, shine; blush, burn, flush, redden. * n blaze, brightness, brilliance, burning, incandescence, luminosity, reddening; ardour, bloom, enthusiasm, fervency, fervour, flush, impetuosity, vehemence, warmth.

**glower** vb frown, glare, lower, scowl, stare. * n frown, glare, scowl.

**glum** adj churlish, crabbed, crestfallen, cross-grained, crusty, depressed, frowning, gloomy, glowering, moody, morose, sour, spleenish, spleeny, sulky, sullen, surly.

**glut** vb block up, cloy, cram, gorge, satiate, stuff. * n excess, saturation, surfeit, surplus.

**glutinous** adj adhesive, clammy, cohesive, gluey, gummy, sticky, tenacious, viscid, viscous.

**glutton** n gobbler, gorger, gourmand, gormandizer, greedy-guts, lurcher, pig.

**gnarled** adj contorted, cross-grained, gnarly, knotted, knotty, snaggy, twisted.

**go** vb advance, move, pass, proceed, progress repair; act, operate; be about, extravagate, fare, journey, roam, rove, travel, walk, wend; depart, disappear, cease; elapse, extend, lead, reach, run; avail, concur, contribute, tend, serve; eventuate, fare, turn out; afford, bet, risk, wager. * n action, business, case, chance, circumstance, doings, turn; custom, fad, fashion, mode, vogue; energy, endurance, power, stamina, verve, vivacity.

**goad** vb annoy, badger, harass, irritate, sting, worry; arouse, impel, incite, instigate, prod, spur, stimulate, urge. * n incentive, incitement, pressure, stimulation.

**goal** n bound, home, limit, mark, mete, post; end, object; aim, design, destination.

**gobble** vb bolt, devour, gorge, gulp, swallow.

**goblin** n apparition, elf, bogey, demon, gnome, hobgoblin, phantom, spectre, sprite.

**god** n almighty, creator, deity, divinity, idol, Jehovah, omnipotence, providence.

**godless** adj atheistic, impious, irreligious, profane, ungodly, wicked.

**godlike** adj celestial, divine, heavenly, supernal.

**godly** adj devout, holy, pious, religious, righteous, saint-like, saintly.

**godsend** n fortune, gift, luck, present, windfall.

**golden** adj aureate, brilliant, bright, gilded, resplendent, shining, splendid; excellent, precious; auspicious, favourable, opportune, propitious; blessed, delightful, glorious, halcyon, happy.

**good** adj advantageous, beneficial, favourable, profitable, serviceable, useful; adequate, appropriate, becoming, convenient, fit, proper, satisfactory, suitable, well-adapted; decorous, dutiful, honest, just, pious, reliable, religious, righteous, true, upright, virtuous, well-behaved, worthy; admirable, capable, excellent, genuine, healthy, precious, sincere, sound, sterling, valid, valuable; benevolent, favourable, friendly, gracious, humane, kind, merciful, obliging, well-disposed; fair, honourable, immaculate, unblemished, unimpeachable, unimpeached, unsullied, untarnished; cheerful, companionable, lively, genial, social; able, competent, dextrous, expert, qualified, ready, skilful, thorough, well-qualified; creditworthy; agreeable, cheering, gratifying, pleasant. * n advantage, benefit, boon, favour, gain, profit, utility; interest, prosperity, welfare, weal; excellence, righteousness, virtue, worth.

**good breeding** n affability, civility, courtesy, good manners, polish, politeness, urbanity.

**goodbye** n adieu, farewell, parting.

**goodly** adj beautiful, comely, good-looking, graceful; agreeable, considerate, desirable, happy, pleasant.

**good-natured** adj amiable, benevolent, friendly, kind, kind-hearted, kindly.

**goodness** n excellence, quality, value, worth; honesty, integrity, morality, principle, probity, righteousness, uprightness, virtue; benevolence, beneficence, benignity, good-will, humaneness, humanity, kindness.

**goods** npl belongings, chattels, effects, furniture, movables; commodities, merchandise, stock, wares.

**goodwill** n benevolence, kindness, good nature; ardour, earnestness, heartiness, willingness, zeal; custom, patronage.

**gore** vb horn, pierce, stab, wound.

**gorge**[1] vb bolt, devour, eat, feed, swallow; cram, fill, glut, gormandize, sate, satiate, stuff, surfeit. * n craw, crop, gullet, throat.

**gorge**[2] n canyon, defile, fissure, notch, ravine.

**gorgeous** adj bright, brilliant, dazzling, fine, glittering, grand, magnificent, resplendent, rich, shining, showy, splendid, superb.

**Gorgon** n bugaboo, fright, hobgoblin, hydra, ogre, spectre.

**gory** adj bloody, ensanguined, sanguinary.

**gospel** n creed, doctrine, message, news, revelation, tidings.

**gossip** vb chat, cackle, clack, gabble, prate, prattle, tattle. * n babbler, busybody, chatterer, gossipmonger, newsmonger, quidnunc, tale-bearer, tattler, telltale; cackle, chat, chit-chat, prate, prattle, tattle.

**gourmet** n connoisseur, epicure, epicurean.

**govern** vb administer, conduct, direct, manage, regulate, reign, rule, superintend, supervise; guide, pilot, steer; bridle, check, command, control, curb, restrain, rule, sway.

**government** n autonomy, command, conduct, control, direction, discipline, dominion, guidance, management, regulation, restraint, rule, rulership, sway; administration, cabinet, commonwealth, polity, sovereignty, state.

**governor** n commander, comptroller, director, head, headmaster, manager, overseer, ruler, superintendent, supervisor; chief magistrate, executive; guardian, instructor, tutor.

**grab** vb capture, clutch, seize, snatch.

**grace** vb adorn, beautify, deck, decorate, embellish; dignify, honour. * n benignity, condescension, favour, good-will, kindness, love; devotion, efficacy, holiness, love, piety, religion, sanctity, virtue; forgiveness, mercy, pardon, reprieve; accomplishment, attractiveness, charm, elegance, polish, propriety, refinement; beauty, comeliness, ease, gracefulness, symmetry; blessing, petition, thanks.

**graceful** *adj* beautiful, becoming, comely, easy, elegant; flowing, natural, rounded, unlaboured; appropriate; felicitous, happy, tactful.

**graceless** *adj* abandoned, corrupt, depraved, dissolute, hardened, incorrigible, irreclaimable, lost, obdurate, profligate, reprobate, repugnant, shameless,

**gracious** *adj* beneficent, benevolent, benign, benignant, compassionate, condescending, favourable, friendly, gentle, good-natured, kind, kindly, lenient, merciful, mild, tender; affable, civil, courteous, easy, familiar, polite.

**grade** *vb* arrange, classify, group, order, rank, sort. * *n* brand, degree, intensity, stage, step, rank; gradient, incline, slope.

**gradual** *adj* approximate, continuous, gentle, progressive, regular, slow, successive.

**graduate** *vb* adapt, adjust, proportion, regulate. * *n* alumna, alumnus, laureate, postgraduate.

**graft** *vb* ingraft, inoculate, insert, transplant. * *n* bud, scion, shoot, slip, sprout; corruption, favouritism, influence, nepotism.

**grain** *n* kernel, ovule, seed; cereals, corn, grist; atom, bit, glimmer, jot, particle, scintilla, scrap, shadow, spark, tittle, trace, whit; disposition, fibre, humour, temper, texture; colour, dye, hue, shade, stain, texture, tincture, tinge.

**granary** *n* corn-house, garner, grange, store-house.

**grand** *adj* august, dignified, elevated, eminent, exalted, great, illustrious, lordly, majestic, princely, stately, sublime; fine, glorious, gorgeous, magnificent, pompous, lofty, noble, splendid, superb; chief, leading, main, pre-eminent, principal, superior.

**grandee** *n* lord, noble, nobleman.

**grandeur** *n* elevation, greatness, immensity, impressiveness, loftiness, vastness; augustness, dignity, eminence, glory, magnificence, majesty, nobility, pomp, splendour, state, stateliness.

**grandiloquent** *adj* bombastic, declamatory, high-minded, high-sounding, inflated, pompous, rhetorical, stilted, swelling, tumid, turgid.

**grant** *vb* accord, admit, allow, sanction; cede, concede, give, impart, indulge; bestow, confer, deign, invest, vouchsafe; convey, transfer, yield. * *n* admission, allowance, benefaction, bestowal, boon, bounty, concession, donation, endowment, gift, indulgence, largesse, present; conveyance, cession.

**graphic** *adj* descriptive, diagrammatic, figural, figurative, forcible, lively, pictorial, picturesque, striking, telling, vivid, well-delineated, well-drawn.

**grapple** *vb* catch, clutch, grasp, grip, hold, hug, seize, tackle, wrestle.

**grasp** *vb* catch, clasp, clinch, clutch, grapple, grip, seize; comprehend, understand. * *n* clasp, grip, hold; comprehension, power, reach, scope, understanding.

**grasping** *adj* acquisitive, avaricious, covetous, exacting, greedy, rapacious, sordid, tight-fisted.

**grate** *vb* abrade, rub, scrape, triturate; comminute, rasp; creak, fret, grind, jar, vex. * *n* bars, grating, latticework, screen; basket, fire bed.

**grateful** *adj* appreciative, beholden, indebted, obliged, sensible, thankful; pleasant, welcome.

**gratification** *n* gratifying, indulgence, indulging, pleasing, satisfaction, satisfying; delight, enjoyment, fruition, pleasure, reward.

**gratify** *vb* delight, gladden, please; humour, fulfil, grant, indulge, requite, satisfy.

**gratifying** *adj* agreeable, delightful, grateful, pleasing, welcome.

**grating** *adj* disagreeable, displeasing, harsh, irritating, offensive. * *n* grate, partition.

**gratis** *adv* freely, gratuitously.

**gratitude** *n* goodwill, gratitude, indebtedness, thankfulness.

**gratuitous** *adj* free, spontaneous, unrewarded, voluntary; assumed, baseless, groundless, unfounded, unwarranted, wanton.

**gratuity** *n* benefaction, bounty, charity, donation, endowment, gift, grant, largesse, present.

**grave**[1] *n* crypt, mausoleum, ossuary, pit, sepulchre, sepulture, tomb, vault.

**grave**[2] *adj* cogent, heavy, important, momentous, ponderous, pressing, serious, weighty; dignified, sage, sedate, serious, slow, solemn, staid, thoughtful; dull, grim, plain, quiet, sober, sombre, subdued; cruel, hard, harsh, severe; despicable, dire, dismal, gross, heinous, infamous, outrageous, scandalous, shameful, shocking; heavy, hollow, low, low-pitched, sepulchral.

**grave**[3] *vb* engrave, impress, imprint, infix; carve, chisel, cut, sculpt.

**gravel** vb bewilder, embarrass, nonplus, perplex, pose, puzzle, stagger. * n ballast, grit, sand, shingle.

**graveyard** n burial ground, cemetery, churchyard, god's acre, mortuary, necropolis.

**gravity** n heaviness, weight; demureness, sedateness, seriousness, sobriety, thoughtfulness; importance, moment, momentousness, weightiness.

**graze** vb brush, glance, scrape, scratch; abrade, shave, skim; browse, crop, feed, pasture. * n abrasion, bruise, scrape, scratch.

**great** adj ample, big, bulky, Cyclopean, enormous, gigantic, Herculean, huge, immense, large, pregnant, vast; decided, excessive, high, much, pronounced; countless, numerous; chief, considerable, grand, important, leading, main, pre-eminent, principal, superior, weighty; celebrated, distinguished, eminent, exalted, excellent, famed, famous, far-famed, illustrious, noted, prominent, renowned; august, dignified, elevated, grand, lofty, majestic, noble, sublime; chivalrous, generous, high-minded, magnanimous; fine, magnificent, rich, sumptuous.

**greatness** n bulk, dimensions, largeness, magnitude, size; distinction, elevation, eminence, fame, importance, renown; augustness, dignity, grandeur, majesty, loftiness, nobility, nobleness, sublimity; chivalry, generosity, magnanimity, spirit.

**greed, greediness** n gluttony, hunger, omnivorousness, ravenousness, voracity; avidity, covetousness, desire, eagerness, longing; avarice, cupidity, graspingness, grasping, rapacity, selfishness.

**greedy** adj devouring, edacious, gluttonous, insatiable, insatiate, rapacious, ravenous, voracious; desirous, eager; avaricious, grasping, selfish.

**green** adj aquamarine, emerald, olive, verdant, verdure, viridescent, viridian; blooming, flourishing, fresh, undecayed; fresh, new, recent; immature, unfledged, unripe; callow, crude, inexpert, ignorant, inexperienced, raw, unskilful, untrained, verdant, young; unseasoned; conservationist, ecological, environmentalist. * n common, grass plot, lawn, sward, turf, verdure.

**greenhorn** n beginner, novice, tyro.

**greet** vb accost, address, complement, hail, receive, salute, welcome.

**greeting** n compliment, salutation, salute, welcome.

**grief** n affliction, agony, anguish, bitterness, distress, dole, heartbreak, misery, regret, sadness, sorrow, suffering, tribulation, mourning, woe; grievance, trial; disaster, failure, mishap.

**grievance** n burden, complaint, hardship, injury, oppression, wrong; affliction, distress, grief, sorrow, trial, woe.

**grieve** vb afflict, aggrieve, agonize, discomfort, distress, hurt, oppress, pain, sadden, wound; bewail, deplore, mourn, lament, regret, sorrow, suffer.

**grievous** adj afflicting, afflictive, burdensome, deplorable, distressing, heavy, lamentable, oppressive, painful, sad, sorrowful; baleful, baneful, calamitous, destructive, detrimental, hurtful, injurious, mischievous, noxious, troublesome; aggravated, atrocious, dreadful, flagitious, flagrant, gross, heinous, iniquitous, intense, intolerable, severe, outrageous, wicked.

**grill** vb broil, griddle, roast, toast; sweat; cross-examine, interrogate, question; torment, torture. * n grating, gridiron; cross-examination, cross-questioning.

**grim** adj cruel, ferocious, fierce, harsh, relentless, ruthless, savage, stern, unyielding; appalling, dire, dreadful, fearful, frightful, grisly, hideous, horrid, horrible, terrific.

**grimace** vb, n frown, scowl, smirk, sneer.

**grime** n dirt, filth, foulness, smut.

**grimy** adj begrimed, defiled, dirty, filthy, foul, soiled, sullied, unclean.

**grind** vb bruise, crunch, crush, grate, grit, pulverize, rub, triturate; sharpen, whet; afflict, harass, oppress, persecute, plague, trouble. * n chore, drudgery, labour, toil.

**grip** vb clasp, clutch, grasp, hold, seize. * n clasp, clutch, control, domination, grasp, hold.

**grisly** adj appalling, frightful, dreadful, ghastly, grim, grey, hideous, horrible, horrid, terrible, terrific.

**grit** vb clench, grate, grind. * n bran, gravel, pebbles, sand; courage, decision, determination, firmness, perseverance, pluck, resolution, spirit.

**groan** vb complain, lament, moan, whine; creak. * n cry, moan, whine; complaint; grouse, grumble.

**groom** vb clean, dress, tidy; brush, tend; coach, educate, nurture, train. * n equerry, hostler, manservant, ostler, servant, stable-hand, valet, waiter.

**groove** n channel, cut, furrow, rabbet, rebate, recess, rut, scoring; routine.

**gross** vb accumulate, earn, make. * adj big, bulky, burly, fat, great, large; dense, dull, stupid, thick; beastly, broad, carnal, coarse, crass, earthy, impure, indelicate, licentious, low, obscene, unbecoming, unrefined, unseemly, vulgar, rough, sensual; aggravated, brutal, enormous, flagrant, glaring, grievous, manifest, obvious, palpable, plain, outrageous, shameful; aggregate, entire, total, whole. * n aggregate, bulk, total, whole.

**grossness** n bigness, bulkiness, greatness; density, thickness; coarseness, ill-breeding, rudeness, vulgarity; bestiality, brutality, carnality, coarseness, impurity, indelicacy, licentiousness, sensuality.

**grotesque** adj bizarre, extravagant, fanciful, fantastic, incongruous, odd, strange, unnatural, whimsical, wild; absurd, antic, burlesque, ludicrous, ridiculous.

**ground** vb fell, place; base, establish, fix, found, set; instruct, train. * n area, clod, distance, earth, loam, mould, sod, soil, turf; country, domain, land, region, territory; acres, estate, field, property; base, basis, foundation, groundwork, support; account, consideration, excuse, gist, motive, opinion, reason.

**groundless** adj baseless, causeless, false, gratuitous, idle, unauthorized, unfounded, unjustifiable, unsolicited, unsought, unwarranted.

**grounds** npl deposit, dregs, grouts, lees, precipitate, sediment, settlings; accounts, arguments, considerations, reasons, support; campus, gardens, lawns, premises, yard.

**group** vb arrange, assemble, dispose, order. * n aggregation, assemblage, assembly, body, combination, class, clump, cluster, collection, order.

**grove** n copse, glade, spinney, thicket, wood, woodland.

**grovel** vb cower, crawl, creep, cringe, fawn, flatter, sneak.

**grovelling** adj creeping, crouching, squat; abject, base, beggarly, cringing, fawning, low, mean, servile, slavish, sneaking, undignified, unworthy, vile.

**grow** vb enlarge, expand, extend, increase, swell; arise, burgeon, develop, germinate, shoot, sprout, vegetate; advance, extend, improve, progress, thrive, wax; cultivate, produce, raise.

**growl** vb complain, crook, find fault, gnarl, groan, grumble, lament, murmur, snarl. * n croak, grown, snarl; complaint.

**growth** n augmentation, development, expansion, extension, growing, increase; burgeoning, excrescence, formation, germination, pollution, shooting, sprouting, vegetation; cultivation, produce, product,

production; advance, advancement, development, improvement, progress; adulthood, maturity.

**grub** vb clear, dig, eradicate, root. * n caterpillar, larvae, maggot; drudge, plodder.

**grudge** vb begrudge, envy, repine; complain, grieve, murmur. * n aversion, dislike, enmity, grievance, hate, hatred, ill-will, malevolence, malice, pique, rancour, resentment, spite, venom.

**gruff** adj bluff, blunt, brusque, churlish, discourteous, grumpy, harsh, impolite, rough, rude, rugged, surly, uncivil, ungracious.

**grumble** vb croak, complain, murmur, repine; gnarl, growl, snarl; roar, rumble. * n growl, murmur, complaint, roar, rumble.

**grumpy** adj crabbed, cross, glum, moody, morose, sour, sullen, surly.

**guarantee** vb assure, insure, pledge, secure, warrant. * n assurance, pledge, security, surety, warrant, warranty.

**guard** vb defend, keep, patrol, protect, safeguard, save, secure, shelter, shield, watch. * n aegis, bulwark, custody, defence, palladium, protection, rampart, safeguard, security, shield; keeper, guardian, patrol, sentinel, sentry, warden, watch, watchman; conduct, convoy, escort; attention, care, caution, circumspection, heed, watchfulness.

**guarded** adj careful, cautious, circumspect, reserved, reticent, wary, watchful.

**guardian** n custodian, defender, guard, keeper, preserver, protector, trustee, warden.

**guerdon** n recompense, remuneration, requital, reward.

**guess** vb conjecture, divine, mistrust, surmise, suspect; fathom, find out, penetrate, solve; believe, fancy, hazard, imagine, reckon, suppose, think. * n conjecture, divination, notion, supposition, surmise.

**guest** n caller, company, visitant.

**guidance** n conduct, control, direction, escort, government, lead, leadership, pilotage, steering.

**guide** vb conduct, escort, lead, pilot; control, direct, govern, manage, preside, regulate, rule, steer, superintend, supervise. * n cicerone, conductor, director, monitor, pilot; adviser, counsellor, instructor, mentor; clew, directory, index, key, thread; guidebook, itinerary, landmark.

**guild** n association, brotherhood, company, corporation, fellowship, fraternity, society, union.

**guile** n art, artfulness, artifice, craft, cunning, deceit, deception, duplicity, fraud, knavery, ruse, subtlety, treachery, trickery, wiles, wiliness.

**guileless** adj artless, candid, frank, honest, ingenuous, innocent, open, pure, simple-minded, sincere, straightforward, truthful, undesigning, unsophisticated.

**guilt** n blame, criminality, culpability, guiltless; ill-desert, iniquity, offensiveness, wickedness, wrong; crime, offence, sin.

**guiltless** adj blameless, immaculate, innocent, pure, sinless, spotless, unpolluted, unspotted, unsullied, untarnished.

**guilty** adj criminal, culpable, evil, sinful, wicked, wrong.

**guise** n appearance, aspect, costume, dress, fashion, figure, form, garb, manner, mode, shape; air, behaviour, demeanour, mien; cover, custom, disguise, habit, pretence, pretext, practice.

**gulf** n abyss, chasm, opening; bay, inlet; whirlpool.

**gull** vb beguile, cheat, circumvent, cozen, deceive, dupe, hoax, overreach, swindle, trick. * n cheat, deception, hoax, imposition, fraud, trick; cat's paw, dupe.

**gullibility** n credulity, naiveness, naivety, overtrustfulness, simplicity, unsophistication.

**gullible** adj confiding, credulous, naive, over-trustful, simple, unsophisticated, unsuspicious.

**gumption** n ability, astuteness, cleverness, capacity,

common sense, discernment, penetration, power, sagacity, shrewdness, skill; courage, guts, spirit.

**gun** n blunderbuss, cannon, carbine, firearm, musket, pistol, revolver, rifle, shotgun.

**gurgle** vb babble, bubble, murmur, purl, ripple. * n babbling, murmur, ripple.

**gush** vb burst, flood, flow, pour, rush, spout, stream; emotionalize, sentimentalize. * n flow, jet, onrush, rush, spurt, surge; effusion, effusiveness, loquacity, loquaciousness, talkativeness.

**gushing** adj flowing, issuing, rushing; demonstrative, effusive, sentimental.

**gust** vb blast, blow, puff. * n blast, blow, squall; burst, fit, outburst, paroxysm.

**gusto** n enjoyment, gust, liking, pleasure, relish, zest.

**gusty** adj blustering, blustery, puffy, squally, stormy, tempestuous, unsteady, windy.

**gut** vb destroy, disembowel, embowel, eviscerate, paunch. * n bowels, entrails, intestines, inwards, viscera.

**gutter** n channel, conduit, kennel, pipe, tube.

**guttural** adj deep, gruff, hoarse, thick, throaty.

**guy** vb caricature, mimic, ridicule. * n boy, man, person; dowdy, eccentric, fright, scarecrow.

**guzzle** vb carouse, drink, gorge, gormandize, quaff, swill, tipple, tope.

**gyrate** vb revolve, rotate, spin, whirl.

# H

**habiliment** n apparel, attire, clothes, costume, dress, garb, garment, habit, raiment, robes, uniform, vesture, vestment.

**habit** vb accoutre, array, attire, clothe, dress, equip, robe. * n condition, constitution, temperament; addiction, custom, habitude, manner, practice, rule, usage, way, wont; apparel, costume, dress, garb, habiliment.

**habitation** n abode, domicile, dwelling, headquarters, home, house, lodging, quarters, residence.

**habitual** adj accustomed, common, confirmed, customary, everyday, familiar, inveterate, ordinary, regular, routine, settled, usual, wonted.

**habituate** vb accustom, familiarize, harden, inure, train, use.

**habitude** n custom, practice, usage, wont.

**hack**[1] vb chop, cut, hew, mangle, mutilate, notch; cough, rasp. * n cut, cleft, incision, notch; cough, rasp.

**hack**[2] vb ride. * adj hired, mercenary; banal, hackneyed, pedestrian, uninspired, unoriginal. * n horse, nag, pony; hireling, mercenary; journalist, scribbler, writer.

**hackneyed** adj banal, common, commonplace, overworked, pedestrian, stale, threadbare, trite.

**hag** n beldame, crone, fury, harridan, jezebel, she-monster, shrew, termagant, virago, vixen, witch.

**haggard** adj intractable, refractory, unruly, untamed, wild, wayward; careworn, emaciated, gaunt, ghastly, lank, lean, meagre, raw, spare, thin, wasted, worn.

**haggle** vb argue, bargain, cavil, chaffer, dispute, higgle, stickle; annoy, badger, bait, fret, harass, tease, worry.

**hail**[1] vb acclaim, greet, salute, welcome; accost, address, call, hallo, signal. * n greeting, salute.

**hail**[2] vb assail, bombard, rain, shower, storm, volley. * n bombardment, rain, shower, storm, volley.

**halcyon** adj calm, golden, happy, palmy, placid, peaceful, quiet, serene, still, tranquil, unruffled, undisturbed.

**hale** adj hardy, healthy, hearty, robust, sound, strong, vigorous, well.

**halfwit** n blockhead, dunce, moron, simpleton.

**halfwitted** adj doltish, dull, dull-witted, feeble-minded, foolish, sappy, shallow, silly, simple, soft, stolid, stupid, thick.

**hall** n chamber, corridor, entrance, entry, hallway, lobby, passage, vestibule; manor, manor-house; auditorium, lecture-room.

**halloo** vb call, cry, shout. * n call, cry, hallo, holla, hollo, shout.

**hallow** vb consecrate, dedicate, devote, revere, sanctify, solemnize; enshrine, honour, respect, reverence, venerate.

**hallowed** adj blessed, holy, honoured, revered, sacred.

**hallucination** n blunder, error, fallacy, mistake; aberration, delusion, illusion, phantasm, phantasy, self-deception, vision.

**halo** n aura, aureole, glory, nimbus.

**halt**[1] vb cease, desist, hold, rest, stand, stop. * n end, impasse, pause, standstill, stop.

**halt**[2] vb hesitate, pause, stammer, waver; falter, hobble, limp. * adj crippled, disabled, lame. * n hobble, limp.

**hammer** vb beat, forge, form, shape; excogitate, contrive, invent.

**hammer and tongs** adv earnestly, energetically, resolutely, strenuously, vigorously, zealously.

**hamper** vb bind, clog, confine, curb, embarrass, encumber, entangle, fetter, hinder, impede, obstruct, prevent, restrain, restrict, shackle, trammel. * n basket, box, crate, picnic basket; embarrassment, encumbrance, fetter, handicap, impediment, obstruction, restraint, trammel.

**hand** vb deliver, give, present, transmit; conduct, guide, lead. * n direction, part, side; ability, dexterity, faculty, skill, talent; course, inning, management, turn; agency, intervention, participation, share; control, possession, power; artificer, artisan, craftsman, employee, labourer, operative, workman; index, indicator, pointer; chirography, handwriting.

**handbook** n guidebook, manual.

**handcuff** vb bind, fetter, manacle, shackle. * n fetter, manacle, shackle.

**handful** n fistful, maniple, smattering.

**handicap** vb encumber, hamper, hinder, restrict. * n disadvantage, encumbrance, hampering, hindrance, restriction.

**handicraft** n hand manufacture, handwork, workmanship.

**handle** vb feel, finger, manhandle, paw, touch; direct, manage, manipulate, use, wield; discourse, discuss, treat. * n haft, helve, hilt, stock.

**handsome** adj admirable, comely, fine-looking, stately, well-formed, well-proportioned; appropriate, suitable, becoming, easy, graceful; generous, gracious, liberal, magnanimous, noble; ample, large, plentiful, sufficient.

**handy** adj adroit, clever, dextrous, expert, ready, skilful, skilled; close, convenient, near.

**hang** vb attach, swing; execute, truss; decline, drop, droop, incline; adorn, drape; dangle, depend, impend, suspend; rely; cling, loiter, rest, stick; float, hover, pay.

**hangdog** adj ashamed, base, blackguard, low, villainous, scurvy, sneaking.

**hanger-on** n dependant, minion, parasite, vassal.

**hanker** vb covet, crave, desire, hunger, long, lust, want, yearn.

**hap** n accident, chance, fate, fortune, lot.

**haphazard** adj aimless, chance, random.

**hapless** adj ill-fated, ill-starred, luckless, miserable, unfortunate, unhappy, unlucky, wretched.

**happen** vb befall, betide, chance, come, occur.

**happily** adv fortunately, luckily; agreeably, delightfully, prosperously, successfully.

**happiness** n brightness, cheerfulness, delight, gaiety, joy, light-heartedness, merriment, pleasure; beatitude, blessedness, bliss, felicity, enjoyment, welfare, well-being.

**happy** adj blessed, blest, blissful, cheerful, contented, joyful, joyous, light-hearted, merry; charmed, delighted, glad, gladdened, gratified, pleased; fortunate, lucky, prosperous, successful; able, adroit, apt, dextrous, expert, ready, skilful; befitting, felicitous, opportune, pertinent, seasonable, well-timed; auspicious, bright, favourable, propitious.

**harangue** vb address, declaim, spout. * n address, bombast, declamation, oration, rant, screed, speech, tirade.

**harass** vb exhaust, fag, fatigue, jade, tire, weary; annoy, badger, distress, gall, heckle, disturb, harry,

molest, pester, plague, tantalize, tease, torment, trouble, vex, worry.

**harbour** vb protect, lodge, shelter; cherish, entertain, foster, indulge. * n asylum, cover, refuge, resting place, retreat, sanctuary, shelter; anchorage, destination, haven, port.

**hard** adj adamantine, compact, firm, flinty, impenetrable, marble, rigid, solid, resistant, stony, stubborn, unyielding; difficult, intricate, knotty, perplexing, puzzling; arduous, exacting, fatiguing, laborious, toilsome, wearying; austere, callous, cruel, exacting, hard-hearted, incorrigible, inflexible, insensible, insensitive, obdurate, oppressive, reprobate, rigorous, severe, unfeeling, unkind, unsusceptible, unsympathetic, unyielding, untender; calamitous, disagreeable, distressing, grievous, painful, unpleasant; acid, alcoholic, harsh, rough, sour; excessive, intemperate. * adv close, near; diligently, earnestly, energetically, incessantly, laboriously; distressfully, painfully, rigorously, severely; forcibly, vehemently, violently.

**harden** vb accustom, discipline, form, habituate, inure, season, train; brace, fortify, indurate, nerve, steel, stiffen, strengthen.

**hardened** adj annealed, case-hardened, tempered, indurated; abandoned, accustomed, benumbed, callous, confirmed, deadened, depraved, habituated, impenitent, incorrigible, inured, insensible, irreclaimable, lost, obdurate, reprobate, seared, seasoned, steeled, trained, unfeeling.

**hard-headed** adj astute, collected, cool, intelligent, sagacious, shrewd, well-balanced, wise.

**hardhearted** adj cruel, fell, implacable, inexorable, merciless, pitiless, relentless, ruthless, unfeeling, uncompassionate, unmerciful, unpitying, unrelenting.

**hardihood** n audacity, boldness, bravery, courage, decision, firmness, fortitude, intrepidity, manhood, mettle, pluck, resolution, stoutness; assurance, audacity, brass, effrontery, impudence.

**hardly** adv barely, scarcely; cruelly, harshly, rigorously, roughly, severely, unkindly.

**hardship** n fatigue, toil, weariness; affliction, burden, calamity, grievance, hardness, injury, misfortune, privation, suffering, trial, trouble.

**hardy** adj enduring, firm, hale, healthy, hearty, inured, lusty, rigorous, robust, rugged, sound, stout, strong, sturdy, tough; bold, brave, courageous, daring, heroic, intrepid, manly, resolute, stout-hearted, valiant.

**harebrained** adj careless, changeable, flighty, giddy,

harum-scarum, headlong, heedless, rash, reckless, unsteady, volatile, wild.

**hark** *interj* attend, hear, hearken, listen.

**harlequin** *n* antic, buffoon, clown, droll, fool, jester, punch, fool.

**harm** *vb* damage, hurt, injure, scathe; abuse, desecrate, ill-use, ill-treat, maltreat, molest. * *n* damage, detriment, disadvantage, hurt, injury, mischief, misfortune, prejudice, wrong.

**harmful** *adj* baneful, detrimental, disadvantageous, hurtful, injurious, mischievous, noxious, pernicious, prejudicial.

**harmless** *adj* innocent, innocuous, innoxious; inoffensive, safe, unoffending.

**harmonious** *adj* concordant, consonant, harmonic; dulcet, euphonious, mellifluous, melodious, musical, smooth, tuneful; comfortable, congruent, consistent, correspondent, orderly, symmetrical; agreeable, amicable, brotherly, cordial, fraternal, friendly, neighbourly.

**harmonize** *vb* adapt, attune, reconcile, unite; accord, agree, blend, chime, comport, conform, correspond, square, sympathize, tally, tune.

**harmony** *n* euphony, melodiousness, melody; accord, accordance, agreement, chime, concord, concordance, consonance, order, unison; adaptation, congruence, congruity, consistency, correspondence, fairness, smoothness, suitableness; amity, friendship, peace.

**harness** *vb* hitch, tackle. * *n* equipment, gear, tackle, tackling; accoutrements, armour, array, mail, mounting.

**harp** *vb* dwell, iterate, reiterate, renew, repeat.

**harping** *n* dwelling, iteration, reiteration, repetition.

**harrow** *vb* harass, lacerate, rend, tear, torment, torture, wound.

**harry** *vb* devastate, pillage, plunder, raid, ravage, rob; annoy, chafe, disturb, fret, gall, harass, harrow, incommode, pester, plague, molest, tease, torment, trouble, vex, worry.

**harsh** *adj* acid, acrid, astringent, biting, caustic, corrosive, crabbed, rough, sharp, sour, tart; cacophonous, discordant, grating, jarring, metallic, raucous, strident, unmelodious; abusive, austere, crabbed, crabby, cruel, disagreeable, hard, ill-natured, ill-tempered, morose, rigorous, severe, stern, unfeeling; bearish, bluff, blunt, brutal, gruff, rude, uncivil, ungracious.

**harshness** *n* roughness; acerbity, asperity, austerity, churlishness, crabbedness, hardness, ill-nature, ill-temper, moroseness, rigour, severity, sternness, unkindness; bluffness, bluntness, churlishness, gruffness, incivility, ungraciousness, rudeness.

**harum-scarum** *adj* hare-brained, precipitate, rash, reckless, volatile, wild.

**harvest** *vb* gather, glean, reap. * *n* crops, produce, yield; consequence, effect, issue, outcome, produce, result.

**haste** *n* alacrity, celerity, dispatch, expedition, nimbleness, promptitude, quickness, rapidity, speed, urgency, velocity; flurry, hurry, hustle, impetuosity, precipitateness, precipitation, press, rashness, rush, vehemence.

**hasten** *vb* haste, hurry; accelerate, dispatch, expedite, precipitate, press, push, quicken, speed, urge.

**hasty** *adj* brisk, fast, fleet, quick, rapid, speedy, swift; cursory, hurried, passing, slight, superficial; ill-advised, rash, reckless; headlong, helter-skelter, pell-mell, precipitate; abrupt, choleric, excitable, fiery, fretful, hot-headed, irascible, irritable, passionate, peevish, peppery, pettish, petulant, testy, touchy, waspish.

**hatch** *vb* brew, concoct, contrive, excogitate, design, devise, plan, plot, project, scheme; breed, incubate.

**hate** *vb* abhor, abominate, detest, dislike, execrate, loathe, nauseate. * *n* abomination, animosity, antipathy, detestation, dislike, enmity, execration, hatred, hostility, loathing.

**hateful** *adj* malevolent, malicious, malign, malignant, rancorous, spiteful; abhorrent, abominable, accursed, damnable, detestable, execrable, horrid, odious, shocking; disgusting, foul, loathsome, nauseous, obnoxious, offensive, repellent, repugnant, repulsive, revolting, vile.

**hatred** *n* animosity, enmity, hate, hostility, ill-will, malevolence, malice, malignity, odium, rancour; abhorrence, abomination, antipathy, aversion, detestation, disgust, execration, horror, loathing, repugnance, revulsion.

**haughtiness** *n* arrogance, contempt, contemptuousness, disdain, hauteur, insolence, loftiness, pride, self-importance, snobbishness, stateliness, superciliousness.

**haughty** *adj* arrogant, assuming, contemptuous, disdainful, imperious, insolent, lofty, lordly, overbearing, overweening, proud, scornful, snobbish, supercilious.

**haul** vb drag, draw, lug, pull, tow, trail, tug. * n heaving, pull, tug; booty, harvest, takings, yield.

**haunt** vb frequent, resort; follow, importune; hover, inhabit, obsess. * n den, resort, retreat.

**hauteur** n arrogance, contempt, contemptuousness, disdain, haughtiness, insolence, loftiness, pride, self-importance, stateliness, superciliousness.

**have** vb cherish, exercise, experience, keep, hold, occupy, own, possess; acquire, gain, get, obtain, receive; accept, take.

**haven** n asylum, refuge, retreat, shelter; anchorage, harbour, port.

**havoc** n carnage, damage, desolation, destruction, devastation, ravage, ruin, slaughter, waste, wreck.

**hawk-eyed** adj eagle-eyed, sharp-sighted.

**hazard** vb adventure, risk, venture; endanger, imperil, jeopardize. * n accident, casualty, chance, contingency, event, fortuity, stake; danger, jeopardy, peril, risk, venture.

**hazardous** adj dangerous, insecure, perilous, precarious, risky, uncertain, unsafe.

**haze** n fog, har, mist, smog; cloud, dimness, fume, miasma, obscurity, pall.

**hazy** adj foggy, misty; cloudy, dim, nebulous, obscure; confused, indefinite, indistinct, uncertain, vague.

**head** vb command, control, direct, govern, guide, lead, rule; aim, point, tend; beat, excel, outdo, precede, surpass. * adj chief, first, grand, highest, leading, main, principal; adverse, contrary. * n acme, summit, top; beginning, commencement, origin, rise, source; chief, chieftain, commander, director, leader, master, principal, superintendent, superior; intellect, mind, thought, understanding; branch, category, class, department, division, section, subject, topic; brain, crown, headpiece, intellect, mind, thought, understanding; cape, headland, point, promontory.

**headiness** n hurry, precipitation, rashness; obstinacy, stubbornness.

**headless** adj acephalous, beheaded; leaderless, undirected; headstrong, heady, imprudent, obstinate, rash, senseless, stubborn.

**headlong** adj dangerous, hasty, heady, impulsive, inconsiderate, perilous, precipitate, rash, reckless, ruinous, thoughtless; perpendicular, precipitous, sheer, steep. * adv hastily, headfirst, helter-skelter, hurriedly, precipitately, rashly, thoughtlessly.

**headstone** n cornerstone, gravestone.

**headstrong** adj cantankerous, cross-grained, dogged, forward, headless, heady, intractable, obstinate, self-willed, stubborn, ungovernable, unruly, violent, wayward.

**heady** adj hasty, headlong, impetuous, impulsive, inconsiderate, precipitate, rash, reckless, rushing, stubborn, thoughtless; exciting, inebriating, inflaming, intoxicating, spirituous, strong.

**heal** vb amend, cure, remedy, repair, restore; compose, harmonize, reconcile, settle, soothe.

**healing** adj curative, palliative, remedial, restoring, restorative; assuaging, assuasive, comforting, composing, gentle, lenitive, mild, soothing.

**health** n healthfulness, robustness, salubrity, sanity, soundness, strength, tone, vigour.

**healthy** adj active, hale, hearty, lusty, sound, vigorous, well; bracing, healthful, health-giving, hygienic, invigorating, nourishing, salubrious, salutary, wholesome.

**heap** vb accumulate, augment, amass, collect, overfill, pile up, store. * n accumulation, collection, cumulus, huddle, lot, mass, mound, pile, stack.

**hear** vb eavesdrop, hearken, heed, listen, overhear; ascertain, discover, gather, learn, understand; examine, judge.

**heart** n bosom, breast; centre, core, essence, interior, kernel, marrow, meaning, pith; affection, benevolence, character, disposition, feeling, inclination, love, mind, passion, purpose, will; affections, ardour, emotion, feeling, love; boldness, courage, fortitude, resolution, spirit.

**heartache** n affliction, anguish, bitterness, distress, dole, grief, heartbreak, sorrow, woe.

**heartbroken** adj broken-hearted, cheerless, comfortless, desolate, disconsolate, forlorn, inconsolable, miserable, woebegone, wretched.

**hearten** vb animate, assure, cheer, comfort, console, embolden, encourage, enhearten, incite, inspire, inspirit, reassure, stimulate.

**heartfelt** adj cordial, deep, deep-felt, hearty, profound, sincere, warm.

**hearth** n fireplace, fireside, forge, hearthstone.

**heartily** adv abundantly, completely, cordially, earnestly, freely, largely, sincerely, vigorously.

**heartless** adj brutal, cold, cruel, hard, harsh, merciless, pitiless, unfeeling, unsympathetic; spiritless, timid, timorous, uncourageous.

**heart-rending** adj affecting, afflicting, anguishing, crushing, distressing.

**hearty** adj cordial, deep, earnest, fervent, heartfelt, profound, sincere, true, unfeigned, warm; active, animated, energetic, fit, vigorous, zealous; convivial, hale, healthy, robust, sound, strong, warm; abundant, full, heavy; nourishing, nutritious, rich.

**heat** vb excite, flush, inflame; animate, rouse, stimulate, stir. * n calorie, caloricity, torridity, warmth; excitement, fever, flush, impetuosity, passion, vehemence, violence; ardour, earnestness, fervency, fervour, glow, intensity, zeal; exasperation, fierceness, frenzy, rage.

**heath** n field, moor, wasteland, plain.

**heathen** adj animist, animistic; pagan, paganical, paganish, paganistic, unconverted; agnostic, atheist, atheistic, gentile, idolatrous, infidel, irreligious; barbarous, cruel, inhuman, savage. * n atheist, gentile, idolater, idolatress, infidel, pagan, unbeliever; barbarian, philistine, savage.

**heave** vb elevate, hoist, lift, raise; breathe, exhale; cast, fling, hurl, send, throw, toss; dilate, expand, pant, rise, swell; retch, throw up; strive, struggle.

**heaven** n empyrean, firmament, sky, welkin; bliss, ecstasy, elysium, felicity, happiness, paradise, rapture, transport.

**heavenly** adj celestial, empyreal, ethereal; angelic, beatific, beatified, cherubic, divine, elysian, glorious, god-like, sainted, saintly, seraphic; blissful, delightful, divine, ecstatic, enrapturing, enravishing, exquisite, golden, rapturous, ravishing, exquisite, transporting.

**heaviness** n gravity, heft, ponderousness, weight; grievousness, oppressiveness, severity; dullness, languor, lassitude, sluggishness, stupidity; dejection, depression, despondency, gloom, melancholy, sadness, seriousness.

**heavy** adj grave, hard, onerous, ponderous, weighty; afflictive, burdensome, crushing, cumbersome, grievous, oppressive, severe, serious; dilatory, dull, inactive, inanimate, indolent, inert, lifeless, listless, sleepy, slow, sluggish, stupid, torpid; chapfallen, crestfallen, crushed, depressed, dejected, despondent, disconsolate, downhearted, gloomy, low-spirited, melancholy, sad, sobered, sorrowful; difficult, laborious, tedious, tiresome, wearisome, weary; burdened, encumbered, loaded; clammy, clayey, cloggy, ill-raised, miry, muddy, soggy; boisterous, deep, energetic, loud, roaring, severe, stormy, strong, tempestuous, violent; cloudy, dark, dense, gloomy, lowering, overcast.

**hebetate** adj blunt; dull, obtuse, sluggish, stupid, stupefied.

**hectic** adj animated, excited, fevered, feverish, flushed, heated, hot.

**hector** vb bluster, boast, bully, menace, threaten; annoy, fret, harass, harry, irritate, provoke, tease, vex, worry. * n blusterer, bully, swaggerer.

**hedge** vb block, encumber, hinder, obstruct, surround; enclose, fence, fortify, guard, protect; disappear, dodge, evade, hide, skulk, temporize. * n barrier, hedgerow, fence, limit.

**heed** vb attend, consider, mark, mind, note, notice, observe, regard. * n attention, care, carefulness, caution, circumspection, consideration, heedfulness, mindfulness, notice, observation, regard, wariness, vigilance, watchfulness.

**heedful** adj attentive, careful, cautious, circumspect, mindful, observant, observing, provident, regardful, watchful, wary.

**heedless** adj careless, inattentive, neglectful, negligent, precipitate, rash, reckless, thoughtless, unmindful, unminding, unobserving, unobservant.

**heft** n handle, haft, helve; bulk, weight.

**hegemony** n ascendancy, authority, headship, leadership, predominance, preponderance, rule.

**height** n altitude, elevation, tallness; acme, apex, climax, eminence, head, meridian, pinnacle, summit, top, vertex, zenith; eminence, hill, mountain; dignity, exaltation, grandeur, loftiness, perfection.

**heighten** vb elevate, raise; ennoble, exalt, magnify, make greater; augment, enhance, improve, increase, strengthen; aggravate, intensify.

**heinous** adj aggravated, atrocious, crying, enormous, excessive, flagitious, flagrant, hateful, infamous, monstrous, nefarious, odious, villainous.

**heir** n child, inheritor, offspring, product.

**helical** adj screw-shaped, spiral, winding.

**hellish** adj abominable, accursed, atrocious, curst, damnable, damned, demoniacal, detestable, devilish, diabolical, execrable, fiendish, infernal, monstrous, nefarious, satanic.

**helm** n rudder, steering-gear, tiller, wheel; command, control, direction, rein, rule.

**help** vb relieve, save, succour; abet, aid, assist, back, cooperate, second, serve, support, sustain, wait; alleviate, ameliorate, better, cure, heal, improve, remedy, restore; control, hinder, prevent, repress, resist, withstand; avoid, forbear, control. * n aid, assistance, succour, support; relief, remedy; assistant, helper, servant.

**helper** adj aider, abettor, ally, assistant, auxiliary, coadjutor, colleague, helpmate, partner, supporter.

**helpful** adj advantageous, assistant, auxiliary, beneficial, contributory, convenient, favourable, kind, profitable, serviceable, useful.

**helpless** adj disabled, feeble, imbecile, impotent, infirm, powerless, prostrate, resourceless, weak; abandoned, defenceless, exposed, unprotected; desperate, irremediable, remediless.

**helpmate** n companion, consort, husband, partner, wife; aider, assistant, associate, helper.

**helter-skelter** adj disorderly, headlong, irregular, pell-mell, precipitate. * adv confusedly, hastily, headlong, higgledy-piggledy, pell-mell, precipitately, wildly.

**hem** vb border, edge, skirt; beset, confine, enclose, environ, surround, sew; hesitate. * n border, edge, trim.

**henchman** n attendant, follower, retainer, servant, supporter.

**herald** vb announce, proclaim, publish. * n announcer, crier, publisher; harbinger, precursor, proclaimer.

**heraldry** n blazonry, emblazonry.

**herbage** n greenery, herb, pasture, plants, vegetation.

**herculean** adj able-bodied, athletic, brawny, mighty, muscular, powerful, puissant, sinewy, stalwart, strong, sturdy, vigorous; dangerous, difficult, hard, laborious, perilous, toilsome, troublesome; colossal, Cyclopean, gigantic, great, large, strapping.

**herd** vb drive, gather, lead, tend; assemble, associate, flock. * n drover, herder, herdsman, shepherd; crowd, multitude, populace, rabble; assemblage, assembly, collection, drove, flock, pack.

**hereditary** adj ancestral, inheritable, inherited, patrimonial, transmitted.

**heresy** n dissent, error, heterodoxy, impiety, recusancy, unorthodoxy.

**heretic** n dissenter, dissident, nonconformist, recusant, schismatic, sectarian, sectary, separatist, unbeliever.

**heretical** adj heterodox, impious, schismatic, schismatical, sectarian, unorthodox.

**heritage** n estate, inheritance, legacy, patrimony, portion.

**hermetic** adj airtight, impervious; cabbalistic, emblematic, emblematical, magical, mysterious, mystic, mystical, occult, secret, symbolic, symbolical.

**hermit** n anchoress, anchoret, anchorite, ascetic, eremite, monk, recluse, solitaire, solitary.

**heroic** adj bold, brave, courageous, daring, dauntless, fearless, gallant, illustrious, intrepid, magnanimous, noble, valiant; desperate, extravagant, extreme, violent.

**heroism** n boldness, bravery, courage, daring, endurance, fearlessness, fortitude, gallantry, intrepidity, prowess, valour.

**hesitate** vb boggle, delay, demur, doubt, pause, scruple, shilly-shally, stickle, vacillate, waver; falter, stammer, stutter.

**hesitation** n halting, misgiving, reluctance; delay, doubt, indecision, suspense, uncertainty, vacillation; faltering, stammering, stuttering.

**heterodox** adj heretical, recusant, schismatic, unorthodox, unsound; apocryphal, uncanonical.

**heterogeneous** adj contrasted, contrary, different, dissimilar, diverse, incongruous, indiscriminate, miscellaneous, mixed, opposed, unhomogeneous, unlike.

**hew** vb chop, cut, fell, hack; fashion, form, shape, smooth.

**hiatus** n blank, break, chasm, gap, interval, lacuna, opening, rift.

**hidden** adj blind, clandestine, cloaked, close, concealed, covered, covert, enshrouded, latent, masked, occult, private, secluded, secret, suppressed, undiscovered, veiled; abstruse, cabbalistic, cryptic, dark, esoteric, hermetic, inward, mysterious, mystic, mystical, obscure, oracular, recondite.

**hide** vb bury, conceal, cover, secrete, suppress, withhold; cloak, disguise, eclipse, hoard, mask, screen, shelter, veil.

**hideous** adj abominable, appalling, awful, dreadful, frightful, ghastly, ghoulish, grim, grisly, horrible, horrid, repulsive, revolting, shocking, terrible, terrifying.

**hie** vb hasten, speed.

**hieratic** adj consecrated, devoted, priestly, sacred, sacerdotal.

**hieroglyph** n picture-writing, rebus, sign, symbol.

**hieroglyphic** adj emblematic, emblematical, figurative, obscure, symbolic, symbolical.

**higgle** vb hawk, peddle; bargain, chaffer, haggle, negotiate.

**higgledy-piggledy** adj chaotic, confused, disorderly, jumbled. * adv confusedly, in disorder, helter-skelter, pell-mell.

**high** adj elevated, high-reaching, lofty, soaring, tall, towering; distinguished, eminent, pre-eminent, prominent, superior; admirable, dignified, exalted, great, noble; arrogant, haughty, lordly, proud, supercilious; boisterous, strong, tumultuous, turbulent, violent; costly, dear, pricey; acute, high-pitched, high-toned, piercing, sharp, shrill; tainted, malodorous. * adv powerfully, profoundly; eminently, loftily; luxuriously, richly.

**high-flown** adj elevated, presumptuous, proud, lofty, swollen; extravagant, high-coloured, lofty, overdrawn, overstrained; bombastic, inflated, pompous, pretentious, strained, swollen, turgid.

**high-handed** adj arbitrary, despotic, dictatorial, domineering, oppressive, overbearing, self-willed, violent, wilful.

**highly strung** adj ardent, excitable, irascible, nervous, quick, tense; high-spirited, sensitive.

**high-minded** adj arrogant, haughty, lofty, proud; elevated, high-toned; generous honourable, magnanimous, noble, spiritual.

**highwayman** n bandit, brigand, footpad, freebooter, marauder, outlaw, robber.

**hilarious** adj boisterous, cheerful, comical, convivial, riotous, uproarious, jovial, joyful, merry, mirthful, noisy.

**hilarity** n cheerfulness, conviviality, exhilarated, gaiety, glee, jollity, joviality, joyousness, merriment, mirth.

**hill** n ascent, ben, elevation, eminence, hillock, knoll, mount, mountain, rise, tor.

**hind** adj back, hinder, hindmost, posterior, rear, rearward.

**hinder** vb bar, check, clog, delay, embarrass, encumber, impede, interrupt, obstruct, oppose, prevent, restrain, retard, stop, thwart.

**hindrance** n check, deterrent, encumbrance, hitch, impediment, interruption, obstacle, obstruction, restraint, stop, stoppage.

**hinge** vb depend, hang, rest, turn.

**hint** vb allude, glance, imply, insinuate, intimate, mention, refer, suggest. * n allusion, clue, implication, indication, innuendo, insinuation, intimation, mention, reminder, suggestion, taste, trace.

**hire** vb buy, rent, secure; charter, employ, engage, lease, let. * n allowance, bribe, compensation, pay, remuneration, rent, reward, salary, stipend, wages.

**hireling** n employee, mercenary, myrmidon.

**hirsute** adj bristled, bristly, hairy, shaggy; boorish, course, ill-bred, loutish, rough, rude, rustic, uncouth, unmannerly.

**hiss** vb shrill, sibilate, whistle, whir, whiz; condemn, damn, ridicule. * n fizzle, hissing, sibilant, sibilation, sizzle.

**historian** n annalist, autobiographer, biographer, chronicler, narrator, recorder.

**history** n account, autobiography, annals, biography, chronicle, genealogy, memoirs, narration, narrative, recital, record, relation, story.

**hit** vb discomfit, hurt, knock, strike; accomplish, achieve, attain, gain, reach, secure, succeed, win; accord, fit, suit; beat, clash, collide, contact, smite. * n blow, collision, strike, stroke; chance, fortune, hazard, success, venture.

**hitch** vb catch, impede, stick, stop; attach, connect, fasten, harness, join, tether, tie, unite, yoke. * n catch, check, hindrance, impediment, interruption, obstacle; knot, noose.

**hoar** adj ancient, grey, hoary, old, white.

**hoard** vb accumulate, amass, collect, deposit, garner, hive, husband, save, store, treasure. * n accumulation, collection, deposit, fund, mass, reserve, savings, stockpile, store.

**hoarse** adj discordant, grating, gruff, guttural, harsh, husky, low, raucous, rough.

**hoary** adj grey, hoar, silvery, white; ancient, old, venerable.

**hoax** vb deceive, dupe, fool, gammon, gull, hoodwink, swindle, trick. * n canard, cheat, deception, fraud, humbug, imposition, imposture, joke, trick, swindle.

**hobble** vb falter, halt, hop, limp; fasten, fetter, hopple, shackle, tie. * n halt, limp; clog, fetter, shackle; embarrassment, difficulty, perplexity, pickle, strait.

**hobgoblin** n apparition, bogey, bugbear, goblin, imp, spectre, spirit, sprite.

**hobnail** n bumpkin, churl, clodhopper, clown, lout, rustic.

**hocus-pocus** n cheater, impostor, juggler, sharper,

swindler, trickster; artifice, cheat, deceit, deception, delusion, hoax, imposition, juggle, trick.

**hodgepodge** n farrago, hash, hotchpotch, jumble, medley, miscellany, mixture, ragout, stew.

**hog** n beast, glutton, pig; grunter, porker, swine.

**hoggish** adj brutish, filthy, gluttonish, piggish, swinish; grasping, greedy, mean, selfish, sordid.

**hoist** vb elevate, heave, lift, raise, rear. * n elevator, lift.

**hold** vb clasp, clinch, clutch, grasp, grip, seize; have, keep, occupy, possess, retain; bind, confine, control, detain, imprison, restrain, restrict; connect, fasten, fix, lock; arrest, check, stay, stop, suspend, withhold; continue, keep up, maintain, manage, prosecute, support, sustain; cherish, embrace, entertain; account, believe, consider, count, deem, entertain, esteem, judge, reckon, regard, think; accommodate, admit, carry, contain, receive, stow; assemble, conduct, convene; endure, last, persist, remain; adhere, cleave, cling, cohere, stick. * n anchor, bite, clasp, control, embrace, foothold, grasp, grip, possession, retention, seizure; prop, stay, support; claim, footing, vantage point; castle, fort, fortification, fortress, stronghold, tower; locker, storage, storehouse.

**hole** n aperture, opening, perforation; abyss, bore, cave, cavern, cavity, chasm, depression, excavation, eye, hollow, pit, pore, void; burrow, cover, lair, retreat; den, hovel, kennel.

**holiday** n anniversary, celebration, feast, festival, festivity, fete, gala, recess, vacation.

**holiness** n blessedness, consecration, devotion, devoutness, godliness, piety, purity, religiousness, righteousness, sacredness, saintliness, sanctity, sinlessness.

**hollow** vb dig, excavate, groove, scoop. * adj cavernous, concave, depressed, empty, sunken, vacant, void; deceitful, faithless, false, false-hearted, hollow-hearted, hypocritical, insincere, pharisaical, treacherous, unfeeling; deep, low, muffled, reverberating, rumbling, sepulchral. * n basin, bowl, depression; cave, cavern, cavity, concavity, dent, dimple, dint, depression, excavation, hole, pit; canal, channel, cup, dimple, dig, groove, pocket, sag.

**holocaust** n carnage, destruction, devastation, genocide, massacre.

**holy** adj blessed, consecrated, dedicated, devoted, hallowed, sacred, sanctified; devout, godly, pious,

pure, religious, righteous, saintlike, saintly, sinless, spiritual.

**homage** n allegiance, devotion, fealty, fidelity, loyalty; court, deference, duty, honour, obeisance, respect, reverence, service; adoration, devotion, worship.

**home** adj domestic, family; close, direct, effective, penetrating, pointed. * n abode, dwelling, seat, quarters, residence.

**homely** adj domestic, familiar, house-like; coarse, commonplace, homespun, inelegant, plain, simple, unattractive, uncomely, unpolished, unpretentious.

**homespun** adj coarse, homely, inelegant, plain, rude, rustic, unpolished.

**homicide** n manslaughter, murder.

**homily** n address, discourse, lecture, sermon.

**homogeneous** adj akin, alike, cognate, kindred, similar, uniform.

**honest** adj equitable, fair, faithful, honourable, open, straight, straightforward; conscientious, equitable, reliable, sound, square, true, trustworthy, trusty, uncorrupted, upright, virtuous; above-board, faithful, genuine, thorough, unadulterated; creditable, decent, proper, reputable, respectable, suitable; chaste, decent; candid, direct, frank, ingenuous, sincere, unreserved.

**honesty** n equity, fairness, faithfulness, fidelity, honour, integrity, justice, probity, trustiness, trustworthiness, uprightness; truth, truthfulness, veracity; genuineness, thoroughness; candour, frankness, ingenuousness, openness, sincerity, straightforwardness, unreserve.

**honorary** adj formal, nominal, titular, unofficial, unpaid.

**honour** vb dignify, exalt, glorify, grace; respect, revere, reverence, venerate; adore, hallow, worship; celebrate, commemorate, keep, observe. * n civility, deference, esteem, homage, respect, reverence, veneration; dignity, distinction, elevation, nobleness; consideration, credit, fame, glory, reputation; high-mindedness, honesty, integrity, magnanimity, probity, uprightness; chastity, purity, virtue; boast, credit, ornament, pride.

**honourable** adj elevated, famous, great, illustrious, noble; admirable, conscientious, fair, honest, just, magnanimous, true, trustworthy, upright, virtuous, worshipful; creditable, esteemed, estimable, equitable, proper, respected, reputable, right.

**honours** npl dignities, distinctions, privilege,

titles; adornments, beauties, decorations, glories; civilities.

**hood** n capuche, coif, cover, cowl, head.

**hoodwink** vb blind, blindfold; cloak, conceal, cover, hide; cheat, circumvent, cozen, deceive, delete, dupe, fool, gull, impose, overreach, trick.

**hook** vb catch, ensnare, entrap, hasp, snare; bend, curve. * n catch, clasp, fastener, hasp; snare, trap; cutter; grass-hook, reaper, reaping-hook, sickle.

**hooked** adj aquiline, bent, crooked, curved, hamate, unciform.

**hoop** vb clasp, encircle, enclose, surround. * n band, circlet, girdle, ring; crinoline, farthingale.

**hoot** vb boo, cry, jeer, shout, yell; condemn, decry, denounce, execrate, hiss. * n boo, cry, jeer, shout, yell.

**hop** vb bound, caper, frisk, jump, leap, skip, spring; dance, trip; halt, hobble, limp. * n bound, caper, dance, jump, leap, skip, spring.

**hope** vb anticipate, await, desire, expect, long; believe, rely, trust. * n confidence, belief, faith, reliance, sanguineness, sanguinity, trust; anticipation, desire, expectancy, expectation.

**hopeful** adj anticipatory, confident, expectant, fond, optimistic, sanguine; cheerful, encouraging, promising.

**hopeless** adj abject, crushed, depressed, despondent, despairing, desperate, disconsolate, downcast, forlorn, pessimistic, woebegone; abandoned, helpless, incurable, irremediable, remediless; impossible, impracticable, unachievable, unattainable.

**horde** n clan, crew, gang, troop; crowd, multitude, pack, throng.

**horn** vb gore, pierce. * n trumpet, wind instrument; beaker, drinking cup, cornucopia; spike, spur; cusp, prong, wing.

**horrid** adj alarming, awful, bristling, dire, dreadful, fearful, frightful, harrowing, hideous, horrible, horrific, horrifying, rough, terrible, terrific; abominable, disagreeable, disgusting, odious, offensive, repulsive, revolting, shocking, unpleasant, vile.

**horrify** vb affright, alarm, frighten, shock, terrify, terrorise.

**horror** n alarm, awe, consternation, dismay, dread, fear, fright, panic; abhorrence, abomination, antipathy, aversion, detestation, disgust, hatred, loathing, repugnance, revulsion; shuddering.

**horse** n charger, cob, colt, courser, filly, gelding, mare, nag, pad, palfrey, pony, stallion, steed; cavalry, horseman; buck, clotheshorse, frame, sawhorse, stand, support.

**horseman** n cavalier, equestrian, rider; cavalryman, chasseur, dragoon, horse-soldier.

**hospitable** adj attentive, bountiful, kind; bountiful, cordial, generous, liberal, open, receptive, sociable, unconstrained, unreserved.

**host**[1] n entertainer, innkeeper, landlord, master of ceremonies, presenter, proprietor, owner, receptionist.

**host**[2] n array, army, legion; assemblage, assembly, horde, multitude, throng.

**host**[3] n altar bread, bread, consecrated bread, loaf, wafer.

**hostile** adj inimical, unfriendly, warlike; adverse, antagonistic, contrary, opposed, opposite, repugnant.

**hostilities** npl conflict, fighting, war, warfare.

**hostility** n animosity, antagonism, enmity, hatred, ill-will, unfriendliness; contrariness, opposition, repugnance, variance.

**hot** adj burning, fiery, scalding; boiling, flaming, heated, incandescent, parching, roasting, torrid; heated, oppressive, sweltering, warm; angry, choleric, excitable, furious, hasty, impatient, impetuous, irascible, lustful, passionate, touchy, urgent, violent; animated, ardent, eager, fervent, fervid, glowing, passionate, vehement; acrid, biting, highly flavoured, highly seasoned, peppery, piquant, pungent, sharp, stinging.

**hotchpotch** n farrago, jumble, hodgepodge, medley, miscellany, stew.

**hotel** n inn, public house, tavern.

**hot-headed** adj furious, headlong, headstrong, hot-brained, impetuous, inconsiderate, passionate, precipitate, rash, reckless, vehement, violent.

**hound** vb drive, incite, spur, urge; bate, chase, goad, harass, harry, hunt, pursue.

**house** vb harbour, lodge, protect, shelter. * n abode, domicile, dwelling, habitation, home, mansion, residence; building, edifice; family, household; kindred, race, lineage, tribe; company, concern, firm, partnership; hotel, inn, public house, tavern.

**housing** n accommodation, dwellings, houses; casing, container, covering, protection, shelter.

**hovel** n cabin, cot, den, hole, hut, shed.

**hover** vb flutter; hang; vacillate, waver.

**however** adv but, however, nevertheless, notwithstanding, still, though, yet.

**howl** vb bawl, cry, lament, ululate, weep, yell, yowl. * n cry, yell, ululation.

**hoyden** n romp, tomboy.

**hoydenish** adj bad-mannered, boisterous, bold, ill-behaved, ill-taught, inelegant, romping, rough, rude, rustic, tomboyish, uncouth, ungenteel, unladylike, unruly.

**hubbub** n clamour, confusion, din, disorder, disturbance, hullabaloo, racket, riot, outcry, tumult, uproar.

**huckster** n hawker, peddler, retailer.

**huddle** vb cluster, crowd, gather; crouch, curl up, nestle, snuggle. * n confusion, crowd, disorder, disturbance, jumble, tumult.

**hue** n cast, colour, complexion, dye, shade, tinge, tint, tone.

**huff** vb blow, breathe, exhale, pant, puff. * n anger, fume, miff, passion, pet, quarrel, rage, temper, tiff.

**hug** vb clasp, cling, cuddle, embrace, grasp, grip, squeeze; cherish, nurse, retain. * n clasp, cuddle, embrace, grasp, squeeze.

**huge** adj bulky, colossal, Cyclopean, elephantine, enormous, gigantic, herculean, immense, stupendous, vast,

**huggermugger** adj clandestine, secret, sly; base, contemptible, mean, unfair; confused, disorderly, slovenly.

**hull** vb husk, peel, shell. * n covering, husk, rind, shell.

**hullabaloo** n clamour, confusion, din, disturbance, hubbub, outcry, racket, vociferation, uproar.

**hum** vb buzz, drone, murmur; croon, sing.

**humane** adj accommodating, benevolent, benign, charitable, clement, compassionate, gentle, good-hearted, kind, kind-hearted, lenient, merciful, obliging, tender, sympathetic; cultivating, elevating, humanizing, refining, rational, spiritual.

**humanity** n benevolence, benignity, charity, fellow-feeling, humaneness, kind-heartedness, kindness, philanthropy, sympathy, tenderness; humankind, mankind, mortality.

**humanize** vb civilize, cultivate, educate, enlighten, improve, polish, reclaim, refine, soften.

**humble** vb abase, abash, break, crush, debase, degrade, disgrace, humiliate, lower, mortify, reduce, sink, subdue. * adj meek, modest, lowly, simple, submissive, unambitious, unassuming, unobtrusive, unostentatious, unpretending; low, obscure, mean, plain, poor, small, undistinguished, unpretentious.

**humbug** vb cheat, cozen, deceive, hoax, swindle,

trick. * n cheat, dodge, gammon, hoax, imposition, imposture, deception, fraud, trick; cant, charlatanism, charlatanry, hypocrisy, mummery, quackery; charlatan, impostor, fake, quack.

**humdrum** adj boring, dronish, dreary, dry, dull, monotonous, prosy, stupid, tedious, tiresome, wearisome.

**humid** adj damp, dank, moist, wet.

**humiliate** vb abase, abash, debase, degrade, depress, humble, mortify, shame.

**humiliation** n abasement, affront, condescension, crushing, degradation, disgrace, dishonouring, humbling, indignity, mortification, self-abasement, submissiveness, resignation.

**humility** n diffidence, humbleness, lowliness, meekness, modesty, self-abasement, submissiveness.

**humorist** n comic, comedian, droll, jester, joker, wag, wit.

**humorous** adj comic, comical, droll, facetious, funny, humorous, jocose, jocular, laughable, ludicrous, merry, playful, pleasant, sportive, whimsical, witty.

**humour** vb favour, gratify, indulge. * n bent, bias, disposition, predilection, prosperity, temper, vein; mood, state; caprice, crotchet, fancy, freak, vagary, whim, whimsy, wrinkle; drollery, facetiousness, fun, jocoseness, jocularity, pleasantry, wit; fluid, moisture, vapour.

**hunch** vb arch, jostle, nudge, punch, push, shove. * n bunch, hump, knob, protuberance; nudge, punch, push, shove; feeling, idea, intuition, premonition.

**hungry** adj covetous, craving, desirous, greedy; famished, starved, starving; barren, poor, unfertile, unproductive.

**hunk** n chunk, hunch, lump, slice.

**hunt** vb chase, drive, follow, hound, pursue, stalk, trap, trail; poach, shoot; search, seek. * n chase, field-sport, hunting, pursuit.

**hurl** vb cast, dart, fling, pitch, project, send, sling, throw, toss.

**hurly-burly** n bustle, commotion, confusion, disturbance, hurl, hurly, uproar, tumult, turmoil.

**hurricane** n cyclone, gale, storm, tempest, tornado, typhoon.

**hurried** adj cursory, hasty, slight, superficial.

**hurry** vb drive, precipitate; dispatch, expedite, hasten, quicken, speed; haste, scurry. * n agitation, bustle, confusion, flurry, flutter, perturbation, precipitation; celerity, haste, dispatch, expedition, promptitude, promptness, quickness.

**hurt** vb damage, disable, disadvantage, harm, impair, injure, mar; bruise, pain, wound; afflict, grieve, offend; ache, smart, throb. * n damage, detriment, disadvantage, harm, injury, mischief; ache, bruise, pain, suffering, wound.

**hurtful** adj baleful, baneful, deleterious, destructive, detrimental, disadvantageous, harmful, injurious, mischievous, noxious, pernicious, prejudicial, unwholesome.

**husband** vb economize, hoard, save, store.

**husbandry** n agriculture, cultivation, farming, geoponics, tillage; economy, frugality, thrift.

**hush** vb quiet, repress, silence, still, suppress; appease, assuage, calm, console, quiet, still. * n quiet, quietness, silence, stillness.

**hypocrite** n deceiver, dissembler, impostor, pretender.

**hypocritical** adj deceiving, dissembling, false, insincere, spurious, two-faced.

**hypothesis** n assumption, proposition, supposition, theory.

**hypothetical** adj assumed, imaginary, supposed, theoretical.

**hysterical** adj frantic, frenzied, overwrought, uncontrollable; comical, uproarious.

# I

**ice** *vb* chill, congeal, freeze. * *n* crystal; frosting, sugar.

**icy** *adj* glacial; chilling, cold, frosty; cold-hearted, distant, frigid, indifferent, unemotional.

**idea** *n* archetype, essence, exemplar, ideal, model, pattern, plan, model; fantasy, fiction, image, imagination; apprehension, conceit, conception, fancy, illusion, impression, thought; belief, judgement, notion, opinion, sentiment, supposition.

**ideal** *adj* intellectual, mental; chimerical, fancied, fanciful, fantastic, illusory, imaginary, unreal, visionary, shadowy; complete, consummate, excellent, perfect; impractical, unattainable, utopian. * *n* criterion, example, model, standard.

**identical** *adj* equivalent, same, selfsame, tantamount.

**identity** *n* existence, individuality, personality, sameness.

**ideology** *n* belief, creed, dogma, philosophy, principle. .

**idiocy** *n* fatuity, feebleness, foolishness, imbecility, insanity.

**idiosyncrasy** *n* caprice, eccentricity, fad, peculiarity, singularity.

**idiot** *n* blockhead, booby, dunce, fool, ignoramus, imbecile, simpleton.

**idiotic** *adj* fatuous, foolish, imbecile, irrational, senseless, sottish, stupid.

**idle** *adj* inactive, unemployed, unoccupied, vacant; indolent, inert, lazy, slothful, sluggish; abortive, bootless, fruitless, futile, groundless, ineffectual, unavailing, useless, vain; foolish, frivolous, trashy, trifling, trivial, unimportant, unprofitable. * *vb* dally, dawdle, laze, loiter, potter, waste; drift, shirk, slack.

**idler** *n* dawdler, doodle, drone, laggard, lazybones, loafer, lounger, slacker, slowcoach, sluggard, trifler.

**idol** *n* deity, god, icon, image, pagan, simulacrum, symbol; delusion, falsity, pretender, sham; beloved, darling, favourite, pet.

**idolater** *n* heathen, pagan; admirer, adorer, worshipper.

**idolize** *vb* canonize, deify; adore, honour, love, reverence, venerate.

**idyll** *n* eclogue, pastoral.

**if** *conj* admitting, allowing, granting, provided, supposing, though, whether. * *n* condition, hesitation, uncertainty.

**igneous** *adj* combustible, combustive, conflagrative, fiery, molten.

**ignite** *vb* burn, inflame, kindle, light, torch.

**ignoble** *adj* base-born, low, low-born, mean, peasant, plebeian, rustic, vulgar; contemptible, degraded, insignificant, mean, worthless; disgraceful, dishonourable, infamous, low, unworthy.

**ignominious** *adj* discreditable, disgraceful, dishonourable, disreputable, infamous, opprobrious, scandalous, shameful; base, contemptible, despicable.

**ignominy** *n* abasement, contempt, discredit, disgrace, dishonour disrepute, infamy, obloquy, odium, opprobrium, scandal, shame.

**ignoramus** *n* blockhead, duffer, dunce, fool, greenhorn, novice, numskull, simpleton.

**ignorance** *n* benightedness, darkness, illiteracy, nescience, rusticity; blindness, unawareness.

**ignorant** *adj* blind, illiterate, nescient, unaware, unconversant, uneducated, unenlightened, uninformed, uninstructed, unlearned, unread, untaught, untutored, unwitting.

**ignore** *vb* disregard, neglect, overlook, reject, skip.

**ill** *adj* bad, evil, faulty, harmful, iniquitous, naughty, unfavourable, unfortunate, unjust, wicked; ailing, diseased, disordered, indisposed, sick, unwell, wrong; crabbed, cross, hateful, malicious, malevolent, peevish, surly, unkind, ill-bred; ill-favoured, ugly, unprepossessing. * *adv* badly, poorly, unfortunately. * *n* badness, depravity, evil, mischief, misfortune, wickedness; affliction, ailment, calamity, harm, misery, pain, trouble.

**ill-advised** *adj* foolish, ill-judged, imprudent, injudicious, unwise.

**ill-bred** *adj* discourteous, ill-behaved, ill-mannered, impolite, rude, uncivil, uncourteous, uncourtly, uncouth.

**illegal** *adj* contraband, forbidden, illegitimate, illicit, prohibited, unauthorized, unlawful, unlicensed.

**illegible** *adj* indecipherable, obscure, undecipherable, unreadable.

**illegitimate** *adj* bastard, misbegotten, natural.

**ill-fated** *adj* ill-starred, luckless, unfortunate, unlucky.

**ill-favoured** *adj* homely, ugly, offensive, plain, unpleasant.

**ill humour** *n* fretfulness, ill-temper, peevishness, petulance, testiness.

**illiberal** *adj* close, close-fisted, covetous, mean, miserly, narrow, niggardly, parsimonious, penurious, selfish, sordid, stingy, ungenerous; bigoted, narrow-minded, uncharitable, ungentlemanly, vulgar.

**illicit** *adj* illegal, illegitimate, unauthorized, unlawful, unlegalized, unlicensed; criminal, guilty, forbidden, improper, wrong.

**illimitable** *adj* boundless, endless, immeasurable, immense, infinite, unbounded, unlimited, vast.

**illiterate** *adj* ignorant, uneducated, uninstructed, unlearned, unlettered, untaught, untutored.

**ill-judged** *adj* foolish, ill-advised, imprudent, injudicious, unwise.

**ill-mannered** *adj* discourteous, ill-behaved, ill-bred, impolite, rude, uncivil, uncourteous, uncourtly, uncouth, unpolished.

**ill-natured** *adj* disobliging, hateful, malevolent, unamiable, unfriendly, unkind; acrimonious, bitter, churlish, crabbed, cross, cross-grained, crusty, ill-tempered, morose, perverse, petulant, sour, spiteful, sulky, sullen, wayward.

**illness** *n* ailing, ailment, complaint, disease, disorder, distemper, indisposition, malady, sickness.

**illogical** *adj* absurd, fallacious, inconsistent, inconclusive, inconsequent, incorrect, invalid, unreasonable, unsound.

**ill-proportioned** *adj* awkward, ill-made, ill-shaped, misshapen, misproportioned, shapeless.

**ill-starred** *adj* ill-fated, luckless, unfortunate, unhappy, unlucky.

**ill temper** *n* bad temper, crabbedness, crossness, grouchiness, ill nature, moroseness, sulkiness, sullenness.

**ill-tempered** *adj* acrimonious, bad-tempered, crabbed, cross, grouchy, ill-natured, morose, sour, sulky, surly.

**ill-timed** *adj* inapposite, inopportune, irrelevant, unseasonable, untimely.

**ill-treat** *vb* abuse, ill-use, injure, maltreat, mishandle, misuse.

**illude** *vb* cheat, deceive, delude, disappoint, mock, swindle, trick.

**illuminate** *vb* illume, illumine, light; adorn, brighten, decorate, depict, edify, enlighten, inform, inspire, instruct, make wise.

**illusion** *n* chimera, deception, delusion, error, fallacy, false appearance, fantasy, hallucination, mockery, phantasm.

**illusive, illusory** *adj* barmecide, deceitful, deceptive, delusive, fallacious, imaginary, make-believe, mock, sham, unsatisfying, unreal, unsubstantial, visionary, tantalizing.

**illustrate** *vb* clarify, demonstrate, elucidate, enlighten, exemplify, explain; adorn, depict, draw.

**illustration** *n* demonstration, elucidation, enlightenment, exemplification, explanation, interpretation; adornment, decoration, picture.

**illustrative** *adj* elucidative, elucidatory, exemplifying.

**illustrious** *adj* bright, brilliant, glorious, radiant, splendid; celebrated, conspicuous, distinguished, eminent, famed, famous, noble, noted, remarkable, renowned, signal.

**ill will** *n* animosity, dislike, enmity, envy, grudge, hate, hatred, hostility, ill nature, malevolence, malice, malignity, rancour, spleen, spite, uncharitableness, unkindness, venom.

**image** *n* idol, statue; copy, effigy, figure, form, imago, likeness, picture, resemblance, representation, shape, similitude, simulacrum, statue, symbol; conception, counterpart, embodiment, idea, reflection.

**imagery** *n* dream, phantasm, phantom, vision.

**imaginable** *adj* assumable, cogitable, conceivable, conjecturable, plausible, possible, supposable, thinkable.

**imaginary** *adj* chimerical, dreamy, fancied, fanciful, fantastic, fictitious, ideal, illusive, illusory, invented, quixotic, shadowy, unreal, utopian, visionary, wild; assumed, conceivable, hypothetical, supposed.

**imagination** *n* chimera, conception, fancy, fantasy, invention, unreality; position; contrivance, device, plot, scheme.

**imaginative** *adj* creative, dreamy, fanciful, inventive, poetical, plastic, visionary.

**imagine** vb conceive, dream, fancy, imagine, picture, pretend; contrive, create, devise, frame, invent, mould, project; assume, suppose, hypothesize; apprehend, assume, believe, deem, guess, opine, suppose, think.

**imbecile** adj cretinous, drivelling, fatuous, feeble, feeble-minded, foolish, helpless, idiotic, imbecilic, inane, infirm, witless. * n dotard, driveller.

**imbecility** n debility, feebleness, helplessness, infirmity, weakness; foolishness, idiocy, silliness, stupidity, weak-mindedness.

**imbibe** vb absorb, assimilate, drink, suck, swallow; acquire, gain, gather, get, receive.

**imbroglio** n complexity, complication, embarrassment, entanglement, misunderstanding.

**imbrue** vb drench, embrue, gain, moisten, soak, stain, steep, wet.

**imbue** vb colour, dye, stain, tincture, tinge, tint; bathe, impregnate, infuse, inoculate, permeate, pervade, provide, saturate, steep.

**imitate** vb copy, counterfeit, duplicate, echo, emulate, follow, forge, mirror, reproduce, simulate; ape, impersonate, mimic, mock, personate; burlesque, parody, travesty.

**imitation** adj artificial, fake, man-made, mock, reproduction, synthetic. * n aping, copying, imitation, mimicking, parroting; copy, duplicate, likeness, resemblance; mimicry, mocking; burlesque, parody, travesty.

**imitative** adj copying, emulative, imitating, mimetic, simulative; apeish, aping, mimicking.

**imitator** n copier, copycat, copyist, echo, impersonator, mimic, mimicker, parrot.

**immaculate** adj clean, pure, spotless, stainless, unblemished, uncontaminated, undefiled, unpolluted, unspotted, unsullied, untainted, untarnished; faultless, guiltless, holy, innocent, pure, saintly, sinless, stainless.

**immanent** adj congenital, inborn, indwelling, inherent, innate, internal, intrinsic, subjective.

**immaterial** adj bodiless, ethereal, extramundane, impalpable, incorporeal, mental, metaphysical, spiritual, unbodied, unfleshly, unsubstantial; inconsequential, insignificant, nonessential, unessential, unimportant.

**immature** adj crude, green, imperfect, raw, rudimental, rudimentary, unfinished, unformed, unprepared, unripe, unripened, youthful; hasty, premature, unseasonable, untimely.

**immaturity** n crudeness, crudity, greenness, imperfection, rawness, unpreparedness, unripeness.

**immeasurable** adj bottomless, boundless, illimitable, immense, infinite, limitless, measureless, unbounded, vast.

**immediate** adj close, contiguous, near, next, proximate; intuitive, primary, unmeditated; direct, instant, instantaneous, present, pressing, prompt.

**immediately** adv closely, proximately; directly, forthwith, instantly, presently, presto, pronto.

**immemorial** adj ancient, hoary, olden.

**immense** adj boundless, illimitable, infinite, interminable, measureless, unbounded, unlimited; colossal, elephantine, enormous, gigantic, huge, large, monstrous, mountainous, prodigious, stupendous, titanic, tremendous, vast.

**immensity** n boundlessness, endlessness, limitlessness, infiniteness, infinitude, infinity; amplitude, enormity, greatness, hugeness, magnitude, vastness.

**immerse** vb baptize, bathe, dip, douse, duck, overwhelm, plunge, sink, souse, submerge; absorb, engage, engross, involve.

**immersion** n dipping, immersing, plunging; absorption, engagement; disappearance; baptism.

**imminent** adj close, impending, near, overhanging, threatening; alarming, dangerous, perilous.

**immobile** adj fixed, immovable, inflexible, motionless, quiescent, stable, static, stationary, steadfast; dull, expressionless, impassive, rigid, stiff, stolid.

**immobility** n fixedness, fixity, immovability, immovableness, motionlessness, stability, steadfastness, unmovableness; dullness, expressionlessness, inflexibility, rigidity, stiffness, stolidity.

**immoderate** adj excessive, exorbitant, extravagant, extreme, inordinate, intemperate, unreasonable.

**immodest** adj coarse, gross, indecorous, indelicate, lewd, shameless; bold, brazen, forward, impudent, indecent; broad, filthy, impure, indecent, obscene, smutty, unchaste.

**immodesty** n coarseness, grossness, indecorum, indelicacy, shamelessness; impurity, lewdness, obscenity, smuttiness, unchastity; boldness, brass, forwardness, impatience.

**immolate** vb kill, sacrifice.

**immoral** adj antisocial, corrupt, loose, sinful, unethical, vicious, wicked, wrong; bad, depraved, dissolute, profligate, unprincipled; abandoned, indecent, licentious.

**immorality** n corruption, corruptness, criminality, demoralization, depravity, impurity, profligacy, sin, sinfulness, vice, wickedness; wrong.

**immortal** adj deathless, ever-living, imperishable, incorruptible, indestructible, indissoluble, never-dying, undying, unfading; ceaseless, continuing, eternal, endless, everlasting, never-ending, perpetual, sempiternal; abiding, enduring, lasting, permanent. * n god, goddess; genius, hero.

**immortality** n deathlessness, incorruptibility, incorruptibleness, indestructibility; perpetuity.

**immortalize** vb apotheosize, enshrine, glorify, perpetuate.

**immovable** adj firm, fixed, immobile, stable, stationary; impassive, steadfast, unalterable, unchangeable, unshaken, unyielding.

**immunity** n exemption, exoneration, freedom, release; charter, franchise, liberty, license, prerogative, privilege, right.

**immure** vb confine, entomb, imprison, incarcerate.

**immutability** n constancy, inflexibility, invariability, invariableness, permanence, stability, unalterableness, unchangeableness.

**immutable** adj constant, fixed, inflexible, invariable, permanent, stable, unalterable, unchangeable, undeviating.

**imp** n demon, devil, elf, flibbertigibbet, hobgoblin, scamp, sprite; graft, scion, shoot.

**impact** vb collide, crash, strike. * n brunt, impression, impulse, shock, stroke, touch; collision, contact, impinging, striking.

**impair** vb blemish, damage, deface, deteriorate, injure, mar, ruin, spoil, vitiate; decrease, diminish, lessen, reduce; enervate, enfeeble, weaken.

**impale** vb hole, pierce, puncture, spear, spike, stab, transfix.

**impalpable** adj attenuated, delicate, fine, intangible; imperceptible, inapprehensible, incorporeal, indistinct, shadowy, unsubstantial.

**impart** vb bestow, confer, give, grant; communicate, disclose, discover, divulge, relate, reveal, share, tell.

**impartial** adj candid, disinterested, dispassionate, equal, equitable, even-handed, fair, honourable, just, unbiased, unprejudiced, unwarped.

**impassable** adj blocked, closed, impenetrable, impermeable, impervious, inaccessible, pathless, unattainable, unnavigable, unreachable.

**impassioned** adj animated, ardent, burning, excited, fervent, fervid, fiery, glowing, impetuous, intense, passionate, vehement, warm, zealous.

**impassive** adj calm, passionless; apathetic, callous, indifferent, insensible, insusceptible, unfeeling, unimpressible, unsusceptible.

**impassivity** n calmness, composure, indifference, insensibility, insusceptibility, passionlessness, stolidity.

**impatience** n disquietude, restlessness, uneasiness; eagerness, haste, impetuosity, precipitation, vehemence; heat, irritableness, irritability, violence.

**impatient** adj restless, uneasy, unquiet; eager, hasty, impetuous, precipitate, vehement; abrupt, brusque, choleric, fretful, hot, intolerant, irritable, peevish, sudden, testy, violent.

**impeach** vb accuse, arraign, charge, indict; asperse, censure, denounce, disparage, discredit, impair, impute, incriminate, lessen.

**impeachment** n accusation, arraignment, indictment; aspersion, censure, disparagement, imputation, incrimination, reproach.

**impeccable** adj faultless, immaculate, incorrupt, innocent, perfect, pure, sinless, stainless, uncorrupt.

**impede** vb bar, block, check, clog, curb, delay, encumber, hinder, interrupt, obstruct, restrain, retard, stop, thwart.

**impediment** n bar, barrier, block, check, curb, difficulty, encumbrance, hindrance, obstacle, obstruction, stumbling block.

**impel** vb drive, push, send, urge; actuate, animate, compel, constrain, embolden, incite, induce, influence, instigate, move, persuade, stimulate.

**impend** vb approach, menace, near, threaten.

**impending** adj approaching, imminent, menacing, near, threatening.

**impenetrable** adj impermeable, impervious, inaccessible; cold, dull, impassive, indifferent, obtuse, senseless, stolid, unsympathetic; dense, proof.

**impenitence** n hardheartedness, impenitency, impenitentness, obduracy, stubbornness.

**impenitent** adj hardened; hard-hearted, incorrigible, irreclaimable, obdurate, recusant, relentless, seared, stubborn, uncontrite, unconverted, unrepentant.

**imperative** adj authoritative, commanding, despotic, domineering, imperious, overbearing, peremptory, urgent; binding, obligatory.

**imperceptible** *adj* inaudible, indiscernible, indistinguishable, invisible; fine, impalpable, inappreciable, gradual, minute.

**imperfect** *adj* abortive, crude, deficient, garbled, incomplete, poor; defective, faulty, impaired.

**imperfection** *n* defectiveness, deficiency, faultiness, incompleteness; blemish, defect, fault, flaw, lack, stain, taint; failing, foible, frailty, limitation, vice, weakness.

**imperial** *adj* kingly, regal, royal, sovereign; august, consummate, exalted, grand, great, kingly, magnificent, majestic, noble, regal, royal, queenly, supreme, sovereign, supreme, consummate.

**imperil** *vb* endanger, expose, hazard, jeopardize, risk.

**imperious** *adj* arrogant, authoritative, commanding, compelling, despotic, dictatorial, domineering, haughty, imperative, lordly, magisterial, overbearing, tyrannical, urgent, compelling.

**imperishable** *adj* eternal, everlasting, immortal, incorruptible, indestructible, never-ending, perennial, unfading.

**impermeable** *adj* impenetrable, impervious.

**impermissible** *adj* deniable, insufferable, objectionable, unallowable, unallowed, unlawful.

**impersonate** *vb* act, ape, enact, imitate, mimic, mock, personate; embody, incarnate, personify, typify.

**impersonation** *n* incarnation, manifestation, personification; enacting, imitation, impersonating, mimicking, personating, representation.

**impertinence** *n* irrelevance, irrelevancy, unfitness, impropriety; assurance, boldness, brass, brazenness, effrontery, face, forwardness, impudence, incivility, insolence, intrusiveness, presumption, rudeness, sauciness, pertness.

**impertinent** *adj* inapplicable, inapposite, irrelevant; bold, forward, impudent, insolent, intrusive, malapert, meddling, officious, pert, rude, saucy, unmannerly.

**imperturbability** *n* calmness, collectedness, composure, dispassion, placidity, placidness, sedateness, serenity, steadiness, tranquility.

**imperturbable** *adj* calm, collected, composed, cool, placid, sedate, serene, tranquil, unmoved, undisturbed, unexcitable, unmoved, unruffled.

**impervious** *adj* impassable, impenetrable, impermeable.

**impetuosity** *n* force, fury, haste, precipitancy, vehemence, violence.

**impetuous** *adj* ardent, boisterous, brash, breakneck, fierce, fiery, furious, hasty, headlong, hot, hot-headed, impulsive, overzealous, passionate, precipitate, vehement, violent.

**impetus** *n* energy, force, momentum, propulsion.

**impiety** *n* irreverence, profanity, ungodliness; iniquity, sacreligiousness, sin, sinfulness, ungodliness, unholiness, unrighteousness, wickedness.

**impinge** *vb* clash, dash, encroach, hit, infringe, strike, touch.

**impious** *adj* blasphemous, godless, iniquitous, irreligious, irreverent, profane, sinful, ungodly, unholy, unrighteous, wicked.

**implacable** *adj* deadly, inexorable, merciless, pitiless, rancorous, relentless, unappeasable, unforgiving, unpropitiating, unrelenting.

**implant** *vb* ingraft, infix, insert, introduce, place.

**implement** *vb* effect, execute, fulfil. * *n* appliance, instrument, tool, utensil.

**implicate** *vb* entangle, enfold; compromise, concern, entangle, include, involve.

**implication** *n* entanglement, involvement, involution; connotation, hint, inference, innuendo, intimation; conclusion, meaning, significance.

**implicit** *adj* implied, inferred, understood; absolute, constant, firm, steadfast, unhesitating, unquestioning, unreserved, unshaken.

**implicitly** *adv* by implication, silently, tacitly, unspokenly, virtually, wordlessly.

**implore** *vb* adjure, ask, beg, beseech, entreat, petition, pray, solicit, supplicate.

**imply** *vb* betoken, connote, denote, import, include, infer, insinuate, involve, mean, presuppose, signify.

**impolicy** *n* folly, imprudence, ill-judgement, indiscretion, inexpediency.

**impolite** *adj* bearish, boorish, discourteous, disrespectful, ill-bred, insolent, rough, rude, uncivil, uncourteous, ungentle, ungentlemanly, ungracious, unmannerly, unpolished, unrefined.

**impoliteness** *n* boorishness, discourteousness, discourtesy, disrespect, ill-breeding, incivility, insolence, rudeness, unmannerliness.

**impolitic** *adj* ill-advised, imprudent, indiscreet, inexpedient, injudicious, unwise.

**import** *vb* bring in, introduce, transport; betoken, denote, imply, mean, purport, signify. * *n* goods, importation, merchandise; bearing, drift, gist, intention, interpretation, matter, meaning, purpose, sense, signification, spirit, tenor; consequence, importance, significance, weight.

**importance** n concern, consequence, gravity, import, moment, momentousness, significance, weight, weightiness; consequence, pomposity, self-importance.

**important** adj considerable, grave, material, momentous, notable, pompous, ponderous, serious, significant, urgent, valuable, weighty; esteemed, influential, prominent, substantial; consequential, pompous, self-important.

**importunate** adj busy, earnest, persistent, pertinacious, pressing, teasing, troublesome, urgent.

**importune** vb ask, beset, dun, ply, press, solicit, urge.

**importunity** n appeal, beseechment, entreaty, petition, plying, prayer, pressing, suit, supplication, urging; contention, insistence; urgency.

**impose** vb lay, place, put, set; appoint, charge, dictate, enjoin, force, inflict, obtrude, prescribe, tax; (with **on, upon**) abuse, cheat, circumvent, deceive, delude, dupe, exploit, hoax, trick, victimize.

**imposing** adj august, commanding, dignified, exalted, grand, grandiose, impressive, lofty, magnificent, majestic, noble, stately, striking.

**imposition** n imposing, laying, placing, putting; burden, charge, constraint, injunction, levy, oppression, tax; artifice, cheating, deception, dupery, fraud, imposture, trickery.

**impossibility** n hopelessness, impracticability, inability, infeasibility, unattainability; inconceivability.

**impossible** adj hopeless, impracticable, infeasible, unachievable, unattainable; inconceivable, self-contradictory, unthinkable.

**impost** n custom, duty, excise, rate, tax, toil, tribute.

**impostor** n charlatan, cheat, counterfeiter, deceiver, double-dealer, humbug, hypocrite, knave, mountebank, pretender, quack, rogue, trickster.

**imposture** n artifice, cheat, deceit, deception, delusion, dodge, fraud, hoax, imposition, ruse, stratagem, trick, wile.

**impotence** n disability, feebleness, frailty, helplessness, inability, incapability, incapacity, incompetence, inefficaciousness, inefficacy, inefficiency, infirmity, powerlessness, weakness.

**impotent** adj disabled, enfeebled, feeble, frail, helpless, incapable, incapacitated, incompetent, inefficient, infirm, nerveless, powerless, unable, weak; barren, sterile.

**impound** vb confine, coop, engage, imprison.

**impoverish** vb beggar, pauperize; deplete, exhaust, ruin.

**impracticability** n impossibility, impracticableness, impracticality, infeasibility, unpracticability.

**impracticable** adj impossible, infeasible; intractable, obstinate, recalcitrant, stubborn, thorny, unmanageable; impassable, insurmountable.

**impracticality** n impossibility, impracticableness, impractibility, infeasibility, unpracticability; irrationality, unpracticalness, unrealism, unreality, unreasonableness.

**imprecate** vb anathematize, curse, execrate, invoke, maledict.

**imprecation** n anathema, curse, denunciation, execration, invocation, malediction.

**imprecatory** adj appealing, beseeching, entreating, imploratory, imploring, imprecatory, pleading; cursing, damnatory, execrating, maledictory.

**impregnable** adj immovable, impenetrable, indestructible, invincible, inviolable, invulnerable, irrefrangible, secure, unconquerable, unassailable, unyielding.

**impregnate** vb fecundate, fertilize, fructify; dye, fill, imbrue, imbue, infuse, permeate, pervade, saturate, soak, tincture, tinge.

**impress** vb engrave, imprint, print, stamp; affect, move, strike; fix, inculcate; draft, enlist, levy, press, requisition. * n impression, imprint, mark, print, seal, stamp; cognizance, device, emblem, motto, symbol.

**impressibility** n affectibility, impressionability, pliancy, receptiveness, responsiveness, sensibility, sensitiveness, susceptibility.

**impressible** adj affectible, excitable, impressionable, pliant, receptive, responsive, sensitive, soft, susceptible, tender.

**impression** n edition, imprinting, printing, stamping; brand, dent, impress, mark, stamp; effect, influence, sensation; fancy, idea, instinct, notion, opinion, recollection.

**impressive** adj affecting, effective, emphatic, exciting, forcible, moving, overpowering, powerful, solemn, speaking, splendid, stirring, striking, telling, touching.

**imprint** vb engrave, mark, print, stamp; impress, inculcate. * n impression, mark, print, sign, stamp.

**imprison** vb confine, jail, immure, incarcerate, shut up.

**imprisonment** n captivity, commitment, confinement, constraint, durance, duress, incarceration, restraint.

**improbability** n doubt, uncertainty, unlikelihood.

**improbable** adj doubtful, uncertain, unlikely, unplausible.

**improbity** n dishonesty, faithlessness, fraud, fraudulence, knavery, unfairness.

**impromptu** adj extempore, improvised, offhand, spontaneous, unpremeditated, unprepared, unrehearsed. * adv extemporaneously, extemporarily, extempore, offhand, ad-lib.

**improper** adj immodest, inapposite, inappropriate, irregular, unadapted, unapt, unfit, unsuitable, unsuited; indecent, indecorous, indelicate, unbecoming, unseemly; erroneous, inaccurate, incorrect, wrong.

**impropriety** n inappropriateness, unfitness, unsuitability, unsuitableness; indecorousness, indecorum, unseemliness.

**improve** vb ameliorate, amend, better, correct, edify, meliorate, mend, rectify, reform; cultivate; gain, mend, progress; enhance, increase, rise.

**improvement** n ameliorating, amelioration, amendment, bettering, improving, meliorating, melioration; advancement, proficiency, progress.

**improvidence** n imprudence, thriftlessness, unthriftiness.

**improvident** adj careless, heedless, imprudent, incautious, inconsiderate, negligent, prodigal, rash, reckless, shiftless, thoughtless, thriftless, unthrifty, wasteful.

**improvisation** n ad-libbing, contrivance, extemporaneousness, extemporariness, extemporization, fabrication, invention; (mus) extempore, impromptu.

**improvise** vb ad-lib, contrive, extemporize, fabricate, imagine, invent.

**imprudence** n carelessness, heedlessness, improvidence, incautiousness, inconsideration, indiscretion, rashness.

**imprudent** adj careless, heedless, ill-advised, ill-judged, improvident, incautious, inconsiderate, indiscreet, rash, unadvised, unwise.

**impudence** n assurance, audacity, boldness, brashness, brass, bumptiousness, cheek, cheekiness, effrontery, face, flippancy, forwardness, front, gall, impertinence, insolence, jaw, lip, nerve, pertness, presumption, rudeness, sauciness, shamelessness.

**impudent** adj bold, bold-faced, brazen, brazen-faced, cool, flippant, forward, immodest, impertinent, insolent, insulting, pert, presumptuous, rude, saucy, shameless.

**impugn** vb assail, attack, challenge, contradict, dispute, gainsay, oppose, question, resist.

**impulse** n force, impetus, impelling, momentum, push, thrust; appetite, inclination, instinct, passion, proclivity; incentive, incitement, influence, instigation, motive, instigation.

**impulsive** adj impelling, moving, propulsive; emotional, hasty, heedless, hot, impetuous, mad-cap, passionate, quick, rash, vehement, violent.

**impunity** n exemption, immunity, liberty, licence, permission, security.

**impure** adj defiled, dirty, feculent, filthy, foul, polluted, unclean; bawdy, coarse, immodest, gross, immoral, indelicate, indecent, lewd, licentious, loose, obscene, ribald, smutty, unchaste; adulterated, corrupt, mixed.

**impurity** n defilement, feculence, filth, foulness, pollution, uncleanness; admixture, coarseness, grossness, immodesty, indecency, indelicacy, lewdness, licentiousness, looseness, obscenity, ribaldry, smut, smuttiness, unchastity, vulgarity.

**imputable** adj ascribable, attributable, chargeable, owing, referable, traceable, owing.

**imputation** n attributing, charging, imputing; accusation, blame, censure, charge, reproach.

**impute** vb ascribe, attribute, charge, consider, imply, insinuate, refer.

**inability** n impotence, incapacity, incapability, incompetence, incompetency, inefficiency; disability, disqualification.

**inaccessible** adj unapproachable, unattainable.

**inaccuracy** n erroneousness, impropriety, incorrectness, inexactness; blunder, defect, error, fault, mistake.

**inaccurate** adj defective, erroneous, faulty, incorrect, inexact, mistaken, wrong.

**inaccurately** adv carelessly, cursorily, imprecisely, incorrectly, inexactly, mistakenly, unprecisely, wrongly.

**inactive** adj inactive; dormant, inert, inoperative, peaceful, quiet, quiescent; dilatory, drowsy, dull, idle, inanimate, indolent, inert, lazy, lifeless, lumpish, passive, slothful, sleepy, stagnant, supine.

**inactivity** n dilatoriness, idleness, inaction, indolence, inertness, laziness, sloth, sluggishness, supineness, torpidity, torpor.

**inadequacy** n inadequateness, insufficiency; defectiveness, imperfection, incompetence, incompetency, incompleteness, insufficiency, unfitness, unsuitableness.

**inadequate** adj disproportionate, incapable, insufficient, unequal; defective, imperfect, inapt, incompetent, incomplete.

**inadmissible** adj improper, incompetent, unacceptable, unallowable, unqualified, unreasonable.

**inadvertence, inadvertency** n carelessness, heedlessness, inattention, inconsiderateness, negligence, thoughtlessness; blunder, error, oversight, slip.

**inadvertent** adj careless, heedless, inattentive, inconsiderate, negligent, thoughtless.

**inadvertently** adv accidently, carelessly, heedlessly, inconsiderately, negligently, thoughtlessly, unintentionally.

**inalienable** adj undeprivable, unforfeitable, untransferable.

**inane** adj empty, fatuous, vacuous, void; foolish, frivolous, idiotic, puerile, senseless, silly, stupid, trifling, vain, worthless.

**inanimate** adj breathless, dead, extinct; dead, dull, inert, lifeless, soulless, spiritless.

**inanition** n emptiness, inanity, vacuity; exhaustion, hunger, malnutrition, starvation, want.

**inanity** n emptiness, foolishness, inanition, vacuity; folly, frivolousness, puerility, vanity, worthlessness.

**inapplicable** adj inapposite, inappropriate, inapt, irrelevant, unfit, unsuitable, unsuited.

**inapposite** adj impertinent, inapplicable, irrelevant, nonpertinent; inappropriate, unfit, unsuitable.

**inappreciable** adj impalpable, imperceptible, inconsiderable, inconspicuous, indiscernible, infinitesimal, insignificant, negligible, undiscernible, unnoticed.

**inappropriate** adj inapposite, unadapted, unbecoming, unfit, unsuitable, unsullied.

**inapt** adj inapposite, unapt, unfit, unsuitable; awkward, clumsy, dull, slow, stolid, stupid.

**inaptitude** n awkwardness, inapplicability, inappropriateness, inaptness, unfitness, unsuitableness.

**inarticulate** adj blurred, indistinct, thick; dumb, mute.

**inartificial** adj artless, direct, guileless, ingenuous, naive, simple, simple-minded, sincere, single-minded.

**inasmuch as** conj considering that, seeing that, since.

**inattention** n absent-mindedness, carelessness, disregard, heedlessness, inadvertence, inapplication, inconsiderateness, neglect, remissness, slip, thoughtlessness, unmindfulness, unobservance

**inattentive** adj absent-minded, careless, disregarding, heedless, inadvertent, inconsiderate, neglectful, remiss, thoughtless, unmindful, unobservant.

**inaudible** adj faint, indistinct, muffled; mute, noiseless, silent, still.

**inaugurate** vb induct, install, introduce, invest; begin, commence, initiate, institute, originate.

**inauguration** n beginning, commencement, initiation, institution, investiture, installation, opening, origination.

**inauspicious** adj bad, discouraging, ill-omened, ill-starred, ominous, unfavourable, unfortunate, unlucky, unpromising, unpropitious, untoward.

**inborn** adj congenital, inbred, ingrained, inherent, innate, instinctive, native, natural.

**incalculable** adj countless, enormous, immense, incalculable, inestimable, innumerable, sumless, unknown, untold.

**incandescence** n candescence, glow, gleam, luminousness, luminosity.

**incandescent** adj aglow, candent, candescent, gleaming, glowing, luminous, luminant, radiant.

**incantation** n charm, conjuration, enchantment, magic, necromancy, sorcery, spell, witchcraft, witchery.

**incapability** n disability, inability, incapacity, incompetence.

**incapable** adj feeble, impotent, incompetent, insufficient, unable, unfit, unfitted, unqualified, weak.

**incapacious** adj cramped, deficient, incommodious, narrow, scant.

**incapacitate** vb cripple, disable; disqualify, make unfit.

**incapacity** n disability, inability, incapability, incompetence; disqualification, unfitness.

**incarcerate** vb commit, confine, immure, imprison, jail, restrain, restrict.

**incarnate** vb body, embody, incorporate, personify. * adj bodied, embodied, incorporated, personified.

**incarnation** n embodiment, exemplification, impersonation, manifestation, personification.

**incautious** adj impolitic, imprudent, indiscreet,

uncircumspect, unwary; careless, headlong, heedless, inconsiderate, negligent, rash, reckless, thoughtless.

**incendiary** adj dissentious, factious, inflammatory, seditious. * n agitator, firebrand, fire-raiser.

**incense**[1] vb anger, chafe, enkindle, enrage, exasperate, excite, heat, inflame, irritate, madden, provoke.

**incense**[2] n aroma, fragrance, perfume, scent; admiration, adulation, applause, laudation.

**incentive** n cause, encouragement, goad, impulse, incitement, inducement, instigation, mainspring, motive, provocation, spur, stimulus.

**inception** n beginning, commencement, inauguration, initiation, origin, rise, start.

**incertitude** n ambiguity, doubt, doubtfulness, indecision, uncertainty.

**incessant** adj ceaseless, constant, continual, continuous, eternal, everlasting, never-ending, perpetual, unceasing, unending, uninterrupted, unremitting.

**inchoate** adj beginning, commencing; inceptive, incipient, initial.

**incident** n circumstance, episode, event, fact, happening, occurrence. * adj happening; belonging, pertaining, appertaining, accessory, relating, natural; falling, impinging.

**incidental** adj accidental, casual, chance, concomitant, contingent, fortuitous, subordinate; adventitious, extraneous, nonessential, occasional.

**incinerate** vb burn, char, conflagrate, cremate, incremate.

**incipient** adj beginning, commencing, inchoate, inceptive, originating, starting.

**incised** adj carved, cut, engraved, gashed, graved, graven.

**incision** n cut, gash, notch, opening, penetration.

**incisive** adj cutting; acute, biting, sarcastic, satirical, sharp; acute, clear, distinct, penetrating, sharp-cut, trenchant.

**incite** vb actuate, animate, arouse, drive, encourage, excite, foment, goad, hound, impel, instigate, prod, prompt, provoke, push, rouse, spur, stimulate, urge.

**incitement** n encouragement, goad, impulse, incentive, inducement, motive, provocative, spur, stimulus.

**incivility** n discourteousness, discourtesy, disrespect, ill-breeding, ill-manners, impoliteness, impudence, inurbanity, rudeness, uncourtliness, unmannerliness.

**inclemency** n boisterousness, cruelty, harshness, rigour, roughness, severity, storminess, tempestuousness, tyranny.

**inclement** adj boisterous, harsh, rigorous, rough, severe, stormy; cruel, unmerciful.

**inclination** n inclining, leaning, slant, slope; trending, verging; aptitude, bent, bias, disposition, penchant, predilection, predisposition, proclivity, proneness, propensity, tendency, turn, twist; desire, fondness, liking, taste, partiality, predilection, wish; bow, nod, obeisance.

**incline** vb lean, slant, slope; bend, nod, verge; tend; bias, dispose, predispose, turn; bow. * n ascent, descent, grade, gradient, rise, slope.

**inclose** see **enclose**.

**include** vb contain, hold; comprehend, comprise, contain, cover, embody, embrace, incorporate, involve, take in.

**inclusive** adj comprehending, embracing, encircling, enclosing, including, taking in.

**incognito, incognita** adj camouflaged, concealed, disguised, unknown. * n camouflage, concealment, disguise.

**incoherent** adj detached, loose, nonadhesive, noncohesive; disconnected, incongruous, inconsequential, inconsistent, uncoordinated; confused, illogical, irrational, rambling, unintelligible, wild.

**income** n earnings, emolument, gains, interest, pay, perquisite, proceeds, profits, receipts, rents, return, revenue, salary, wages.

**incommensurate** adj disproportionate, inadequate, insufficient, unequal.

**incommode** vb annoy, discommode, disquiet, disturb, embarrass, hinder, inconvenience, molest, plague, trouble, upset, vex.

**incommodious** adj awkward, cumbersome, cumbrous, inconvenient, unhandy, unmanageable, unsuitable, unwieldy; annoying, disadvantageous, harassing, irritating, vexatious.

**incommunicative** adj exclusive, unsociable, unsocial, reserved.

**incomparable** adj matchless, inimitable, peerless, surpassing, transcendent, unequalled, unparalleled, unrivalled.

**incompatibility** n contrariety, contradictoriness, discrepancy, incongruity, inconsistency, irreconcilability, unsuitability, unsuitableness

**incompatible** adj contradictory, incongruous, inconsistent, inharmonious, irreconcilable, unadapted, unsuitable.

**incompetence** n inability, incapability, incapacity, incompetency; inadequacy, insufficiency; disqualification, unfitness.

**incompetent** adj incapable, unable; inadequate, insufficient; disqualified, incapacitated, unconstitutional, unfit, unfitted.

**incomplete** adj defective, deficient, imperfect, partial; inexhaustive, unaccompanied, uncompleted, unexecuted, unfinished.

**incomprehensible** adj inconceivable, inexhaustible, unfathomable, unimaginable; inconceivable, unintelligible, unthinkable.

**incomputable** adj enormous, immense, incalculable, innumerable, prodigious.

**inconceivable** adj incomprehensible, incredible, unbelievable, unimaginable, unthinkable.

**inconclusive** adj inconsequent, inconsequential, indecisive, unconvincing. illogical, unproved, unproven.

**incongruity** n absurdity, contradiction, contradictoriness, contrariety, discordance, discordancy, discrepancy, impropriety, inappropriateness, incoherence, incompatibility, inconsistency, unfitness, unsuitableness.

**incongruous** adj absurd, contradictory, contrary, disagreeing, discrepant, inappropriate, incoherent, incompatible, inconsistent, inharmonious, unfit, unsuitable.

**inconsequent** adj desultory, disconnected, fragmentary, illogical, inconclusive, inconsistent, irrelevant, loose.

**inconsiderable** adj immaterial, insignificant, petty, slight, small, trifling, trivial, unimportant.

**inconsiderate** adj intolerant, uncharitable, unthoughtful; careless, heedless, giddy, hare-brained, hasty, headlong, imprudent, inadvertent, inattentive, indifferent, indiscreet, light-headed, negligent, rash, thoughtless.

**inconsistency** n incoherence, incompatibility, incongruity, unsuitableness; contradiction, contrariety; changeableness, inconstancy, instability, vacillation, unsteadiness.

**inconsistent** adj different, discrepant, illogical, incoherent, incompatible, incongruous, inconsequent, inconsonant, irreconcilable, unsuitable; contradictory, contrary; changeable, fickle, inconstant, unstable, unsteady, vacillating, variable.

**inconsolable** adj comfortless, crushed, disconsolate, forlorn, heartbroken, hopeless, woebegone.

**inconstancy** n changeableness, mutability, variability, variation, fluctuation, faithlessness, fickleness, capriciousness, vacillation, uncertainty, unsteadiness, volatility.

**inconstant** adj capricious, changeable, faithless, fickle, fluctuating, mercurial, mutable, unsettled, unsteady, vacillating, variable, varying, volatile, wavering; mutable, uncertain, unstable.

**incontestable** adj certain, incontrovertible, indisputable, indubitable, irrefrangible, sure, undeniable, unquestionable.

**incontinence** n excess, extravagance, indulgence, intemperance, irrepressibility, lasciviousness, lewdness, licentiousness, prodigality, profligacy, riotousness, unrestraint, wantonness, wildness.

**incontinent** adj debauched, lascivious, lewd, licentious, lustful, prodigal, unchaste, uncontrolled, unrestrained.

**incontrovertible** adj certain, incontestable, indisputable, indubitable, irrefutable, sure, undeniable, unquestionable.

**inconvenience** vb discommode; annoy, disturb, molest, trouble, vex. * n annoyance, disadvantage, disturbance, molestation, trouble, vexation; awkwardness, cumbersomeness, incommodiousness, unwieldiness; unfitness, unseasonableness, unsuitableness.

**inconvenient** adj annoying, awkward, cumbersome, cumbrous, disadvantageous, incommodious, inopportune, troublesome, uncomfortable, unfit, unhandy, unmanageable, unseasonable, unsuitable, untimely, unwieldy, vexatious.

**incorporate** vb affiliate, amalgamate, associate, blend, combine, consolidate, include, merge, mix, unite; embody, incarnate. * adj incorporeal, immaterial, spiritual, supernatural; blended, consolidated, merged, united.

**incorporation** n affiliation, alignment, amalgamation, association, blend, blending, combination, consolidation, fusion, inclusion, merger, mixture, unification, union, embodiment, incarnation, personification.

**incorporeal** adj bodiless, immaterial, impalpable, incorporate, spiritual, supernatural, unsubstantial.

**incorrect** adj erroneous, false, inaccurate, inexact,

untrue, wrong; faulty, improper, mistaken, ungrammatical, unbecoming, unsound.

**incorrectness** n error, inaccuracy, inexactness, mistake.

**incorrigible** adj abandoned, graceless, hardened, irreclaimable, lost, obdurate, recreant, reprobate, shameless; helpless, hopeless, irremediable, irrecoverable, irreparable, irretrievable, irreversible, remediless.

**incorruptibility** n unpurchasableness; deathlessness, immortality, imperishableness, incorruptibleness, incorruption, indestructibility.

**incorruptible** adj honest, unbribable; imperishable, indestructible, immortal, undying, deathless, everlasting.

**increase** vb accrue, advance, augment, enlarge, extend, grow, intensify, mount, wax; multiply; enhance, greaten, heighten, raise, reinforce; aggravate, prolong. * n accession, accretion, accumulation, addition, augmentation, crescendo, development, enlargement, expansion, extension, growth, heightening, increment, intensification, multiplication, swelling; gain, produce, product, profit; descendants, issue, offspring, progeny.

**incredible** adj absurd, inadmissible, nonsensical, unbelievable.

**incredulity** n distrust, doubt, incredulousness, scepticism, unbelief.

**incredulous** adj distrustful, doubtful, dubious, sceptical, unbelieving.

**increment** n addition, augmentation, enlargement, increase.

**incriminate** vb accuse, blame, charge, criminate, impeach.

**incubate** vb brood, develop, hatch, sit.

**inculcate** vb enforce, implant, impress, infix, infuse, ingraft, inspire, instil.

**inculpable** adj blameless, faultless, innocent, irreprehensible, irreproachable, irreprovable, sinless, unblamable, unblameable.

**inculpate** vb accuse, blame, censure, charge, incriminate, impeach, incriminate.

**inculpatory** adj criminatory, incriminating.

**incumbent** adj binding, devolved, devolving, laid, obligatory; leaning, prone, reclining, resting. * n holder, occupant.

**incur** vb acquire, bring, contract.

**incurable** adj cureless, hopeless, irrecoverable, remediless; helpless, incorrigible, irremediable, irreparable, irretrievable, remediless.

**incurious** adj careless, heedless, inattentive, indifferent, uninquisitive, unobservant, uninterested.

**incursion** n descent, foray, raid, inroad, irruption.

**incursive** adj aggressive, hostile, invasive, predatory, raiding.

**incurvate** vb bend, bow, crook, curve. * adj (bot) aduncous, arcuate, bowed, crooked, curved, hooked.

**indebted** adj beholden, obliged, owing.

**indecency** n impropriety, indecorum, offensiveness, outrageousness, unseemliness; coarseness, filthiness, foulness, grossness, immodesty, impurity, obscenity, vileness.

**indecent** adj bold, improper, indecorous, offensive, outrageous, unbecoming, unseemly; coarse, dirty, filthy, gross, immodest, impure, indelicate, lewd, nasty, obscene, pornographic, salacious, shameless, smutty, unchaste.

**indecipherable** adj illegible, undecipherable, undiscoverable, inexplicable, obscure, unintelligible, unreadable.

**indecision** n changeableness, fickleness, hesitation, inconstancy, irresolution, unsteadiness, vacillation.

**indecisive** adj dubious, hesitating, inconclusive, irresolute, undecided, unsettled, vacillating, wavering.

**indecorous** adj coarse, gross, ill-bred, impolite, improper, indecent, rude, unbecoming, uncivil, unseemly.

**indecorum** n grossness, ill-breeding, ill manners, impoliteness, impropriety, incivility, indecency, indecorousness.

**indeed** adv absolutely, actually, certainly, in fact, in truth, in reality, positively, really, strictly, truly, verily, veritably. * interj really! you don't say so! is it possible!

**indefatigable** adj assiduous, never-tiring, persevering, persistent, sedulous, tireless, unflagging, unremitting, untiring, unwearied.

**indefeasible** adj immutable, inalienable, irreversible, irrevocable, unalterable.

**indefensible** adj censurable, defenceless, faulty, unpardonable, untenable; inexcusable, insupportable, unjustifiable, unwarrantable, wrong.

**indefinite** adj confused, doubtful, equivocal, general, imprecise, indefinable, indecisive, indeterminate, indistinct, inexact, inexplicit, lax, loose, nondescript, obscure, uncertain, undefined, undetermined, unfixed, unsettled, vague.

**indelible** adj fast, fixed, ineffaceable, ingrained, permanent.

**indelicacy** n coarseness, grossness, indecorousness, indecorum, impropriety, offensiveness, unseemliness, vulgarity; immodesty, indecency, lewdness, unchastity; foulness, obscenity.

**indelicate** adj broad, coarse, gross, indecorous, intrusive, rude, unbecoming, unseemly; foul, immodest, indecent, lewd, obscene, unchaste, vulgar.

**indemnification** n compensation, reimbursement, remuneration, security.

**indemnify** vb compensate, reimburse, remunerate, requite, secure.

**indent** vb bruise, jag, notch, pink, scallop, serrate; bind, indenture.

**indentation** n bruise, dent, depression, jag, notch.

**indenture** vb bind, indent. * n contract, instrument; indentation.

**independence** n freedom, liberty, self-direction; distinctness, nondependence, separation; competence, ease.

**independent** adj absolute, autonomous, free, self-directing, uncoerced, unrestrained, unrestricted, voluntary; (person) self-reliant, unconstrained, unconventional.

**indescribable** adj ineffable, inexpressible, nameless, unutterable.

**indestructible** adj abiding, endless, enduring, everlasting, fadeless, imperishable, incorruptible, undecaying.

**indeterminate** adj indefinite, uncertain, undetermined, unfixed.

**index** vb alphabetize, catalogue, codify, earmark, file, list, mark, tabulate. * n catalogue, list, register, tally; indicator, lead, mark, pointer, sign, signal, token; contents, table of contents; forefinger; exponent.

**indicate** vb betoken, denote, designate, evince, exhibit, foreshadow, manifest, mark, point out, prefigure, presage, register, show, signify, specify, tell; hint, imply, intimate, sketch, suggest.

**indication** n hint, index, manifestation, mark, note, sign, suggestion, symptom, token.

**indicative** adj significant, suggestive, symptomatic; (gram) affirmative, declarative.

**indict** vb (law) accuse, charge, present.

**indictment** n (law) indicting, presentment; accusation, arraignment, charge, crimination, impeachment.

**indifference** n apathy, carelessness, coldness, coolness, heedlessness, inattention, insignificance, negligence, unconcern, unconcernedness, uninterestedness; disinterestedness, impartiality, neutrality.

**indifferent** adj apathetic, cold, cool, dead, distant, dull, easy-going, frigid, heedless, inattentive, incurious, insensible, insouciant, listless, lukewarm, nonchalant, perfunctory, regardless, stoical, unconcerned, uninterested, unmindful, unmoved; equal; fair, medium, middling, moderate, ordinary, passable, tolerable; mediocre, so-so; immaterial, unimportant; disinterested, impartial, neutral, unbiased.

**indigence** n destitution, distress, necessity, need, neediness, pauperism, penury, poverty, privation, want.

**indigenous** adj aboriginal, home-grown, inborn, inherent, native.

**indigent** adj destitute, distressed, insolvent, moneyless, necessitous, needy, penniless, pinched, poor, reduced.

**indigested** adj unconcocted, undigested; crude, ill-advised, ill-considered, ill-judged; confused, disorderly, ill-arranged, unmethodical.

**indigestion** n dyspepsia, dyspepsy.

**indignant** adj angry, exasperated, incensed, irate, ireful, provoked, roused, wrathful, wroth.

**indignation** n anger, choler, displeasure, exasperation, fury, ire, rage, resentment, wrath.

**indignity** n abuse, affront, contumely, dishonour, disrespect, ignominy, insult, obloquy, opprobrium, outrage, reproach, slight.

**indirect** adj circuitous, circumlocutory, collateral, devious, oblique, roundabout, sidelong, tortuous; deceitful, dishonest, dishonorable, unfair; mediate, remote, secondary, subordinate.

**indiscernible** adj imperceptible, indistinguishable, invisible, undiscernible, undiscoverable.

**indiscipline** n laxity, insubordination.

**indiscreet** adj foolish, hasty, headlong, heedless, imprudent, incautious, inconsiderate, injudicious, rash, reckless, unwise.

**indiscretion** n folly, imprudence, inconsiderateness, rashness; blunder, faux pas, lapse, mistake, misstep.

**indiscriminate** adj confused, heterogeneous,

indistinct, mingled, miscellaneous, mixed, promiscuous, undiscriminating, undistinguishable, undistinguishing.

**indispensable** *adj* essential, expedient, necessary, needed, needful, requisite.

**indisputable** *adj* certain, incontestable, indubitable, infallible, sure, undeniable, undoubted, unmistakable, unquestionable.

**indisposed** *adj* ailing, ill, sick, unwell; averse, backward, disinclined, loath, reluctant, unfriendly, unwilling.

**indisposition** *n* ailment, illness, sickness; aversion, backwardness, dislike, disinclination, reluctance, unwillingness.

**indisputable** *adj* certain, incontestable, indutitable, infallible, sure, undeniable, undoubted, unmistakable, unquestionable.

**indissoluble** *adj* abiding, enduring, firm, imperishable, incorruptible, indestructible, lasting, stable, unbreakable.

**indistinct** *adj* ambiguous, doubtful, uncertain; blurred, dim, dull, faint, hazy, misty, nebulous, obscure, shadowy, vague; confused, inarticulate, indefinite, indistinguishable, undefined, undistinguishable.

**indistinguishable** *adj* imperceptible, indiscernible, unnoticeable, unobservable; chaotic, confused, dim, indistinct, obscure, vague.

**indite** *vb* compose, pen, write.

**individual** *adj* characteristic, distinct, identical, idiosyncratic, marked, one, particular, personal, respective, separate, single, singular, special, unique; peculiar, proper; decided, definite, independent, positive, self-guided, unconventional. * *n* being, character, party, person, personage, somebody, someone; type, unit.

**individuality** *n* definiteness, indentity, personality; originality, self-direction, self-determination, singularity, uniqueness.

**individualize** *vb* individuate, particularize, singularize, specify.

**indivisible** *adj* incommensurable, indissoluble, inseparable, unbreakable, unpartiable.

**indocile** *adj* cantankerous, contumacious, dogged, froward, inapt, headstrong, intractable, mulish, obstinate, perverse, refractory, stubborn, ungovernable, unmanageable, unruly, unteachable.

**indoctrinate** *vb* brainwash, imbue, initiate, instruct, rehabilitate, teach.

**indoctrination** *n* grounding, initiation, instruction, rehabilitation.

**indolence** *n* idleness, inactivity, inertia, inertness, laziness, listlessness, sloth, slothfulness, sluggishness.

**indolent** *adj* easy, easy-going, inactive, inert, lazy, listless, lumpish, otiose, slothful, sluggish, supine.

**indomitable** *adj* invincible, unconquerable, unyielding.

**indorse** *see* **endorse**.

**indubitable** *adj* certain, evident, incontestable, incontrovertible, indisputable, sure, undeniable, unquestionable.

**induce** *vb* actuate, allure, bring, draw, drive, entice, impel, incite, influence, instigate, move, persuade, prevail, prompt, spur, urge; bring on, cause, effect, motivate, lead, occasion, produce.

**inducement** *n* allurement, draw, enticement, instigation, persuasion; cause, consideration, impulse, incentive, incitement, influence, motive, reason, spur, stimulus.

**induct** *vb* inaugurate, initiate, install, institute, introduce, invest.

**induction** *n* inauguration, initiation, institution, installation, introduction; conclusion, generalization, inference.

**indue** *vb* assume, endow, clothe, endue, invest, supply.

**indulge** *vb* gratify, license, revel, satisfy, wallow, yield to; coddle, cosset, favour, humour, pamper, pet, spoil; allow, cherish, foster, harbour, permit, suffer.

**indulgence** *n* gratification, humouring, pampering; favour, kindness, lenience, lenity, liberality, tenderness; (*theol*) absolution, remission.

**indulgent** *adj* clement, easy, favouring, forbearing, gentle, humouring, kind, lenient, mild, pampering, tender, tolerant.

**indurate** *vb* harden, inure, sear, strengthen.

**induration** *n* hardening, obduracy.

**industrious** *adj* assiduous, diligent, hard-working, laborious, notable, operose, sedulous; brisk, busy, persevering, persistent.

**industry** *n* activity, application, assiduousness, assiduity, diligence; perseverance, persistence, sedulousness, vigour; effort, labour, toil.

**inebriated** *adj* drunk, intoxicated, stupefied.

**ineffable** *adj* indescribable, inexpressible, unspeakable, unutterable.

**ineffaceable** adj indelible, indestructible, inerasable, inexpungeable, ingrained.

**ineffectual** adj abortive, bootless, fruitless, futile, inadequate, inefficacious, ineffective, inoperative, useless, unavailing, vain; feeble, inefficient, powerless, impotent, weak.

**inefficacy** n ineffectualness, inefficiency.

**inefficient** adj feeble, incapable, ineffectual, ineffective, inefficacious, weak.

**inelastic** adj flabby, flaccid, inductile, inflexible, irresilient.

**inelegant** adj abrupt, awkward, clumsy, coarse, constrained, cramped, crude, graceless, harsh, homely, homespun, rough, rude, stiff, tasteless, uncourtly, uncouth, ungainly, ungraceful, unpolished, unrefined.

**ineligible** adj disqualified, unqualified; inexpedient, objectionable, unadvisable, undesirable.

**inept** adj awkward, improper, inapposite, inappropriate, unapt, unfit, unsuitable; null, useless, void, worthless; foolish, nonsensical, pointless, senseless, silly, stupid.

**ineptitude** n inappositeness, inappropriateness, inaptitude, unfitness, unsuitability, unsuitable-ness; emptiness, nullity, uselessness, worthlessness; folly, foolishness, nonsense, pointlessness, senselessness, silliness, stupidity.

**inequality** n disproportion, inequitableness, injustice, unfairness; difference, disparity, dissimilarity, diversity, imparity, irregularity, roughness, unevenness; inadequacy, incompetency, insufficiency.

**inequitable** adj unfair, unjust.

**inert** adj comatose, dead, inactive, lifeless, motionless, quiescent, passive; apathetic, dronish, dull, idle, indolent, lazy, lethargic, lumpish, phlegmatic, slothful, sluggish, supine, torpid.

**inertia** n apathy, inertness, lethargy, passiveness, passivity, slothfulness, sluggishness.

**inestimable** adj incalculable, invaluable, precious, priceless, valuable.

**inevitable** adj certain, necessary, unavoidable, undoubted.

**inexact** adj imprecise, inaccurate, incorrect; careless, crude, loose.

**inexcusable** adj indefensible, irremissible, unallowable, unjustifiable, unpardonable.

**inexhaustible** adj boundless, exhaustless, indefatigable, unfailing, unlimited.

**inexorable** adj cruel, firm, hard, immovable, implacable, inflexible, merciless, pitiless, relentless, severe, steadfast, unbending, uncompassionate, unmerciful, unrelenting, unyielding.

**inexpedient** adj disadvantageous, ill-judged, impolitic, imprudent, indiscreet, injudicious, inopportune, unadvisable, unprofitable, unwise.

**inexperience** n greenness, ignorance, rawness.

**inexperienced** adj callow, green, raw, strange, unacquainted, unconversant, undisciplined, uninitiated, unpractised, unschooled, unskilled, untrained, untried, unversed, young.

**inexpert** adj awkward, bungling, clumsy, inapt, maladroit, unhandy, unskilful, unskilled.

**inexpiable** adj implacable, inexorable, irreconcilable, unappeasable; irremissible, unatonable, unpardonable.

**inexplicable** adj enigmatic, enigmatical, incomprehensible, inscrutable, mysterious, strange, unaccountable, unintelligible.

**inexpressible** adj indescribable, ineffable, unspeakable, unutterable; boundless, infinite, surpassing.

**inexpressive** adj blank, characterless, dull, unexpressive.

**inextinguishable** adj unquenchable.

**in extremis** adv moribund.

**inextricable** adj entangled, intricate, perplexed, unsolvable.

**infallibility** n certainty, infallibleness, perfection.

**infallible** adj certain, indubitable, oracular, sure, unerring, unfailing.

**infamous** adj abominable, atrocious, base, damnable, dark, detestable, discreditable, disgraceful, dishonorable, disreputable, heinous, ignominious, nefarious, odious, opprobrious, outrageous, scandalous, shameful, shameless, vile, villainous, wicked.

**infamy** n abasement, discredit, disgrace, dishonour, disrepute, ignominy, obloquy, odium, opprobrium, scandal, shame; atrocity, detestableness, disgracefulness, dishonorableness, odiousness, scandalousness, shamefulness, villainy, wickedness.

**infancy** n beginning, commencement; babyhood, childhood, minority, nonage, pupillage.

**infant** n babe, baby, bairn, bantling, brat, chit, minor, nursling, papoose, suckling, tot.

**infantile** adj childish, infantine, newborn, tender, young; babyish, childish, weak; babylike, childlike.

**infatuate** vb befool, besot, captivate, delude, prepossess, stultify.

**infatuation** n absorption, besottedness, folly, foolishness, prepossession, stupefaction.

**infeasible** adj impractical, unfeasible.

**infect** vb affect, contaminate, corrupt, defile, poison, pollute, taint, vitiate.

**infection** n affection, bane, contagion, contamination, corruption, defilement, pest, poison, pollution, taint, virus, vitiation.

**infectious** adj catching, communicable, contagious, contaminating, corrupting, defiling, demoralizing, pestiferous, pestilential, poisoning, polluting, sympathetic, vitiating.

**infecund** adj barren, infertile, sterile, unfruitful, unproductive, unprolific.

**infecundity** n unfruitfulness.

**infelicitous** adj calamitous, miserable, unfortunate, unhappy, wretched; inauspicious, unfavourable, unpropitious; ill-chosen, inappropriate, unfitting.

**infer** vb collect, conclude, deduce, derive, draw, gather, glean, guess, presume, reason.

**inference** n conclusion, consequence, corollary, deduction, generalization, guess, illation, implication, induction, presumption.

**inferior** adj lower, nether; junior, minor, secondary, subordinate; bad, base, deficient, humble, imperfect, indifferent, mean, mediocre, paltry, poor, second-rate, shabby.

**inferiority** n juniority, subjection, subordination, mediocrity; deficiency, imperfection, inadequacy, shortcoming.

**infernal** adj abominable, accursed, atrocious, damnable, dark, demoniacal, devilish, diabolical, fiendish, fiendlike, hellish, malicious, nefarious, satanic, Stygian.

**infertility** n barrenness, infecundity, sterility, unfruitfulness, unproductivity.

**infest** vb annoy, disturb, harass, haunt, molest, plague, tease, torment, trouble, vex, worry; beset, overrun, possess, swarm, throng.

**infidel** n agnostic, atheist, disbeliever, heathen, heretic, sceptic, unbeliever.

**infidelity** n adultery, disloyalty, faithlessness, treachery, unfaithfulness; disbelief, scepticism, unbelief.

**infiltrate** vb absorb, pervade, soak.

**infinite** adj boundless, endless, illimitable, immeasurable, inexhaustible, interminable, limitless, measureless, perfect, unbounded, unlimited; enormous, immense, stupendous, vast; absolue, eternal, self-determined, self-existent, unconditioned.

**infinitesimal** adj infinitely small; microscopic, miniscule.

**infinity** n absoluteness, boundlessness, endlessness, eternity, immensity, infiniteness, infinitude, interminateness, self-determination, self-existence, vastness.

**infirm** adj ailing, debilitated, enfeebled, feeble, frail, weak, weakened; faltering, irresolute, vacillating, wavering; insecure, precarious, unsound, unstable.

**infirmity** n ailment, debility, feebleness, frailness, frailty, weakness; defect, failing, fault, foible, weakness.

**infix** vb fasten, fix, plant, set; implant, inculcate, infuse, ingraft, instil.

**inflame** vb animate, arouse, excite, enkindle, fire, heat, incite, inspirit, intensify, rouse, stimulate; aggravate, anger, chafe, embitter, enrage, exasperate, incense, infuriate, irritate, madden, nettle, provoke.

**inflammability** n combustibility, combustibleness, inflammableness.

**inflammable** adj combustible, ignitible; excitable.

**inflammation** n burning, conflagration; anger, animosity, excitement, heat, rage, turbulence, violence.

**inflammatory** adj fiery, inflaming; dissentious, incendiary, seditious.

**inflate** vb bloat, blow up, distend, expand, swell, sufflate; elate, puff up; enlarge, increase.

**inflated** adj bloated, distended, puffed-up, swollen, bombastic, declamatory, grandiloquent, high-flown, magniloquent, overblown, pompous, rhetorical, stilted, tumid, turgid.

**inflation** n enlargement, increase, overenlargement, overissue; bloatedness, distension, expansion, sufflation; bombast, conceit, conceitedness, self-conceit, self-complacency, self-importance, self-sufficiency, vaingloriousness, vainglory.

**inflect** vb bend, bow, curve, turn; (gram) conjugate, decline, vary.

**inflection** n bend, bending, crook, curvature, curvity, flexure; (gram) accidence, conjugation, declension, variation; (mus) modulation.

**inflexibility** n inflexibleness, rigidity, stiffness; doggedness, obstinacy, perinacity, stubbornness; firmness, perseverance, resolution, tenacity.

**inflexible** adj rigid, rigorous, stiff, unbending; cantankerous, cross-grained, dogged, headstrong, heady, inexorable, intractable, obdurate, obstinant, pertinacious, refractory, stubborn, unyielding, wilful; firm, immovable, persevering, resolute, steadfast, unbending.

**inflict** vb bring, impose, lay on.

**infliction** n imposition, inflicting; judgment, punishment.

**inflorescence** n blooming, blossoming, flowering.

**influence** vb affect, bias, control, direct, lead, modify, prejudice, prepossess, sway; actuate, arouse, impel, incite, induce, instigate, move, persuade, prevail upon, rouse. * n ascendancy, authority, control, mastery, potency, predominance, pull, rule, sway; credit, reputation, weight; inflow, inflowing, influx; magnetism, power, spell.

**influential** adj controlling, effective, effectual, potent, powerful, strong; authoritative, momentous, substantial, weighty.

**influx** n flowing in, introduction.

**infold** see **enfold**.

**inform** vb animate, inspire, quicken; acquaint, advise, apprise, enlighten, instruct, notify, teach, tell, tip, warn.

**informal** adj unceremonious, unconventional, unofficial; easy, familiar, natural, simple; irregular, nonconformist, unusual.

**informality** n unceremoniousness; unconventionality; ease, familiarity, naturalness, simplicity; noncomformity, irregularity, unusualness.

**informant** n advertiser, adviser, informer, intelligencer, newsmonger, notifier, relator; accuser, complainant, informer.

**information** n advice, data, intelligence, knowledge, notice; advertisement, enlightenment, instruction, message, tip, word, warning; accusation, complaint, denunciation.

**informer** n accuser, complainant, informant, snitch.

**infraction** n breach, breaking, disobedience, encroachment, infringement, nonobservance, transgression, violation.

**infrangible** adj inseparable, inviolable, unbreakable.

**infrequency** n rareness, rarity, uncommonness, unusualness.

**infrequent** adj rare, uncommon, unfrequent, unusual; occasional, scant, scarce, sporadic.

**infringe** vb break, contravene, disobey, intrude, invade, transgress, violate.

**infringement** n breach, breaking, disobedience, infraction, nonobservance, transgression, violation.

**infuriated** adj angry, enraged, furious, incensed, maddened, raging, wild.

**infuse** vb breathe into, implant, inculcate, ingraft, insinuate, inspire, instil, introduce; macerate, steep.

**infusion** n inculcation, instillation, introduction; infusing, macerating, steeping.

**ingathering** n harvest.

**ingenious** adj able, adroit, artful, bright, clever, fertile, gifted, inventive, ready, sagacious, shrewd, witty.

**ingenuity** n ability, acuteness, aptitude, aptness, capacity, capableness, cleverness, faculty, genius, gift, ingeniousness, inventiveness, knack, readiness, skill, turn.

**ingenuous** adj artless, candid, childlike, downright, frank, generous, guileless, honest, innocent, naive, open, open-hearted, plain, simple-minded, sincere, single-minded, straightforward, transparent, truthful, unreserved.

**ingenuousness** n artlessness, candour, childlikeness, frankness, guilelessness, honesty, naivety, open-heartedness, openness, sincerity, single-mindedness, truthfulness.

**inglorious** adj humble, lowly, mean, nameless, obscure, undistinguished, unhonoured, unknown, unmarked, unnoted; discreditable, disgraceful, humiliating, ignominous, scandalous, shameful.

**ingloriousness** n humbleness, lowliness, meanness, namelessness, obscurity; abasement, discredit, disgrace, dishonour, disrepute, humiliation, infamy, ignominousness, ignominy, obloquy, odium, opprobrium, shame.

**ingraft** vb graft, implant, inculcate, infix, infuse, instil.

**ingrain** vb dye, imbue, impregnate.

**ingratiate** vb insinuate.

**ingratitude** n thanklessness, ungratefulness, unthankfulness.

**ingredient** n component, constituent, element.

**ingress** n entrance, entré, entry, introgression.

**ingulf** see **engulf**.

**inhabit** vb abide, dwell, live, occupy, people, reside, sojourn.

**inhabitable** adj habitable, livable.

**inhabitant** n citizen, denizen, dweller, inhabiter, resident.

**inhalation** n breath, inhaling, inspiration; sniff, snuff.

**inhale** vb breathe in, draw in, inbreathe, inspire.

**inharmonious** adj discordant, inharmonic, out of tune, unharmonious, unmusical.

**inhere** vb cleave to, stick, stick fast; abide, belong, exist, lie, pertain, reside.

**inherent** adj essential, immanent, inborn, inbred, indwelling, ingrained, innate, inseparable, intrinsic, native, natural, proper; adhering, sticking.

**inherit** vb get, receive.

**inheritance** n heritage, legacy, patrimony; inheriting.

**inheritor** n heir, (low) parcener.

**inhibit** vb bar, check, debar, hinder, obstruct, prevent, repress, restrain, stop; forbid, interdict, prohibit.

**inhibition** n check, hindrance, impediment, obstacle, obstruction, restraint; disallowance, embargo, interdict, interdiction, prevention, prohibition.

**inhospitable** adj cool, forbidding, unfriendly, unkind; bigoted, illiberal, intolerant, narrow, prejudiced, ungenerous, unreceptive; barren, wild.

**inhospitality** n inhospitableness, unkindness; illiberality, narrowness.

**inhuman** adj barbarous, brutal, cruel, fell, ferocious, merciless, pitiless, remorseless, ruthless, savage, unfeeling; nonhuman.

**inhumanity** n barbarity, brutality, cruelty, ferocity, savageness; hard-heartedness, unkindness.

**inhume** vb bury, entomb, inter.

**inimical** adj antagonistic, hostile, unfriendly; adverse, contrary, harmful, hurtful, noxious, opposed, pernicious, repugnant, unfavourable.

**inimitable** adj incomparable, matchless, peerless, unequalled, unexampled, unmatched, unparagoned, unparalleled, unrivalled, unsurpassed.

**iniquitous** adj atrocious, criminal, flagitious, heinous, inequitable, nefarious, sinful, wicked, wrong, unfair, unjust, unrighteous.

**iniquity** n injustice, sin, sinfulness, unrighteousness, wickedness, wrong; crime, misdeed, offence.

**initial** adj first; beginning, commencing, incipient, initiatory, introductory, opening, original; elementary, inchoate, rudimentary.

**initiate** vb begin, commence, enter upon, inaugurate, introduce, open; ground, indoctrinate, instruct, prime, teach.

**initiation** n beginning, commencement, inaugura-tion, opening; admission, entrance, introduction; indoctrinate, instruction.

**initiative** n beginning; energy, enterprise.

**initiatory** adj inceptive, initiative.

**inject** vb force in, interject, insert, introduce, intromit.

**injudicious** adj foolish, hasty, ill-advised, ill-judged, imprudent, incautious, inconsiderate, indiscreet, rash, unwise.

**injunction** n admonition, bidding, command, mandate, order, precept.

**injure** vb damage, disfigure, harm, hurt, impair, mar, spoil, sully, wound; abuse, aggrieve, wrong; affront, dishonour, insult.

**injurious** adj baneful, damaging, deadly, deleterious, destructive, detrimental, disadvantageous, evil, fatal, hurtful, mischievous, noxious, pernicious, prejudicial, ruinous; inequitable, iniquitous, unjust, wrongful; contumelious, detractory, libellous, slanderous.

**injury** n evil, ill, injustice, wrong; damage, detriment, harm, hurt, impairment, loss, mischief, prejudice.

**injustice** n inequity, unfairness; grievance, iniquity, injury, wrong.

**inkhorn** n inkbottle, inkstand.

**inkling** n hint, intimation, suggestion, whisper.

**inky** adj atramentous, black, murky.

**inland** adj domestic, hinterland, home, upcountry; interior, internal.

**inlet** n arm, bay, bight, cove, creek; entrance, ingress, passage.

**inmate** n denizen, dweller, guest, intern, occupant.

**inmost** adj deepest, innermost.

**inn** n hostel, hostelry, hotel, pub, public house, tavern.

**innate** adj congenital, constitutional, inborn, inbred, indigenous, inherent, inherited, instinctive, native, natural, organic.

**inner** adj interior, internal.

**innermost** adj deepest, inmost.

**innkeeper** n host, innholder, landlady, landlord, tavernkeeper.

**innocence** n blamelessness, chastity, guilelessness, guiltlessness, purity, simplicity, sinlessness, stainlessness; harmlessness, innocuousness, innoxiousness, inoffensiveness.

**innocent** adj blameless, clean, clear, faultless, guiltless, immaculate, pure, sinless, spotless, unfallen, upright; harmless, innocuous, innoxious, inoffensive;

lawful, legitimate, permitted; artless, guileless, ignorant, ingenuous, simple. * n babe, child, ingénue, naif, naive, unsophisticate.

**innocuous** adj harmless, innocent, inoffensive, safe.

**innovate** vb change, introduce.

**innovation** n change, introduction; departure, novelty.

**innuendo** n allusion, hint, insinuation, intimation, suggestion.

**innumerable** adj countless, numberless.

**inoculate** vb infect, vaccinate.

**inoffensive** adj harmless, innocent, innocuous, innoxious, unobjectionable, unoffending.

**inoperative** adj inactive, ineffectual, inefficacious, not in force.

**inopportune** adj ill-timed, inexpedient, infelicitous, mistimed, unfortunate, unhappy, unseasonable, untimely.

**inordinate** adj excessive, extravagant, immoderate, intemperate, irregular.

**inorganic** adj inanimate, unorganized; mineral.

**inquest** n inquiry, inquisition, investigation, quest, search.

**inquietude** n anxiety, disquiet, disquietude, disturbance, restlessness, uneasiness.

**inquire, enquire** vb ask, catechize, interpellate, interrogate, investigate, query, question, quiz.

**inquiry, enquiry** n examination, exploration, investigation, research, scrutiny, study; interrogation, query, question, quiz.

**inquisition** n examination, inquest, inquiry, investigation, search.

**inquisitive** adj curious, inquiring, scrutinizing; curious, meddlesome, peeping, peering, prying.

**inroad** n encroachment, foray, incursion, invasion, irruption, raid.

**insalubrious** adj noxious, unhealthful, unhealthy, unwholesome.

**insane** adj abnormal, crazed, crazy, delirious, demented, deranged, distracted, lunatic, mad, maniacal, unhealthy, unsound.

**insanity** n craziness, delirium, dementia, derangement, lunacy, madness, mania, mental aberration, mental alienation.

**insatiable** adj greedy, rapacious, voracious; insatiate, unappeasable.

**inscribe** vb emblaze, endorse, engrave, enroll, impress, imprint, letter, mark, write; address, dedicate.

**inscrutable** adj hidden, impenetrable, incomprehensible, inexplicable, mysterious, undiscover-able, unfathomable, unsearchable.

**inscrutableness** n impenetrability, incomprehensibility, incomprehensibleness, inexplicability, inscrutability, mysteriousness, mystery, unfathomableness, unsearchableness.

**insecure** adj risky, uncertain, unconfident, unsure; exposed, ill-protected, unprotected, unsafe; dangerous, hazardous, perilous; infirm, shaking, shaky, tottering, unstable, weak, wobbly.

**insecurity** n riskiness, uncertainty; danger, hazardousness, peril; instability, shakiness, weakness, wobbliness.

**insensate** adj dull, indifferent, insensible, torpid; brutal, foolish, senseless, unwise; inanimate, insensible, insentient, nonpercipient, unconscious, unperceiving.

**insensibility** n dullness, insentience, lethargy, torpor; apathy, indifference, insusceptibility, unfeelingness, dullness, stupidity; anaesthesia, coma, stupor, unconsciousness.

**insensible** adj imperceivable, imperceptible, undiscoverable; blunted, brutish, deaf, dull, insensate, numb, obtuse, senseless, sluggish, stolid, stupid, torpid, unconscious; apathetic, callous, phlegmatic, impassive, indifferent, insensitive, insentient, unfeeling, unimpressible, unsusceptible.

**insensibly** adv imperceptibly.

**insentient** adj inert, nonsentient, senseless; inanimate, insensible, insensate, nonpercipient, unconscious, unperceiving.

**inseparable** adj close, friendly, intimate, together; indissoluble, indivisible, inseverable.

**insert** vb infix, inject, intercalate, interpolate, introduce, inweave, parenthesize, place, put, set.

**inside** adj inner, interior, internal; confidential, exclusive, internal, private, secret. * adv indoors, within. * n inner part, interior; nature.

**insidious** adj creeping, deceptive, gradual, secretive; arch, artful, crafty, crooked, cunning, deceitful, designing, diplomatic, foxy, guileful, intriguing, Machiavellian, sly, sneaky, subtle, treacherous, trickish, tricky, wily.

**insight** n discernment, intuition, penetration, perception, perspicuity, understanding.

**insignia** npl badges, marks.

**insignificance** n emptiness, nothingenss, paltriness, triviality, unimportance.

**insignificant** adj contemptible, empty, immaterial, inconsequential, inconsiderable, inferior, meaningless, paltry, petty, small, sorry, trifling, trivial, unessential, unimportant.

**insincere** adj deceitful, dishonest, disingenuous, dissembling, dissimulating, double-faced, double-tongued, duplicitous, empty, faithless, false, hollow, hypocritical, pharisaical, truthless, uncandid, untrue.

**insincerity** n bad faith, deceitfulness, dishonesty, disingenuousness, dissimulation, duplicity, falseness, faithlessness, hypocrisy.

**insinuate** vb hint, inculcate, infuse, ingratiate, instil, intimate, introduce, suggest.

**insipid** adj dead, dull, flat, heavy, inanimate, jejune, lifeless, monotonous, pointless, prosaic, prosy, spiritless, stupid, tame, unentertaining, uninteresting; mawkish, savourless, stale, tasteless, vapid, zestless.

**insipidity, insipidness** n dullness, heaviness, lifelessness, prosiness, stupidity, tameness; flatness, mawkishness, staleness, tastlessness, unsavouriness, vapidness, zestlessness.

**insist** vb demand, maintain, urge.

**insistence** n importunity, solicitousness, urging, urgency.

**insnare** see **ensnare**.

**insolence** n impertinence, impudence, malapertness, pertness, rudeness, sauciness; contempt, contumacy, contumely, disrespect, frowardness, insubordination.

**insolent** adj abusive, contemptuous, contumelious, disrespectful, domineering, insulting, offensive, overbearing, rude, supercilious; cheeky, impertinent, impudent, malapert, pert, saucy; contumacious, disobedient, froward, insubordinate.

**insoluble** adj indissoluble, indissolvable, irreducible; inexplicable, insolvable.

**insolvable** adj inexplicable.

**insolvent** adj bankrupt, broken, failed, ruined.

**insomnia** n sleeplessness, wakefulness.

**inspect** vb examine, investigate, look into, pry into, scrutinize; oversee, superintend, supervise.

**inspection** n examination, investigation, scrutiny; oversight, superintendence, supervision.

**inspector** n censor, critic, examiner, visitor; boss, overseer, superintendent, supervisor.

**inspiration** n breathing, inhalation; afflatus, fire, inflatus; elevation, exaltation; enthusiasm.

**inspire** vb breathe, inhale; infuse, instil; animate, cheer, enliven, inspirit; elevate, exalt, stimulate; fill, imbue, impart, inform, quicken.

**inspirit** vb animate, arouse, cheer, comfort, embolden, encourage, enhearten, enliven, fire, hearten, incite, invigorate, quicken, rouse, stimulate.

**instable** see **unstable**.

**instability** n changeableness, fickleness, inconstancy, insecurity, mutability.

**install, instal** vb inaugurate, induct, introduce; establish, place, set up.

**installation** n inauguration, induction, instalment, investiture.

**instalment** n earnest, payment, portion.

**instance** vb adduce, cite, mention, specify. * n case, example, exemplification, illustration, occasion; impulse, incitement, instigation, motive, prompting, request, solicitation.

**instant** adj direct, immediate, instantaneous, prompt, quick; current, present; earnest, fast, imperative, importunate, pressing, urgent; ready cooked. * n flash, jiffy, moment, second, trice, twinkling; hour, time.

**instantaneous** adj abrupt, immediate, instant, quick, sudden.

**instantaneously** adv forthwith, immediately, presto, quickly, right away.

**instauration** n reconstitution, reconstruction, redintegration, re-establishment, rehabilitation, reinstatement, renewal, renovation, restoration.

**instead** adv in lieu, in place, rather.

**instigate** vb actuate, agitate, encourage, impel, incite, influence, initiate, move, persuade, prevail upon, prompt, provoke, rouse, set on, spur on, stimulate, stir up, tempt, urge.

**instigation** n encouragement, incitement, influence, instance, prompting, solicitation, urgency.

**instil, instill** vb enforce, implant, impress, inculcate, ingraft; impart, infuse, insinuate.

**instillation** n infusion, insinuation, introduction.

**instinct** n natural impulse.

**instinctive** adj automatic, inherent, innate, intuitive, involuntary, natural, spontaneous; impulsive, unreflecting.

**institute**[1] n academy, college, foundation, guild, institution, school; custom, doctrine, dogma, law, maxim, precedent, principle, rule, tenet.

**institute**[2] vb begin, commence, constitute, establish, found, initial, install, introduce, organize, originate, start.

**institution** n enactment, establishment, foundation, institute, society; investiture; custom, law, practice.

**instruct** vb discipline, educate, enlighten, exercise, guide, indoctrinate, inform, initiate, school, teach, train; apprise, bid, command, direct, enjoin, order, prescribe to.

**instruction** n breeding, discipline, education, indoctrination, information, nurture, schooling, teaching, training, tuition; advice, counsel, precept; command, direction, mandate, order.

**instructor** n educator, master, preceptor, schoolteacher, teacher, tutor.

**instrument** n appliance, apparatus, contrivance, device, implement, musical instrument, tool, utensil; agent, means, medium; charter, deed, document, indenture, writing.

**instrumental** adj ancillary, assisting, auxiliary, conducive, contributory, helpful, helping, ministerial, ministrant, serviceable, subservient, subsidiary.

**instrumentality** n agency, intermediary; intervention, means, mediation.

**insubordinate** adj disobedient, disorderly, mutinous, refractory, riotous, seditious, turbulent, ungovernable, unruly.

**insubordination** n disobedience, insurrection, mutiny, revolt, riotousness, sedition; indiscipline, laxity.

**insufferable** adj intolerable, unbearable, unendurable, insupportable; abominable, detestable, disgusting, execrable, outrageous.

**insufficiency** n dearth, defectiveness, deficiency, lack, inadequacy, inadequateness, incapability, incompetence, paucity, shortage.

**insufficient** adj deficient, inadequate, incommensurate, incompetent, scanty; incapable, incompetent, unfitted, unqualified, unsuited, unsatisfactory.

**insular** adj contracted, illiberal, limited, narrow, petty, prejudiced, restricted; isolated, remote.

**insulate** vb detach, disconnect, disengage, disunite, isolate, separate.

**insulation** n disconnection, disengagement, isolation, separation.

**insult** vb abuse, affront, injure, offend, outrage, slander, slight. * n abuse, affront, cheek, contumely, indignity, insolence, offence, outrage, sauce, slight.

**insulting** adj abusive, arrogant, contumelious, impertinent, impolite, insolent, rude, vituperative.

**insuperable** adj impassable, insurmountable.

**insupportable** adj insufferable, intolerable, unbearable, unendurable.

**insuppressible** adj irrepressible, uncontrollable.

**insurance** n assurance, security.

**insure** vb assure, guarantee, indemnify, secure, underwrite.

**insurgent** adj disobedient, insubordinate, mutinous, rebellious, revolting, revolutionary, seditious. * n mutineer, rebel, revolter, revolutionary.

**insurmountable** adj impassable, insuperable.

**insurrection** n insurgence, mutiny, rebellion, revolt, revolution, rising, sedition, uprising.

**intact** adj scathless, unharmed, unhurt, unimpaired, uninjured, untouched; complete, entire, integral, sound, unbroken, undiminished, whole.

**intangible** adj dim, impalpable, imperceptible, indefinite, insubstantial, intactile, shadowy, vague; aerial, phantom, spiritous.

**intangibility** n imperceptibility, insubstantiality, intangibleness, shadowiness, vagueness.

**integral** adj complete, component, entire, integrant, total, whole.

**integrity** n goodness, honesty, principle, probity, purity, rectitude, soundness, uprightness, virtue; completeness, entireness, entirety, wholeness.

**integument** n coat, covering, envelope, skin, tegument.

**intellect** n brains, cognitive faculty, intelligence, mind, rational faculty, reason, reasoning, faculty, sense, thought, understanding, wit.

**intellectual** adj cerebral, intelligent, mental, scholarly, thoughtful. * n academic, highbrow, pundit, savant, scholar.

**intelligence** n acumen, apprehension, brightness, discernment, imagination, insight, penetration, quickness, sagacity, shrewdness, understanding, wits; information, knowledge; advice, instruction, news, notice, notification, tidings; brains, intellect, mentality, sense, spirit.

**intelligent** adj acute, alert, apt, astute, brainy, bright, clear-headed, clear-sighted, clever, discerning, keen-eyed, keen-sighted, knowing, long-headed, quick, quick-sighted, sagacious, sensible, sharp-sighted, sharp-witted, shrewd, understanding.

**intelligibility** n clarity, comprehensibility, intelligibleness, perspicuity.

**intelligible** adj clear, comprehensible, distinct, evident, lucid, manifest, obvious, patent, perspicuous, plain, transparent, understandable.

**intemperate** adj drunken; excessive, extravagant, extreme, immoderate, inordinate, unbridled, uncontrolled, unrestrained; self-indulgent.

**intend** vb aim at, contemplate, design, determine, drive at, mean, meditate, propose, purpose, think of.

**intendant** n inspector, overseer, superintendent, supervisor.

**intense** adj ardent, earnest, fervid, passionate, vehement; close, intent, severe, strained, stretched, strict; energetic, forcible, keen, potent, powerful, sharp, strong, vigorous, violent; acute, deep, extreme, exquisite, grievous, poignant.

**intensify** vb aggravate, concentrate, deepen, enhance, heighten, quicken, strengthen, whet.

**intensity** n closeness, intenseness, severity, strictness; excess, extremity, violence; activity, energy, force, power, strength, vigour; ardour, earnestness, vehemence.

**intensive** adj emphatic, intensifying.

**intent** adj absorbed, attentive, close, eager, earnest, engrossed, occupied, pre-occupied, zealous; bent, determined, decided, resolved, set. * n aim, design, drift, end, import, intention, mark, meaning, object, plan, purport, purpose, purview, scope, view.

**intention** n aim, design, drift, end, import, intent, mark, meaning, object, plan, purport, purpose, purview, scope, view.

**intentional** adj contemplated, deliberate, designed, intended, preconcerted, predetermined, premeditated, purposed, studied, voluntary, wilful.

**inter** vb bury, commit to the earth, entomb, inhume, inurn.

**intercalate** vb insert, interpolate.

**intercede** vb arbitrate, interpose, mediate; entreat, plead, supplicate.

**intercept** vb cut off, interrupt, obstruct, seize.

**intercession** n interposition, intervention, mediation; entreaty, pleading, prayer, supplication.

**intercessor** n interceder, mediator.

**interchange** vb alternate, change, exchange, vary. * n alternation.

**interchangeableness** n interchangeability.

**interchangeably** adv alternately.

**intercourse** n commerce, communication, communion, connection, converse, correspondence, dealings, fellowship, truck; acquaintance, intimacy.

**interdict** vb debar, forbid, inhibit, prohibit, prescribe, proscribe, restrain from. * n ban, decree, interdiction, prohibition.

**interest** vb affect, concern, touch; absorb, attract, engage, enlist, excite, grip, hold, occupy. * n advantage, benefit, good, profit, weal; attention, concern, regard, sympathy; part, participation, portion, share, stake; discount, premium, profit.

**interested** adj attentive, concerned, involved, occupied; biassed, patial, prejudiced; selfish, self-seeking.

**interesting** adj attractive, engaging, entertaining, pleasing.

**interfere** vb intermeddle, interpose, meddle; clash, collide, conflict.

**interference** n intermeddling, interposition; clashing, collision, interfering, opposition.

**interim** n intermediate time, interval, meantime.

**interior** adj inmost, inner, internal, inward; inland, remote; domestic, home. * n inner part, inland, inside.

**interjacent** adj intermediate, interposed, intervening, parenthetical.

**interject** vb comment, inject, insert, interpose.

**interjection** n exclamation.

**interlace** vb bind, complicate, entwine, intersperse, intertwine, interweave, inweave, knit, mix, plait, twine, twist, unite.

**interlard** vb difersify, interminate, intersperse, intertwine, mix, vary.

**interline** vb insert, write between.

**interlineal** adj interlinear, interlined.

**interlink, interlock** vb connect, interchain, interrelate, join.

**interlocution** n colloquy, conference, dialogue, interchange.

**interlocutor** n respondent, speaker.

**interloper** n intruder, meddler.

**intermeddle** vb interfere, interpose, meddle.

**intermediary** n go-between, mediator.

**intermediate** adj interjacent, interposed, intervening, mean, median, middle, transitional.

**interment** n burial, entombment, inhumation, sepulture.

**interminable** adj boundless, endless, illimitable,

immeasurable, infinite, limitless, unbounded, unlimited; long-drawn-out, tedious, wearisome.

**intermingle** vb blend, commingle, commix, intermix, mingle, mix.

**intermission** n cessation, interruption, interval, lull, pause, remission, respite, rest, stop, stoppage, suspension.

**intermit** vb interrupt, intervene, stop, suspend; discontinue, give over, leave off; abate, subside.

**intermittent** adj broken, capricious, discontinuous, fitful, flickering, intermitting, periodic, recurrent, remittent, spasmodic.

**intermix** vb blend, commingle, commix, intermingle, mingle, mix.

**internal** adj inner, inside, interior, inward; incorporeal, mental, spiritual; deeper, emblematic, hidden, higher, metaphorical, secret, symbolical, under; genuine, inherent, intrinsic, real, true; domestic, home, inland, inside.

**international** adj cosmopolitan, universal.

**internecine** adj deadly, destructive, exterminating, exterminatory, interneciary, internecinal, internecive, mortal.

**interpellate** vb interrogate, question.

**interpellation** n interruption; intercession, interposition; interrogation, questioning.

**interplay** n interaction.

**interpolate** vb add, foist, insert, interpose; (math) intercalate, introduce.

**interpose** vb arbitrate, intercede, intervene, mediate; interfere, intermeddle, interrupt, meddle, tamper; insert, interject, put in, remark, sandwich, set between; intrude, thurst in.

**interposition** n intercession, interpellation, intervention, mediation.

**interpret** vb decipher, decode, define, elucidate, explain, expound, solve, unfold, unravel; construe, render, translate.

**interpretation** n meaning, sense, signification; elucidation, explanation, explication, exposition; construction, rendering, rendition, translation, version.

**interpreter** n expositor, expounder, translator.

**interrogate** vb ask, catechize, examine, inquire of, interpellate, question.

**interrogation** n catechizing, examination, examining, interpellation, interrogating, questioning; inquiry, query, question.

**interrogative** adj interrogatory, questioning.

**interrupt** vb break, check, disturb, hinder, intercept, interfere with, obstruct, pretermit, stop; break, cut, disconnect, disjoin, dissever, dissolve, disunite, divide, separate, sever, sunder; break off, cease, discontinue, intermit, leave off, suspend.

**interruption** n hindrance, impediment, obstacle, obstruction, stop, stoppage; cessation, discontinuance, intermission, pause, suspension; break, breaking, disconnecting, disconnection, disjunction, dissolution, disunion, disuniting, division, separation, severing, sundering.

**intersect** vb cross, cut, decussate, divide, interrupt.

**intersection** n crossing.

**interspace** n interlude, interstice, interval.

**intersperse** vb intermingle, scatter, sprinkle; diversify, interlard, mix.

**interstice** n interspace, interval, space; chink, crevice.

**interstitial** adj intermediate, intervening.

**intertwine** vb interlace, intertwine, interweave, inweave, twine.

**interval** n interim, interlude, interregnum, pause, period, recess, season, space, spell, term; interstice, skip.

**intervene** vb come between, interfere, mediate; befall, happen, occur.

**intervening** adj interjacent, intermediate; interstitial.

**intervention** n interference, interposition; agency, mediation.

**interview** n conference, consultation, parley; meeting.

**interweave** vb interlace, intertwine, inweave, weave; intermingle, intermix, mingle, mix.

**intestinal** adj domestic, interior, internal.

**intestines** npl bowels, entrails, guts, insides, inwards, viscera.

**intimacy** n close acquaintance, familiarity, fellowship; friendship; closeness, nearness.

**intimate**[1] adj close, near; familiar, friendly; bosom, chummy, close, dear, homelike, special; confidential, personal, private, secret; detailed, exhaustive, first-hand, immediate, penetrating, profound; cosy, warm. * n chum, confidant, companion, crony, friend.

**intimate**[2] vb allude to, express, hint, impart, indicate, insinuate, signify, suggest, tell.

**intimately** adv closely, confidentially, familiarly, nearly, thoroughly.

**intimation** n allusion, hint, innuendo, insinuation, suggestion.

**intimidate** vb abash, affright, alarm, appal, browbeat, bully, cow, daunt, dishearten, dismay, frighten, overawe, scare, subdue, terrify, terrorize.

**intimidation** n fear, intimidating, terror, terrorism.

**intolerable** adj insufferable, insupportable, unbearable, unendurable.

**intolerance** n bigotry, narrowness; impatience, rejection.

**intolerant** adj bigoted, narrow, proscriptive; dictatorial, impatient, imperious, overbearing, supercilious.

**intonation** n cadence, modulation, tone; musical recitation.

**in toto** adv entirely, wholly.

**intoxicate** vb fuddle, inebriate, muddle.

**intoxicated** adj boozy, drunk, drunken, fuddled, inebriated, maudlin, mellow, muddled, stewed, tight, tipsy.

**intoxication** n drunkenness, ebriety, inebriation, inebriety; excitement, exhilaration, infatuation.

**intractability** n cantankerousness, contrariety, inflexibility, intractableness, obduracy, obstinacy, perverseness, perversity, pig-headedness, stubbornness, wilfulness.

**intractable** adj cantankerous, contrary, contumacious, cross-grained, dogged, froward, headstrong, indocile, inflexible, mulish, obdurate, obstinate, perverse, pig-headed, refractory, restive, stubborn, tough, uncontrollable, ungovernable, unmanageable, unruly, unyielding, wilful.

**intrench** see **entrench**.

**intrenchment** see **entrenchment**.

**intrepid** adj bold, brave, chivalrous, courageous, daring, dauntless, doughty, fearless, gallant, heroic, unappalled, unawed, undaunted, undismayed, unterrified, valiant, valorous.

**intrepidity** n boldness, bravery, courage, daring, dauntlessness, fearlessness, gallantry, heroism, intrepidness, prowess, spirit, valour.

**intricacy** n complexity, complication, difficulty, entanglement, intricateness, involution, obscurity, perplexity.

**intricate** adj complicated, difficult, entangled, involved, mazy, obscure, perplexed.

**intrigue** vb connive, conspire, machinate, plot, scheme; beguile, bewitch, captivate, charm, fascinate. * n artifice, cabal, conspiracy, deception, finesse, Machiavelianism, machination, manoeuvre, plot, ruse, scheme, stratagem, wile; amour, liaison, love affair.

**intriguing** adj arch, artful, crafty, crooked, cunning, deceitful, designing, diplomatic, foxy, Machiavelian, insidious, politic, sly, sneaky, subtle, tortuous, trickish, tricky, wily.

**intrinsic** adj essential, genuine, real, sterling, true; inborn, inbred, ingrained, inherent, internal, inward, native, natural.

**intrinsically** adv essentially, really, truly; inherently, naturally.

**introduce** vb bring in, conduct, import, induct, inject, insert, lead in, usher in; present; begin, broach, commence, inaugurate, initiate, institute, start.

**introduction** n exordium, preface, prelude, proem; introducing, ushering in; presentation.

**introductory** adj precursory, prefatory, preliminary, proemial.

**introspection** n introversion, self-contemplation.

**intrude** vb encroach, impose, infringe, interfere, interlope, obtrude, trespass.

**intruder** n interloper, intermeddler, meddler, stranger.

**intrusion** n encroachment, infringement, intruding, obtrusion.

**intrusive** adj obtrusive, trespassing.

**intuition** n apprehension, cognition, insight, instinct; clairvoyance, divination, presentiment.

**intuitive** adj instinctive, intuitional, natural; clear, distinct, full, immediate.

**intumesce** vb bubble up, dilate, expand, swell.

**intumescence** n inturgescence, swelling, tumefaction, turgescence.

**inundate** vb deluge, drown, flood, glut, overflow, overwhelm, submerge.

**inundation** n cataclysm, deluge, flood, glut, overflow, superfluity.

**inure** vb accustom, discipline, familiarize, habituate, harden, toughen, train, use.

**inutile** adj bootless, ineffectual, inoperative, unavailing, unprofitable, useless.

**invade** vb encroach upon, infringe, violate; attack, enter in, march into.

**invalid**[1] adj baseless, fallacious, false, inoperative, nugatory, unfounded, unsound, untrue, worthless; (law) null, void.

**invalid**[2] *adj* ailing, bedridden, feeble, frail, ill, infirm, sick, sickly, valetudinary, weak, weakly. * *n* convalescent, patient, valetudinarian.

**invalidate** *vb* abrogate, annul, cancel, nullify, overthrow, quash, repeal, reverse, undo, unmake, vitiate.

**invalidity** *n* baselessness, fallaciousness, fallacy, falsity, unsoundness.

**invaluable** *adj* inestimable; priceless.

**invariable** *adj* changeless, constant, unchanging, uniform, unvarying; changeless, immutable, unalterable, unchangeable.

**invariableness** *n* changelessness, constancy, uniformity, unvaryingness; changelessness, immutability, unchangeableness, invariability.

**invasion** *n* encroachment, incursion, infringement, inroad; aggression, assault, attack, foray, raid.

**invective** *n* abuse, censure, contumely, denunciation, diatribe, railing, reproach, sarcasm, satire, vituperation.

**inveigh** *vb* blame, censure, condemn, declaim against, denounce, exclaim against, rail at, reproach, vituperate.

**inveigle** *vb* contrive, devise; concoct, conceive, create, design, excogitate, frame, imagine, originate; coin, fabricate, forge, spin.

**invent** *vb* concoct, contrive, design, devise, discover, fabricate, find out, frame, originate.

**invention** *n* creation, discovery, ingenuity, inventing, origination; contrivance, design, device; coinage, fabrication, fiction, forgery.

**inventive** *adj* creative, fertile, ingenious.

**inventor** *n* author, contriver, creator, originator.

**inventory** *n* account, catalogue, list, record, roll, register, schedule.

**inverse** *adj* indirect, inverted, opposite, reversed.

**inversion** *n* inverting, reversing, transposal, transposition.

**invert** *vb* capsize, overturn; reverse, transpose.

**invertebrate** *adj* invertebral; spineless.

**invest** *vb* put money into; confer, endow, endue; (*mil*) beset, besiege, enclose, surround; array, clothe, dress.

**investigate** *vb* canvass, consider, dissect, examine, explore, follow up, inquire into, look into, overhaul, probe, question, research, scrutinize, search into, search out, sift, study.

**investigation** *n* examination, exploration, inquiry, inquisition, overhauling, research, scrutiny, search, sifting, study.

**investiture** *n* habilitation, induction, installation, ordination.

**investment** *n* money invested; endowment; (*mil*) beleaguerment, siege; clothes, dress, garments, habiliments, robe, vestment.

**inveteracy** *n* inverateness, obstinacy.

**inveterate** *adj* accustomed, besetting, chronic, confirmed, deep-seated, habitual, habituated, hardened, ingrained, long-established, obstinate.

**invidious** *adj* disagreeable, envious, hateful, odious, offensive, unfair.

**invigorate** *vb* animate, brace, energize, fortify, harden, nerve, quicken, refresh, stimulate, strengthen, vivify.

**invincible** *adj* impregnable, indomitable, ineradicable, insuperable, insurmountable, irrepressible, unconquerable, unsubduable, unyielding.

**inviolable** *adj* hallowed, holy, inviolate, sacramental, sacred, sacrosanct, stainless.

**inviolate** *adj* unbroken, unviolated; pure, stainless, unblemished, undefiled, unhurt, uninjured, unpolluted, unprofaned, unstained; inviolable, sacred.

**invisibility** *n* imperceptibility, indistinctness, invisibleness, obscurity.

**invisible** *adj* impalpable, imperceptible, indistinguishable, intangible, unapparent, undiscernable, unperceivable, unseen.

**invitation** *n* bidding, call, challenge, solicitation, summons.

**invite** *vb* ask, bid, call, challenge, request, solicit, summon; allure, attract, draw on, entice, lead, persuade, prevail upon.

**inviting** *adj* alluring, attractive, bewitching, captivating, engaging, fascinating, pleasing, winning; prepossessing, promising.

**invocation** *n* conjuration, orison, petition, prayer, summoning, supplication.

**invoice** *vb* bill, list. * *n* bill, inventory, list, schedule.

**invoke** *vb* adjure, appeal to, beseech, beg, call upon, conjure, entreat, implore, importune, pray, pray to, solicit, summon, supplicate.

**involuntary** *adj* automatic, blind, instinctive, mechanical, reflex, spontaneous, unintentional; compulsory, reluctant, unwilling.

**involve** *vb* comprise, contain, embrace, imply, include, lead to; complicate, compromise, embarrass, entangle, implicate, incriminate, inculpate; cover, envelop, enwrap, surround, wrap; blend, conjoin, connect, join, mingle; entwine, interlace, intertwine, interweave, inweave.

**invulnerability** n invincibility, invulnerableness.

**invulnerable** adj incontrovertible, invincible, unassailable, irrefragable.

**inward**[1] adj incoming, inner, interior, internal; essential, hidden, mental, spiritual; private, secret.

**inward**[2], **inwards** adv inwardly, towards the inside, within.

**inweave** vb entwine, interlace, intertwine, interweave, weave together.

**iota** n atom, bit, glimmer, grain, jot, mite, particle, scintilla, scrap, shadow, spark, tittle, trace, whit.

**irascibility** n hastiness, hot-headedness, impatience, irascibleness, irritability, peevishness, petulance, quickness, spleen, testiness, touchiness.

**irascible** adj choleric, cranky, hasty, hot, hot-headed, impatient, irritable, nettlesome, peevish, peppery, pettish, petulant, quick, splenetic, snappish, testy, touchy, waspish.

**irate** adj angry, incensed, ireful, irritated, piqued.

**ire** n anger, choler, exasperation, fury, indignation, passion, rage, resentment, wrath.

**ireful** adj angry, furious, incensed, irate, raging, passionate.

**iridescent** adj irisated, nacreous, opalescent, pavonine, prismatic, rainbow-like.

**iris** n rainbow; (bot) fleur-de-lis, flower-de-luce; diaphragm of the eye.

**irksome** adj annoying, burdensome, humdrum, monotonous, tedious, tiresome, wearisome, weary, wearying.

**iron** adj ferric, ferrous.

**ironic, ironical** adj mocking, sarcastic.

**irons** npl chains, fetters, gyves, hampers, manacles, shackles.

**irony** n mockery, raillery, ridicule, sarcasm, satire.

**irradiate** vb brighten, illume, illuminate, illumine, light up, shine upon.

**irrational** adj absurd, extravagant, foolish, injudicious, preposterous, ridiculous, silly, unwise; unreasonable, unreasoning, unthinking; brute, brutish; aberrant, alienated, brainless, crazy, demented, fantastic, idiotic, imbecilic, insane, lunatic.

**irrationality** n absurdity, folly, foolishness, unreasonableness; brutishness.

**irreclaimable** adj hopeless, incurable, irrecoverable, irreparable, irretrievable, irreversible, remediless;

abandoned, graceless, hardened, impenitent, incorrigible, lost, obdurate, profligate, recreant, reprobate, shameless, unrepentant.

**irreconcilable** adj implacable, inexorable, inexpiable, unappeasable; incompatible, incongruous, inconsistent.

**irrecoverable** adj hopeless, incurable, irremediable, irreparable, irretrievable, remediless.

**irrefragable** adj impregnable, incontestable, incontrovertible, indisputable, invincible, irrefutable, irresistible, unanswerable, unassailable, undeniable.

**irrefutable** adj impregnable, incontestable, incontrovertible, indisputable, invincible, irrefragable, irresistible, unanswerable, unassailable, undeniable.

**irregular** adj aberrant, abnormal, anomalistic, anomalous, crooked, devious, eccentric, erratic, exceptional, heteromorphous, raged, tortuous, unconformable, unusual; capricious, changeable, desultory, fitful, spasmodic, uncertain, unpunctual, unsettled, variable; disordered, disorderly, improper, uncanonical, unparliamentary, unsystematic; asymmetric, uneven, unsymmetrical; disorderly, dissolute, immoral, loose, wild. * n casual, freelance, hireling, mercenary.

**irregularity** n aberration, abnormality, anomaly, anomalousness, singularity; capriciousness, changeableness, uncertainty, variableness; asymmetry; disorderliness, dissoluteness, immorality, laxity, looseness, wildness.

**irrelevance, irrelevancy** n impertinency, inapplicability, nonpertinency.

**irrelevant** adj extraneous, foreign, illogical, impertinent, inapplicable, inapposite, inappropriate, inconsequent, unessential, unrelated.

**irreligion** n atheism, godlessness, impiety, ungodliness.

**irreligious** adj godless, ungodly, undevout; blasphemous, disrespectful, impious, irreverent, profane, ribald, wicked.

**irremediable** adj hopeless, incurable, immedicable, irrecoverable, irreparable, remediless.

**irremissible** adj binding, inexpiable, obligatory, unatonable, unpardonable.

**irreparable** adj irrecoverable, irremediable, irretrievable, remediless.

**irreprehensible** adj blameless, faultless, inculpable, innocent, irreproachable, irreprovable, unblamable.

**irrepressible** *adj* insuppressible, uncontrollable, unquenchable, unsmotherable.

**irreproachable** *adj* blameless, faultless, inculpable, innocent, irreprehensible, irreprovable, unblamable.

**irresistible** *adj* irrefragable, irrepressible, overpowering, overwhelming, resistless.

**irresolute** *adj* changeable, faltering, fickle, hesitant, hesitating, inconstant, mutable, spineless, uncertain, undecided, undetermined, unsettled, unstable, unsteady, vacillating, wavering.

**irrespective** *adj* independent, regardless.

**irresponsible** *adj* unaccountable; untrustworthy.

**irretrievable** *adj* incurable, irrecoverable, irremediable, irreparable, remediless.

**irreverence** *n* blasphemy, impiety, profaneness, profanity; disesteem, disrespect.

**irreverent** *adj* blasphemous, impious, irreligious, profane; disrespectful, slighting.

**irreversible** *adj* irrepealable, irrevocable, unalterable, unchangeable; changeless, immutable, invariable.

**irrevocable** *adj* irrepealable, irreversible, unalterable, unchangeable.

**irrigate** *vb* moisten, wash, water, wet.

**irrigation** *n* watering.

**irritability** *n* excitability, fretfulness, irascibility, peevishness, petulance, snappishness, susceptibility, testiness.

**irritable** *adj* captious, choleric, excitable, fiery, fretful, hasty, hot, irascible, passionate, peppery, peevish, pettish, petulant, snappish, splenetic, susceptible, testy, touchy, waspish.

**irritate** *vb* anger, annoy, chafe, enrage, exacerbate, exasperate, fret, incense, jar, nag, nettle, offend, provoke, rasp, rile, ruffle, vex; gall, tease; (*med*) excite, inflame, stimulate.

**irritation** *n* irritating; anger, exacerbation, exasperation, excitement, indignation, ire, passion, provocation, resentment, wrath; (*med*) excitation, inflammation, stimulation; burn, itch.

**irruption** *n* breaking in, bursting in; foray, incursion, inroad, invasion, raid.

**island** *n* atoll, isle, islet, reef.

**isochronal** *adj* isochronous, uniform.

**isolate** *vb* detach, dissociate, insulate, quarantine, segregate, separate, set apart.

**isolated** *adj* detached, separate, single, solitary.

**isolation** *n* detachment, disconnection, insulation, quarantine, segregation, separation; loneliness, solitariness, solitude.

**issue** *vb* come out, flow out, flow forth, gush, run, rush out, spout, spring, spurt, well; arise, come, emanate, ensue, flow, follow, originate, proceed, spring; end, eventuate, result, terminate; appear, come out, deliver, depart, debouch, discharge, emerge, emit, put forth, send out; distribute, give out; publish, utter. * *n* conclusion, consequence, consummation, denouement, end, effect, event, finale, outcome, result, termination, upshot; antagonism, contest, controversy; debouchment, delivering, delivery, discharge, emergence, emigration, emission, issuance; flux, outflow, outpouring, stream; copy, edition, number; egress, exit, outlet, passage out, vent, way out; escape, sally, sortie; children, offspring, posterity, progeny.

**itch** *vb* tingle. * *n* itching; burning, coveting, importunate craving, teasing desire, uneasy hankering.

**itching** *n* itch; craving, longing, importunate craving, desire, appetite, hankering.

**item** *adv* also, in like manner. * *n* article, detail, entry, particular, point.

**iterate** *vb* reiterate, repeat.

**itinerant** *adj* nomadic, peripatetic, roaming, roving, travelling, unsettled, wandering.

**itinerary** *n* guide, guidebook; circuit, route.

# J

**jabber** vb chatter, gabble, prate, prattle.

**jacket** n casing, cover, sheath; anorak, blazer coat, doublet, jerkin.

**jaded** adj dull, exhausted, fatigued, satiated, tired, weary.

**jagged** adj cleft, divided, indented, notched, serrated, ragged, uneven.

**jail, gaol** n bridewell, (sl) clink, dungeon, lockup, (sl) nick, penitentiary, prison.

**jam** vb block, crowd, crush, press. * n block, crowd, crush, mass, pack, press.

**jangle** vb bicker, chatter, dispute, gossip, jar, quarrel, spar, spat, squabble, tiff, wrangle. * n clang, clangour, clash, din, dissonance.

**jar**[1] vb clash, grate, interfere, shake; bicker, contend, jangle, quarrel, spar, spat, squabble, tiff, wrangle; agitate, jolt, jounce, shake. * n clash, conflict, disaccord, discord, jangle, dissonance; agitation, jolt, jostle, shake, shaking, shock, start.

**jar**[2] n can, crock, cruse, ewer, flagon.

**jarring** adj conflicting, discordant, inconsistent, inconsonant, wrangling.

**jargon** n gabble, gibberish, nonsense, rigmarole; argot, cant, lingo, slang; chaos, confusion, disarray, disorder, jumble.

**jaundiced** adj biased, envious, prejudiced.

**jaunt** n excursion, ramble, tour, trip.

**jaunty** adj airy, cheery, garish, gay, fine, fluttering, showy, sprightly, unconcerned.

**jealous** adj distrustful, envious, suspicious; anxious, apprehensive, intolerant, solicitous, zealous.

**jealousy** n envy, suspicion, watchfulness.

**jeer** vb deride, despise, flout, gibe, jape, jest, mock, scoff, sneer, spurn, rail, ridicule, taunt. * n abuse, derision, mockery, sneer, ridicule, taunt.

**jeopardize** vb endanger, hazard, imperil, risk, venture.

**jeopardy** n danger, hazard, peril, risk, venture.

**jerk** vb, n flip, hitch, pluck, tweak, twitch, yank.

**jest** vb banter, joke, quiz. * n fun, joke, pleasantry, raillery, sport.

**jester** n humorist, joker, wag; buffoon, clown, droll, fool, harlequin, punch.

**jibe** see **gibe**.

**jiffy** n instant, moment, second, twinkling, trice.

**jilt** vb break with, deceive, disappoint, discard. * n coquette, flirt, light-o'-love.

**jingle** vb chink, clink, jangle, rattle, tinkle. * n chink, clink, jangle, rattle, tinkle; chorus, ditty, melody, song.

**jocose** adj comical, droll, facetious, funny, humorous, jesting, jocular, merry, sportive, waggish, witty.

**jocund** adj airy, blithe, cheerful, debonair, frolicsome, jolly, joyful, joyous, lively, merry, playful.

**jog** vb jostle, notify, nudge, push, remind, warn; canter, run, trot. * n push, reminder.

**join** vb add, annex, append, attach; cement, combine, conjoin, connect, couple, dovetail, link, unite, yoke; amalgamate, assemble, associate, confederate, consolidate.

**joint** vb fit, join, unite. * adj combined, concerted, concurrent, conjoint. * n connection, junction, juncture, hinge, splice.

**joke** vb banter, jest, frolic, rally. * n crank, jest, quip, quirk, witticism.

**jolly** adj airy, blithe, cheerful, frolicsome, gamesome, facetious, funny, gay, jovial, joyous, merry, mirthful, jocular, jocund, playful, sportive, sprightly, waggish; bouncing, chubby, lusty, plump, portly, stout.

**jolt** vb jar, shake, shock. * n jar, jolting, jounce, shaking.

**jostle** vb collide, elbow, hustle, joggle, shake, shoulder, shove.

**jot** n ace, atom, bit, corpuscle, iota, grain, mite, particle, scrap, whit.

**journal** n daybook, diary, log; gazette, magazine, newspapers, periodical.

**journey** vb ramble, roam, rove, travel; fare, go, proceed. * n excursion, expedition, jaunt, passage, pilgrimage, tour, travel, trip, voyage.

**jovial** adj airy, convivial, festive, jolly, joyous, merry, mirthful.

**joy** n beatification, beatitude, delight, ecstasy, exultation, gladness, glee, mirth, pleasure, rapture, ravishment, transport; bliss, felicity, happiness.

**joyful** *adj* blithe, blithesome, buoyant, delighted, elate, elated, exultant, glad, happy, jocund, jolly, joyous, merry, rejoicing.

**jubilant** *adj* exultant, exulting, rejoicing, triumphant.

**judge** *vb* conclude, decide, decree, determine, pronounce; adjudicate, arbitrate, condemn, doom, sentence, try, umpire; account, apprehend, believe, consider, deem, esteem, guess, hold, imagine, measure, reckon, regard, suppose, think; appreciate, estimate. * *n* adjudicator, arbiter, arbitrator, bencher, justice, magistrate, moderator, referee, umpire, connoisseur, critic.

**judgment, judgement** *n* brains, ballast, circumspection, depth, discernment, discretion, discrimination, intelligence, judiciousness, penetration, prudence, sagacity, sense, sensibility, taste, understanding, wisdom, wit; conclusion, consideration, decision, determination, estimation, notion, opinion, thought; adjudication, arbitration, award, censure, condemnation, decree, doom, sentence.

**judicious** *adj* cautious, considerate, cool, critical, discriminating, discreet, enlightened, provident, politic, prudent, rational, reasonable, sagacious, sensible, sober, solid, sound, staid, wise.

**jug** *n* cruse, ewer, flagon, pitcher, vessel.

**juicy** *adj* lush, moist, sappy, succulent, watery; entertaining, exciting, interesting, lively, racy, spicy.

**jumble** *vb* confound, confuse, disarrange, disorder, mix, muddle. * *n* confusion, disarrangement, disorder, medley, mess, mixture, muddle.

**jump** *vb* bound, caper, clear, hop, leap, skip, spring, vault. * *n* bound, caper, hop, leak, skip, spring, vault; fence, hurdle, obstacle; break, gap, interruption, space; advance, boost, increase, rise; jar, jolt, shock, start, twitch.

**junction** *n* combination, connection, coupling, hook-up, joining, linking, seam, union; conjunction, joint, juncture.

**junta** *n* cabal, clique, combination, confederacy, coterie, faction, gang, league, party, set.

**just** *adj* equitable, lawful, legitimate, reasonable, right, rightful; candid, even-handed, fair, fair-minded, impartial; blameless, conscientious, good, honest, honourable, pure, square, straightforward, virtuous; accurate, correct, exact, normal, proper, regular, true; condign, deserved, due, merited, suitable.

**justice** *n* accuracy, equitableness, equity, fairness, honesty, impartiality, justness, right; judge, justiciary.

**justifiable** *adj* defensible, fit, proper, right, vindicable, warrantable.

**justification** *n* defence, exculpation, excuse, exoneration, reason, vindication, warrant.

**justify** *vb* approve, defend, exculpate, excuse, exonerate, maintain, vindicate, support, warrant.

**justness** *n* accuracy, correctness, fitness, justice, precision, propriety.

**juvenile** *adj* childish, immature, puerile, young, youthful. * *n* boy, child, girl, youth.

**juxtaposition** *n* adjacency, contiguity, contact, proximity.

# K

**keen**[1] *adj* ardent, eager, earnest, fervid, intense, vehement, vivid; acute, sharp; cutting; acrimonious, biting, bitter, caustic, poignant, pungent, sarcastic, severe; astute, discerning, intelligent, quick, sagacious, sharp-sighted, shrewd.

**keen**[2] *vb* bemoan, bewail, deplore, grieve, lament, mourn, sorrow, weep. * *n* coronach, dirge, elegy, lament, lamentation, monody, plaint, requiem, threnody.

**keenness** *n* ardour, eagerness, fervour, vehemence, zest; acuteness, sharpness; rigour, severity, sternness; acrimony, asperity, bitterness, causticity, causticness, pungency; astuteness, sagacity, shrewdness.

**keep** *vb* detain, hold, retain; continue, preserve; confine, detain, reserve, restrain, withhold; attend, guard, preserve, protect; adhere to, fulfil; celebrate, commemorate, honour, observe, perform, solemnize; maintain, support, sustain; husband, save, store; abide, dwell, lodge, stay, remain; endure, last. * *n* board, maintenance, subsistence, support; donjon, dungeon, stronghold, tower.

**keeper** *n* caretaker, conservator, curator, custodian, defender, gaoler, governor, guardian, jailer, superintendent, warden, warder, watchman.

**keeping** *n* care, charge, custody, guard, possession; feed, maintenance, support; agreement, conformity, congruity, consistency, harmony.

**keepsake** *n* memento, souvenir, token.

**ken** *n* cognizance, sight, view.

**key** *adj* basic, crucial, essential, important, major, principal. * *n* lock-opener, opener; clue, elucidation, explanation, guide, solution, translation; (*mus*) keynote, tonic; clamp, lever, wedge.

**kick** *vb* boot, punt; oppose, rebel, resist, spurn. * *n* force, intensity, power, punch, vitality; excitement, pleasure, thrill.

**kidnap** *vb* abduct, capture, carry off, remove, steal away.

**kill** *vb* assassinate, butcher, dispatch, destroy, massacre, murder, slaughter, slay.

**kin** *adj* akin, allied, cognate, kindred, related. * *n* affinity, consanguinity, relationship; connections, family, kindred, kinsfolk, relations, relatives, siblings.

**kind**[1] *adj* accommodating, amiable, beneficent, benevolent, benign, bland, bounteous, brotherly, charitable, clement, compassionate, complaisant, gentle, good, good-natured, forbearing, friendly, generous, gracious, humane, indulgent, lenient, mild, obliging, sympathetic, tender, tender-hearted.

**kind**[2] *n* breed, class, family, genus, race, set, species, type; brand, character, colour, denomination, description, form; make, manner, nature, persuasion, sort, stamp, strain, style,

**kindle** *vb* fire, ignite, inflame, light; animate, awaken, bestir, exasperate, excite, foment, incite, provoke, rouse, stimulate, stir, thrill, warm.

**kindliness** *n* amiability, benevolence, benignity, charity, compassion, friendliness, humanity, kindness, sympathy; gentleness, mildness, softness.

**kindly** *adj* appropriate, congenial, kindred, natural, proper; benevolent, considerate, friendly, gracious, humane, sympathetic, well-disposed. * *adv* agreeably, graciously, humanely, politely, thoughtfully.

**kindness** *n* benefaction, charity, favour; amiability, beneficence, benevolence, benignity, clemency, generosity, goodness, grace, humanity, kindliness, mildness, philanthropy, sympathy, tenderness.

**kindred** *adj* akin, allied, congenial, connected, related, sympathetic. * *n* affinity, consanguinity, flesh, relationship; folks, kin, kinsfolk, kinsmen, relations, relatives.

**king** *n* majesty, monarch, sovereign.

**kingdom** *n* dominion, empire, monarchy, rule, sovereignty, supremacy; region, tract; division, department, domain, province, realm.

**kingly** *adj* imperial, kinglike, monarchical, regal, royal, sovereign; august, glorious, grand, imperial, imposing, magnificent, majestic, noble, splendid.

**kink** *n* cramp, crick, curl, entanglement, knot, loop, twist; crochet, whim, wrinkle.

**kinsfolk** *n* kin, kindred, kinsmen, relations, relatives.

**kit** *n* equipment, implements, outfit, set, working.

**knack** *n* ability, address, adroitness, aptitude, aptness;

dexterity, dextrousness, expertness, facility, quickness, readiness, skill.

**knave** n caitiff, cheat, miscreant, rascal, rogue, scamp, scapegrace, scoundrel, sharper, swindler, trickster, villain.

**knavery** n criminality, dishonesty, fraud, knavishness, rascality, scoundrelism, trickery, villainy.

**knavish** adj dishonest, fraudulent, rascally, scoundrelly, unprincipled, roguish, trickish, tricky, villainous.

**knell** vb announce, peal, ring, toll. * n chime, peal, ring, toll.

**knife** vb cut, slash, stab. * n blade, jackknife, lance.

**knit** vb connect, interlace, join, unite, weave.

**knob** n boss, bunch, hunch, lump, protuberance, stud.

**knock** vb clap, cuff, hit, rap, rattle, slap, strike, thump; beat, blow, box. * n blow, slap, smack, thump; blame, criticism, rejection, setback.

**knoll** n hill, hillock, mound.

**knot** vb complicate, entangle, gnarl, kink, tie, weave. * n complication, entanglement; connection, tie; joint, node, knag; bunch, rosette, tuft; band, cluster, clique, crew, gang, group, pack, set, squad.

**knotty** adj gnarled, hard, knaggy, knurled, knotted, rough, rugged; complex, difficult, harassing, intricate, involved, perplexing, troublesome.

**know** vb apprehend, comprehend, cognize, discern, perceive, recognize, see, understand; discriminate, distinguish.

**knowing** adj accomplished, competent, experienced, intelligent, proficient, qualified, skilful, well-informed; aware, conscious, percipient, sensible, thinking; cunning, expressive, significant.

**knowingly** adv consciously, intentionally, purposely, wittingly.

**knowledge** n apprehension, command, comprehension, discernment, judgment, perception, understanding, wit; acquaintance, acquirement, attainments, enlightenment, erudition, information, learning, lore, mastery, scholarship, science; cognition, cognizance, consciousness, ken, notice, prescience, recognition.

**knowledgeable** adj aware, conscious, experienced, well-informed; educated, intelligent, learned, scholarly.

**knuckle** vb cringe, crouch, stoop, submit, yield.

# L

**laborious** adj assiduous, diligent, hardworking, indefatigable, industrious, painstaking, sedulous, toiling; arduous, difficult, fatiguing, hard, Herculean, irksome, onerous, tiresome, toilsome, wearisome.

**labour** vb drudge, endeavour, exert, strive, toil, travail, work. * n drudgery, effort, exertion, industry, pains, toil, work; childbirth, delivery, parturition.

**labyrinth** n entanglement, intricacy, maze, perplexity, windings.

**labyrinthine** adj confused, convoluted, intricate, involved, labyrinthian, labyrinthic, perplexing, winding.

**lace** vb attach, bind, fasten, intertwine, tie, twine. * n filigree, lattice, mesh, net, netting, network, openwork, web.

**lacerate** vb claw, cut, lancinate, mangle, rend, rip, sever, slash, tear, wound; afflict, harrow, rend, torture, wound.

**lack** vb need, want. * n dearth, default, defectiveness, deficiency, deficit, destitution, insufficiency, need, scantiness, scarcity, shortcoming, shortness, want.

**lackadaisical** adj languishing, sentimental, pensive.

**laconic** adj brief, compact, concise, pithy, sententious, short, succinct, terse.

**lad** n boy, schoolboy, stripling, youngster, youth.

**lading** n burden, cargo, freight, load.

**ladylike** adj courtly, genteel, refined, well-bred.

**lag** vb dawdle, delay, idle, linger, loiter, saunter, tarry.

**laggard** n idler, lingerer, loiterer, lounger, saunterer, sluggard.

**lair** n burrow, couch, den, form, resting place.

**lambent** adj flickering, gliding, gleaming, licking, touching, twinkling.

**lame** vb cripple, disable, hobble. * adj crippled, defective, disabled, halt, hobbling, limping; feeble, insufficient, poor, unsatisfactory, weak.

**lament** vb complain, grieve, keen, moan, mourn, sorrow, wail, weep; bemoan, bewail, deplore, regret. * n complaint, lamentation, moan, moaning, plaint, wailing; coronach, dirge, elegy, keen, monody, requiem, threnody.

**lamentable** adj deplorable, doleful, grievous, lamented, melancholy, woeful; contemptible, miserable, pitiful, poor, wretched.

**lamentation** n dirge, grief, lament, moan, moaning, mourning, plaint, ululation, sorrow, wailing.

**lampoon** vb calumniate, defame, lash, libel, parody, ridicule, satirize, slander. * n calumny, defamation, libel, parody, pasquinade, parody, satire, slander.

**land** vb arrive, debark, disembark. * n earth, ground, soil; country, district, province, region, reservation, territory, tract, weald.

**landlord** n owner, proprietor; host, hotelier, innkeeper.

**landscape** n prospect, scene, view.

**language** n dialect, speech, tongue, vernacular; conversation; expression, idiom, jargon, parlance, phraseology, slang, style, terminology; utterance, voice.

**languid** adj drooping, exhausted, faint, feeble, flagging, languishing, pining, weak; dull, heartless, heavy, inactive, listless, lukewarm, slow, sluggish, spiritless, torpid.

**languish** vb decline, droop, fade, fail, faint, pine, sicken, sink, wither.

**languor** n debility, faintness, feebleness, languidness, languishment, weakness; apathy, ennui, heartlessness, heaviness, lethargy, listlessness, torpidness, torpor, weariness.

**lank** adj attenuated, emaciated, gaunt, lean, meagre, scraggy, slender, skinny, slim, starveling, thin.

**lap**[1] vb drink, lick, mouth, tongue; plash, ripple, splash, wash; quaff, sip, sup, swizzle, tipple. * n draught, dram, drench, drink, gulp, lick, swig, swill, quaff, sip, sup, suck; plash, splash, wash.

**lap**[2] vb cover, enfold, fold, turn, twist, swaddle, wrap; distance, pass, outdistance, overlap. * n fold, flap, lappet, lapel, ply, plait; ambit, beat, circle, circuit, cycle, loop, orbit, revolution, round, tour, turn, walk.

**lapse** vb glide, sink, slide, slip; err, fail, fall. * n course, flow, gliding; declension, decline, fall; error, fault, indiscretion, misstep, shortcoming, slip.

**larceny** n pilfering, robbery, stealing, theft, thievery.

**large** *adj* big, broad, bulky, colossal, elephantine, enormous, heroic, great, huge, immense, vast; broad, expanded, extensive, spacious, wide; abundant, ample, copious, full, liberal, plentiful; capacious, comprehensive.

**lascivious** *adj* concupiscent, immodest, incontinent, goatish, lecherous, lewd, libidinous, loose, lubricious, lustful, prurient, salacious, sensual, unchaste, voluptuous, wanton.

**lash**[1] *vb* belay, bind, strap, tie; fasten, join, moor, pinion, secure.

**lash**[2] *vb* beat, castigate, chastise, flagellate, flail, flay, flog, goad, scourge, swinge, thrash, whip; assail, censure, excoriate, lampoon, satirize, trounce. * *n* scourge, strap, thong, whip; cut, slap, smack, stroke, stripe.

**lass** *n* damsel, girl, lassie, maiden, miss.

**lassitude** *n* dullness, exhaustion, fatigue, languor, languidness, prostration, tiredness, weariness.

**last**[1] *vb* abide, carry on, continue, dwell, endure, extend, maintain, persist, prevail, remain, stand, stay, survive.

**last**[2] *adj* hindermost, hindmost, latest; conclusive, final, terminal, ultimate; eventual, endmost, extreme, farthest, ultimate; greatest, highest, maximal, maximum, most, supreme, superlative, utmost; latest, newest; aforegoing, foregoing, latter, preceding; departing, farewell, final, leaving, parting, valedictory. * *n* conclusion, consummation, culmination, end, ending, finale, finis, finish, termination.

**last**[3] *n* cast, form, matrix, mould, shape, template.

**lasting** *adj* abiding, durable, enduring, fixed, perennial, permanent, perpetual, stable.

**lastly** *adv* conclusively, eventually, finally, ultimately.

**late** *adj* behindhand, delayed, overdue, slow, tardy; deceased, former; recent. * *adv* lately, recently, sometime; tardily.

**latent** *adj* abeyant, concealed, hidden, invisible, occult, secret, unseen, veiled.

**latitude** *n* amplitude, breadth, compass, extent, range, room, scope; freedom, indulgence, liberty; laxity.

**latter** *adj* last, latest, modern, recent.

**lattice** *n* espalier, grating, latticework, trellis.

**laud** *vb* approve, celebrate, extol, glorify, magnify, praise.

**laudable** *adj* commendable, meritorious, praiseworthy.

**laugh** *vb* cackle, chortle, chuckle, giggle, guffaw, snicker, snigger, titter. * *n* chortle, chuckle, giggle, guffaw, laughter, titter.

**laughable** *adj* amusing, comical, diverting, droll, farcical, funny, ludicrous, mirthful, ridiculous.

**laughter** *n* cackle, chortle, chuckle, glee, giggle, guffaw, laugh, laughing.

**launch** *vb* cast, dart, dispatch, hurl, lance, project, throw; descant, dilate, enlarge, expiate; begin, commence, inaugurate, open, start.

**lavish** *vb* dissipate, expend, spend, squander, waste. * *adj* excessive, extravagant, generous, immoderate, overliberal, prodigal, profuse, thriftless, unrestrained, unstinted, unthrifty, wasteful.

**law** *n* act, code, canon, command, commandment, covenant, decree, edict, enactment, order, precept, principle, statute, regulation, rule; jurisprudence; litigation, process, suit.

**lawful** *adj* constitutional, constituted, legal, legalized, legitimate; allowable, authorized, permissible, warrantable; equitable, rightful, just, proper, valid.

**lawless** *adj* anarchic, anarchical, chaotic, disorderly, insubordinate, rebellious, reckless, riotous, seditious, wild.

**lawyer** *n* advocate, attorney, barrister, counsel, counsellor, pettifogger, solicitor.

**lax** *adj* loose, relaxed, slow; drooping, flabby, soft; neglectful, negligent, remiss; dissolute, immoral, licentious, seditious, wild.

**lay**[1] *vb* deposit, establish, leave, place, plant, posit, put, set, settle, spread; arrange, dispose, locate, organize, position; bear, produce; advance, lodge, offer, submit; allocate, allot, ascribe, assign, attribute, charge, impute; concoct, contrive, design, plan, plot, prepare; apply, burden, encumber, impose, saddle, tax; bet, gamble, hazard, risk, stake, wager; allay, alleviate, appease, assuage, calm, relieve, soothe, still, suppress; disclose, divulge, explain, reveal, show, unveil; acquire, grab, grasp, seize; assault, attack, beat up; discover, find, unearth; bless, confirm, consecrate, ordain. * *n* arrangement, array, form, formation; attitude, aspect, bearing, demeanour, direction, lie, pose, position, posture, set.

**lay**[2] *adj* amateur, inexpert, nonprofessional; civil, laic, laical, nonclerical, nonecclesiastical, nonreligious, secular, temporal, unclerical.

**lay**[3] *n* ballad, carol, ditty, lied, lyric, ode, poem, rhyme, round, song, verse.

**layer** n bed, course, lay, seam, stratum.

**laziness** n idleness, inactivity, indolence, slackness, sloth, fulness, sluggishness, tardiness.

**lazy** adj idle, inactive, indolent, inert, slack, slothful, slow, sluggish, supine, torpid.

**lead** vb conduct, deliver, direct, draw, escort, guide; front, head, precede; advance, excel, outstrip, pass; allure, entice, induce, persuade, prevail; conduce, contribute, serve, tend. * adj chief, first, foremost, main, primary, prime, principal. * n direction, guidance, leadership; advance; precedence, priority.

**leader** n conductor, director, guide; captain, chief, chieftain, commander, head; superior, dominator, victor.

**leading** adj governing, ruling; capital, chief, first, foremost, highest, principal, superior.

**league** vb ally, associate, band, combine, confederate, unite. * n alliance, association, coalition, combination, combine, confederacy, confederation, consortium, union.

**leak** vb drip, escape, exude, ooze, pass, percolate, spill. * n chink, crack, crevice, hole, fissure, oozing, opening; drip, leakage, leaking, percolation.

**lean**[1] adj bony, emaciated, gaunt, lank, meagre, poor, skinny, thin; dull, barren, jejune, meagre, tame; inadequate, pitiful, scanty, slender; bare, barren, infertile, unproductive.

**lean**[2] vb incline, slope; bear, recline, repose, rest; confide, depend, rely, trust.

**leaning** n aptitude, bent, bias, disposition, inclination, liking, predilection, proneness, propensity, tendency.

**leap** vb bound, clear, jump, spring, vault; caper, frisk, gambol, hop, skip. * n bound, jump, spring, vault; caper, frisk, gambol, hop, skip.

**learn** vb acquire, ascertain, attain, collect, gain, gather, hear, memorize.

**learned** adj erudite, lettered, literate, scholarly, well-read; expert, experienced, knowing, skilled, versed, well-informed.

**learner** n beginner, novice, pupil, student, tyro.

**learning** n acquirements, attainments, culture, education, information, knowledge, lore, scholarship, tuition.

**least** adj meanest, minutest, smallest, tiniest.

**leave**[1] vb abandon, decamp, go, quit, vacate, withdraw; desert, forsake, relinquish, renounce; commit, consign; refer; cease, desist from, discontinue, refrain,

stop; allow, let, let alone, permit; bequeath, demise, desist, will.

**leave**[2] n allowance, liberty, permission, licence, sufferance; departure, retirement, withdrawal; adieu, farewell, goodbye.

**leaven** vb ferment, lighten, raise; colour, elevate, imbue, inspire, lift, permeate, tinge; infect, vitiate. * n barm, ferment, yeast; influence, inspiration.

**leavings** npl bits, dregs, fragments, leftovers, pieces, relics, remains, remnants, scraps.

**lecherous** adj carnal, concupiscent, incontinent, lascivious, lewd, libidinous, lubricious, lustful, wanton, salacious, unchaste.

**lechery** n concupiscence, lasciviousness, lewdness, lubriciousness, lubricity, lust, salaciousness, salacity.

**lecture** vb censure, chide, reprimand, reprove, scold, sermonize; address, harangue, teach. * n censure, lecturing, lesson, reprimand, reproof, scolding; address, discourse, prelection.

**ledge** n projection, ridge, shelf.

**lees** npl dregs, precipitate, refuse, sediment, settlings.

**leg** n limb, prop.

**legacy** n bequest, gift, heirloom; heritage, inheritance, tradition.

**legal** adj allowable, authorized, constitutional, lawful, legalized, legitimate, proper, sanctioned.

**legalize** vb authorize, legitimate, legitimatize, legitimize, permit, sanction.

**legend** n fable, fiction, myth, narrative, romance, story, tale.

**legendary** adj fabulous, fictitious, mythical, romantic.

**legible** adj clear, decipherable, fair, distinct, plain, readable; apparent, discoverable, recognizable, manifest.

**legion** n army, body, cohort, column, corps, detachment, detail, division, force, maniple, phalanx, platoon; squad; army, horde, host, multitude, number, swarm, throng. * adj many, multitudinous, myriad, numerous.

**legislate** vb enact, ordain.

**legitimacy** n lawfulness, legality; genuineness.

**legitimate** adj authorized, lawful, legal, sanctioned; genuine, valid; correct, justifiable, logical, reasonable, warrantable, warranted.

**leisure** n convenience, ease, freedom, liberty, opportunity, recreation, retirement, vacation.

**lend** vb advance, afford, bestow, confer, furnish, give, grant, impart, loan, supply.

**lengthen** vb elongate, extend, produce, prolong, stretch; continue, protract.

**lengthy** adj diffuse, lengthened, long, long-drawn-out, prolix, prolonged, protracted.

**lenience, leniency** n clemency, compassion, forbearance, gentleness, lenity, mercy, mildness, tenderness.

**lenient** adj assuasive, lenitive, mitigating, mitigative, softening, soothing; clement, easy, forbearing, gentle, humouring, indulgent, long-suffering, merciful, mild, tender, tolerant.

**lesion** n derangement, disorder, hurt, injury.

**less** adj baser, inferior, lower, smaller; decreased, fewer, lesser, reduced, smaller, shorter; * adv barely, below, least, under; decreasingly. * prep excepting, lacking, minus, sans, short of, without.

**lessen** vb abate, abridge, contract, curtail, decrease, diminish, narrow, reduce, shrink; degrade, lower; dwindle, weaken.

**lesson** n exercise, task; instruction, precept; censure, chiding, lecture, lecturing, rebuke, reproof, scolding.

**let**[1] vb admit, allow, authorize, permit, suffer; charter, hire, lease, rent.

**let**[2] vb hinder, impede, instruct, prevent. * n hindrance, impediment, interference, obstacle, obstruction, restriction.

**lethal** adj deadly, destructive, fatal, mortal, murderous.

**lethargic** adj apathetic, comatose, drowsy, dull, heavy, inactive, inert, sleepy, stupid, stupefied, torpid.

**lethargy** n apathy, coma, drowsiness, dullness, hypnotism, inactiveness, inactivity, inertia, sleepiness, sluggishness, stupefaction, stupidity, stupor, torpor.

**letter** n epistle, missive, note.

**lettered** adj bookish, educated, erudite, learned, literary, versed, well-read.

**levee** n ceremony, entertainment, reception, party, soiree; embankment.

**level** vb equalize, flatten, horizontalize, smooth; demolish, destroy, raze; aim, direct, point. * adj equal, even, flat, flush, horizontal, plain, plane, smooth. * n altitude, degree, equality, evenness, plain, plane, smoothness; deck, floor, layer, stage, storey, tier.

**levity** n buoyancy, facetiousness, fickleness, flighti-ness, flippancy, frivolity, giddiness, inconstancy, levity, volatility.

**levy** vb collect, exact, gather, tax; call, muster, raise, summon. * n duty, tax.

**lewd** adj despicable, impure, lascivious, libidinous, licentious, loose, lustful, profligate, unchaste, vile, wanton, wicked.

**liability** n accountableness, accountability, duty, obligation, responsibility, tendency; exposedness; debt, indebtedness, obligation.

**liable** adj accountable, amenable, answerable, bound, responsible; exposed, likely, obnoxious, subject.

**liaison** n amour, intimacy, intrigue; connection, relation, union.

**libel** vb calumniate, defame, lampoon, satirize, slander, vilify. * n calumny, defamation, lampoon, satire, slander, vilification, vituperation.

**liberal** adj beneficent, bountiful, charitable, disinterested, free, generous, munificent, open-hearted, princely, unselfish; broad-minded, catholic, chivalrous, enlarged, high-minded, honourable, magnanimous, tolerant, unbiased, unbigoted; abundant, ample, bounteous, full, large, plentiful, unstinted; humanizing, liberalizing, refined, refining.

**liberality** n beneficence, bountifulness, bounty, charity, disinterestedness, generosity, kindness, munificence; benefaction, donation, gift, gratuity, present; broad-mindedness, catholicity, candour, impartiality, large-mindedness, magnanimity, toleration.

**liberate** vb deliver, discharge, disenthral, emancipate, free, manumit, ransom, release.

**libertine** adj corrupt, depraved, dissolute, licentious, profligate, rakish. * n debauchee, lecher, profligate, rake, roue, voluptuary.

**liberty** n emancipation, freedom, independence, liberation, self-direction, self-government; franchise, immunity, privilege; leave, licence, permission.

**libidinous** adj carnal, concupiscent, debauched, impure, incontinent, lascivious, lecherous, lewd, loose, lubricious, lustful, salacious, sensual, unchaste, wanton, wicked.

**licence** n authorization, leave, permission, privilege, right; certificate, charter, dispensation, imprimatur, permit, warrant; anarchy, disorder, freedom, lawlessness, laxity, liberty.

**license** vb allow, authorize, grant, permit, warrant; suffer, tolerate.

**licentious** adj disorderly, riotous, uncontrolled, uncurbed, ungovernable, unrestrained, unruly, wanton; debauched, dissolute, lax, libertine, loose, profligate, rakish; immoral, impure, lascivious, lecherous, lewd, libertine, libidinous, lustful, sensual, unchaste, wicked.

**lick** vb beat, flog, spank, thrash; lap, taste. * n blow, slap, stroke; salt-spring.

**lie**[1] vb couch, recline, remain, repose, rest; consist, pertain.

**lie**[2] vb equivocate, falsify, fib, prevaricate, romance. * n equivocation, falsehood, falsification, fib, misrepresentation, prevarication, untruth; delusion, illusion.

**lief** adv freely, gladly, willingly.

**life** n activity, alertness, animation, briskness, energy, sparkle, spirit, sprightliness, verve, vigour, vivacity; behaviour, conduct, deportment; being, duration, existence, lifetime; autobiography, biography, curriculum vitae, memoirs, story. ·

**lifeless** adj dead, deceased, defunct, extinct, inanimate; cold, dull, flat, frigid, inert, lethargic, passive, pulseless, slow, sluggish, tame, torpid.

**lift** vb elevate, exalt, hoist, raise, uplift. * n aid, assistance, help; elevator.

**light**[1] vb alight, land, perch, settle. * adj porous, sandy, spongy, well-leavened; loose, sandy; free, portable, unburdened, unencumbered; inconsiderable, moderate, negligible, slight, small, trifling, trivial, unimportant; ethereal, feathery, flimsy, gossamer, insubstantial, weightless; easy, effortless, facile; fickle, frivolous, unsettled, unsteady, volatile; airy, buoyant, carefree, light-hearted, lightsome; unaccented, unstressed, weak.

**light**[2] vb conflagrate, fire, ignite, inflame, kindle; brighten, illume, illuminate, illumine, luminate, irradiate, lighten. * adj bright, clear, fair, lightsome; luminous, pale, pearly, whitish. * n dawn, day, daybreak, sunrise; blaze, brightness, effulgence, gleam, illumination, luminosity, phosphorescence, radiance, ray; candle, lamp, lantern, lighthouse, taper, torch; comprehension, enlightenment, information, insight, instruction, knowledge; elucidation, explanation, illustration; attitude, construction, interpretation, observation, reference, regard, respect, view.

**lighten**[1] vb allay, alleviate, ease, mitigate, palliate; disburden, disencumber, relieve, unburden, unload.

**lighten**[2] vb brighten, gleam, shine; light, illume, illuminate, illumine, irradiate; enlighten, inform; emit, flash.

**light-headed** adj dizzy, giddy, vertiginous; confused, delirious, wandering; addle-pated, frivolous, giddy, heedless, indiscreet, light, rattle-brained, thoughtless, volatile.

**light-hearted** adj blithe, blithesome, carefree, cheerful, frolicsome, gay, glad, gladsome, gleeful, happy, jocund, jovial, joyful, lightsome, merry.

**lightness** n flightiness, frivolity, giddiness, levity, volatility; agility, buoyancy, facility.

**like**[1] vb approve, please; cherish, enjoy, love, relish; esteem, fancy, regard; choose, desire, elect, list, prefer, select, wish. * n liking, partiality, preference.

**like**[2] adj alike, allied, analogous, cognate, corresponding, parallel, resembling, similar; equal, same; likely, probable. * adv likely, probably. * n counterpart, equal, match, peer, twin.

**likelihood** n probability, verisimilitude.

**likely** adj credible, liable, possible, probable; agreeable, appropriate, convenient, likable, pleasing, suitable, well-adapted, well-suited. * adv doubtlessly, presumably, probably.

**likeness** n appearance, form, parallel, resemblance, semblance, similarity, similitude; copy, counterpart, effigy, facsimile, image, picture, portrait, representation.

**liking** n desire, fondness, partiality, wish; appearance, bent, bias, disposition, inclination, leaning, penchant, predisposition, proneness, propensity, tendency, turn.

**limb** n arm, extremity, leg, member; bough, branch, offshoot.

**limit** vb bound, circumscribe, define; check, condition, hinder, restrain, restrict. * n bound, boundary, bourn, confine, frontier, march, precinct, term, termination, terminus; check, hindrance, obstruction, restraint, restriction.

**limitation** n check, constraint, restraint, restriction.

**limitless** adj boundless, endless, eternal, illimitable, immeasurable, infinite, never-ending, unbounded, undefined, unending, unlimited.

**limp**[1] vb halt, hitch, hobble, totter. * n hitch, hobble, shamble, shuffle, totter.

**limp**[2] adj drooping, droopy, floppy, sagging, weak; flabby, flaccid, flexible, limber, pliable, relaxed, slack, soft.

**limpid** adj bright, clear, crystal, crystalline, lucid, pellucid, pure, translucent, transparent.

**line** vb align, line up, range, rank, regiment; border, bound, edge, fringe, hem, interline, march, rim, verge; seam, stripe, streak, striate, trace; carve, chisel, crease, cut, crosshatch; define, delineate, describe. * n mark, streak, stripe; cable, cord, rope, string, thread; rank, row; ancestry, family, lineage, race, succession; course, method; business, calling, employment, job, occupation, post, pursuit.

**lineage** n ancestry, birth, breed, descendants, descent, extraction, family, forebears, forefathers, genealogy, house, line, offspring, progeny, race.

**lineament** n feature, line, outline, trait.

**linen** n cloth, fabric, flax, lingerie.

**linger** vb dally, dawdle, delay, idle, lag, loiter, remain, saunter, stay, tarry, wait.

**link** vb bind, conjoin, connect, fasten, join, tie, unite. * n bond, connection, connective, copula, coupler, joint, juncture; division, member, part, piece.

**liquefy** vb dissolve, fuse, melt, thaw.

**liquid** adj fluid; clear, dulcet, flowing, mellifluous, mellifluent, melting, soft. * n fluid, liquor.

**list**[1] vb alphabetize, catalogue, chronicle, codify, docket, enumerate, file, index, inventory, record, register, tabulate, tally; enlist, enroll; choose, desire, elect, like, please, prefer, wish. * n catalogue, enumeration, index, inventory, invoice, register, roll, schedule, scroll, series, table, tally; border, bound, limit; border, edge, selvedge, strip, stripe; fillet, listel.

**list**[2] vb cant, heel, incline, keel, lean, pitch, tilt, tip. * n cant, inclination, incline, leaning, pitch, slope, tilt, tip.

**listen** vb attend, eavesdrop, hark, hear, hearken, heed, obey, observe.

**listless** adj apathetic, careless, heedless, impassive, inattentive, indifferent, indolent, languid, torpid, vacant, supine, thoughtless, vacant.

**listlessness** n apathy, carelessness, heedlessness, impassivity, inattention, indifference, indolence, languidness, languor, supineness, thoughtlessness, torpor, torpidity, vacancy.

**literally** adv actually, really; exactly, precisely, rigorously, strictly.

**literary** adj bookish, book-learned, erudite, instructed, learned, lettered, literate, scholarly, well-read.

**literature** n erudition, learning, letters, lore, writings.

**lithe** adj flexible, flexile, limber, pliable, pliant, supple.

**litigation** n contending, contest, disputing, lawsuit.

**litigious** adj contentious, disputatious, quarrelsome; controvertible, disputable.

**litter** vb derange, disarrange, disorder, scatter, strew; bear. * n bedding, couch, palanquin, sedan, stretcher; confusion, disarray, disorder, mess, untidiness; fragments, rubbish, shreds, trash.

**little** adj diminutive, infinitesimal, minute, small, tiny, wee; brief, short, small; feeble, inconsiderable, insignificant, moderate, petty, scanty, slender, slight, trivial, unimportant, weak; contemptible, illiberal, mean, narrow, niggardly, paltry, selfish, stingy. * n handful, jot, modicum, pinch, pittance, trifle, whit.

**live**[1] vb be, exist; continue, endure, last, remain, survive; abide, dwell, reside; fare, feed, nourish, subsist, support; continue, lead, pass.

**live**[2] adj alive, animate, living, quick; burning, hot, ignited; bright, brilliant, glowing, lively, vivid; active, animated, earnest, glowing, wide-awake.

**livelihood** n living, maintenance, subsistence, support, sustenance.

**liveliness** n activity, animation, briskness, gaiety, spirit, sprightliness, vivacity.

**lively** adj active, agile, alert, brisk, energetic, nimble, quick, smart, stirring, supple, vigorous, vivacious; airy, animated, blithe, blithesome, buoyant, frolicsome, gleeful, jocund, jolly, merry, spirited, sportive, sprightly, spry; bright, brilliant, clear, fresh, glowing, strong, vivid; dynamic, forcible, glowing, impassioned, intense, keen, nervous, piquant, racy, sparkling, strenuous, vigorous.

**living** adj alive, breathing, existing, live, organic, quick; active, lively, quickening. * n livelihood, maintenance, subsistence, support; estate, keeping; benefice.

**load** vb freight, lade; burden, cumber, encumber, oppress, weigh. * n burden, freightage, pack, weight; cargo, freight, lading; clog, deadweight, encumbrance, incubus, oppression, pressure.

**loafer** n (sl) bum, idler, lounger, vagabond, vagrant.

**loath** adj averse, backward, disinclined, indisposed, reluctant, unwilling.

**loathe** vb abhor, abominate, detest, dislike, hate, recoil.

**loathing** n abhorrence, abomination, antipathy, aversion, detestation, disgust, hatred, horror, repugnance, revulsion.

**loathsome** adj disgusting, nauseating, nauseous, offensive, palling, repulsive, revolting, sickening; abominable, abhorrent, detestable, execrable, hateful, odious, shocking.

**local** adj limited, neighbouring, provincial, regional, restricted, sectional, territorial, topical.

**locality** n location, neighbourhood, place, position, site, situation, spot.

**locate** vb determine, establish, fix, place, set, settle.

**lock**[1] vb bolt, fasten, padlock, seal; confine; clog, impede, restrain, stop; clasp, embrace, encircle, enclose, grapple, hug, join, press. * n bolt, fastening, padlock; embrace, grapple, hug.

**lock**[2] n curl, ringlet, tress, tuft.

**lodge** vb deposit, fix, settle; fix, place, plant; accommodate, cover, entertain, harbour, quarter, shelter; abide, dwell, inhabit, live, reside, rest; remain, rest, sojourn, stay, stop. * n cabin, cot, cottage, hovel, hut, shed; cave, den, haunt, lair; assemblage, assembly, association club, group, society.

**lodging** n abode, apartment, dwelling, habitation, quarters, residence; cover, harbour, protection, refuge, shelter.

**loftiness** n altitude, elevation, height; arrogance, haughtiness, pride, vanity; dignity, grandeur, sublimity.

**lofty** adj elevated, high, tall, towering; arrogant, haughty, proud; eminent, exalted, sublime; dignified, imposing, majestic, stately.

**logical** adj close, coherent, consistent, dialectical, sound, valid; discriminating, rational, reasoned.

**loiter** vb dally, dawdle, delay, dilly-dally, idle, lag, linger, saunter, stroll, tarry.

**loneliness** n isolation, retirement, seclusion, solitariness, solitude; desolation, dreariness, forlornness.

**lonely** adj apart, dreary, isolated, lonesome, remote, retired, secluded, separate, sequestrated, solitary; alone, lone, companionless, friendless, unaccompanied; deserted, desolate, forlorn, forsaken, withdrawn.

**lonesome** adj cheerless, deserted, desolate, dreary, gloomy, lone, lonely.

**long**[1] vb anticipate, await, expect; aspire, covet, crave, desire, hanker, lust, pine, wish, yearn.

**long**[2] adj drawn-out, extended, extensive, far-reaching, lengthy, prolonged, protracted, stretched; diffuse, long-winded, prolix, tedious, wearisome; backward, behindhand, dilatory, lingering, slack, slow, tardy.

**longing** n aspiration, coveting, craving, desire, hankering, hunger, pining, yearning.

**long-suffering** adj enduring, forbearing, patient. * n clemency, endurance, forbearing.

**look** vb behold, examine, notice, see, search; consider, inspect, investigate, observe, study, contemplate, gaze, regard, scan, survey, view; anticipate, await, expect; heed, mind, watch; face, front; appear, seem. * n examination, gaze, glance, peep, peer, search; appearance, aspect, complexion; air, aspect, manner, mien.

**loophole** n aperture, crenellation, loop, opening; excuse, plea, pretence, pretext, subterfuge.

**loose** vb free, liberate, release, unbind, undo, unfasten, unlash, unlock, untie; ease, loosen, relax, slacken; detach, disconnect, disengage. * adj unbound, unconfined, unfastened, unsewn, untied; disengaged, free, unattached; relaxed; diffuse, diffusive, prolix, rambling, unconnected; ill-defined, indefinite, indeterminate, indistinct, vague; careless, heedless, negligent, lax, slack; debauched, dissolute, immoral, licentious, unchaste, wanton.

**loosen** vb liberate, relax, release, separate, slacken, unbind, unloose, untie.

**looseness** n easiness, slackness; laxity, levity; lewdness, unchastity, wantonness, wickedness; diarrhoea, flux.

**loot** vb pillage, plunder, ransack, rifle, rob, sack. * n booty, plunder, spoil.

**lop** vb cut, truncate; crop, curtail, dock, prune; detach, dissever, sever.

**loquacious** adj garrulous, talkative, voluble, wordy; noisy, speaking, talking; babbling, blabbing, tattling, tell-tale.

**loquacity** n babbling, chattering, gabbling, garrulity, loquaciousness, talkativeness, volubility.

**lord** n earl, noble, nobleman, peer, viscount; governor, king, liege, master, monarch, prince, ruler, seigneur, seignior, sovereign, superior; husband, spouse.

**lordly** adj aristocratic, dignified, exalted, grand, lofty, majestic, noble; arrogant, despotic, domineering, haughty, imperious, insolent, masterful, overbearing, proud, tyrannical; large, liberal.

**lordship** n authority, command, control, direction, domination, dominion, empire, government, rule, sovereignty, sway; manor, domain, seigneury, seigniory.

**lore** n erudition, knowledge, learning, letters, scholarship; admonition, advice, counsel, doctrine, instruction, lesson, teaching, wisdom.

**lose** vb deprive, dispossess, forfeit, miss; dislodge, displace, mislay, misspend, squander, waste; decline, fall, succumb, yield.

**loss** n deprivation, failure, forfeiture, privation; casualty, damage, defeat, destruction, detriment, disadvantage, injury, overthrow, ruin; squandering, waste.

**lost** adj astray, missing; forfeited, missed, unredeemed; dissipated, misspent, squandered, wasted; bewildered, confused, distracted, perplexed, puzzled; absent, absent-minded, abstracted, dreamy, napping, preoccupied; abandoned, corrupt, debauched, depraved, dissolute, graceless, hardened, incorrigible, irreclaimable, licentious, profligate, reprobate, shameless, unchaste, wanton; destroyed, ruined.

**lot** n allotment, apportionment, destiny, doom, fate; accident, chance, fate, fortune, hap, haphazard, hazard; division, parcel, part, portion.

**loth** adj averse, disinclined, disliking, reluctant, unwilling

**loud** adj high-sounding, noisy, resounding, sonorous; deafening, stentorian, strong, stunning; boisterous, clamorous, noisy, obstreperous, tumultuous, turbulent, uproarious, vociferous; emphatic, impressive, positive, vehement; flashy, gaudy, glaring, loud, ostentatious, showy, vulgar.

**lounge** vb loll, recline, sprawl; dawdle, idle, loaf, loiter.

**love** vb adore, like, worship. * n accord, affection, amity, courtship, delight, fondness, friendship, kindness, regard, tenderness, warmth; adoration, amour, ardour, attachment, passion; devotion, inclination, liking; benevolence, charity, goodwill.

**lovely** adj beautiful, charming, delectable, delightful, enchanting, exquisite, graceful, pleasing, sweet, winning; admirable, adorable, amiable.

**loving** adj affectionate, dear, fond, kind, tender.

**low**[1] vb bellow, moo.

**low**[2] adj basal, depressed, profound; gentle, grave, soft, subdued; cheap, humble, mean, plebeian, vulgar; abject, base, base-minded, degraded, dirty, grovelling, ignoble, low-minded, menial, scurvy, servile, shabby, slavish, vile; derogatory, disgraceful, dishonourable, disreputable, unbecoming, undignified, ungentlemanly, unhandsome, unmanly; exhausted, feeble, reduced, weak; frugal, plain, poor, simple, spare; lowly, reverent, submissive; dejected, depressed, dispirited.

**lower**[1] vb depress, drop, sink, subside; debase, degrade, disgrace, humble, humiliate, reduce; abate, decrease, diminish, lessen. * adj baser, inferior, less, lesser, shorter, smaller; subjacent, under.

**lower**[2] vb blacken, darken, frown, glower, threaten.

**lowering** adj dark, clouded, cloudy, lurid, murky, overcast, threatening.

**lowliness** n humbleness, humility, meekness, self-abasement, submissiveness.

**lowly** adj gentle, humble, meek, mild, modest, plain, poor, simple, unassuming, unpretending, unpretentious; low-born, mean, servile.

**loyal** adj constant, devoted, faithful, patriotic, true.

**loyalty** n allegiance, constancy, devotion, faithfulness, fealty, fidelity, patriotism.

**lubricious** adj slippery, smooth; uncertain, unstable, wavering; impure, incontinent, lascivious, lecherous, lewd, libidinous, licentious, lustful, salacious, unchaste, wanton.

**lucid** adj beaming, bright, brilliant, luminous, radiant, resplendent, shining, clear, crystalline, diaphanous, limpid, lucent, pellucid, pure, transparent; clear, distinct, evident, intelligible, obvious, perspicuous, plain; reasonable, sane, sober, sound.

**luck** n accident, casualty, chance, fate, fortune, hap, haphazard, hazard, serendipity, success.

**luckless** adj ill-fated, ill-starred, unfortunate, unhappy, unlucky, unpropitious, unprosperous, unsuccessful.

**lucky** adj blessed, favoured, fortunate, happy, successful; auspicious, favourable, propitious, prosperous.

**lucrative** adj advantageous, gainful, paying, profitable, remunerative.

**ludicrous** adj absurd, burlesque, comic, comical, droll, farcical, funny, laughable, odd, ridiculous, sportive.

**lugubrious** adj complaining, doleful, gloomy, melancholy, mournful, sad, serious, sombre, sorrowful.

**lukewarm** adj blood-warm, tepid, thermal; apathetic, cold, dull, indifferent, listless, unconcerned, torpid.

**lull** vb calm, compose, hush, quiet, still, tranquillize;

abate, cease, decrease, diminish, subside. * n calm, calmness, cessation.

**lumber**[1] vb rumble, shamble, trudge.

**lumber**[2] n refuse, rubbish, trash, trumpery; wood.

**luminous** adj effulgent, incandescent, radiant, refulgent, resplendent, shining; bright, brilliant, clear; clear, lucid, lucent, perspicuous, plain.

**lunacy** n aberration, craziness, dementia, derangement, insanity, madness, mania.

**lunatic** adj crazy, demented, deranged, insane, mad, psychopathic. * n madman, maniac, psychopath.

**lurch** vb appropriate, filch, pilfer, purloin, steal; deceive, defeat, disappoint, evade; ambush, lurk, skulk; contrive, dodge, shift, trick; pitch, sway.

**lure** vb allure, attract, decoy, entice, inveigle, seduce, tempt. * n allurement, attraction, bait, decoy, enticement, temptation.

**lurid** adj dismal, ghastly, gloomy, lowering, murky, pale, wan; glaring, sensational, startling, unrestrained.

**lurk** vb hide, prowl, skulk, slink, sneak, snoop.

**luscious** adj delicious, delightful, grateful, palatable, pleasing, savoury, sweet.

**lush** adj fresh, juicy, luxuriant, moist, sappy, succulent, watery.

**lust** vb covet, crave, desire, hanker, need, want, yearn. * n cupidity, desire, longing; carnality, concupiscence, lasciviousness, lechery, lewdness, lubricity, salaciousness, salacity, wantonness.

**lustful** adj carnal, concupiscent, hankering, lascivious, lecherous, licentious, libidinous, lubricious, salacious.

**lustily** adv strongly, vigorously.

**lustiness** n hardihood, power, robustness, stoutness, strength, sturdiness, vigour.

**lustre** n brightness, brilliance, brilliancy, splendour.

**lusty** adj healthful, lively, robust, stout, strong, sturdy, vigorous; bulky, burly, corpulent, fat, large, stout.

**luxuriance** n exuberance, profusion, superabundance.

**luxuriant** adj exuberant, plenteous, plentiful, profuse, superabundant.

**luxuriate** vb abound, delight, enjoy, flourish, indulge, revel.

**luxurious** adj epicurean, opulent, pampered, self-indulgent, sensual, sybaritic, voluptuous.

**luxury** n epicureanism, epicurism, luxuriousness, opulence, sensuality, voluptuousness; delight, enjoyment, gratification, indulgence, pleasure; dainty, delicacy, treat.

**lying** adj equivocating, false, mendacious, untruthful, untrue.

**lyric** adj dulcet, euphonious, lyrical, mellifluous, mellifluent, melodic, melodious, musical, poetic, silvery, tuneful.

**lyrical** adj ecstatic, enthusiastic, expressive, impassion; dulcet, lyric, mellifluous, mellifluent, melodic, melodious, musical, poetic.

# M

**macabre** *adj* cadaverous, deathlike, deathly, dreadful, eerie, frightening, frightful, ghoulish, grim, grisly, gruesome, hideous, horrid, morbid, unearthly, weird.

**mace** *n* baton, staff, truncheon.

**macerate** *vb* harass, mortify, torture; digest, soak, soften, steep.

**Machiavellian** *adj* arch, artful, astute, crafty, crooked, cunning, deceitful, designing, diplomatic, insidious, intriguing, shrewd, sly, subtle, tricky, wily.

**machination** *n* artifice, cabal, conspiracy, contrivance, design, intrigue, plot, scheme, stratagem, trick.

**machine** *n* instrument, puppet, tool; machinery, organization, system; engine.

**mad** *adj* crazed, crazy, delirious, demented, deranged, distracted, insane, irrational, lunatic, maniac, maniacal; enraged, furious, rabid, raging, violent; angry, enraged, exasperated, furious, incensed, provoked, wrathful; distracted, infatuated, wild; frantic, frenzied, raving.

**madden** *vb* annoy, craze, enrage, exasperate, inflame, infuriate, irritate, provoke.

**madness** *n* aberration, craziness, dementia, derangement, insanity, lunacy, mania; delirium, frenzy, fury, rage.

**magazine** *n* depository, depot, entrepot, receptacle, repository, storehouse, warehouse; pamphlet, paper, periodical.

**magic** *adj* bewitching, charming, enchanting, fascinating, magical, miraculous, spellbinding. * *n* conjuring, enchantment, necromancy, sorcery, thaumaturgy, voodoo, witchcraft; char, fascination, witchery.

**magician** *n* conjurer, enchanter, juggler, magus, necromancer, shaman, sorcerer, wizard.

**magisterial** *adj* august, dignified, majestic, pompous; authoritative, despotic, domineering, imperious, dictatorial.

**magnanimity** *n* chivalry, disinterestedness, forbearance, high-mindedness, generosity, nobility.

**magnificence** *n* brilliance, éclat, grandeur, luxuriousness, luxury, majesty, pomp, splendour.

**magnificent** *adj* elegant, grand, majestic, noble, splendid, superb; brilliant, gorgeous, imposing, lavish, luxurious, pompous, showy, stately.

**magnify** *vb* amplify, augment, enlarge; bless, celebrate, elevate, exalt, extol, glorify, laud, praise; exaggerate.

**magnitude** *n* bulk, dimension, extent, mass, size, volume; consequence, greatness, importance; grandeur, loftiness, sublimity.

**maid** *n* damsel, girl, lass, lassie, maiden, virgin; maidservant, servant.

**maiden** *adj* chaste, pure, undefiled, virgin; fresh, new, unused. * *n* girl, maid, virgin.

**maidenly** *adj* demure, gentle, modest, maidenlike, reserved.

**maim** *vb* cripple, disable, disfigure, mangle, mar, mutilate. * *n* crippling, disfigurement, mutilation; harm, hurt, injury, mischief.

**main**[1] *adj* capital, cardinal, chief, leading, principal; essential, important, indispensable, necessary, requisite, vital; enormous, huge, mighty, vast; pure, sheer; absolute, direct, entire, mere. * *n* channel, pipe; force, might, power, strength, violence.

**main**[2] *n* high seas, ocean; continent, mainland.

**maintain** *vb* keep, preserve, support, sustain, uphold; hold, possess; defend, vindicate, justify; carry on, continue, keep up; feed, provide, supply; allege, assert, declare; affirm, aver, contend, hold, say.

**maintenance** *n* defence, justification, preservation, support, sustenance, vindication; bread, food, livelihood, provisions, subsistence, sustenance, victuals.

**majestic** *adj* august, dignified, imperial, imposing, lofty, noble, pompous, princely, stately, regal, royal; grand, magnificent, splendid, sublime.

**majesty** *n* augustness, dignity, elevation, grandeur, loftiness, stateliness.

**majority** *n* bulk, greater, mass, more, most, plurality, preponderance, superiority; adulthood, manhood.

**make** *vb* create; fashion, figure, form, frame, mould, shape; cause, construct, effect, establish, fabricate, produce; do, execute, perform, practice; acquire, gain, get, raise, secure; cause, compel, constrain, force, occasion; compose, constitute; go, journey, move, proceed, tend, travel; conduce, contribute, effect, favour, operate; estimate, judge, reckon, suppose, think. * n brand, build, constitution, construction, form, shape, structure.

**maker** n creator, god; builder, constructor, fabricator, framer, manufacturer; author, composer, poet, writer.

**maladministration** n malversation, misgovernment, misrule.

**maladroit** adj awkward, bungling, clumsy, inept, inexpert, unhandy, unskilful, unskilled.

**malady** n affliction, ailment, complaint, disease, disorder, illness, indisposition, sickness.

**malcontent** adj discontented, dissatisfied, insurgent, rebellious, resentful, uneasy, unsatisfied. * n agitator, complainer, fault-finder, grumbler, spoilsport.

**malediction** n anathema, ban, curse, cursing, denunciation, execration, imprecation, malison.

**malefactor** n convict, criminal, culprit, delinquent, evildoer, felon, offender, outlaw.

**malevolence** n hate, hatred, ill-will, malice, malignity, rancour, spite, spitefulness, vindictiveness.

**malevolent** adj evil-minded, hateful, hostile, ill-natured, malicious, malignant, mischievous, rancorous, spiteful, venomous. vindictive.

**malice** n animosity, bitterness, enmity, grudge, hate, ill-will, malevolence, maliciousness, malignity, pique, rancour, spite, spitefulness, venom, vindictiveness.

**malicious** adj bitter, envious, evil-minded, ill-disposed, ill-natured, invidious, malevolent, malignant, mischievous, rancorous, resentful, spiteful, vicious.

**malign** vb abuse, asperse, blacken, calumniate, defame, disparage, revile, scandalize, slander, traduce, vilify. * adj malevolent, malicious, malignant, ill-disposed; baneful, injurious, pernicious, unfavourable, unpropitious.

**malignant** adj bitter, envious, hostile, inimical, malevolent, malicious, malign, spiteful, rancorous, resentful, virulent; heinous, pernicious; ill-boding, unfavourable, unpropitious; dangerous, fatal.

**malignity** n animosity, hatred, ill-will, malice, malevolence, maliciousness, rancour, spite; deadliness, destructiveness, fatality, harmfulness, malignancy, perniciousness, virulence; enormity, evilness, heinousness.

**malpractice** n dereliction, malversation, misbehaviour, misconduct, misdeed, misdoing, sin, transgression.

**maltreat** vb abuse, harm, hurt, ill-treat, ill-use, injure.

**mammoth** adj colossal, enormous, gigantic, huge, immense, vast.

**man** vb crew, garrison, furnish; fortify, reinforce, strengthen. * n adult, being, body, human, individual, one, person, personage, somebody, soul; humanity, humankind, mankind; attendant, butler, dependant, liege, servant, subject, valet, vassal; employee, workman.

**manacle** vb bind, chain, fetter, handcuff, restrain, shackle, tie. * n bond, chain, handcuff, gyve, hand-fetter, shackle.

**manage** vb administer, conduct, direct, guide, handle, operate, order, regulate, superintend, supervise, transact, treat; control, govern, rule; handle, manipulate, train, wield; contrive, economize, husband, save.

**manageable** adj controllable, docile, easy, governable, tamable, tractable.

**management** n administration, care, charge, conduct, control, direction, disposal, economy, government, guidance, superintendence, supervision, surveillance, treatment.

**manager** n comptroller, conductor, director, executive, governor, impresario, overseer; superintendent, supervisor.

**mandate** n charge, command, commission, edict, injunction, order, precept, requirement.

**manful** adj bold, brave, courageous, daring, heroic, honourable, intrepid, noble, stout, strong, undaunted, vigorous.

**mangily** adv basely, foully, meanly, scabbily, scurvily, vilely.

**mangle**[1] vb hack, lacerate, mutilate, rend, tear; cripple, crush, destroy, maim, mar, spoil.

**mangle**[2] vb calender, polish, press, smooth.

**manhood** n virility; bravery, courage, firmness, fortitude, hardihood, manfulness, manliness, resolution; human nature, humanity; adulthood, maturity.

**mania** n aberration, craziness, delirium, dementia, derangement, frenzy, insanity, lunacy, madness; craze, desire, enthusiasm, fad, fanaticism.

**manifest** vb declare, demonstrate, disclose, discover, display, evidence, evince, exhibit, express, reveal, show. * adj apparent, clear, conspicuous, distinct, evident, glaring, indubitable, obvious, open, palpable, patent, plain, unmistakable, visible.

**manifestation** n disclosure, display, exhibition, exposure, expression, revelation.

**manifold** adj complex, diverse, many, multifarious, multiplied, multitudinous, numerous, several, sundry, varied, various.

**manipulate** vb handle, operate, work.

**manliness** n boldness, bravery, courage, dignity, fearlessness, firmness, heroism, intrepidity, nobleness, resolution, valour.

**manly** adj bold, brave, courageous, daring, dignified, firm, heroic, intrepid, manful, noble, stout, strong, undaunted, vigorous; male, masculine, virile.

**manner** n fashion, form, method, mode, style, way; custom, habit, practice; degree, extent, measure; kind, kinds, sort, sorts; air, appearance, aspect, behaviour, carriage, demeanour, deportment, look, mien; mannerism, peculiarity; behaviour, conduct, habits, morals; civility, deportment.

**mannerly** adj ceremonious, civil, complaisant, courteous, polite, refined, respectful, urbane, well-behaved, well-bred.

**manners** npl conduct, habits, morals; air, bearing, behaviour, breeding, carriage, comportment, deportment, etiquette.

**manoeuvre** vb contrive, finesse, intrigue, manage, plan, plot, scheme. * n evolution, exercise, movement, operation; artifice, finesse, intrigue, plan, plot, ruse, scheme, stratagem, trick.

**mansion** n abode, dwelling, dwelling house, habitation, hall, residence, seat.

**mantle** vb cloak, cover, discover, obscure; expand, spread; bubble, cream, effervesce, foam, froth, sparkle. * n chasuble, cloak, toga; cover, covering, hood.

**manufacture** vb build, compose, construct, create, fabricate, forge, form, make, mould, produce, shape. * n constructing, fabrication, making, production.

**manumission** n deliverance, emancipation, enfranchisement, freedom, liberation, release.

**manumit** vb deliver, emancipate, enfranchise, free, liberate, release.

**manure** vb enrich, fertilize. * n compost, dressing, fertilizer, guano, muck.

**many** adj abundant, diverse, frequent, innumerable, manifold, multifarious, multifold, multiplied, multitudinous, numerous, sundry, varied, various. * n crowd, multitude, people.

**map** vb chart, draw up, plan, plot, set out, sketch. * n chart, diagram, outline, plot, sketch.

**mar** vb blot, damage, harm, hurt, impair, injure, ruin, spoil, stain; deface, deform, disfigure, maim, mutilate.

**marauder** n bandit, brigand, desperado, filibuster, freebooter, outlaw, pillager, plunderer, ravager, robber, rover.

**march** vb go, pace, parade, step, tramp, walk. * n hike, tramp, walk; parade, procession; gait, step, stride; advance, evolution, progress.

**marches** npl borders, boundaries, confines, frontiers, limits, precincts.

**margin** n border, brim, brink, confine, edge, limit, rim, skirt, verge; latitude, room, space, surplus.

**marine** adj oceanic, pelagic, saltwater, sea; maritime, naval, nautical. * n navy, shipping; sea-dog, sea soldier, soldier; sea piece, seascape.

**mariner** n navigator, sailor, salt, seafarer, seaman, tar.

**marital** adj connubial, conjugal, matrimonial.

**maritime** adj marine, naval, nautical, oceanic, sea, seafaring, seagoing; coastal, seaside.

**mark** vb distinguish, earmark, label; betoken, brand, characterize, denote, designate, engrave, impress, imprint, indicate, print, stamp; evince, heed, note, notice, observe, regard, remark, show, spot. * n brand, character, characteristic, impression, impress, line, note, print, sign, stamp, symbol, token, race; evidence, indication, proof, symptom, trace, track, vestige; badge; footprint; bull's-eye, butt, object, target; consequence, distinction, eminence, fame, importance, notability, position, preeminence, reputation, significance.

**marked** adj conspicuous, distinguished, eminent, notable, noted, outstanding, prominent, remarkable.

**marriage** n espousals, nuptials, spousals, wedding; matrimony, wedlock; union; alliance, association, confederation.

**marrow** n medulla, pith; cream, essence, quintessence, substance.

**marsh** n bog, fen, mire, morass, quagmire, slough, swamp.

**marshal** vb arrange, array, dispose, gather, muster, range, order, rank; guide, herald, lead. * n conductor, director, master of ceremonies, regulator; harbinger, herald, pursuivant.

**marshy** adj boggy, miry, mossy, swampy, wet.

**martial** adj brave, heroic, military, soldier-like, warlike.

**marvel** vb gape, gaze, goggle, wonder. * n miracle,

prodigy, wonder; admiration, amazement, astonishment, surprise.

**marvellous** adj amazing, astonishing, extraordinary, miraculous, prodigious, strange, stupendous, wonderful, wondrous; improbable, incredible, surprising, unbelievable.

**masculine** adj bold, hardy, manful, manlike, manly, mannish, virile; potent, powerful, robust, strong, vigorous; bold, coarse, forward.

**mask** vb cloak, conceal, cover, disguise, hide, screen, shroud, veil. * n blind, cloak, disguise, screen, veil; evasion, pretence, plea, pretext, ruse, shift, subterfuge, trick; masquerade; bustle, mummery.

**masquerade** vb cover, disguise, hide, mask, revel, veil. * n mask, mummery, revel, revelry.

**Mass** n communion, Eucharist.

**mass** vb accumulate, amass, assemble, collect, gather, rally, throng. * adj extensive, general, large-scale, widespread. * n cake, clot, lump; assemblage, collection, combination, congeries, heap; bulk, dimension, magnitude, size; accumulation, aggregate, body, sum, total, totality, whole.

**massacre** vb annihilate, butcher, exterminate, kill, murder, slaughter, slay. * n annihilation, butchery, carnage, extermination, killing, murder, pogrom, slaughter.

**massive** adj big, bulky, colossal, enormous, heavy, huge, immense, ponderous, solid, substantial, vast, weighty.

**master** vb conquer, defeat, direct, govern, overcome, overpower, rule, subdue, subjugate, vanquish; acquire, learn. * adj cardinal, chief, especial, grand, great, main, leading, prime, principal; adept, expert, proficient. * n director, governor, lord, manager, overseer, superintendent, ruler; captain, commander; instructor, pedagogue, preceptor, schoolteacher, teacher, tutor; holder, owner, possessor, proprietor; chief, head, leader, principal.

**masterly** adj adroit, clever, dextrous, excellent, expert, finished, skilful, skilled; arbitrary, despotic, despotical, domineering, imperious.

**mastery** n command, dominion, mastership, power, rule, supremacy, sway; ascendancy, conquest, leadership, preeminence, superiority, upper-hand, victory; acquisition, acquirement, attainment; ability, cleverness, dexterity, proficiency, skill.

**masticate** vb chew, eat, munch.

**match** vb equal, rival; adapt, fit, harmonize, propor-

tion, suit; marry, mate; combine, couple, join, sort; oppose, pit; correspond, suit, tally. * n companion, equal, mate, tally; competition, contest, game, trial; marriage, union.

**matchless** adj consummate, excellent, exquisite, incomparable, inimitable, peerless, perfect, surpassing, unequalled, unmatched, unparalleled, unrivalled.

**mate** vb marry, match, wed; compete, equal, vie; appal, confound, crush, enervate, subdue, stupefy. * n associate, companion, compeer, consort, crony, friend, fellow, intimate; companion, equal, match; assistant, subordinate; husband, spouse, wife.

**material** adj bodily, corporeal, nonspiritual, physical, temporal; essential, important, momentous, relevant, vital, weighty. * n body, element, stuff, substance.

**maternal** adj motherlike, motherly.

**matrimonial** adj conjugal, connubial, espousal, hymeneal, marital, nuptial, spousal.

**matrimony** n marriage, wedlock.

**matter** vb import, signify, weigh. * n body, content, sense, substance; difficulty, distress, trouble; material, stuff; question, subject, subject matter, topic; affair, business, concern, event; consequence, import, importance, moment, significance; discharge, purulence, pus.

**mature** vb develop, perfect, ripen. * adj complete, fit, full-grown, perfect; ripe; completed, prepared, ready, well-considered, well-digested.

**maturity** n completeness, completion, matureness, perfection, ripeness.

**mawkish** adj disgusting, flat, insipid, nauseous, sickly, stale, tasteless, vapid; emotional, feeble, maudlin, sentimental.

**maxim** n adage, aphorism, apothegm, axiom, byword, dictum, proverb, saw, saying, truism.

**maze** vb amaze, bewilder, confound, confuse, perplex. * n intricacy, labyrinth, meander; bewilderment, embarrassment, intricacy, perplexity, puzzle, uncertainty.

**mazy** adj confused, confusing, intricate, labyrinthian, labyrinthic, labyrinthine, perplexing, winding.

**meagre** adj emaciated, gaunt, lank, lean, poor, skinny, starved, spare, thin; barren, poor, sterile, unproductive; bold, barren, dry, dull, mean, poor, prosy, feeble, insignificant, jejune, scanty, small, tame, uninteresting, vapid.

**mean**[1] vb contemplate, design, intend, purpose;

connote, denote, express, imply, import, indicate, purport, signify, symbolize.

**mean²** *adj* average, medium, middle; intermediate, intervening. * *n* measure, mediocrity, medium, moderation; average; agency, instrument, instrumentality, means, measure, method, mode, way.

**mean³** *adj* coarse, common, humble, ignoble, low, ordinary, plebeian, vulgar; abject, base, base-minded, beggarly, contemptible, degraded, dirty, dishonourable, disingenuous, grovelling, low-minded, pitiful, rascally, scurvy, servile, shabby, sneaking, sorry, spiritless, unfair, vile; illiberal, mercenary, miserly, narrow, narrow-minded, niggardly, parsimonious, penurious, selfish, sordid, stingy, ungenerous, unhandsome; contemptible, despicable, diminutive, insignificant, paltry, petty, poor, small, wretched.

**meaning** *n* acceptation, drift, import, intention, purport, purpose, sense, signification.

**means** *npl* instrument, method, mode, way; appliance, expedient, measure, resource, shift, step; estate, income, property, resources, revenue, substance, wealth, wherewithal.

**measure** *vb* mete; adjust, gauge, proportion; appraise, appreciate, estimate, gauge, value. * *n* gauge, meter, rule, standard; degree, extent, length, limit; allotment, share, proportion; means, step; foot, metre, rhythm, tune, verse.

**measureless** *adj* boundless, endless, immeasurable, immense, limitless, unbounded, unlimited, vast.

**meat** *n* aliment, cheer, diet, fare, feed, flesh, food, nourishment, nutriment, provision, rations, regimen, subsistence, sustenance, viands, victuals.

**mechanic** *n* artificer, artisan, craftsman, hand, handicraftsman, machinist, operative, workman.

**meddle** *vb* interfere, intermeddle, interpose, intrude.

**meddlesome** *adj* interfering, intermeddling, intrusive, officious, prying.

**mediate** *vb* arbitrate, intercede, interpose, intervene, settle. * *adj* interposed, intervening, middle.

**mediation** *n* arbitration, intercession, interposition, intervention.

**mediator** *n* advocate, arbitrator, interceder, intercessor, propitiator, umpire.

**medicine** *n* drug, medicament, medication, physic; therapy.

**mediocre** *adj* average, commonplace, indifferent, mean, medium, middling, ordinary.

**meditate** *vb* concoct, contrive, design, devise, intend, plan, purpose, scheme; chew, contemplate, ruminate, study; cogitate, muse, ponder, think.

**meditation** *n* cogitation, contemplation, musing, pondering, reflection, ruminating, study, thought.

**meditative** *adj* contemplative, pensive, reflective, studious, thoughtful.

**medium** *adj* average, mean, mediocre, middle. * *n* agency, channel, intermediary, instrument, instrumentality, means, organ; conditions, environment, influences; average, means.

**medley** *n* confusion, farrago, hodgepodge, hotchpotch, jumble, mass, melange, miscellany, mishmash, mixture.

**meed** *n* award, guerdon, premium, prize, recompense, remuneration, reward.

**meek** *adj* gentle, humble, lowly, mild, modest, pacific, soft, submissive, unassuming, yielding.

**meekness** *n* gentleness, humbleness, humility, lowliness, mildness, modesty, submission, submissiveness.

**meet** *vb* cross, intersect, transact; confront, encounter, engage; answer, comply, fulfil, gratify, satisfy; converge, join, unite; assemble, collect, convene, congregate, forgather, muster, rally. * *adj* adapted, appropriate, befitting, convenient, fit, fitting, proper, qualified, suitable, suited.

**meeting** *n* encounter, interview; assemblage, assembly, audience, company, concourse, conference, congregation, convention, gathering; assignation, encounter, introduction, rendezvous; confluence, conflux, intersection, joining, junction, union; collision.

**melancholy** *adj* blue, dejected, depressed, despondent, desponding, disconsolate, dismal, dispirited, doleful, down, downcast, downhearted, gloomy, glum, hypochondriac, low-spirited, lugubrious, moody, mopish, sad, sombre, sorrowful, unhappy; afflictive, calamitous, unfortunate, unlucky; dark, gloomy, grave, quiet. * *n* blues, dejection, depression, despondency, dismals, dumps, gloom, gloominess, hypochondria, sadness, vapours.

**melee** *n* affray, brawl, broil, contest, fight, fray, scuffle.

**mellifluous, mellifluent** *adj* dulcet, euphonic, euphonical, euphonious, mellow, silver-toned, silvery, smooth, soft, sweet.

**mellow** *vb* mature, ripen; improve, smooth, soften, tone;

pulverize; perfect. * adj mature, ripe; dulcet, mellifluous, mellifluent, rich, silver-toned, silvery, smooth, soft; delicate; genial, good-humoured, jolly, jovial, matured, softened; mellowy, loamy, unctuous; perfected, well-prepared; disguised, fuddled, intoxicated, tipsy.

**melodious** adj arioso, concordant, dulcet, euphonious, harmonious, mellifluous, mellifluent, musical, silvery, sweet, tuneful.

**melody** n air, descant, music, plainsong, song, theme, tune.

**melt** vb dissolve, fuse, liquefy, thaw; mollify, relax, soften, subdue; dissipate, waste; blend, pass, shade.

**member** n arm, leg, limb, organ; component, constituent, element, part, portion; branch, clause, division, head.

**memento** n memorial, remembrance, reminder, souvenir.

**memoir** n account, autobiography, biography, journal, narrative, record, register.

**memorable** adj celebrated, distinguished, extraordinary, famous, great, illustrious, important, notable, noteworthy, remarkable, signal, significant.

**memorandum** n minute, note, record.

**memorial** adj commemorative, monumental. * n cairn, commemoration, memento, monument, plaque, record, souvenir; memorandum, remembrance.

**memory** n recollection, remembrance, reminiscence; celebrity, fame, renown, reputation; commemoration, memorial.

**menace** vb alarm, frighten, intimidate, threaten. * n danger, hazard, peril, threat, warning; nuisance, pest, troublemaker.

**menage** n household, housekeeping, management.

**mend** vb darn, patch, rectify, refit, repair, restore, retouch; ameliorate, amend, better, correct, emend, improve, meliorate, reconcile, rectify, reform; advance, help; augment, increase.

**mendacious** adj deceitful, deceptive, fallacious, false, lying, untrue, untruthful.

**mendacity** n deceit, deceitfulness, deception, duplicity, falsehood, lie, untruth.

**mendicant** n beggar, pauper, tramp.

**menial** adj base, low, mean, servile, vile. * n attendant, bondsman, domestic, flunkey, footman, lackey, serf, servant, slave, underling, valet, waiter.

**mensuration** n measurement, measuring; survey, surveying.

**mental** adj ideal, immaterial, intellectual, psychiatric, subjective.

**mention** vb acquaint, allude, cite, communicate, declare, disclose, divulge, impart, inform, name, report, reveal, state, tell. * n allusion, citation, designation, notice, noting, reference.

**mentor** n adviser, counsellor, guide, instructor, monitor.

**mephitic** adj baleful, baneful, fetid, foul, mephitical, noisome, noxious, poisonous, pestilential.

**mercantile** adj commercial, marketable, trading.

**mercenary** adj hired, paid, purchased, venal; avaricious, covetous, grasping, mean, niggardly, parsimonious, penurious, sordid, stingy. * n hireling, soldier.

**merchandise** n commodities, goods, wares.

**merchant** n dealer, retailer, shopkeeper, trader, tradesman.

**merciful** adj clement, compassionate, forgiving, gracious, lenient, pitiful; benignant, forbearing, gentle, humane, kind, mild, tender, tender-hearted.

**merciless** adj barbarous, callous, cruel, fell, hard-hearted, inexorable, pitiless, relentless, remorseless, ruthless, savage, severe, uncompassionate, unfeeling, unmerciful, unrelenting, unrepenting, unsparing.

**mercurial** adj active, lively, nimble, prompt, quick, sprightly; cheerful, light-hearted; changeable, fickle, flighty, inconstant, mobile, volatile.

**mercy** n benevolence, clemency, compassion, gentleness, kindness, lenience, leniency, lenity, mildness, pity, tenderness; blessing, favour, grace; discretion, disposal; forgiveness, pardon.

**mere** adj bald, bare, naked, plain, sole, simple; absolute, entire, pure, sheer, unmixed. * n lake, pond, pool.

**meretricious** adj deceitful, brummagem, false, gaudy, make-believe, sham, showy, spurious, tawdry.

**merge** vb bury, dip, immerse, involve, lose, plunge, sink, submerge.

**meridian** n acme, apex, climax, culmination, summit, zenith; midday, noon, noontide.

**merit** vb deserve, earn, incur; acquire, gain, profit, value. * n claim, right; credit, desert, excellence, goodness, worth, worthiness.

**meritorious** adj commendable, deserving, excellent, good, worthy.

**merriment** n amusement, frolic, gaiety, hilarity,

jocularity, jollity, joviality, laughter, liveliness, mirth, sport, sportiveness.

**merry** *adj* agreeable, brisk, delightful, exhilarating, lively, pleasant, stirring; airy, blithe, blithesome, buxom, cheerful, comical, droll, facetious, frolicsome, gladsome, gleeful, hilarious, jocund, jolly, jovial, joyous, light-hearted, lively, mirthful, sportive, sprightly, vivacious.

**mess** *n* company, set; farrago, hodgepodge, hotch-potch, jumble, medley, mass, melange, miscellany, mishmash, mixture; confusion, muddle, perplexity, pickle, plight, predicament.

**message** *n* communication, dispatch, intimation, letter, missive, notice, telegram, wire, word.

**messenger** *n* carrier, courier, emissary, envoy, express, mercury, nuncio; forerunner, harbinger, herald, precursor.

**metamorphic** *adj* changeable, mutable, variable.

**metamorphose** *vb* change, mutate, transfigure, transform, transmute.

**metamorphosis** *n* change, mutation, transfiguration, transformation, transmutation.

**metaphorical** *adj* allegorical, figurative, symbolic, symbolical.

**metaphysical** *adj* abstract, allegorical, figurative, general, intellectual, parabolic, subjective, unreal.

**mete** *vb* dispense, distribute, divide, measure, ration, share. * *n* bound, boundary, butt, limit, measure, term, terminus.

**meteor** *n* aerolite, falling star, shooting star.

**method** *n* course, manner, means, mode, procedure, process, rule, way; arrangement, classification, disposition, order, plan, regularity, scheme, system.

**methodical** *adj* exact, orderly, regular, systematic, systematical.

**metropolis** *n* capital, city, conurbation.

**mettle** *n* constitution, element, material, stuff; character, disposition, spirit, temper; ardour, courage, fire, hardihood, life, nerve, pluck, sprightliness, vigour.

**mettlesome** *adj* ardent, brisk, courageous, fiery, frisky, high-spirited, lively, spirited, sprightly.

**mew** *vb* confine, coop, encase, enclose, imprison; cast, change, mould, shed.

**microscopic** *adj* infinitesimal, minute, tiny.

**middle** *adj* central, halfway, mean, medial, mid; intermediate, intervening. * *n* centre, halfway, mean, midst.

**middleman** *n* agent, broker, factor, go-between, intermediary.

**mien** *n* air, appearance, aspect, bearing, behaviour, carriage, countenance, demeanour, deportment, look, manner.

**might** *n* ability, capacity, efficacy, efficiency, force, main, power, prowess, puissance, strength.

**mighty** *adj* able, bold, courageous, potent, powerful, puissant, robust, strong, sturdy, valiant, valorous, vigorous; bulky, enormous, huge, immense, monstrous, stupendous, vast.

**migratory** *adj* nomadic, roving, shifting, strolling, unsettled, wandering, vagrant.

**mild** *adj* amiable, clement, compassionate, gentle, good-natured, indulgent, kind, lenient, meek, merciful, pacific, tender; bland, pleasant, soft, suave; calm, kind, placid, temperate, tranquil; assuasive, compliant, demulcent, emollient, lenitive, mollifying, soothing.

**mildness** *n* amiability, clemency, gentleness, indulgence, kindness, meekness, moderation, softness, tenderness, warmth.

**mildew** *n* blight, blast, mould, must, mustiness, smut, rust.

**milieu** *n* background, environment, sphere, surroundings.

**militant** *adj* belligerent, combative, contending, fighting.

**military** *adj* martial, soldier, soldierly, warlike. * *n* army, militia, soldiers.

**mill** *vb* comminute, crush, grate, grind, levigate, powder, pulverize. * *n* factory, manufactory; grinder; crowd, throng.

**mimic** *vb* ape, counterfeit, imitate, impersonate, mime, mock, parody. * *adj* imitative, mock, simulated. * *n* imitator, impersonator, mime, mocker, parodist, parrot.

**mince**[1] *vb* chop, cut, hash, shatter. * *n* forcemeat, hash, mash, mincemeat.

**mince**[2] *vb* attenuate, diminish, extenuate, mitigate, palliate, soften; pose, sashay, simper, smirk.

**mind**[1] *vb* attend, heed, mark, note, notice, regard, tend, watch; obey, observe, submit; design, incline, intend, mean; recall, recollect, remember, remind; beware, look out, watch out. * *n* soul, spirit; brains, common sense, intellect, reason, sense, understanding; belief, consideration, contemplation, judgement, opinion, reflection, sentiment, thought;

memory, recollection, remembrance; bent, desire, disposition, inclination, intention, leaning, purpose, tendency, will.

**mind**[2] vb balk, begrudge, grudge, object, resent.

**mindful** adj attentive, careful, heedful, observant, regardful, thoughtful.

**mindless** adj dull, heavy, insensible, senseless, sluggish, stupid, unthinking; careless, forgetful, heedless, neglectful, negligent, regardless.

**mine** vb dig, excavate, quarry, unearth; sap, undermine, weaken; destroy, ruin. * n colliery, deposit, lode, pit, shaft.

**mingle** vb blend, combine, commingle, compound, intermingle, intermix, join, mix, unite.

**miniature** adj bantam, diminutive, little, small, tiny.

**minion** n creature, dependant, favourite, hanger-on, parasite, sycophant; darling, favourite, flatterer, pet.

**minister** vb administer, afford, furnish, give, supply; aid, assist, contribute, help, succour. * n agent, assistant, servant, subordinate, underling; administrator, executive; ambassador, delegate, envoy, plenipotentiary; chaplain, churchman, clergyman, cleric, curate, divine, ecclesiastic, parson, pastor, preacher, priest, rector, vicar.

**ministry** n agency, aid, help, instrumentality, interposition, intervention, ministration, service, support; administration, cabinet, council, government.

**minor** adj less, smaller; inferior, junior, secondary, subordinate, younger; inconsiderable, petty, unimportant, small.

**minstrel** n bard, musician, singer, troubadour.

**mint** vb coin, stamp; fabricate, fashion, forge, invent, make, produce. * adj fresh, new, perfect, undamaged. * n die, punch, seal, stamp; fortune, (inf) heap, million, pile, wad.

**minute**[1] adj diminutive, fine, little, microscopic, miniature, slender, slight, small, tiny; circumstantial, critical, detailed, exact, fussy, meticulous, nice, particular, precise.

**minute**[2] n account, entry, item, memorandum, note, proceedings, record; instant, moment, second, trice, twinkling.

**miracle** n marvel, prodigy, wonder.

**miraculous** adj supernatural, thaumaturgic, thaumaturgical; amazing, extraordinary, incredible, marvellous, unaccountable, unbelievable, wondrous.

**mirror** vb copy, echo, emulate, reflect, show. * n looking-glass, reflector, speculum; archetype, exemplar, example, model, paragon, pattern, prototype.

**mirth** n cheerfulness, festivity, frolic, fun, gaiety, gladness, glee, hilarity, festivity, jollity, joviality, joyousness, laughter, merriment, merry-making, rejoicing, sport.

**mirthful** adj cheery, cheery, festive, frolicsome, hilarious, jocund, jolly, merry, jovial, joyous, lively, playful, sportive, vivacious; comic, droll, humorous, facetious, funny, jocose, jocular, ludicrous, merry, waggish, witty.

**misadventure** n accident, calamity, catastrophe, cross, disaster, failure, ill-luck, infelicity, mischance, misfortune, mishap, reverse.

**misanthrope** n cynic, egoist, egotist, man-hater, misanthropist.

**misapply** vb abuse, misuse, pervert.

**misapprehend** vb misconceive, mistake, misunderstand.

**misbehaviour** n ill-behaviour, ill-conduct, incivility, miscarriage, misconduct, misdemeanour, naughtiness, rudeness.

**miscarriage** n calamity, defeat, disaster, failure, mischance, mishap; misbehaviour, misconduct, ill-behaviour.

**miscellaneous** adj confused, diverse, diversified, heterogeneous, indiscriminate, jumbled, many, mingled, mixed, promiscuous, stromatic, stromatous, various.

**miscellany** n collection, diversity, farrago, gallimaufry, hodgepodge, hotchpotch, jumble, medley, mishmash, melange, miscellaneous, mixture, variety.

**mischance** n accident, calamity, disaster, ill-fortune, ill-luck, infelicity, misadventure, misfortune, mishap.

**mischief** n damage, detriment, disadvantage, evil, harm, hurt, ill, injury, prejudice; ill-consequence, misfortune, trouble; devilry, wrong-doing.

**mischievous** adj destructive, detrimental, harmful, hurtful, injurious, noxious, pernicious; malicious, sinful, vicious, wicked; annoying, impish, naughty, troublesome, vexatious.

**misconceive** vb misapprehend, misjudge, mistake, misunderstand.

**misconduct** vb botch, bungle, misdirect, mismanage. * n bad conduct, ill-conduct, misbehaviour, misdemeanour, rudeness, transgression; ill-management, mismanagement.

**misconstrue** vb misread, mistranslate; misapprehend, misinterpret, mistake, misunderstand.

**miscreant** adj corrupt, criminal, evil, rascally, unprincipled, vicious, villainous, wicked. * n caitiff, knave, ragamuffin, rascal, rogue, ruffian, scamp, scoundrel, vagabond, villain.

**misdemeanour** n fault, ill-behaviour, misbehaviour, misconduct, misdeed, offence, transgression, trespass.

**miser** n churl, curmudgeon, lickpenny, money-grabber, niggard, penny-pincher, pinch-fist, screw, scrimp, skinflint.

**miserable** adj afflicted, broken-hearted, comfortless, disconsolate, distressed, forlorn, heartbroken, unhappy, wretched; calamitous, hapless, ill-starred, pitiable, unfortunate, unlucky; poor, valueless, worthless; abject, contemptible, despicable, low, mean, worthless.

**miserly** adj avaricious, beggarly, close, close-fisted, covetous, grasping, mean, niggardly, parsimonious, penurious, sordid, stingy, tight-fisted.

**misery** n affliction, agony, anguish, calamity, desolation, distress, grief, heartache, heavy-heartedness, misfortune, sorrow, suffering, torment, torture, tribulation, unhappiness, woe, wretchedness.

**misfortune** n adversity, affliction, bad luck, blow, calamity, casualty, catastrophe, disaster, distress, hardship, harm, ill, infliction, misadventure, mischance, mishap, reverse, scourge, stroke, trial, trouble, visitation.

**misgiving** n apprehension, distrust, doubt, hesitation, suspicion, uncertainty.

**mishap** n accident, calamity, disaster, ill luck, misadventure, mischance, misfortune.

**misinterpret** vb distort, falsify, misapprehend, misconceive, misconstrue, misjudge.

**mislead** vb beguile, deceive, delude, misdirect, misguide.

**mismanage** vb botch, fumble, misconduct, mishandle, misrule.

**misprize** vb slight, underestimate, underrate, undervalue.

**misrepresent** vb belie, caricature, distort, falsify, misinterpret, misstate, pervert.

**misrule** n anarchy, confusion, disorder, malad-ministration, misgovernment, mismanagement.

**miss**[1] vb blunder, err, fail, fall short, forgo, lack, lose, miscarry, mistake, omit, overlook, trip; avoid, escape, evade, skip, slip; feel the loss of, need, want, wish. * n blunder, error, failure, fault, mistake, omission, oversight, slip, trip; loss, want.

**miss**[2] n damsel, girl, lass, maid, maiden.

**misshapen** adj deformed, ill-formed, ill-shaped, ill-proportioned, misformed, ugly, ungainly.

**missile** n projectile, weapon.

**mission** n commission, legation; business, charge, duty, errand, office, trust; delegation, deputation, embassy.

**missive** n communication, epistle, letter, message, note.

**mist** vb cloud, drizzle, mizzle, smog. * n cloud, fog, haze; bewilderment, obscurity, perplexity.

**mistake** vb misapprehend, miscalculate, misconceive, misjudge, misunderstand; confound, take; blunder, err. * n misapprehension, miscalculation, misconception, mistaking, misunderstanding; blunder, error, fault, inaccuracy, oversight, slip, trip.

**mistaken** adj erroneous, inaccurate, incorrect, misinformed, wrong.

**mistrust** vb distrust, doubt, suspect; apprehend, fear, surmise, suspect. * n doubt, distrust, misgiving, suspicion.

**misty** adj cloudy, clouded, dark, dim, foggy, obscure, overcast.

**misunderstand** vb misapprehend, misconceive, misconstrue, mistake.

**misunderstanding** n error, misapprehension, misconception, mistake; difference, difficulty, disagreement, discord, dissension, quarrel.

**misuse** vb desecrate, misapply, misemploy, pervert, profane; abuse, ill-treat, maltreat, ill-use; fritter, squander, waste. * n abuse, perversion, profanation, prostitution; ill-treatment, ill-use, ill-usage, misusage; misapplication, solecism.

**mitigate** vb abate, alleviate, assuage, diminish, extenuate, lessen, moderate, palliate, relieve; allay, appease, calm, mollify, pacify, quell, quiet, reduce, soften, soothe; moderate, temper.

**mitigation** n abatement, allaying, alleviation, assuagement, diminution, moderation, palliation, relief.

**mix** vb alloy, amalgamate, blend, commingle, combine, compound, incorporate, interfuse, interlard, mingle, unite; associate, join. * n alloy, amalgam, blend, combination, compound, mixture.

**mixture** n admixture, association, intermixture, union; compound, farrago, hash, hodgepodge, hotchpotch, jumble, medley, melange, mishmash; diversity, miscellany, variety.

**moan** vb bemoan, bewail, deplore, grieve, groan, lament, mourn, sigh, weep. * n groan, lament, lamentation, sigh, wail.

**mob** vb crowd, jostle, surround, swarm, pack, throng. * n assemblage, crowd, rabble, multitude, throng, tumult; dregs, canaille, populace, rabble, riffraff, scum.

**mobile** adj changeable, fickle, expressive, inconstant, sensitive, variable, volatile.

**mock** vb ape, counterfeit, imitate, mimic, take off; deride, flout, gibe, insult, jeer, ridicule, taunt; balk, cheat, deceive, defeat, disappoint, dupe, elude, illude, mislead. * adj assumed, clap-trap, counterfeit, fake, false, feigned, make-believe, pretended, spurious. * n fake, imitation, phoney, sham; gibe, insult, jeer, scoff, taunt.

**mockery** n contumely, counterfeit, deception, derision, imitation, jeering, mimicry, ridicule, scoffing, scorn, sham, travesty.

**mode** n fashion, manner, method, style, way; accident, affection, degree, graduation, modification, quality, variety.

**model** vb design, fashion, form, mould, plan, shape. * adj admirable, archetypal, estimable, exemplary, ideal, meritorious, paradigmatic, perfect, praiseworthy, worthy. * n archetype, design, mould, original, pattern, protoplast, prototype, type; dummy, example, form; copy, facsimile, image, imitation, representation.

**moderate** vb abate, allay, appease, assuage, blunt, dull, lessen, soothe, mitigate, mollify, pacify, quell, quiet, reduce, repress, soften, still, subdue; diminish, qualify, slacken, temper; control, govern, regulate. * adj abstinent, frugal, sparing, temperate; limited, mediocre; abstemious, sober; calm, cool, judicious, reasonable, steady; gentle, mild, temperate, tolerable.

**moderation** n abstemiousness, forbearance, frugality, restraint, sobriety, temperance; calmness, composure, coolness, deliberateness, equanimity, mildness, sedateness.

**modern** adj fresh, late, latest, new, novel, present, recent, up-to-date.

**modest** adj bashful, coy, diffident, humble, meek, reserved, retiring, shy, unassuming, unobtrusive, unostentatious, unpretending, unpretentious; chaste, proper, pure, virtuous; becoming, decent, moderate.

**modesty** n bashfulness, coyness, diffidence, humility, meekness, propriety, prudishness, reserve, shyness, unobtrusiveness; chastity, purity, virtue; decency, moderation.

**modification** n alteration, change, qualification, reformation, variation; form, manner, mode, state.

**modify** vb alter, change, qualify, reform, shape, vary; lower, moderate, qualify, soften.

**modish** adj fashionable, stylish; ceremonious, conventional, courtly, genteel.

**modulate** vb attune, harmonize, tune; inflect, vary; adapt, adjust, proportion.

**moiety** n half; part, portion, share.

**moil** vb drudge, labour, toil; bespatter, daub, defile, soil, splash, spot, stain; fatigue, weary, tire.

**moist** adj damp, dank, humid, marshy, muggy, swampy, wet.

**moisture** n dampness, dankness, humidity, wetness.

**mole** n breakwater, dike, dyke, jetty, mound, pier, quay.

**molecule** n atom, monad, particle.

**molest** vb annoy, badger, bore, bother, chafe, discommode, disquiet, disturb, harass, harry, fret, gull, hector, incommode, inconvenience, irritate, oppress, pester, plague, tease, torment, trouble, vex, worry.

**mollify** vb soften; appease, calm, compose, pacify, quiet, soothe, tranquillize; abate, allay, assuage, blunt, dull, ease, lessen, mitigate, moderate, relieve, temper; qualify, tone down.

**moment** n flash, instant, jiffy, second, trice, twinkling, wink; avail, consequence, consideration, force, gravity, importance, significance, signification, value, weight; drive, force, impetus, momentum.

**momentous** adj grave, important, serious, significant, vital, weighty.

**momentum** n impetus, moment.

**monarch** n autocrat, despot; chief, dictator, emperor, king, potentate, prince, queen, ruler, sovereign.

**monastery** n abbey, cloister, convent, lamasery, nunnery, priory.

**monastic** adj coenobitic, coenobitical, conventual, monkish, secluded.

**money** n banknotes, cash, coin, currency, riches, specie, wealth.

**moneyed, monied** adj affluent, opulent, rich, well-off, well-to-do.

**monitor** vb check, observe, oversee, supervise, watch. * n admonisher, admonitor, adviser, counsellor, instructor, mentor, overseer.

**monomania** n delusion, hallucination, illusion, insanity, self-deception.

**monopolize** vb control, dominate, engross, forestall.

**monotonous** adj boring, dull, tedious, tiresome, undiversified, uniform, unvaried, unvarying, wearisome.

**monotony** n boredom, dullness, sameness, tedium, tiresomeness, uniformity, wearisomeness.

**monster** adj enormous, gigantic, huge, immense, mammoth, monstrous. * n enormity, marvel, prodigy, wonder; brute, demon, fiend, miscreant, ruffian, villain, wretch.

**monstrous** adj abnormal, preternatural, prodigious, unnatural; colossal, enormous, extraordinary, huge, immense, stupendous, vast; marvellous, strange, wonderful; bad, base, dreadful, flagrant, frightful, hateful, hideous, horrible, shocking, terrible.

**monument** n memorial, record, remembrance, testimonial; cairn, cenotaph, gravestone, mausoleum, memorial, pillar, tomb, tombstone.

**mood** n disposition, humour, temper, vein.

**moody** adj capricious, humoursome, variable; angry, crabbed, crusty, fretful, ill-tempered, irascible, irritable, passionate, pettish, peevish, petulant, snappish, snarling, sour, testy; cross-grained, dogged, frowning, glowering, glum, intractable, morose, perverse, spleeny, stubborn, sulky, sullen, wayward; abstracted, gloomy, melancholy, pensive, sad, saturnine.

**moonshine** n balderdash, fiction, flummery, fudge, fustian, nonsense, pretence, stuff, trash, twaddle, vanity.

**moor**[1] vb anchor, berth, fasten, fix, secure, tie.

**moor**[2] n bog, common, heath, moorland, morass, moss, wasteland.

**moot** vb agitate, argue, debate, discuss, dispute. * adj arguable, debatable, doubtful, unsettled.

**mopish** adj dejected, depressed, desponding, downcast, down-hearted, gloomy, glum, sad.

**moral** adj ethical, good, honest, honourable, just, upright, virtuous; abstract, ideal, intellectual, mental. * n intent, meaning, significance.

**morals** npl ethics, morality; behaviour, conduct, habits, manners.

**morass** n bog, fen, marsh, quagmire, slough, swamp.

**morbid** adj ailing, corrupted, diseased, sick, sickly, tainted, unhealthy, unsound, vitiated; depressed, downcast, gloomy, pessimistic, sensitive.

**mordacious** adj acrid, biting, cutting, mordant, pungent, sharp, stinging; caustic, poignant, satirical, sarcastic, scathing, severe.

**mordant** adj biting, caustic, keen, mordacious, nipping, sarcastic.

**moreover** adv, conj also, besides, further, furthermore, likewise, too.

**morning** n aurora, daybreak, dawn, morn, morningtide, sunrise.

**morose** adj austere, churlish, crabbed, crusty, dejected, desponding, downcast, downhearted, gloomy, glum, melancholy, moody, sad, severe, sour, sullen, surly.

**morsel** n bite, mouthful, titbit; bit, fragment, part, piece, scrap.

**mortal** adj deadly, destructive, fatal, final, human, lethal, perishable, vital. * n being, earthling, human, man, person, woman.

**mortality** n corruption, death, destruction, fatality.

**mortification** n chagrin, disappointment, discontent, dissatisfaction, displeasure, humiliation, trouble, shame, vexation; humility, penance, self-abasement, self-denial; gangrene, necrosis.

**mortify** vb annoy, chagrin, depress, disappoint, displease, disquiet, dissatisfy, harass, humble, plague, vex, worry; abase, abash, confound, humiliate, restrain, shame, subdue; corrupt, fester, gangrene, putrefy.

**mortuary** n burial place, cemetery, churchyard, graveyard, necropolis; charnel house, morgue.

**mostly** adv chiefly, customarily, especially, generally, mainly, particularly, principally.

**mote** n atom, corpuscle, flaw, mite, particle, speck, spot.

**motherly** adj affectionate, kind, maternal, paternal, tender.

**motion** vb beckon, direct, gesture, signal. * n action, change, drift, flux, movement, passage, stir, transit; air, gait, port; gesture, impulse, prompting, suggestion; proposal, proposition.

**motionless** adj fixed, immobile, quiescent, stable, stagnant, standing, stationary, still, torpid, unmoved.

**motive** adj activating, driving, moving, operative.
* n cause, consideration, ground, impulse, incentive, incitement, inducement, influence, occasion, prompting, purpose, reason, spur, stimulus.

**motley** adj coloured, dappled, mottled, speckled, spotted, variegated; composite, diversified, heterogeneous, mingled, mixed.

**mottled** adj dappled, motley, piebald, speckled, spotted, variegated.

**mould**[1] vb carve, cast, fashion, form, make, model, shape. * n cast, character, fashion, form, matrix, pattern, shape; material, matter, substance.

**mould**[2] n blight, mildew, mouldiness, must, mustiness, rot; fungus, lichen, mushroom, puffball, rust, smut, toadstool; earth, loam, soil.

**moulder** vb crumble, decay, perish, waste.

**mouldy** adj decaying, fusty, mildewed, musty.

**mound** n bank, barrow, hill, hillock, knoll, tumulus; bulwark, defence, rampart.

**mount**[1] n hill, mountain, peak.

**mount**[2] vb arise, ascend, climb, rise, soar, tower; escalate, scale; embellish, ornament; bestride, get upon. * n charger, horse, ride, steed.

**mountain** n alp, height, hill, mount, peak; abundance, heap, mound, stack.

**mountebank** n charlatan, cheat, impostor, pretender, quack.

**mourn** vb bemoan, bewail, deplore, grieve, lament, sorrow, wail.

**mournful** adj afflicting, afflictive, calamitous, deplorable, distressed, grievous, lamentable, sad, woeful; doleful, heavy, heavy-hearted, lugubrious, melancholy, sorrowful, tearful.

**mouth** vb clamour, declaim, rant, roar, vociferate. * n chaps, jaws; aperture, opening, orifice; entrance, inlet; oracle, mouthpiece, speaker, spokesman.

**movables** npl chattels, effects, furniture, goods, property, wares.

**move** vb dislodge, drive, impel, propel, push, shift, start, stir; actuate, incite, instigate, rouse; determine, incline, induce, influence, persuade, prompt; affect, impress, touch, trouble; agitate, awaken, excite, incense, irritate; propose, recommend, suggest; go, march, proceed, walk; act, live; flit, remove. * n action, motion, movement.

**movement** n change, move, motion, passage; emotion; crusade, drive.

**moving** adj impelling, influencing, instigating, persuading, persuasive; affecting, impressive, pathetic, touching.

**mucous** adj glutinous, gummy, mucilaginous, ropy, slimy, viscid.

**mud** n dirt, mire, muck, slime.

**muddle** vb confuse, disarrange, disorder; fuddle, inebriate, stupefy; muff, mull, spoil. * n confusion, disorder, mess, plight, predicament.

**muddy** vb dirty, foul, smear, soil; confuse, obscure. * adj dirty, foul, impure, slimy, soiled, turbid; bothered, confused, dull, heavy, stupid; incoherent, obscure, vague.

**muffle** vb cover, envelop, shroud, wrap; conceal, disguise, involve; deaden, soften, stifle, suppress.

**mulish** adj cross-grained, headstrong, intractable, obstinate, stubborn.

**multifarious** adj different, divers, diverse, diversified, manifold, multiform, multitudinous, various.

**multiloquence** n garrulity, loquacity, loquaciousness, talkativeness.

**multiply** vb augment, extend, increase, spread.

**multitude** n numerousness; host, legion; army, assemblage, assembly, collection, concourse, congregation, crowd, horde, mob, swarm, throng; commonality, herd, mass, mob, pack, populace, rabble.

**mundane** adj earthly, secular, sublunary, temporal, terrene, terrestrial, worldly.

**munificence** n benefice, bounteousness, bountifulness, bounty, generosity, liberality.

**munificent** adj beneficent, bounteous, bountiful, free, generous, liberal, princely.

**murder** vb assassinate, butcher, destroy, dispatch, kill, massacre, slaughter, slay; abuse, mar, spoil. * n assassination, butchery, destruction, homicide, killing, manslaughter, massacre.

**murderer** n assassin, butcher, cut-throat, killer, manslaughterer, slaughterer, slayer.

**murderous** adj barbarous, bloodthirsty, bloody, cruel, fell, sanguinary, savage.

**murky** adj cheerless, cloudy, dark, dim, dusky, gloomy, hazy, lowering, lurid, obscure, overcast.

**murmur** vb croak, grumble, mumble, mutter; hum, whisper. * n complaint, grumble, mutter, plaint, whimper; hum, undertone, whisper.

**muscular** adj sinewy; athletic, brawny, powerful, lusty, stalwart, stout, strong, sturdy, vigorous.

**muse** vb brood, cogitate, consider, contemplate, deliberate, dream, meditate, ponder, reflect, ruminate, speculate, think. * n abstraction, musing, reverie.

**music** n harmony, melody, symphony.

**musical** adj dulcet, harmonious, melodious, sweet, sweet-sounding, symphonious, tuneful.

**musing** adj absent-minded, meditative, preoccupied. * n absent-mindedness, abstraction, contemplation, daydreaming, meditation, muse, reflection, reverie, rumination.

**muster** vb assemble, collect, congregate, convene, convoke, gather, marshal, meet, rally, summon. * n assemblage, assembly, collection, congregation, convention, convocation, gathering, meeting, rally.

**musty** adj fetid, foul, fusty, mouldy, rank, sour, spoiled; hackneyed, old, stale, threadbare, trite; ill-favoured, insipid, vapid; dull, heavy, rusty, spiritless.

**mutable** adj alterable, changeable; changeful, fickle, inconstant, irresolute, mutational, unsettled, unstable, unsteady, vacillating, variable, wavering.

**mutation** n alteration, change, variation.

**mute** vb dampen, lower, moderate, muffle, soften. * adj dumb, voiceless; silent, speechless, still, taciturn.

**mutilate** vb cripple, damage, disable, disfigure, hamstring, injure, maim, mangle, mar.

**mutinous** adj contumacious, insubordinate, rebellious, refractory, riotous, tumultuous, turbulent, unruly; insurgent, seditious.

**mutiny** vb rebel, revolt, rise, resist. * n insubordination, insurrection, rebellion, revolt, revolution, riot, rising, sedition, uprising.

**mutter** vb grumble, muffle, mumble, murmur.

**mutual** adj alternate, common, correlative, interchangeable, interchanged, reciprocal, requited.

**myopic** adj near-sighted, purblind, short-sighted.

**myriad** adj innumerable, manifold, multitudinous, uncounted. * n host, million(s), multitude, score(s), sea, swarm, thousand(s).

**mysterious** adj abstruse, cabbalistic, concealed, cryptic, dark, dim, enigmatic, enigmatical, hidden, incomprehensible, inexplicable, inscrutable, mystic, mystical, obscure, occult, puzzling, recondite, secret, sphinx-like, unaccountable, unfathomable, unintelligible, unknown.

**mystery** n enigma, puzzle, riddle, secret; art, business, calling, trade.

**mystical** adj abstruse, cabbalistic, dark, enigmatical, esoteric, hidden, inscrutable, mysterious, obscure, occult, recondite, transcendental; allegorical, emblematic, emblematical, symbolic, symbolical.

**mystify** vb befog, bewilder, confound, confuse, dumbfound, embarrass, obfuscate, perplex, pose, puzzle.

**myth** n fable, legend, tradition; allegory, fiction, invention, parable, story; falsehood, fancy, figment, lie, untruth.

**mythical** adj allegorical, fabled, fabulous, fanciful, fictitious, imaginary, legendary, mythological.

# N

**nab** vb catch, clutch, grasp, seize.

**nag¹** vb carp, fuss, hector, henpeck, pester, torment, worry. * n nagger, scold, shrew, tartar.

**nag²** n bronco, crock, hack, horse, pony, scrag.

**naive** adj artless, candid, ingenuous, natural, plain, simple, unaffected, unsophisticated.

**naked** adj bare, nude, uncovered; denuded, unclad, unclothed, undressed; defenceless, exposed, open, unarmed, unguarded, unprotected; evident, manifest, plain, stark, unconcealed, undisguised; mere, sheer, simple; bare, destitute, rough, rude, unfurnished, unprovided; uncoloured, unexaggerated, unvarnished.

**name** vb call, christen, denounce, dub, entitle, phrase, style, term; mention; denominate, designate, indicate, nominate, specify. * n appellation, cognomen, denomination, designation, epithet, nickname, surname, sobriquet, title; character, credit, reputation, repute; celebrity, distinction, eminence, fame, honour, note, praise, renown.

**narcotic** adj stupefacient, stupefactive, stupefying. * n anaesthetic, anodyne, dope, opiate, sedative, stupefacient, tranquillizer.

**narrate** vb chronicle, describe, detail, enumerate, recite, recount, rehearse, relate, tell.

**narration** n account, description, chronicle, history, narrative, recital, rehearsal, relation, story, tale.

**narrow** vb confine, contract, cramp, limit, restrict, straiten. * adj circumscribed, confined, contracted, cramped, incapacious, limited, pinched, scanty, straitened; bigoted, hidebound, illiberal, ungenerous; close, near.

**nastiness** n defilement, dirtiness, filth, filthiness, foulness, impurity, pollution, squalor, uncleanness; indecency, grossness, obscenity, pornography, ribaldry, smut, smuttiness.

**nasty** adj defiled, dirty, filthy, foul, impure, loathsome, polluted, squalid, unclean; gross, indecent, indelicate, lewd, loose, obscene, smutty, vile; disagreeable, disgusting, nauseous, odious, offensive, repulsive, sickening; aggravating, annoying, pesky, pestering, troublesome.

**nation** n commonwealth, realm, state; community, people, population, race, stock, tribe.

**native** adj aboriginal, autochthonal, autochthonous, domestic, home, indigenous, vernacular; genuine, intrinsic, natural, original, real; congenital, inborn, inbred, inherent, innate, natal. * n aborigine, autochthon, inhabitant, national, resident.

**natty** adj dandyish, fine, foppish, jaunty, neat, nice, spruce, tidy.

**natural** adj indigenous, innate, native, original; characteristic, essential; legitimate, normal, regular; artless, authentic, genuine, ingenious, unreal, simple, spontaneous, unaffected; bastard, illegitimate.

**nature** n universe, world; character, constitution, essence; kind, quality, species, sort; disposition, grain, humour, mood, temper; being, intellect, intelligence, mind.

**naughty** adj bad, corrupt, mischievous, perverse, worthless.

**nausea** n queasiness, seasickness; loathing, qualm, aversion, disgust, repugnance.

**nauseous** adj abhorrent, disgusting, distasteful, loathsome, offensive, repulsive, revolting, sickening.

**naval** adj marine, maritime, nautical.

**navigate** vb cruise, direct, guide, pilot, plan, sail, steer.

**navy** n fleet, shipping, vessels.

**near** vb approach, draw close. * adj adjacent, approximate, close, contiguous, neighbouring, nigh; approaching, forthcoming, imminent, impending; dear, familiar, friendly, intimate; direct, immediate, short, straight; accurate, literal; narrow, parsimonious.

**nearly** adv almost, approximately, well-nigh; closely, intimately, pressingly; meanly, parsimoniously, penuriously, stingily.

**neat** adj clean, cleanly, orderly, tidy, trim, unsoiled; nice, smart, spruce; chaste, pure, simple; excellent, pure, unadulterated; adroit, clever, exact, finished; dainty, nice.

**nebulous** adj cloudy, hazy, misty.

**necessary** adj inevitable, unavoidable; essential, expedient, indispensable, needful, requisite; compelling, compulsory, involuntary. * n essential, necessity, requirement, requisite.

**necessitate** vb compel, constrain, demand, force, impel, oblige.

**necessitous** adj destitute, distressed, indigent, moneyless, needy, penniless, pinched, poor, poverty-stricken; narrow, pinching.

**necessity** n inevitability, inevitableness, unavoidability, unavoidableness; compulsion, destiny, fatality, fate; emergency, urgency; exigency, indigence, indispensability, indispensableness, need, needfulness, poverty, want; essentiality, essentialness, requirement, requisite.

**necromancy** n conjuration, divination, enchantment, magic, sorcery, witchcraft, wizardry.

**necropolis** n burial ground, cemetery, churchyard, crematorium, graveyard, mortuary.

**need** vb demand, lack, require, want. * n emergency, exigency, extremity, necessity, strait, urgency, want; destitution, distress, indigence, neediness, penury, poverty, privation.

**needful** adj distressful, necessitous, necessary; essential, indispensable, requisite.

**needless** adj superfluous, unnecessary, useless.

**needy** adj destitute, indigent, necessitous, poor.

**nefarious** adj abominable, atrocious, detestable, dreadful, execrable, flagitious, heinous, horrible, infamous, iniquitous, scandalous, vile, wicked.

**negation** n denial, disavowal, disclaimer, rejection, renunciation.

**neglect** vb condemn, despise, disregard, forget, ignore, omit, overlook, slight. * n carelessness, default, failure, heedlessness, inattention, omission, remissness; disregard, disrespect, slight; indifference, negligence.

**negligence** n carelessness, disregard, heedlessness, inadvertency, inattention, indifference, neglect, remissness, slackness, thoughtlessness; defect, fault, inadvertence, omission, shortcoming.

**negligent** adj careless, heedless, inattentive, indifferent, neglectful, regardless, thoughtless.

**negotiate** vb arrange, bargain, deal, debate, sell, settle, transact, treat.

**neighbourhood** n district, environs, locality, vicinage, vicinity; adjacency, nearness, propinquity, proximity.

**neighbourly** adj attentive, civil, friendly, kind, obliging, social.

**neophyte** n beginner, catechumen, convert, novice, pupil, tyro.

**nerve** vb brace, energize, fortify, invigorate, strengthen. * n force, might, power, strength, vigour; coolness, courage, endurance, firmness, fortitude, hardihood, manhood, pluck, resolution, self-command, steadiness.

**nervous** adj forcible, powerful, robust, strong, vigorous; irritable, fearful, shaky, timid, timorous, weak, weakly.

**nestle** vb cuddle, harbour, lodge, nuzzle, snug, snuggle.

**nettle** vb chafe, exasperate, fret, harass, incense, irritate, provoke, ruffle, sting, tease, vex.

**neutral** adj impartial, indifferent; colourless, mediocre.

**neutralize** vb cancel, counterbalance, counterpoise, invalidate, offset.

**nevertheless** adv however, nonetheless, notwithstanding, yet.

**new** adj fresh, latest, modern, novel, recent, unused; additional, another, further; reinvigorated, renovated, repaired.

**news** n advice, information, intelligence, report, tidings, word.

**nice** adj accurate, correct, critical, definite, delicate, exact, exquisite, precise, rigorous, strict; dainty, difficult, exacting, fastidious, finical, punctilious, squeamish; discerning, discriminating, particular, precise, scrupulous; neat, tidy, trim; fine, minute, refined, subtle; delicate, delicious, luscious, palatable, savoury, soft, tender; agreeable, delightful, good, pleasant.

**nicety** n accuracy, exactness, niceness, precision, truth, daintiness, fastidiousness, squeamishness; discrimination, subtlety.

**niggard** n churl, curmudgeon, miser, screw, scrimp, skinflint.

**niggardly** adj avaricious, close, close-fisted, illiberal, mean, mercenary, miserly, parsimonious, penurious, skinflint, sordid, stingy.

**nigh** adj adjacent, adjoining, contiguous, near; present, proximate. * adv almost, near, nearly.

**nimble** adj active, agile, alert, brisk, lively, prompt, quick, speedy, sprightly, spry, swift, tripping.

**nobility** n aristocracy, dignity, elevation, eminence, grandeur, greatness, loftiness, magnanimity, nobleness, peerage, superiority, worthiness.

**noble** adj dignified, elevated, eminent, exalted, generous, great, honourable, illustrious, magnanimous, superior, worthy; choice, excellent; aristocratic, gentle, high-born, patrician; grand, lofty, lordly, magnificent, splendid, stately. * n aristocrat, grandee, lord, nobleman, peer.

**noctambulist** n sleepwalker, somnambulist.

**noise** vb bruit, gossip, repeat, report, rumour. * n ado, blare, clamour, clatter, cry, din, fuss, hubbub, hullabaloo, outcry, pandemonium, racket, row, sound, tumult, uproar, vociferation.

**noiseless** adj inaudible, quiet, silent, soundless.

**noisome** adj bad, baneful, deleterious, disgusting, fetid, foul, hurtful, injurious, mischievous, nocuous, noxious, offensive, pernicious, pestiferous, pestilential, poisonous, unhealthy, unwholesome.

**noisy** adj blatant, blustering, boisterous, brawling, clamorous, loud, uproarious, riotous, tumultuous, vociferous.

**nomadic** adj migratory, pastoral, vagrant, wandering.

**nominal** adj formal, inconsiderable, minimal, ostensible, pretended, professed, so-called, titular.

**nominate** vb appoint, choose, designate, name, present, propose.

**nonchalant** adj apathetic, careless, cool, indifferent, unconcerned.

**nondescript** adj amorphous, characterless, commonplace, dull, indescribable, odd, ordinary, unclassifiable, uninteresting, unremarkable.

**nonentity** n cipher, futility, inexistence, inexistency, insignificance, nobody, nonexistence, nothingness.

**nonplus** vb astonish, bewilder, confound, confuse, discomfit, disconcert, embarrass, floor, gravel, perplex, pose, puzzle.

**nonsensical** adj absurd, foolish, irrational, senseless, silly, stupid.

**norm** n model, pattern, rule, standard.

**normal** adj analogical, legitimate, natural, ordinary, regular, usual; erect, perpendicular, vertical.

**notable** adj distinguished, extraordinary, memorable, noted, remarkable, signal; conspicuous, evident, noticeable, observable, plain, prominent, striking; notorious, rare, well-known. * n celebrity, dignitary, notability, worthy.

**note** vb heed, mark, notice, observe, regard, remark; record, register; denote, designate. * n memorandum, minute, record; annotation, comment, remark, scholium; indication, mark, sign, symbol, token; account, bill, catalogue, reckoning; billet, epistle, letter; consideration, heed, notice, observation; celebrity, consequence, credit, distinction, eminence, fame, notability, notedness, renown, reputation, respectability; banknote, bill, promissory note; song, strain, tune, voice.

**noted** adj celebrated, conspicuous, distinguished, eminent, famed, famous, illustrious, notable, notorious, remarkable, renowned, well-known.

**nothing** n inexistence, nonentity, nonexistence, nothingness, nullity; bagatelle, trifle.

**notice** vb mark, note, observe, perceive, regard, see; comment on, mention, remark; attend to, heed. * n cognizance, heed, note, observation, regard; advice, announcement, information, intelligence, mention, news, notification; communication, intimation, premonition, warning; attention, civility, consideration, respect; comments, remarks.

**notify** vb advertise, announce, declare, publish, promulgate; acquaint, apprise, inform.

**notion** n concept, conception, idea; apprehension, belief, conceit, conviction, expectation, estimation, impression, judgement, opinion, sentiment, view.

**notoriety** n celebrity, fame, figure, name, note, publicity, reputation, repute, vogue.

**notorious** adj apparent, egregious, evident, notable, obvious, open, overt, manifest, patent, well-known; celebrated, conspicuous, distinguished, famed, famous, flagrant, infamous, noted, remarkable, renowned.

**notwithstanding** conj despite, however, nevertheless, yet. * prep despite.

**nourish** vb feed, nurse, nurture; maintain, supply, support; breed, educate, instruct, train; cherish, encourage, foment, foster, promote, succour.

**nourishment** n aliment, diet, food, nutriment, nutrition, sustenance.

**novel** adj fresh, modern, new, rare, recent, strange, uncommon, unusual. * n fiction, romance, story, tale.

**novice** n convert, proselyte; initiate, neophyte, novitiate, probationer; apprentice, beginner, learner, tyro.

**noxious** adj baneful, deadly, deleterious, destructive, detrimental, hurtful, injurious, insalubrious, mischievous, noisome, pernicious, pestilent, poisonous, unfavourable, unwholesome.

**nude** adj bare, denuded, exposed, naked, uncovered, unclothed, undressed.

**nugatory** *adj* frivolous, insignificant, trifling, trivial, vain, worthless; bootless, ineffectual, inefficacious, inoperative, null, unavailing, useless.

**nuisance** *n* annoyance, bore, bother, infliction, offence, pest, plague, trouble.

**null** *adj* ineffectual, invalid, nugatory, useless, void; characterless, colourless.

**nullify** *vb* abolish, abrogate, annul, cancel, invalidate, negate, quash, repeal, revoke.

**numb** *vb* benumb, deaden, stupefy. * *adj* benumbed, deadened, dulled, insensible, paralysed.

**number** *vb* calculate, compute, count, enumerate, numerate, reckon, tell; account, reckon. * *n* digit, figure, numeral; horde, multitude, numerousness, throng; aggregate, collection, sum, total.

**numerous** *adj* abundant, many, numberless.

**nuncio** *n* ambassador, legate, messenger.

**nunnery** *n* abbey, cloister, convent, monastery.

**nuptial** *adj* bridal, conjugal, connubial, hymeneal, matrimonial.

**nuptials** *npl* espousal, marriage, wedding.

**nurse** *vb* nourish, nurture; rear, suckle; cherish, encourage, feed, foment, foster, pamper, promote, succour; economize, manage; caress, dandle, fondle. * *n* auxiliary, orderly, sister; amah, *au pair*, babysitter, nanny, nursemaid, nurserymaid,

**nurture** *vb* feed, nourish, nurse, tend; breed, discipline, educate, instruct, rear, school, train. * *n* diet, food, nourishment; breeding, discipline, education, instruction, schooling, training, tuition; attention, nourishing, nursing.

**nutriment** *n* aliment, food, nourishment, nutrition, pabulum, subsistence, sustenance.

**nutrition** *n* diet, food, nourishment, nutriment.

**nutritious** *adj* invigorating, nourishing, strengthening, supporting, sustaining.

**nymph** *n* damsel, dryad, lass, girl, maid, maiden, naiad.

# O

**oaf** n blockhead, dolt, dunce, fool, idiot, simpleton.

**oath** n blasphemy, curse, expletive, imprecation, malediction; affirmation, pledge, promise, vow.

**obduracy** n contumacy, doggedness, obstinacy, stubbornness, tenacity; depravity, impenitence.

**obdurate** adj hard, harsh, rough, rugged; callous, cantankerous, dogged, firm, hardened, inflexible, insensible, obstinate, pigheaded, unfeeling, stubborn, unbending, unyielding; depraved, graceless, lost, reprobate, shameless, impenitent, incorrigible, irreclaimable.

**obedience** n acquiescence, agreement, compliance, duty, respect, reverence, submission, submissiveness, subservience.

**obedient** adj acquiescent, compliant, deferential, duteous, dutiful, observant, regardful, respectful, submissive, subservient, yielding.

**obeisance** n bow, courtesy, curtsy, homage, reverence, salutation.

**obelisk** n column, pillar.

**obese** adj corpulent, fat, fleshy, gross, plump, podgy, portly, stout.

**obesity** n corpulence, corpulency, embonpoint, fatness, fleshiness, obeseness, plumpness.

**obey** vb comply, conform, heed, keep, mind, observe, submit, yield.

**obfuscate** vb cloud, darken, obscure; bewilder, confuse, muddle.

**object**[1] vb cavil, contravene, demur, deprecate, disapprove of, except to, impeach, oppose, protest, refuse.

**object**[2] n particular, phenomenon, precept, reality, thing; aim, butt, destination, end, mark, recipient, target; design, drift, goal, intention, motive, purpose, use, view.

**objection** n censure, difficulty, doubt, exception, protest, remonstrance, scruple.

**objurgate** vb chide, reprehend, reprove.

**oblation** n gift, offering, sacrifice.

**obligation** n accountability, accountableness, responsibility; agreement, bond, contract, covenant, engagement, stipulation; debt, indebtedness, liability.

**obligatory** adj binding, coercive, compulsory, enforced, necessary, unavoidable.

**oblige** vb bind, coerce, compel, constrain, force, necessitate, require; accommodate, benefit, convenience, favour, gratify, please; obligate, bind.

**obliging** adj accommodating, civil, complaisant, considerate, kind, friendly, polite.

**oblique** adj aslant, inclined, sidelong, slanting; indirect, obscure.

**obliterate** vb cancel, delete, destroy, efface, eradicate, erase, expunge.

**oblivious** adj careless, forgetful, heedless, inattentive, mindless, negligent, neglectful.

**obloquy** n aspersion, backbiting, blame, calumny, censure, contumely, defamation, detraction, disgrace, odium, reproach, reviling, slander, traducing.

**obnoxious** adj blameworthy, censurable, faulty, reprehensible; hateful, objectionable, obscene, odious, offensive, repellent, repugnant, repulsive, unpleasant, unpleasing.

**obscene** adj broad, coarse, filthy, gross, immodest, impure, indecent, indelicate, ribald, unchaste, lewd, licentious, loose, offensive, pornographic, shameless, smutty; disgusting, dirty, foul.

**obscure** vb becloud, befog, blur, cloud, darken, eclipse, dim, obfuscate, obnubilate, shade; conceal, cover, equivocate, hide. * adj dark, darksome, dim, dusky, gloomy, lurid, murky, rayless, shadowy, sombre, unenlightened, unilluminated; abstruse, blind, cabbalistic, difficult, doubtful, enigmatic, high, incomprehensible, indefinite, indistinct, intricate, involved, mysterious, mystic, recondite, undefined, unintelligible, vague; remote, secluded; humble, inglorious, nameless, renownless, undistinguished, unhonoured, unknown, unnoted, unnoticed.

**obsequious** adj cringing, deferential, fawning, flattering, servile, slavish, supple, subservient, sycophantic, truckling.

**observant** adj attentive, heedful, mindful, perceptive, quick, regardful, vigilant, watchful.

**observation** n attention, cognition, notice, observance; annotation, note, remark; experience, knowledge.

**observe** vb eye, mark, note, notice, remark, watch;

behold, detect, discover, perceive, see; express, mention, remark, say, utter; comply, conform, follow, fulfil, obey; celebrate, keep, regard, solemnize.

**obsolete** adj ancient, antiquated, antique, archaic, disused, neglected, old, old-fashioned, obsolescent, out-of-date, past, passé, unfashionable.

**obstacle** n barrier, check, difficulty, hindrance, impediment, interference, interruption, obstruction, snag, stumbling block.

**obstinacy** n contumacy, doggedness, headiness, firmness, inflexibility, intractability, obduracy, persistence, perseverance, perversity, resoluteness, stubbornness, tenacity, wilfulness.

**obstinate** adj cross-grained, contumacious, dogged, firm, headstrong, inflexible, immovable, intractable, mulish, obdurate, opinionated, persistent, pertinacious, perverse, resolute, self-willed, stubborn, tenacious, unyielding, wilful.

**obstreperous** adj boisterous, clamorous, loud, noisy, riotous, tumultuous, turbulent, unruly, uproarious, vociferous.

**obstruct** vb bar, barricade, block, blockade, block up, choke, clog, close, glut, jam, obturate, stop; hinder, impede, oppose, prevent; arrest, check, curb, delay, embrace, interrupt, retard, slow.

**obstruction** n bar, barrier, block, blocking, check, difficulty, hindrance, impediment, obstacle, stoppage; check, clog, embarrassment, interruption, obturation.

**obtain** vb achieve, acquire, attain, bring, contrive, earn, elicit, gain, get, induce, procure, secure; hold, prevail, stand, subsist.

**obtrude** vb encroach, infringe, interfere, intrude, trespass.

**obtrusive** adj forward, interfering, intrusive, meddling, officious.

**obtuse** adj blunt; blockish, doltish, dull, dull-witted, heavy, stockish, stolid, stupid, slow, unintellectual, unintelligent.

**obviate** vb anticipate, avert, counteract, preclude, prevent, remove.

**obvious** adj exposed, liable, open, subject; apparent, clear, distinct, evident, manifest, palatable, patent, perceptible, plain, self-evident, unmistakable, visible.

**occasion** vb breed, cause, create, originate, produce; induce, influence, move, persuade. * n casualty, event, incident, occurrence; conjuncture, convenience,

juncture, opening, opportunity; condition, necessity, need, exigency, requirement, want; cause, ground, reason; inducement, influence; circumstance, exigency.

**occasional** adj accidental, casual, incidental, infrequent, irregular, uncommon; causative, causing.

**occasionally** adv casually, sometimes.

**occult** adj abstruse, cabbalistic, hidden, latent, secret, invisible, mysterious, mystic, mystical, recondite, shrouded, undetected, undiscovered, unknown, unrevealed, veiled. * n magic, sorcery, witchcraft.

**occupation** n holding, occupancy, possession, tenure, use; avocation, business, calling, craft, employment, engagement, job, post, profession, trade, vocation.

**occupy** vb capture, hold, keep, possess; cover, fill, garrison, inhabit, take up, tenant; engage, employ, use.

**occur** vb appear, arise, offer; befall, chance, eventuate, happen, result, supervene.

**occurrence** n accident, adventure, affair, casualty, event, happening, incident, proceeding, transaction.

**odd** adj additional, redundant, remaining; casual, incidental; inappropriate, queer, unsuitable; comical, droll, erratic; extravagant, extraordinary, fantastic, grotesque, irregular, peculiar, quaint, singular, strange, uncommon, uncouth, unique, unusual, whimsical.

**odds** npl difference, disparity, inequality; advantage, superiority, supremacy.

**odious** adj abominable, detestable, execrable, hateful, shocking; hated, obnoxious, unpopular; disagreeable, forbidding, loathsome, offensive.

**odium** n abhorrence, detestation, dislike, enmity, hate, hatred; odiousness, repulsiveness; obloquy, opprobrium, reproach, shame.

**odorous** adj aromatic, balmy, fragrant, perfumed, redolent, scented, sweet-scented, sweet-smelling.

**odour** n aroma, fragrance, perfume, redolence, scent, smell.

**offal** n carrion, dregs, garbage, refuse, rubbish, waste.

**offence** n aggression, attack, assault; anger, displeasure, indignation, pique, resentment, umbrage, wrath; affront, harm, injury, injustice, insult, outrage, wrong; crime, delinquency, fault, misdeed, misdemeanour, sin, transgression, trespass.

**offend** vb affront, annoy, chafe, displease, fret, gall,

irritate, mortify, nettle, provoke, vex; molest, pain, shock, wound; fall, sin, stumble, transgress.

**offender** n convict, criminal, culprit, delinquent, felon, malefactor, sinner, transgressor, trespasser.

**offensive** adj aggressive, attacking, invading; disgusting, loathsome, nauseating, nauseous, repulsive, sickening; abominable, detestable, disagreeable, displeasing, execrable, hateful, obnoxious, repugnant, revolting, shocking, unpalatable, unpleasant; abusive, disagreeable, impertinent, insolent, insulting, irritating, opprobrious, rude, saucy, unpleasant. * n attack, onslaught.

**offer** vb present, proffer, tender; exhibit; furnish, propose, propound, show; volunteer; dare, essay, endeavour, venture. * n overture, proffering, proposal, proposition, tender, overture; attempt, bid, endeavour, essay.

**offhand** adj abrupt, brusque, casual, curt, extempore, impromptu, informal, unpremeditated, unstudied. * adv carelessly, casually, clumsily, haphazardly, informally, slapdash; ad-lib, extemporaneously, extemporarily, extempore, impromptu.

**office** n duty, function, service, work; berth, place, position, post, situation; business, capacity, charge, employment, trust; bureau, room.

**officiate** vb act, perform, preside, serve.

**officious** adj busy, dictatorial, forward, impertinent, interfering, intermeddling, meddlesome, meddling, obtrusive, pushing, pushy.

**offset** vb balance, counteract, counterbalance, counterpoise. * n branch, offshoot, scion, shoot, slip, sprout, twig; counterbalance, counterpoise, set-off, equivalent.

**offspring** n brood, children, descendants, issue, litter, posterity, progeny; cadet, child, scion.

**often** adv frequently, generally, oftentimes, repeatedly.

**ogre** n bugbear, demon, devil, goblin, hobgoblin, monster, spectre.

**old** adj aged, ancient, antiquated, antique, archaic, elderly, obsolete, olden, old-fashioned, superannuated; decayed, done, senile, worn-out; original, primitive, pristine; former, preceding, pre-existing.

**oleaginous** adj adipose, fat, fatty, greasy, oily, sebaceous, unctuous.

**omen** n augury, auspice, foreboding, portent, presage, prognosis, sign, warning.

**ominous** adj inauspicious, monitory, portentous, premonitory, threatening, unpropitious.

**omission** n default, failure, forgetfulness, neglect, oversight.

**omit** vb disregard, drop, eliminate, exclude, miss, neglect, overlook, skip.

**omnipotent** adj almighty, all-powerful.

**omniscient** adj all-knowing, all-seeing, all-wise.

**oneness** n individuality, singleness, unity.

**onerous** adj burdensome, difficult, hard, heavy, laborious, oppressive, responsible, weighty.

**one-sided** adj partial, prejudiced, unfair, unilateral, unjust.

**only** adj alone, single, sole, solitary. * adv barely, merely, simply.

**onset** n assault, attack, charge, onslaught, storm, storming.

**onus** n burden, liability, load, responsibility.

**ooze** vb distil, drip, drop, shed; drain, exude, filter, leak, percolate, stain, transude. * n mire, mud, slime.

**opaque** adj dark, dim, hazy, muddy; abstruse, cryptic, enigmatic, enigmatical, obscure, unclear.

**open** vb expand, spread; begin, commence, initiate; disclose, exhibit, reveal, show; unbar, unclose, uncover, unlock, unseal, untie. * adj expanded, extended, unclosed, spread wide; aboveboard, artless, candid, cordial, fair, frank, guileless, hearty, honest, sincere, openhearted, single-minded, undesigning, undisguised, undissembling, unreserved; bounteous, bountiful, free, generous, liberal, munificent; ajar, uncovered; exposed, undefended, unprotected; clear, unobstructed; accessible, public, unenclosed; unrestricted; mild, moderate; apparent, debatable, evident, obvious, patent, plain, undetermined.

**opening** adj commencing, first, inaugural, initiatory, introductory. * n aperture, breach, chasm, cleft, fissure, flaw, gap, gulf, hole, interspace, loophole, orifice, perforation, rent, rift; beginning, commencement, dawn; chance, opportunity, vacancy.

**openly** adv candidly, frankly, honestly, plainly, publicly.

**openness** n candour, frankness, honesty, ingenuousness, plainness, unreservedness.

**operate** vb act, function, work; cause, effect, occasion, produce; manipulate, use, run.

**operation** n manipulation, performance, procedure, proceeding, process; action, affair, manoeuvre, motion, movement.

**operative** adj active, effective, effectual, efficient,

serviceable, vigorous; important, indicative, influential, significant. * n artisan, employee, labourer, mechanic, worker, workman.

**opiate** adj narcotic, sedative, soporiferous, soporific. * n anodyne, drug, narcotic, sedative, tranquillizer.

**opine** vb apprehend, believe, conceive, fancy, judge, suppose, presume, surmise, think.

**opinion** n conception, idea, impression, judgment, notion, sentiment, view; belief, persuasion, tenet; esteem, estimation, judgment.

**opinionated** adj biased, bigoted, cocksure, conceited, dictatorial, dogmatic, opinionative, prejudiced, stubborn.

**opponent** adj adverse, antagonistic, contrary, opposing, opposite, repugnant. * n adversary, antagonist, competitor, contestant, counteragent, enemy, foe, opposite, opposer, party, rival.

**opportune** adj appropriate, auspicious, convenient, favourable, felicitous, fit, fitting, fortunate, lucky, propitious, seasonable, suitable, timely, well-timed.

**opportunity** n chance, convenience, moment, occasion.

**oppose** vb combat, contravene, counteract, dispute, obstruct, oppugn, resist, thwart; withstand; check, prevent; confront, counterpoise.

**opposite** adj facing, fronting; conflicting, contradictory, contrary, different, diverse, incompatible, inconsistent, irreconcilable; adverse, antagonistic, hostile, inimical, opposed, opposing, repugnant. * n contradiction, contrary, converse, reverse.

**opposition** n antagonism, antinomy, contrariety, inconsistency, repugnance; counteraction, counterinfluence, hostility, resistance; hindrance, obstacle, obstruction, oppression, prevention.

**oppress** vb burden, crush, depress, harass, load, maltreat, overburden, overpower, overwhelm, persecute, subdue, suppress, tyrannize, wrong.

**oppression** n abuse, calamity, cruelty, hardship, injury, injustice, misery, persecution, severity, suffering, tyranny; depression, dullness, heaviness, lassitude.

**oppressive** adj close, muggy, stifling, suffocating, sultry.

**opprobrious** adj abusive, condemnatory, contemptuous, damnatory, insolent, insulting, offensive, reproachable, scandalous, scurrilous, vituperative; despised, dishonourable, disreputable, hateful, infamous, shameful.

**opprobrium** n contumely, scurrility; calumny, disgrace, ignominy, infamy, obloquy, odium, reproach.

**oppugn** vb assail, argue, attack, combat, contravene, oppose, resist, thwart, withstand.

**option** n choice, discretion, election, preference, selection.

**optional** adj discretionary, elective, nonobligatory, voluntary.

**opulence** n affluence, fortune, independence, luxury, riches, wealth.

**opulent** adj affluent, flush, luxurious, moneyed, plentiful, rich, sumptuous, wealthy.

**oracular** adj ominous, portentous, prophetic; authoritative, dogmatic, magisterial, positive; aged, grave, wise; ambiguous, blind, dark, equivocal, obscure.

**oral** adj nuncupative, spoken, verbal, vocal.

**oration** n address, declamation, discourse, harangue, speech.

**orb** n ball, globe, sphere; circle, circuit, orbit, ring; disk, wheel.

**orbit** vb circle, encircle, revolve around. * n course, path, revolution, track.

**ordain** vb appoint, call, consecrate, elect, experiment, constitute, establish, institute, regulate; decree, enjoin, enact, order, prescribe.

**order** vb adjust, arrange, methodize, regulate, systematize; carry on, conduct, manage; bid, command, direct, instruct, require. * n arrangement, disposition, method, regularity, symmetry, system; law, regulation, rule; discipline, peace, quiet; command, commission, direction, injunction, instruction, mandate, prescription; class, degree, grade, kind, rank; family, tribe; brotherhood, community, fraternity, society; sequence, succession.

**orderly** adj methodical, regular, systematic; peaceable, quiet, well-behaved; neat, shipshape, tidy.

**ordinance** n appointment, command, decree, edict, enactment, law, order, prescript, regulation, rule, statute; ceremony, observance, sacrament, rite, ritual.

**ordinary** adj accustomed, customary, established, everyday, normal, regular, settled, wonted, everyday, regular; common, frequent, habitual, usual; average, commonplace, indifferent, inferior, mean, mediocre, second-rate, undistinguished; homely, plain.

**organization** n business, construction, constitution, organism, structure, system.

**organize** vb adjust, constitute, construct, form, make,

shape; arrange, coordinate, correlate, establish, systematize.

**orgy** *n* carousal, debauch, debauchery, revel, saturnalia.

**orifice** *n* aperture, hole, mouth, perforation, pore, vent.

**origin** *n* beginning, birth, commencement, cradle, derivation, foundation, fountain, fountainhead, original, rise, root, source, spring, starting point; cause, occasion; heritage, lineage, parentage.

**original** *adj* aboriginal, first, primary, primeval, primitive, primordial, pristine; fresh, inventive, novel; eccentric, odd, peculiar. * *n* cause, commencement, origin, source, spring; archetype, exemplar, model, pattern, prototype, protoplast, type.

**originate** *vb* arise, begin, emanate, flow, proceed, rise, spring; create, discover, form, invent, produce.

**originator** *n* author, creator, former, inventor, maker, parent.

**orison** *n* petition, prayer, solicitation, supplication.

**ornament** *vb* adorn, beautify, bedeck, bedizen, decorate, deck, emblazon, garnish, grace. * *n* adornment, bedizenment, decoration, design, embellishment, garnish, ornamentation.

**ornate** *adj* beautiful, bedecked, decorated, elaborate, elegant, embellished, florid, flowery, ornamental, ornamented.

**orthodox** *adj* conventional, correct, sound, true.

**oscillate** *vb* fluctuate, sway, swing, vacillate, vary, vibrate.

**ostensible** *adj* apparent, assigned, avowed, declared, exhibited, manifest, presented, visible; plausible, professed, specious.

**ostentation** *n* dash, display, flourish, pageantry, parade, pomp, pomposity, pompousness, show, vaunting; appearance, semblance, showiness.

**ostentatious** *adj* boastful, dashing, flaunting, pompous, pretentious, showy, vain, vainglorious; gaudy.

**ostracize** *vb* banish, boycott, exclude, excommunicate, exile, expatriate, expel, evict.

**oust** *vb* dislodge, dispossess, eject, evict, expel.

**outbreak** *n* ebullition, eruption, explosion, outburst; affray, broil, conflict, commotion, fray, riot, row; flare-up, manifestation.

**outcast** *n* exile, expatriate; castaway, pariah, reprobate, vagabond.

**outcome** *n* conclusion, consequence, event, issue, result, upshot.

**outcry** *n* cry, scream, screech, yell; bruit, clamour, noise, tumult, vociferation.

**outdo** *vb* beat, exceed, excel, outgo, outstrip, outvie, surpass.

**outlandish** *adj* alien, exotic, foreign, strange; barbarous, bizarre, uncouth.

**outlaw** *vb* ban, banish, condemn, exclude, forbid, make illegal, prohibit. * *n* bandit, brigand, crook, freebooter, highwayman, lawbreaker, marauder, robber, thief.

**outlay** *n* disbursement, expenditure, outgoings.

**outline** *vb* delineate, draft, draw, plan, silhouette, sketch. * *n* contour, profile; delineation, draft, drawing, plan, rough draft, silhouette, sketch.

**outlive** *vb* last, live longer, survive.

**outlook** *n* future, prospect, sight, view; lookout, watch-tower.

**outrage** *vb* abuse, injure, insult, maltreat, offend, shock, injure. * *n* abuse, affront, indignity, insult, offence.

**outrageous** *adj* abusive, frantic, furious, frenzied, mad, raging, turbulent, violent, wild; atrocious, enormous, flagrant, heinous, monstrous, nefarious, villainous; enormous, excessive, extravagant, unwarrantable.

**outré** *adj* excessive, exorbitant, extravagant, immoderate, inordinate, overstrained, unconventional.

**outrun** *vb* beat, exceed, outdistance, outgo, outstrip, outspeed, surpass.

**outset** *n* beginning, commencement, entrance, opening, start, starting point.

**outshine** *vb* eclipse, outstrip, overshadow, surpass.

**outspoken** *adj* abrupt, blunt, candid, frank, plain, plainspoken, unceremonious, unreserved.

**outstanding** *adj* due, owing, uncollected, ungathered, unpaid, unsettled; conspicuous, eminent, prominent, striking.

**outward** *adj* exterior, external, outer, outside.

**outwit** *vb* cheat, circumvent, deceive, defraud, diddle, dupe, gull, outmanoeuvre, overreach, swindle, victimize.

**overawe** *vb* affright, awe, browbeat, cow, daunt, frighten, intimidate, scare, terrify.

**overbalance** *vb* capsize, overset, overturn, tumble, upset; outweigh, preponderate.

**overbearing** *adj* oppressive, overpowering; arrogant, dictatorial, dogmatic, domineering, haughty, imperious, overweening, proud, supercilious.

**overcast** vb cloud, darken, overcloud, overshadow, shade, shadow. *adj cloudy, darkened, hazy, murky, obscure.

**overcharge** vb burden, oppress, overburden, overload, surcharge; crowd, overfill; exaggerate, overstate, overstrain.

**overcome** vb beat, choke, conquer, crush, defeat, discomfit, overbear, overmaster, overpower, overthrow, overturn, overwhelm, prevail, rout, subdue, subjugate, surmount, vanquish.

**overflow** vb brim over, fall over, pour over, pour out, shower, spill; deluge, inundate, submerge. * n deluge, inundation, profusion, superabundance.

**overhaul** vb overtake; check, examine, inspect, repair, survey. * n check, examination, inspection.

**overlay** vb cover, spread over; overlie, overpress, smother; crush, overpower, overwhelm; cloud, hide, obscure, overcast. * n appliqué, covering, decoration, veneer.

**overlook** vb inspect, oversee, superintend, supervise; disregard, miss, neglect, slight; condone, excuse, forgive, pardon, pass over.

**overpower** vb beat, conquer, crush, defeat, discomfit, overbear, overcome, overmaster, overturn, overwhelm, subdue, subjugate, vanquish.

**overreach** vb exceed, outstrip, overshoot, pass, surpass; cheat, circumvent, deceive, defraud.

**override** vb outride, outweigh, pass, quash, supersede, surpass.

**overrule** vb control, govern, sway; annul, cancel, nullify, recall, reject, repeal, repudiate, rescind, revoke, reject, set aside, supersede, suppress.

**oversight** n care, charge, control, direction, inspection, management, superintendence, supervision, surveillance; blunder, error, fault, inadvertence, inattention, lapse, miss, mistake, neglect, omission, slip, trip.

**overt** adj apparent, glaring, open, manifest, notorious, patent, public, unconcealed.

**overthrow** vb overturn, upset, subvert; demolish, destroy, level; beat, conquer, crush, defeat, discomfit, foil, master, overcome, overpower, overwhelm, rout, subjugate, vanquish, worst. * n downfall, fall, prostration, subversion; destruction, demolition, ruin; defeat, discomfiture, dispersion, rout.

**overturn** vb invert, overthrow, reverse, subvert, upset.

**overture** n invitation, offer, proposal, proposition.

**overweening** adj arrogant, conceited, consequential, egotistical, haughty, opinionated, proud, supercilious, vain, vainglorious.

**overwhelm** vb drown, engulf, inundate, overflow, submerge, swallow up, swamp; conquer, crush, defeat, overbear, overcome, overpower, subdue, vanquish.

**overwrought** adj overdone, overelaborate; agitated, excited, overexcited, overworked, stirred.

**own**[1] vb have, hold, possess; avow, confess; acknowledge, admit, allow, concede.

**own**[2] adj particular, personal, private.

**owner** n freeholder, holder, landlord, possessor, proprietor.

# P

**pace** vb go, hasten, hurry, move, step, walk. * n amble, gait, step, walk.

**pacific** adj appeasing, conciliatory, ironic, mollifying, placating, peacemaking, propitiatory; calm, gentle, peaceable, peaceful, quiet, smooth, tranquil, unruffled.

**pacify** vb appease, conciliate, harmonize, tranquillize; allay, appease, assuage, calm, compose, hush, lay, lull, moderate, mollify, placate, propitiate, quell, quiet, smooth, soften, soothe, still.

**pack** vb compact, compress, crowd, fill; bundle, burden, load, stow. * n bale, budget, bundle, package, packet, parcel; burden, load; assemblage, assembly, assortment, collection, set; band, bevy, clan, company, crew, gang, knot, lot, party, squad.

**pact** n agreement, alliance, bargain, bond, compact, concordat, contract, convention, covenant, league, stipulation.

**pagan** adj heathen, heathenish, idolatrous, irreligious, paganist, paganistic. * n gentile, heathen, idolater.

**pageantry** n display, flourish, magnificence, parade, pomp, show, splendour, state.

**pain** vb agonize, bite, distress, hurt, rack, sting, torment, torture; afflict, aggrieve, annoy, bore, chafe, displease, disquiet, fret, grieve, harass, incommode, plague, tease, trouble, vex, worry; rankle, smart, shoot, sting, twinge. * n ache, agony, anguish, discomfort, distress, gripe, hurt, pang, smart, soreness, sting, suffering, throe, torment, torture, twinge; affliction, anguish, anxiety, bitterness, care, chagrin, disquiet, dolour, grief, heartache, misery, punishment, solicitude, sorrow, trouble, uneasiness, unhappiness, vexation, woe, wretchedness.

**painful** adj agonizing, distressful, excruciating, racking, sharp, tormenting, torturing; afflicting, afflictive, annoying, baleful, disagreeable, displeasing, disquieting, distressing, dolorous, grievous, provoking, troublesome, unpleasant, vexatious; arduous, careful, difficult, hard, severe, sore, toilsome.

**pains** npl care, effort, labour, task, toilsomeness, trouble; childbirth, labour, travail.

**painstaking** adj assiduous, careful, conscientious, diligent, hardworking, industrious, laborious, persevering, plodding, sedulous, strenuous.

**paint** vb delineate, depict, describe, draw, figure, pencil, portray, represent, sketch; adorn, beautify, deck, embellish, ornament. * n colouring, dye, pigment, stain; cosmetics, greasepaint, make-up.

**pair** vb couple, marry, mate, match. * n brace, couple, double, duo, match, twosome.

**pal** n buddy, chum, companion, comrade, crony, friend, mate, mucker.

**palatable** adj acceptable, agreeable, appetizing, delicate, delicious, enjoyable, flavourful, flavoursome, gustative, gustatory, luscious, nice, pleasant, pleasing, savoury, relishable, tasteful, tasty, toothsome.

**palaver** vb chat, chatter, converse, patter, prattle, say, speak, talk; confer, parley; blandish, cajole, flatter, wheedle. * n chat, chatter, conversation, discussion, language, prattle, speech, talk; confab, confabulation, conference, conclave, parley, powwow; balderdash, cajolery, flummery, gibberish.

**pale** vb blanch, lose colour, whiten. * adj ashen, ashy, blanched, bloodless, pallid, sickly, wan, white; blank, dim, obscure, spectral. * n picket, stake; circuit, enclosure; district, region, territory; boundary, confine, fence, limit.

**pall**[1] n cloak, cover, curtain, mantle, pallium, shield, shroud, veil.

**pall**[2] vb cloy, glut, gorge, satiate, surfeit; deject, depress, discourage, dishearten, dispirit; cloak, cover, drape, invest, overspread, shroud.

**palliate** vb cloak, conceal, cover, excuse, extenuate, hide, gloss, lessen; abate, allay, alleviate, assuage, blunt, diminish, dull, ease, mitigate, moderate, mollify, quell, quiet, relieve, soften, soothe, still.

**pallid** adj ashen, ashy, cadaverous, colourless, pale, sallow, wan, whitish.

**palm**[1] vb foist, impose, obtrude, pass off; handle, touch.

**palm**[2] n bays, crown, laurels, prize, trophy, victory.

**palmy** adj flourishing, fortunate, glorious, golden, halcyon, happy, joyous, prosperous, thriving, victorious.

**palpable** adj corporeal, material, tactile, tangible; evident, glaring, gross, intelligible, manifest, obvious, patent, plain, unmistakable.

**palpitate** vb flutter, pulsate, throb; quiver, shiver, tremble.

**palter** vb dodge, equivocate, evade, haggle, prevaricate, quibble, shift, shuffle, trifle.

**paltry** adj diminutive, feeble, inconsiderable, insignificant, little, miserable, petty, slender, slight, small, sorry, trifling, trivial, unimportant, wretched.

**pamper** vb baby, coddle, fondle, gratify, humour, spoil.

**panacea** n catholicon, cure-all, medicine, remedy.

**panegyric** adj commendatory, encomiastic, encomiastical, eulogistic, eulogistical, laudatory, panegyrical. * n eulogy, laudation, praise, paean, tribute.

**pang** n agony, anguish, distress, gripe, pain, throe, twinge.

**panic** vb affright, alarm, scare, startle, terrify; become terrified, overreact. * n alarm, consternation, fear, fright, jitters, terror.

**pant** vb blow, gasp, puff; heave, palpitate, pulsate, throb; languish; desire, hunger, long, sigh, thirst, yearn. * n blow, gasp, puff.

**parable** n allegory, fable, story.

**paraclete** n advocate, comforter, consoler, intercessor, mediator.

**parade** vb display, flaunt, show, vaunt. * n ceremony, display, flaunting, ostentation, pomp, show; array, pageant, review, spectacle; mall, promenade.

**paradox** n absurdity, contradiction, mystery.

**paragon** n flower, ideal, masterpiece, model, nonpareil, pattern, standard.

**paragraph** n clause, item, notice, passage, section, sentence, subdivision.

**parallel** vb be alike, compare, conform, correlate, match. * adj abreast, concurrent; allied, analogous, correspondent, equal, like, resembling, similar. * n conformity, likeness, resemblance, similarity; analogue, correlative, counterpart.

**paramount** adj chief, dominant, eminent, pre-eminent, principal, superior, supreme.

**paraphernalia** n accoutrements, appendages, appurtenances, baggage, belongings, effects, equipage, equipment, ornaments, trappings.

**parasite** n bloodsucker, fawner, flatterer, flunky, hanger-on, leech, spaniel, sycophant, toady, wheedler.

**parcel** vb allot, apportion, dispense, distribute, divide. * n budget, bundle, package; batch, collection, group, lot, set; division, part, patch, pierce, plot, portion, tract.

**parched** adj arid, dry, scorched, shrivelled, thirsty.

**pardon** vb condone, forgive, overlook, remit; absolve, acquit, clear, discharge, excuse, release. * n absolution, amnesty, condonation, discharge, excuse, forgiveness, grace, mercy, overlook, release.

**parentage** n ancestry, birth, descent, extraction, family, lineage, origin, parenthood, pedigree, stock.

**pariah** n outcast, wretch.

**parish** n community, congregation, parishioners; district, subdivision.

**parity** n analogy, correspondence, equality, equivalence, likeness, sameness, similarity.

**parody** vb burlesque, caricature, imitate, lampoon, mock, ridicule, satirize, travesty. * n burlesque, caricature, imitation, ridicule, satire, travesty.

**paroxysm** n attack, convulsion, exacerbation, fit, outburst, seizure, spasm, throe.

**parsimonious** adj avaricious, close, close-fisted, covetous, frugal, grasping, grudging, illiberal, mean, mercenary, miserly, near, niggardly, penurious, shabby, sordid, sparing, stingy, tightfisted.

**parson** n churchman, clergyman, divine, ecclesiastic, incumbent, minister, pastor, priest, rector.

**part** vb break, dismember, dissever, divide, sever, subdivide, sunder; detach, disconnect, disjoin, dissociate, disunite, separate; allot, apportion, distribute, divide, mete, share; secrete. * n crumb, division, fraction, fragment, moiety, parcel, piece, portion, remnant, scrap, section, segment, subdivision; component, constituent, element, ingredient, member, organ; lot, share; concern, interest, participation; allotment, apportionment, dividend; business, charge, duty, function, office, work; faction, party, side; character, cue, lines, role; clause, paragraph, passage.

**partake** vb engage, participate, share; consume, eat, take; evince, evoke, show, suggest.

**partial** adj component, fractional, imperfect, incomplete, limited; biased, influential, interested, one-sided, prejudiced, prepossessed, unfair, unjust, warped; fond, indulgent.

**participate** vb engage in, partake, perform, share.

**particle** n atom, bit, corpuscle, crumb, drop, glimmer, grain, granule, iota, jot, mite, molecule, morsel, mote, scrap, shred, snip, spark, speck, whit.

**particular** adj especial, special, specific; distinct, individual, respective, separate, single; characteristic, distinctive, peculiar; individual, intimate, own, personal, private; notable, noteworthy; circumstantial, definite, detailed, exact, minute, narrow, precise; careful, close, conscientious, critical, fastidious, nice, scrupulous, strict; marked, odd, singular, strange, uncommon. * n case, circumstance, count, detail, feature, instance, item, particularity; point, regard, respect.

**parting** adj breaking, dividing, separating; final, last, valedictory; declining, departing. * n breaking, disruption, rupture, severing; detachment, division, separation; death, departure, farewell, leave-taking.

**partisan** adj biased, factional, interested, partial, prejudiced. * n adherent, backer, champion, disciple, follower, supporter, votary; baton, halberd, pike, quarterstaff, truncheon, staff.

**partition** vb apportion, distribute, divide, portion, separate, share. * n division, separation; barrier, division, screen, wall; allotment, apportionment, distribution.

**partner** n associate, colleague, copartner, partaker, participant, participator; accomplice, ally, coadjutor, confederate; companion, consort, spouse.

**partnership** n association, company, copartnership, firm, house, society; connection, interest, participation, union.

**parts** npl abilities, accomplishments, endowments, faculties, genius, gifts, intellect, intelligence, mind, qualities, powers, talents; districts, regions.

**party** n alliance, association, cabal, circle, clique, combination, confederacy, coterie, faction, group, junta, league, ring, set; body, company, detachment, squad, troop; assembly, gathering; partaker, participant, participator, sharer; defendant, litigant, plaintiff; individual, one, person, somebody; cause, division, interest, side.

**pass**[1] vb devolve, fall, go, move, proceed; change, elapse, flit, glide, lapse, slip; cease, die, fade, expire, vanish; happen, occur; convey, deliver, send, transmit, transfer; disregard, ignore, neglect; exceed, excel, surpass; approve, ratify, sanction; answer, do, succeed, suffice, suit; express, pronounce, utter; beguile, wile.

**pass**[2] n avenue, ford, road, route, way; defile, gorge, passage, ravine; authorization, licence, passport, permission, ticket; condition, conjecture, plight, situation, state; lunge, push, thrust, tilt; transfer, trick.

**passable** adj admissible, allowable, mediocre, middling, moderate, ordinary, so-so, tolerable; acceptable, current, receivable; navigable, traversable.

**passage** n going, passing, progress, transit; evacuation, journey, migration, transit, voyage; avenue, channel, course, pass, path, road, route, thoroughfare, vennel, way; access, currency, entry, reception; act, deed, event, feat, incidence, occurrence, passion; corridor, gallery, gate, hall; clause, paragraph, sentence, text; course, death, decease, departure, expiration, lapse; affair, brush, change, collision, combat, conflict, contest, encounter, exchange, joust, skirmish, tilt.

**passenger** n fare, itinerant, tourist, traveller, voyager, wayfarer.

**passionate** adj animated, ardent, burning, earnest, enthusiastic, excited, fervent, fiery, furious, glowing, hot-blooded, impassioned, impetuous, impulsive, intense, vehement, warm, zealous; hot-headed, irascible, quick-tempered, tempestuous, violent.

**passive** adj inactive, inert, quiescent, receptive; apathetic, enduring, long-suffering, nonresistant, patient, stoical, submissive, suffering, unresisting.

**past** adj accomplished, elapsed, ended, gone, spent; ancient, bygone, former, obsolete, outworn. * adv above, extra, beyond, over. * prep above, after, beyond, exceeding. * n antiquity, heretofore, history, olden times, yesterday.

**pastime** n amusement, diversion, entertainment, hobby, play, recreation, sport.

**pastor** n clergyman, churchman, divine, ecclesiastic, minister, parson, priest, vicar.

**pat**[1] vb dab, hit, rap, tap; caress, chuck, fondle, pet. * n dab, hit, pad, rap, tap; caress.

**pat**[2] adj appropriate, apt, fit, pertinent, suitable. * adv aptly, conveniently, fitly, opportunely, seasonably.

**patch** vb mend, repair. * n repair; parcel, plot, tract.

**patent** adj expanded, open, spreading; apparent, clear, conspicuous, evident, glaring, indisputable, manifest, notorious, obvious, public, open, palpable, plain, unconcealed, unmistakable. * n copyright, privilege, right.

**paternity** n derivation, descent, fatherhood, origin.

**path** n access, avenue, course, footway, passage, pathway, road, route, track, trail, way.

**pathetic** adj affecting, melting, moving, pitiable, plaintive, sad, tender, touching.

**patience** n endurance, fortitude, long-sufferance, resignation, submission, sufferance; calmness, composure, quietness; forbearance, indulgence, leniency; assiduity, constancy, diligence, indefatigability, indefatigableness, perseverance, persistence.

**patient** adj meek, passive, resigned, submissive, uncomplaining, unrepining; calm, composed, contented, quiet; indulgent, lenient, long-suffering; assiduous, constant, diligent, indefatigable, persevering, persistent. * n case, invalid, subject, sufferer.

**patrician** adj aristocratic, blue-blooded, highborn, noble, senatorial, well-born. * n aristocrat, blue blood, nobleman.

**patron** n advocate, defender, favourer, guardian, helper, protector, supporter.

**patronize** vb aid, assist, befriend, countenance, defend, favour, maintain, support; condescend, disparage, scorn.

**pattern** vb copy, follow, imitate. * n archetype, exemplar, last, model, original, paradigm, plan, prototype; example, guide, sample, specimen; mirror, paragon; design, figure, shape, style, type.

**paucity** n deficiency, exiguity, insufficiency, lack, poverty, rarity, shortage.

**paunch** n abdomen, belly, gut, stomach.

**pauperism** n beggary, destitution, indigence, mendicancy, mendicity, need, poverty, penury, want.

**pause** vb breathe, cease, delay, desist, rest, stay, stop, wait; delay, forbear, intermit, stay, stop, tarry, wait; deliberate, demur, hesitate, waver. * n break, caesura, cessation, halt, intermission, interruption, interval, remission, rest, stop, stoppage, stopping, suspension; hesitation, suspense, uncertainty; paragraph.

**pawn**[1] n cat's-paw, dupe, plaything, puppet, stooge, tool, toy.

**pawn**[2] vb bet, gage, hazard, lay, pledge, risk, stake, wager. * n assurance, bond, guarantee, pledge, security.

**pay** vb defray, discharge, discount, foot, honour, liquidate, meet, quit, settle; compensate, recompense, reimburse, requite, reward; punish, revenge; give, offer, render. * n allowance, commission, compensation, emolument, hire, recompense, reimbursement, remuneration, requital, reward, salary, wages.

**peace** n calm, calmness, quiet, quietness, repose, stillness; accord, amity, friendliness, harmony; composure, equanimity, imperturbability, placidity, quietude, tranquillity; agreement, armistice.

**peaceable** adj pacific, peaceful; amiable, amicable, friendly, gentle, inoffensive, mild; placid, quiet, serene, still, tranquil, undisturbed, unmoved.

**peaceful** adj quiet, undisturbed; amicable, concordant, friendly, gentle, harmonious, mild; pacific, peaceable; calm, composed, placid, serene, still.

**peak** vb climax, culminate, top; dwindle, thin. * n acme, apex, crest, crown, pinnacle, summit, top, zenith.

**peaked** adj piked, pointed, thin.

**peasant** n boor, countryman, clown, hind, labourer, rustic, swain.

**peculate** vb appropriate, defraud, embezzle, misappropriate, pilfer, purloin, rob, steal.

**peculiar** adj appropriate, idiosyncratic, individual, proper; characteristic, eccentric, exceptional, extraordinary, odd, queer, rare, singular, strange, striking, uncommon, unusual; individual, especial, particular, select, special, specific.

**peculiarity** n appropriateness, distinctiveness, individuality, speciality; characteristic, idiosyncrasy, oddity, peculiarity, singularity.

**pedantic** adj conceited, fussy, officious, ostentatious, over-learned, particular, pedagogical, pompous, pragmatical, precise, pretentious, priggish, stilted.

**pedlar** n chapman, costermonger, hawker, packman, vendor.

**pedigree** adj purebred, thoroughbred. * n ancestry, breed, descent, extraction, family, genealogy, house, line, lineage, race, stock, strain.

**peer**[1] vb gaze, look, peek, peep, pry, squinny, squint; appear, emerge.

**peer**[2] n associate, co-equal, companion, compeer, equal, equivalent, fellow, like, mate, match; aristocrat, baron, count, duke, earl, grandee, lord, marquis, noble, nobleman, viscount.

**peerless** adj excellent, incomparable, matchless, outstanding, superlative, unequalled, unique, unmatched, unsurpassed.

**peevish** adj acrimonious, captious, churlish, complaining, crabbed, cross, crusty, discontented, fretful, ill-natured, ill-tempered, irascible, irritable, pettish, petulant, querulous, snappish, snarling, splenetic, spleeny, testy, waspish; forward, headstrong, obstinate, self-willed, stubborn; childish, silly, thoughtless, trifling.

**pellucid** adj bright, clear, crystalline, diaphanous, limpid, lucid, transparent.

**pelt**[1] vb assail, batter, beat, belabour, bombard, pepper, stone, strike; cast, hurl, throw; hurry, rush, speed, tear.

**pelt**[2] n coat, hide, skin.

**pen**[1] vb compose, draft, indite, inscribe, write.

**pen**[2] vb confine, coop, encage, enclose, impound, imprison, incarcerate. * n cage, coop, corral, crib, hutch, enclosure, paddock, pound, stall, sty.

**penalty** n chastisement, fine, forfeiture, mulct, punishment, retribution.

**penance** n humiliation, maceration, mortification, penalty, punishment.

**penchant** n bent, bias, disposition, fondness, inclination, leaning, liking, predilection, predisposition, proclivity, proneness, propensity, taste, tendency, turn.

**penetrate** vb bore, burrow, cut, enter, invade, penetrate, percolate, perforate, pervade, pierce, soak, stab; affect, sensitize, touch; comprehend, discern, perceive, understand.

**penetrating** adj penetrative, permeating, piercing, sharp, subtle; acute, clear-sighted, discerning, intelligent, keen, quick, sagacious, sharp-witted, shrewd.

**penetration** n acuteness, discernment, insight, sagacity.

**penitence** n compunction, contrition, qualms, regret, remorse, repentance, sorrow.

**penitent** adj compunctious, conscience-stricken, contrite, regretful, remorseful, repentant, sorrowing, sorrowful. * n penance-doer, penitentiary, repentant.

**penniless** adj destitute, distressed, impecunious, indigent, moneyless, pinched, poor, necessitous, needy, pensive, poverty-stricken, reduced.

**pensive** adj contemplative, dreamy, meditative, reflective, sober, thoughtful; grave, melancholic, melancholy, mournful, sad, serious, solemn.

**penurious** adj inadequate, ill-provided, insufficient, meagre, niggardly, poor, scanty, stinted; avaricious, close, close-fisted, covetous, illiberal, grasping, grudging, mean, mercenary, miserly, near, niggardly, parsimonious, sordid, stingy, tightfisted.

**penury** n beggary, destitution, indigence, need, poverty, privation, want.

**people** vb colonize, inhabit, populate. * n clan, country, family, nation, race, state, tribe; folk, humankind, persons, population, public; commons, community, democracy, populace, proletariat; mob, multitude, rabble.

**perceive** vb behold, descry, detect, discern, discover, discriminate, distinguish, note, notice, observe, recognize, remark, see, spot; appreciate, comprehend, know, understand.

**perceptible** adj apparent, appreciable, cognizable, discernible, noticeable, perceivable, understandable, visible.

**perception** n apprehension, cognition, discernment, perceiving, recognition, seeing; comprehension, conception, consciousness, perceptiveness, perceptivity, understanding, feeling.

**perchance** adv haply, maybe, mayhap, peradventure, perhaps, possibly, probably.

**percolate** vb drain, drip, exude, filter, filtrate, ooze, penetrate, stain, transude.

**percussion** n collision, clash, concussion, crash, encounter, shock.

**perdition** n damnation, demolition, destruction, downfall, hell, overthrow, ruin, wreck.

**peremptory** adj absolute, authoritative, categorical, commanding, decisive, express, imperative, imperious, positive; determined, resolute, resolved; arbitrary, dogmatic, incontrovertible.

**perennial** adj ceaseless, constant, continual, deathless, enduring, immortal, imperishable, lasting, never-failing, permanent, perpetual, unceasing, undying, unfailing, uninterrupted.

**perfect** vb accomplish, complete, consummate, elaborate, finish. * adj completed, finished; complete, entire, full, unqualified, utter, whole; capital, consummate, excellent, exquisite, faultless, ideal; accomplished, disciplined, expert, skilled; blameless, faultless, holy, immaculate, pure, spotless, unblemished.

**perfection** n completeness, completion, consummation, correctness, excellence, faultlessness, finish, maturity, perfection, perfectness, wholeness; beauty, quality.

**perfidious** adj deceitful, dishonest, disloyal, double-faced, faithless, false, false-hearted, traitorous, treacherous, unfaithful, untrustworthy, venal.

**perfidy** n defection, disloyalty, faithlessness, infidelity, perfidiousness, traitorousness, treachery, treason.

**perforate** vb bore, drill, penetrate, pierce, pink, prick, punch, riddle, trepan.

**perform** vb accomplish, achieve, còmpass, consummate, do, effect, transact; complete, discharge, execute, fulfil, meet, observe, satisfy; act, play, represent.

**performance** n accomplishment, achievement, completion, consummation, discharge, doing, execution, fulfilment; act, action, deed, exploit, feat, work; composition, production; acting, entertainment, exhibition, play, representation, hold; execution, playing.

**perfume** n aroma, balminess, bouquet, fragrance, incense, odour, redolence, scent, smell, sweetness.

**perfunctory** adj careless, formal, heedless, indifferent, mechanical, negligent, reckless, slight, slovenly, thoughtless, unmindful.

**perhaps** adv haply, peradventure, perchance, possibly.

**peril** vb endanger, imperil, jeopardize, risk. * n danger, hazard, insecurity, jeopardy, pitfall, risk, snare, uncertainty.

**perilous** adj dangerous, hazardous, risky, unsafe.

**period** n aeon, age, cycle, date, eon, epoch, season, span, spell, stage, term, time; continuance, duration; bound, conclusion, determination, end, limit, term, termination; clause, phrase, proposition, sentence.

**periodical** adj cyclical, incidental, intermittent, recurrent, recurring, regular, seasonal, systematic. * n magazine, paper, review, serial, weekly.

**periphery** n boundary, circumference, outside, perimeter, superficies, surface.

**perish** vb decay, moulder, shrivel, waste, wither; decease, die, expire, vanish.

**perishable** adj decaying, decomposable, destructible; dying, frail, mortal, temporary.

**perjured** adj false, forsworn, perfidious, traitorous, treacherous, untrue.

**permanent** adj abiding, constant, continuing, durable, enduring, fixed, immutable, invariable, lasting, perpetual, persistent, stable, standing, steadfast, unchangeable, unchanging, unfading, unmovable.

**permissible** adj admissible, allowable, free, lawful, legal, legitimate, proper, sufferable, unprohibited.

**permission** n allowance, authorization, consent, dispensation, leave, liberty, licence, permit, sufferance, toleration, warrant.

**permit** vb agree, allow, endure, let, suffer, tolerate; admit, authorize, consent, empower, license, warrant. * n leave, liberty, licence, passport, permission, sanction, warrant.

**pernicious** adj baleful, baneful, damaging, deadly, deleterious, destructive, deftrimental, disadvantageous, fatal, harmful, hurtful, injurious, malign, mischievous, noisome, noxious, prejudicial, ruinous; evil-hearted, malevolent, malicious, malignant, mischief-making, wicked.

**perpetrate** vb commit, do, execute, perform.

**perpetual** adj ceaseless, continual, constant, endless, enduring, eternal, ever-enduring, everlasting, incessant, interminable, never-ceasing, never-ending, perennial, permanent, sempiternal, unceasing, unending, unfailing, uninterrupted.

**perplex** vb complicate, encumber, entangle, involve, snarl, tangle; beset, bewilder, confound, confuse, corner, distract, embarrass, fog, mystify, nonplus, pother, puzzle, set; annoy, bother, disturb, harass, molest, pester, plague, tease, trouble, vex, worry.

**persecute** vb afflict, distress, harass, molest, oppress, worry; annoy, beset, importune, pester, solicit, tease.

**perseverance** n constancy, continuance, doggedness, indefatigableness, persistence, persistency, pertinacity, resolution, steadfastness, steadiness, tenacity.

**persevere** vb continue, determine, endure, maintain, persist, remain, resolve, stick.

**persist** vb continue, endure, last, remain; insist, persevere.

**persistent** adj constant; continuing, enduring, fixed, immovable, persevering, persisting, steady, tenacious; contumacious, dogged, indefatigable, obdurate, obstinate, pertinacious, perverse, pigheaded, stubborn.

**personable** adj comely, good-looking, graceful, seemly, well-turned-out.

**personal** adj individual, peculiar, private, special; bodily, corporal, corporeal, exterior, material, physical.

**personate** vb act, impersonate, personify, play, represent; disguise, mast; counterfeit, feign, simulate.

**perspective** n panorama, prospect, view, vista; proportion, relation.

**perspicacious** adj keen-sighted, quick-sighted, sharp-sighted; acute, clever, discerning, keen, penetrating, sagacious, sharp-witted, shrewd.

**perspicacity** n acumen, acuteness, astuteness, discernment, insight, penetration, perspicaciousness, sagacity, sharpness, shrewdness.

**perspicuity** n clearness, distinctness, explicitness, intelligibility, lucidity, lucidness, perspicuousness, plainness, transparency.

**perspicuous** adj clear, distinct, explicit, intelligible, lucid, obvious, plain, transparent, unequivocal.

**perspire** vb exhale, glow, sweat, swelter.

**persuade** vb allure, actuate, entice, impel, incite, induce, influence, lead, move, prevail upon, urge; advise, counsel; convince, satisfy; inculcate, teach.

**persuasion** n exhortation, incitement, inducement, influence; belief, conviction, opinion; creed, doctrine, dogma, tenet; kind, sort, variety.

**persuasive** adj cogent, convincing, inducing, inducible, logical, persuading, plausible, sound, valid, weighty.

**pert** adj brisk, dapper, lively, nimble, smart, sprightly, perky; bold, flippant, forward, free, impertinent, impudent, malapert, presuming, smart, saucy.

**pertain** vb appertain, befit, behove, belong, concern, refer, regard, relate.

**pertinacious** adj constant, determined, firm, obdurate, persevering, resolute, staunch, steadfast, steady; dogged, headstrong, inflexible, mulish, intractable, obstinate, perverse, stubborn, unyielding, wayward, wilful.

**pertinent** adj adapted, applicable, apposite, appropriate, apropos, apt, fit, germane, pat, proper, relevant, suitable; appurtenant, belonging, concerning, pertaining, regarding.

**perturb** vb agitate, disquiet, distress, disturb, excite, trouble, unsettle, upset, vex, worry; confuse.

**pervade** vb affect, animate, diffuse, extend, fill, imbue, impregnate, infiltrate, penetrate, permeate.

**perverse** adj bad, disturbed, oblique, perverted; contrary, dogged, headstrong, mulish, obstinate, pertinacious, perversive, stubborn, ungovernable, intractable, unyielding, wayward, wilful; cantankerous, churlish, crabbed, cross, cross-grained, crusty, cussed, morose, peevish, petulant, snappish, snarling, spiteful, spleeny, surly, testy, touchy, wicked, wrong-headed; inconvenient, troublesome, untoward, vexatious.

**perversion** n abasement, corruption, debasement, impairment, injury, prostitution, vitiation.

**perverted** adj corrupt, debased, distorted, evil, impaired, misguiding, vitiated, wicked.

**pessimistic** adj cynical, dark, dejected, depressed, despondent, downhearted, gloomy, glum, melancholy, melancholic, morose, sad.

**pest** n disease, epidemic, infection, pestilence, plague; annoyance, bane, curse, infliction, nuisance, scourge, trouble.

**pestilent** adj contagious, infectious, malignant, pestilential; deadly, evil, injurious, malign, mischievous, noxious, poisonous; annoying, corrupt, pernicious, troublesome, vexatious.

**petition** vb ask, beg, crave, entreat, pray, solicit, sue, supplicate. * n address, appeal, application, entreaty, prayer, request, solicitation, supplication, suit.

**petrify** vb calcify, fossilize, lapidify; benumb, deaden; amaze, appal, astonish, astound, confound, dumbfound, paralyse, stun, stupefy.

**petty** adj diminutive, frivolous, inconsiderable, inferior, insignificant, little, mean, slight, small, trifling, trivial, unimportant.

**petulant** adj acrimonious, captious, cavilling, censorious, choleric, crabbed, cross, crusty, forward, fretful, hasty, ill-humoured, ill-tempered, irascible, irritable, peevish, perverse, pettish, querulous, snappish, snarling, testy, touchy, waspish.

**phantom** n apparition, ghost, illusion, phantasm, spectre, vision, wraith.

**pharisaism** n cant, formalism, hypocrisy, phariseeism, piety, sanctimoniousness, self-righteousness.

**phenomenal** adj marvellous, miraculous, prodigious, wondrous.

**philanthropy** n alms-giving, altruism, benevolence, charity, grace, humanitarianism, humanity, kindness.

**philosophical, philosophic** adj rational, reasonable, sound, wise; calm, collected, composed, cool, imperturbable, sedate, serene, stoical, tranquil, unruffled.

**phlegmatic** adj apathetic, calm, cold, cold-blooded, dull, frigid, heavy, impassive, indifferent, inert, sluggish, stoical, tame, unfeeling.

**phobia** n aversion, detestation, dislike, distaste, dread, fear, hatred.

**phrase** vb call, christen, denominate, designate, describe, dub, entitle, name, style. * n diction, expression, phraseology, style.

**phraseology** n diction, expression, language, phrasing, style.

**physical** adj material, natural; bodily, corporeal, external, substantial, tangible, sensible.

**physiognomy** n configuration, countenance, face, look, visage.

**picaroon** n adventurer, cheat, rogue; buccaneer, corsair, freebooter, marauder, pirate, plunderer, sea-rover.

**pick** vb peck, pierce, strike; cut, detach, gather, pluck; choose, cull, select; acquire, collect, get; pilfer, steal. * n pickaxe, pike, spike, toothpick.

**picture** vb delineate, draw, imagine, paint, represent. * n drawing, engraving, painting, print; copy, counterpart, delineation, embodiment, illustration, image, likeness, portraiture, portrayal, semblance, representation, resemblance, similitude; description.

**picturesque** adj beautiful, charming, colourful, graphic, scenic, striking, vivid.

**piece** vb mend, patch, repair; augment, complete, enlarge, increase; cement, join, unite. * n amount, bit, chunk, cut, fragment, hunk, part, quantity, scrap, shred, slice; portion; article, item, object; composition, lucubration, work, writing.

**pied** adj irregular, motley, mottled, particoloured, piebald, spotted, variegated.

**pierce** vb gore, impale, pink, prick, stab, transfix; bore, drill, excite, penetrate, perforate, puncture; affect, move, rouse, strike, thrill, touch.

**piety** n devotion, devoutness, holiness, godliness, grace, religion, sanctity.

**pile**[1] vb accumulate, amass; collect, gather, heap, load. * n accumulation, collection, heap, mass, stack; fortune, wad; building, edifice, erection, fabric, pyramid, skyscraper, structure, tower; reactor, nuclear reactor.

**pile**[2] n beam, column, pier, pillar, pole, post.

**pile**[3] n down, feel, finish, fur, fluff, fuzz, grain, nap, pappus, shag, surface, texture.

**pilfer** vb filch, purloin, rob, steal, thieve.

**pilgrim** n journeyer, sojourner, traveller, wanderer, wayfarer; crusader, devotee, palmer.

**pilgrimage** n crusade, excursion, expedition, journey, tour, trip.

**pillage** vb despoil, loot, plunder, rifle, sack, spoil, strip. * n depredation, destruction, devastation, plundering, rapine, spoliation; despoilation, plunder, rifling, sack, spoils.

**pillar** n column, pier, pilaster, post, shaft, stanchion; maintainer, prop, support, supporter, upholder.

**pilot** vb conduct, control, direct, guide, navigate, steer. * adj experimental, model, trial. * n helmsman, navigator, steersman; airman, aviator, conductor, director, flier, guide.

**pinch** vb compress, contract, cramp, gripe, nip, squeeze; afflict, distress, famish, oppress, straiten, stint; frost, nip; apprehend, arrest; economize, spare, stint. * n gripe, nip; pang, throe; crisis, difficulty, emergency, exigency, oppression, pressure, push, strait, stress.

**pine** vb decay, decline, droop, fade, flag, languish, waste, wilt, wither; desire, long, yearn.

**pinion** vb bind, chain, fasten, fetter, maim, restrain, shackle. * n pennon, wing; feather, quill, pen, plume, wing; fetter.

**pinnacle** n minaret, turret; acme, apex, height, peak, summit, top, zenith.

**pious** adj filial; devout, godly, holy, religious, reverential, righteous, saintly.

**piquant** adj biting, highly flavoured, piercing, prickling, pungent, sharp, stinging; interesting, lively, racy, sparkling, stimulating; cutting, keen, pointed, severe, strong, tart.

**pique** vb goad, incite, instigate, spur, stimulate, urge; affront, chafe, displease, fret, incense, irritate, nettle, offend, provoke, sting, vex, wound. * n annoyance, displeasure, irritation, offence, resentment, vexation.

**pirate** vb copy, crib, plagiarize, reproduce, steal. * n buccaneer, corsair, freebooter, marauder, picaroon, privateer, seadog, sea-robber, sea-rover, sea wolf.

**pit** vb match, oppose; dent, gouge, hole, mark, nick, notch, scar. * n cavity, hole, hollow; crater, dent, depression, dint, excavation, well; abyss, chasm, gulf; pitfall, snare, trap: auditorium, orchestra.

**pitch** vb fall, lurch, plunge, reel; light, settle, rest; cast, dart, fling, heave, hurl, lance, launch, send, toss, throw; erect, establish, fix, locate, place, plant, set, settle, station. * n degree, extent, height, intensity, measure, modulation, rage, rate; declivity, descent, inclination, slope; cast, jerk, plunge, throw, toss; place, position, spot; field, ground; line, patter.

**piteous** adj affecting, distressing, doleful, grievous, mournful, pathetic, rueful, sorrowful, woeful; deplorable, lamentable, miserable, pitiable, wretched; compassionate, tender.

**pith** n chief, core, essence, heart, gist, kernel, marrow, part, quintessence, soul, substance; importance, moment, weight; cogency, force, energy, strength, vigour.

**pithy** adj cogent, energetic, forcible, powerful; compact, concise, brief, laconic, meaty, pointed, short, sententious, substantial, terse; corky, porous.

**pitiable** *adj* deplorable, lamentable, miserable, pathetic, piteous, pitiable, woeful, wretched; abject, base, contemptible, despicable, disreputable, insignificant, low, paltry, mean, rascally, sorry, vile, worthless.

**pitiably** *adv* deplorably, distressingly, grievously, lamentably, miserably, pathetically, piteously, woefully, wretchedly.

**pitiful** *adj* compassionate, kind, lenient, merciful, mild, sympathetic, tender, tenderhearted; deplorable, lamentable, miserable, pathetic, piteous, pitiable, wretched; abject, base, contemptible, despicable, disreputable, insignificant, mean, paltry, rascally, sorry, vile, worthless.

**pitiless** *adj* cruel, hardhearted, implacable, inexorable, merciless, unmerciful, relentless, remorseless, unfeeling, unpitying, unrelenting, unsympathetic.

**pittance** *n* allowance, allotment, alms, charity, dole, gift; driblet, drop, insufficiency, mite, modicum, trifle.

**pity** *vb* commiserate, condole, sympathize. * *n* clemency, commiseration, compassion, condolence, fellow-feeling, grace, humanity, leniency, mercy, quarter, sympathy, tenderheartedness.

**pivot** *vb* depend, hinge, turn. * *n* axis, axle, centre, focus, hinge, joint.

**place** *vb* arrange, bestow, commit, deposit, dispose, fix, install, lay, locate, lodge, orient, orientate, pitch, plant, pose, put, seat, set, settle, situate, stand, station, rest; allocate, arrange, class, classify, identify, order, organize, recognize; appoint, assign, commission, establish, induct, nominate. * *n* area, courtyard, square; bounds, district, division, locale, locality, location, part, position, premises, quarter, region, scene, site, situation, spot, station, tract, whereabouts; calling, charge, employment, function, occupation, office, pitch, post; calling, condition, grade, precedence, rank, sphere, stakes, standing; abode, building, dwelling, habitation, mansion, residence, seat; city, town, village; fort, fortress, stronghold; paragraph, part, passage, portion; ground, occasion, opportunity, reason, room; lieu, stead.

**placid** *adj* calm, collected, composed, cool, equable, gentle, peaceful, quiet, serene, tranquil, undisturbed, unexcitable, unmoved, unruffled; halcyon, mild, serene.

**plague** *vb* afflict, annoy, badger, bore, bother, pester, chafe, disquiet, distress, disturb, embarrass, harass, fret, gall, harry, hector, incommode, irritate, molest, perplex, tantalize, tease, torment, trouble, vex, worry. * *n* disease, pestilence, pest; affliction, annoyance, curse, molestation, nuisance, thorn, torment, trouble, vexation, worry.

**plain** *adj* dull, even, flat, level, plane, smooth, uniform; clear, open, unencumbered, uninterrupted; apparent, certain, conspicuous, evident, distinct, glaring, manifest, notable, notorious, obvious, overt, palpable, patent, prominent, pronounced, staring, transparent, unmistakable, visible; explicit, intelligible, perspicuous, unambiguous, unequivocal; homely, ugly; aboveboard, blunt, crude, candid, direct, downright, frank, honest, ingenuous, open, openhearted, sincere, single-minded, straightforward, undesigning, unreserved, unsophisticated; artless, common, natural, simple, unaffected, unlearned; absolute, mere, unmistakable; clear, direct, easy; audible, articulate, definite; frugal, homely; unadorned, unfigured, unornamented, unvariegated. * *n* expanse, flats, grassland, pampas, plateau, prairie, steppe, stretch.

**plaint** *n* complaint, cry, lament, lamentation, moan, wail.

**plaintiff** *n* accuser, prosecutor.

**plaintive** *adj* dirge-like, doleful, grievous, melancholy, mournful, piteous, rueful, sad, sorrowful, woeful.

**plan** *vb* arrange, calculate, concert, delineate, devise, diagram, figure, premeditate, project, represent, study; concoct, conspire, contrive, design, digest, hatch, invent, manoeuvre, machinate, plot, prepare, scheme. * *n* chart, delineation, diagram, draught, drawing, layout, map, plot, sketch; arrangement, conception, contrivance, design, device, idea, method, programme, project, proposal, proposition, scheme, system; cabal, conspiracy, intrigue, machination; custom, process, way.

**plane** *vb* even, flatten, level, smooth; float, fly, glide, skate, skim, soar. * *adj* even, flat, horizontal, level, smooth. * *n* degree, evenness, level, levelness, smoothness; aeroplane, aircraft; groover, jointer, rabbet, rebate, scraper.

**plant** *vb* bed, sow; breed, engender; direct, point, set; colonize, furnish, inhabit, settle; establish, introduce; deposit, establish, fix, found, hide. * *n* herb, organism, vegetable; establishment, equipment, factory, works.

**plaster** vb bedaub, coat, cover, smear, spread. * n cement, gypsum, mortar, stucco.

**plastic** adj ductile, flexible, formative, mouldable, pliable, pliant, soft.

**platitude** n dullness, flatness, insipidity, mawkishness; banality, commonplace, truism; balderdash, chatter, flummery, fudge, jargon, moonshine, nonsense, palaver, stuff, trash, twaddle, verbiage.

**plaudit** n acclaim, acclamation, applause, approbation, clapping, commendation, encomium, praise.

**plausible** adj believable, credible, probable, reasonable; bland, fair-spoken, glib, smooth, suave.

**play** vb caper, disport, frisk, frolic, gambol, revel, romp, skip, sport; dally, flirt, idle, toy, trifle, wanton; flutter, hover, wave; act, impersonate, perform, personate, represent; bet, gamble, stake, wager. * n amusement, exercise, frolic, gambols, game, jest, pastime, prank, romp, sport; gambling, gaming; act, comedy, drama, farce, performance, tragedy; action, motion, movement; elbowroom, freedom, latitude, movement, opportunity, range, scope, sweep, swing, use.

**playful** adj frisky, frolicsome, gamesome, jolly, kittenish, merry, mirthful, rollicking, sportive; amusing, arch, humorous, lively, mischievous, roguish, skittish, sprightly, vivacious.

**plead** vb answer, appeal, argue, reason; argue, defend, discuss, reason, rejoin; beg, beseech, entreat, implore, petition, sue, supplicate.

**pleasant** adj acceptable, agreeable, delectable, delightful, enjoyable, grateful, gratifying, nice, pleasing, pleasurable, prepossessing, seemly, welcome; cheerful, enlivening, good-humoured, gracious, likable, lively, merry, sportive, sprightly, vivacious, facetious, humorous, jocose, jocular, sportive, witty.

**please** vb charm, delight, elate, gladden, gratify, pleasure, rejoice; content, oblige, satisfy; choose, like, prefer.

**pleasure** n cheer, comfort, delight, delectation, elation, enjoyment, exhilaration, joy, gladness, gratifying, gusto, relish, satisfaction, solace; amusement, diversion, entertainment, indulgence, refreshment, treat; gratification, luxury, sensuality, voluptuousness; choice, desire, preference, purpose, will, wish; favour, kindness.

**plebeian** adj base, common, ignoble, low, lowborn, mean, obscure, popular, vulgar. * n commoner, peasant, proletarian.

**pledge** vb hypothecate, mortgage, pawn, plight; affiance, bind, contract, engage, plight, promise. * n collateral, deposit, gage, pawn; earnest, guarantee, security; hostage, security.

**plenipotentiary** n ambassador, envoy, legate, minister.

**plenitude** n abundance, completeness, fullness, plenteousness, plentifulness, plenty, plethora, profusion, repletion.

**plentiful** adj abundant, ample, copious, full, enough, exuberant, fruitful, luxuriant, plenteous, productive, sufficient.

**plenty** n abundance, adequacy, affluence, amplitude, copiousness, enough, exuberance, fertility, fruitfulness, fullness, overflow, plenteousness, plentifulness, plethora, profusion, sufficiency, supply.

**pleonastic** adj circumlocutory, diffuse, redundant, superfluous, tautological, verbose, wordy.

**plethora** n fullness, plenitude, repletion; excess, redundance, redundancy, superabundance, superfluity, surfeit.

**pliable** adj flexible, limber, lithe, lithesome, pliable, pliant, supple; adaptable, compliant, docile, ductile, facile, manageable, obsequious, tractable, yielding.

**plight**[1] n case, category, complication, condition, dilemma, imbroglio, mess, muddle, pass, predicament, scrape, situation, state, strait.

**plight**[2] vb avow, contract, covenant, engage, honour, pledge, promise, propose, swear, vow. * n avowal, contract, covenant, oath, pledge, promise, troth, vow, word; affiancing, betrothal, engagement.

**plod** vb drudge, lumber, moil, persevere, persist, toil, trudge.

**plot**[1] vb connive, conspire, intrigue, machinate, scheme; brew, concoct, contrive, devise, frame, hatch, compass, plan, project; chart, map. * n blueprint, chart, diagram, draft, outline, plan, scenario, skeleton; cabal, combination, complicity, connivance, conspiracy, intrigue, plan, project, scheme, stratagem; script, story, subject, theme, thread, topic.

**plot**[2] n field, lot, parcel, patch, piece, plat, section, tract.

**pluck**[1] vb cull, gather, pick; jerk, pull, snatch, tear, tug, twitch.

**pluck**[2] n backbone, bravery, courage, daring, determination, energy, force, grit, hardihood, heroism, indomitability, indomitableness, manhood, mettle, nerve, resolution, spirit, valour.

**plump**[1] adj bonny, bouncing, buxom, chubby, corpulent, fat, fleshy, full-figured, obese, portly, rotund, round, sleek, stout, well-rounded; distended, full, swollen, tumid.

**plump**[2] vb dive, drop, plank, plop, plunge, plunk, put; choose, favour, support * adj blunt, complete, direct, downright, full, unqualified, unreserved.

**plunder** vb desolate, despoil, devastate, fleece, forage, harry, loot, maraud, pillage, raid, ransack, ravage, rifle, rob, sack, spoil, spoliate, plunge. * n freebooting, devastation, harrying, marauding, rapine, robbery, sack; booty, pillage, prey, spoil.

**ply**[1] vb apply, employ, exert, manipulate, wield; exercise, practise; assail, belabour, beset, press; importune, solicit, urge; offer, present.

**ply**[2] n fold, layer, plait, twist; bent, bias, direction, turn.

**pocket** vb appropriate, steal; bear, endure, suffer, tolerate. * n cavity, cul-de-sac, hollow, pouch, receptacle.

**poignant** adj bitter, intense, penetrating, pierce, severe, sharp; acrid, biting, mordacious, piquant, prickling, pungent, sharp, stinging; caustic, irritating, keen, mordant, pointed, satirical, severe.

**point** vb acuminate, sharpen; aim, direct, level; designate indicate, show; punctuate. * n apex, needle, nib, pin, prong, spike, stylus, tip; cape, headland, projection, promontory; eve, instant, moment, period, verge; place, site, spot, stage, station; condition, degree, grade, state; aim, design, end, intent, limit, object, purpose; nicety, pique, punctilio, trifle; position, proposition, question, text, theme, thesis; aspect, matter, respect; characteristic, peculiarity, trait; character, mark, stop; dot, jot, speck; epigram, quip, quirk, sally, witticism; poignancy, sting.

**point-blank** adj categorical, direct, downright, explicit, express, plain, straight. * adv categorically, directly, flush, full, plainly, right, straight.

**pointless** adj blunt, obtuse; aimless, dull, flat, fruitless, futile, meaningless, vague, vapid, stupid.

**poise** vb balance, float, hang, hover, support, suspend. * n aplomb, balance, composure, dignity, equanimity, equilibrium, equipoise, serenity.

**poison** vb adulterate, contaminate, corrupt, defile, embitter, envenom, impair, infect, intoxicate, pollute, taint, vitiate. * adj deadly, lethal, poisonous,

toxic. * n bane, canker, contagion, pest, taint, toxin, venom, virulence, virus.

**poisonous** adj baneful, corruptive, deadly, fatal, noxious, pestiferous, pestilential, toxic, venomous.

**poke** vb jab, jog, punch, push, shove, thrust; interfere, meddle, pry, snoop. * n jab, jog, punch, push, shove, thrust; bag, pocket, pouch, sack.

**pole**[1] n caber, mast, post, rod, spar, staff, stick; bar, beam, pile, shaft; oar, paddle, scull.

**pole**[2] n axis, axle, hub, pivot, spindle.

**poles** npl antipodes, antipoles, counterpoles, opposites.

**policy** n administration, government, management, rule; plan, plank, platform, role; art, address, cunning, discretion, prudence, shrewdness, skill, stratagem, strategy, tactics; acumen, astuteness, wisdom, wit.

**polish** vb brighten, buff, burnish, furbish, glaze, gloss, scour, shine, smooth; civilize, refine. * n brightness, brilliance, brilliancy, lustre, splendour; accomplishment, elegance, finish, grace, refinement.

**polished** adj bright, burnished, glossed, glossy, lustrous, shining, smooth; accomplished, cultivated, elegant, finished, graceful, polite, refined.

**polite** adj attentive, accomplished, affable, chivalrous, civil, complaisant, courtly, courteous, cultivated, elegant, gallant, genteel, gentle, gentlemanly, gracious, mannerly, obliging, polished, refined, suave, urbane, well, well-bred, well-mannered.

**politic** adj civic, civil, political; astute, discreet, judicious, long-headed, noncommittal, provident, prudent, prudential, sagacious, wary, wise; artful, crafty, cunning, diplomatic, expedient, foxy, ingenious, intriguing, Machiavellian, shrewd, skilful, sly, subtle, strategic, timeserving, unscrupulous, wily; well-adapted, well-devised.

**political** adj civic, civil, national, politic, public.

**pollute** vb defile, foul, soil, taint; contaminate, corrupt, debase, demoralize, deprave, impair, infect, pervert, poison, stain, tarnish, vitiate; desecrate, profane; abuse, debauch, defile, deflower, dishonour, ravish, violate.

**pollution** n abomination, contamination, corruption, defilement, foulness, impurity, pollutedness, taint, uncleanness, vitiation.

**poltroon** n coward, crave, dastard, milksop, recreant, skulk, sneak.

**pomp** n display, flourish, grandeur, magnificence,

ostentation, pageant, pageantry, parade, pompousness, pride, show, splendour, state, style.

**pompous** adj august, boastful, bombastic, dignified, gorgeous, grand, inflated, lofty, magisterial, ostentatious, pretentious, showy, splendid, stately, sumptuous, superb, vainglorious.

**ponder** vb cogitate, consider, contemplate, deliberate, examine, meditate, muse, reflect, study, weigh.

**ponderous** adj bulky, heavy, massive, weighty; dull, laboured, slow-moving; important, momentous; forcible, mighty.

**poniard** n dagger, dirk, stiletto.

**poor** adj indigent, necessitous, needy, pinched, straitened; destitute, distressed, embarrassed, impecunious, impoverished, insolvent, moneyless, penniless, poverty-stricken, reduced, seedy, unprosperous; emaciated, gaunt, spare, lank, lean, shrunk, skinny, spare, thin; barren, fruitless, sterile, unfertile, unfruitful, unproductive, unprolific; flimsy, inadequate, insignificant, insufficient, paltry, slender, slight, small, trifling, trivial, unimportant, valueless, worthless; decrepit, delicate, feeble, frail, infirm, unsound, weak; inferior, shabby, valueless, worthless; bad, beggarly, contemptible, despicable, humble, inferior, low, mean, pitiful, sorry; bald, cold, dry, dull, feeble, frigid, jejune, languid, meagre, prosaic, prosing, spiritless, tame, vapid, weak; ill-fated, ill-starred, inauspicious, indifferent, luckless, miserable, pitiable, unfavourable, unfortunate, unhappy, unlucky, wretched; deficient, imperfect, inadequate, insufficient, mediocre, scant, scanty; faulty, unsatisfactory; feeble.

**populace** n citizens, crowd, inhabitants, masses, people, public, throng.

**popular** adj lay, plebeian, public; comprehensible, easy, familiar, plain; acceptable, accepted, accredited, admired, approved, favoured, liked, pleasing, praised, received; common, current, prevailing, prevalent; cheap, inexpensive.

**pore**[1] n hole, opening, orifice, spiracle.

**pore**[2] vb brood, consider, dwell, examine, gaze, read, study.

**porous** adj honeycombed, light, loose, open, penetrable, perforated, permeable, pervious, sandy.

**porridge** n broth, gruel, mush, pap, pottage, soup.

**port**[1] n anchorage, harbour, haven, shelter; door, entrance, gate, passageway; embrasure, porthole.

**port**[2] n air, appearance, bearing, behaviour, carriage, demeanour, deportment, mien, presence.

**portable** adj convenient, handy, light, manageable, movable, portative, transmissible.

**portend** vb augur, betoken, bode, forebode, foreshadow, foretoken, indicate, presage, procrastinate, signify, threaten.

**portent** n augury, omen, presage, prognosis, sign, warning; marvel, phenomenon, wonder.

**portion** vb allot, distribute, divide, parcel; endow, supply. * n bit, fragment, morsel, part, piece, scrap, section; allotment, contingent, dividend, division, lot, measure, quantity, quota, ration, share; inheritance.

**portly** adj dignified, grand, imposing, magisterial, majestic, stately; bulky, burly, corpulent, fleshy, large, plump, round, stout.

**portray** vb act, draw, depict, delineate, describe, paint, picture, represent, pose, position, sketch.

**pose** vb arrange, place, set; bewilder, confound, dumbfound, embarrass, mystify, nonplus, perplex, place, puzzle, set, stagger; affect, attitudinize. * n attitude, posture; affectation, air, facade, mannerism, pretence, role.

**position** vb arrange, array, fix, locate, place, put, set, site, stand. * n locality, place, post, site, situation, spot, station; relation; attitude, bearing, posture; affirmation, assertion, doctrine, predication, principle, proposition, thesis; caste, dignity, honour, rank, standing, status; circumstance, condition, phase, place, state; berth, billet, incumbency, place, post, situation.

**positive** adj categorical, clear, defined, definite, direct, determinate, explicit, express, expressed, precise, unequivocal, unmistakable, unqualified; absolute, actual, real, substantial, true, veritable; assured, certain, confident, convinced, sure; decisive, incontrovertible, indisputable, indubitable, inescapable; imperative, unconditional, undeniable; decided, dogmatic, emphatic, obstinate, overbearing, overconfident, peremptory, stubborn, tenacious.

**possess** vb control, have, hold, keep, obsess, obtain, occupy, own, seize.

**possession** n monopoly, ownership, proprietorship; control, occupation, occupancy, retention, tenancy, tenure; bedevilment, lunacy, madness, obsession; (pl) assets, effects, estate, property, wealth.

**possessor** n owner, proprietor.

**possible** adj conceivable, contingent, imaginable, potential; accessible, feasible, likely, practical, practicable, workable.

**possibly** adv haply, maybe, mayhap, peradventure, perchance, perhaps.

**post**[1] vb advertise, announce, inform, placard, publish; brand, defame, disgrace, vilify; enter, slate, record, register. * n column, picket, pier, pillar, stake, support.

**post**[2] vb establish, fix, place, put, set, station. * n billet, employment, office, place, position, quarter, seat, situation, station.

**post**[3] vb drop, dispatch, mail. * n carrier, courier, express, mercury, messenger, postman; dispatch, haste, hurry, speed.

**posterior** adj after, ensuing, following, later, latter, postprandial, subsequent. * n back, buttocks, hind, hinder, rump.

**posterity** n descendants, offspring, progeny, seed; breed, brood, children, family, heirs, issue.

**postpone** vb adjourn, defer, delay, procrastinate, prorogue, retard.

**postscript** n addition, afterthought, appendix, supplement.

**postulate** vb assume, presuppose; beseech, entreat, solicit, supplicate. * n assumption, axiom, conjecture, hypothesis, proposition, speculation, supposition, theory.

**posture** vb attitudinize, pose. * n attitude, pose, position; condition, disposition, mood, phase, state.

**pot** n kettle, pan, saucepan, skillet; can, cup, mug, tankard; crock, jar, jug.

**potency** n efficacy, energy, force, intensity, might, power, strength, vigour; authority, control, influence, sway.

**potent** adj efficacious, forceful, forcible, intense, powerful, strong, virile; able, authoritative, capable, efficient, mighty, puissant, strong; cogent, influential.

**potentate** n emperor, king, monarch, prince, sovereign, ruler.

**potential** adj able, capable, inherent, latent, possible. * n ability, capability, dynamic, possibility, potentiality, power.

**pother** vb beset, bewilder, confound, confuse, embarrass, harass, perplex, pose, puzzle, tease. * n bustle, commotion, confusion, disturbance, flutter, fuss, huddle, hurly-burly, rumpus, tumult, turbulence, turmoil.

**pound**[1] vb beat, strike, thump; bray, bruise, comminute, crush, levigate, pulverize, triturate; confound, coop, enclose, impound.

**pound**[2] n enclosure, fold, pen.

**pour** vb cascade, emerge, flood, flow, gush, issue, rain, shower, stream.

**pouting** adj bad-tempered, cross, ill-humoured, moody, morose, sulky, sullen.

**poverty** n destitution, difficulties, distress, impecuniosity, impecuniousness, indigence, necessity, need, neediness, penury, privation, straits, want; beggary, mendicancy, pauperism, pennilessness; dearth, jejuneness, lack, scantiness, sparingness, meagreness; exiguity, paucity, poorness, smallness; humbleness, inferiority, lowliness; barrenness, sterility, unfruitfulness, unproductiveness.

**power** n ability, ableness, capability, cogency, competency, efficacy, faculty, might, potency, validity, talent; energy, force, strength, virtue; capacity, susceptibility; endowment, faculty, gift, talent; ascendancy, authoritativeness, authority, carte blanche, command, control, domination, dominion, government, influence, omnipotence, predominance, prerogative, pressure, proxy, puissance, rule, sovereignty, sway, warrant; governor, monarch, potentate, ruler, sovereign; army, host, troop.

**powerful** adj mighty, potent, puissant; able-bodied, herculean, muscular, nervous, robust, sinewy, strong, sturdy, vigorous, vivid; able, commanding, dominating, forceful, forcible, overpowering; cogent, effective, effectual, efficacious, efficient, energetic, influential, operative, valid.

**practicable** adj achievable, attainable, bearable, feasible, performable, possible, workable; operative, passable, penetrable.

**practical** adj hardheaded, matter-of-fact, pragmatic, pragmatical; able, experienced, practised, proficient, qualified, trained, skilled, thoroughbred, versed; effective, useful, virtual, workable.

**practice** n custom, habit, manner, method, repetition; procedure, usage, use; application, drill, exercise, pursuit; action, acts, behaviour, conduct, dealing, proceeding.

**practise** vb apply, do, exercise, follow, observe, perform, perpetrate, pursue.

**practised** adj able, accomplished, experienced, instructed, practical, proficient, qualified, skilled, thoroughbred, trained, versed.

**pragmatic** adj impertinent, intermeddling, interfering, intrusive, meddlesome, meddling, obtrusive, officious, over-busy; earthy, hard-headed, matter-of-fact, practical, pragmatical, realistic, sensible, stolid.

**praise** vb approbate, acclaim, applaud, approve, commend; celebrate, compliment, eulogize, extol, flatter, laud; adore, bless, exalt, glorify, magnify, worship. * n acclaim, approbation, approval, commendation; encomium, eulogy, glorification, laud, laudation, panegyric; exaltation, extolling, glorification, homage, tribute, worship; celebrity, distinction, fame, glory, honour, renown; desert, merit, praiseworthiness.

**praiseworthy** adj commendable, creditable, good, laudable, meritorious.

**prank** n antic, caper, escapade, frolic, gambol, trick.

**prate** vb babble, chatter, gabble, jabber, palaver, prattle, tattle. * n chatter, gabble, nonsense, palaver, prattle, twaddle.

**pray** vb ask, beg, beseech, conjure, entreat, implore, importune, invoke, petition, request, solicit, supplicate.

**prayer** n beseeching, entreaty, imploration, petition, request, solicitation, suit, supplication; adoration, devotion(s), litany, invocation, orison, praise, suffrage.

**preach** vb declare, deliver, proclaim, pronounce, publish; inculcate, press, teach, urge; exhort, lecture, moralize, sermonize.

**preamble** n foreword, introduction, preface, prelude, prologue.

**precarious** adj critical, doubtful, dubious, equivocal, hazardous, insecure, perilous, unassured, riskful, risky, uncertain, unsettled, unstable, unsteady.

**precaution** n care, caution, circumspection, foresight, forethought, providence, prudence, safeguard, wariness; anticipation, premonition, provision.

**precautionary** adj preservative, preventative, provident.

**precede** vb antedate, forerun, head, herald, introduce, lead, utter.

**precedence** n advantage, antecedence, lead, pre-eminence, preference, priority, superiority, supremacy.

**precedent** n antecedent, authority, custom, example, instance, model, pattern, procedure, standard, usage.

**precept** n behest, bidding, canon, charge, command, commandment, decree, dictate, edict, injunction, instruction, law, mandate, ordinance, ordination, order, regulation; direction, doctrine, maxim, principle, teaching, rubric, rule.

**preceptor** n instructor, lecturer, master, pedagogue, professor, schoolteacher, teacher, tutor.

**precinct** n border, bound, boundary, confine, environs, frontier, enclosure, limit, list, march, neighbourhood, purlieus, term, terminus; area, district.

**precious** adj costly, inestimable, invaluable, priceless, prized, valuable; adored, beloved, cherished, darling, dear, idolized, treasured; fastidious, overnice, overrefined, precise.

**precipice** n bluff, cliff, crag, steep.

**precipitate** vb advance, accelerate, dispatch, expedite, forward, further, hasten, hurry, plunge, press, quicken, speed. * adj hasty, hurried, headlong, impetuous, indiscreet, overhasty, rash, reckless; abrupt, sudden, violent.

**precipitous** adj abrupt, cliffy, craggy, perpendicular, uphill, sheer, steep.

**precise** adj accurate, correct, definite, distinct, exact, explicit, express, nice, pointed, severe, strict, unequivocal, well-defined; careful, scrupulous; ceremonious, finical, formal, prim, punctilious, rigid, starched, stiff.

**precision** n accuracy, correctness, definiteness, distinctness, exactitude, exactness, nicety, preciseness.

**preclude** vb bar, check, debar, hinder, inhibit, obviate, prevent, prohibit, restrain, stop.

**precocious** adj advanced, forward, overforward, premature.

**preconcert** vb concoct, prearrange, predetermine, premeditate, prepare.

**precursor** n antecedent, cause, forerunner, predecessor; harbinger, herald, messenger, pioneer; omen, presage, sign.

**precursory** adj antecedent, anterior, forerunning, precedent, preceding, previous, prior; initiatory, introductory, precursive, prefatory, preliminary, prelusive, prelusory, premonitory, preparatory, prognosticative.

**predatory** adj greedy, pillaging, plundering, predacious, rapacious, ravaging, ravenous, voracious.

**predestination** n doom, fate, foredoom, foreordainment, foreordination, necessity, predetermination, preordination.

**predicament** n attitude, case, condition, plight, position, posture, situation, state; corner, dilemma, emergency, exigency, fix, hole, impasse, mess, pass, pinch, push, quandary, scrape.

**predict** vb augur, betoken, bode, divine, forebode,

forecast, foredoom, foresee, forespeak, foretell, foretoken, forewarn, portend, prognosticate, prophesy, read, signify, soothsay.

**predilection** n bent, bias, desire, fondness, inclination, leaning, liking, love, partiality, predisposition, preference, prejudice, prepossession.

**predisposition** n aptitude, bent, bias, disposition, inclination, leaning, proclivity, proneness, propensity, willingness.

**predominant** adj ascendant, controlling, dominant, overruling, prevailing, prevalent, reigning, ruling, sovereign, supreme.

**predominate** vb dominate, preponderate, prevail, rule.

**pre-eminent** adj chief, conspicuous, consummate, controlling, distinguished, excellent, excelling, paramount, peerless, predominant, renowned, superior, supreme, surpassing, transcendent, unequalled.

**preface** vb begin, introduce, induct, launch, open, precede. * n exordium, foreword, induction, introduction, preamble, preliminary, prelude, prelusion, premise, proem, prologue, prolusion.

**prefatory** adj antecedent, initiative, introductory, precursive, precursory, preliminary, prelusive, prelusory, preparatory, proemial.

**prefer** vb address, offer, present, proffer, tender; advance, elevate, promote, raise; adopt, choose, elect, fancy, pick, select, wish.

**preference** n advancement, choice, election, estimation, precedence, priority, selection.

**preferment** n advancement, benefice, dignity, elevation, exaltation, promotion.

**pregnant** adj big, enceinte, parturient; fraught, full, important, replete, significant, weighty; fecund, fertile, fruitful, generative, potential, procreant, procreative, productive, prolific.

**prejudice** vb bias, incline, influence, turn, warp; damage, diminish, hurt, impair, injure. * n bias, intolerance, partiality, preconception, predilection, prejudgement, prepossession, unfairness; damage, detriment, disadvantage, harm, hurt, impairment, injury, loss, mischief.

**prejudiced** adj biased, bigoted, influenced, one-sided, partial, partisan, unfair.

**preliminary** adj antecedent, initiatory, introductory, precedent, precursive, precursory, prefatory, prelusive, prelusory, preparatory, previous, prior,

proemial. * n beginning, initiation, introduction, opening, preamble, preface, prelude, start.

**prelude** n introduction, opening, overture, prelusion, preparation, voluntary; exordium, preamble, preface, preliminary, proem.

**premature** adj hasty, ill-considered, precipitate, unmatured, unprepared, unripe, unseasonable, untimely.

**premeditation** n deliberation, design, forethought, intention, prearrangement, predetermination, purpose.

**premise** vb introduce, preamble, preface, prefix. * n affirmation, antecedent, argument, assertion, assumption, basis, foundation, ground, hypothesis, position, premiss, presupposition, proposition, support, thesis, theorem.

**premium** n bonus, bounty, encouragement, fee, gift, guerdon, meed, payment, prize, recompense, remuneration, reward; appreciation, enhancement.

**premonition** n caution, foreboding, foreshadowing, forewarning, indication, omen, portent, presage, presentiment, sign, warning.

**preoccupied** adj absent, absentminded, abstracted, dreaming, engrossed, inadvertent, inattentive, lost, musing, unobservant.

**prepare** vb adapt, adjust, fit, qualify; arrange, concoct, fabricate, make, order, plan, procure, provide.

**preponderant** adj outweighing, overbalancing, preponderating.

**prepossessing** adj alluring, amiable, attractive, bewitching, captivating, charming, engaging, fascinating, inviting, taking, winning.

**preposterous** adj absurd, excessive, exorbitant, extravagant, foolish, improper, irrational, monstrous, nonsensical, perverted, ridiculous, unfit, unreasonable, wrong.

**prerogative** n advantage, birthright, claim, franchise, immunity, liberty, privilege, right.

**presage** vb divine, forebode; augur, betoken, bode, foreshadow, foretell, foretoken, indicate, portend, predict, prognosticate, prophesy, signify, soothsay. * n augury, auspice, boding, foreboding, foreshowing, indication, omen, portent, prognostication, sign, token; foreknowledge, precognition, prediction, premonition, presentiment, prophecy.

**prescribe** vb advocate, appoint, command, decree, dictate, direct, enjoin, establish, institute, ordain, order.

**presence** n attendance, company, inhabitance,

inhabitancy, nearness, neighbourhood, occupancy, propinquity, proximity; residence, ubiquity, vicinity; air, appearance, carriage, demeanour, mien, personality.

**present**[1] *adj* near; actual, current, existing, happening, immediate, instant, living; available, quick, ready; attentive, favourable. * *n* now, time being, today.

**present**[2] *n* benefaction, boon, donation, favour, gift, grant, gratuity, largesse, offering.

**present**[3] *vb* introduce, nominate; exhibit, offer; bestow, confer, give, grant; deliver, hand; advance, express, prefer, proffer, tender.

**presentiment** *n* anticipation, apprehension, foreboding, forecast, foretaste, forethought, prescience.

**presently** *adv* anon, directly, forthwith, immediately, shortly, soon.

**preservation** *n* cherishing, conservation, curing, maintenance, protection, support; safety, salvation, security; integrity, keeping, soundness.

**preserve** *vb* defend, guard, keep, protect, rescue, save, secure, shield; maintain, uphold, sustain, support; conserve, economize, husband, retain. * *n* comfit, compote, confection, confiture, conserve, jam, jelly, marmalade, sweetmeat; enclosure, warren.

**preside** *vb* control, direct, govern, manage, officiate.

**press** *vb* compress, crowd, crush, squeeze; flatten, iron, smooth; clasp, embrace, hug; force, compel, constrain; emphasize, enforce, enjoin, inculcate, stress, urge; hasten, hurry, push, rush; crowd, throng; entreat, importune, solicit. * *n* crowd, crush, multitude, throng; hurry, pressure, urgency; case, closet, cupboard, repository.

**pressing** *adj* constraining, critical, distressing, imperative, importunate, persistent, serious, urgent, vital.

**pressure** *n* compressing, crushing, squeezing; influence, force; compulsion, exigency, hurry, persuasion, press, stress, urgency; affliction, calamity, difficulty, distress, embarrassment, grievance, oppression, straits; impression, stamp.

**prestidigitation** *n* conjuring, juggling, legerdemain, sleight-of-hand.

**prestige** *n* credit, distinction, importance, influence, reputation, weight.

**presume** *vb* anticipate, apprehend, assume, believe, conjecture, deduce, expect, infer, surmise, suppose, think; consider, presuppose; dare, undertake, venture.

**presumption** *n* anticipation, assumption, belief, concession, conclusion, condition, conjecture, deduction, guess, hypothesis, inference, opinion, supposition, understanding; arrogance, assurance, audacity, boldness, brass, effrontery, forwardness, haughtiness, presumptuousness; probability.

**presumptuous** *adj* arrogant, assuming, audacious, bold, brash, forward, irreverent, insolent, intrusive, presuming; foolhardy, overconfident, rash.

**pretence** *n* affectation, cloak, colour, disguise, mask, semblance, show, simulation, veil, window-dressing; excuse, evasion, fabrication, feigning, makeshift, pretext, sham, subterfuge; claim, pretension.

**pretend** *vb* affect, counterfeit, deem, dissemble, fake, falsify, feign, sham, simulate; act, imagine, lie, profess; aspire, claim.

**pretension** *n* assertion, assumption, claim, demand, pretence; affectation, airs, conceit, ostentation, pertness, pretentiousness, priggishness, vanity.

**pretentious** *adj* affected, assuming, conceited, conspicuous, ostentatious, presuming, priggish, showy, tawdry, unnatural, vain.

**preternatural** *adj* abnormal, anomalous, extraordinary, inexplicable, irregular, miraculous, mysterious, odd, peculiar, strange, unnatural.

**pretext** *n* affectation, appearance, blind, cloak, colour, guise, mask, pretence, semblance, show, simulation, veil; excuse, justification, plea, vindication.

**pretty** *adj* attractive, beautiful, bonny, comely, elegant, fair, handsome, neat, pleasing, trim; affected, foppish. * *adv* fairly, moderately, quite, rather, somewhat.

**prevail** *vb* overcome, succeed, triumph, win; obtain, predominate, preponderate, reign, rule.

**prevailing** *adj* controlling, dominant, effectual, efficacious, general, influential, operative, overruling, persuading, predominant, preponderant, prevalent, ruling, successful.

**prevalent** *adj* ascendant, compelling, efficacious, governing, predominant, prevailing, successful, superior; extensive, general, rife, widespread.

**prevaricate** *vb* cavil, deviate, dodge, equivocate, evade, palter, pettifog, quibble, shift, shuffle, tergiversate.

**prevent** *vb* bar, check, debar, deter, forestall, help, hinder, impede, inhibit, intercept, interrupt, obstruct, obviate, preclude, prohibit, restrain, save, stop, thwart.

**prevention** n anticipation, determent, deterrence, deterrent, frustration, hindrance, interception, interruption, obstruction, preclusion, prohibition, restriction, stoppage.

**previous** adj antecedent, anterior, earlier, foregoing, foregone, former, precedent, preceding, prior.

**prey** vb devour, eat, feed on, live off; exploit, intimidate, terrorize; burden, distress, haunt, oppress, trouble, worry. * n booty, loot, pillage, plunder, prize, rapine, spoil; food, game, kill, quarry, victim; depredation, ravage.

**price** vb assess, estimate, evaluate, rate, value. * n amount, cost, expense, outlay, value; appraisal, charge, estimation, excellence, figure, rate, quotation, valuation, value, worth; compensation, guerdon, recompense, return, reward.

**priceless** adj dear, expensive, precious, inestimable, invaluable, valuable; amusing, comic, droll, funny, humorous, killing, rich.

**prick** vb perforate, pierce, puncture, stick; drive, goad, impel, incite, spur, urge; cut, hurt, mark, pain, sting, wound; hasten, post, ride. * n mark, perforation, point, puncture; prickle, sting, wound.

**pride** vb boast, brag, crow, preen, revel in. * n conceit, egotism, self-complacency, self-esteem, self-exaltation, self-importance, self-sufficiency, vanity; arrogance, assumption, disdain, haughtiness, hauteur, insolence, loftiness, lordliness, pomposity, presumption, superciliousness, vainglory; decorum, dignity, elevation, self-respect; decoration, glory, ornament, show, splendour.

**priest** n churchman, clergyman, divine, ecclesiastic, minister, pastor, presbyter.

**prim** adj demure, formal, nice, precise, prudish, starch, starched, stiff, strait-laced.

**primary** adj aboriginal, earliest, first, initial, original, prime, primitive, primeval, primordial, pristine; chief, main, principal; basic, elementary, fundamental, preparatory: radical.

**prime**[1] adj aboriginal, basic, first, initial, original, primal, primary, primeval, primitive, primordial, pristine; chief, foremost, highest, leading, main, paramount, principal; blooming, early; capital, cardinal, dominant, predominant; excellent, first-class, first-rate, optimal, optimum, quintessential, superlative; beginning, opening. * n beginning, dawn, morning, opening; spring, springtime, youth; bloom, cream, flower, height,

heyday, optimum, perfection, quintessence, zenith.

**prime**[2] vb charge, load, prepare, undercoat; coach, groom, train, tutor.

**primeval** adj original, primitive, primordial, pristine.

**primitive** adj aboriginal, first, fundamental, original, primal, primary, prime, primitive, primordial, pristine; ancient, antiquated, crude, old-fashioned, quaint, simple, uncivilized, unsophisticated.

**prince** n monarch, potentate, ruler, sovereign; dauphin, heir apparent, infant; chief, leader, potentate.

**princely** adj imperial, regal, royal; august, generous, grand, liberal, magnanimous, magnificent, majestic, munificent, noble, pompous, splendid, superb, titled; dignified, elevated, high-minded, lofty, noble, stately.

**principal** adj capital, cardinal, chief, essential, first, foremost, highest, leading, main, pre-eminent, prime. * n chief, head, leader; head teacher; master.

**principally** adv chiefly, essentially, especially, mainly, particularly.

**principle** n cause, fountain, fountainhead, groundwork, mainspring, nature, origin, source, spring; basis, constituent, element, essence, substratum; assumption, axiom, law, maxim, postulation; doctrine, dogma, impulse, maxim, opinion, precept, rule, tenet, theory; conviction, ground, motive, reason; equity, goodness, honesty, honour, incorruptibility, integrity, justice, probity, rectitude, righteousness, trustiness, truth, uprightness, virtue, worth; faculty, power.

**prink** vb adorn, deck, decorate; preen, primp, spruce.

**print** vb engrave, impress, imprint, mark, stamp; issue, publish. * n book, periodical, publication; copy, engraving, photograph, picture; characters, font, fount, lettering, type, typeface.

**prior** adj antecedent, anterior, earlier, foregoing, precedent, preceding, precursory, previous, superior.

**priority** n antecedence, anteriority, precedence, pre-eminence, pre-existence; superiority.

**priory** n abbey, cloister, convent, monastery, nunnery.

**prison** n confinement, dungeon, gaol, jail, keep, lockup, penitentiary, reformatory; can, clink, cooler, jug.

**pristine** adj ancient, earliest, first, former, old, original, primary, primeval, primitive, primordial.

**privacy** n concealment, secrecy; retirement, retreat, seclusion, solitude.

**private** *adj* retired, secluded, sequestrated, solitary; individual, own, particular, peculiar, personal, special, unofficial; confidential, privy; clandestine, concealed, hidden, secret. * *n* GI, soldier, tommy.

**privation** *n* bereavement, deprivation, dispossession, loss; destitution, distress, indigence, necessity, need, want; absence, negation; degradation.

**privilege** *n* advantage, charter, claim, exemption, favour, franchise, immunity, leave, liberty, licence, permission, prerogative, right.

**privy** *adj* individual, particular, peculiar, personal, private, special; clandestine, secret; retired, sequestrated.

**prize**[1] *vb* appreciate, cherish, esteem, treasure, value.

**prize**[2] *adj* best, champion, first-rate, outstanding, winning. * *n* guerdon, honours, meed, premium, reward; cup, decoration, medal, laurels, palm, trophy; booty, capture, lot, plunder, spoil; advantage, gain, privilege.

**probability** *n* chance, prospect, likelihood, presumption; appearance, credibility, credibleness, likeliness, verisimilitude.

**probable** *adj* apparent, credible, likely, presumable, reasonable.

**probably** *adv* apparently, likely, maybe, perchance, perhaps, presumably, possibly, seemingly.

**probation** *n* essay, examination, ordeal, proof, test, trial; novitiate.

**probe** *vb* examine, explore, fathom, investigate, measure, prove, scrutinize, search, sift, sound, test, verify. * *n* examination, exploration, inquiry, investigation, scrutiny, study.

**probity** *n* candour, conscientiousness, equity, fairness, faith, goodness, honesty, honour, incorruptibility, integrity, justice, loyalty, morality, principle, rectitude, righteousness, sincerity, soundness, trustworthiness, truth, truthfulness, uprightness, veracity, virtue, worth.

**problem** *adj* difficult, intractable, uncontrollable, unruly. * *n* dilemma, dispute, doubt, enigma, exercise, proposition, puzzle, riddle, theorem.

**problematic** *adj* debatable, disputable, doubtful, dubious, enigmatic, problematical, puzzling, questionable, suspicious, uncertain, unsettled.

**procedure** *n* conduct, course, custom, management, method, operation, policy, practice, process; act, action, deed, measure, performance, proceeding, step, transaction.

**proceed** *vb* advance, continue, go, pass, progress; accrue, arise, come, emanate, ensue, flow, follow, issue, originate, result, spring.

**proceeds** *npl* balance, earnings, effects, gain, income, net, produce, products, profits, receipts, returns, yield.

**process** *vb* advance, deal with, fulfil, handle, progress; alter, convert, refine, transform. * *n* advance, course, progress, train; action, conduct, management, measure, mode, operation, performance, practice, procedure, proceeding, step, transaction, way; action, case, suit, trial; outgrowth, projection, protuberance.

**procession** *n* cavalcade, cortege, file, march, parade, retinue, train.

**proclaim** *vb* advertise, announce, blazon, broach, broadcast, circulate, cry, declare, herald, promulgate, publish, trumpet; ban, outlaw, proscribe.

**proclamation** *n* advertisement, announcement, blazon, declaration, promulgation, publication; ban, decree, edict, manifesto, ordinance.

**proclivity** *n* bearing, bent, bias, determination, direction, disposition, drift, inclination, leaning, predisposition, proneness, propensity, tendency, turn; aptitude, facility, readiness.

**procrastinate** *vb* adjourn, defer, delay, postpone, prolong, protract, retard; neglect, omit; lag, loiter.

**procrastination** *n* delay, dilatoriness, postponement, protraction, slowness, tardiness.

**procreate** *vb* beget, breed, engender, generate, produce, propagate.

**procurable** *adj* acquirable, compassable, obtainable.

**procurator** *n* agent, attorney, deputy, proctor, proxy, representative, solicitor.

**procure** *vb* acquire, gain, get, obtain; cause, compass, contrive, effect.

**procurer** *n* bawd, pander, pimp.

**prodigal** *adj* abundant, dissipated, excessive, extravagant, generous, improvident, lavish, profuse, reckless, squandering, thriftless, unthrifty, wasteful. * *n* spendthrift, squanderer, waster, wastrel.

**prodigality** *n* excess, extravagance, lavishness, profusion, squandering, unthriftiness, waste, wastefulness.

**prodigious** adj amazing, astonishing, astounding, extraordinary, marvellous, miraculous, portentous, remarkable, startling, strange, surprising, uncommon, wonderful, wondrous; enormous, huge, immense, monstrous, vast.

**prodigy** n marvel, miracle, phenomenon, portent, sign, wonder; curiosity, monster, monstrosity.

**produce** vb exhibit, show; bear, beget, breed, conceive, engender, furnish, generate, hatch, procreate, yield; accomplish, achieve, cause, create, effect, make, occasion, originate; accrue, afford, give, impart, make, render; extend, lengthen, prolong, protract; fabricate, fashion, manufacture. * n crop, fruit, greengrocery, harvest, product, vegetables, yield.

**producer** n creator, inventor, maker, originator; agriculturalist, farmer, greengrocer, husbandman, raiser.

**product** n crops, fruits, harvest, outcome, proceeds, produce, production, returns, yield; consequence, effect, fruit, issue, performance, production, result, work.

**production** n fruit, produce, product; construction, creation, erection, fabrication, making, performance; completion, fruition; birth, breeding, development, growth, propagation; opus, publication, work; continuation, extension, lengthening, prolongation.

**productive** adj copious, fertile, fruitful, luxuriant, plenteous, prolific, teeming; causative, constructive, creative, efficient, life-giving, producing.

**proem** n exordium, foreword, introduction, preface, prelims, prelude, prolegomena.

**profane** vb defile, desecrate, pollute, violate; abuse, debase. * adj blasphemous, godless, heathen, idolatrous, impious, impure, pagan, secular, temporal, unconsecrated, unhallowed, unholy, unsanctified, worldly, unspiritual; impure, polluted, unholy.

**profanity** n blasphemy, impiety, irreverence, profaneness, sacrilege.

**profess** vb acknowledge, affirm, allege, aver, avouch, avow, confess, declare, own, proclaim, state; affect, feign, pretend.

**profession** n acknowledgement, assertion, avowal, claim, declaration; avocation, evasion, pretence, pretension, protestation, representation; business, calling, employment, engagement, occupation, office, trade, vocation.

**proffer** vb offer, propose, propound, suggest, tender, volunteer. * n offer, proposal, suggestion, tender.

**proficiency** n advancement, forwardness, improvement; accomplishment, aptitude, competency, dexterity, mastery, skill.

**proficient** adj able, accomplished, adept, competent, conversant, dextrous, expert, finished, masterly, practised, skilled, skilful, thoroughbred, trained, qualified, well-versed. * n adept, expert, master, master-hand.

**profit** vb advance, benefit, gain, improve. * n aid, clearance, earnings, emolument, fruit, gain, lucre, produce, return; advancement, advantage, benefit, interest, perquisite, service, use, utility, weal.

**profitable** adj advantageous, beneficial, desirable, gainful, productive, useful; lucrative, remunerative.

**profitless** adj bootless, fruitless, unprofitable, useless, valueless, worthless.

**profligate** adj abandoned, corrupt, corrupted, degenerate, depraved, dissipated, dissolute, graceless, immoral, shameless, vicious, vitiated, wicked. * n debauchee, libertine, rake, reprobate, roué.

**profound** adj abysmal, deep, fathomless; heavy, undisturbed; erudite, learned, penetrating, sagacious, skilled; deeply felt, far-reaching, heartfelt, intense, lively, strong, touching, vivid; low, submissive; abstruse, mysterious, obscure, occult, subtle, recondite; complete, thorough.

**profundity** n deepness, depth, profoundness.

**profuse** adj abundant, bountiful, copious, excessive, extravagant, exuberant, generous, improvident, lavish, overabundant, plentiful, prodigal, wasteful.

**profusion** n abundance, bounty, copiousness, excess, exuberance, extravagance, lavishness, prodigality, profuseness, superabundance, waste.

**progenitor** n ancestor, forebear, forefather.

**progeny** n breed, children, descendants, family, issue, lineage, offshoot, offspring, posterity, race, scion, stock, young.

**prognostic** adj foreshadowing, foreshowing, foretokening. * n augury, foreboding, indication, omen, presage, prognostication, sign, symptom, token; foretelling, prediction, prophecy.

**prognosticate** vb foretell, predict, prophesy; augur, betoken, forebode, foreshadow, foreshow, foretoken, indicate, portend, presage.

**prognostication** n foreknowledge, foreshowing, foretelling, prediction, presage; augury, foreboding, foretoken, indication, portent, prophecy.

**progress** vb advance, continue, proceed; better, gain,

improve, increase. * n advance, advancement, progression; course, headway, ongoing, passage; betterment, development, growth, improvement, increase, reform; circuit, procession.

**prohibit** vb debar, hamper, hinder, preclude, prevent; ban, disallow, forbid, inhibit, interdict.

**prohibition** n ban, bar, disallowance, embargo, forbiddance, inhibition, interdict, interdiction, obstruction, prevention, proscription, taboo, veto.

**prohibitive** adj forbidding, prohibiting, refraining, restrictive.

**project** vb cast, eject, fling, hurl, propel, shoot, throw; brew, concoct, contrive, design, devise, intend, plan, plot, purpose, scheme; delineate, draw, exhibit; bulge, extend, jut, protrude. * n contrivance, design, device, intention, plan, proposal, purpose, scheme.

**projectile** n bullet, missile, shell.

**projection** n delivery, ejection, emission, propulsion, throwing; contriving, designing, planning, scheming; bulge, extension, outshoot, process, prominence, protuberance, salience, saliency, salient, spur; delineation, map, plan.

**proletarian** adj mean, plebeian, vile, vulgar. * n commoner, plebeian.

**proletariat** n commonality, hoi polloi, masses, mob, plebs, working class.

**prolific** adj abundant, fertile, fruitful, generative, productive, teeming.

**prolix** adj boring, circumlocutory, discursive, diffuse, lengthy, long, long-winded, loose, prolonged, protracted, prosaic, rambling, tedious, tiresome, verbose, wordy.

**prologue** n foreword, introduction, preamble, preface, preliminary, prelude, proem.

**prolong** vb continue, extend, lengthen, protract, sustain; defer, postpone.

**promenade** vb saunter, walk. * n dance, stroll, walk; boulevard, esplanade, parade, walkway.

**prominent** adj convex, embossed, jutting, projecting, protuberant, raised, relieved; celebrated, conspicuous, distinguished, eminent, famous, foremost, influential, leading, main, noticeable, outstanding; conspicuous, distinctive, important, manifest, marked, principal, salient.

**promiscuous** adj confused, heterogeneous, indiscriminate, intermingled, mingled, miscellaneous, mixed; abandoned, dissipated, dissolute, immoral, licentious, loose, unchaste, wanton.

**promise** vb covenant, engage, pledge, subscribe, swear, underwrite, vow; assure, attest, guarantee, warrant; agree, bargain, engage, stipulate, undertake. * n agreement, assurance, contract, engagement, oath, parole, pledge, profession, undertaking, vow, word.

**promising** adj auspicious, encouraging, hopeful, likely, propitious.

**promote** vb advance, aid, assist, cultivate, encourage, further, help, promote; dignify, elevate, exalt, graduate, honour, pass, prefer, raise.

**promotion** n advancement, encouragement, furtherance; elevation, exaltation, preferment.

**prompt** vb actuate, dispose, impel, incite, incline, induce, instigate, stimulate, urge; remind; dictate, hint, influence, suggest. * adj active, alert, apt, quick, ready; forward, hasty; disposed, inclined, prone; early, exact, immediate, instant, precise, punctual, seasonable, timely. * adv apace, directly, forthwith, immediately, promptly. * n cue, hint, prompter, reminder, stimulus.

**promptly** adv apace, directly, expeditiously, forthwith, immediately, instantly, pronto, punctually, quickly, speedily, straightway, straightaway, summarily, swiftly.

**promptness** n activity, alertness, alacrity, promptitude, readiness, quickness.

**promulgate** vb advertise, announce, broadcast, bruit, circulate, declare, notify, proclaim, publish, spread, trumpet.

**prone** adj flat, horizontal, prostrate, recumbent; declivitous, inclined, inclining, sloping; apt, bent, disposed, inclined, predisposed, tending; eager, prompt, ready.

**pronounce** vb articulate, enunciate, frame, say, speak, utter; affirm, announce, assert, declare, deliver, state.

**proof** adj firm, fixed, impenetrable, stable, steadfast. * n essay, examination, ordeal, test, trial; attestation, certification, conclusion, conclusiveness, confirmation, corroboration, demonstration, evidence, ratification, substantiation, testimony, verification.

**prop** vb bolster, brace, buttress, maintain, shore, stay, support, sustain, truss, uphold. * n support, stay; buttress, fulcrum, pin, shore, strut.

**propaganda** n inculcation, indoctrination, promotion.

**propagate** vb continue, increase, multiply; circulate,

diffuse, disseminate, extend, promote, promulgate, publish, spread, transmit; beget, breed, engender, generate, originate, procreate.

**propel** vb drive, force, impel, push, urge; cast, fling, hurl, project, throw.

**propensity** n aptitude, bent, bias, disposition, inclination, ply, proclivity, proneness, tendency.

**proper** adj individual, inherent, natural, original, particular, peculiar, special, specific; adapted, appropriate, becoming, befitting, convenient, decent, decorous, demure, fit, fitting, legitimate, meet, pertinent, respectable, right, seemly, suitable; accurate, correct, exact, fair, fastidious, formal, just, precise; actual, real.

**property** n attribute, characteristic, disposition, mark, peculiarity, quality, trait, virtue; appurtenance, assets, belongings, chattels, circumstances, effects, estate, goods, possessions, resources, wealth; ownership, possession, proprietorship, tenure; claim, copyright, interest, participation, right, title.

**prophecy** n augury, divination, forecast, foretelling, portent, prediction, premonition, presage, prognostication; exhortation, instruction; preaching.

**prophesy** vb augur, divine, foretell, predict, prognosticate.

**propinquity** n adjacency, contiguity, nearness, neighbourhood, proximity, vicinity; affinity, connection, consanguinity, kindred, relationship.

**propitiate** vb appease, atone, conciliate, intercede, mediate, pacify, reconcile, satisfy.

**propitious** adj benevolent, benign, friendly, gracious, kind, merciful; auspicious, encouraging, favourable, fortunate, happy, lucky, opportune, promising, prosperous, thriving, timely, well-disposed.

**proportion** vb adjust, graduate, regulate; form, shape. * n arrangement, relation; adjustment, commensuration, dimension, distribution, symmetry; extent, lot, part, portion, quota, ratio, share.

**proposal** n design, motion, offer, overture, proffer, proposition, recommendation, scheme, statement, suggestion, tender.

**propose** vb move, offer, pose, present, propound, proffer, put, recommend, state, submit, suggest, tender; design, intend, mean, purpose.

**proposition** vb accost, proffer, solicit. * n offer, overture, project, proposal, suggestion, tender, undertaking; affirmation, assertion, axiom, declaration,

dictum, doctrine, position, postulation, predication, statement, theorem, thesis.

**proprietor** n lord, master, owner, possessor, proprietary.

**propriety** n accuracy, adaptation, appropriation, aptness, becomingness, consonance, correctness, fitness, justness, reasonableness, rightness, seemliness, suitableness; conventionality, decency, decorum, demureness, fastidiousness, formality, modesty, properness, respectability.

**prorogation** n adjournment, continuance, postponement.

**prosaic** adj commonplace, dull, flat, humdrum, matter-of-fact, pedestrian, plain, prolix, prosing, sober, stupid, tame, tedious, tiresome, unentertaining, unimaginative, uninspired, uninteresting, unromantic, vapid.

**proscribe** vb banish, doom, exile, expel, ostracize, outlaw; exclude, forbid, interdict, prohibit; censure, condemn, curse, denounce, reject.

**prosecute** vb conduct, continue, exercise; follow, persist, pursue; arraign, indict, sue, summon.

**prospect** vb explore, search, seek, survey. * n display, field, landscape, outlook, perspective, scene, show, sight, spectacle, survey, view, vision, vista; picture, scenery; anticipation, calculation, contemplation, expectance, expectancy, expectation, foreseeing, foresight, hope, presumption, promise, trust; likelihood, probability.

**prospectus** n announcement, conspectus, description, design, outline, plan, programme, sketch, syllabus.

**prosper** vb aid, favour, forward, help; advance, flourish, grow rich, thrive, succeed; batten, increase.

**prosperity** n affluence, blessings, happiness, felicity, good luck, success, thrift, weal, welfare, well-being; boom, heyday.

**prosperous** adj blooming, flourishing, fortunate, golden, halcyon, rich, successful, thriving; auspicious, booming, bright, favourable, good, golden, lucky, promising, propitious, providential, rosy.

**prostrate** vb demolish, destroy, fell, level, overthrow, overturn, ruin; depress, exhaust, overcome, reduce. * adj fallen, prostrated, prone, recumbent, supine; helpless, powerless.

**prostration** n demolition, destruction, overthrow; dejection, depression, exhaustion.

**prosy** adj prosaic, unpoetic, unpoetical; dull, flat,

jejune, stupid, tedious, tiresome, unentertaining, unimaginative, uninteresting.

**protect** vb cover, defend, guard, shield; fortify, harbour, house, preserve, save, screen, secure, shelter; champion, countenance, foster, patronize.

**protector** n champion, custodian, defender, guardian, patron, warden.

**protest** vb affirm, assert, asseverate, attest, aver, avow, declare, profess, testify; demur, expostulate, object, remonstrate, repudiate. * n complaint, declaration, disapproval, objection, protestation.

**prototype** n archetype, copy, exemplar, example, ideal, model, original, paradigm, precedent, protoplast, type.

**protract** vb continue, extend, lengthen, prolong; defer, delay, postpone.

**protrude** vb beetle, bulge, extend, jut, project.

**protuberance** n bulge, bump, elevation, excrescence, hump, lump, process, projection, prominence, roundness, swelling, tumour.

**proud** adj assuming, conceited, contended, egotistical, overweening, self-conscious, self-satisfied, vain; arrogant, boastful, haughty, high-spirited, highly strung, imperious, lofty, lordly, presumptuous, supercilious, uppish, vainglorious.

**prove** vb ascertain, conform, demonstrate, establish, evidence, evince, justify, manifest, show, substantiate, sustain, verify; assay, check, examine, experiment, test, try.

**proverb** n adage, aphorism, apothegm, byword, dictum, maxim, precept, saw, saying.

**proverbial** adj acknowledged, current, notorious, unquestioned.

**provide** vb arrange, collect, plan, prepare, procure; gather, keep, store; afford, contribute, feed, furnish, produce, stock, supply, yield; cater, purvey; agree, bargain, condition, contract, covenant, engage, stipulate.

**provided, providing** conj granted, if, supposing.

**provident** adj careful, cautious, considerate, discreet, farseeing, forecasting, forehanded, foreseeing, prudent; economical, frugal, thrifty.

**province** n district, domain, region, section, territory, tract; colony, dependency; business, calling, capacity, charge, department, duty, employment, function, office, part, post, sphere; department, division, jurisdiction.

**provincial** adj annexed, appendant, outlying; bucolic, countrified, rude, rural, rustic, unpolished, unrefined;

insular, local, narrow. * n peasant, rustic, yokel.

**provision** n anticipation, providing; arrangement, care, preparation, readiness; equipment, fund, grist, hoard, reserve, resources, stock, store, supplies, supply; clause, condition, prerequisite, proviso, reservation, stipulation.

**provisions** npl eatables, fare, food, provender, supplies, viands, victuals.

**proviso** n clause, condition, provision, stipulation.

**provocation** n incentive, incitement, provocativeness, stimulant, stimulus; affront, indignity, insult, offence; angering, vexation.

**provoke** vb animate, arouse, awaken, excite, impel, incite, induce, inflame, instigate, kindle, move, rouse, stimulate; affront, aggravate, anger, annoy, chafe, enrage, exacerbate, exasperate, incense, infuriate, irritate, nettle, offend, pique, vex; cause, elicit, evoke, instigate, occasion, produce, promote.

**provoking** adj aggravating, annoying, exasperating, irritating, offensive, tormenting, vexatious, vexing.

**prowess** n bravery, courage, daring, fearlessness, gallantry, heroism, intrepidity, valour; aptitude, dexterity, expertness, facility.

**proximity** n adjacency, contiguity, nearness, neighbourhood, propinquity, vicinage, vicinity.

**proxy** n agent, attorney, commissioner, delegate, deputy, lieutenant, representative, substitute.

**prudence** n carefulness, caution, circumspection, common sense, considerateness, discretion, forecast, foresight, judgment, judiciousness, policy, providence, sense, tact, wariness, wisdom.

**prudent** adj cautious, careful, circumspect, considerate, discreet, foreseeing, heedful, judicious, politic, provident, prudential, wary, wise.

**prudish** adj coy, demure, modest, precise, prim, reserved, strait-laced.

**prune** vb abbreviate, clip, cut, dock, lop, thin, trim; dress, preen.

**prurient** adj covetous, craving, desiring, hankering, itching, lascivious, libidinous, longing, lustful.

**pry** vb examine, ferret, inspect, investigate, peep, peer, question, scrutinize, search; force, lever, prise.

**public** adj civil, common, countrywide, general, national, political, state; known, notorious, open, popular, published, well-known. * n citizens, community, country, everyone, general public, masses, nation, people, population; audience, buyers, following, supporters.

**publication** n advertisement, announcement, disclosure, divulgement, divulgence, proclamation, promulgation, report; edition, issue, issuance, printing.

**publicity** n daylight, currency, limelight, notoriety, spotlight; outlet, vent.

**publish** vb advertise, air, bruit, announce, blaze, blazon, broach, communicate, declare, diffuse, disclose, disseminate, impart, placard, post, proclaim, promulgate, reveal, tell, utter, vent, ventilate.

**pucker** vb cockle, contract, corrugate, crease, crinkle, furrow, gather, pinch, purse, shirr, wrinkle. * n crease, crinkle, fold, furrow, wrinkle.

**puerile** adj boyish, childish, infantile, juvenile, youthful; foolish, frivolous, idle, nonsensical, petty, senseless, silly, simple, trifling, trivial, weak.

**puffy** adj distended, swelled, swollen, tumid, turgid; bombastic, extravagant, inflated, pompous.

**pugnacious** adj belligerent, bellicose, contentious, fighting, irascible, irritable, petulant, quarrelsome.

**puissant** adj forcible, mighty, potent, powerful, strong.

**pull** vb drag, draw, haul, row, tow, tug; cull, extract, gather, pick, pluck; detach, rend, tear, wrest. * n pluck, shake, tug, twitch, wrench; contest, struggle; attraction, gravity, magnetism; graft, influence, power.

**pulsate** vb beat, palpitate, pant, throb, thump, vibrate.

**pulverize** vb bruise, comminute, grind, levigate, triturate.

**pun** vb assonate, alliterate, play on words. * n assonance, alliteration, clinch, conceit, double-meaning, paranomasia, play on words, quip, rhyme, witticism, wordplay.

**punctilious** adj careful, ceremonious, conscientious, exact, formal, nice, particular, precise, punctual, scrupulous, strict.

**punctual** adj exact, nice, precise, punctilious; early, prompt, ready, regular, seasonable, timely.

**puncture** vb bore, penetrate, perforate, pierce, prick. * n bite, hole, sting, wound.

**pungent** adj acid, acrid, biting, burning, caustic, hot, mordant, penetrating, peppery, piercing, piquant, prickling, racy, salty, seasoned, sharp, smart, sour, spicy, stimulating, stinging; acute, acrimonious, cutting, distressing, irritating, keen, painful, peevish, poignant, pointed, satirical, severe, tart, trenchant, waspish.

**punish** vb beat, castigate, chasten, chastise, correct, discipline, flog, lash, scourge, torture, whip.

**punishment** n castigation, chastening, chastisement, correction, discipline, infliction, retribution, scourging, trial; judgment, nemesis, penalty.

**puny** adj feeble, inferior, weak; dwarf, dwarfish, insignificant, diminutive, little, petty, pygmy, small, stunted, tiny, underdeveloped, undersized.

**pupil** n beginner, catechumen, disciple, learner, neophyte, novice, scholar, student, tyro.

**pupillage** n minority, nonage, tutelage, wardship.

**puppet** n doll, image, manikin, marionette; cat's-paw, pawn, tool.

**purchase** vb buy, gain, get, obtain, pay for, procure; achieve, attain, earn, win. * n acquisition, buy, gain, possession, property; advantage, foothold, grasp, hold, influence, support.

**pure** adj clean, clear, fair, immaculate, spotless, stainless, unadulterated, unalloyed, unblemished, uncorrupted, undefiled, unpolluted, unspotted, unstained, unsullied, untainted, untarnished; chaste, continent, guileless, guiltless, holy, honest, incorrupt, innocent, modest, sincere, true, uncorrupt, upright, virgin, virtuous; genuine, perfect, real, simple, true, unadorned; absolute, essential, mere, sheer, thorough; classic, classical.

**purge** vb cleanse, clear, purify; clarify, defecate, evacuate; deterge, scour; absolve, pardon, shrive. * n elimination, eradication, expulsion, removal, suppression; cathartic, emetic, enema, laxative, physic.

**purify** vb clean, cleanse, clear, depurate, expurgate, purge, refine, wash; clarify, fine.

**puritanical** adj ascetic, narrow-minded, overscrupulous, prim, prudish, rigid, severe, strait-laced, strict.

**purity** n clearness, fineness; cleanness, correctness, faultlessness, immaculacy, immaculateness; guilelessness, guiltlessness, holiness, honesty, innocence, integrity, piety, simplicity, truth, uprightness, virtue; excellence, genuineness; homogeneity, simpleness; chasteness, chastity, continence, modesty, pudency, virginity.

**purlieus** npl borders, bounds, confines, environs, limits, neighbourhood, outskirts, precincts, suburbs, vicinage, vicinity.

**purloin** vb abstract, crib, filch, pilfer, rob, steal, thieve.

**purport** vb allege, assert, claim, maintain, pretend, profess; denote, express, imply, indicate, mean, signify, suggest. * n bearing, current, design, drift, gist, import, intent, meaning, scope, sense, significance, signification, spirit, tendency, tenor.

**purpose** vb contemplate, design, intend, mean, meditate; determine, resolve. * n aim, design, drift, end, intent, intention, object, resolution, resolve, view; plan, project; meaning, purport, sense; consequence, effect.

**pursue** vb chase, dog, follow, hound, hunt, shadow, track; conduct, continue, cultivate, maintain, practise, prosecute; seek, strive; accompany, attend.

**pursuit** n chase, hunt, race; conduct, cultivation, practice, prosecution, pursuance; avocation, calling, business, employment, fad, hobby, occupation, vocation.

**pursy** adj corpulent, fat, fleshy, plump, podgy, pudgy, short, thick; short-breathed, short-winded; opulent, rich.

**purview** n body, compass, extent, limit, reach, scope, sphere, view.

**push** vb elbow, crowd, hustle, impel, jostle, shoulder, shove, thrust; advance, drive, hurry, propel, urge; importune, persuade, tease. * n pressure, thrust; determination, perseverance; emergency, exigency, extremity, pinch, strait, test, trial; assault, attack, charge, endeavour, onset.

**pusillanimous** adj chicken, chicken-hearted, cowardly, dastardly, faint-hearted, feeble, lily-livered, mean-spirited, spiritless, timid, recreant, timorous, weak.

**pustule** n abscess, blain, blister, blotch, boil, fester, gathering, pimple, sore, ulcer.

**put** vb bring, collocate, deposit, impose, lay, locate, place, set; enjoin, impose, inflict, levy; offer, present, propose, state; compel, constrain, force, oblige; entice, incite, induce, urge; express, utter.

**putative** adj deemed, reckoned, reported, reputed, supposed.

**putrefy** vb corrupt, decay, decompose, fester, rot, stink.

**putrid** adj corrupt, decayed, decomposed, fetid, rank, rotten, stinking.

**puzzle** vb bewilder, confound, confuse, embarrass, gravel, mystify, nonplus, perplex, pose, stagger; complicate, entangle. * n conundrum, enigma, labyrinth, maze, paradox, poser, problem, riddle; bewilderment, complication, confusion, difficulty, dilemma, embarrassment, mystification, perplexity, point, quandary, question.

**pygmy** adj diminutive, dwarf, dwarfish, Lilliputian, little, midget, stunted, tiny. * n dwarf, Lilliputian, midget.

# Q

**quack**[1] vb, n cackle, cry, squeak.

**quack**[2] adj fake, false, sham. * n charlatan, empiric, humbug, impostor, mountebank, pretender.

**quadruple** adj fourfold, quadruplicate.

**quagmire** n bog, fen, marsh, morass, slough, swamp; difficulty, impasse, muddle, predicament.

**quail** vb blench, cower, droop, faint, flinch, shrink, tremble.

**quaint** adj antiquated, antique, archaic, curious, droll, extraordinary, fanciful, odd, old-fashioned, queer, singular, uncommon, unique, unusual; affected, fantastic, far-fetched, whimsical; artful, ingenious.

**quake** vb quiver, shake, shiver, shudder; move, vibrate. * n earthquake, shake, shudder.

**qualification** n ability, accomplishment, capability, competency, eligibility, fitness, suitability; condition, exception, limitation, modification, proviso, restriction, stipulation; abatement, allowance, diminution, mitigation.

**qualified** adj accomplished, certificated, certified, competent, fitted, equipped, licensed, trained; adapted, circumscribed, conditional, limited, modified, restricted.

**qualify** vb adapt, capacitate, empower, entitle, equip, fit; limit, modify, narrow, restrain, restrict; abate, assuage, ease, mitigate, moderate, reduce, soften; diminish, modulate, temper, regulate, vary.

**quality** n affection, attribute, characteristic, colour, distinction, feature, flavour, mark, nature, peculiarity, property, singularity, timbre, tinge, trait; character, condition, disposition, humour, mood, temper; brand, calibre, capacity, class, description, excellence, grade, kind, rank, sort, stamp, standing, station, status, virtue; aristocracy, gentility, gentry, noblesse, nobility.

**qualm** n agony, pang, throe; nausea, queasiness, sickness; compunction, remorse, uneasiness, twinge.

**quandary** n bewilderment, difficulty, dilemma, doubt, embarrassment, perplexity, pickle, plight, predicament, problem, puzzle, strait, uncertainty.

**quantity** n content, extent, greatness, measure, number, portion, share, size; aggregate, batch, amount, bulk, lot, mass, quantum, store, sum, volume; duration, length.

**quarrel** vb altercate, bicker, brawl, carp, cavil, clash, contend, differ, dispute, fight, jangle, jar, scold, scuffle, spar, spat, squabble, strive, wrangle. * n altercation, affray, bickering, brawl, breach, breeze, broil, clash, contention, contest, controversy, difference, disagreement, discord, dispute, dissension, disturbance, feud, fight, fray, imbroglio, jar, miff, misunderstanding, quarrelling, row, rupture, spat, squabble, strife, tiff, tumult, variance, wrangle.

**quarrelsome** adj argumentative, choleric, combative, contentious, cross, discordant, disputatious, dissentious, fiery, irascible, irritable, petulant, pugnacious, ugly, wranglesome.

**quarter** vb billet, lodge, post, station; allot, furnish, share. * n abode, billet, dwelling, habitation, lodgings, posts, quarters, stations; direction, district, locality, location, lodge, position, region, territory; clemency, mercy, mildness.

**quash** vb abate, abolish, annul, cancel, invalidate, nullify, overthrow; crush, extinguish, repress, stop, subdue, suppress.

**queasy** adj nauseated, pukish, seasick, sick, squeamish.

**queer** vb botch, harm, impair, mar, spoil. * adj curious, droll, extraordinary, fantastic, odd, peculiar, quaint, singular, strange, uncommon, unusual, whimsical; gay, homosexual.

**quell** vb conquer, crush, overcome, overpower, subdue; bridle, check, curb, extinguish, lay, quench, rein in, repress, restrain, stifle; allay, calm, compose, hush, lull, pacify, quiet, quieten, still, tranquillize; alleviate, appease, blunt, deaden, dull, mitigate, mollify, soften, soothe.

**quench** vb extinguish, put out; check, destroy, repress, satiate, stifle, still, suppress; allay, cool, dampen, extinguish, slake.

**querulous** adj .bewailing, complaining, cross, discontented, dissatisfied, fretful, fretting, irritable, mourning, murmuring, peevish, petulant, plaintive, touchy, whining.

**query** vb ask, enquire, inquire, question; dispute, doubt. * n enquiry, inquiry, interrogatory, issue, problem, question.

**quest** n expedition, journey, search, voyage; pursuit, suit; examination, enquiry, inquiry; demand, desire, invitation, prayer, request, solicitation.

**question** vb ask, catechize, enquire, examine, inquire, interrogate, quiz, sound out; doubt, query; challenge, dispute. * n examination, enquiry, inquiry, interpellation, interrogation; enquiry, inquiry, interrogatory, query; debate, discussion, disquisition, examination, investigation, issue, trial; controversy, dispute, doubt; motion, mystery, point, poser, problem, proposition, puzzle, topic.

**questionable** adj ambiguous, controversial, controvertible, debatable, doubtful, disputable, equivocal, problematic, problematical, suspicious, uncertain, undecided.

**quibble** vb cavil, equivocate, evade, prevaricate, shuffle. * n equivocation, evasion, pretence, prevarication, quirk, shift, shuffle, sophism, subtlety, subterfuge.

**quick** adj active, agile, alert, animated, brisk, lively, nimble, prompt, ready, smart, sprightly; expeditious, fast, fleet, flying, hurried, rapid, speedy, swift; adroit, apt, clever, dextrous, expert, skilful; choleric, hasty, impetuous, irascible, irritable, passionate, peppery, petulant, precipitate, sharp, unceremonious, testy, touchy, waspish; alive, animate, live, living.

**quicken** vb animate, energize, resuscitate, revivify, vivify; cheer, enliven, invigorate, reinvigorate, revive, whet; accelerate, dispatch, expedite, hasten, hurry, speed; actuate, excite, incite, kindle, refresh, sharpen, stimulate; accelerate, live, take effect.

**quickly** adv apace, fast, immediately, nimbly, quick, rapidly, readily, soon, speedily, swiftly.

**quickness** n celerity, dispatch, expedition, haste, rapidity, speed, swiftness, velocity; agility, alertness, activity, briskness, liveliness, nimbleness, promptness, readiness, smartness; adroitness, aptitude, aptness, dexterity, facility, knack; acumen, acuteness, keenness, penetration, perspicacity, sagacity, sharpness, shrewdness.

**quiescent** adj at rest, hushed, motionless, quiet, resting, still; calm, mute, placid, quiet, serene, still, tranquil, unagitated, undisturbed, unruffled.

**quiet** adj hushed, motionless, quiescent, still, unmoved; calm, contented, gentle, mild, meek, modest, peaceable, peaceful, placid, silent, smooth, tranquil, undemonstrative, unobtrusive, unruffled; patient; retired, secluded. * n calmness, peace, repose, rest, silence, stillness.

**quieten** vb arrest, discontinue, intermit, interrupt, still, stop, suspend; allay, appease, calm, compose, lull, pacify, sober, soothe, tranquillize; hush, silence; alleviate, assuage, blunt, dull, mitigate, moderate, mollify, soften.

**quip** n crank, flout, gibe, jeer, mock, quirk, repartee, retort, sarcasm, sally, scoff, sneer, taunt, witticism.

**quit** vb absolve, acquit, deliver, free, release; clear, deliver, discharge from, free, liberate, relieve; acquit, behave, conduct; carry through, perform; discharge, pay, repay, requite; relinquish, renounce, resign, stop, surrender; depart from, leave, withdraw from; abandon, desert, forsake, forswear. * adj absolved, acquitted, clear, discharged, free, released.

**quite** adv completely, entirely, exactly, perfectly, positively, precisely, totally, wholly.

**quiver** vb flicker, flutter, oscillate, palpitate, quake, play, shake, shiver, shudder, tremble, twitch, vibrate. * n shake, shiver, shudder, trembling.

**quixotic** adj absurd, chimerical, fanciful, fantastic, fantastical, freakish, imaginary, mad, romantic, utopian, visionary, wild.

**quiz** vb examine, question, test; peer at; banter, hoax, puzzle, ridicule. * n enigma, hoax, jest, joke, puzzle; jester, joker, hoax.

**quota** n allocation, allotment, apportionment, contingent, portion, proportion, quantity, share.

**quotation** n citation, clipping, cutting, extract, excerpt, reference, selection; estimate, rate, tender.

**quote** vb adduce, cite, excerpt, extract, illustrate, instance, name, repeat, take; estimate, tender.

# R

**rabble** n commonality, horde, mob, populace, riffraff, rout, scum, trash.

**rabid** adj frantic, furious, mad, raging, wild; bigoted, fanatical, intolerant, irrational, narrow-minded, rampant.

**race**[1] n ancestry, breed, family, generation, house, kindred, line, lineage, pedigree, stock, strain; clan, folk, nation, people, tribe; breed, children, descendants, issue, offspring, progeny, stock.

**race**[2] vb career, compete, contest, course, hasten, hurry, run, speed. * n career, chase, competition, contest, course, dash, heat, match, pursuit, run, sprint; flavour, quality, smack, strength, taste.

**rack** vb agonize, distress, excruciate, rend, torment, torture, wring; exhaust, force, harass, oppress, strain, stretch, wrest. * n agony, anguish, pang, torment, torture; crib, manger; neck, crag; dampness, mist, moisture, vapour.

**racket** n clamour, clatter, din, dissipation, disturbance, fracas, frolic, hubbub, noise, outcry, tumult, uproar; game, graft, scheme, understanding.

**racy** adj flavoursome, palatable, piquant, pungent, rich, spicy, strong; forcible, lively, pungent, smart, spirited, stimulating, vigorous, vivacious.

**radiance** n brightness, brilliance, brilliancy, effluence, efflux, emission, glare, glitter, light, lustre, refulgence, resplendence, shine, splendour.

**radiant** adj beaming, brilliant, effulgent, glittering, glorious, luminous, lustrous, resplendent, shining, sparkling, splendid; ecstatic, happy, pleased.

**radiate** vb beam, gleam, glitter, shine; emanate, emit; diffuse, spread.

**radical** adj constitutional, deep-seated, essential, fundamental, ingrained, inherent, innate, native, natural, organic, original, uncompromising; original, primitive, simple, uncompounded, underived; complete, entire, extreme, fanatic, insurgent, perfect, rebellious, thorough, total. * n etymon, radix, root; fanatic, revolutionary.

**rage** vb bluster, boil, chafe, foam, fret, fume, ravage, rave. * n excitement, frenzy, fury, madness, passion, rampage, raving, vehemence, wrath; craze, fashion, mania, mode, style, vogue.

**ragged** adj rent, tattered, torn; contemptible, mean, poor, shabby; jagged, rough, rugged, shaggy, uneven; discordant, dissonant, inharmonious, unmusical.

**raid** vb assault, forage, invade, pillage, plunder. * n attack, foray, invasion, inroad, plunder.

**rail** vb abuse, censure, inveigh, scoff, scold, sneer, upbraid.

**raillery** n banter, chaff, irony, joke, pleasantry, ridicule, satire.

**raiment** n array, apparel, attire, clothes, clothing, costume, dress, garb, garments, habiliment, habit, vestments, vesture.

**rain** vb drizzle, drop, fall, pour, shower, sprinkle, teem; bestow, lavish. * n cloudburst, downpour, drizzle, mist, shower, sprinkling.

**raise** vb boost, construct, erect, heave, hoist, lift, uplift, upraise, rear; advance, elevate, ennoble, exalt, promote; aggravate, amplify, augment, enhance, heighten, increase, invigorate; arouse, awake, cause, effect, excite, originate, produce, rouse, stir up, occasion, start; assemble, collect, get, levy, obtain; breed, cultivate, grow, propagate, rear; ferment, leaven, work.

**rake**[1] vb collect, comb, gather, scratch; ransack, scour.

**rake**[2] n debauchee, libertine, profligate, roué.

**rakish** adj debauched, dissipated, dissolute, lewd, licentious; cavalier, jaunty.

**ramble** vb digress, maunder, range, roam, rove, saunter, straggle, stray, stroll, wander. * n excursion, rambling, roving, tour, trip, stroll, wandering.

**rambling** adj discursive, irregular; straggling, strolling, wandering.

**ramification** n arborescence, branching, divarication, forking, radiation; branch, division, offshoot, subdivision; consequence, upshot.

**ramify** vb branch, divaricate, extend, separate.

**rampant** adj excessive, exuberant, luxuriant, rank, wanton; boisterous, dominant, headstrong, impetuous, predominant, raging, uncontrollable, unbridled, ungovernable, vehement, violent.

**rampart** n bulwark, circumvallation, defence, fence, fortification, guard, security, wall.

**rancid** adj bad, fetid, foul, fusty, musty, offensive, rank, sour, stinking, tainted.

**rancorous** adj bitter, implacable, malevolent, malicious, malign, malignant, resentful, spiteful, vindictive, virulent.

**rancour** n animosity, antipathy, bitterness, enmity, gall, grudge, hate, hatred, ill-will, malevolence, malice, malignity, spite, venom, vindictiveness.

**random** adj accidental, casual, chance, fortuitous, haphazard, irregular, stray, wandering.

**range** vb course, cruise, extend, ramble, roam, rove, straggle, stray, stroll, wander; bend, lie, run; arrange, class, dispose, rank. * n file, line, row, rank, tier; class, kind, order, sort; excursion, expedition, ramble, roving, wandering; amplitude, bound, command, compass, distance, extent, latitude, reach, scope, sweep, view; register.

**rank**[1] vb arrange, class, classify, range. * n file, line, order, range, row, tier; class, division, group, order, series; birth, blood, caste, degree, estate, grade, position, quality, sphere, stakes, standing; dignity, distinction, eminence, nobility.

**rank**[2] adj dense, exuberant, luxuriant, overabundant, overgrown, vigorous, wild; excessive, extreme, extravagant, flagrant, gross, rampant, sheer, unmitigated, utter, violent; fetid, foul, fusty, musty, offensive, rancid; fertile, productive, rich; coarse, disgusting.

**ransack** vb pillage, plunder, ravage, rifle, sack, strip; explore, overhaul, rummage, search thoroughly.

**ransom** vb deliver, emancipate, free, liberate, redeem, rescue, unfetter. * n money, payment pay-off, price; deliverance, liberation, redemption, release.

**rant** vb declaim, mouth, spout, vociferate. * n bombast, cant, exaggeration, fustian.

**rapacious** adj predacious, preying, raptorial; avaricious, grasping, greedy, ravenous, voracious.

**rapid** adj fast, fleet, quick, swift; brisk, expeditious, hasty, hurried, quick, speedy.

**rapine** n depredation, pillage, plunder, robbery, spoliation.

**rapt** adj absorbed, charmed, delighted, ecstatic, engrossed, enraptured, entranced, fascinated, inspired, spellbound.

**rapture** vb enrapture, ravish, transport. * n delight, exultation, enthusiasm, rhapsody; beatification, beatitude, bliss, ecstasy, felicity, happiness, joy, spell, transport.

**rare**[1] adj sparse, subtle, thin; extraordinary, infrequent, scarce, singular, strange, uncommon, unique, unusual; choice, excellent, exquisite, fine, incomparable, inimitable.

**rare**[2] adj bloody, underdone.

**rarity** n attenuation, ethereality, etherealness, rarefaction, rareness, tenuity, tenuousness, thinness; infrequency, scarcity, singularity, sparseness, uncommonness, unwontedness.

**rascal** n blackguard, caitiff, knave, miscreant, rogue, reprobate, scallywag, scapegrace, scamp, scoundrel, vagabond, villain.

**rash**[1] adj adventurous, audacious, careless, foolhardy, hasty, headlong, headstrong, heedless, incautious, inconsiderate, indiscreet, injudicious, impetuous, impulsive, incautious, precipitate, quick, rapid, reckless, temerarious, thoughtless, unguarded, unwary, venturesome.

**rash**[2] n breaking-out, efflorescence, eruption; epidemic, flood, outbreak, plague, spate.

**rashness** n carelessness, foolhardiness, hastiness, heedlessness, inconsideration, indiscretion, precipitation, recklessness, temerity, venturesomeness.

**rate**[1] vb appraise, compute, estimate, value. * n cost, price; class, degree, estimate, rank, value, valuation, worth; proportion, ration; assessment, charge, impost, tax.

**rate**[2] vb abuse, berate, censure, chide, criticize, find fault, reprimand, reprove, scold.

**ratify** vb confirm, corroborate, endorse, establish, seal, settle, substantiate; approve, bind, consent, sanction.

**ration** vb apportion, deal, distribute, dole, restrict. * n allowance, portion, quota, share.

**rational** adj intellectual, reasoning; equitable, fair, fit, just, moderate, natural, normal, proper, reasonable, right; discreet, enlightened, intelligent, judicious, sagacious, sensible, sound, wise.

**raucous** adj harsh, hoarse, husky, rough.

**ravage** vb consume, desolate, despoil, destroy, devastate, harry, overrun, pillage, plunder, ransack, ruin, sack, spoil, strip, waste. * n desolation, despoilment, destruction, devastation, havoc, pillage, plunder, rapine, ruin, spoil, waste.

**ravenous** adj devouring, ferocious, gluttonous, greedy, insatiable, omnivorous, ravening, rapacious, voracious.

**ravine** n canyon, cleft, defile, gap, gorge, gulch, gully, pass.

**raving** adj delirious, deranged, distracted, frantic, frenzied, furious, infuriated, mad, phrenetic, raging. * n delirium, frenzy, fury, madness, rage.

**ravish** vb abuse, debauch, defile, deflower, force, outrage, violate; captivate, charm, delight, enchant, enrapture, entrance, overjoy, transport; abduct, kidnap, seize, snatch, strip.

**raw** adj fresh, inexperienced, unpractised, unprepared, unseasoned, untried, unskilled; crude, green, immature, unfinished, unripe; bare, chafed, excoriated, galled, sensitive, sore; bleak, chilly, cold, cutting, damp, piercing, windswept; uncooked.

**ray** n beam, emanation, gleam, moonbeam, radiance, shaft, streak, sunbeam.

**raze** vb demolish, destroy, dismantle, extirpate, fell, level, overthrow, ruin, subvert; efface, erase, obliterate.

**reach** vb extend, stretch; grasp, hit, strike, touch; arrive at, attain, gain, get, obtain, win. * n capability, capacity, grasp.

**readily** adv easily, promptly, quickly; cheerfully, willingly.

**readiness** n alacrity, alertness, expedition, quickness, promptitude, promptness; aptitude, aptness, dexterity, easiness, expertness, facility, quickness, skill; preparation, preparedness, ripeness; cheerfulness, disposition, eagerness, ease, willingness.

**ready** vb arrange, equip, organize, prepare. * adj alert, expeditious, prompt, quick, punctual, speedy; adroit, apt, clever, dextrous, expert, facile, handy, keen, nimble, prepared, prompt, ripe, quick, sharp, skilful, smart; cheerful, disposed, eager, free, inclined, willing; accommodating, available, convenient, near, handy; easy, facile, fluent, offhand, opportune, short, spontaneous.

**real** adj absolute, actual, certain, literal, positive, practical, substantial, substantive, veritable; authentic, genuine, true; essential, internal, intrinsic.

**realize** vb accomplish, achieve, discharge, effect, effectuate, perfect, perform; apprehend, comprehend, experience, recognize, understand; externalize, substantiate; acquire, earn, gain, get, net, obtain, produce, sell.

**reality** n actuality, certainty, fact, truth, verity.

**really** adv absolutely, actually, certainly, indeed, positively, truly, verily, veritably.

**reap** vb acquire, crop, gain, gather, get, harvest, obtain, receive.

**rear**[1] adj aft, back, following, hind, last. * n background, reverse, setting; heel, posterior, rear end, rump, stern, tail; path, trail, train, wake.

**rear**[2] vb construct, elevate, erect, hoist, lift, raise; cherish, educate, foster, instruct, nourish, nurse, nurture, train; breed, grow; rouse, stir up.

**reason** vb argue, conclude, debate, deduce, draw from, infer, intellectualize, syllogize, think, trace. * n faculty, intellect, intelligence, judgement, mind, principle, sanity, sense, thinking, understanding; account, argument, basis, cause, consideration, excuse, explanation, gist, ground, motive, occasion, pretence, proof; aim, design, end, object, purpose; argument, reasoning; common sense, reasonableness, wisdom; equity, fairness, justice, right; exposition, rationale, theory.

**reasonable** adj equitable, fair, fit, honest, just, proper, rational, right, suitable; enlightened, intelligent, judicious, sagacious, sensible, wise; considerable, fair, moderate, tolerable; credible, intellectual, plausible, well-founded; sane, sober, sound; cheap, inexpensive, low-priced.

**rebate** vb abate, bate, blunt, deduct, diminish, lessen, reduce; cut, pare, rabbet. * n decrease, decrement, diminution, lessening; allowance, deduction, discount, reduction.

**rebel** vb mutiny, resist, revolt, strike. * adj insubordinate, insurgent, mutinous, rebellious. * n insurgent, mutineer, traitor.

**rebellion** n anarchy, insubordination, insurrection, mutiny, resistance, revolt, revolution, uprising.

**rebellious** adj contumacious, defiant, disloyal, disobedient, insubordinate, intractable, obstinate, mutinous, rebel, refractory, seditious.

**rebuff** vb check, chide, oppose, refuse, reject, repel, reprimand, resist, snub. * n check, defeat, discouragement, opposition, rejection, resistance, snub.

**rebuke** vb blame, censure, chide, lecture, upbraid, reprehend, reprimand, reprove, scold, silence. * n blame, censure, chiding, expostulation, remonstrance, reprimand, reprehension, reproach, reproof, reproval; affliction, chastisement, punishment.

**recall** vb abjure, abnegate, annul, cancel, countermand, deny, nullify, overrule, recant, repeal, repudiate, rescind, retract, revoke, swallow, withdraw; commemorate, recollect, remember, retrace, review, revive. * n abjuration, abnegation, annulment, cancellation, nullification, recantation, repeal, repudiation, rescindment, retraction, revocation, withdrawal; memory, recollection, remembrance, reminiscence.

**recant** vb abjure, annul, disavow, disown, recall, renounce, repudiate, retract, revoke, unsay.

**recapitulate** vb epitomize, recite, rehearse, reiterate, repeat, restate, review, summarize.

**recede** vb desist, ebb, retire, regress, retreat, retrograde, return, withdraw.

**receive** vb accept, acquire, derive, gain, get, obtain, take; admit, shelter, take in; entertain, greet, welcome; allow, permit, tolerate; adopt, approve, believe, credit, embrace, follow, learn, understand; accommodate, carry, contain, hold, include, retain; bear, encounter, endure, experience, meet, suffer, sustain.

**recent** adj fresh, new, novel; latter, modern, young; deceased, foregoing, late, preceding, retiring.

**reception** n acceptance, receipt, receiving; entertainment, greeting, welcome; levee, soiree, party; admission, credence; belief, credence, recognition.

**recess** n alcove, corner, depth, hollow, niche, nook, privacy, retreat, seclusion; break, holiday, intermission, interval, respite, vacation; recession, retirement, retreat, withdrawal.

**reciprocal** adj alternate, commutable, complementary, correlative, correspondent, mutual.

**recital** n rehearsal, repetition, recitation; account, description, detail, explanation, narration, relation, statement, telling.

**recite** vb declaim, deliver, rehearse, repeat; describe, mention, narrate, recount, relate, tell; count, detail, enumerate, number, recapitulate.

**reckless** adj breakneck, careless, desperate, devil-may-care, flighty, foolhardy, giddy, harebrained, headlong, heedless, inattentive, improvident, imprudent, inconsiderate, indifferent, indiscreet, mindless, negligent, rash, regardless, remiss, thoughtless, temerarious, uncircumspect, unconcerned, unsteady, volatile, wild.

**reckon** vb calculate, cast, compute, consider, count, enumerate, guess, number; account, class, esteem, estimate, regard, repute, value.

**reckoning** n calculation, computation, consideration, counting; account, bill, charge, estimate, register, score; arrangement, settlement.

**reclaim** vb amend, correct, reform; recover, redeem,

regenerate, regain, reinstate, restore; civilize, tame.

**recline** vb couch, lean, lie, lounge, repose, rest.

**recluse** adj anchoritic, anchoritical, cloistered, eremitic, eremitical, hermitic, hermitical, reclusive, solitary. * n anchorite, ascetic, eremite, hermit, monk, solitary.

**reclusive** adj recluse, retired, secluded, sequestered, sequestrated, solitary.

**recognition** n identification, memory, recollection, remembrance; acknowledgement, appreciation, avowal, comprehension, confession, notice; allowance, concession.

**recognize** vb apprehend, identify, perceive, remember; acknowledge, admit, avow, confess, own; allow, concede, grant; greet, salute.

**recoil** vb react, rebound, reverberate; retire, retreat, withdraw; blench, fail, falter, quail, shrink. * n backstroke, boomerang, elasticity, kick, reaction, rebound, repercussion, resilience, revulsion, ricochet, shrinking.

**recollect** vb recall, remember, reminisce.

**recollection** n memory, remembrance, reminiscence.

**recommend** vb approve, commend, endorse, praise, sanction; commit; advise, counsel, prescribe, suggest.

**recommendation** n advocacy, approbation, approval, commendation, counsel, credential, praise, testimonial.

**recompense** vb compensate, remunerate, repay, requite, reward, satisfy; indemnify, redress, reimburse. * n amends, compensation, indemnification, indemnity, remuneration, repayment, reward, satisfaction; requital, retribution.

**reconcilable** adj appeasable, forgiving, placable; companionable, congruous, consistent.

**reconcile** vb appease, conciliate, pacify, placate, propitiate, reunite; content, harmonize, regulate; adjust, compose, heal, settle.

**recondite** adj concealed, dark, hidden, mystic, mystical, obscure, occult, secret, transcendental.

**record** vb chronicle, enter, note, register. * n account, annals, archive, chronicle, diary, docket, enrolment, entry, file, list, minute, memoir, memorandum, memorial, note, proceedings, register, registry, report, roll, score; mark, memorial, relic, trace, track, trail, vestige; memory, remembrance; achievement, career, history.

**recount** vb describe, detail, enumerate, mention, narrate, particularize, portray, recite, relate, rehearse, report, tell.

**recover** vb recapture, reclaim, regain; rally, recruit, repair, retrieve; cure, heal, restore, revive; redeem, rescue, salvage, save; convalesce, recuperate.

**recreant** adj base, cowardly, craven, dastardly, faint-hearted, mean-spirited, pusillanimous, yielding; apostate, backsliding, faithless, false, perfidious, treacherous, unfaithful, untrue. * n coward, dastard; apostate, backslider, renegade.

**recreation** n amusement, cheer, diversion, entertainment, fun, game, leisure, pastime, play, relaxation, sport.

**recreational** adj amusing, diverting, entertaining, refreshing, relaxing, relieving.

**recruit** vb repair, replenish; recover, refresh, regain, reinvigorate, renew, renovate, restore, retrieve, revive, strengthen, supply. * n auxiliary, beginner, helper, learner, novice, tyro.

**rectify** vb adjust, amend, better, correct, emend, improve, mend, redress, reform, regulate, straighten.

**rectitude** n conscientiousness, equity, goodness, honesty, integrity, justice, principle, probity, right, righteousness, straightforwardness, uprightness, virtue.

**recumbent** adj leaning, lying, prone, prostrate, reclining; idle, inactive, listless, reposing.

**recur** vb reappear, resort, return, revert.

**recusancy** n dissent, heresy, heterodoxy, nonconformity.

**redeem** vb reform, regain, repurchase, retrieve; free, liberate, ransom, rescue, save; deliver, reclaim, recover, reinstate; atone, compensate for, recompense; discharge, fulfil, keep, perform, satisfy.

**redemption** n buying, compensation, recovery, repurchase, retrieval; deliverance, liberation, ransom, release, rescue, salvation; discharge, fulfilment, performance.

**redolent** adj aromatic, balmy, fragrant, odoriferous, odorous, scented, sweet, sweet-smelling.

**redoubtable** adj awful, doughty, dreadful, formidable, terrible, valiant.

**redound** vb accrue, conduce, contribute, result, tend.

**redress** vb amend, correct, order, rectify, remedy, repair; compensate, ease, relieve. * n abatement, amends, atonement, compensation, correction,

cure, indemnification, rectification, repair, righting, remedy, relief, reparation, satisfaction.

**reduce** vb bring; form, make, model, mould, remodel, render, resolve, shape; abate, abbreviate, abridge, attenuate, contract, curtail, decimate, decrease, diminish, lessen, minimize, shorten, thin; abase, debase, degrade, depress, dwarf, impair, lower, weaken; capture, conquer, master, overpower, overthrow, subject, subdue, subjugate, vanquish; impoverish, ruin; resolve, solve.

**redundant** adj copious, excessive, exuberant, fulsome, inordinate, lavish, needless, overflowing, overmuch, plentiful, prodigal, superabundant, replete, superfluous, unnecessary, useless; diffuse, periphrastic, pleonastic, tautological, verbose, wordy.

**reel**[1] n capstan, winch, windlass; bobbin, spool.

**reel**[2] vb falter, flounder, heave, lurch, pitch, plunge, rear, rock, roll, stagger, sway, toss, totter, tumble, wallow, welter, vacillate; spin, swing, turn, twirl, wheel, whirl. * n gyre, pirouette, spin, turn, twirl, wheel, whirl.

**re-establish** vb re-found, rehabilitate, reinstall, reinstate, renew, renovate, replace, restore.

**refer** vb commit, consign, direct, leave, relegate, send, submit; ascribe, assign, attribute, impute; appertain, belong, concern, pertain, point, relate, respect, touch; appeal, apply, consult; advert, allude, cite, quote.

**referee** vb arbitrate, judge, umpire. * n arbiter, arbitrator, judge, umpire.

**reference** n concern, connection, regard, respect; allusion, ascription, citation, hint, intimation, mark, reference, relegation.

**refine** vb clarify, cleanse, defecate, fine, purify; cultivate, humanize, improve, polish, rarefy, spiritualize.

**refined** adj courtly, cultured, genteel, polished, polite; discerning, discriminating, fastidious, sensitive; filtered, processed, purified.

**refinement** n clarification, filtration, purification, sublimation; betterment, improvement; delicacy, cultivation, culture, elegance, elevation, finish, gentility, good breeding, polish, politeness, purity, spirituality, style.

**reflect** vb copy, imitate, mirror, reproduce; cogitate, consider, contemplate, deliberate, meditate, muse, ponder, ruminate, study, think.

**reflection** n echo, shadow; cogitation, consideration, contemplation, deliberation, idea, meditation, musing, opinion, remark, rumination, thinking, thought; aspersion, blame, censure, criticism, disparagement, reproach, slur.

**reflective** adj reflecting, reflexive; cogitating, deliberating, musing, pondering, reasoning, thoughtful.

**reform** vb amend, ameliorate, better, correct, improve, mend, meliorate, rectify, reclaim, redeem, regenerate, repair, restore; reconstruct, remodel, reshape. * n amendment, correction, progress, reconstruction, rectification, reformation.

**reformation** n amendment, emendation, improvement, reform; adoption, conversion, redemption; refashioning, regeneration, reproduction, reconstruction.

**refractory** adj cantankerous, contumacious, cross-grained, disobedient, dogged, headstrong, heady, incoercible, intractable, mulish, obstinate, perverse, recalcitrant, self-willed, stiff, stubborn, sullen, ungovernable, unmanageable, unruly, unyielding.

**refrain**[1] vb abstain, cease, desist, forbear, stop, withhold.

**refrain**[2] n chorus, song, undersong.

**refresh** vb air, brace, cheer, cool, enliven, exhilarate, freshen, invigorate, reanimate, recreate, recruit, reinvigorate, revive, regale, slake.

**refreshing** adj comfortable, cooling, grateful, invigorating, pleasant, reanimating, restful, reviving.

**refuge** n asylum, covert, harbour, haven, protection, retreat, safety, sanction, security, shelter.

**refulgent** adj bright, brilliant, effulgent, lustrous, radiant, resplendent, shining.

**refund** vb reimburse, repay, restore, return. * n reimbursement, repayment.

**refuse**[1] n chaff, discard, draff, dross, dregs, garbage, junk, leavings, lees, litter, lumber, offal, recrement, remains, rubbish, scoria, scum, sediment, slag, sweepings, trash, waste.

**refuse**[2] vb decline, deny, withhold; disallow, disavow, exclude, rebuff, reject, renege, renounce, repel, repudiate, repulse, revoke, veto.

**refute** vb confute, defeat, disprove, overcome, overthrow, rebut, repel, silence.

**regain** vb recapture, recover, re-obtain, repossess, retrieve.

**regal** adj imposing, imperial, kingly, noble, royal, sovereign.

**regale** vb delight, entertain, gratify, refresh; banquet, feast.

**regard** vb behold, gaze, look, notice, mark, observe, remark, see, view, watch; attend to, consider, heed, mind, respect; esteem, honour, revere, reverence, value; account, believe, estimate, deem, hold, imagine, reckon, suppose, think, treat, use. * n aspect, gaze, look, view; attention, attentiveness, care, concern, consideration, heed, notice, observance; account, reference, relation, respect; admiration, affection, attachment, deference, esteem, estimation, favour, honour, interest, liking, love, respect, reverence, sympathy, value; account, eminence, note, reputation, repute; condition, matter, point.

**regardful** adj attentive, careful, considerate, deferential, heedful, mindful, observing, thoughtful, watchful.

**regarding** prep concerning, respecting, touching.

**regardless** adj careless, disregarding, heedless, inattentive, indifferent, mindless, neglectful, negligent, unconcerned, unmindful, unobservant. * adv however, irrespectively, nevertheless, nonetheless, notwithstanding.

**regenerate** vb reproduce; renovate, revive; change, convert, renew, sanctify. * adj born-again, converted, reformed, regenerated.

**regime** n administration, government, rule.

**region** n climate, clime, country, district, division, latitude, locale, locality, province, quarter, scene, territory, tract; area, neighbourhood, part, place, portion, spot, space, sphere, terrain, vicinity.

**register** vb delineate, portray, record, show. * n annals, archive, catalogue, chronicle, list, record, roll, schedule; clerk, registrar, registry; compass, range.

**regret** vb bewail, deplore, grieve, lament, repine, sorrow; bemoan, repent, mourn, rue. * n concern, disappointment, grief, lamentation, rue, sorrow, trouble; compunction, contrition, penitence, remorse, repentance, repining, self-condemnation, self-reproach.

**regular** adj conventional, natural, normal, ordinary, typical; correct, customary, cyclic, established, fixed, habitual, periodic, periodical, recurring, reasonable, rhythmic, seasonal, stated, usual; steady, constant, uniform, even; just, methodical, orderly, punctual, systematic, unvarying; complete, genuine, indubitable, out-and-out, perfect, thorough; balanced, consistent, symmetrical.

**regulate** vb adjust, arrange, dispose, methodize, order, organize, settle, standardize, time, systematize; conduct, control, direct, govern, guide, manage, rule.

**regulation** adj customary, mandatory, official, required, standard. * n adjustment, arrangement, control, disposal, disposition, law, management, order, ordering, precept, rule, settlement.

**rehabilitate** vb reinstate, re-establish, restore; reconstruct, reconstitute, reintegrate, reinvigorate, renew, renovate.

**rehearsal** n drill, practice, recital, recitation, repetition; account, history, mention, narration, narrative, recounting; relation, statement, story, telling.

**rehearse** vb recite, repeat; delineate, depict, describe, detail, enumerate, narrate, portray, recapitulate, recount, relate, tell.

**reign** vb administer, command, govern, influence, predominate, prevail, rule. * n control, dominion, empire, influence, power, royalty, sovereignty, power, rule, sway.

**reimburse** vb refund, repay, restore; compensate, indemnify, requite, satisfy.

**rein** vb bridle, check, control, curb, guide, harness, hold, restrain, restrict. * n bridle, check, curb, harness, restraint, restriction.

**reinforce** vb augment, fortify, strengthen.

**reinstate** vb re-establish, rehabilitate, reinstall, replace, restore.

**reject** vb cashier, discard, dismiss, eject, exclude, pluck; decline, deny, disallow, despise, disapprove, disbelieve, rebuff, refuse, renounce, repel, repudiate, scout, slight, spurn, veto. * n cast-off, discard, failure, refusal, repudiation.

**rejoice** vb cheer, delight, enliven, enrapture, exhilarate, gladden, gratify, please, transport; crow, exult, delight, gloat, glory, jubilate, triumph, vaunt.

**rejoin** vb answer, rebut, respond, retort.

**relate** vb describe, detail, mention, narrate, recite, recount, rehearse, report, tell; apply, connect, correlate.

**relation** n account, chronicle, description, detail, explanation, history, mention, narration, narrative, recital, rehearsal, report, statement, story, tale; affinity, application, bearing, connection, correlation, dependency, pertinence, relationship; concern, reference, regard, respect; alliance, nearness, propinquity, rapport; blood, consanguinity, cousinship, kin, kindred, kinship, relationship; kinsman, kinswoman, relative.

**relax** vb loose, loosen, slacken, unbrace, unstrain; debilitate, enervate, enfeeble, prostrate, unbrace, unstring, weaken; abate, diminish, lessen, mitigate, reduce, remit; amuse, divert, ease, entertain, recreate, unbend.

**release** vb deliver, discharge, disengage, exempt, extricate, free, liberate, loose, unloose; acquit, discharge, quit, relinquish, remit. * n deliverance, discharge, freedom, liberation; absolution, dispensation, excuse, exemption, exoneration; acquaintance, clearance.

**relentless** adj cruel, hard, impenitent, implacable, inexorable, merciless, obdurate, pitiless, rancorous, remorseless, ruthless, unappeasable, uncompassionate, unfeeling, unforgiving, unmerciful, unpitying, unrelenting, unyielding, vindictive.

**relevant** adj applicable, appropriate, apposite, apt, apropos, fit, germane, pertinent, proper, relative, suitable.

**reliable** adj authentic, certain, constant, dependable, sure, trustworthy, trusty, unfailing.

**reliance** n assurance, confidence, credence, dependence, hope, trust.

**relic** n keepsake, memento, memorial, remembrance, souvenir, token, trophy; trace, vestige.

**relics** npl fragments, leavings, remainder, remains, remnants, ruins, scraps; body, cadaver, corpse, remains.

**relict** n dowager, widow.

**relief** n aid, alleviation, amelioration, assistance, assuagement, comfort, deliverance, ease, easement, help, mitigation, reinforcement, respite, rest, succour, softening, support; indemnification, redress, remedy; embossment, projection, prominence, protrusion; clearness, distinction, perspective, vividness.

**relieve** vb aid, comfort, help, spell, succour, support, sustain; abate, allay, alleviate, assuage, cure, diminish, ease, lessen, lighten, mitigate, remedy, remove, soothe; indemnify, redress, right, repair; disengage, free, release, remedy, rescue.

**religious** adj devotional, devout, god-fearing, godly, holy, pious, prayerful, spiritual; conscientious, exact, rigid, scrupulous, strict; canonical, divine, theological.

**relinquish** vb abandon, desert, forsake, forswear, leave, quit, renounce, resign, vacate; abdicate, cede, forbear, forgo, give up, surrender, yield.

**relish** vb appreciate, enjoy, like, prefer; season,

flavour, taste. * n appetite, appreciation, enjoyment, fondness, gratification, gusto, inclination, liking, partiality, predilection, taste, zest; cast, flavour, manner, quality, savour, seasoning, sort, tang, tinge, touch; appetizer, condiment.

**reluctance** n aversion, backwardness, disinclination, dislike, loathing, repugnance, unwillingness.

**reluctant** adj averse, backward, disinclined, hesitant, indisposed, loath, unwilling.

**rely** vb confide, count, depend, hope, lean, reckon, repose, trust.

**remain** vb abide, continue, endure, last; exceed, persist, survive; abide, continue, dwell, halt, inhabit, rest, sojourn, stay, stop, tarry, wait.

**remainder** n balance, excess, leavings, remains, remnant, residue, rest, surplus.

**remark** vb heed, notice, observe, regard; comment, express, mention, observe, say, state, utter. * n consideration, heed, notice, observation, regard; annotation, comment, gloss, note, stricture; assertion, averment, comment, declaration, saying, statement, utterance.

**remarkable** adj conspicuous, distinguished, eminent, extraordinary, famous, notable, noteworthy, noticeable, pre-eminent, rare, singular, strange, striking, uncommon, unusual, wonderful.

**remedy** vb cure, heal, help, palliate, relieve; amend, correct, rectify, redress, repair, restore, retrieve. * n antidote, antitoxin, corrective, counteractive, cure, help, medicine, nostrum, panacea, restorative, specific; redress, reparation, restitution, restoration; aid, assistance, relief.

**remembrance** n recollection, reminiscence, retrospection; keepsake, memento, memorial, memory, reminder, souvenir, token; consideration, regard, thought.

**reminiscence** n memory, recollection, remembrance, retrospective.

**remiss** adj backward, behindhand, dilatory, indolent, languid, lax, lazy, slack, slow, tardy; careless, dilatory, heedless, idle, inattentive, neglectful, negligent, shiftless, slothful, thoughtless.

**remission** n abatement, decrease, diminution, lessening, mitigation, moderation, reduction, relaxation; cancellation, discharge, release, relinquishment; intermission, interruption, pause, rest, stop, stoppage, suspense, suspension; absolution, acquittal, excuse, exoneration, forgiveness, indulgence, pardon.

**remit** vb replace, restore, return; abate, bate, diminish, relax; release; absolve, condone, excuse, forgive, overlook, pardon; relinquish, resign, surrender; consign, forward, refer, send, transmit. * n authorization, brief, instructions, orders.

**remnant** n remainder, remains, residue, rest, trace; fragment, piece, scrap.

**remorse** n compunction, contrition, penitence, qualm, regret, repentance, reproach, self-reproach, sorrow.

**remorseless** adj cruel, barbarous, hard, harsh, implacable, inexorable, merciless, pitiless, relentless, ruthless, savage, uncompassionate, unmerciful, unrelenting.

**remote** adj distant, far, out-of-the-way; alien, far-fetched, foreign, inappropriate, unconnected, unrelated; abstracted, separated; inconsiderable, slight; isolated, removed, secluded, sequestrated.

**removal** n abstraction, departure, dislodgement, displacement, relegation, remove, shift, transference; elimination, extraction, withdrawal; abatement, destruction; discharge, dismissal, ejection, expulsion.

**remove** vb carry, dislodge, displace, shift, transfer, transport; abstract, extract, withdraw; abate, banish, destroy, suppress; cashier, depose, discharge, dismiss, eject, expel, oust, retire; depart, move.

**remunerate** vb compensate, indemnify, pay, recompense, reimburse, repay, requite, reward, satisfy.

**remuneration** n compensation, earnings, indemnity, pay, payment, recompense, reimbursement, reparation, repayment, reward, salary, wages.

**remunerative** adj gainful, lucrative, paying, profitable; compensatory, recompensing, remuneratory, reparative, requiting, rewarding.

**rend** vb break, burst, cleave, crack, destroy, dismember, dissever, disrupt, divide, fracture, lacerate, rive, rupture, sever, shiver, snap, split, sunder, tear.

**render** vb restore, return, surrender; assign, deliver, give, present; afford, contribute, furnish, supply, yield; construe, interpret, translate.

**rendition** n restitution, return, surrender; delineation, exhibition, interpretation, rendering, representation, reproduction; translation, version.

**renegade** adj apostate, backsliding, disloyal, false, outlawed, rebellious, recreant, unfaithful. * n apostate, backslider, recreant, turncoat; deserter, outlaw, rebel, revolter; traitor; vagabond, wretch.

**renew** vb rebuild, recreate, re-establish, refit, refresh, rejuvenate, renovate, repair, replenish, restore, resuscitate, revive; continue, recommence, repeat; iterate, reiterate; regenerate, transform.

**renounce** vb abjure, abnegate, decline, deny, disclaim, disown, forswear, neglect, recant, repudiate, reject, slight; abandon, abdicate, drop, forgo, forsake, desert, leave, quit, relinquish, resign.

**renovate** vb reconstitute, re-establish, refresh, refurbish, renew, restore, revamp; reanimate, recreate, regenerate, reproduce, resuscitate, revive, revivify.

**renown** n celebrity, distinction, eminence, fame, figure, glory, honour, greatness, name, note, notability, notoriety, reputation, repute.

**renowned** adj celebrated, distinguished, eminent, famed, famous, honoured, illustrious, remarkable, wonderful.

**rent**[1] n breach, break, crack, cleft, crevice, fissure, flaw, fracture, gap, laceration, opening, rift, rupture, separation, split, tear; schism.

**rent**[2] vb hire, lease, let. * n income, rental, revenue.

**repair**[1] vb mend, patch, piece, refit, retouch, tinker, vamp; correct, recruit, restore, retrieve. * n mending, refitting, renewal, reparation, restoration.

**repair**[2] vb betake oneself, go, move, resort, turn.

**repairable** adj curable, recoverable, reparable, restorable, retrievable.

**reparable** adj curable, recoverable, repairable, restorable, retrievable.

**reparation** n renewal, repair, restoration; amends, atonement, compensation, correction, indemnification, recompense, redress, requital, restitution, satisfaction.

**repay** vb refund, reimburse, restore, return; compensate, recompense, remunerate, reward, satisfy; avenge, retaliate, revenge.

**repeal** vb abolish, annul, cancel, recall, rescind, reverse; revoke. * n abolition, abrogation, annulment, cancellation, rescission, reversal, revocation.

**repeat** vb double, duplicate, iterate; cite, narrate, quote, recapitulate, recite, rehearse; echo, renew, reproduce. * n duplicate, duplication, echo, iteration, recapitulation, reiteration, repetition.

**repel** vb beat, disperse, repulse, scatter; check, confront, oppose, parry, rebuff, resist, withstand; decline, refuse, reject; disgust, revolt, sicken.

**repellent** adj abhorrent, disgusting, forbidding, repelling, repugnant, repulsive, revolting, uninviting.

**repent** vb atone, regret, relent, rue, sorrow.

**repentance** n compunction, contriteness, contrition,

penitence, regret, remorse, self-accusation, self-condemnation, self-reproach.

**repentant** adj contrite, penitent, regretful, remorseful, rueful, sorrowful, sorry.

**repercussion** n rebound, recoil, reverberation; backlash, consequence, result.

**repetition** n harping, iteration, recapitulation, reiteration; diffuseness, redundancy, tautology, verbosity; narration, recital, rehearsal, relation, retailing; recurrence, renewal.

**repine** vb croak, complain, fret, grumble, long, mope, murmur.

**replace** vb re-establish, reinstate, reset; refund, repay, restore; succeed, supersede, supplant.

**replenish** vb fill, refill, renew, re-supply; enrich, furnish, provide, store, supply.

**replete** adj abounding, charged, exuberant, fraught, full, glutted, gorged, satiated, well-stocked.

**repletion** n abundance, exuberance, fullness, glut, profusion, satiation, satiety, surfeit.

**replica** n autograph, copy, duplicate, facsimile, reproduction.

**reply** vb answer, echo, rejoin, respond. * n acknowledgement, answer, rejoinder, repartee, replication, response, retort.

**report** vb announce, annunciate, communicate, declare; advertise, broadcast, bruit, describe, detail, herald, mention, narrate, noise, promulgate, publish, recite, relate, rumour, state, tell; minute, record. * n account, announcement, communication, declaration, statement; advice, description, detail, narration, narrative, news, recital, story, tale, talk, tidings; gossip, hearsay, rumour; clap, detonation, discharge, explosion, noise, repercussion, sound; fame, reputation, repute; account, bulletin, minute, note, record, statement.

**repose**[1] vb compose, recline, rest, settle; couch, lie, recline, sleep, slumber; confide, lean. * n quiet, recumbence, recumbency, rest, sleep, slumber; breathing time, inactivity, leisure, respite, relaxation; calm, ease, peace, peacefulness, quietness, quietude, stillness, tranquillity.

**repose**[2] vb place, put, stake; deposit, lodge, reposit, store.

**repository** n conservatory, depository, depot, magazine, museum, receptacle, repertory, storehouse, storeroom, thesaurus, treasury, vault.

**reprehend** vb accuse, blame, censure, chide, rebuke, reprimand, reproach, reprove, upbraid.

**reprehensible** *adj* blameable, blameworthy, censurable, condemnable, culpable, reprovable.

**reprehension** *n* admonition, blame, censure, condemnation, rebuke, reprimand, reproof.

**represent** *vb* exhibit, express, show; delineate, depict, describe, draw, portray, sketch; act, impersonate, mimic, personate, personify; exemplify, illustrate, image, reproduce, symbolize, typify.

**representation** *n* delineation, exhibition, show; impersonation, personation, simulation; account, description, narration, narrative, relation, statement; image, likeness, model, portraiture, resemblance, semblance; sight, spectacle; expostulation, remonstrance.

**representative** *adj* figurative, illustrative, symbolic, typical; delegated, deputed, representing. * *n* agent, commissioner, delegate, deputy, emissary, envoy, legate, lieutenant, messenger, proxy, substitute.

**repress** *vb* choke, crush, dull, overcome, overpower, silence, smother, subdue, suppress, quell; bridle, chasten, chastise, check, control, curb, restrain; appease, calm, quiet.

**reprimand** *vb* admonish, blame, censure, chide, rebuke, reprehend, reproach, reprove, upbraid. * *n* admonition, blame, censure, rebuke, reprehension, reproach, reprobation, reproof, reproval.

**reprint** *vb* republish. * *n* reimpression, republication; copy.

**reproach** *vb* blame, censure, rebuke, reprehend, reprimand, reprove, upbraid; abuse, accuse, asperse, condemn, defame, discredit, disparage, revile, traduce, vilify. * *n* abuse, blame, censure, condemnation, contempt, contumely, disapprobation, disapproval, expostulation, insolence, invective, railing, rebuke, remonstrance, reprobation, reproof, reviling, scorn, scurrility, upbraiding, vilification; abasement, discredit, disgrace, dishonour, disrepute, indignity, ignominy, infamy, insult, obloquy, odium, offence, opprobrium, scandal, shame, slur, stigma.

**reproachful** *adj* abusive, censorious, condemnatory, contemptuous, contumelious, damnatory, insolent, insulting, offensive, opprobrious, railing, reproving, sacrifice, scolding, scornful, scurrilous, upbraiding, vituperative; base, discreditable, disgraceful, dishonourable, disreputable, infamous, scandalous, shameful, vile.

**reprobate** *vb* censure, condemn, disapprove, discard,

reject, reprehend; disallow; abandon, disown. * *adj* abandoned, base, castaway, corrupt, depraved, graceless, hardened, irredeemable, lost, profligate, shameless, vile, vitiated, wicked. * *n* caitiff, castaway, miscreant, outcast, rascal, scamp, scoundrel, sinner, villain.

**reproduce** *vb* copy, duplicate, emulate, imitate, print, repeat, represent; breed, generate, procreate, propagate.

**reproof** *n* admonition, animadversion, blame, castigation, censure, chiding, condemnation, correction, criticism, lecture, monition, objurgation, rating, rebuke, reprehension, reprimand, reproach, reproval, upbraiding.

**reprove** *vb* admonish, blame, castigate, censure, chide, condemn, correct, criticize, inculpate, lecture, objurgate, rate, rebuke, reprimand, reproach, scold, upbraid.

**reptilian** *adj* abject, crawling, creeping, grovelling, low, mean, treacherous, vile, vulgar.

**repudiate** *vb* abjure, deny, disavow, discard, disclaim, disown, nullify, reject, renounce.

**repugnance** *n* contrariety, contrariness, incompatibility, inconsistency, irreconcilability, irreconcilableness, unsuitability, unsuitableness; contest, opposition, resistance, struggle; antipathy, aversion, detestation, dislike, hatred, hostility, reluctance, repulsion, unwillingness.

**repugnant** *adj* incompatible, inconsistent, irreconcilable; adverse, antagonistic, contrary, hostile, inimical, opposed, opposing, unfavourable; detestable, distasteful, offensive, repellent, repulsive.

**repulse** *vb* check, defeat, refuse, reject, repel. * *n* repelling, repulsion; denial, refusal; disappointment, failure.

**repulsion** *n* abhorrence, antagonism, anticipation, aversion, discard, disgust, dislike, hatred, hostility, loathing, rebuff, rejection, repugnance, repulse, spurning.

**repulsive** *adj* abhorrent, cold, disagreeable, disgusting, forbidding, frigid, harsh, hateful, loathsome, nauseating, nauseous, odious, offensive, repellent, repugnant, reserved, revolting, sickening, ugly, unpleasant.

**reputable** *adj* creditable, estimable, excellent, good, honourable, respectable, worthy.

**reputation** *n* account, character, fame, mark, name, repute; celebrity, credit, distinction, eclat, esteem,

**repute** estimation, glory, honour, prestige, regard, renown, report, respect; notoriety.

**repute** vb account, consider, deem, esteem, estimate, hold, judge, reckon, regard, think.

**request** vb ask, beg, beseech, call, claim, demand, desire, entreat, pray, solicit, supplicate. * n asking, entreaty, importunity, invitation, petition, prayer, requisition, solicitation, suit, supplication.

**require** vb beg, beseech, bid, claim, crave, demand, dun, importune, invite, pray, requisition, request, sue, summon; need, want; direct, enjoin, exact, order, prescribe.

**requirement** n claim, demand, exigency, market, need, needfulness, requisite, requisition, request, urgency, want; behest, bidding, charge, command, decree, exaction, injunction, mandate, order, precept.

**requisite** adj essential, imperative, indispensable, necessary, needful, needed, required. * n essential, necessity, need, requirement.

**requite** vb compensate, pay, remunerate, reciprocate, recompense, repay, reward, satisfy; avenge, punish, retaliate, satisfy.

**rescind** vb abolish, abrogate, annul, cancel, countermand, quash, recall, repeal, reverse, revoke, vacate, void.

**rescue** vb deliver, extricate, free, liberate, preserve, ransom, recapture, recover, redeem, release, retake, save. * n deliverance, extrication, liberation, redemption, release, salvation.

**research** vb analyse, examine, explore, inquire, investigate, probe, study. * n analysis, examination, exploration, inquiry, investigation, scrutiny, study.

**resemblance** n affinity, agreement, analogy, likeness, semblance, similarity, similitude; counterpart, facsimile, image, representation.

**resemble** vb compare, liken; copy, counterfeit, imitate.

**resentful** adj angry, bitter, choleric, huffy, hurt, irascible, irritable, malignant, revengeful, sore, touchy.

**resentment** n acrimony, anger, annoyance, bitterness, choler, displeasure, dudgeon, fury, gall, grudge, heartburning, huff, indignation, ire, irritation, pique, rage, soreness, spleen, sulks, umbrage, vexation, wrath.

**reservation** n reserve, suppression; appropriation, booking, exception, restriction, saving; proviso, salvo; custody, park, reserve, sanctuary.

**reserve** vb hold, husband, keep, retain, store. * adj alternate, auxiliary, spare, substitute. * n reservation; aloofness, backwardness, closeness, coldness, concealment, constraint, suppression, reservedness, retention, restraint, reticence, uncommunicativeness, unresponsiveness; coyness, demureness, modesty, shyness, taciturnity; park, reservation, sanctuary.

**reserved** adj coy, demure, modest, shy, taciturn; aloof, backward, cautious, cold, distant, incommunicative, restrained, reticent, self-controlled, unsociable, unsocial; bespoken, booked, excepted, held, kept, retained, set apart, taken, withheld.

**reside** vb abide, domicile, domiciliate, dwell, inhabit, live, lodge, remain, room, sojourn, stay.

**residence** n inhabitance, inhabitancy, sojourn, stay, stop, tarrying; abode, domicile, dwelling, habitation, home, house, lodging, mansion.

**residue** n leavings, remainder, remains, remnant, residuum, rest; excess, overplus, surplus.

**resign** vb abandon, abdicate, abjure, cede, commit, disclaim, forego, forsake, leave, quit, relinquish, renounce, surrender, yield.

**resignation** n abandonment, abdication, relinquishment, renunciation, retirement, surrender; acquiescence, compliance, endurance, forbearance, fortitude, long-sufferance, patience, submission, sufferance.

**resist** vb assail, attack, baffle, block, check, confront, counteract, disappoint, frustrate, hinder, impede, impugn, neutralize, obstruct, oppose, rebel, rebuff, stand against, stem, stop, strive, thwart, withstand.

**resolute** adj bold, constant, decided, determined, earnest, firm, fixed, game, hardy, inflexible, persevering, pertinacious, relentless, resolved, staunch, steadfast, steady, stout, stouthearted, sturdy, tenacious, unalterable, unbending, undaunted, unflinching, unshaken, unwavering, unyielding.

**resolution** n boldness, disentanglement, explication, unravelling; backbone, constancy, courage, decision, determination, earnestness, energy, firmness, fortitude, grit, hardihood, inflexibility, intention, manliness, pluck, perseverance, purpose, relentlessness, resolve, resoluteness, stamina, steadfastness, steadiness, tenacity.

**resolve** vb analyse, disperse, scatter, separate, reduce; change, dissolve, liquefy, melt, reduce, transform; decipher, disentangle, elucidate, explain, interpret, unfold, solve, unravel; conclude, decide, determine, fix, intend, purpose, will. * n conclusion, decision, determination, intention, will; declaration, resolution.

**resonant** adj booming, clangorous, resounding, reverberating, ringing, roaring, sonorous, thundering, vibrant.

**resort** vb frequent, haunt; assemble, congregate, convene, go, repair. * n application, expedient, recourse; haunt, refuge, rendezvous, retreat, spa; assembling, confluence, concourse, meeting; recourse, reference.

**resound** vb echo, re-echo, reverberate, ring; celebrate, extol, praise, sound.

**resource** n dependence, resort; appliance, contrivance, device, expedient, instrumentality, means, resort.

**resources** npl capital, funds, income, money, property, reserve, supplies, wealth.

**respect** vb admire, esteem, honour, prize, regard, revere, reverence, spare, value, venerate; consider, heed, notice, observe. * n attention, civility, courtesy, consideration, deference, estimation, homage, honour, notice, politeness, recognition, regard, reverence, veneration; consideration, favour, goodwill, kind; aspect, bearing, connection, feature, matter, particular, point, reference, regard, relation.

**respects** npl compliments, greetings, regards.

**respectable** adj considerable, estimable, honourable, presentable, proper, upright, worthy; adequate, moderate; tolerable.

**respectful** adj ceremonious, civil, complaisant, courteous, decorous, deferential, dutiful, formal, polite.

**respire** vb breathe, exhale, live.

**respite** vb delay, relieve, reprieve. * n break, cessation, delay, intermission, interval, pause, recess, rest, stay, stop; forbearance, postponement, reprieve.

**resplendent** adj beaming, bright, brilliant, effulgent, lucid, glittering, glorious, gorgeous, luminous, lustrous, radiant, shining, splendid.

**respond** vb answer, reply, rejoin; accord, correspond, suit.

**response** n answer, replication, rejoinder, reply, retort.

**responsible** adj accountable, amenable, answerable, liable, trustworthy.

**rest**[1] vb cease, desist, halt, hold, pause, repose, stop; breathe, relax, unbend; repose, sleep, slumber; lean, lie, lounge, perch, recline, ride; acquiesce, confide, trust; confide, rely, trust; calm, comfort, ease. * n

fixity, immobility, inactivity, motionlessness, quiescence, quiet, repose; hush, peace, peacefulness, quietness, relief, security, stillness, tranquillity; cessation, intermission, interval, lull, pause, relaxation, respite, stop, stay; siesta, sleep, slumber; death; brace, stay, support; axis, fulcrum, pivot.

**rest**[2] vb be left, remain. * n balance, remainder, remnant, residuum; overplus, surplus.

**restaurant** n bistro, café, cafeteria, chophouse, eatery, eating house, pizzeria, trattoria.

**restitution** n restoration, return; amends, compensation, indemnification, recompense, rehabilitation, remuneration, reparation, repayment, requital, satisfaction.

**restive** adj mulish, obstinate, stopping, stubborn, unwilling; impatient, recalcitrant, restless, uneasy, unquiet.

**restless** adj disquieted, disturbed, restive, sleepless, uneasy, unquiet, unresting; changeable, inconstant, irresolute, unsteady, vacillating; active, astatic, roving, transient, unsettled, unstable, wandering; agitated, fidgety, fretful, turbulent.

**restoration** n recall, recovery, re-establishment, reinstatement, reparation, replacement, restitution, return; reconsideration, redemption, reintegration, renewal, renovation, repair, resuscitation, revival; convalescence, cure, recruitment, recuperation.

**restorative** adj curative, invigorating, recuperative, remedial, restoring, stimulating. * n corrective, curative, cure, healing, medicine, remedy, reparative, stimulant.

**restore** vb refund, repay, return; caulk, cobble, emend, heal, mend, patch, reintegrate, re-establish, rehabilitate, reinstate, renew, repair, replace, retrieve; cure, heal, recover, revive; resuscitate.

**restrain** vb bridle, check, coerce, confine, constrain, curb, debar, govern, hamper, hinder, hold, keep, muzzle, picket, prevent, repress, restrict, rule, subdue, tie, withhold; abridge, circumscribe, narrow.

**restraint** n bridle, check, coercion, control, compulsion, constraint, curb, discipline, repression, suppression; arrest, deterrence, hindrance, inhibition, limitation, prevention, prohibition, restriction, stay, stop; confinement, detention, imprisonment, shackles; constraint, stiffness, reserve, unnaturalness.

**restrict** vb bound, circumscribe, confine, limit, qualify, restrain, straiten.

**restriction** n confinement, limitation; constraint, restraint; reservation, reserve.

**result** vb accrue, arise, come, ensue, flow, follow, issue, originate, proceed, spring, rise; end, eventuate, terminate. * n conclusion, consequence, deduction, inference, outcome; corollary, effect, end, event, eventuality, fruit, harvest, issue, product, sequel, termination; decision, determination, finding, resolution, resolve, solution, verdict.

**resume** vb continue, recommence, renew, restart, summarize.

**résumé** n abstract, curriculum vitae, epitome, recapitulation, summary, synopsis.

**resuscitate** vb quicken, reanimate, renew, resurrect, restore, revive, revivify.

**retain** vb detain, hold, husband, keep, preserve, recall, recollect, remember, reserve, save, withhold; engage, maintain.

**retainer** n adherent, attendant, dependant, follower, hanger-on, servant.

**retaliate** vb avenge, match, repay, requite, retort, return, turn.

**retaliation** n boomerang, counterstroke, punishment, repayment, requital, retribution, revenge.

**retard** vb check, clog, hinder, impede, obstruct, slacken; adjourn, defer, delay, postpone, procrastinate.

**reticent** adj close, reserved, secretive, silent, taciturn, uncommunicative.

**retinue** n bodyguard, cortege, entourage, escort, followers, household, ménage, suite, tail, train.

**retire** vb discharge, shelve, superannuate, withdraw; depart, leave, resign, retreat.

**retired** adj abstracted, removed, withdrawn; apart, private, secret, sequestrated, solitary.

**retirement** n isolation, loneliness, privacy, retreat, seclusion, solitude, withdrawal.

**retiring** adj coy, demure, diffident, modest, reserved, retreating, shy, withdrawing.

**retort** vb answer, rejoin, reply, respond. * n answer, rejoinder, repartee, reply, response; crucible, jar, vessel, vial.

**retract** vb reverse, withdraw; abjure, cancel, disavow, recall, recant, revoke, unsay.

**retreat** vb recoil, retire, withdraw; recede. * n departure, recession, recoil, retirement, withdrawal; privacy, seclusion, solitude; asylum, cove, den, habitat, haunt, niche, recess, refuge, resort, shelter.

**retrench** vb clip, curtail, cut, delete, dock, lop, mutilate, pare, prune; abridge, decrease, diminish, lessen; confine, limit; economize, encroach.

**retribution** n compensation, desert, judgement, nemesis, penalty, recompense, repayment, requital, retaliation, return, revenge, reward, vengeance.

**retrieve** vb recall, recover, recoup, recruit, re-establish, regain, repair, restore.

**retrograde** vb decline, degenerate, recede, retire, retrocede. * adj backward, inverse, retrogressive, unprogressive.

**retrospect** n recollection, re-examination, reminiscence, re-survey, review, survey.

**return** vb reappear, recoil, recur, revert; answer, reply, respond; recriminate, retort; convey, give, communicate, reciprocate, recompense, refund, remit, repay, report, requite, send, tell, transmit; elect. * n payment, reimbursement, remittance, repayment; recompense, recovery, recurrence, renewal, repayment, requital, restitution, restoration, reward; advantage, benefit, interest, profit, rent, yield.

**reunion** n assemblage, assembly, gathering, meeting, re-assembly; rapprochement, reconciliation.

**reveal** vb announce, communicate, confess, declare, disclose, discover, display, divulge, expose, impart, open, publish, tell, uncover, unmask, unseal, unveil.

**revel** vb carouse, disport, riot, roister, tipple; delight, indulge, luxuriate, wanton. * n carousal, feast, festival, saturnalia, spree.

**revelry** n bacchanal, carousal, carouse, debauch, festivity, jollification, jollity, orgy, revel, riot, rout, saturnalia, wassail.

**revenge** vb avenge, repay, requite, retaliate, vindicate. * n malevolence, rancour, reprisal, requital, retaliation, retribution, vengeance, vindictiveness.

**revengeful** adj implacable, malevolent, malicious, malignant, resentful, rancorous, spiteful, vengeful, vindictive.

**revenue** n fruits, income, produce, proceeds, receipts, return, reward, wealth.

**reverberate** vb echo, re-echo, resound, return.

**revere** vb adore, esteem, hallow, honour, reverence, venerate, worship.

**reverence** vb adore, esteem, hallow, honour, revere, venerate, worship. * n adoration, awe, deference, homage, honour, respect, veneration, worship.

**reverential** adj deferential, humble, respectful, reverent, submissive.

**reverse** vb invert, transpose; overset, overthrow, overturn, quash, subvert, undo, unmake; annul, countermand, repeal, rescind, retract, revoke; back, back up, retreat. * adj back, converse, contrary, opposite, verso. * n back, calamity, check, comedown, contrary, counterpart, defeat, opposite, tail; change, vicissitude; adversity, affliction, hardship, misadventure, mischance, misfortune, mishap, trial.

**revert** vb repel, reverse; backslide, lapse, recur, relapse, return.

**review** vb inspect, overlook, reconsider, re-examine, retrace, revise, survey; analyse, criticize, discuss, edit, judge, scrutinize, study. * n reconsideration, re-examination, re-survey, retrospect, survey; analysis, digest, synopsis; commentary, critique, criticism, notice, review, scrutiny, study.

**revile** vb abuse, asperse, backbite, calumniate, defame, execrate, malign, reproach, slander, traduce, upbraid, vilify.

**revise** vb reconsider, re-examine, review; alter, amend, correct, edit, overhaul, polish.

**revive** vb reanimate, reinspire, reinspirit, reinvigorate, resuscitate, revitalize, revivify; animate, cheer, comfort, invigorate, quicken, reawaken, recover, refresh, renew, renovate, rouse, strengthen; reawake, recall.

**revocation** n abjuration, recall, recantation, repeal, retraction, reversal.

**revoke** vb abolish, abrogate, annul, cancel, countermand, invalidate, quash, recall, recant, repeal, repudiate, rescind, retract.

**revolt** vb desert, mutiny, rebel, rise; disgust, nauseate, repel, sicken. * n defection, desertion, faithlessness, inconstancy; disobedience, insurrection, mutiny, outbreak, rebellion, sedition, strike, uprising.

**revolting** adj abhorrent, abominable, disgusting, hateful, monstrous, nauseating, nauseous, objectionable, obnoxious, offensive, repulsive, shocking, sickening; insurgent, mutinous, rebellious.

**revolution** n coup, disobedience, insurrection, mutiny, outbreak, rebellion, sedition, strike, uprising; change, innovation, reformation, transformation, upheaval; circle, circuit, cycle, lap, orbit, rotation, spin, turn..

**revolve** vb circle, circulate, rotate, swing, turn, wheel; devolve, return; consider, mediate, ponder, ruminate, study.

**revulsion** n abstraction, shrinking, withdrawal; change, reaction, reversal, transition; abhorrence, disgust, loathing, repugnance.

**reward** vb compensate, gratify, indemnify, pay, punish, recompense, remember, remunerate, requite. * n compensation, gratification, guerdon, indemnification, pay, recompense, remuneration, requital; bounty, bonus, fee, gratuity, honorarium, meed, perquisite, premium, remembrance, tip; punishment, retribution.

**rhythm** n cadence, lilt, pulsation, swing; measure, metre, number.

**ribald** adj base, blue, coarse, filthy, gross, indecent, lewd, loose, low, mean, obscene, vile.

**rich** adj affluent, flush, moneyed, opulent, prosperous, wealthy; costly, estimable, gorgeous, luxurious, precious, splendid, sumptuous, superb, valuable; delicious, luscious, savoury; abundant, ample, copious, enough, full, plentiful, plenteous, sufficient; fertile, fruitful, luxuriant, productive, prolific; bright, dark, deep, exuberant, vivid; harmonious, mellow, melodious, soft, sweet; comical, funny, humorous, laughable.

**riches** npl abundance, affluence, fortune, money, opulence, plenty, richness, wealth, wealthiness.

**rickety** adj broken, imperfect, shaky, shattered, tottering, tumbledown, unsteady, weak.

**rid** vb deliver, free, release; clear, disburden, disencumber, scour, sweep; disinherit, dispatch, dissolve, divorce, finish, sever.

**riddance** n deliverance, disencumberment, extrication, escape, freedom, release, relief.

**riddle**¹ vb explain, solve, unriddle. * n conundrum, enigma, mystery, puzzle, rebus.

**riddle**² vb sieve, sift, perforate, permeate, spread. * n colander, sieve, strainer.

**ridge** n chine, hogback, ledge, saddle, spine, rib, watershed, weal, wrinkle.

**ridicule** vb banter, burlesque, chaff, deride, disparage, jeer, mock, lampoon, rally, satirize, scout, taunt. * n badinage, banter, burlesque, chaff, derision, game, gibe, irony, jeer, mockery, persiflage, quip, raillery, sarcasm, satire, sneer, squib, wit.

**ridiculous** adj absurd, amusing, comical, droll, eccentric, fantastic, farcical, funny, laughable, ludicrous, nonsensical, odd, outlandish, preposterous, queer, risible, waggish.

**rife** adj abundant, common, current, general, numerous, plentiful, prevailing, prevalent, replete.

**riffraff** n horde, mob, populace, rabble, scum, trash.

**rifle** vb despoil, fleece, pillage, plunder, ransack, rob, strip.

**rift** vb cleave, rive, split. * n breach, break, chink, cleft, crack, cranny, crevice, fissure, fracture, gap, opening, reft, rent.

**rig** vb accoutre, clothe, dress. * n costume, dress, garb; equipment, team.

**right** vb adjust, correct, regulate, settle, straighten, vindicate. * adj direct, rectilinear, straight; erect, perpendicular, plumb, upright; equitable, even-handed, fair, just, justifiable, honest, lawful, legal, legitimate, rightful, square, unswerving; appropriate, becoming, correct, conventional, fit, fitting, meet, orderly, proper, reasonable, seemly, suitable, well-done; actual, genuine, real, true, unquestionable; dexter, dextral, right-handed. * adv equitably, fairly, justly, lawfully, rightfully, rightly; correctly, fitly, properly, suitably, truly; actually, exactly, just, really, truly, well. * n authority, claim, liberty, permission, power, privilege, title; equity, good, honour, justice, lawfulness, legality, propriety, reason, righteousness, truth.

**righteous** adj devout, godly, good, holy, honest, incorrupt, just, pious, religious, saintly, uncorrupt, upright, virtuous; equitable, fair, right, rightful.

**righteousness** n equity, faithfulness, godliness, goodness, holiness, honesty, integrity, justice, piety, purity, right, rightfulness, sanctity, uprightness, virtue.

**rightful** adj lawful, legitimate, true; appropriate, correct, deserved, due, equitable, fair, fitting, honest, just, legal, merited, proper, reasonable, suitable.

**rigid** adj firm, hard, inflexible, permanent, stiff, stiffened, unbending, unpliant, unyielding; bristling, erect, precipitous, steep; austere, conventional, correct, exact, formal, harsh, meticulous, precise, rigorous, severe, sharp, stern, strict, unmitigated; cruel.

**rigmarole** n balderdash, flummery, gibberish, gobbledegook, jargon, nonsense, palaver, trash, twaddle, verbiage.

**rigour** n hardness, inflexibility, rigidity, rigidness, stiffness; asperity, austerity, harshness, severity, sternness; evenness, strictness; inclemency.

**rile** vb anger, annoy, irritate, upset, vex.

**rim** n brim, brink, border, confine, curb, edge, flange, girdle, margin, ring, skirt.

**ring**[1] vb circle, encircle, enclose, girdle, surround. * n circle, circlet, girdle, hoop, round, whorl; cabal, clique, combination, confederacy, coterie, gang, junta, league, set.

**ring**[2] vb chime, clang, jingle, knell, peal, resound, reverberate, sound, tingle, toll; call, phone, telephone. * n chime, knell, peal, tinkle, toll; call, phone call, telephone call.

**riot** vb carouse, luxuriate, revel. * n affray, altercation, brawl, broil, commotion, disturbance, fray, outbreak, pandemonium, quarrel, squabble, tumult, uproar; dissipation, excess, luxury, merrymaking, revelry.

**riotous** adj boisterous, luxurious, merry, revelling, unrestrained, wanton; disorderly, insubordinate, lawless, mutinous, rebellious, refractory, seditious, tumultuous, turbulent, ungovernable, unruly, violent.

**ripe** adj advanced, grown, mature, mellow, seasoned, soft; fit, prepared, ready; accomplished, complete, consummate, finished, perfect, perfected.

**ripen** vb burgeon, develop, mature, prepare.

**rise** vb arise, ascend, clamber, climb, levitate, mount; excel, succeed; enlarge, heighten, increase, swell, thrive; revive; grow, kindle, wax; begin, flow, head, originate, proceed, spring, start; mutiny, rebel, revolt; happen, occur. * n ascension, ascent, rising; elevation, grade, hill, slope; beginning, emergence, flow, origin, source, spring; advance, augmentation, expansion, increase.

**risible** adj amusing, comical, droll, farcical, funny, laughable, ludicrous, ridiculous.

**risk** vb bet, endanger, hazard, jeopardize, peril, speculate, stake, venture, wager. * n chance, danger, hazard, jeopardy, peril, venture.

**rite** n ceremonial, ceremony, form, formulary, ministration, observance, ordinance, ritual, rubric, sacrament, solemnity.

**ritual** adj ceremonial, conventional, formal, habitual, routine, stereotyped. * n ceremonial, ceremony, liturgy, observance, rite, sacrament, service; convention, form, formality, habit, practice, protocol.

**rival** vb emulate, match, oppose. * adj competing, contending, emulating, emulous, opposing. * n antagonist, competitor, emulator, opponent.

**rive** vb cleave, rend, split.

**river** n affluent, current, reach, stream, tributary.

**road** n course, highway, lane, passage, path, pathway, roadway, route, street, thoroughfare, track, trail, turnpike, way.

**roam** vb jaunt, prowl, ramble, range, rove, straggle, stray, stroll, wander.

**roar** vb bawl, bellow, cry, howl, vociferate, yell; boom, peal, rattle, resound, thunder. * n bellow, roaring; rage, resonance, storm, thunder; cry, outcry, shout; laugh, laughter, shout.

**rob** vb despoil, fleece, pilfer, pillage, plunder, rook, strip; appropriate, deprive, embezzle, plagiarize.

**robber** n bandit, brigand, desperado, depredator, despoiler, footpad, freebooter, highwayman, marauder, pillager, pirate, plunderer, rifler, thief.

**robbery** n depredation, despoliation, embezzlement, freebooting, larceny, peculation, piracy, plagiarism, plundering, spoliation, theft.

**robe** vb array, clothe, dress, invest. * n attire, costume, dress, garment, gown, habit, vestment; bathrobe, dressing gown, housecoat.

**robust** adj able-bodied, athletic, brawny, energetic, firm, forceful, hale, hardy, hearty, iron, lusty, muscular, powerful, seasoned, self-assertive, sinewy, sound, stalwart, stout, strong, sturdy, vigorous.

**rock**[1] n boulder, cliff, crag, reef, stone; asylum, defence, foundation, protection, refuge, strength, support; gneiss, granite, marble, slate, etc.

**rock**[2] vb calm, cradle, lull, quiet, soothe, still, tranquillize; reel, shake, sway, teeter, totter, wobble.

**rogue** n beggar, vagabond, vagrant; caitiff, cheat, knave, rascal, scamp, scapegrace, scoundrel, sharper, swindler, trickster, villain.

**roguish** adj dishonest, fraudulent, knavish, rascally, scoundrelly, trickish, tricky; arch, sportive, mischievous, puckish, waggish, wanton.

**role** n character, function, impersonation, part, task.

**roll** vb gyrate, revolve, rotate, turn, wheel; curl, muffle, swathe, wind; bind, involve, enfold, envelop; flatten, level, smooth, spread; bowl, drive, trundle, wheel; gybe, lean, lurch, stagger, sway, yaw; billow, swell, undulate; wallow, welter; flow, glide, run. * n document, scroll, volume; annals, chronicle, history, record, rota; catalogue, inventory, list, register, schedule; booming, resonance, reverberation, thunder; cylinder, roller.

**rollicking** adj frisky, frolicking, frolicsome, jolly, jovial, lively, swaggering.

**romance** vb exaggerate, fantasize. * n fantasy, fiction, legend, novel, story, tale; exaggeration, falsehood, lie; ballad, idyll, song.

**romantic** adj extravagant, fanciful, fantastic, ideal, imaginative, sentimental, wild; chimerical, fabulous, fantastic, fictitious, imaginary, improbable, legendary, picturesque, quixotic, sentimental. * n dreamer, idealist, sentimentalist, visionary.

**romp** vb caper, gambol, frisk, sport. * n caper, frolic, gambol.

**room** n accommodation, capacity, compass, elbowroom, expanse, extent, field, latitude, leeway, play, scope, space, swing; place, stead; apartment, chamber, lodging; chance, occasion, opportunity.

**roomy** adj ample, broad, capacious, comfortable, commodious, expansive, extensive, large, spacious, wide.

**root**[1] vb anchor, embed, fasten, implant, place, settle; confirm, establish. * n base, bottom, foundation; cause, occasion, motive, origin, reason, source; etymon, radical, radix, stem.

**root**[2] vb destroy, eradicate, extirpate, exterminate, remove, unearth, uproot; burrow, dig, forage, grub, rummage; applaud, cheer, encourage.

**rooted** adj chronic, confirmed, deep, established, fixed, radical.

**roseate** adj blooming, blushing, rose-coloured, rosy, rubicund; hopeful.

**rostrum** n platform, stage, stand, tribune.

**rosy** adj auspicious, blooming, blushing, favourable, flushed, hopeful, roseate, ruddy, sanguine.

**rot** vb corrupt, decay, decompose, degenerate, putrefy, spoil, taint. * n corruption, decay, decomposition, putrefaction.

**rotary** adj circular, rotating, revolving, rotatory, turning, whirling.

**rotten** adj carious, corrupt, decomposed, fetid, putrefied, putrescent, putrid, rank, stinking; defective, unsound; corrupt, deceitful, immoral, treacherous, unsound, untrustworthy.

**rotund** adj buxom, chubby, full, globular, obese, plump, round, stout; fluent, grandiloquent.

**roué** n debauchee, libertine, profligate, rake.

**rough** vb coarsen, roughen; manhandle, mishandle, molest. * adj bumpy, craggy, irregular, jagged, rugged, scabrous, scraggy, scratchy, stubby, uneven; approximate, cross-grained, crude, formless, incomplete, knotty, rough-hewn, shapeless, sketchy, uncut, unfashioned, unfinished, unhewn, unpolished, unwrought, vague; bristly, bushy, coarse, disordered, hairy, hirsute, ragged, shaggy, unkempt; austere, bearish, bluff, blunt, brusque, burly, churlish, discourteous, gruff, harsh, impolite, indelicate, rude, surly, uncivil, uncourteous, ungracious, unpolished, unrefined; harsh, severe, sharp, violent; astringent, crabbed, hard, sour, tart; discordant, grating, inharmonious, jarring, raucous, scabrous, unmusical; boisterous, foul, inclement, severe, stormy, tempestuous, tumultuous, turbulent, untamed, violent, wild; acrimonious, brutal, cruel, disorderly, riotous, rowdy, severe, uncivil, unfeeling, ungentle. * n bully, rowdy, roughneck, ruffian; draft, outline, sketch, suggestion; unevenness.

**round** vb curve; circuit, encircle, encompass, surround. * adj bulbous, circular, cylindrical, globular, orbed, orbicular, rotund, spherical; complete, considerable, entire, full, great, large, unbroken, whole; chubby, corpulent, plump, stout, swelling; continuous, flowing, harmonious, smooth; brisk, quick; blunt, candid, fair, frank, honest, open, plain, upright. * adv around, circularly, circuitously. * prep about, around. * n bout, cycle, game, lap, revolution, rotation, succession, turn; canon, catch, dance; ball, circle, circumference, cylinder, globe, sphere; circuit, compass, perambulation, routine, tour, watch.

**roundabout** adj circuitous, circumlocutory, indirect, tortuous; ample, broad, extensive; encircling, encompassing.

**rouse** vb arouse, awaken, raise, shake, wake, waken; animate, bestir, brace, enkindle, excite, inspire, kindle, rally, stimulate, stir, whet; startle, surprise.

**rout** vb beat, conquer, defeat, discomfit, overcome, overpower, overthrow, vanquish; chase away, dispel, disperse, scatter. * n defeat, discomfiture, flight, ruin; concourse, multitude, rabble; brawl, disturbance, noise, roar, uproar.

**route** vb direct, forward, send, steer. * n course, circuit, direction, itinerary, journey, march, road, passage, path, way.

**routine** adj conventional, familiar, habitual, ordinary, standard, typical, usual; boring, dull, humdrum, predictable, tiresome. * n beat, custom, groove, method, order, path, practice, procedure, round, rut.

**rove** vb prowl, ramble, range, roam, stray, struggle, stroll, wander.

**row**[1] n file, line, queue, range, rank, series, string, tier; alley, street, terrace.

**row**[2] vb argue, dispute, fight, quarrel, squabble. * n affray, altercation, brawl, broil, commotion, dispute, disturbance, noise, outbreak, quarrel, riot, squabble, tumult, uproar.

**royal** adj august, courtly, dignified, generous, grand, imperial, kingly, kinglike, magnanimous, magnificent, majestic, monarchical, noble, princely, regal, sovereign, splendid, superb.

**rub** vb abrade, chafe, grate, graze, scrape; burnish, clean, massage, polish, scour, wipe; apply, put, smear, spread. * n caress, massage, polish, scouring, shine, wipe; catch, difficulty, drawback, impediment, obstacle, problem.

**rubbish** n debris, detritus, fragments, refuse, ruins, waste; dregs, dross, garbage, litter, lumber, scoria, scum, sweepings, trash, trumpery.

**rubicund** adj blushing, erubescent, florid, flushed, red, reddish, ruddy.

**rude** adj coarse, crude, ill-formed, rough, rugged, shapeless, uneven, unfashioned, unformed, unwrought; artless, barbarous, boorish, clownish, ignorant, illiterate, loutish, raw, savage, uncivilized, uncouth, uncultivated, undisciplined, unpolished, ungraceful, unskilful, unskilled, untaught, untrained, untutored, vulgar; awkward, barbarous, bluff, blunt, boorish, brusque, brutal, churlish, gruff, ill-bred, impertinent, impolite, impudent, insolent, insulting, ribald, saucy, uncivil, uncourteous, unrefined; boisterous, fierce, harsh, severe, tumultuous, turbulent, violent; artless, inelegant, rustic, unpolished; hearty, robust.

**rudimentary** adj elementary, embryonic, fundamental, initial, primary, rudimental, undeveloped.

**rue** vb deplore, grieve, lament, regret, repent.

**rueful** adj dismal, doleful, lamentable, lugubrious, melancholic, melancholy, mournful, penitent, regretful, sad, sorrowful, woeful.

**ruffian** n bully, caitiff, cutthroat, hoodlum, miscreant, monster, murderer, rascal, robber, roisterer, rowdy, scoundrel, villain, wretch.

**ruffle** vb damage, derange, disarrange, dishevel, disorder, ripple, roughen, rumple; agitate, confuse, discompose, disquiet, disturb, excite, harass, irritate, molest, plague, perturb, torment, trouble, vex, worry; cockle, flounce, pucker, wrinkle. * n edging, frill, ruff; agitation, bustle, commotion, confusion, contention, disturbance, excitement, fight, fluster, flutter, flurry, perturbation, tumult.

**rugged** adj austere, bristly, coarse, crabbed, cragged, craggy, hard, hardy, irregular, ragged, robust, rough, rude, scraggy, severe, seamed, shaggy, uneven, unkempt, wrinkled; boisterous, inclement, stormy, tempestuous, tumultuous, turbulent, violent; grating, harsh, inharmonious, unmusical, scabrous.

**ruin** vb crush, damn, defeat, demolish, desolate, destroy, devastate, overthrow, overturn, overwhelm, seduce, shatter, smash, subvert, wreck; beggar, impoverish. * n damnation, decay, defeat, demolition, desolation, destruction, devastation, discomfiture, downfall, fall, loss, perdition, prostration, rack, ruinatton, shipwreck, subversion, undoing, wrack, wreck; bane, mischief, pest.

**ruination** n demolition, destruction, overthrow, ruin, subversion.

**ruinous** adj decayed, demolished, dilapidated; baneful, calamitous, damnatory, destructive, disastrous, mischievous, noisome, noxious, pernicious, subversive, wasteful.

**rule** vb bridle, command, conduct, control, direct, domineer, govern, judge, lead, manage, reign, restrain; advise, guide, persuade; adjudicate, decide, determine, establish, settle; obtain, prevail, predominate. * n authority, command, control, direction, domination, dominion, empire, government, jurisdiction, lordship, mastery, mastership, regency, reign, sway; behaviour, conduct; habit, method, order, regularity, routine, system; aphorism, canon, convention, criterion, formula, guide, law, maxim, model, precedent, precept, standard, system, test, touchstone; decision, order, prescription, regulation, ruling.

**ruler** n chief, governor, king, lord, master, monarch, potentate, regent, sovereign; director, head, manager, president; controller, guide, rule; straight-edge.

**ruminate** vb brood, chew, cogitate, consider, contemplate, meditate, muse, ponder, reflect, think.

**rumour** vb bruit, circulate, report, tell. * n bruit, gossip, hearsay, report, talk; news, report, story, tidings; celebrity, fame, reputation, repute.

**rumple** vb crease, crush, corrugate, crumple, disarrange, dishevel, pucker, ruffle, wrinkle. * n crease, corrugation, crumple, fold, pucker, wrinkle.

**run** vb bolt, career, course, gallop, haste, hasten, hie, hurry, lope, post, race, scamper, scour, scud, scuttle, speed, trip; flow, glide, go, move, proceed, stream; fuse, liquefy, melt; advance, pass, proceed, vanish; extend, lie, spread, stretch; circulate, pass, press; average, incline, tend; flee; pierce, stab; drive, force, propel, push, thrust, turn; cast, form, mould, shape; follow, perform, pursue, take; discharge, emit; direct, maintain, manage. * n race, running; course, current, flow, motion, passage, progress, way, wont; continuance, currency, popularity; excursion, gallop, journey, trip, trot; demand, pressure; brook, burn, flow, rill, rivulet, runlet, runnel, streamlet.

**rupture** vb break, burst, fracture, sever, split. * n breach, break, burst, disruption, fracture, split; contention, faction, feud, hostility, quarrel, schism.

**rural** adj agrarian, bucolic, country, pastoral, rustic, sylvan.

**ruse** n artifice, deception, deceit, fraud, hoax, imposture, manoeuvre, sham, stratagem, trick, wile.

**rush** vb attack, career, charge, dash, drive, gush, hurtle, precipitate, surge, sweep, tear. * n dash, onrush, onset, plunge, precipitance, precipitancy, rout, stampede, tear.

**rust** vb corrode, decay, degenerate. * n blight, corrosion, crust, mildew, must, mould, mustiness.

**rustic** adj country, rural; awkward, boorish, clownish, countrified, loutish, outlandish, rough, rude, uncouth, unpolished, untaught; coarse, countrified, homely, plain, simple, unadorned; artless, honest, unsophisticated. * n boor, bumpkin, clown, countryman, peasant, swain, yokel.

**ruthless** adj barbarous, cruel, fell, ferocious, hardhearted, inexorable, inhuman, merciless, pitiless, relentless, remorseless, savage, truculent, uncompassionate, unmerciful, unpitying, unrelenting, unsparing.

# S

**sable** adj black, dark, dusky, ebony, sombre.

**sabulous** adj gritty, sabulose, sandy.

**sack**[1] n bag, pouch.

**sack**[2] vb despoil, devastate, pillage, plunder, ravage, spoil. * n desolation, despoliation, destruction, devastation, havoc, ravage, sacking, spoliation, waste; booty, plunder, spoil.

**sacred** adj consecrated, dedicated, devoted, divine, hallowed, holy; inviolable, inviolate; sainted, venerable.

**sacrifice** vb forgo, immolate, surrender. * n immolation, oblation, offering; destruction, devotion, loss, surrender.

**sacrilege** n desecration, profanation, violation.

**sacrilegious** adj desecrating, impious, irreverent, profane.

**sad** adj grave, pensive, sedate, serious, sober, sombre, staid.

**saddle** vb burden, charge, clog, encumber, load.

**sadly** adv grievously, miserable, mournfully, sorrowfully; afflictively, badly, calamitously; darkly; gravely, seriously, soberly.

**sadness** n dejection, depression, despondency, melancholy, mournful, sorrow, sorrowfulness; dolefulness, gloominess, grief, mournfulness, sorrow; gravity, sedateness, seriousness.

**safe** adj undamaged, unharmed, unhurt, unscathed; guarded, protected, secure, snug, unexposed; certain, dependable, reliable, sure, trustworthy; good, harmless, sound, whole. * n chest, coffer, strongbox.

**safeguard** vb guard, protect. * n defence, protection, security; convoy, escort, guard, safe-conduct; pass, passport.

**sagacious** adj acute, apt, astute, clear-sighted, discerning, intelligent, judicious, keen, penetrating, perspicacious, rational, sage, sharp-witted, wise, shrewd.

**sagacity** n acuteness, astuteness, discernment, ingenuity, insight, penetration, perspicacity, quickness, readiness, sense, sharpness, shrewdness, wisdom.

**sage** adj acute, discerning, intelligent, prudent, sagacious, sapient, sensible, shrewd, wise; judicious, well-judged; grave, serious, solemn. * n philosopher, pundit, savant.

**sailor** n mariner, navigator, salt, seafarer, seaman, tar.

**saintly** adj devout, godly, holy, pious, religious.

**sake** n end, cause, purpose, reason; account, consideration, interest, regard, respect, score.

**saleable** adj marketable, merchantable, vendible.

**salacious** adj carnal, concupiscent, incontinent, lascivious, lecherous, lewd, libidinous, loose, lustful, prurient, unchaste, wanton.

**salary** n allowance, hire, pay, stipend, wages.

**salient** adj bounding, jumping, leaping; beating, springing, throbbing; jutting, projecting, prominent; conspicuous, remarkable, striking.

**saline** adj briny, salty.

**sally** vb issue, rush. * n digression, excursion, sortie, run, trip; escapade, frolic; crank, fancy, jest, joke, quip, quirk, sprightly, witticism.

**salt** adj saline, salted, salty; bitter, pungent, sharp. * n flavour, savour, seasoning, smack, relish, taste; humour, piquancy, poignancy, sarcasm, smartness, wit, zest; mariner, sailor, seaman, tar.

**salubrious** adj beneficial, benign, healthful, healthy, salutary, sanitary, wholesome.

**salutary** adj healthy, healthful, helpful, safe, salubrious, wholesome; advantageous, beneficial, good, profitable, serviceable, useful.

**salute** vb accost, address, congratulate, greet, hail, welcome. * n address, greeting, salutation.

**salvation** n deliverance, escape, preservation, redemption, rescue, saving.

**same** adj ditto, identical, selfsame; corresponding, like, similar.

**sample** vb savour, sip, smack, sup, taste; test, try; demonstrate, exemplify, illustrate, instance. * adj exemplary, illustrative, representative. * n demonstration, exemplification, illustration, instance, piece, specimen; example, model, pattern.

**sanctify** vb consecrate, hallow, purify; justify, ratify, sanction.

**sanctimonious** adj affected, devout, holy, hypocritical, pharisaical, pious, self-righteous.

**sanction** *vb* authorize, countenance, encourage, support; confirm, ratify. * *n* approval, authority, authorization, confirmation, countenance, endorsement, ratification, support, warranty; ban, boycott, embargo, penalty.

**sanctity** *n* devotion, godliness, goodness, grace, holiness, piety, purity, religiousness, saintliness.

**sanctuary** *n* altar, church, shrine, temple; asylum, protection, refuge, retreat, shelter.

**sane** *adj* healthy, lucid, rational, reasonable, sober, sound.

**sang-froid** *n* calmness, composure, coolness, imperturbability, indifference, nonchalance, phlegm, unconcern.

**sanguinary** *adj* bloody, gory, murderous; barbarous, bloodthirsty, *cruel, fell, pitiless, savage, ruthless.

**sanguine** *adj* crimson, florid, red; animated, ardent, cheerful, lively, warm; buoyant, confident, enthusiastic, hopeful, optimistic; full-blooded.

**sanitary** *adj* clean, curative, healing, healthy, hygienic, remedial, therapeutic, wholesome.

**sanity** *n* normality, rationality, reason, saneness, soundness.

**sapient** *adj* acute, discerning, intelligent, knowing, sagacious, sage, sensible, shrewd, wise.

**sarcastic** *adj* acrimonious, biting, cutting, mordacious, mordant, sardonic, satirical, sharp, severe, sneering, taunting.

**sardonic** *adj* bitter, derisive, ironical, malevolent, malicious, malignant, sarcastic.

**satanic** *adj* devilish, diabolical, evil, false, fiendish, hellish, infernal, malicious.

**satellite** *adj* dependent, subordinate, tributary, vassal. * *n* attendant, dependant, follower, hanger-on, retainer, vassal.

**satiate** *vb* fill, sate, satisfy, suffice; cloy, glut, gorge, overfeed, overfill, pall, surfeit.

**satire** *n* burlesque, diatribe, invective, fling, irony, lampoon, pasquinade, philippic, ridicule, sarcasm, skit, squib.

**satirical** *adj* abusive, biting, bitter, censorious, cutting, invective, ironical, keen, mordacious, poignant, reproachful, sarcastic, severe, sharp, taunting.

**satirize** *vb* abuse, censure, lampoon, ridicule.

**satisfaction** *n* comfort, complacency, contentment, ease, enjoyment, gratification, pleasure, satiety; amends, appeasement, atonement, compensation, indemnification, recompense, redress, remuneration, reparation, requital, reward.

**satisfactory** *adj* adequate, conclusive, convincing, decisive, sufficient; gratifying, pleasing.

**satisfy** *vb* appease, content, fill, gratify, please, sate, satiate, suffice; indemnify, compensate, liquidate, pay, recompense, remunerate, requite; discharge, settle; assure, convince, persuade; answer, fulfil, meet.

**saturate** *vb* drench, fill, fit, imbue, soak, steep, wet.

**saturnine** *adj* dark, dull, gloomy, grave, heavy, leaden, morose, phlegmatic, sad, sedate, sombre; melancholic, mournful, serious, unhappy; mischievous, naughty, troublesome, vexatious, wicked.

**sauce** *n* cheekiness, impudence, insolence; appetizer, compound, condiment, relish, seasoning.

**saucy** *adj* bold, cavalier, disrespectful, flippant, forward, immodest, impertinent, impudent, insolent, pert, rude.

**saunter** *vb* amble, dawdle, delay, dilly-dally, lag, linger, loiter, lounge, stroll, tarry. * *n* amble, stroll, walk.

**savage** *vb* attack, lacerate, mangle, maul. * *adj* rough, uncultivated, wild; rude, uncivilized, unpolished, untaught; bloodthirsty, feral, ferine, ferocious, fierce, rapacious, untamed, vicious; beastly, bestial, brutal, brutish, inhuman; atrocious, barbarous, barbaric, bloody, brutal, cruel, fell, fiendish, hardhearted, heathenish, merciless, murderous, pitiless, relentless, ruthless, sanguinary, truculent; native, rough, rugged. * *n* barbarian, brute, heathen, vandal.

**save** *vb* keep, liberate, preserve, rescue; salvage, recover, redeem; economize, gather, hoard, husband, reserve, store; hinder, obviate, prevent, spare. * *prep* but, deducting, except.

**saviour** *n* defender, deliverer, guardian, protector, preserver, rescuer, saver.

**savour** *vb* affect, appreciate, enjoy, like, partake, relish; flavour, season. * *n* flavour, gusto, relish, smack, taste; fragrance, odour, smell, scent.

**savoury** *adj* agreeable, delicious, flavourful, luscious, nice, palatable, piquant, relishing.

**saw** *n* adage, aphorism, apothegm, axiom, byword, dictum, maxim, precept, proverb, sententious saying.

**say** *vb* declare, express, pronounce, speak, tell, utter; affirm, allege, argue; recite, rehearse, repeat; assume, presume, suppose. * n affirmation, declaration, speech, statement; decision, voice, vote.

**saying** n declaration, expression, observation, remark, speech, statement; adage, aphorism, byword, dictum, maxim, proverb, saw.

**scale**[1] n basin, dish, pan; balance.

**scale**[2] n flake, lamina, lamella, layer, plate.

**scale**[3] vb ascend, climb, escalate, mount. * n graduation.

**scamp** n cheat, knave, rascal, rogue, scapegrace, scoundrel, swindler, trickster, villain.

**scamper** vb haste, hasten, hie, run, scud, speed, trip.

**scan** vb examine, investigate, scrutinize, search, sift.

**scandal** vb asperse, defame, libel, traduce. * n aspersion, calumny, defamation, obloquy, reproach; discredit, disgrace, dishonour, disrepute, ignominy, infamy, odium, opprobrium, offence, shame.

**scandalize** vb offend; asperse, backbite, calumniate, decry, defame, disgust, lampoon, libel, reproach, revile, satirize, slander, traduce, vilify.

**scandalous** adj defamatory, libellous, opprobrious, slanderous; atrocious, disgraceful, disreputable, infamous, inglorious, ignominious, odious, shameful.

**scanty** adj insufficient, meagre, narrow, scant, small; hardly, scarce, short, slender; niggardly, parsimonious, penurious, scrimpy, skimpy, sparing.

**scar**[1] vb hurt, mark, wound. * n cicatrice, cicatrix, seam; blemish, defect, disfigurement, flaw, injury, mark.

**scar**[2] n bluff, cliff, crag, precipice.

**scarce** adj deficient, wanting; infrequent, rare, uncommon. * adv barely, hardly, scantily.

**scarcely** adv barely, hardly, scantily.

**scarcity** n dearth, deficiency, insufficiency, lack, want; infrequency, rareness, rarity, uncommonness.

**scare** vb affright, alarm, appal, daunt, fright, frighten, intimidate, shock, startle, terrify. * n alarm, fright, panic, shock, terror.

**scathe** vb blast, damage, destroy, injure, harm, haste. * n damage, harm, injury, mischief, waste.

**scatter** vb broadcast, sprinkle, strew; diffuse, disperse, disseminate, dissipate, distribute, separate, spread; disappoint, dispel, frustrate, overthrow.

**scene** n display, exhibition, pageant, representation, show, sight, spectacle, view; place, situation, spot, arena, stage.

**scent** vb breathe in, inhale, nose, smell, sniff;

detect, smell out, sniff out; aromatize, perfume. * n aroma, balminess, fragrance, odour, perfume, smell, redolence.

**sceptic** n doubter, freethinker, questioner, unbeliever.

**sceptical** adj doubtful, doubting, dubious, hesitating, incredulous, questioning, unbelieving.

**scepticism** n doubt, dubiety, freethinking, incredulity, unbelief.

**schedule** vb line up, list, plan, programme, tabulate. * n document, scroll; catalogue, inventory, list, plan, record, register, roll, table, timetable.

**scheme** vb contrive, design, frame, imagine, plan, plot, project. * n plan, system, theory; cabal, conspiracy, contrivance, design, device, intrigue, machination, plan, plot, project, stratagem; arrangement, draught, diagram, outline.

**schism** n division, separation, split; discord, disunion, division, faction, separation.

**scholar** n disciple, learner, pupil, student; don, fellow, intellectual, pedant, savant.

**scholarship** n accomplishments, acquirements, attainments, erudition, knowledge, learning; bursary, exhibition, foundation, grant, maintenance.

**scholastic** adj academic, bookish, lettered, literary; formal, pedantic.

**school** vb drill, educate, exercise, indoctrinate, instruct, teach, train; admonish, control, chide, discipline, govern, reprove, tutor. * adj academic, collegiate, institutional, scholastic, schoolish. * n academy, college, gymnasium, institute, institution, kindergarten, lyceum, manège, polytechnic, seminary, university; adherents, camarilla, circle, clique, coterie, disciples, followers; body, order, organization, party, sect.

**schooling** n discipline, education, instruction, nurture, teaching, training, tuition.

**scintillate** vb coruscate, flash, gleam, glisten, glitter, sparkle, twinkle.

**scoff** vb deride, flout, jeer, mock, ridicule, taunt; gibe, sneer. * n flout, gibe, jeer, sneer, mockery, taunt; derision, ridicule.

**scold** vb berate, blame, censure, chide, rate, reprimand, reprove; brawl, rail, rate, reprimand, upbraid, vituperate. * n shrew, termagant, virago, vixen.

**scope** n aim, design, drift, end, intent, intention, mark, object, purpose, tendency, view; amplitude, field, latitude, liberty, margin, opportunity, purview, range, room, space, sphere, vent; extent, length, span, stretch, sweep.

**scorch** vb blister, burn, char, parch, roast, sear, shrivel, singe.

**score** vb cut, furrow, mark, notch, scratch; charge, note, record; impute, note; enter, register. * n incision, mark, notch; account, bill, charge, debt, reckoning; consideration, ground, motive, reason.

**scorn** vb condemn, despise, disregard, disdain, scout, slight, spurn. * n contempt, derision, disdain, mockery, slight, sneer; scoff.

**scornful** adj contemptuous, defiant, disdainful, contemptuous, regardless.

**scot-free** adj untaxed; clear, unhurt, uninjured, safe.

**scoundrel** n cheat, knave, miscreant, rascal, reprobate, rogue, scamp, swindler, trickster, villain.

**scour**[1] vb brighten, buff, burnish, clean, cleanse, polish, purge, scrape, scrub, rub, wash, whiten; rake; efface, obliterate, overrun.

**scour**[2] vb career, course, range, scamper, scud, scuttle; comb, hunt, rake, ransack, rifle, rummage, search.

**scourge** vb lash, whip; afflict, chasten, chastise, correct, punish; harass, torment. * n cord, cowhide, lash, strap, thong, whip; affliction, bane, curse, infliction, nuisance, pest, plague, punishment.

**scout** vb contemn, deride, disdain, despise, ridicule, scoff, scorn, sneer, spurn; investigate, probe, search. * n escort, lookout, precursor, vanguard.

**scowl** vb frown, glower, lower. * n frown, glower, lower.

**scraggy** adj broken, craggy, rough, rugged, scabrous, scragged, uneven; attenuated, bony, emaciated, gaunt, lank, lean, meagre, scrawny, skinny, thin.

**scrap**[1] vb discard, junk, trash. * n bit, fragment, modicum, particle, piece, snippet; bite, crumb, morsel, mouthful; debris, junk, litter, rubbish, rubble, trash, waste.

**scrap**[2] vb altercate, bicker, dispute, clash, fight, hassle, quarrel, row, spat, squabble, tiff, tussle, wrangle. * n affray, altercation, bickering, clash, dispute, fight, fray, hassle, melee, quarrel, row, run-in, set-to, spat, squabble, tiff, tussle, wrangle.

**scrape** vb bark, grind, rasp, scuff; accumulate, acquire, collect, gather, save; erase, remove. * n difficulty, distress, embarrassment, perplexity, predicament.

**scream** vb screech, shriek, squall, ululate. * n cry, outcry, screech, shriek, shrill, ululation.

**screen** vb cloak, conceal, cover, defend, fence, hide, mask, protect, shelter, shroud. * n blind, curtain, lattice, partition; defence, guard, protection, shield; cloak, cover, veil, disguise; riddle, sieve.

**screw** vb force, press, pressurize, squeeze, tighten, twist, wrench; oppress, rack; distort. * n extortioner, extortionist, miser, scrimp, skinflint; prison guard; sexual intercourse.

**scrimmage** n brawl, melee, riot, scuffle, skirmish.

**scrimp** vb contract, curtail, limit, pinch, reduce, scant, shorten, straiten.

**scrimpy** adj contracted, deficient, narrow, scanty.

**scroll** n inventory, list, parchment, roll, schedule.

**scrub**[1] adj contemptible, inferior, mean, niggardly, scrubby, shabby, small, stunted. * n brushwood, underbrush, underwood.

**scrub**[2] vb clean, cleanse, rub, scour, scrape, wash.

**scruple** vb boggle, demur, falter, hesitate, object, pause, stickle, waver. * n delicacy, hesitancy, hesitation, nicety, perplexity, qualm.

**scrupulous** adj conscientious, fastidious, nice, precise, punctilious, rigorous, strict; careful, cautious, circumspect, exact, vigilant.

**scrutinize** vb canvass, dissect, examine, explore, investigate, overhaul, probe, search, sift, study.

**scrutiny** n examination, exploration, inquisition, inspection, investigation, search, searching, sifting.

**scud** vb flee, fly, haste, hasten, hie, post, run, scamper, speed, trip.

**scuffle** vb contend, fight, strive, struggle. * n altercation, brawl, broil, contest, encounter, fight, fray, quarrel, squabble, struggle, wrangle.

**sculpt** vb carve, chisel, cut, sculpture; engrave, grave.

**scurrilous** adj abusive, blackguardly, contumelious, foul, foul-mouthed, indecent, infamous, insolent, insulting, offensive, opprobrious, reproachful, ribald, vituperative; coarse, gross, low, mean, obscene, vile, vulgar.

**scurry** vb bustle, dash, hasten, hurry, scamper, scud, scutter. * n burst, bustle, dash, flurry, haste, hurry, scamper, scud, spurt.

**scurvy** adj scabbed, scabby, scurfy; abject, bad, base, contemptible, despicable, low, mean, pitiful, sorry, vile, vulgar, worthless; malicious, mischievous, offensive.

**scuttle**[1] vb hurry, hustle, run, rush, scamper, scramble, scud, scurry. * n dash, drive, flurry, haste, hurry, hustle, race, rush, scamper, scramble, scud, scurry.

**scuttle**[2] vb capsize, founder, go down, sink, overturn, upset. * n hatch, hatchway.

**seal** vb close, fasten, secure; attest, authenticate, confirm, establish, ratify, sanction; confine, enclose, imprison. * n fastening, stamp, wafer, wax; assurance, attestation, authentication, confirmation, pledge, ratification.

**seamy** adj disreputable, nasty, seedy, sordid, unpleasant.

**sear** vb blight, brand, cauterize, dry, scorch, wither. * adj dried up, dry, sere, withered.

**search** vb examine, explore, ferret, inspect, investigate, overhaul, probe, ransack, scrutinize, sift; delve, hunt, forage, inquire, look, rummage. * n examination, exploration, hunt, inquiry, inspection, investigation, pursuit, quest, research, seeking, scrutiny.

**searching** adj close, keen, penetrating, trying; examining, exploring, inquiring, investigating, probing, seeking.

**seared** adj callous, graceless, hardened, impenitent, incorrigible, obdurate, shameless, unrepentant.

**season** vb acclimatize, accustom, form, habituate, harden, inure, mature, qualify, temper, train; flavour, spice. * n interval, period, spell, term, time, while.

**seasonable** adj appropriate, convenient, fit, opportune, suitable, timely.

**seasoning** n condiment, flavouring, relish, salt, sauce.

**seat** vb establish, fix, locate, place, set, station. * n place, site, situation, station; abode, capital, dwelling, house, mansion, residence; bottom, fundament; bench, chair, pew, settle, stall, stool.

**secede** vb apostatize, resign, retire, withdraw.

**secluded** adj close, covert, embowered, isolated, private, removed, retired, screened, sequestrated, withdrawn.

**seclusion** n obscurity, privacy, retirement, secrecy, separation, solitude, withdrawal.

**second**[1] n instant, jiffy, minute, moment, trice.

**second**[2] vb abet, advance, aid, assist, back, encourage, forward, further, help, promote, support, sustain; approve, favour. * adj inferior, second-rate, secondary; following, next, subsequent; additional, extra, other; double, duplicate. * n another, other; assistant, backer, supporter.

**secondary** adj collateral, inferior, minor, subsidiary, subordinate. * n delegate, deputy, proxy.

**secrecy** n clandestineness, concealment, furtiveness, stealth, surreptitiousness.

**secret** adj close, concealed, covered, covert, cryptic, hid, hidden, mysterious, privy, shrouded, veiled, unknown, unrevealed, unseen; cabbalistic, clandestine, furtive, privy, sly, stealthy, surreptitious, underhand; confidential, private, retired, secluded, unseen; abstruse, latent, mysterious, obscure, occult, recondite, unknown. * n confidence, enigma, key, mystery.

**secretary** n clerk, scribe, writer; escritoire, writing-desk.

**secrete**[1] vb bury, cache, conceal, disguise, hide, shroud, stash; screen, separate.

**secrete**[2] vb discharge, emit, excrete, exude, release, secern.

**secretive** adj cautious, close, reserved, reticent, taciturn, uncommunicative, wary.

**sect** n denomination, faction, schism, school.

**section** n cutting, division, fraction, part, piece, portion, segment, slice.

**secular** adj civil, laic, laical, lay, profane, temporal, worldly.

**secure** vb guard, protect, safeguard; assure, ensure, guarantee, insure; fasten; acquire, gain, get, obtain, procure. * adj assured, certain, confident, sure; insured, protected, safe; fast, firm, fixed, immovable, stable; careless, easy, undisturbed, unsuspecting; heedless, inattentive, incautious, negligent, overconfident.

**security** n bulwark, defence, guard, palladium, protection, safeguard, safety, shelter; bond, collateral, deposit, guarantee, pawn, pledge, stake, surety, warranty; carelessness, heedlessness, overconfidence, negligence; assurance, assuredness, certainty, confidence, ease.

**sedate** adj calm, collected, composed, contemplative, cool, demure, grave, placid, philosophical, quiet, serene, serious, sober, still, thoughtful, tranquil, undisturbed, unemotional, unruffled.

**sedative** adj allaying, anodyne, assuasive, balmy, calming, composing, demulcent, lenient, lenitive, soothing, tranquillizing. * n anaesthetic, anodyne, hypnotic, narcotic, opiate.

**sedentary** adj inactive, motionless, sluggish, torpid.

**sediment** n dregs, grounds, lees, precipitate, residue, residuum, settlings.

**sedition** n insurgence, insurrection, mutiny, rebellion, revolt, riot, rising, treason, tumult, uprising, uproar.

**seditious** adj factious, incendiary, insurgent, mutinous, rebellious, refractory, riotous, tumultuous, turbulent.

**seduce** vb allure, attract, betray, corrupt, debauch, deceive, decoy, deprave, ensnare, entice, inveigle, lead, mislead.

**seductive** adj alluring, attractive, enticing, tempting.

**sedulous** adj active, assiduous, busy, diligent, industrious, laborious, notable, painstaking, persevering, unremitting, untiring.

**see** vb behold, contemplate, descry, glimpse, sight, spot, survey; comprehend, conceive, distinguish, espy, know, notice, observe, perceive, recognize, remark, understand; beware, consider, envisage, regard, visualize; experience, feel, suffer; examine, inspire, notice, observe; discern, look; call on, visit.

**seed** n semen, sperm; embryo, grain, kernel, matured ovule; germ, original; children, descendants, offspring, progeny; birth, generation, race.

**seedy** adj faded, old, shabby, worn; destitute, distressed, indigent, needy, penniless, pinched, poor.

**seek** vb hunt, look, search; court, follow, prosecute, pursue, solicit; attempt, endeavour, strive, try.

**seem** vb appear, assume, look, pretend.

**seeming** adj apparent, appearing, ostensible, specious. * n appearance, colour, guise, look, semblance.

**seemly** adj appropriate, becoming, befitting, congruous, convenient, decent, decorous, expedient, fit, fitting, meet, proper, right, suitable; beautiful, comely, fair, good-looking, graceful, handsome, pretty, well-favoured.

**seer** n augur, diviner, foreteller, predictor, prophet, soothsayer.

**segment** n bit, division, part, piece, portion, section, sector.

**segregate** vb detach, disconnect, disperse, insulate, part, separate.

**segregation** n apartheid, discrimination, insulation, separation.

**seize** vb capture, catch, clutch, grab, grapple, grasp, grip, snatch; confiscate, impress, impound; apprehend, comprehend; arrest, take.

**seldom** adv infrequently, occasionally, rarely.

**select** vb choose, cull, pick, prefer. * adj choice, chosen, excellent, exquisite, good, picked, rare, selected.

**selection** n choice, election, pick, preference.

**self-conscious** adj awkward, diffident, embarrassed, insecure, nervous.

**self-control** n restraint, willpower.

**self-important** adj assuming, consequential, proud, haughty, lordly, overbearing, overweening.

**selfish** adj egoistic, egotistical, greedy, illiberal, mean, narrow, self-seeking, ungenerous.

**self-possessed** adj calm, collected, composed, cool, placid, sedate, undisturbed, unexcited, unruffled.

**self-willed** adj contumacious, dogged, headstrong, obstinate, pig-headed, stubborn, uncompliant, wilful.

**sell** vb barter, exchange, hawk, market, peddle, trade, vend.

**semblance** n likeness, resemblance, similarity; air, appearance, aspect, bearing, exterior, figure, form, mien, seeming, show; image, representation, similitude.

**seminal** adj important, original; germinal, radical, rudimental, rudimentary, unformed.

**seminary** n academy, college, gymnasium, high school, institute, school, university.

**send** vb cast, drive, emit, fling, hurl, impel, lance, launch, project, propel, throw, toss; delegate, depute, dispatch; forward, transmit; bestow, confer, give, grant.

**senile** adj aged, doddering, superannuated; doting, imbecile.

**senior** adj elder, older; higher.

**seniority** n eldership, precedence, priority, superiority.

**sensation** n feeling, sense, perception; excitement, impression, thrill.

**sensational** adj exciting, melodramatic, startling, thrilling.

**sense** vb appraise, appreciate, estimate, notice, observe, perceive, suspect, understand. * n brains, intellect, intelligence, mind, reason, understanding; appreciation, apprehension, discernment, feeling, perception, recognition, tact; connotation, idea, implication, judgment, notion, opinion, sentiment, view; import, interpretation, meaning, purport, significance; sagacity, soundness, substance, wisdom.

**senseless** adj apathetic, inert, insensate, unfeeling; absurd, foolish, ill-judged, nonsensical, silly, unmeaning, unreasonable, unwise; doltish, foolish, simple, stupid, witless, weak-minded.

**sensible** *adj* apprehensible, perceptible; aware, cognizant, conscious, convinced, persuaded, satisfied; discreet, intelligent, judicious, rational, reasonable, sagacious, sage, sober, sound, wise; observant, understanding; impressionable, sensitive.

**sensitive** *adj* perceptive, sentient; affected, impressible, impressionable, responsive, susceptible; delicate, tender, touchy.

**sensual** *adj* animal, bodily, carnal, voluptuous; gross, lascivious, lewd, licentious, unchaste.

**sentence** *vb* condemn, doom, judge. * *n* decision, determination, judgment, opinion, verdict; doctrine, dogma, opinion, tenet; condemnation, conviction, doom; period, proposition.

**sententious** *adj* compendious, compact, concise, didactic, laconic, pithy, pointed, succinct, terse.

**sentiment** *n* judgment, notion, opinion; maxim, saying; emotion, tenderness; disposition, feeling, thought.

**sentimental** *adj* impressible, impressionable, overemotional, romantic, tender.

**sentinel** *n* guard, guardsman, patrol, picket, sentry, watchman.

**separate** *vb* detach, disconnect, disjoin, disunite, dissever, divide, divorce, part, sever, sunder; eliminate, remove, withdraw; cleave, open. * *adj* detached, disconnected, disjoined, disjointed, dissociated, disunited, divided, parted, severed; discrete, distinct, divorced, unconnected; alone, segregated, withdrawn.

**separation** *n* disjunction, disjuncture, dissociation; disconnection, disseverance, disseveration, disunion, division, divorce; analysis, decomposition.

**sepulchral** *adj* deep, dismal, funereal, gloomy, grave, hollow, lugubrious, melancholy, mournful, sad, sombre, woeful.

**sepulchre** *n* burial place, charnel house, grave, ossuary, sepulture, tomb.

**sequel** *n* close, conclusion, denouement, end, termination; consequence, event, issue, result, upshot.

**sequence** *n* following, graduation, progression, succession; arrangement, series, train.

**sequestrated** *adj* hidden, private, retired, secluded, unfrequented, withdrawn; seized.

**seraphic** *adj* angelic, celestial, heavenly, sublime; holy, pure, refined.

**serene** *adj* calm, collected, placid, peaceful, quiet, tranquil, sedate, undisturbed, unperturbed, unruffled; bright, calm, clear, fair, unclouded.

**serenity** *n* calm, calmness, collectedness, composure, coolness, imperturbability, peace, peacefulness, quiescence, sedateness, tranquillity; brightness, calmness, clearness, fairness, peace, quietness, stillness.

**serf** *n* bondman, servant, slave, thrall, villein.

**serfdom** *n* bondage, enslavement, enthralment, servitude, slavery, subjection, thraldom.

**series** *n* chain, concatenation, course, line, order, progression, sequence, succession, train.

**serious** *adj* earnest, grave, demure, pious, resolute, sedate, sober, solemn, staid, thoughtful; dangerous, great, important, momentous, weighty.

**sermon** *n* discourse, exhortation, homily, lecture.

**serpentine** *adj* anfractuous, convoluted, crooked, meandering, sinuous, spiral, tortuous, twisted, undulating, winding.

**servant** *n* attendant, dependant, factotum, helper, henchman, retainer, servitor, subaltern, subordinate, underling; domestic, drudge, flunky, lackey, menial, scullion, slave.

**serve** *vb* aid, assist, attend, help, minister, oblige, succour; advance, benefit, forward, promote; content, satisfy, supply; handle, officiate, manage, manipulate, work.

**service** *vb* check, maintain, overhaul, repair. * *n* labour, ministration, work; attendance, business, duty, employ, employment, office; advantage, benefit, good, gain, profit; avail, purpose, use, utility; ceremony, function, observance, rite, worship.

**serviceable** *adj* advantageous, available, beneficial, convenient, functional, handy, helpful, operative, profitable, useful.

**servile** *adj* dependent, menial; abject, base, beggarly, cringing, fawning, grovelling, low, mean, obsequious, slavish, sneaking, sycophantic, truckling.

**servility** *n* bondage, dependence, slavery; abjection, abjectness, baseness, fawning, meanness, obsequiousness, slavishness, sycophancy.

**servitor** *n* attendant, dependant, footman, lackey, retainer, servant, squire, valet, waiter.

**servitude** *n* bondage, enslavement, enthralment, serfdom, service, slavery, thraldom.

**set**[1] *vb* lay, locate, mount, place, put, stand, station; appoint, determine, establish, fix, settle; risk, stake, wager; adapt, adjust, regulate; adorn, stud, variegate; arrange, dispose, pose, post; appoint, assign, predetermine, prescribe; estimate, prize, rate, value; embarrass, perplex, pose; contrive, produce; decline, sink; congeal, concern, consolidate, harden, solidify; flow, incline, run, tend; (with **about**) begin, commence; (with **apart**) appropriate, consecrate, dedicate, devote, reserve, set aside; (with **aside**) abrogate, annul, omit, reject; reserve, set apart; (with **before**) display, exhibit; (with **down**) chronicle, jot down, record, register, state, write down; (with **forth**) display, exhibit, explain, expound, manifest, promulgate, publish, put forward, represent, show; (with **forward**) advance, further, promote; (with **free**) acquit, clear, emancipate, liberate, release; (with **off**) adorn, decorate, embellish; define, portion off; (with **on**) actuate, encourage, impel, influence, incite, instigate, prompt, spur, urge; attack, assault, set upon; (with **out**) display, issue, publish, proclaim, prove, recommend, show; (with **right**) correct, put in order; (with **to rights**) adjust, regulate; (with **up**) elevate, erect, exalt, raise; establish, found, institute; (with **upon**) assail, assault, attack, fly at, rush upon. * adj appointed, established, formal, ordained, prescribed, regular, settled; determined, fixed, firm, obstinate, positive, stiff, unyielding; immovable, predetermined; located, placed, put. * n attitude, position, posture; scene, scenery, setting.

**set²** n assortment, collection, suit; class, circle, clique, cluster, company, coterie, division, gang, group, knot, party, school, sect.

**setback** n blow, hitch, hold-up, rebuff; defeat, disappointment, reverse.

**set-off** n adornment, decoration, embellishment, ornament; counterbalance, counterclaim, equivalent.

**settle** vb adjust, arrange, compose, regulate; account, balance, close up, conclude, discharge, liquidate, pay, pay up, reckon, satisfy, square; allay, calm, compose, pacify, quiet, repose, rest, still, tranquillize; confirm, decide, determine, make clear; establish, fix, set; fall, gravitate, sink, subside; abide, colonize, domicile, dwell, establish, inhabit, people, place, plant, reside; (with **on**) determine on, fix on, fix upon; establish. * n bench, seat, stool.

**settled** adj established, fixed, stable; decided, deep-rooted, steady, unchanging; adjusted, arranged; methodical, orderly, quiet; common, customary, everyday, ordinary, usual, wonted.

**set-to** n combat, conflict, contest, fight.

**sever** vb divide, part, rend, separate, sunder; detach, disconnect, disjoin, disunite.

**several** adj individual, single, particular; distinct, exclusive, independent, separate; different, divers, diverse, manifold, many, sundry, various.

**severance** n partition, separation.

**severe** adj austere, bitter, dour, hard, harsh, inexorable, morose, painful, relentless, rigid, rigorous, rough, sharp, stern, stiff, strait-laced, unmitigated, unrelenting, unsparing; accurate, exact, methodical, strict; chaste, plain, restrained, simple, unadorned; biting, caustic, cruel, cutting, harsh, keen, sarcastic, satirical, trenchant; acute, afflictive, distressing, excruciating, extreme, intense, stringent, violent; critical, exact.

**severity** n austerity, gravity, harshness, rigour, seriousness, sternness, strictness; accuracy, exactness, niceness; chasteness, plainness, simplicity; acrimony, causticity, keenness, sharpness; afflictiveness, extremity, keenness, stringency, violence; cruelty.

**sew** vb baste, bind, hem, stitch, tack.

**sex** n gender, femininity, masculinity, sexuality; coitus, copulation, fornication, love-making.

**shabby** adj faded, mean, poor, ragged, seedy, threadbare, worn, worn-out; beggarly, mean, paltry, penurious, stingy, ungentlemanly, unhandsome.

**shackle** vb chain, fetter, gyve, hamper, manacle; bind, clog, confine, cumber, embarrass, encumber, impede, obstruct, restrict, trammel. * n chain, fetter, gyve, hamper, manacle.

**shade** vb cloud, darken, dim, eclipse, obfuscate, obscure; cover, ensconce, hide, protect, screen, shelter. * n darkness, dusk, duskiness, gloom, obscurity, shadow; cover, protection, shelter; awning, blind, curtain, screen, shutter, veil; degree, difference, kind, variety; cast, colour, complexion, dye, hue, tinge, tint, tone; apparition, ghost, manes, phantom, shadow, spectre, spirit.

**shadow** vb becloud, cloud, darken, obscure, shade; adumbrate, foreshadow, symbolize, typify; conceal, cover, hide, protect, screen, shroud. * n penumbra, shade, umbra, umbrage; darkness, gloom, obscurity; cover, protection, security, shelter; adumbration, foreshadowing, image, prefiguration, representation; apparition, ghost, phantom, shade, spirit; image, portrait, reflection, silhouette.

**shadowy** adj shady, umbrageous; dark, dim, gloomy, murky, obscure; ghostly, imaginary, impalpable, insubstantial, intangible, spectral, unreal, unsubstantial, visionary.

**shady** adj shadowy, umbrageous; crooked.

**shaft** n arrow, missile, weapon; handle, helve; pole, tongue; axis, spindle; pinnacle, spire; stalk, stem, trunk.

**shaggy** adj rough, rugged.

**shake** vb quake, quaver, quiver, shiver, shudder, totter, tremble; agitate, convulse, jar, jolt, stagger; daunt, frighten, intimidate; endanger, move, weaken; oscillate, vibrate, wave; move, put away, remove, throw off. * n agitation, concussion, flutter, jar, jolt, quaking, shaking, shivering, shock, trembling, tremor.

**shaky** adj jiggly, quaky, shaking, tottering, trembling.

**shallow** adj flimsy, foolish, frivolous, puerile, trashy, trifling, trivial; empty, ignorant, silly, slight, simple, superficial, unintelligent.

**sham** vb ape, feign, imitate, pretend; cheat, deceive, delude, dupe, impose, trick. * adj assumed, counterfeit, false, feigned, mock, make-believe, pretended, spurious. * n delusion, feint, fraud, humbug, imposition, imposture, pretence, trick.

**shamble** vb hobble, shuffle.

**shambles** npl abattoir, slaughterhouse; confusion, disorder, mess.

**shame** vb debase, degrade, discredit, disgrace, dishonour, stain, sully, taint, tarnish; abash, confound, confuse, discompose, disconcert, humble, humiliate; deride, flout, jeer, mock, ridicule, sneer. * n contempt, degradation, derision, discredit, disgrace, dishonour, disrepute, ignominy, infamy, obloquy, odium, opprobrium; abashment, chagrin, confusion, embarrassment, humiliation, mortification; reproach, scandal; decency, decorousness, decorum, modesty, propriety, seemliness.

**shamefaced** adj bashful, diffident, overmodest.

**shameful** adj atrocious, base, disgraceful, dishonourable, disreputable, heinous, ignominious, infamous, nefarious, opprobrious, outrageous, scandalous, vile, villainous, wicked; degrading, indecent, unbecoming.

**shameless** adj assuming, audacious, bold-faced, brazen, brazen-faced, cool, immodest, impudent, indecent, indelicate, insolent, unabashed, unblushing; abandoned, corrupt, depraved, dissolute, graceless, hardened, incorrigible, irreclaimable,

lost, obdurate, profligate, reprobate, sinful, unprincipled, vicious.

**shape** vb create, form, make, produce; fashion, model, mould; adjust, direct, frame, regulate; conceive, conjure up, figure, image, imagine. * n appearance, aspect, fashion, figure, form, guise, make; build, cast, cut, model, mould, pattern; apparition, image.

**shapeless** adj amorphous, formless; grotesque, irregular, rude, uncouth, unsymmetrical.

**shapely** adj comely, symmetrical, trim, well-formed.

**share** vb apportion, distribute, divide, parcel out, portion, split; partake, participate; experience, receive. * n part, portion, quantum; allotment, allowance, contingent, deal, dividend, division, interest, lot, proportion, quantity, quota.

**sharer** n communicant, partaker, participator.

**sharp** adj acute, cutting, keen, keen-edged, knife-edged, razor-edged, trenchant; acuminate, needle-shaped, peaked, pointed, ridged; apt, astute, canny, clear-sighted, clever, cunning, discerning, discriminating, ingenious, inventive, keen-witted, penetrating, perspicacious, quick, ready, sagacious, sharp-witted, shrewd, smart, subtle, witty; acid, acrid, biting, bitter, burning, high-flavoured, high-seasoned, hot, mordacious, piquant, poignant, pungent, sour, stinging; acrimonious, biting, caustic, cutting, harsh, mordant, sarcastic, severe, tart, trenchant; cruel, hard, rigid; afflicting, distressing, excruciating, intense, painful, piercing, shooting, sore, violent; nipping, pinching; ardent, eager, fervid, fierce, fiery, impetuous, strong; high, screeching, shrill; attentive, vigilant; severe; close, exacting, shrewd, cold, crisp, freezing, icy wintry. * adv abruptly, sharply, suddenly; exactly, precisely, punctually.

**sharp-cut** adj clear, distinct, well-defined.

**sharpen** vb edge, intensify, point.

**sharper** n cheat, deceiver, defrauder, knave, rogue, shark, swindler, trickster.

**sharply** adv rigorously, roughly, severely; acutely, keenly; vehemently, violently; accurately, exactly, minutely, trenchantly, wittily; abruptly, steeply.

**sharpness** n acuteness, keenness, trenchancy; acuity, spinosity; acumen, cleverness, discernment, ingenuity, quickness, sagacity, shrewdness, smartness, wit; acidity, acridity, piquancy, pungency, sting, tartness; causticness, incisiveness, pungency, sarcasm, satire, severity; afflictiveness, intensity, painfulness, poignancy;

ardour, fierceness, violence; discordance, dissonance, highness, screechiness, squeakiness, shrillness.

**sharp-sighted** adj clear-sighted, keen, keen-eyed, keen-sighted.

**sharp-witted** adj acute, clear-sighted, cunning, discerning, ingenious, intelligent, keen, keen-sighted, long-headed, quick, sagacious, sharp, shrewd.

**shatter** vb break, burst, crack, rend, shiver, smash, splinter, split; break up, derange, disorder, overthrow.

**shave** vb crop, cut off, mow, pare; slice; graze, skim, touch.

**shaver** n boy, child, youngster; bargainer, extortioner, sharper.

**shear** vb clip, cut, fleece, strip; divest; break off.

**sheath** n case, casing, covering, envelope, scabbard, sheathing.

**sheathe** vb case, cover, encase, enclose.

**shed**[1] n cabin, cot, hovel, hut, outhouse, shack, shelter.

**shed**[2] vb effuse, let fall, pour out, spill; diffuse, emit, give out, scatter, spread; cast, let fall, put off, slough, throw off.

**sheen** n brightness, gloss, glossiness, shine, spendour.

**sheep** n ewe, lamb, ram.

**sheepish** adj bashful, diffident, overmodest, shame-faced, timid, timorous.

**sheer**[1] adj perpendicular, precipitous, steep, vertical; clear, downright, mere, pure, simple, unadulterated, unmingled, unmixed, unqualified, utter; clear; fine, transparent. * adv outright; perpendicularly, steeply.

**sheer**[2] vb decline, deviate, move aside, swerve. * n bow, curve.

**shelf** n bracket, console, ledge, mantelpiece.

**shell** vb exfoliate, fall off, peel off; bombard. * n carapace, case, covering, shard; bomb, grenade, sharpnel; framework.

**shelter** vb cover, defend, ensconce, harbour, hide, house, protect, screen, shield, shroud. * n asylum, cover, covert, harbour, haven, hideaway, refuge, retreat, sanctuary; defence, protection, safety, screen, security, shield; guardian, protector.

**shelve** vb dismiss, put aside; incline, slope.

**shepherd** vb escort, guide, marshal, usher; direct, drive, drove, herd, lead; guard, tend, watch over. * n drover, grazier, herder, herdsman; chaplain, churchman, clergyman, cleric, divine, ecclesiastic,

minister, padre, parson, pastor; chaperon, duenna, escort, guide, squire, usher.

**shield** vb cover, defend, guard, protect, shelter; repel, ward off; avert, forbid, forfend. * n aegis, buckler, escutcheon, scutcheon, targe; bulwark, cover, defence, guard, palladium, protection, rampart, safeguard, security, shelter.

**shift** vb alter, change, fluctuate, move, vary; chop, dodge, swerve, veer; contrive, devise, manage, plan, scheme, shuffle. * n change, substitution, turn; contrivance, expedient, means, resort, resource; artifice, craft, device, dodge, evasion, fraud, mask, ruse, stratagem, subterfuge, trick, wile; chemise, smock.

**shiftless** adj improvident, imprudent, negligent, slack, thriftless, unresourceful.

**shifty** adj tricky, undependable, wily.

**shillyshally** vb hesitate, waver. * n hesitation, irresolute, wavering.

**shimmer** vb flash, glimmer, glisten, shine. * n blink, glimmer, glitter, twinkle.

**shin** vb climb, swarm. * n shinbone, tibia.

**shindy** n disturbance, riot, roughhouse, row, spree, uproar.

**shine** vb beam, blaze, coruscate, flare, give light, glare, gleam, glimmer, glisten, glitter, glow, lighten, radiate, sparkle; excel. * n brightness, brilliancy, glaze, gloss, polish, sheen.

**shining** adj beaming, bright, brilliant, effulgent, gleaming, glowing, glistening, glittering, luminous, lustrous, radiant, resplendent, splendid; conspicuous, distinguished, illustrious.

**shiny** adj bright, clear, luminous, sunshiny, unclouded; brilliant, burnished, glassy, glossy, polished.

**ship** n boat, craft, steamer, vessel.

**shipshape** adj neat, orderly, tidy, trim, well-arranged.

**shipwreck** vb cast away, maroon, strand, wreck. * n demolition, destruction, miscarriage, overthrow, perdition, ruin, subversion, wreck.

**shirk** vb avoid, dodge, evade, malinger, quit, slack; cheat, shark, trick.

**shiver**[1] vb break, shatter, splinter. * n bit, fragment, piece, slice, sliver, splinter.

**shiver**[2] vb quake, quiver, shake, shudder, tremble. * n shaking, shivering, shuddering, tremor.

**shivery**[1] adj brittle, crumbly, frangible, friable, shatterable, splintery.

**shivery**[2] adj quaking, quavering, quivering, shaky, trembly, tremulous; chilly, shivering.

**shoal**[1] vb crowd, throng. * n crowd, horde, multitude, swarm, throng.

**shoal**[2] n sandbank, shallows; danger.

**shock** vb appall, horrify; disgust, disquiet, disturb, nauseate, offend, outrage, revolt, scandalize, sicken; astound, stagger, stun; collide with, jar, jolt, shake, strike against; encounter, meet. * n agitation, blow, offence, stroke, trauma; assault, brunt, conflict; clash, collision, concussion, impact, percussion.

**shocking** adj abominable, detestable, disgraceful, disgusting, execrable, foul, hateful, loathsome, obnoxious, odious, offensive, repugnant, repulsive, revolting; appalling, awful, dire, dreadful, fearful, frightful, ghastly, hideous, horrible, horrid, horrific, monstrous, terrible.

**shoot** vb catapult, expel, hurl, let fly, propel; discharge, fire, let off; dart, fly, pass, pelt; extend, jut, project, protrude, protuberate, push, put forth, send forth, stretch; bud, germinate, sprout; (with **up**) grow increase, spring up, run up, start up. * n branch, offshoot, scion, sprout, twig.

**shop** n emporium, market, mart, store; workshop.

**shore**[1] n beach, brim, coast, seabord, seaside, strand, waterside.

**shore**[2] vb brace, buttress, prop, stay, support. * n beam, brace, buttress, prop, stay, support.

**shorn** adj cut-off; deprived.

**short** adj brief, curtailed; direct, near, straight; compendious, concise, condensed, laconic, pithy, terse, sententious, succinct, summary; abrupt, curt, petulant, pointed, sharp, snappish, uncivil; defective, deficient, inadequate, insufficient, niggardly, scanty, scrimpy; contracted, desitute, lacking, limited, minus, wanting; dwarfish, squat, undersized; brittle, crisp, crumbling, friable. * adv abruptly, at once, forthwith, suddenly.

**shortcoming** n defect, deficiency, delinquency, error, failing, failure, fault, imperfection, inadequacy, remissness, slip, weakness.

**shorten** vb abbreviate, abridge, curtail, cut short; abridge, contract, diminish, lessen, retrench, reduce; cut off, dock, lop, trim; confine, hinder, restrain, restrict.

**shortening** n abbreviation, abridgment, contraction, curtailment, diminution, retrenchment, reduction.

**shorthand** n brachygraphy, stenography, tachygraphy.

**short-lived** adj emphemeral, transient, transitory.

**shortly** adv quickly, soon; briefly, concisely, succinctly, tersely.

**short-sighted** adj myopic, nearsighted, purblind; imprudent, indiscreet.

**shot**[1] n discharge; ball, bullet, missile, projectile; marksman, shooter.

**shot**[2] adj chatoyant, iridescent, irisated, moiré, watered; intermingled, interspersed, interwoven.

**shoulder** vb bear, bolster, carry, hump, maintain, pack, support, sustain, tote; crowd, elbow, jostle, press forward, push, thrust. * n projection, protuberance.

**shoulder blade** n blade bone, omoplate, scapula, shoulder bone.

**shout** vb bawl, cheer, clamour, exclaim, halloo, roar, vociferate, whoop, yell. * n cheer, clamour, exclamation, halloo, hoot, huzza, outcry, roar, vociferation, whoop, yell.

**shove** vb jostle, press against, propel, push, push aside; (with **off**) push away, thrust away.

**show** vb blazon, display, exhibit, flaunt, parade, present; indicate, mark, point out; disclose, discover, divulge, explain, make clear, make known, proclaim, publish, reveal, unfold; demonstrate, evidence, manifest, prove, verify; conduct, guide, usher; direct, inform, instruct, teach; expound, elucidate, interpret; (with **off**) display, exhibit, make a show, set off; (with **up**) expose. * n array, exhibition, representation, sight, spectacle; blazonry, bravery, ceremony, dash, demonstration, display, flourish, ostentation, pageant, pageantry, parade, pomp, splendour, splurge; likeness, resemblance, semblance; affectation, appearance, colour, illusion, mask, plausibility, pose, pretence, pretext, simulation, speciousness; entertainment, production.

**showy** adj bedizened, dressy, fine, flashy, flaunting, garish, gaudy, glaring, gorgeous, loud, ornate, smart, swanky, splendid; grand, magnificent, ostentatious, pompous, pretentious, stately, sumptuous.

**shred** vb tear. * n bit, fragment, piece, rag, scrap, strip, tatter.

**shrew** n brawler, fury, scold, spitfire, termagant, virago, vixen.

**shrewd** adj arch, artful, astute, crafty, cunning, Machiavellian, sly, subtle, wily; acute, astute, canny, discerning, discriminating, ingenious, keen, knowing, penetrating, sagacious, sharp, sharp-sighted.

**shrewdness** n address, archness, art, artfulness, astuteness, craft, cunning, policy, skill, slyness, subtlety; acumen, acuteness, discernment, ingenuity, keenness, penetration, perspicacity, sagacity, sharpness, wit.

**shrewish** *adj* brawling, clamorous, froward, peevish, petulant, scolding, vixenish.

**shriek** *vb* scream, screech, squeal, yell, yelp. * *n* cry, scream, screech, yell.

**shrill** *adj* acute, high, high-toned, high-pitched, piercing, piping, sharp.

**shrine** *n* reliquary, sacred tomb; altar, hallowed place, sacred place.

**shrink** *vb* contract, decrease, dwindle, shrivel, wither; balk, blench, draw back, flinch, give way, quail, recoil, retire, swerve, wince, withdraw.

**shrivel** *vb* dry, dry up, parch; contract, decrease, dwindle, shrink, wither, wrinkle.

**shroud** *vb* bury, cloak, conceal, cover, hide, mask, muffle, protect, screen, shelter, veil. * *n* covering, garment; grave clothes, winding sheet.

**shrub** *n* bush, dwarf tree, low tree.

**shrubby** *adj* bushy.

**shudder** *vb* quake, quiver, shake, shiver, tremble. * *n* shaking, shuddering, trembling, tremor.

**shuffle** *vb* confuse, disorder, intermix, jumble, mix, shift; cavil, dodge, equivocate, evade, prevaricate, quibble, vacillate; struggle. * *n* artifice, cavil, evasion, fraud, pretence, pretext, prevarication, quibble, ruse, shuffling, sophism, subterfuge, trick.

**shun** *vb* avoid, elude, eschew, escape, evade, get clear of.

**shut** *vb* close, close up, stop; confine, coop up, enclose, imprison, lock up, shut up; (*with* **in**) confine, enclose; (*with* **off**) bar, exclude, intercept; (*with* **up**) close up, shut; confine, enclose, fasten in, imprison, lock in, lock up.

**shy** *vb* cast, chuck, fling, hurl, jerk, pitch, sling, throw, toss; boggle, sheer, start aside. * *adj* bashful, coy, diffident, reserved, retiring, sheepish, shrinking, timid; cautious, chary, distrustful, heedful, wary. * *n* start; fling, throw.

**sibilant** *adj* buzzing, hissing, sibilous.

**sick** *adj* ailing, ill, indisposed, laid-up, unwell, weak; nauseated, queasy; disgusted, revolted, tired, weary; diseased, distempered, disordered, feeble, morbid, unhealthy, unsound, weak; languishing, longing, pining.

**sicken** *vb* ail, disease, fall sick, make sick; nauseate; disgust, weary; decay, droop, languish, pine.

**sickening** *adj* nauseating, nauseous, palling, sickish; disgusting, distasteful, loathsome, offensive, repulsive, revolting.

**sickly** *adj* ailing, diseased, faint, feeble, infirm, languid, languishing, morbid, unhealthy, valetudinary, weak, weakly.

**sickness** *n* ail, ailment, complaint, disease, disorder, distemper, illness, indisposition, invalidism, malady, morbidity; nausea, qualmishness, queasiness.

**side** *vb* border, bound, edge, flank, frontier, march, rim, skirt, verge; avert, turn aside; (*with* **with**) befriend, favour, flock to, join with, second, support. * *adj* flanking, later, skirting; indirect, oblique; extra, odd, off, spare. * *n* border, edge, flank, margin, verge; cause, faction, interest, party, sect.

**sideboard** *n* buffet, dresser.

**side by side** abreast, alongside, by the side.

**sidelong** *adj* lateral, oblique. * *adv* laterally, obliquely; on the side.

**sidewalk** *n* footpath, footway, pavement.

**sideways, sidewise** *adv* laterally. * *adv* athwart, crossways, crosswise, laterally, obliquely, sidelong, sidewards.

**siesta** *n* doze, nap.

**sift** *vb* part, separate; bolt, screen, winnow; analyse, canvass, discuss, examine, fathom, follow up, inquire into, investigate, probe, scrutinze, sound, try.

**sigh** *vb* complain, grieve, lament, mourn. * *n* long breath, sough, suspiration.

**sight** *vb* get sight of, perceive, see. * *n* cognizance, ken, perception, view; beholding, eyesight, seeing, vision; exhibition, prospect, representation, scene, show, spectacle, wonder; consideration, estimation, knowledge; examination, inspection.

**sightless** *adj* blind, eyeless, unseeing.

**sightly** *adj* beautiful, comely, handsome.

**sign** *vb* indicate, signal, signify; countersign, endorse, subscribe. * *n* emblem, index, indication, manifestation, mark, note, proof, signal, signification, symbol, symptom, token; beacon; augury, auspice, foreboding, miracle, omen, portent, presage, prodigy, prognostic, wonder; type; countersign, password.

**signal** *vb* flag, glance, hail, nod, nudge, salute, sign, signalize, sound, speak, touch, wave, wink. * *adj* conspicuous, eminent, extraordinary, memorable, notable, noteworthy, remarkable. * *n* cue, indication, mark, sign, token.

**signalize** vb celebrate, distinguish, make memorable.

**signature** n mark, sign, stamp; autograph, hand.

**significance** n implication, import, meaning, purport, sense; consequence, importance, moment, portent, weight; emphasis, energy, expressiveness, force, impressiveness.

**significant** adj betokening, expressive, indicative, significative, signifying; important, material, momentous, portentous, weighty; forcible, emphatic, expressive, telling.

**signification** n expression; acceptation, import, meaning, purport, sense.

**signify** vb betoken, communication, express, indicate, intimate; denote, imply, import, mean, purport, suggest; announce, declare, give notice of, impart, make known, manifest, proclaim, utter; augur, foreshadow, indicate, portend, represent; matter, weigh.

**silence** vb hush, muzzle, still; allay, calm, quiet. * interj be silent, be still, hush, soft, tush, tut, whist. * n calm, hush, lull, noiselessness, peace, quiet, quietude, soundlessness, stillness; dumbness, mumness, muteness, reticence, speechlessness, taciturnity.

**silent** adj calm, hushed, noiseless, quiet, soundless, still; dumb, inarticulate, mum, mute, nonvocal, speechless, tacit; reticent, taciturn, uncommunicative.

**silken** adj flossy, silky, soft.

**silkiness** n smoothness, softness.

**silly** adj brainless, childish, foolish, inept, senseless, shallow, simple, stupid, weak-minded, witless; absurd, extravagant, frivolous, imprudent, indiscreet, nonsensical, preposterous, trifling, unwise. * n ass, duffer, goose, idiot, simpleton.

**silt** n alluvium, deposit, deposition, residue, settlement, settlings, sediment.

**silver** adj argent, silvery; bright, silvery, white; clear, mellifluous, soft.

**similar** adj analogous, duplicate, like, resembling, twin; homogeneous, uniform.

**similarity** n agreement, analogy, correspondence, likeness, parallelism, parity, resemblance, sameness, semblance, similitude.

**simile** n comparison, metaphor, similitude.

**similitude** n image, likeness, resemblance; comparison, metaphor, simile.

**simmer** vb boil, bubble, seethe, stew.

**simper** vb smile, smirk.

**simple** adj bare, elementary, homogeneous, incomplex, mere, single, unalloyed, unblended, uncombined, uncompounded, unmingled, unmixed; chaste, plain, homespun, inornate, natural, neat, unadorned, unaffected, unembellished, unpretentious, unstudied, unvarnished; artless, downright, frank, guileless, inartificial, ingenuous, naive, open, simple-hearted, simple-minded, sincere, single-minded, straightforward, true, unconstrained, undesigning, unsophisticated; credulous, fatuous, foolish, shallow, silly, unwise, weak; clear, intelligible, understandable, uninvolved, unmistakable.

**simple-hearted** adj artless, frank, ingenuous, open, simple, single-hearted.

**simpleton** n fool, greenhorn, nincompoop, ninny.

**simplicity** n chasteness, homeliness, naturalness, neatness, plainness; artlessness, frankness, naivety, openness, simplesse, sincerity; clearness; gullibility, folly, silliness, weakness.

**simply** adv artlessly, plainly, sincerely, unaffectedly; barely, merely, of itself, solely; absolutely, alone.

**simulate** vb act, affect, ape, assume, counterfeit, dissemble, feign, mimic, pretend, sham.

**simulation** n counterfeiting, feigning, personation, pretence.

**simultaneous** adj coeval, coincident, concomitant, concurrent, contemporaneous, synchronous.

**sin** vb do wrong, err, transgress, trespass. * n delinquency, depravity, guilt, iniquity, misdeed, offence, transgression, unrighteousness, wickedness, wrong.

**since** conj as, because, considering, seeing that. * adv ago, before this; from that time. * prep after, from the time of, subsequently to.

**sincere** adj pure, unmixed; genuine, honest, inartificial, real, true, unaffected, unfeigned, unvarnished; artless, candid, direct, frank, guileless, hearty, honest, ingenuous, open, plain, single, straightforward, truthful, undissembling, upright, whole-hearted.

**sincerity** n artlessness, candour, earnestness, frankness, genuineness, guilelessness, honesty, ingenuousness, probity, truth, truthfulness, unaffectedness, veracity.

**sinew** n ligament, tendon; brawn, muscle, nerve, strength.

**sinewy** adj able-bodied, brawny, firm, Herculean, muscular, nervous, powerful, robust, stalwart, strapping, strong, sturdy, vigorous, wiry.

**sinful** adj bad, criminal, depraved, immoral, iniquitous, mischievous, peccant, transgressive, unholy, unrighteous, wicked, wrong.

**sinfulness** n corruption, criminality, depravity, iniquity, irreligion, ungodliness, unholiness, unrighteousness, wickedness.

**sing** vb cantillate, carol, chant, hum, hymn, intone, lilt, troll, warble, yodel.

**singe** vb burn, scorch, sear.

**singer** n cantor, caroler, chanter, gleeman, prima donna, minstrel, psalmodist, songster, vocalist.

**single** vb (with **out**) choose, pick, select, single. * adj alone, isolated, one only, sole, solitary; individual, particular, separate; celibate, unmarried, unwedded; pure, simple, uncompounded, unmixed; honest, ingenuous, sincere, unbiased, uncorrupt, upright.

**single-handed** adj alone, by one's self, unaided, unassisted.

**single-minded** adj artless, candid, guileless, ingenuous, sincere.

**singleness** n individuality, unity; purity, simplicity; ingenuousness, integrity, sincerity, uprightness.

**singular** adj eminent, exceptional, extraordinary, rare, remarkable, strange, uncommon, unusual, unwonted; particular, unexampled, unparalleled, unprecedented; unaccountable; bizarre, curious, eccentric, fantastic, odd, peculiar, queer; individual, single; not complex, single, uncompounded, unique.

**singularity** n aberration, abnormality, irregularity, oddness, rareness, rarity, strangeness, uncommonness; characteristic, idiosyncrasy, individuality, particularity, peculiarity; eccentricity, oddity.

**sinister** adj baleful, injurious, untoward; boding ill, inauspicious, ominous, unlucky; left, on the left hand.

**sink** vb droop, drop, fall, founder, go down, submerge, subside; enter, penetrate; collapse, fail; decay, decline, decrease, dwindle, give way, languish, lose strength; engulf, immerse, merge, submerge, submerse; dig, excavate, scoop out; abase, bring down, crush, debase, degrade, depress, diminish, lessen, lower, overbear; destroy, overthrow, overwhelm, reduce, ruin, swamp, waste. * n basin, cloaca, drain.

**sinless** adj faultless, guiltless, immaculate, impeccable, innocent, spotless, unblemished, undefiled, unspotted, unsullied, untarnished.

**sinner** n criminal, delinquent, evildoer, offender, reprobate, wrongdoer.

**sinuosity** n crook, curvature, flexure, sinus, tortuosity, winding.

**sinuous** adj bending, crooked, curved, curvilinear, flexuous, serpentine, sinuate, sinuated, tortuous, undulating, wavy, winding.

**sip** vb drink, suck up, sup; absorb, drink in. * n small draught, taste.

**sire** vb father, reproduce; author, breed, conceive, create, generate, originate, produce, propagate. * n father, male parent, progenitor; man, male person; sir, sirrah; author, begetter, creator, father, generator, originator.

**siren** adj alluring, bewitching, fascinating, seducing, tempting. * n mermaid; charmer, Circe, seducer, seductress, tempter, temptress.

**sit** vb be, remain, repose, rest, stay; bear on, lie, rest; abide, dwell, settle; perch; brood, incubate; become, be suited, fit.

**site** vb locate, place, position, situate, station. * n ground, locality, location, place, position, seat, situation, spot, station, whereabouts.

**sitting** n meeting, session.

**situation** n ground, locality, location, place, position, seat, site, spot, whereabouts; case, category, circumstances, condition, juncture, plight, predicament, state; employment, office, place, post, station.

**size** n amplitude, bigness, bulk, dimensions, expanse, greatness, largeness, magnitude, mass, volume.

**skeleton** n framework; draft, outline, sketch.

**sketch** vb design, draft, draw out; delineate, depict, paint, portray, represent. * n delineation, design, draft, drawing, outline, plan, skeleton.

**sketchy** adj crude, incomplete, unfinished.

**skilful** adj able, accomplished, adept, adroit, apt, clever, competent, conversant, cunning, deft, dexterous, dextrous, expert, handy, ingenious, masterly, practised, proficient, qualified, quick, ready, skilled, trained, versed, well-versed.

**skill** n ability, address, adroitness, aptitude, aptness, art, cleverness, deftness, dexterity, expertise, expertness, facility, ingenuity, knack, quickness, readiness, skilfulness; discernment, discrimination, knowledge, understanding, wit.

**skim** vb brush, glance, graze, kiss, scrape, scratch, sweep, touch lightly; coast, flow, fly, glide, sail, scud, whisk; dip into, glance at, scan, skip, thumb over, touch upon.

**skin** vb pare, peel; decorticate, excoriate, flay. * n

cuticle, cutis, derm, epidermis, hide, integument, pellicle, pelt; hull, husk, peel, rind.

**skinflint** n churl, curmudgeon, lickpenny, miser, niggard, scrimp.

**skinny** adj emaciated, lank, lean, poor, shrivelled, shrunk, thin.

**skip** vb bound, caper, frisk, gambol, hop, jump, leap, spring; disregard, intermit, miss, neglect, omit, pass over, skim. * n bound, caper, frisk, gambol, hop, jump, leap, spring.

**skirmish** vb battle, brush, collide, combat, contest, fight, scuffle, tussle. * n affair, affray, battle, brush, collision, combat, conflict, contest, encounter, fight, scuffle, tussle.

**skirt** vb border, bound, edge, fringe, hem, march, rim; circumnavigate, circumvent, flank, go along. * n border, boundary, edge, margin, rim, verge; flap, kilt, overskirt, petticoat.

**skittish** adj changeable, fickle, inconstant; hasty, volatile, wanton; shy, timid, timorous.

**skulk** vb hide, lurk, slink, sneak.

**skulker** n lurker, sneak; shirk, slacker, malingerer.

**skull** n brain pan, cranium.

**sky** n empyrean, firmament, heaven, heavens, welkin.

**sky-blue** adj azure, cerulean, sapphire, sky-coloured.

**skylarking** n carousing, frolicking, sporting.

**slab** adj slimy, thick, viscous. * n beam, board, layer, panel, plank, slat, table, tablet; mire, mud, puddle, slime.

**slabber** vb drivel, slaver, slobber; drop, let fall, shed, spill.

**slack** vb ease off, let up; abate, ease up, relax, slacken; malinger, shirk; choke, damp, extinguish, smother, stifle. * adj backward, careless, inattentive, lax, negligent, remiss; abated, dilatory, diminished, lingering, slow, tardy; loose, relaxed; dull, idle, inactive, quiet, sluggish. * n excess, leeway, looseness, play; coal dust, culm, residue.

**slacken** vb abate, diminish, lessen, lower, mitigate, moderate, neglect, remit, relieve, retard, slack; loosen, relax; flag, slow down; bridle, check, control, curb, repress, restrain.

**slackness** n looseness; inattention, negligence, remissness; slowness, tardiness.

**slander** vb asperse, backbite, belie, brand, calumniate, decry, defame, libel, malign, reproach, scandalize,

traduce, vilify; detract from, disparage. * n aspersion, backbiting, calumny, defamation, detraction, libel, obloquy, scandal, vilification.

**slanderous** adj calumnious, defamatory, false, libellous, malicious, maligning.

**slang** n argo, cant, jargon, lingo.

**slant** vb incline, lean, lie obliquely, list, slope. * n inclination, slope, steep, tilt.

**slap** vb dab, clap, pat, smack, spank, strike. * adv instantly, quickly, plumply. * n blow, clap.

**slapdash** adv haphazardly, hurriedly, precipitately.

**slash** vb cut, gash, slit. * n cut, gash, slit.

**slashed** adj cut, slit; (bot) jagged, laciniate, multifid.

**slattern** adj slatternly, slovenly, sluttish. * n drab, slut, sloven, trollop.

**slatternly** adj dirty, slattern, slovenly, sluttish, unclean, untidy. * adv carelessly, negligently, sluttishly.

**slaughter** vb butcher, kill, massacre, murder, slay. * n bloodshed, butchery, carnage, havoc, killing, massacre, murder, slaying.

**slaughterer** n assassin, butcher, cutthroat, destroyer, killer, murderer, slayer.

**slave** vb drudge, moil, toil. * n bondmaid, bondservant, bondslave, bondman, captive, dependant, henchman, helot, peon, serf, thrall, vassal, villein; drudge, menial.

**slavery** n bondage, bond-service, captivity, enslavement, enthralment, serfdom, servitude, thraldom, vassalage, villeinage; drudgery, mean labour.

**slavish** adj abject, beggarly, base, cringing, fawning, grovelling, low, mean, obsequious, servile, sycophantic; drudging, laborious, menial, servile.

**slay** vb assassinate, butcher, dispatch, kill, massacre, murder, slaughter; destroy, ruin.

**slayer** n assassin, destroyer, killer, murderer, -slaughterer.

**sledge** n drag, sled; cutter, pung, sleigh.

**sleek** adj glossy, satin, silken, silky, smooth.

**sleekly** adv evenly, glossily, nicely, smoothly.

**sleep** vb catnap, doze, drowse, nap, slumber. * n dormancy, hypnosis, lethargy, repose, rest, slumber.

**sleeping** adj dormant, inactive, quiescent.

**sleepwalker** n night-walker, noctambulist, somnambulist.

**sleepwalking** n somnambulism.

**sleepy** adj comatose, dozy, drowsy, heavy, lethargic,

nodding, somnolent; narcotic, opiate, slumberous, somniferous, somnific, soporiferous, soporific; dull, heavy, inactive, lazy, slow, sluggish, torpid.

**sleight** n adroitness, dexterity, manoeuvring.

**sleight of hand** n conjuring, hocus-pocus, jugglery, legerdemain, prestidigitation.

**slender** adj lank, lithe, narrow, skinny, slim, spindly, thin; feeble, fine, flimsy, fragile, slight, tenuous, weak; inconsiderable, moderate, small, trivial; exiguous, inadequate, insufficient, lean, meagre, pitiful, scanty; abstemious, light, simple, spare, sparing.

**slice** vb cut, divide, part, section; cut off, sever. * n chop, collop, piece.

**slick** adj glassy, glossy, polished, sleek, smooth; alert, clever, cunning, shrewd, slippery, unctuous. vb burnish, gloss, lacquer, polish, shine, sleek, varnish; grease, lubricate, oil.

**slide** vb glide, move smoothly, slip. * n glide, glissade, skid, slip.

**sliding** adj gliding, slippery, uncertain. * n backsliding, falling, fault, lapse, transgression.

**slight** vb cold-shoulder, disdain, disregard, neglect, snub; overlook; scamp, skimp, slur. * adj inconsiderable, insignificant, little, paltry, petty, small, trifling, trivial, unimportant, unsubstantial; delicate, feeble, frail, gentle, weak; careless, cursory, desultory, hasty, hurried, negligent, scanty, superficial; flimsy, perishable; slender, slim. * n discourtesy, disregard, disrespect, inattention, indignity, neglect.

**slightingly** adv contemptuously, disrespectfully, scornfully, slightly.

**slightly** adv inconsiderably, little, somewhat; feebly, slenderly, weakly; cursorily, hastily, negligently, superficially.

**slim** vb bant, diet, lose weight, reduce, slenderize. * adj gaunt, lank, lithe, narrow, skinny, slender, spare; inconsiderable, paltry, poor, slight, trifling, trivial, unsubstantial, weak; insufficient, meagre.

**slime** n mire, mud, ooze, sludge.

**slimy** adj miry, muddy, oozy; clammy, gelatinous, glutinous, gummy, lubricious, mucilaginous, mucous, ropy, slabby, viscid, viscous.

**sling** vb cast, fling, hurl, throw; hang up, suspend.

**slink** vb skulk, slip away, sneak, steal away.

**slip** vb glide, slide; err, mistake, trip; lose, omit; disengage, throw off; escape, let go, loose, loosen, release. * n glide, slide, slipping; blunder, lapse, misstep, mistake, oversight, peccadillo, trip; backsliding,

error, fault, impropriety, indiscretion, transgression; desertion, escape; cord, leash, strap, string; case, covering, wrapper.

**slippery** adj glib, slithery, smooth; changeable, insecure, mutable, perilous, shaky, uncertain, unsafe, unstable, unsteady; cunning, dishonest, elusive, faithless, false, knavish, perfidious, shifty, treacherous.

**slipshod** adj careless, shuffling, slovenly, untidy.

**slit** vb cut; divide, rend, slash, split, sunder. * n cut, gash.

**slobber** vb drivel, drool, slabber, slaver; daub, obscure, smear, stain.

**slobbery** adj dank, floody, moist, muddy, sloppy, wet.

**slope** vb incline, slant, tilt. * n acclivity, cant, declivity, glacis, grade, gradient, incline, inclination, obliquity, pitch, ramp.

**sloping** adj aslant, bevelled, declivitous, inclining, oblique, shelving, slanting.

**sloppy** adj muddy, plashy, slabby, slobbery, splashy, wet.

**sloth** n dilatoriness, slowness, tardiness; idleness, inaction, inactivity, indolence, inertness, laziness, lumpishness, slothfulness, sluggishness, supineness, torpor.

**slothful** adj dronish, idle, inactive, indolent, inert, lazy, lumpish, slack, sluggish, supine, torpid.

**slouch** vb droop, loll, slump; shamble, shuffle. * n malingerer, shirker, slacker; shamble, shuffle, stoop.

**slouching** adj awkward, clownish, loutish, lubberly, uncouth, ungainly.

**slough**[1] n bog, fen, marsh, morass, quagmire; dejection, depression, despondence, despondency.

**slough**[2] vb cast, desquamate, excuviate, moult, shed, throw off; cast off, discard, divest, jettison, reject. * n cast, desquamation.

**sloven** n slattern, slob, slouch, slut.

**slovenly** adj unclean, untidy; blowsy, disorderly, dowdy, frowsy, loose, slatternly, tacky, unkempt, untidy; careless, heedless, lazy, negligent, perfunctory.

**slow** vb abate, brake, check, decelerate, diminish, lessen, mitigate, moderate, modulate, reduce, weaken; delay, detain, retard; ease, ease up, relax, slack, slacken, slack off. * adj deliberate, gradual; dead, dull, heavy, inactive, inert, sluggish, stupid; behindhand, late, tardy, unready; delaying, dilatory, lingering, slack.

**sludge** n mire, mud; slosh, slush.

**sluggard** n dawdler, drone, idler, laggard, lounger, slug.

**sluggish** adj dronish, drowsy, idle, inactive, indolent, inert, languid, lazy, listless, lumpish, phlegmatic, slothful, torpid; slow; dull, stupid, supine, tame.

**sluice** vb drain, drench, flood, flush, irrigate. * n floodgate, opening, vent.

**slumber** vb catnap, doze, nap, repose, rest, sleep. * n catnap, doze, nap, repose, rest, siesta, sleep.

**slumberous** adj drowsy, sleepy, somniferous, somnific, soporific.

**slump** vb droop, drop, fall, flop, founder, sag, sink, sink down; decline, depreciate, deteriorate, ebb, fail, fall away, lose ground, recede, slide, slip, subside, wane. * n droop, drop, fall, flop, lowering, sag, sinkage; decline, depreciation, deterioration, downturn, downtrend, subsidence, ebb, falling off, wane; crash, recession, smash.

**slur** vb asperse, calumniate, disparage, depreciate, reproach, traduce; conceal, disregard, gloss over, obscure, pass over, slight. * n mark, stain; brand, disgrace, reproach, stain, stigma; innuendo.

**slush** n slosh, sludge.

**slushy** vb plashy, sloppy, sloshy, sludgy.

**slut** n drab, slattern, sloven, trollop.

**sluttish** adj careless, dirty, disorderly, unclean, untidy.

**sly** adj artful, crafty, cunning, insidious, subtle, wily; astute, cautious, shrewd; arch, knowing, clandestine, secret, stealthy, underhand.

**smack**[1] vb smell, taste. * n flavour, savour, tang, taste, tincture; dash, infusion, little, space, soupçon, sprinkling, tinge, touch; smattering.

**smack**[2] vb slap, strike; crack, slash, snap; buss, kiss. * n crack, slap, slash, snap; buss, kiss.

**small** adj diminutive, Lilliputian, little, miniature, petite, pygmy, tiny, wee; infinitesimal, microscopic, minute; inappreciable, inconsiderable, insignificant, petty, trifling, trivial, unimportant; moderate, paltry, scanty, slender; faint, feeble, puny, slight, weak; illiberal, mean, narrow, narrow-minded, paltry, selfish, sorded, ungenerous, unworthy.

**small talk** n chat, conversation, gossip.

**smart**[1] vb hurt, pain, sting; suffer. * adj keen, painful, poignant, pricking, pungent, severe, sharp, stinging.

**smart**[2] adj active, agile, brisk, fresh, lively, nimble, quick, spirited, sprightly, spry; effective, efficient, energetic, forcible, vigorous; adroit, alert, clever, dexterous, dextrous, expert, intelligent, stirring; acute, apt, pertinent, ready, witty; chic, dapper, fine, natty, showy, spruce, trim.

**smartness** n acuteness, keenness, poignancy, pungency, severity, sharpness; efficiency, energy, force, vigour; activity, agility, briskness, liveliness, nimbleness, sprightliness, spryness, vivacity; alertness, cleverness, dexterity, expertise, expertness, intelligence, quickness; acuteness, aptness, pertinency, wit, wittiness; chic, nattiness, spruceness, trimness.

**smash** vb break, crush, dash, mash, shatter. * n crash, debacle, destruction, ruin; bankruptcy, failure.

**smattering** n dabbling, smatter, sprinkling.

**smear** vb bedaub, begrime, besmear, daub, plaster, smudge; contaminate, pollute, smirch, smut, soil, stain, sully, tarnish. * n blot, blotch, daub, patch, smirch, smudge, spot, stain; calumny, defamation, libel, slander.

**smell** vb scent, sniff, stench, stink. * n aroma, bouquet, fragrance, fume, odour, perfume, redolence, scent, stench, stink; sniff, snuff.

**smelt** vb fuse, melt.

**smile** vb grin, laugh, simper, smirk. * n grin, simper, smirk.

**smite** vb beat, box, collide, cuff, knock, strike, wallop, whack; destroy, kill, slay; afflict, chasten, punish; blast, destroy.

**smitten** adj attracted, captivated, charmed, enamoured, fascinated, taken; destroyed, killed, slain; smit, struck; afflicted, chastened, punished.

**smock** n chemise, shift, slip; blouse, gaberdine.

**smoke** vb emit, exhale, reek, steam; fumigate, smudge; discover, find out, smell out. * n effluvium, exhalation, fume, mist, reek, smother, steam, vapour; fumigation, smudge.

**smoky** adj fuliginous, fumid, fumy, smudgy; begrimed, blackened, dark, reeky, sooty, tanned.

**smooth** vb flatten, level, plane; ease, lubricate; extenuate, palliate, soften; allay, alleviate, assuage, calm, mitigate, mollify. * adj even, flat, level, plane, polished, unruffled, unwrinkled; glabrous, glossy, satiny, silky, sleek, soft, velvet; euphonious, flowing, liquid, mellifluent; fluent, glib, voluble; bland, flattering, ingratiating, insinuating, mild, oily, smooth-tongued, soothing, suave, unctuous.

**smoothly** adv evenly; easily, readily, unobstructedly;

blandly, flatteringly, gently, mildly, pleasantly, softly, soothingly.

**smooth-tongued** *adj* adulatory, cozening, flattering, plausible, smooth, smooth-spoken.

**smother** *vb* choke, stifle, suffocate; conceal, deaden, extinguish, hide, keep down, repress, suppress; smoke, smoulder.

**smudge** *vb* besmear, blacken, blur, smear, smut, smutch, soil, spot, stain. * *n* blur, blot, smear, smut, spot, stain.

**smug** *adj* complacent, self-satisfied; neat, nice, spruce, trim.

**smuggler** *n* contrabandist, runner.

**smut** *vb* blacken, smouch, smudge, soil, stain, sully, taint, tarnish. * *n* dirt, smudge, smutch, soot; nastiness, obscenity, ribaldry, smuttiness; pornography.

**smutty** *adj* coarse, gross, immodest, impure, indecent, indelicate, loose, nasty; dirty, foul, nasty, soiled, stained.

**snack** *n* bite, light meal, nibble.

**snag** *vb* catch, enmesh, entangle, hook, snare, sniggle, tangle. * *n* knarl, knob, knot, projection, protuberance, snub; catch, difficulty, drawback, hitch, rub, shortcoming, weakness; obstacle.

**snaky** *adj* serpentine, snaking, winding; artful, cunning, deceitful, insinuating, sly, subtle.

**snap** *vb* break, fracture; bite, catch at, seize, snatch at, snip; crack; crackle, crepitate, decrepitate, pop. * *adj* casual, cursory, hasty, offhand, sudden, superficial. * *n* bite, catch, nip, seizure; catch, clasp, fastening, lock; crack, fillip, flick, flip, smack; briskness, energy, verve, vim.

**snappish** *adj* acrimonious, captious, churlish, crabbed, cross, crusty, froward, irascible, ill-tempered, peevish, perverse, pettish, petulant, snarling, splenetic, surly, tart, testy, touchy, waspish.

**snare** *vb* catch, ensnare, entangle, entrap. * *n* catch, gin, net, noose, springe, toil, trap, wile.

**snarl**[1] *vb* girn, gnarl, growl, grumble, murmur. * *n* growl, grumble.

**snarl**[2] *vb* complicate, disorder, entangle, knot; confuse, embarrass, ensnare. * *n* complication, disorder, entanglement, tangle; difficulty, embarrassment, intricacy.

**snatch** *vb* catch, clutch, grasp, grip, pluck, pull, seize, snip, twich, wrest, wring. * *n* bit, fragment, part, portion; catch, effort.

**sneak** *vb* lurk, skulk, slink, steal; crouch, truckle. * *adj*

clandestine, concealed, covert, hidden, secret, sly, underhand. * *n* informer, telltale; lurker, shirk.

**sneaky** *adj* furtive, skulking, slinking; abject, crouching, grovelling, mean; clandestine, concealed, covert, hidden, secret, sly, underhand.

**sneer** *vb* flout, gibe, jeer, mock, rail, scoff; (*with* **at**) deride, despise, disdain, laugh at, mock, rail at, scoff, spurn. * *n* flouting, gibe, jeer, scoff.

**snicker** *vb* giggle, laugh, snigger, titter.

**sniff** *vb* breathe, inhale, snuff; scent, smell.

**snip** *vb* clip, cut, nip; snap, snatch. * *n* bit, fragment, particle, piece, shred; share, snack.

**snivel** *vb* blubber, cry, fret, sniffle, snuffle, weep, whimper, whine.

**snivelly** *adj* snotty; pitiful, whining.

**snob** *n* climber, toady.

**snooze** *vb* catnap, doze, drowse, nap, sleep, slumber. * *n* catnap, nap, sleep, slumber.

**snout** *n* muzzle, nose; nozzle.

**snowy** *adj* immaculate, pure, spotless, unblemished, unstained, unsullied, white.

**snub**[1] *vb* abash, cold-shoulder, cut, discomfit, humble, humiliate, mortify, slight, take down. * *n* check, rebuke, slight.

**snub**[2] *vb* check, clip, cut short, dock, nip, prune, stunt. * *adj* pug, retroussé, snubbed, squashed, squat, stubby, turned-up.

**snuff**[1] *vb* breathe, inhale, sniff; scent, smell; snort.

**snuff**[2] *vb* (*with* **out**) annihilate, destroy, efface, extinguish, obliterate.

**snuffle** *vb* sniffle; snort, snuff.

**snug** *adj* close, concealed; comfortable, compact, convenient, neat, trim.

**snuggle** *vb* cuddle, nestle, nuzzle.

**so** *adv* thus, with equal reason; in such a manner; in this way, likewise; as it is, as it was, such; for this reason, therefore; be it so, thus be it. * *conj* in case that, on condition that, provided that.

**soak** *vb* drench, moisten, permeate, saturate, wet; absorb, imbibe; imbue, macerate, steep.

**soar** *vb* ascend, fly aloft, glide, mount, rise, tower.

**sob** *vb* cry, sigh convulsively, weep.

**sober** *vb* (*with* **up**) calm down, collect oneself, compose oneself, control oneself, cool off, master, moderate, simmer down. * *adj* abstemious, abstinent, temperate, unintoxicated; rational, reasonable, sane, sound; calm, collected, composed, cool, dispassionate, moderate, rational, reasonabler, regular, restrained, steady, temperate, unimpassioned, unruffled, well-regulated; demure, grave, quiet, sedate, serious, solemn, sombre, staid; dark, drab, dull-looking, quiet, sad, subdued.

**sobriety** n abstemiousness, abstinence, soberness, temperance; calmness, coolness, gravity, sedateness, sober-mindedness, staidness, thoughtfulness; gravity, seriousness, solemnity.

**sobriquet** n appellation, nickname, nom de plume, pseudonym.

**sociability** n companionableness, comradeship, good fellowship, sociality.

**sociable** adj accessible, affable, communicative, companionable, conversable, friendly, genial, neighbourly, social.

**social** adj civic, civil; accessible, affable, communicative, companionable, familiar, friendly, hospitable, neighbourly, sociable; convivial, festive, gregarious. * n conversazione, gathering, get-together, party, reception, soiree.

**society** n association, companionship, company, converse, fellowship; the community, populace, the public, the world; élite, monde; body, brotherhood, copartnership, corporation, club, fraternity, partnership, sodality, union.

**sodden** adj drenched, saturated, soaked, steeped, wet; boiled, decocted, seethed, stewed.

**sofa** n couch, davenport, divan, ottoman, settee.

**soft** adj impressible, malleable, plastic, pliable, yielding; downy, fleecy, velvety, mushy, pulpy, squashy; compliant, facile, irresolute, submissive, undecided, weak; bland, mild, gentle, kind, lenient, soft-hearted, tender; delicate, easy, even, quiet, smooth-going, steady; effeminate, luxurious, unmanly; dulcet, fluty, mellifluous, melodious, smooth. * interj hold, stop.

**soften** vb intenerate, mellow, melt, tenderize; abate, allay, alleviate, appease, assuage, attemper, balm, blunt, calm, dull, ease, lessen, make easy, mitigate, moderate, mollify, milden, qualify, quell, quiet, relent, relieve, soothe, still, temper; extenuate, modify, palliate, qualify; enervate, weaken.

**soil**[1] n earth, ground loam, mould; country, land.

**soil**[2] vb bedaub, begrime, bemire, besmear, bespatter, contaminate, daub, defile, dirty, foul, pollute, smirch, stain, sully, taint, tarnish. * n blemish, defilement, dirt, filth, foulness; blot, spot, stain, taint, tarnish.

**sojourn** vb abide, dwell, live, lodge, remain, reside, rest, stay, stop, tarry, visit. * n residence, stay.

**solace** vb cheer, comfort, console, soothe; allay, assuage, mitigate, relieve, soften. * n alleviation, cheer, comfort, consolation, relief.

**soldier** n fighting man, man-at-arms, warrior; GI, private.

**soldierly** adj martial, military, warlike; brave, courageous, gallant, heroic, honourable, intrepid, valiant.

**sole** adj alone, individual, one, only, single, solitary, unique.

**solecism** n barbarism, blunder, error, faux pas, impropriety, incongruity, mistake, slip.

**solemn** adj ceremonial, formal, ritual; devotional, devout, religious, reverential, sacred; earnest, grave, serious, sober; august, awe-inspiring, awful, grand, imposing, impressive, majestic, stately, venerable.

**solemnity** n celebration, ceremony, observance, office, rite; awfulness, sacredness, sanctity; gravity, impressiveness, seriousness.

**solemnize** vb celebrate, commemorate, honour, keep, observe.

**solicit** vb appeal to, ask, beg, beseech, conjure, crave, entreat, implore, importune, petition, pray, press, request, supplicate, urge; arouse, awaken, entice, excite, invite, summon; canvass, seek.

**solicitation** n address, appeal, asking, entreaty, imploration, importunity, insistence, petition, request, suit, supplication, urgency; bidding, call, invitation, summons.

**solicitor** n attorney, law agent, lawyer; asker, canvasser, drummer, petitioner, solicitant.

**solicitous** adj anxious, apprehensive, careful, concerned, disturbed, eager, troubled, uneasy.

**solicitude** n anxiety, care, carefulness, concern, perplexity, trouble.

**solid** adj congealed, firm, hard, impenetrable, rock-like; compact, dense, impermeable, massed; cubic; sound, stable, stout, strong, substantial; just, real, true, valid, weighty; dependable, faithful, reliable, safe, staunch, steadfast, trustworthy, well established.

**solidarity** n communion of interests, community, consolidation, fellowship, joint interest, mutual responsibility.

**solidify** vb compact, congeal, consolidate, harden, petrify.

**solidity** n compactness, consistency, density, firmness, hardness, solidness; fullness; massiveness, stability, strength; dependability, gravity, justice, reliability, soundness, steadiness, validity, weight; cubic content, volume.

**soliloquy** n monologue.

**solitariness** n isolation, privacy, recluseness, retirement, seclusion; loneliness, solitude.

**solitary** adj alone, companionless, lone, lonely, only, separate, unaccompanied; individual, single, sole; desert, deserted, desolate, isolated, lonely, remote, retired, secluded, unfrequented.

**solitude** n isolation, loneliness, privacy, recluseness, retiredness, retirement, seclusion, solitariness; desert, waste, wilderness.

**solution** n answer, clue, disentanglement, elucidation, explication, explanation, key, resolution, unravelling, unriddling; disintegration, dissolution, liquefaction, melting, resolution, separation; breach, disconnection, discontinuance, disjunction, disruption.

**solve** vb clear, clear up, disentangle, elucidate, explain, expound, interpret, make plain, resolve, unfold.

**solvent** n diluent, dissolvent, menstruum.

**somatic** adj bodily, corporeal.

**sombre** adj cloudy, dark, dismal, dull, dusky, gloomy, murky, overcast, rayless, shady, sombrous, sunless; doleful, funereal, grave, lugubrious, melancholy, mournful, sad, sober.

**some** adj a, an, any, one; about, near; certain, little, moderate, part, several.

**somebody** n one, someone, something; celebrity, VIP.

**somehow** adv in some way.

**something** n part, portion, thing; somebody; affair, event, matter.

**sometime** adj former, late. * adv formerly, once; now and then, at one time or other, sometimes.

**sometimes** adv at intervals, at times, now and then, occasionally; at a past period, formerly, once.

**somewhat** adv in some degree, more or less, rather, something. * n something, a little, more or less, part.

**somewhere** adv here and there, in one place or another, in some place.

**somnambulism** n sleepwalking, somnambulation.

**somnambulist** n night-walker, noctambulist, sleep-walker, somnambulator, somnambule.

**somniferous** adj narcotic, opiate, slumberous, somnific, soporific, soporiferous.

**somnolence** n doziness, drowsiness, sleepiness, somnolency.

**somnolent** adj dozy, drowsy, sleepy.

**son** n cadet, heir, junior, scion.

**song** n aria, ballad, canticle, carol, ditty, glee, lay, lullaby, snatch; descant, melody; anthem, hymn, poem, psalm, strain; poesy, poetry, verse.

**sonorous** adj full-toned, resonant, resounding, ringing, sounding; high-sounding, loud.

**soon** adv anon, before long, by and by, in a short time, presently, shortly; betimes, early, forthwith, promptly, quick; gladly, lief, readily, willingly.

**soot** n carbon, crock, dust.

**soothe** vb cajole, flatter, humour; appease, assuage, balm, calm, compose, lull, mollify, pacify, quiet, soften, still, tranquillize; allay, alleviate, blunt, check, deaden, dull, ease, lessen, mitigate, moderate, palliate, qualify, relieve, repress, soften, subdue, temper.

**soothsayer** n augur, diviner, foreteller, necromancer, predictor, prophet, seer, sorcerer, vaticinator.

**sooty** adj black, dark, dusky, fuliginous, murky, sable.

**sophism** n casuistry, fallacy, paralogism, paralogy, quibble, specious argument.

**sophist** n quibbler.

**sophistical** adj casuistical, fallacious, illogical, quibbling, subtle, unsound.

**soporific** adj dormitive, hypnotic, narcotic, opiate, sleepy, slumberous, somnific, somniferous, soporiferous, soporous.

**soppy** adj drenched, saturated, soaked, sopped; emotional, mawkish, sentimental.

**soprano** n (mus) descant, discant, treble.

**sorcerer** n charmer, conjurer, diviner, enchanter, juggler, magician, necromancers, seer, shaman, soothsayer, thaumaturgist, wizard.

**sorcery** n black art, charm, divination, enchantment, necromancy, occultism, shamanism, spell, thaumaturgy, voodoo, witchcraft.

**sordid** adj base, degraded, low, mean, vile; avaricious, close-fisted, covetous, illiberal, miserly, niggardly, penurious, stingy, ungenerous.

**sore** adj irritated, painful, raw, tender, ulcerated; aggrieved, galled, grieved, hurt, irritable, vexed; afflictive, distressing, severe, sharp, violent. * n abscess, boil, fester, gathering, imposthume, pustule, ulcer; affliction, grief, pain, sorrow, trouble.

**sorely** adv greatly, grievously, severely, violently.

**sorrily** adv despicably, meanly, pitiably, poorly, wretchedly.

**sorrow** vb bemoan, bewail, grieve, lament, mourn, weep. * n affliction, dolour, grief, heartache, mourning, sadness, trouble, woe.

**sorrowful** adj afflicted, dejected, depressed, grieved, grieving, heartsore, sad; baleful, distressing, grievous, lamentable, melancholy, mournful, painful; disconsolate, dismal, doleful, dolorous, drear, dreary, lugubrious, melancholy, piteous, rueful, woebegone, woeful.

**sorry** adj afflicted, dejected, grieved, pained, poor, sorrowful; distressing, pitiful; chagrined, mortified, pained, regretful, remorseful, sad, vexed; abject, base, beggarly, contemptible, despicable, low, mean, paltry, insignificant, miserable, shabby, worthless, wretched.

**sort** vb arrange, assort, class, classify, distribute, order; conjoin, join, put together; choose, elect, pick out, select; associate, consort, fraternize; accord, agree with, fit, suit. * n character, class, denomination, description, kind, nature, order, race, rank, species, type; manner, way.

**sortie** n attack, foray, raid, sally.

**so-so** adj indifferent, mediocre, middling, ordinary, passable, tolerable.

**sot** n blockhead, dolt, dullard, dunce, fool, simpleton; drunkard, tippler, toper.

**sottish** adj doltish, dull, foolish, senseless, simple, stupid; befuddled, besotted, drunken, insensate, senseless, tipsy.

**sotto voce** adv in a low voice, in an undertone, softly.

**sough** n murmur, sigh; breath, breeze, waft.

**soul** n mind, psyche, spirit; being, person; embodiment, essence, personification, spirit, vital principle; ardour, energy, fervour, inspiration, vitality.

**soulless** adj dead, expressionless, lifeless, unfeeling.

**sound**[1] adj entire, intact, unbroken, unhurt, unimpaired, uninjured, unmutilated, whole; hale, hardy, healthy, hearty, vigorous; good, perfect, undecayed; sane, well-balanced; correct, orthodox, right, solid, valid, well-founded; legal; deep, fast, profound, unbroken, undisturbed; forcible, lusty, severe, stout.

**sound**[2] n channel, narrows, strait.

**sound**[3] vb resound; appear, seem; play on; express,

pronounce, utter; announce, celebrate, proclaim, publish, spread. * n noise, note, tone, voice, whisper.

**sound**[4] vb fathom, gauge, measure, test; examine, probe, search, test, try.

**sounding** adj audible, resonant, resounding, ringing, sonorous; imposing, significant.

**soundless** adj dumb, noiseless, silent; abysmal, bottomless, deep, profound, unfathomable, unsounded.

**soundly** adv satisfactorily, thoroughly, well; healthily, heartily; forcibly, lustily, severely, smartly, stoutly; correctly, rightly, truly; firmly, strongly; deeply, fast, profoundly.

**soundness** n entireness, entirety, integrity, wholeness; healthiness, vigour, saneness, sanity; correctness, orthodoxy, rectitude, reliability, truth, validity; firmness, solidity, strength, validity.

**soup** n broth, consommé, purée.

**sour** vb acidulate; embitter, envenom. * adj acetose, acetous, acid, astringent, pricked, sharp, tart, vinegary; acrimonious, crabbed, cross, crusty, fretful, glum, ill-humoured, ill-natured, ill-tempered, peevish, pettish, petulant, snarling, surly; bitter, disagreeable, unpleasant; austere, dismal, gloomy, morose, sad, sullen; bad, coagulated, curdled, musty, rancid, turned.

**source** n beginning, fountain, fountainhead, head, origin, rise, root, spring, well; cause, original.

**sourness** n acidity, sharpness, tartness; acrimony, asperity, churlishness, crabbedness, crossness, discontent, harshness, moroseness, peevishness.

**souse** vb pickle; dip, douse, immerse, plunge, submerge.

**souvenir** n keepsake, memento, remembrance, reminder.

**sovereign** adj imperial, monarchical, princely, regal, royal, supreme; chief, commanding, excellent, highest, paramount, predominant, principal, supreme, utmost; efficacious, effectual. * n autocrat, monarch, suzerain; emperor, empress, king, lord, potentate, prince, princess, queen, ruler.

**sovereignty** n authority, dominion, empire, power, rule, supremacy, sway.

**sow** vb scatter, spread, strew; disperse, disseminate, propagate, spread abroad; plant; besprinkle, scatter.

**space** n expanse, expansion, extension, extent,

proportions, spread; accommodation, capacity, room, place; distance, interspace, interval.

**spacious** *adj* extended, extensive, vast, wide; ample, broad, capacious, commodious, large, roomy, wide.

**span** *vb* compass, cross, encompass, measure, overlay. * *n* brief period, spell; pair, team, yoke.

**spank** *vb* slap, strike.

**spar**[1] *n* beam, boom, pole, sprit, yard.

**spar**[2] *vb* box, fight; argue, bicker, contend, dispute, quarrel, spat, squabble, wrangle.

**spare** *vb* lay aside, lay by, reserve, save, set apart, set aside; dispense with, do without, part with; forbear, omit, refrain, withhold; exempt, forgive, keep from; afford, allow, give, grant; save; economize, pinch. * *adj* frugal, scanty, sparing, stinted; chary, parsimonious; emaciated, gaunt, lank, lean, meagre, poor, thin, scraggy, skinny, raw-boned; additional, extra, supernumerary.

**sparing** *adj* little, scanty, scarce; abstemious, meagre, spare; chary, economical, frugal, parsimonious, saving; compassionate, forgiving, lenient, merciful.

**spark** *vb* scintillate, sparkle; begin, fire, incite, instigate, kindle, light, set off, start, touch off, trigger. * *n* scintilla, scintillation, sparkle; beginning, element, germ, seed.

**sparkle** *vb* coruscate, flash, gleam, glisten, glister, glitter, radiate, scintillate, shine, twinkle; bubble, effervesce, foam, froth. * *n* glint, scintillation, spark; luminosity, lustre.

**sparkling** *adj* brilliant, flashing, glistening, glittering, glittery, twinkling; bubbling, effervescing, eloquent, foaming, frothing, mantling; brilliant, glowing, lively, nervous, piquant, racy, spirited, sprightly, witty.

**sparse** *adj* dispersed, infrequent, scanty, scattered, sporadic, thin.

**spartan** *adj* bold, brave, chivalric, courageous, daring, dauntless, doughty, fearless, hardy, heroic, intrepid, lion-hearted, undaunted, valiant, valorous; austere, exacting, hard, severe, tough, unsparing; enduring, long-suffering, self-controlled, stoic.

**spasm** *n* contraction, cramp, crick, twitch; fit, paroxysm, seizure, throe.

**spasmodic** *adj* erratic, fitful, intermittent, irregular, sporadic; convulsive, paroxysmal, spasmodical, violent.

**spat** *vb* argue, bicker, dispute, jangle, quarrel, spar, squabble, wrangle.

**spatter** *vb* bespatter, besprinkle, plash, splash, sprinkle; spit, sputter.

**spawn** *vb* bring forth, generate, produce. * *n* eggs, roe; fruit, offspring, product.

**speak** *vb* articulate, deliver, enunciate, express, pronounce, utter; announce, confer, declare, disclose, mention, say, tell; celebrate, make known, proclaim, speak abroad; accost, address, greet, hail; exhibit; argue, converse, dispute, talk; declaim, discourse, hold forth, harangue, orate, plead, spout, treat.

**speaker** *n* discourse, elocutionist, orator, prolocutor, spokesman; chairman, presiding officer.

**speaking** *adj* rhetorical, talking; eloquent, expressive, lifelike. * *n* discourse, talk, utterance; declamation, elocution, oratory.

**spear** *n* dart, gaff, harpoon, javelin, lance, pike; shoot, spire.

**special** *adj* specific, specifical; especial, individual, particular, peculiar; unique; exceptional, extraordinary, marked, particular, uncommon; appropriate, express.

**speciality, specialty** *n* particularity; feature, forte, pet subject.

**species** *n* assemblage, class, collection, group; description, kind, sort, variety; (*law*) fashion, figure, form, shape.

**specific** *adj* characteristic, especial, particular, peculiar; definite, limited, precise, specified.

**specification** *n* characterization, designation; details, particularization.

**specify** *vb* define, designate, detail, indicate, individualize, name, show, particularize.

**specimen** *n* copy, example, model, pattern, sample.

**specious** *adj* manifest, obvious, open, showy; flimsy, illusory, ostensible, plausible, sophistical.

**speck** *n* blemish, blot, flaw, speckle, spot, stain; atom, bit, corpuscle, mite, mote, particle, scintilla.

**spectacle** *n* display, exhibition, pageant, parade, representation, review, scene, show, sight; curiosity, marvel, phenomenon, wonder.

**spectacles** *npl* glasses, goggles, shades.

**spectator** *n* beholder, bystander, observer, onlooker, witness.

**spectral** *adj* eerie, ghostlike, ghostly, phantomlike, shadowy, spooky, weird, wraithlike.

**spectre, specter** *n* apparition, banshee, ghost, goblin, hobgoblin, phantom, shade, shadow, spirit, sprite, wraith.

**spectrum** n appearance, image, representation.

**speculate** vb cogitate, conjecture, contemplate, imagine, meditate, muse, ponder, reflect, ruminate, theorize, think; bet, gamble, hazard, risk, trade, venture.

**speculation** n contemplation, intellectualization; conjecture, hypothesis, scheme, supposition, reasoning, reflection, theory, view.

**speculative** adj contemplative, philosophical, speculatory, unpractical; ideal, imaginary, theoretical; hazardous, risky, unsecured.

**speculator** n speculatist, theorist, theorizer; adventurer, dealer, gambler, trader.

**speech** n articulation, language, words; dialect, idiom, locution, tongue; conversation, oral communication, parlance, talk, verbal intercourse; mention, observation, remark, saying; address, declaration, discourse, harangue, oration, palaver.

**speechless** adj dumb, gagged, inarticulate, mute, silent; dazed, dumbfounded, flabbergasted, shocked.

**speed** vb hasten, hurry, rush, scurry; flourish, prosper, succeed, thrive; accelerate, expedite, hasten, hurry, quicken, press forward, urge on; carry through, dispatch, execute; advance, aid, assist, help; favour. * n acceleration, celerity, dispatch, expedition, fleetness, haste, hurry, quickness, rapidity, swiftness, velocity; good fortune, good luck, prosperity, success; impetuosity.

**speedy** adj fast, fleet, flying, hasty, hurried, hurrying, nimble, quick, rapid, swift; expeditious, prompt, quick; approaching, early, near.

**spell**[1] n charm, exorcism, hoodoo, incantation, jinx, witchery; allure, bewitchment, captivation, enchantment, entrancement, fascination.

**spell**[2] vb decipher, interpret, read, unfold, unravel, unriddle.

**spell**[3] n fit, interval, period, round, season, stint, term, turn.

**spellbound** adj bewitched, charmed, enchanted, entranced, enthralled, fascinated.

**spend** vb disburse, dispose of, expend, lay out, part with; consume, dissipate, exhaust, lavish, squander, use up, wear, waste; apply, bestow, devote, employ, pass.

**spendthrift** n prodigal, spender, squanderer, waster.

**spent** adj exhausted, fatigued, played out, used up, wearied, worn out.

**spew** vb cast up, puke, throw up, vomit; cast forth, eject.

**spheral** adj complete, perfect, symmetrical.

**sphere** n ball, globe, orb, spheroid; ambit, beat, bound, circle, circuit, compass, department, function, office, orbit, province, range, walk; order, rank, standing; country, domain, quarter, realm, region.

**spherical** adj bulbous, globated, globous, globular, orbicular, rotund, round, spheroid; planetary.

**spice** n flavour, flavouring, relish, savour, taste; admixture, dash, grain, infusion, particle, smack, soupçon, sprinkling, tincture.

**spicily** adv pungently, wittily.

**spicy** adj aromatic, balmy, fragrant; keen, piquant, pointed, pungent, sharp; indelicate, off-colour, racy, risqué, sensational, suggestive.

**spill** vb effuse, pour out, shed. * n accident, fall, tumble.

**spin** vb twist; draw out, extend; lengthen, prolong, protract, spend; pirouette, turn, twirl, whirl. * n drive, joyride, ride; autorotation, gyration, loop, revolution, rotation, turning, wheeling; pirouette, reel, turn, wheel, whirl.

**spindle** n axis, shaft.

**spine** n barb, prickle, thorn; backbone; ridge.

**spinose** adj briery, spinous, spiny, thorny.

**spiny** adj briery, prickly, spinose, spinous, thorny; difficult, perplexed, troublesome.

**spiracle** n aperture, blowhole, orifice, pore, vent.

**spiral** adj cochlear, cochleated, curled, helical, screw-shaped, spiry, winding. * n helix, winding, worm.

**spire** n curl, spiral, twist, wreath; steeple; blade, shoot, spear, stalk; apex, summit.

**spirit** vb animate, encourage, excite, inspirit; carry off, kidnap. * n immaterial substance, life, vital essence; person, soul; angel, apparition, demon, elf, fairy, genius, ghost, phantom, shade, spectre, sprite; disposition, frame of mind, humour, mood, temper; spirits; ardour, cheerfulness, courage, earnestness, energy, enterprise, enthusiasm, fire, force, mettle, resolution, vigour, vim, vivacity, zeal; animation, cheerfulness, enterprise, esprit, glow, liveliness, piquancy, spice, spunk, vivacity, warmth; drift, gist, intent, meaning, purport, sense, significance, tenor; character, characteristic, complexion, essence, nature, quality, quintessence; alcohol, liquor; (with **the**) Comforter, Holy Ghost, Paraclete.

**spirited** adj active, alert, animated, ardent, bold,

brisk, courageous, earnest, frisky, high-mettled, high-spirited, high-strung, lively, mettlesome, sprightly, vivacious.

**spiritless** adj breathless, dead, extinct, lifeless; dejected, depressed, discouraged, dispirited, low-spirited; apathetic, cold, dull, feeble, languid, phlegmatic, sluggish, soulless, torpid, unenterprising; dull, frigid, heavy, insipid, prosaic, prosy, stupid, tame, uninteresting.

**spiritual** adj ethereal, ghostly, immaterial incorporeal, psychical, supersensible; ideal, moral, unwordly; divine, holy, pure, sacred; ecclesiastical.

**spiritualize** vb elevate, etherealize, purify, refine.

**spirituous** adj alcoholic, ardent, spiritous.

**spit**[1] vb impale, thrust through, transfix.

**spit**[2] vb eject, throw out; drivel, drool, expectorate, salivate, slobber, spawl, splutter. * n saliva, spawl, spittle, sputum.

**spite** vb injure, mortify, thwart; annoy, offend, vex. * n grudge, hate, hatred, ill-nature, ill-will, malevolence, malice, maliciousness, malignity, pique, rancour, spleen, venom, vindictiveness.

**spiteful** adj evil-minded, hateful, ill-disposed, ill-natured, malevolent, malicious, malign, malignant, rancorous.

**spittoon** n cuspidor.

**splash** vb dabble, dash, plash, spatter, splurge, swash, swish. * n blot, daub, spot.

**splay** adj broad, spreading out, turned out, wide.

**spleen** n anger, animosity, chagrin, gall, grudge, hatred, ill-humour, irascibility, malevolence, malice, malignity, peevishness, pique, rancour, spite.

**spleeny** adj angry, fretful, ill-tempered, irritable, peevish, spleenish, splenetic.

**splendid** adj beaming, bright, brilliant, effulgent, glowing, lustrous, radiant, refulgent, resplendent, shining; dazzling, gorgeous, imposing, kingly, magnificent, pompous, showy, sumptuous, superb; celebrated, conspicuous, distinguished, eminent, excellent, famous, glorious, illustrious, noble, pre-eminent, remarkable, signal; grand, heroic, lofty, noble, sublime.

**splendour** n brightness, brilliance, brilliancy, lustre, radiance, refulgence; display, éclat, gorgeousness, grandeur, magnificence, parade, pomp, show, showiness, stateliness; celebrity, eminence, fame, glory, grandeur, renown; grandeur, loftiness, nobleness, sublimity.

**splenetic** adj choleric, cross, fretful, irascible, irritable, peevish, pettish, petulant, snappish, testy, touchy, waspish; churlish, crabbed, morose, sour, sulky, sullen; gloomy, jaundiced.

**splice** vb braid, connect, join, knit, mortise.

**splinter** vb rend, shiver, sliver, split. * n fragment, piece.

**split** vb cleave, rive; break, burst, rend, splinter; divide, part, separate, sunder. * n crack, fissure, rent; breach, division, separation.

**splotch** n blot, daub, smear, spot, stain.

**splutter** vb sputter, stammer, stutter.

**spoil** vb despoil, fleece, loot, pilfer, plunder, ravage, rob, steal, strip; waste; corrupt, damage, destroy, disfigure, harm, impair, injure, mar, ruin, vitiate; decay, decompose. * n booty, loot, pillage, plunder, prey; rapine, robbery, spoliation, waste.

**spoiler** n pillager, plunderer, robber; corrupter, destroyer.

**spokesman** n mouthpiece, prolocutor, speaker.

**spoliate** vb despoil, destroy, loot, pillage, plunder, rob, spoil.

**spoliation** n depradation, deprivation, despoliation, destruction, robbery; destruction, devastation, pillage, plundering, rapine, ravagement.

**sponge** vb cleanse, wipe; efface, expunge, obliterate, rub out, wipe out.

**sponger** n hanger-on, parasite.

**spongy** adj absorbent, porous, spongeous; rainy, showery, wet; drenched, marshy, saturated, soaked, wet.

**sponsor** vb back, capitalize, endorse, finance, guarantee, patronize, promote, support, stake, subsidize, take up, underwrite. * n angel, backer, guarantor, patron, promoter, supporter, surety, underwriter; godfather, godmother, godparent.

**spontaneity** n improvisation, impulsiveness, spontaneousness.

**spontaneous** adj free, gratuitous, impulsive, improvised, instinctive, self-acting, self-moving, unbidden, uncompelled, unconstrained, voluntary, willing.

**sporadic** adj dispersed, infrequent, isolated, rare, scattered, separate, spasmodic.

**sport** vb caper, disport, frolic, gambol, have fun, make merry, play, romp, skip; trifle; display, exhibit. * n amusement, diversion, entertainment, frolic, fun, gambol, game, jollity, joviality, merriment, merry-making, mirth, pastime, pleasantry, prank, recreation; jest, joke; derision, jeer, mockery, ridicule; monstrosity.

**sportive** *adj* frisky, frolicsome, gamesome, hilarious, lively, merry, playful, prankish, rollicking, sprightly, tricksy; comic, facetious, funny, humorous, jocose, jocular, lively, ludicrous, mirthful, vivacious, waggish.

**spot** *vb* besprinkle, dapple, dot, speck, stud, variegate; blemish, disgrace, soil, splotch, stain, sully, tarnish; detect, discern, espy, make out, observe, see, sight. * *n* blot, dapple, fleck, freckle, maculation, mark, mottle, patch, pip, speck, speckle; blemish, blotch, flaw, pock, splotch, stain, taint; locality, place, site.

**spotless** *adj* perfect, undefaced, unspotted; blameless, immaculate, innocent, irreproachable, pure, stainless, unblemished, unstained, untainted, untarnished.

**spotted** *adj* bespeckled, bespotted, dotted, flecked, freckled, maculated, ocellated, speckled, spotty.

**spousal** *adj* bridal, conjugal, connubial, hymeneal, marital, matrimonial, nuptial, wedded.

**spouse** *n* companion, consort, husband, mate, partner, wife.

**spout** *vb* gush, jet, pour out, spirit, spurt, squirt; declaim, mouth, speak, utter. * *n* conduit, tube; beak, nose, nozzle, waterspout.

**sprain** *vb* overstrain, rick, strain, twist, wrench, wrick.

**spray**[1] *vb* atomize, besprinkle, douche, gush, jet, shower, splash, splatter, spout, sprinkle, squirt. * *n* aerosol, atomizer, douche, foam, froth, shower, sprinkler, spume.

**spray**[2] *n* bough, branch, shoot, sprig, twig.

**spread** *vb* dilate, expand, extend, mantle, stretch; diffuse, disperse, distribute, radiate, scatter, sprinkle, strew; broadcast, circulate, disseminate, divulge, make known, make public, promulgate, propagate, publish; open, unfold, unfurl; cover, extend over, overspread. * *n* compass, extent, range, reach, scope, stretch; expansion, extension; circulation, dissemination, propagation; cloth, cover; banquet, feast, meal.

**spree** *n* bacchanal, carousal, debauch, frolic, jollification, orgy, revel, revelry, saturnalia.

**sprig** *n* shoot, spray, twig; lad, youth.

**sprightliness** *n* animation, activity, briskness, cheerfulness, frolicsomeness, gaiety, life, liveliness, nimbleness, vigour, vivacity.

**sprightly** *adj* airy, animated, blithe, blithesome, brisk, buoyant, cheerful, debonair, frolicsome, joyous, lively, mercurial, vigorous, vivacious.

**spring** *vb* bound, hop, jump, leap, prance, vault; arise, emerge, grow, issue, proceed, put forth, shoot forth, stem; derive, descend, emanate, flow, originate, rise, start; fly back, rebound, recoil; bend, warp; grow, thrive, wax. * *adj* hopping, jumping, resilient, springy. * *n* bound, hop, jump, leap, vault; elasticity, flexibility, resilience, resiliency, springiness; fount, fountain, fountainhead, geyser, springhead, well; cause, origin, original, principle, source; seed time, springtime.

**springe** *n* gin, net, noose, snare, trap.

**springiness** *n* elasticity, resilience, spring; sponginess, wetness.

**springy** *adj* bouncing, bounding, elastic, rebounding, recoiling, resilient.

**sprinkle** *vb* scatter, strew; bedew, besprinkle, dust, powder, sand, spatter; wash, cleanse, purify, shower.

**sprinkling** *n* affusion, baptism, bedewing, spattering, splattering, spraying, wetting; dash, scattering, seasoning, smack, soupçon, suggestion, tinge, touch, trace, vestige.

**sprite** *n* apparition, elf, fairy, ghost, goblin, hobgoblin, phantom, pixie, shade, spectre, spirit.

**sprout** *vb* burgeon, burst forth, germinate, grow, pullulate, push, put forth, ramify, shoot, shoot forth. * *n* shoot, sprig.

**spruce** *vb* preen, prink; adorn, deck, dress, smarten, trim. * *adj* dandyish, dapper, fine, foppish, jaunty, natty, neat, nice, smart, tidy, trig, trim.

**spry** *adj* active, agile, alert, brisk, lively, nimble, prompt, quick, ready, smart, sprightly, stirring, supple.

**spume** *n* foam, froth, scum, spray.

**spumy** *adj* foamy, frothy, spumous.

**spur** *vb* gallop, hasten, press on, prick; animate, arouse, drive, goad, impel, incite, induce, instigate, rouse, stimulate, urge forward. * *n* goad, point, prick, rowel; fillip, impulse, incentive, incitement, inducement, instigation, motive, provocation, stimulus, whip; gnarl, knob, knot, point, projection, snag.

**spurious** *adj* bogus, counterfeit, deceitful, false, feigned, fictitious, make-believe, meretricious, mock, pretended, sham, supposititious, unauthentic.

**spurn** *vb* drive away, kick; contemn, despise,

disregard, flout, scorn, slight; disdain, reject, repudiate.

**spurt** vb gush, jet, spirt, spout, spring out, stream out, well. * n gush, jet, spout, squirt; burst, dash, rush.

**sputter** vb spawl, spit, splutter, stammer.

**spy** vb behold, discern, espy, see; detect, discover, search out; explore, inspect, scrutinize, search; shadow, trail, watch. * n agent, detective, double agent, mole, scout, undercover agent.

**squabble** vb brawl, fight, quarrel, scuffle, struggle, wrangle; altercate, bicker, contend, dispute, jangle. * n brawl, dispute, fight, quarrel, rumpus, scrimmage.

**squad** n band, bevy, crew, gang, knot, lot, relay, set.

**squalid** adj dirty, filthy, foul, mucky, slovenly, unclean, unkempt.

**squalidness** n filthiness, foulness, squalidity, squalor.

**squall** vb bawl, cry, cry out, scream, yell. * n bawl, cry, outcry, scream, yell; blast, flurry, gale, gust, hurricane, storm, tempest.

**squally** adj blustering, blustery, gusty, stormy, tempestuous, windy.

**squander** vb dissipate, expend, lavish, lose, misuse, scatter, spend, throw away, waste.

**squanderer** n lavisher, prodigal, spendthrift, waster.

**square** vb make square, quadrate; accommodate, adapt, fit, mould, regulate, shape, suit; adjust, balance, close, make even, settle; accord, chime in, cohere, comport, fall in, fit, harmonize, quadrate, suit. * adj four-square, quadrilateral, quadrate; equal, equitable, exact, fair, honest, just, upright; adjusted, balanced, even, settled; true, suitable. * n four-sided figure, quadrate, rectangle, tetragon; open area, parade, piazza, plaza.

**squash** vb crush, mash.

**squashy** adj pulpy, soft.

**squat** vb cower, crouch; occupy, plant, settle. * adj cowering, crouching; dumpy, pudgy, short, stocky, stubby, thickset.

**squeal** vb creak, cry, howl, scream, screech, shriek, squawk, yell; betray, inform on. * n creak, cry, howl, scream, screech, shriek, squawk, yell.

**squeamish** adj nauseated, qualmish, queasy, sickish; dainty, delicate, fastidious, finical, hypercritical, nice, over-nice, particular, priggish.

**squeeze** vb clutch, compress, constrict, grip, nip, pinch, press; drive, force; crush, harass, oppress;

crowd, force through; press; (with **out**) extract. * n congestion, crowd, crush, throng; compression.

**squelch** vb crush, quash, quell, silence, squash, suppress.

**squib** n firework, fuse; lampoon, pasquinade, satire.

**squint** vb look askance, look obliquely, peer. * adj askew, aslant, crooked, oblique, skew, skewed, twisted.

**squire** vb accompany, attend, escort, wait on.

**squirm** vb twist, wriggle, writhe.

**squirt** vb eject, jet, splash, spurt.

**stab** vb broach, gore, jab, pierce, pink, spear, stick, transfix, transpierce; wound. * n cut, jab, prick, thrust; blow, dagger-stroke, injury, wound.

**stability** n durability, firmness, fixedness, immovability, permanence, stableness, steadiness; constancy, firmness, reliability.

**stable** adj established, fixed, immovable, immutable, invariable, permanent, unalterable, unchangeable; constant, firm, staunch, steadfast, steady, unwavering; abiding, durable, enduring, fast, lasting, permanent, perpetual, secure, sure.

**staff** n baton, cane, pole, rod, stick, wand; bat, bludgeon, club, cudgel, mace; prop, stay, support; employees, personnel, team, workers, work force.

**stage** vb dramatize, perform, present, produce, put on. * n dais, platform, rostrum, scaffold, staging, stand; arena, field; boards, playhouse, theatre; degree, point, step; diligence, omnibus, stagecoach.

**stagey** adj bombastic, declamatory, dramatic, melodramatic, ranting, theatrical.

**stagger** vb reel, sway, totter; alternate, fluctuate, overlap, vacillate, vary; falter, hesitate, waver; amaze, astonish, astound, confound, dumbfound, nonplus, pose, shock, surprise.

**stagnant** adj close, motionless, quiet, standing; dormant, dull, heavy, inactive, inert, sluggish, torpid.

**stagnate** vb decay, deteriorate, languish, rot, stand still, vegetate.

**staid** adj calm, composed, demure, grave, sedate, serious, settled, sober, solemn, steady, unadventurous.

**stain** vb blemish, blot, blotch, discolour, maculate, smirch, soil, splotch, spot, sully, tarnish; colour, dye, tinge; contaminate, corrupt, debase, defile, deprave, disgrace, dishonour, pollute, taint. * n blemish, blot, defect, discoloration, flaw, imperfection, spot, tarnish; contamination, disgrace, dishonour, infamy, pollution, reproach, shame, taint, tarnish.

**stainless** adj spotless, unspotted, untarnished; blameless, faultless, innocent, guiltless, pure, spotless, uncorrupted, unsullied.

**stairs** npl flight of steps, staircase, stairway.

**stake**[1] vb brace, mark, prop, secure, support. * n pale, palisade, peg, picket, post, stick.

**stake**[2] vb finance, pledge, wager; hazard, imperil, jeopardize, peril, risk, venture. * n bet, pledge, wager; adventure, hazard, risk, venture.

**stale** adj flat, fusty, insipid, mawkish, mouldy, musty, sour, tasteless, vapid; decayed, effete, faded, old, time-worn, worn-out; common, commonplace, hackneyed, stereotyped, threadbare, trite.

**stalk**[1] n culm, pedicel, peduncle, petiole, shaft, spire, stem, stock.

**stalk**[2] vb march, pace, stride, strut, swagger; follow, hunt, shadow, track, walk stealthily.

**stall**[1] n stable; cell, compartment, recess; booth, kiosk, shop, stand.

**stall**[2] vb block, delay, equivocate, filibuster, hinder, postpone, procrastinate, temporize; arrest, check, conk out, die, fail, halt, stick, stop.

**stalwart** adj able-bodied, athletic, brawny, lusty, muscular, powerful, robust, sinewy, stout, strapping, strong, sturdy, vigorous; bold, brave, daring, gallant, indomitable, intrepid, redoubtable, resolute, valiant, valorous. * n backer, member, partisan, supporter.

**stamina** n energy, force, lustiness, power, stoutness, strength, sturdiness, vigour.

**stammer** vb falter, hesitate, stutter. * n faltering, hesitation, stutter.

**stamp** vb brand, impress, imprint, mark, print. * n brand, impress, impression, print; cast, character, complexion, cut, description, fashion, form, kind, make, mould, sort, type.

**stampede** vb charge, flee, panic. * n charge, flight, rout, running away, rush.

**stanch** see **staunch**[1].

**stanchion** n prop, shore, stay, support.

**stand** vb be erect, remain upright; abide, be fixed, continue, endure, hold good, remain; halt, pause, stop; be firm, be resolute, stand ground, stay; be valid, have force; depend, have support, rest; bear, brook, endure, suffer, sustain, weather; abide, admit, await, submit, tolerate, yield; fix, place, put, set upright; (with **against**) oppose, resist, withstand; (with **by**) be near, be present; aid, assist, defend, help, side with, support; defend, make good, justify,

maintain, support, vindicate; (naut) attend, be ready; (with **fast**) be fixed, be immovable; (with **for**) mean, represent, signify; aid, defend, help, maintain, side with, support; (with **off**) keep aloof, keep off; not to comply; (with **out**) be prominent, jut, project, protrude; not comply, not yield, persist; (with **up for**) defend, justify, support, sustain, uphold; (with **with**) agree. * n place, position, post, standing place, station; halt, stay, stop; dais, platform, rostrum; booth, stall; opposition, resistance.

**standard**[1] n banner, colours, ensign, flag, gonfalon, pennon, streamer.

**standard**[2] adj average, conventional, customary, normal, ordinary, regular, usual; accepted, approved, authoritative, orthodox, received; formulary, prescriptive, regulation. * n canon, criterion, model, norm, rule, test, type; gauge, measure, model, scale; support, upright.

**standing** adj established, fixed, immovable, settled; durable, lasting, permanent; motionless, stagnant. * n position, stand, station; continuance, duration, existence; footing, ground, hold; condition, estimation, rank, reputation, status.

**standpoint** n point of view, viewpoint.

**standstill** n cessation, interruption, stand, stop; deadlock.

**stanza** n measure, staff, stave, strophe, verse.

**staple** adj basic, chief, essential, fundamental, main, primary, principal. * n fibre, filament, pile, thread; body, bulk, mass, substance.

**star** vb act, appear, feature, headline, lead, perform, play; emphasize, highlight, stress, underline. * adj leading, main, paramount, principal; celebrated, illustrious, well-known. * n heavenly body, luminary; asterisk, pentacle, pentagram; destiny, doom, fate, fortune, lot; diva, headliner, hero, heroine, lead, leading lady, leading man, prima ballerina, prima donna, principal, protagonist.

**starchy** adj ceremonious, exact, formal, precise, prim, punctilious, rigid, starched, stiff.

**stare** vb gape, gaze, look intently, watch.

**stark** adj rigid, stiff; absolute, bare, downright, entire, gross, mere, pure, sheer, simple. * adv absolutely, completely, entirely, fully, wholly.

**starry** adj astral, sidereal, star-spangled, stellar; bright, brilliant, lustrous, shining, sparkling, twinkling.

**start** vb begin, commence, inaugurate, initiate,

institute; discover, invent; flinch, jump, shrink, startle, wince; alarm, disturb, fright, rouse, scare; depart, set off, take off; arise, call forth, evoke, raise; dislocate, move suddenly, spring. * n beginning, commencement, inauguration, outset; fit, jump, spasm, twitch; impulse, sally.

**startle** vb flinch, shrink, start, wince; affright, alarm, fright, frighten, scare, shock; amaze, astonish, astound.

**startling** adj abrupt, alarming, astonishing, shocking, sudden, surprising, unexpected, unforeseen, unheard of.

**starvation** n famine, famishment.

**starve** vb famish, perish; be in need, lack, want; kill, subdue.

**starveling** adj attenuated, emaciated, gaunt, hungry, lank, lean, meagre, scraggy, skinny, thin. * n beggar, mendicant, pauper.

**state** vb affirm, assert, aver, declare, explain, expound, express, narrate, propound, recite, say, set forth, specify, voice. * adj civic, national, public. * n case, circumstances, condition, pass, phase, plight, position, posture, predicament, situation, status; condition, guise, mode, quality, rank; dignity, glory, grandeur, magnificence, pageantry, parade, pomp, spendour; body politic, civil community, commonwealth, nation, realm.

**statecraft** n diplomacy, political subtlety, state management, statesmanship.

**stated** adj established, fixed, regular, settled; detailed, set forth, specified.

**stately** adj august, dignified, elevated, grand, imperial, imposing, lofty, magnificent, majestic, noble, princely, royal; ceremonious, formal, magisterial, pompous, solemn.

**statement** n account, allegation, announcement, communiqué, declaration, description, exposition, mention, narration, narrative, recital, relation, report, specification; assertion, predication, proposition, pronouncement, thesis.

**statesman** n politician.

**station** vb establish, fix, locate, place, post, set. * n location, place, position, lost, seat, situation; business, employment, function, occupation, office; character, condition, degree, dignity, footing, rank, standing, state, status; depot, stop, terminal.

**stationary** adj fixed, motionless, permanent, quiescent, stable, standing, still.

**statuary** n carving, sculpture, statues.

**statue** n figurine, image, statuette.

**stature** n height, physique, size, tallness; altitude, consequence, elevation, eminence, prominence.

**status** n caste, condition, footing, position, rank, standing, station.

**statute** n act, decree, edict, enactment, law, ordinance, regulation.

**staunch**[1], **stanch** vb arrest, block, check, dam, plug, stem, stop.

**staunch**[2] adj firm, sound, stout, strong; constant, faithful, firm, hearty, loyal, resolute, stable, steadfast, steady, strong, trustworthy, trusty, unwavering, zealous.

**stave** vb break, burst; (with **off**) adjourn, defer, delay, postpone, procrastinate, put off, waive.

**stay** vb abide, dwell, lodge, rest, sojourn, tarry; continue, halt, remain, stand still, stop; attend, delay, linger, wait; arrest, check, curb, hold, keep in, prevent, rein in, restrain, withhold; delay, detain, hinder, obstruct; hold up, prop, shore up, support, sustain, uphold. * n delay, repose, rest, sojourn; halt, stand, stop; bar, check, curb, hindrance, impediment, interruption, obstacle, obstruction, restraint, stumbling block; buttress, dependence, prop, staff, support, supporter.

**stead** n place, room.

**steadfast** adj established, fast, firm, fixed, stable; constant, faithful, implicit, persevering, pertinacious, resolute, resolved, staunch, steady, unhesitating, unreserved, unshaken, unwavering, wholehearted.

**steadiness** n constancy, firmness, perseverance, persistence, resolution, steadfastness; fixedness, stability.

**steady** vb balance, counterbalance, secure, stabilize, support. * adj firm, fixed, stable; constant, equable, regular, undeviating, uniform, unremitting; persevering, resolute, staunch, steadfast, unchangeable, unwavering.

**steal** vb burglarize, burgle, crib, embezzle, filch, peculate, pilfer, plagiarize, poach, purloin, shoplift, thieve; creep, sneak, pass stealthily.

**stealing** n burglary, larceny, peculation, shoplifting, robbery, theft, thievery.

**stealth** n secrecy, slyness, stealthiness.

**stealthy** adj clandestine, furtive, private, secret, skulking, sly, sneaking, surreptitious, underhand.

**steam** vb emit vapour, fume; evaporate, vaporize; coddle, cook, poach; navigate, sail; be hot, sweat.

* *n* vapour; effluvium, exhalation, fume, mist, reek, smoke.

**steamboat** *n* steamer, steamship.

**steamy** *adj* misty, moist, vaporous; erotic, voluptuous.

**steed** *n* charger, horse, mount.

**steel** *vb* case-harden, edge; brace, fortify, harden, make firm, nerve, strengthen.

**steep**[1] *adj* abrupt, declivitous, precipitous, sheer, sloping, sudden. * *n* declivity, precipice.

**steep**[2] *vb* digest, drench, imbrue, imbue, macerate, saturate, soak.

**steeple** *n* belfry, spire, tower, turret.

**steer** *vb* direct, conduct, govern, guide, pilot, point.

**steersman** *n* conductor, guide, helmsman, pilot.

**stellar** *adj* astral, starry, star-spangled, stellary.

**stem**[1] *vb* (*with* **from**) bud, descend, generate, originate, spring, sprout. * *n* axis, stipe, trunk; pedicel, peduncle, petiole, stalk; branch, descendant, offspring, progeny, scion, shoot; ancestry, descent, family, generation, line, lineage, pedigree, race, stock; (*naut*) beak, bow, cutwater, forepart, prow; helm, lookout; etymon, radical, radix, origin, root.

**stem**[2] *vb* breast, oppose, resist, withstand; check, dam, oppose, staunch, stay, stop.

**stench** *n* bad smell, fetor, offensive odour, stink.

**stenography** *n* brachygraphy, shorthand, tachygraphy.

**stentorian** *adj* loud-voiced, powerful, sonorous, thundering, trumpet-like.

**step** *vb* pace, stride, tramp, tread, walk. * *n* footstep, pace, stride; stair, tread; degree, gradation, grade, interval; advance, advancement, progression; act, action, deed, procedure, proceeding; footprint, trace, track, vestige; footfall, gait, pace, walk; expedient, means, measure, method; round, rundle, rung.

**steppe** *n* pampa, prairie, savannah.

**sterile** *adj* barren, infecund, unfruitful, unproductive, unprolific; bare, dry, empty, poor; (*bot*) acarpous, male, staminate.

**sterility** *n* barrenness, fruitlessness, infecundity, unfruitfulness, unproductiveness.

**sterling** *adj* genuine, positive, pure, real, sound, standard, substantial, true.

**stern**[1] *adj* austere, dour, forbidding, grim, severe; bitter, cruel, hard, harsh, inflexible, relentless, rigid, rigorous, severe, strict, unrelenting; immovable, incorruptible, steadfast, uncompromising.

**stern**[2] *n* behind, breach, hind part, posterior, rear, tail; (*naut*) counter, poop, rudderpost, tailpost; butt, buttocks, fundament, rump.

**sternness** *n* austerity, rigidity, severity; asperity, cruelty, harshness, inflexibility, relentlessness, rigour.

**sternum** *n* (*anat*) breastbone, sternon.

**stertorous** *adj* hoarsely breathing, snoring.

**stew** *vb* boil, seethe, simmer, stive. * *n* ragout; confusion, difficulty, mess, scrape.

**steward** *n* chamberlain; majordomo, seneschal; maniple, purveyor.

**stick**[1] *vb* gore, penetrate, pierce, puncture, spear, stab, transfix; infix, insert, thrust; attach, cement, glue, paste; fix in, set; adhere, cleave, cling, hold; abide, persist, remain, stay, stop; doubt, hesitate, scruple, stickle, waver; (*with* **by**) adhere to, be faithful, support. * *n* prick, stab, thrust.

**stick**[2] *n* birch, rod, switch; bat, bludgeon, club, cudgel, shillelah; cane, staff, walking stick; cue, pole, spar, stake.

**stickiness** *n* adhesiveness, glutinousness, tenacity, viscosity, viscousness.

**stickle** *vb* altercate, contend, contest, struggle; doubt, hesitate, scruple, stick, waver.

**sticky** *adj* adhesive, clinging, gluey, glutinous, gummy, mucilaginous, tenacious, viscid, viscous.

**stiff** *adj* inflexible, rigid, stark, unbending, unyielding; firm, tenacious, thick; obstinate, pertinacious, strong, stubborn; absolute, austere, dogmatic, inexorable, peremptory, positive, rigorous, severe, straitlaced, strict, stringent, uncompromising; ceremonious, chilling, constrained, formal, frigid, prim, punctilious, stately, starchy, stilted; abrupt, cramped, crude, graceless, harsh, inelegant.

**stiff-necked** *adj* contumacious, cross-grained, dogged, headstrong, intractable, mulish, obdurate, obstinate, stubborn, unruly.

**stiffness** *n* hardness, inflexibility, rigidity, rigidness, rigour, starkness; compactness, consistence, denseness, density, thickness; contumaciousness, inflexibility, obstinacy, pertinacity, stubbornness; austerity, harshness, rigorousness, severity, sternness, strictness; constraint, formality, frigidity, precision, primness, tenseness.

**stifle** *vb* choke, smother, suffocate; check, deaden, destroy, extinguish, quench, repress, stop, suppress; conceal, gag, hush, muffle, muzzle, silence, smother, still.

**stigma** n blot, blur, brand, disgrace, dishonour, reproach, shame, spot, stain, taint, tarnish.

**stigmatize** vb brand, defame, discredit, disgrace, dishonour, post, reproach, slur, villify.

**stiletto** n dagger, dirk, poniard, stylet; bodkin, piercer.

**still**[1] vb hush, muffle, silence, stifle; allay, appease, calm, compose, lull, pacify, quiet, smooth, tranquillize; calm, check, immobilize, restrain, stop, subdue, suppress. * adj hushed, mum, mute, noiseless, silent; calm, placid, quiet, serene, stilly, tranquil, unruffled; inert, motionless, quiescent, stagnant, stationary. * n hush, lull, peace, quiet, quietness, quietude, silence, stillness, tranquillity; picture, photograph, shot.

**still**[2] n distillery, still-house; distillatory, retort, stillatory.

**still**[3] adv, conj till now, to this time, yet; however, nevertheless, notwithstanding; always, continually, ever, habitually, uniformly; after that, again, in continuance.

**stilted** adj bombastic, fustian, grandiloquent, grandiose, high-flown, high-sounding, inflated, magniloquent, pompous, pretentious, stilty, swelling, tumid, turgid.

**stimulant** adj exciting, stimulating, stimulative. * n bracer, cordial, pick-me-up, tonic; fillip, incentive, provocative, spur, stimulus.

**stimulate** vb animate, arouse, awaken, brace, encourage, energize, excite, fire, foment, goad, impel, incite, inflame, inspirit, instigate, kindle, prick, prompt, provoke, rally, rouse, set on, spur, stir up, urge, whet, work up.

**stimulus** n encouragement, fillip, goad, incentive, incitement, motivation, motive, provocation, spur, stimulant.

**sting** vb hurt, nettle, prick, wound; afflict, cut, pain.

**stinging** adj acute, painful, piercing; biting, nipping, pungent, tingling.

**stingy** adj avaricious, close, close-fisted, covetous, grudging, mean, miserly, narrow-hearted, niggardly, parsimonious, penurious.

**stink** vb emit a stench, reek, smell bad. * n bad smell, fetor, offensive odour, stench.

**stint** vb bound, confine, limit, restrain; begrudge, pinch, scrimp, skimp, straiten; cease, desist, stop. * n bound, limit, restraint; lot, period, project, quota, share, shift, stretch, task, time, turn.

**stipend** n allowance, compensation, emolument, fee, hire, honorarium, pay, remuneration, salary, wages.

**stipulate** vb agree, bargain, condition, contract, covenant, engage, provide, settle terms.

**stipulation** n agreement, bargain, concordat, condition, contract, convention, covenant, engagement, indenture, obligation, pact.

**stir** vb budge, change place, go, move; agitate, bestir, disturb, prod; argue, discuss, moot, raise, start; animate, arouse, awaken, excite, goad, incite, instigate, prompt, provoke, quicken, rouse, spur, stimulate; appear, happen, turn up; get up, rise; (with **up**) animate, awaken, incite, instigate, move, provoke, quicken, rouse, stimulate. * n activity, ado, agitation, bustle, confusion, excitement, fidget, flurry, fuss, hurry, movement; commotion, disorder, disturbance, tumult, uproar.

**stirring** adj active, brisk, diligent, industrious, lively, smart; animating, arousing, awakening, exciting, quickening, stimulating.

**stitch** vb backstitch, baste, bind, embroider, fell, hem, seam, sew, tack, whip.

**stive** vb stow, stuff; boil, seethe, stew; make close, hot or sultry.

**stock** vb fill, furnish, store, supply; accumulate, garner, hoard, lay in, reposit, reserve, save, treasure up. * adj permanent, standard, standing. * n assets, capital, commodities, fund, principal, shares; accumulation, hoard, inventory, merchandise, provision, range, reserve, store, supply; ancestry, breed, descent, family, house, line, lineage, parentage, pedigree, race; cravat, neckcloth; butt, haft, hand; block, log, pillar, post, stake; stalk, stem, trunk.

**stockholder** n shareholder.

**stocking** n hose, sock.

**stock market** n stock exchange; cattle market.

**stocks** npl funds, public funds, public securities; shares.

**stockstill** adj dead-still, immobile, motionless, stationary, still, unmoving.

**stocky** adj chubby, chunky, dumpy, plump, short, stout, stubby, thickset.

**stoic, stoical** adj apathetic, cold-blooded, impassive, imperturbable, passionless, patient, philosophic, philosophical, phlegmatic, unimpassioned.

**stoicism** n apathy, coldness, coolness, impassivity, indifference, insensibility, nonchalance, phlegm.

**stolen** adj filched, pilfered, purloined; clandestine, furtive, secret, sly, stealthy, surreptitious.

**stolid** adj blockish, doltish, dull, foolish, heavy, obtuse, slow, stockish, stupid.

**stolidity** n doltishness, dullness, foolishness, obtuseness, stolidness, stupidity.

**stomach** vb abide, bear, brook, endure, put up with, stand, submit to, suffer, swallow, tolerate. * n abdomen, belly, gut, paunch, pot, tummy; appetite, desire, inclination, keenness, liking, relish, taste.

**stone** vb cover, face, slate, tile; lapidate, pelt. * n boulder, cobble, gravel, pebble, rock; gem, jewel, precious stone; cenotaph, gravestone, monument, tombstone; nut, pit; adamant, agate, flint, gneiss, granite, marble, slate, etc.

**stony** adj gritty, hard, lapidose, lithic, petrous, rocky; adamantine, flinty, hard, inflexible, obdurate; cruel, hard-hearted, inexorable, pitiless, stony-hearted, unfeeling, unrelenting.

**stoop** vb bend forward, bend down, bow, lean, sag, slouch, slump; abase, cower, cringe, give in, submit, succumb, surrender; condescend, deign, descend, vouchsafe; fall, sink. * n bend, inclination, sag, slouch, slump; descent, swoop.

**stop** vb block, blockade, close, close up, obstruct, occlude; arrest, check, halt, hold, pause, stall, stay; bar, delay, embargo, hinder, impede, intercept, interrupt, obstruct, preclude, prevent, repress, restrain, staunch, suppress, thwart; break off, cease, desist, discontinue, forbear, give over, leave off, refrain from; intermit, quiet, quieten, terminate; lodge, tarry. * n halt, intermission, pause, respite, rest, stoppage, suspension, truce; block, cessation, check, hindrance, interruption, obstruction, repression; bar, impediment, obstacle; full stop, point.

**stopcock** n cock, faucet, tap.

**stoppage** n arrest, block, check, closure, hindrance, interruption, obstruction, prevention.

**stopper** n cork, plug, stopple.

**store** vb accumulate, amass, cache, deposit, garner, hoard, husband, lay by, lay in, lay up, put by, reserve, save, store up, stow away, treasure up; furnish, provide, replenish, stock, supply. * n accumulation, cache, deposit, fund, hoard, provision, reserve, stock, supply, treasure, treasury; abundance, plenty; storehouse; emporium, market, shop.

**storehouse** n depository, depot, godown, magazine, repository, store, warehouse.

**storm** vb assail, assault, attack; blow violently; fume, rage, rampage, rant, rave, tear. * n blizzard, gale, hurricane, squall, tempest, tornado, typhoon, whirlwind; agitation, clamour, commotion, disturbance, insurrection, outbreak, sedition, tumult, turmoil; adversity, affliction, calamity, distress; assault, attack, brunt, onset, onslaught; violence.

**storminess** n inclemency, roughness, tempestuousness.

**stormy** adj blustering, boisterous, gusty, squally, tempestuous, windy; passionate, riotous, rough, turbulent, violent, wild; agitated, furious.

**story** n annals, chronicle, history, record; account, narration, narrative, recital, record, rehearsal, relation, report, statement, tale; fable, fiction, novel, romance; anecdote, incident, legend, tale; canard, fabrication, falsehood, fib, figure, invention, lie, untruth.

**storyteller** n bard, chronicler, narrator, raconteur.

**stout** adj able-bodied, athletic, brawny, lusty, robust, sinewy, stalwart, strong, sturdy, vigorous; courageous, hardy, indomitable, stouthearted; contumacious, obstinate, proud, resolute, stubborn; compact, firm, solid, staunch; bouncing, bulky, burly, chubby, corpulent, fat, heavy, jolly, large, obese, plump, portly, stocky, strapping, thickset.

**stouthearted** adj fearless, heroic, redoubtable; bold, brave, courageous, dauntless, doughty, firm, gallant, hardy, indomitable, intrepid, resolute, valiant, valorous.

**stow** vb load, pack, put away, store, stuff.

**straddle** vb bestride.

**straggle** vb rove, wander; deviate, digress, ramble, range, roam, stray, stroll.

**straggling** adj rambling, roving, straying, strolling, wandering; scattered.

**straight** adj direct, near, rectilinear, right, short, undeviating, unswerving; erect, perpendicular, plumb, right, upright, vertical; equitable, fair, honest, honourable, just, square, straightforward. * adv at once, directly, forthwith, immediately, straightaway, straightway, without delay.

**straightaway, straightway** adv at once, directly, forthwith, immediately, speedily, straight, suddenly, without delay.

**straighten** vb arrange, make straight, neaten, order, tidy.

**straight-laced** see **strait-laced**.

**strain**[1] vb draw tightly, make tense, stretch, tighten;

injure, sprain, wrench; exert, overexert, overtax, rack; embrace, fold, hug, press, squeeze; compel, constrain, force; dilute, distill, drain, filter, filtrate, ooze, percolate, purify, separate; fatigue, overtask, overwork, task, tax, tire. * n stress, tenseness, tension, tensity; effort, exertion, force, overexertion; burden, task, tax; sprain, wrench; lay, melody, movement, snatch, song, stave, tune.

**strain**[2] n manner, style, tone, vein; disposition, tendency, trait, turn; descent, extraction, family, lineage, pedigree, race, stock.

**strait** adj close, confined, constrained, constricted, contracted, narrow; rigid, rigorous, severe, strict; difficult, distressful, grievous, straitened. * n channel, narrows, pass, sound.

**straits** npl crisis, difficulty, dilemma, distress, embarrassment, emergency, exigency, extremity, hardship, pass, perplexity, pinch, plight, predicament.

**straiten** vb confine, constrain, constrict, contract, limit; narrow; intensify, stretch; distress, embarrass, perplex, pinch, press.

**straitened** adj distressed, embarrassed limited, perplexed, pinched.

**strait-laced, straight-laced** adj.austere, formal, prim, rigid, rigorous, stern, stiff, strict, uncompromising.

**straitness** n narrowness, rigour, severity, strictness; difficulty, distress, trouble; insufficiency, narrowness, scarcity, want.

**strand**[1] vb abandon, beach, be wrecked, cast away, go aground, ground, maroon, run aground, wreck. * n beach, coast, shore.

**strand**[2] n braid, cord, fibre, filament, line, rope, string, tress.

**stranded** adj aground, ashore, cast away, lost, shipwrecked, wrecked.

**strange** adj alien, exotic, far-fetched, foreign, outlandish, remote; new, novel; curious, exceptional, extraordinary, irregular, odd, particular, peculiar, rare, singular, surprising, uncommon, unusual; abnormal, anomalous, extraordinary, inconceivable, incredible, inexplicable, marvellous, mysterious, preternatural, unaccountable, unbelievable, unheard of, unique, unnatural, wonderful; bizarre, droll, grotesque, quaint, queer; inexperienced, unacquainted, unfamiliar, unknown; bashful, distant, distrustful, reserved, shy, uncommunicative.

**strangeness** n foreignness; bashfulness, coldness, distance, reserve, shyness, uncommunicativeness;

eccentricity, grotesqueness, oddness, singularity, uncommonness, uncouthness.

**stranger** n alien, foreigner, newcomer, immigrant, outsider; guest, visitor.

**strangle** vb choke, contract, smother, squeeze, stifle, suffocate, throttle, tighten; keep back, quiet, repress, still, suppress.

**strap** vb beat, thrash, whip; bind, fasten, sharpen, strop. * n thong; band, ligature, strip, tie; razorstrap, strop.

**strapping** adj big, burly, large, lusty, stalwart, stout, strong, tall.

**stratagem** n artifice, cunning, device, dodge, finesse, intrigue, machination, manoeuvre, plan, plot, ruse, scheme, trick, wile.

**strategic, strategical** adj calculated, deliberate, diplomatic, manoeuvering, planned, politic, tactical; critical, decisive, key, vital.

**strategy** n generalship, manoeuvering, plan, policy, stratagem, strategetics, tactics.

**stratum** n band, bed, layer.

**straw** n culm, stalk, stem; button, farthing, fig, penny, pin, rush, snap.

**stray** vb deviate, digress, err, meander, ramble, range, roam, rove, straggle, stroll, swerve, transgress, wander. * adj abandoned, lost, strayed, wandering; accidental, erratic, random, scattered.

**streak** vb band, bar, striate, stripe, vein; dart, dash, flash, hurtle, run, speed, sprint, stream, tear. * n band, bar, belt, layer, line, strip, stripe, thread, trace, vein; cast, grain, tone, touch, vein; beam, bolt, dart, dash, flare, flash, ray, stream.

**streaky** adj streaked, striped, veined.

**stream** vb course, flow, glide, pour, run, spout; emit, pour out, shed; emanate, go forth, issue, radiate; extend, float, stretch out, wave. * n brook, burn, race, rill, rivulet, run, runlet, runnel, trickle; course, current, flow, flux, race, rush, tide, torrent, wake, wash; beam, gleam, patch, radiation, ray, streak.

**streamer** n banner, colours, ensign, flag, pennon, standard.

**street** n avenue, highway, road, way.

**strength** n force, might, main, nerve, potency, power, vigour; hardness, solidity, toughness; impregnability, proof; brawn, grit, healthy, lustiness, muscle, robustness, sinew, stamina, thews, vigorousness; animation, courage, determination, firmness, fortitude, resolution, spirit; cogency, efficacy, soundness, validity;

emphasis, energy; security, stay, support; brightness, brilliance, clearness, intensity, vitality, vividness; body, excellence, virtue; impetuosity, vehemence, violence; boldness.

**strengthen** vb buttress, recruit, reinforce; fortify; brace, energize, harden, nerve, steel, stimulate; freshen, invigorate, vitalize; animate, encourage; clench, clinch, confirm, corroborate, establish, fix, justify, sustain, support.

**strenuous** adj active, ardent, eager, earnest, energetic, resolute, vigorous, zealous; bold, determined, doughty, intrepid, resolute, spirited, strong, valiant.

**stress** vb accent, accentuate, emphasize, highlight, point up, underline, underscore; bear, bear upon, press, pressurize; pull, rack, strain, stretch, tense, tug. * n accent, accentuation, emphasis; effort, force, pull, strain, tension, tug; boisterousness, severity, violence; pressure, urgency.

**stretch** vb brace, screw, strain, tense, tighten; elongate, extend, lengthen, protract, pull; display, distend, expand, spread, unfold, widen; sprain, strain; distort, exaggerate, misrepresent. * n compass, extension, extent, range, reach, scope; effort, exertion, strain, struggle; course, direction.

**strict** adj close, strained, tense, tight; accurate, careful, close, exact, literal, particular, precise, scrupulous; austere, inflexible, harsh, orthodox, puritanical, rigid, rigorous, severe, stern, strait-laced, stringent, uncompromising, unyielding.

**stricture** n animadversion, censure, denunciation, criticism, compression, constriction, contraction.

**strife** n battle, combat, conflict, contention, contest, discord, quarrel, struggle, warfare.

**strike** vb bang, beat, belabour, box, buffet, cudgel, cuff, hit, knock, lash, pound, punch, rap, slap, slug, smite, thump, whip; impress, imprint, stamp; afflict, chastise, deal, give, inflict, punish; affect, astonish, electrify, stun; clash, collide, dash, touch; surrender, yield; mutiny, rebel, rise.

**stringent** adj binding, contracting, rigid, rigorous, severe, strict.

**strip**¹ n piece, ribbon, shred, slip.

**strip**² vb denude, hull, skin, uncover; bereave, deprive, deforest, desolate, despoil, devastate, disarm, dismantle, disrobe, divest, expose, fleece, loot, shave; plunder, pillage, ransack, rob, sack, spoil; disrobe, uncover, undress.

**strive** vb aim, attempt, endeavour, exert, labour,

strain, struggle, toil; contend, contest, fight, tussle, wrestle; compete, cope.

**stroke**¹ n blow, glance, hit, impact, knock, lash, pat, percussion, rap, shot, switch, thump; attack, paralysis, stroke; affliction, damage, hardship, hurt, injury, misfortune, reverse, visitation; dash, feat, masterstroke, touch.

**stroke**² vb caress, feel, palpate, pet, knead, massage, nuzzle, rub, touch.

**stroll** vb loiter, lounge, ramble, range, rove, saunter, straggle, stray, wander. * n excursion, promenade, ramble, rambling, roving, tour, trip, walk, wandering.

**strong** adj energetic, forcible, powerful, robust, sturdy; able, enduring; cogent, firm, valid.

**structure** vb arrange, constitute, construct, make, organize. * n arrangement, conformation, configuration, constitution, construction, form, formation, make, organization; anatomy, composition, texture; building, edifice, fabric, framework, pile.

**struggle** vb aim, endeavour, exert, labour, strive, toil, try; battle, contend, contest, fight, wrestle; agonize, flounder, writhe. * n effort, endeavour, exertion, labour, pains; battle, conflict, contention, contest, fight, strife; agony, contortions, distress.

**stubborn** adj contumacious, dogged, headstrong, heady, inflexible, intractable, mulish, obdurate, obstinate, perverse, positive, refractory, ungovernable, unmanageable, unruly, unyielding, willful; constant, enduring, firm, hardy, persevering, persistent, steady, stoical, uncomplaining, unremitting; firm, hard, inflexible, stiff, strong, tough, unpliant, studied.

**studious** adj contemplative, meditative, reflective, thoughtful; assiduous, attentive, desirous, diligent, eager, lettered, scholarly, zealous.

**study** vb cogitate, lucubrate, meditate, muse, ponder, reflect, think; analyze, contemplate, examine, investigate, ponder, probe, scrutinize, search, sift, weigh. * n exercise, inquiry, investigation, reading, research, stumble; cogitation, consideration, contemplation, examination, meditation, reflection, thought; stun; model, object, representation, sketch; den, library, office, studio.

**stunning** adj deafening, stentorian; dumbfounding, stupefying.

**stunted** adj checked, diminutive, dwarfed, dwarfish, lilliputian, little, nipped, small, undersized.

**stupendous** adj amazing, astonishing, astounding,

marvellous, overwhelming, surprising, wonderful; enormous, huge, immense, monstrous, prodigious, towering, tremendous, vast.

**stupid** adj brainless, crass, doltish, dull, foolish, idiotic, inane, inept, obtuse, pointless, prosaic, senseless, simple, slow, sluggish, stolid, tedious, tiresome, witless.

**stupor** n coma, confusion, daze, lethargy, narcosis, numbness, stupefaction, torpor.

**sturdy** adj bold, determined, dogged, firm, hardy, obstinate, persevering, pertinacious, resolute, stiff, stubborn, sturdy; athletic, brawny, forcible, lusty, muscular, powerful, robust, stalwart, stout, strong, thickset, vigorous, well-set.

**style** vb address, call, characterize, denominate, designate, dub, entitle, name, term. * n dedication, expression, phraseology, turn; cast, character, fashion, form, genre, make, manner, method, mode, model, shape, vogue, way; appellation, denomination, designation, name, title; chic, elegance, smartness; pen, pin, point, stylus.

**stylish** adj chic, courtly, elegant, fashionable, genteel, modish, polished, smart.

**suave** adj affable, agreeable, amiable, bland, courteous, debonair, delightful, glib, gracious, mild, pleasant, smooth, sweet, oily, unctuous, urbane.

**subdue** vb beat, bend, break, bow, conquer, control, crush, defeat, discomfit, foil, master, overbear, overcome, overpower, overwhelm, quell, rout, subject, subjugate, surmount, vanquish, worst; allay, choke, curb, mellow, moderate, mollify, reduce, repress, restrain, soften, suppress, temper.

**subject** vb control, master, overcome, reduce, subdue, subjugate, tame; enslave, enthral; abandon, refer, submit, surrender. * adj beneath, subjacent, underneath; dependent, enslaved, inferior, servile, subjected, subordinate, subservient; conditional, obedient, submissive; disposed, exposed to, liable, obnoxious, prone. * n dependent, henchman, liegeman, slave, subordinate; matter, point, subject matter, theme, thesis, topic; nominative, premise; case, object, patient, recipient; ego, mind, self, thinking.

**subjoin** vb add, affix, annex, append, join, suffix.

**subjugate** vb conquer, enslave, enthral, master, overcome, overpower, overthrow, subdue, subject, vanquish.

**sublimate** vb alter, change, repress.

**sublime** adj aloft, elevated, high, sacred; eminent,

exalted, grand, great, lofty, mighty; august, glorious, magnificent, majestic, noble, stately, solemn, sublunary; elated, elevated, eloquent, exhilarated, raised.

**submission** n capitulation, cession, relinquishment, surrender, yielding; acquiescence, compliance, obedience, resignation; deference, homage, humility, lowliness, obeisance, passiveness, prostration, self-abasement, submissiveness.

**submissive** adj amenable, compliant, docile, pliant, tame, tractable, yielding; acquiescent, long-suffering, obedient, passive, patient, resigned, unassertive, uncomplaining, unrepining; deferential, humble, lowly, meek, obsequious, prostrate, self-abasing.

**submit** vb cede, defer, endure, resign, subject, surrender, yield; commit, propose, refer; offer; acquiesce, bend, capitulate, comply, stoop, succumb.

**subordinate** adj ancillary, dependent, inferior, junior, minor, secondary, subject, subservient, subsidiary. * n assistant, dependant, inferior, subject, underling.

**subscribe** vb accede, approve, agree, assent, consent, yield; contribute, donate, give, offer, promise.

**subscription** n aid, assistance, contribution, donation, gift, offering.

**subsequent** adj after, attendant, ensuing, later, latter, following, posterior, sequent, succeeding.

**subservient** adj inferior, obsequious, servile, subject, subordinate; accessory, aiding, auxiliary, conducive, contributory, helpful, instrumental, serviceable, useful.

**subside** vb settle, sink; abate, decline, decrease, diminish, drop, ebb, fall, intermit, lapse, lessen, lower, lull, wane.

**subsidence** n settling, sinking; abatement, decline, decrease, descent, ebb, diminution, lessening.

**subsidiary** adj adjutant, aiding, assistant, auxiliary, cooperative, corroborative, helping, subordinate, subservient.

**subsidize** vb aid, finance, fund, sponsor, support, underwrite.

**subsidy** n aid, bounty, grant, subvention, support, underwriting.

**subsist** vb be, breathe, consist, exist, inhere, live, prevail; abide, continue, endure, persist, remain; feed, maintain, ration, support.

**subsistence** n aliment, food, livelihood, living, maintenance, meat, nourishment, nutriment, provision, rations, support, sustenance, victuals.

**substance** n actuality, element, groundwork, hypostasis, reality, substratum; burden, content, core, drift, essence, gist, heart, import, meaning, pith, sense, significance, solidity, soul, sum, weight; estate, income, means, property, resources, wealth.

**substantial** adj actual, considerable, essential, existent, hypostatic, pithy, potential, real, subsistent, virtual; concrete, durable, positive, solid, tangible, true; corporeal, bodily, material; bulky, firm, goodly, heavy, large, massive, notable, significant, sizable, solid, sound, stable, stout, strong, well-made; cogent, just, efficient, influential, valid, weighty.

**substantially** adv adequately, essentially, firmly, materially, positively, really, truly.

**substantiate** vb actualize, confirm, corroborate, establish, prove, ratify, verify.

**subterfuge** n artifice, evasion, excuse, expedient, mask, pretence, pretext, quirk, shift, shuffle, sophistry, trick.

**subtle** adj arch, artful, astute, crafty, crooked, cunning, designing, diplomatic, intriguing, insinuating, sly, tricky, wily; clever, ingenious; acute, deep, discerning, discriminating, keen, profound, sagacious, shrewd; airy, delicate, ethereal, light, nice, rare, refined, slender, subtle, thin, volatile.

**subtlety** n artfulness, artifice, astuteness, craft, craftiness, cunning, guile, subtleness; acumen, acuteness, cleverness, discernment, intelligence, keenness, sagacity, sharpness, shrewdness; attenuation, delicacy, fitness, nicety, rareness, refinement.

**subtract** vb deduct, detract, diminish, remove, take, withdraw.

**suburbs** npl environs, confines, neighbourhood, outskirts, precincts, purlieus, vicinage.

**subversive** adj destructive, overthrowing, pervasive, ruining, upsetting. * n collaborator, dissident, insurrectionist, saboteur, terrorist, traitor.

**subvert** vb invert, overset, overthrow, overturn, reverse, upset; demolish, destroy, extinguish, raze, ruin; confound, corrupt, injure, pervert.

**succeed** vb ensue, follow, inherit, replace; flourish, gain, hit, prevail, prosper, thrive, win.

**success** n attainment, issue, result; fortune, happiness, hit, luck, prosperity, triumph.

**successful** adj auspicious, booming, felicitous, fortunate, happy, lucky, prosperous, victorious, winning.

**succession** n chain, concatenation, cycle, consecution, following, procession, progression, rotation, round, sequence, series, suite; descent, entail, inheritance, lineage, race, reversion.

**succinct** adj brief, compact, compendious, concise, condensed, curt, laconic, pithy, short, summary, terse.

**succour** vb aid, assist, help, relieve; cherish, comfort, encourage, foster, nurse. * n aid, assistance, help, relief, support.

**succulent** adj juicy, luscious, lush, nutritive, sappy.

**succumb** vb capitulate, die, submit, surrender, yield.

**sudden** adj abrupt, hasty, hurried, immediate, instantaneous, rash, unanticipated, unexpected, unforeseen, unusual; brief, momentary, quick, rapid.

**sue** vb charge, court, indict, prosecute, solicit, summon, woo; appeal, beg, demand, entreat, implore, petition, plead, pray, supplicate.

**suffer** vb feel, undergo; bear, endure, sustain, tolerate; admit, allow, indulge, let, permit.

**sufferable** adj allowable, bearable, endurable, permissible, tolerable.

**sufferance** n endurance, inconvenience, misery, pain, suffering; long-suffering, moderation, patience, submission; allowance, permission, toleration.

**suffice** vb avail, content, satisfy, serve.

**sufficient** adj adequate, ample, commensurate, competent, enough, full, plenteous, satisfactory; able, equal, fit, qualified, responsible.

**suffocate** vb asphyxiate, choke, smother, stifle, strangle.

**suffrage** n ballot, franchise, voice, vote; approval, attestation, consent, testimonial, witness.

**suggest** vb advise, allude, hint, indicate, insinuate, intimate, move, present, prompt, propose, propound, recommend.

**suggestion** n allusion, hint, indication, insinuation, intimation, presentation, prompting, proposal, recommendation, reminder.

**suit** vb accommodate, adapt, adjust, fashion, fit, level, match; accord, become, befit, gratify, harmonize, please, satisfy, tally. * n appeal, entreaty, invocation, petition, prayer, request, solicitation, supplication; courtship, wooing; action, case, cause, process, prosecution, trial; clothing, costume, habit.

**suitable** adj adapted, accordant, agreeable, answerable, apposite, applicable, appropriate, apt, becoming, befitting, conformable, congruous, convenient, consonant, correspondent, decent, due, eligible, expedient, fit, fitting, just, meet, pertinent, proper, relevant, seemly, worthy.

**suite** n attendants, bodyguard, convoy, cortege, court, escort, followers, staff, retainers, retinue, train; collection, series, set, suit; apartment, rooms.

**sulky** adj aloof, churlish, cross, cross-grained, dogged, grouchy, ill-humoured, ill-tempered, moody, morose, perverse, sour, spleenish, spleeny, splenetic, sullen, surly, vexatious, wayward.

**sullen** adj cross, crusty, glum, grumpy, ill-tempered, moody, morose, sore, sour, sulky; cheerless, cloudy, dark, depressing, dismal, foreboding, funereal, gloomy, lowering, melancholy, mournful, sombre; dull, heavy, slow, sluggish; intractable, obstinate, perverse, refractory, stubborn, vexatious; baleful, evil, inauspicious, malign, malignant, sinister, unlucky, unpropitious.

**sully** vb blemish, blot, contaminate, deface, defame, dirty, disgrace, dishonour, foul, smirch, soil, slur, spot, stain, tarnish.

**sultry** adj close, damp, hot, humid, muggy, oppressive, stifling, stuffy, sweltering.

**sum** vb add, calculate, compute, reckon; collect, comprehend, condense, epitomize, summarize. * n aggregate, amount, total, totality, whole; compendium, substance, summary; acme, completion, height, summit.

**summary** adj brief, compendious, concise, curt, laconic, pithy, short, succinct, terse; brief, quick, rapid. * n abridgement, abstract, brief, compendium, digest, epitome, precis, résumé, syllabus, synopsis.

**summit** n acme, apex, cap, climax, crest, crown, pinnacle, top, vertex, zenith.

**summon** vb arouse, bid, call, cite, invite, invoke, rouse; convene, convoke; charge, indict, prosecute, subpoena, sue.

**sumptuous** adj costly, dear, expensive, gorgeous, grand, lavish, luxurious, magnificent, munificent, pompous, prodigal, rich, showy, splendid, stately, superb.

**sunburnt** adj bronzed, brown, ruddy, tanned.

**sunder** vb break, disconnect, disjoin, dissociate, dissever, disunited, divide, part, separate, sever.

**sundry** adj different, divers, several, some, various.

**sunny** adj bright, brilliant, clear, fine, luminous, radiant, shining, unclouded, warm; cheerful, genial, happy, joyful, mild, optimistic, pleasant, smiling.

**superannuated** adj aged, anile, antiquated, decrepit, disqualified, doting, effete, imbecile, passé, retired, rusty, time-worn, unfit.

**superb** adj august, beautiful, elegant, exquisite, grand, gorgeous, imposing, magnificent, majestic, noble, pompous, rich, showy, splendid, stately, sumptuous.

**supercilious** adj arrogant, condescending, contemptuous, dictatorial, domineering, haughty, high, imperious, insolent, intolerant, lofty, lordly, magisterial, overbearing, overweening, proud, scornful, vainglorious.

**superficial** adj external, flimsy, shallow, untrustworthy.

**superfluity** n excess, exuberance, redundancy, superabundance, surfeit.

**superfluous** adj excessive, redundant, unnecessary.

**superintend** vb administer, conduct, control, direct, inspect, manage, overlook, oversee, supervise.

**superintendence** n care, charge, control, direction, guidance, government, inspection, management, oversight, supervision, surveillance.

**superior** adj better, greater, high, higher, finer, paramount, supreme, ultra, upper; chief, foremost, principal; distinguished, matchless, noble, pre-eminent, preferable, sovereign, surpassing, unrivalled, unsurpassed; predominant, prevalent. * n boss, chief, director, head, higher-up, leader, manager, principal, senior, supervisor.

**superiority** n advantage, ascendency, lead, odds, predominance, pre-eminence, prevalence, transcendence; excellence, nobility, worthiness.

**superlative** adj consummate, greatest, incomparable, peerless, pre-eminent, supreme, surpassing, transcendent.

**supernatural** adj abnormal, marvellous, metaphysical, miraculous, otherworldly, preternatural, unearthly.

**supernumerary** adj excessive, odd, redundant, superfluous.

**supersede** vb annul, neutralize, obviate, overrule, suspend; displace, remove, replace, succeed, supplant.

**supervise** vb administer, conduct, control, direct, inspect, manage, overlook, oversee, superintend.

**supine** adj apathetic, careless, drowsy, dull, idle, indifferent, indolent, inert, languid, lethargic, listless, lumpish, lazy, negligent, otiose, prostrate, recumbent, sleepy, slothful, sluggish, spineless, torpid.

**supplant** vb overpower, overthrow, undermine; displace, remove, replace, supersede.

**supple** adj elastic, flexible, limber, lithe, pliable, pliant; compliant, humble, submissive, yielding; adulatory, cringing, fawning, flattering, grovelling, obsequious, oily, parasitical, servile, slavish, sycophantic.

**supplement** vb add, augment, extend, reinforce, supply. * n addendum, addition, appendix, codicil, complement, continuation, postscript.

**suppliant** adj begging, beseeching, entreating, imploring, precative, precatory, praying, suing, supplicating. * n applicant, petitioner, solicitor, suitor, supplicant.

**supplicate** vb beg, beseech, crave, entreat, implore, importune, petition, pray, solicit.

**supplication** n invocation, orison, petition, prayer; entreaty, petition, prayer, request, solicitation.

**supply** vb endue, equip, furnish, minister, outfit, provide, replenish, stock, store; afford, accommodate, contribute, furnish, give, grant, yield. * n hoard, provision, reserve, stock, store.

**support** vb brace, cradle, pillow, prop, sustain, uphold; bear, endure, undergo, suffer, tolerate; cherish, keep, maintain, nourish, nurture; act, assume, carry, perform, play, represent; accredit, confirm, corroborate, substantiate, verify; abet, advocate, aid, approve, assist, back, befriend, champion, countenance, encourage, favour, float, hold, patronize, relieve, reinforce, succour, vindicate. * n bolster, brace, buttress, foothold, guy, hold, prop, purchase, shore, stay, substructure, supporter, underpinning; groundwork, mainstay, staff; base, basis, bed, foundation; keeping, living, livelihood, maintenance, subsistence, sustenance; confirmation, evidence; aid, assistance, backing, behalf, championship, comfort, countenance, encouragement, favour, help, patronage, succour.

**suppose** vb apprehend, believe, conceive, conclude, consider, conjecture, deem, imagine, judge, presume, presuppose, think; assume, hypothesize; imply, posit, predicate, think; fancy, opine, speculate, surmise, suspect, theorize, wean.

**supposition** n conjecture, guess, guesswork, presumption, surmise; assumption, hypothesis, postulation, theory, thesis; doubt, uncertainty.

**suppress** vb choke, crush, destroy, overwhelm, overpower, overthrow, quash, quell, quench, smother,

stifle, subdue, withhold; arrest, inhibit, obstruct, repress, restrain, stop; conceal, extinguish, keep, retain, secret, silence, stifle, strangle.

**supremacy** n ascendancy, domination, headship, lordship, mastery, predominance, pre-eminence, primacy, sovereignty.

**supreme** adj chief, dominant, first, greatest, highest, leading, paramount, predominant, pre-eminent, principal, sovereign.

**sure** adj assured, certain, confident, positive; accurate, dependable, effective, honest, infallible, precise, reliable, trustworthy, undeniable, undoubted, unmistakable, well-proven; guaranteed, inevitable, irrevocable; fast, firm, safe, secure, stable, steady.

**surely** adv assuredly, certainly, infallibly, sure, undoubtedly; firmly, safely, securely, steadily.

**surety** n bail, bond, certainty, guarantee, pledge, safety, security.

**surfeit** vb cram, gorge, overfeed, sate, satiate; cloy, nauseate, pall. * n excess, fullness, glut, oppression, plethora, satiation, satiety, superabundance, superfluity.

**surge** vb billow, rise, rush, sweep, swell, swirl, tower. * n billow, breaker, roller, wave, white horse.

**surly** adj churlish, crabbed, cross, crusty, discourteous, fretful, gruff, grumpy, harsh, ill-natured, ill-tempered, morose, peevish, perverse, pettish, petulant, rough, rude, snappish, snarling, sour, sullen, testy, touchy, uncivil, ungracious, waspish; dark, tempestuous.

**surmise** vb believe, conclude, conjecture, consider, divine, fancy, guess, imagine, presume, suppose, think, suspect. * n conclusion, conjecture, doubt, guess, notion, possibility, supposition, suspicion, thought.

**surmount** vb clear, climb, crown, overtop, scale, top, vault; conquer, master, overcome, overpower, subdue, vanquish; exceed, overpass, pass, surpass, transcend.

**surpass** vb beat, cap, eclipse, exceed, excel, outdo, outmatch, outnumber, outrun, outstrip, override, overshadow, overtop, outshine, surmount, transcend.

**surplus** adj additional, leftover, remaining, spare, superfluous, supernumerary, supplementary. * n balance, excess, overplus, remainder, residue, superabundance, surfeit.

**surprise** vb amaze, astonish, astound, bewilder,

confuse, disconcert, dumbfound, startle, stun. * n amazement, astonishment, blow, shock, wonder.

**surprising** adj amazing, astonishing, astounding, extraordinary, marvellous, unexpected, remarkable, startling, strange, unexpected, wonderful.

**surrender** vb cede, sacrifice, yield; abdicate, abandon, forgo, relinquish, renounce, resign, waive; capitulate, comply, succumb. * n abandonment, capitulation, cession, delivery, relinquishment, renunciation, resignation, yielding.

**surreptitious** adj clandestine, fraudulent, furtive, secret, sly, stealthy, unauthorized, underhand.

**surround** vb beset, circumscribe, compass, embrace, encircle, encompass, environ, girdle, hem, invest, loop.

**surveillance** n care, charge, control, direction, inspection, management, oversight, superintendence, supervision, surveyorship, vigilance, watch.

**survey** vb contemplate, observe, overlook, reconnoitre, review, scan, scout, view; examine, inspect, scrutinize; oversee, supervise; estimate, measure, plan, plot, prospect. * n prospect, retrospect, sight, view; examination, inspection, reconnaissance, review; estimating, measuring, planning, plotting, prospecting, work-study.

**survive** vb endure, last, outlast, outlive.

**susceptible** adj capable, excitable, impressible, impressionable, inclined, predisposed, receptive, sensitive.

**suspect** vb believe, conclude, conjecture, fancy, guess, imagine, judge, suppose, surmise, think; distrust, doubt, mistrust. * adj doubtful, dubious, suspicious.

**suspend** vb append, hang, sling, swing; adjourn, arrest, defer, delay, discontinue, hinder, intermit, interrupt, postpone, stay, withhold; debar, dismiss, rusticate.

**suspicion** n assumption, conjecture, dash, guess, hint, inkling, suggestion, supposition, surmise, trace; apprehension, distrust, doubt, fear, jealousy, misgiving, mistrust.

**suspicious** adj distrustful, jealous, mistrustful, suspect, suspecting; doubtful, questionable.

**sustain** vb bear, bolster, fortify, prop, strengthen, support, uphold; maintain, nourish, perpetuate, preserve; aid, assist, comfort, relieve; brave, endure, suffer, undergo; approve, confirm, ratify, sanction, validate; confirm, establish, justify, prove.

**sustenance** n maintenance, subsistence, support; aliment, bread, food, nourishment, nutriment, nutrition, provisions, supplies, victuals.

**swagger** vb bluster, boast, brag, bully, flourish, hector, ruffle, strut, swell, vapour. * n airs, arrogance, bluster, boastfulness, braggadocio, ruffling, strut.

**swain** n clown, countryman, hind, peasant, rustic; adorer, gallant, inamorata, lover, suitor, wooer.

**swallow** vb bolt, devour, drink, eat, englut, engorge, gobble, gorge, gulp, imbibe, ingurgitate, swamp; absorb, appropriate, arrogate, devour, engulf, submerge; consume, employ, occupy; brook, digest, endure, pocket, stomach; recant, renounce, retract. * n gullet, oesophagus, throat; inclination, liking, palate, relish, taste; deglutition, draught, gulp, ingurgitation, mouthful, taste.

**swamp** vb engulf, overwhelm, sink; capsize, embarrass, overset, ruin, upset, wreck. * n bog, fen, marsh, morass, quagmire, slough.

**sward** n grass, lawn, sod, turf.

**swarm** vb abound, crowd, teem, throng. * n cloud, concourse, crowd, drove, flock, hive, horde, host, mass, multitude, press, shoal, throng.

**swarthy** adj black, brown, dark, dark-skinned, dusky, tawny.

**sway** vb balance, brandish, move, poise, rock, roll, swing, wave, wield; bend, bias, influence, persuade, turn, urge; control, dominate, direct, govern, guide, manage, rule; hoist, raise; incline, lean, lurch, yaw. * n ascendency, authority, command, control, domination, dominion, empire, government, mastership, mastery, omnipotence, predominance, power, rule, sovereignty; bias, direction, influence, weight; preponderance, preponderation; oscillation, sweep, swing, wag, wave.

**swear** vb affirm, attest, avow, declare, depose, promise, say, state, testify, vow; blaspheme, curse.

**sweep** vb clean, brush; graze, touch; rake, scour, traverse. * n amplitude, compass, drive, movement, range, reach, scope; destruction, devastation, havoc, ravage; curvature, curve.

**sweeping** adj broad, comprehensive, exaggerated, extensive, extravagant, general, unqualified, wholesale.

**sweet** adj candied, cloying, honeyed, luscious, nectareous, nectarous, sugary, saccharine; balmy, fragrant, odorous, redolent, spicy; harmonious, dulcet, mellifluous, mellow, melodious, musical, pleasant, soft, tuneful, silver-toned, silvery; beautiful, fair, lovely; agreeable, charming, delightful, grateful, gratifying; affectionate, amiable, attractive, engaging, gentle, mild, lovable, winning; benignant, serene; clean, fresh, pure, sound. * n fragrance, perfume, redolence; blessing, delight, enjoyment, gratification, joy, pleasure; candy, treat.

**swell** vb belly, bloat, bulge, dilate, distend, expand, inflate, intumesce, puff, swell, tumefy; augment, enlarge, increase; heave, rise, surge; strut, swagger. * n swelling; augmentation, excrescence, protuberance; ascent, elevation, hill, rise; force, intensity, power; billows, surge, undulation, waves; beau, blade, buck, coxcomb, dandy, exquisite, fop, popinjay.

**swerve** vb deflect, depart, deviate, stray, turn, wander; bend, incline, yield; climb, swarm, wind.

**swift** adj expeditious, fast, fleet, flying, quick, rapid, speedy; alert, eager, forward, prompt, ready, zealous; instant, sudden.

**swiftness** n celerity, expedition, fleetness, quickness, rapidity, speed, velocity.

**swindle** vb cheat, con, cozen, deceive, defraud, diddle, dupe, embezzle, forge, gull, hoax, overreach, steal, trick, victimize. * n cheat, con, deceit, deception, fraud, hoax, imposition, knavery, roguery, trickery.

**swindler** n blackleg, cheat, defaulter, embezzler, faker, fraud, impostor, jockey, knave, peculator, rogue, sharper, trickster.

**swing** vb oscillate, sway, vibrate, wave; dangle, depend, hang; brandish, flourish, whirl; administer, manage. * n fluctuation, oscillation, sway, undulation, vibration; elbow-room, freedom, margin, play, range, scope, sweep; bias, tendency.

**swoop** vb descend, pounce, rush, seize, stoop, sweep. * n clutch, pounce, seizure; stoop, descent.

**sword** n brand, broadsword, claymore, cutlass, epee, falchion, foil, hanger, rapier, sabre, scimitar.

**sybarite** n epicure, voluptuary.

**sycophancy** n adulation, cringing, fawning, flattery, grovelling, obsequiousness, servility.

**sycophant** n cringer, fawner, flunky, hanger-on, lickspittle, parasite, spaniel, toady, wheedler.

**syllabus** n abridgement, abstract, breviary, brief, compendium, digest, epitome, outline, summary, synopsis.

**symbol** n badge, emblem, exponent, figure, mark, picture, representation, representative, sign, token, type.

**symbolic, symbolical** adj emblematic, figurative, hieroglyphic, representative, significant, typical.

**symmetry** n balance, congruity, evenness, harmony, order, parallelism, proportion, regularity, shapeliness.

**sympathetic** adj affectionate, commiserating, compassionate, condoling, kind, pitiful, tender.

**sympathy** n accord, affinity, agreement, communion, concert, concord, congeniality, correlation, correspondence, harmony, reciprocity, union; commiseration, compassion, condolence, fellow-feeling, kindliness, pity, tenderness, thoughtfulness.

**symptom** n diagnostic, indication, mark, note, prognostic, sign, token.

**symptomatic** adj characteristic, indicative, symbolic, suggestive.

**synonymous** adj equipollent, equivalent, identical, interchangeable, similar, tantamount.

**synopsis** n abridgement, abstract, compendium, digest, epitome, outline, precis, résumé, summary, syllabus.

**system** n method, order, plan.

**systematic** adj methodic, methodical, orderly, regular.

# T

**tabernacle** n pavilion, tent; cathedral, chapel, church, minster, synagogue, temple.

**table** vb enter, move, propose, submit, suggest. * n plate, slab, tablet; board, counter, desk, stand; catalogue, chart, compendium, index, list, schedule, syllabus, synopsis, tabulation; diet, fare, food, victuals.

**tableau** n picture, scene, representation.

**taboo** vb forbid, interdict, prohibit, proscribe. * adj banned, forbidden, inviolable, outlawed, prohibited, proscribed. * n ban, interdict, prohibition, proscription.

**tacit** adj implicit, implied, inferred, silent, understood, unexpressed, unspoken.

**taciturn** adj close, dumb; laconic, mum, reserved, reticent, silent, tight-lipped, uncommunicative.

**tack** vb add, affix, append, attach, fasten, tag; gybe, yaw, zigzag. * n nail, pin, staple; bearing, course, direction, heading, path, plan, procedure.

**tackle** vb attach, grapple, seize; attempt, try, undertake. * n apparatus, cordage, equipment, furniture, gear, harness, implements, rigging, tackling, tools, weapons.

**tact** n address, adroitness, cleverness, dexterity, diplomacy, discernment, finesse, insight, knack, perception, skill, understanding.

**tail** vb dog, follow, shadow, stalk, track. * adj abridged, curtailed, limited, reduced. * n appendage, conclusion, end, extremity, stub; flap, skirt; queue, retinue, train.

**taint** vb imbue, impregnate; contaminate, corrupt, defile, inflect, mildew, pollute, poison, spoil, touch; blot, stain, sully, tarnish. * n stain, tincture, tinge, touch; contamination, corruption, defilement, depravation, infection, pollution; blemish, defect, fault, flaw, spot.

**take** vb accept, obtain, procure, receive; clasp, clutch, grasp, grip, gripe, seize, snatch; filch, misappropriate, pilfer, purloin, steal; abstract, apprehend, appropriate, arrest, bag, capture, ensnare, entrap; attack, befall, smite; capture, carry off, conquer, gain, win; allure, attract, bewitch, captivate, charm, delight, enchant, engage, fascinate, interest, please; consider, hold, interrupt, suppose, regard, understand; choose, elect, espouse, select; employ, expend, use; claim, demand, necessitate, require; bear, endure, experience, feel, perceive, tolerate; deduce, derive, detect, discover, draw; carry, conduct, convey, lead, transfer; clear, surmount; drink, eat, imbibe, inhale, swallow. * n proceeds, profits, return, revenue, takings, yield.

**tale** n account, fable, legend, narration, novel, parable, recital, rehearsal, relation, romance, story, yarn; catalogue, count, enumeration, numbering, reckoning, tally.

**talent** n ableness, ability, aptitude, capacity, cleverness, endowment, faculty, forte, genius, gift, knack, parts, power, turn.

**talk** vb chatter, communicate, confer, confess, converse, declaim, discuss, gossip, pontificate, speak. * n chatter, communication, conversation, diction, gossip, jargon, language, rumour, speech, utterance.

**talkative** adj chatty, communicative, garrulous, loquacious, voluble.

**tally** vb accord, agree, conform, coincide, correspond, harmonize, match, square, suit. * n match, mate; check, counterpart, muster, roll call; account, reckoning.

**tame** vb domesticate, reclaim, train; conquer, master, overcome, repress, subdue, subjugate. * adj docile, domestic, domesticated, gentle, mild, reclaimed; broken, crushed, meek, subdued, unresisting, submissive; barren, commonplace, dull, feeble, flat, insipid, jejune, languid, lean, poor, prosaic, prosy, spiritless, tedious, uninteresting, vapid.

**tamper** vb alter, conquer, dabble, damage, interfere, meddle; intrigue, seduce, suborn.

**tang** n aftertaste, flavour, relish, savour, smack, taste; keenness, nip, sting.

**tangible** adj corporeal, material, palpable, tactile, touchable; actual, certain, embodied, evident, obvious, open, perceptible, plain, positive, real, sensible, solid, stable, substantial.

**tangle** vb complicate, entangle, intertwine, interweave, mat, perplex, snarl; catch, ensnare, entrap, involve, catch; embarrass, embroil, perplex. * n complication, disorder, intricacy, jumble, perplexity, snarl; dilemma, embarrassment, quandary, perplexity.

**tantalize** vb balk, disappoint, frustrate, irritate, provoke, tease, torment, vex.

**tantamount** adj equal, equivalent, synonymous.

**tantrum** n fit, ill-humour, outburst, paroxysm, temper, whim.

**tap**[1] vb knock, pat, rap, strike, tip, touch. * n pat, tip, rap, touch.

**tap**[2] vb broach, draw off, extract, pierce; draw on, exploit, mine, use, utilize; bug, eavesdrop, listen in. * n faucet, plug, spigot, spout, stopcock, valve; bug, listening device, transmitter.

**tardiness** n delay, dilatoriness, lateness, procrastination, slackness, slowness.

**tardy** adj slow, sluggish, snail-like; backward, behindhand, dilatory, late, loitering, overdue, slack.

**tarn** n bog, fen, marsh, morass, swamp.

**tarnish** vb blemish, deface, defame, dim, discolour, dull, slur, smear, soil, stain, sully. * n blemish, blot, soiling, spot, stain.

**tarry** vb delay, dally, linger, loiter, remain, stay, stop, wait; defer; abide, lodge, rest, sojourn.

**tart** adj acid, acidulous, acrid, astringent, piquant, pungent, sharp, sour; acrimonious, caustic, crabbed, curt, harsh, ill-humoured, ill-tempered, keen, petulant, sarcastic, severe, snappish, testy.

**task** vb burden, overwork, strain, tax. * n drudgery, labour, toil, work; business, charge, chore, duty, employment, enterprise, job, mission, stint, undertaking; assignment, exercise, lesson.

**taste** vb experience, feel, perceive, undergo; relish, savour, sip. * n flavour, gusto, relish, savour, smack, piquancy; admixture, bit, dash, fragment, hint, infusion, morsel, mouthful, sample, shade, sprinkling, suggestion, tincture; appetite, desire, fondness, liking, partiality, predilection; acumen, cultivation, culture, delicacy, discernment, discrimination, elegance, fine-feeling, grace, judgement, polish, refinement; manner, style.

**tasteful** adj appetizing, delicious, flavoursome, palatable, savoury, tasty, toothsome; aesthetic, artistic, attractive, elegant.

**tasteless** adj flat, insipid, savourless, stale, watery; dull, mawkish, uninteresting, vapid.

**tattle** vb babble, chat, chatter, jabber, prate, prattle; blab, gossip, inform. * n gabble, gossip, prate, prattle, tittle-tattle, twaddle.

**taunt** vb censure, chaff, deride, flout, jeer, mock, scoff, sneer, revile, reproach, ridicule, twit, upbraid. * n censure, derision, gibe, insult, jeer, quip, quirk, reproach, ridicule, scoff.

**taut** adj strained, stretched, tense, tight.

**tautology** n iteration, pleonasm, redundancy, reiteration, repetition, verbosity, wordiness.

**tavern** n bar, chophouse, hostelry, inn, pub, public house.

**tawdry** adj flashy, gaudy, garish, glittering, loud, meretricious, ostentatious, showy.

**tax** vb burden, demand, exact, load, overtax, require, strain, task; accuse, charge. * n assessment, custom, duty, excise, impost, levy, rate, taxation, toll, tribute; burden, charge, demand, requisition, strain; accusation, censure.

**teach** vb catechize, coach, discipline, drill, edify, educate, enlighten, inform, indoctrinate, initiate, instruct, ground, prime, school, train, tutor; communicate, disseminate, explain, expound, impart, implant, inculcate, infuse, instil, interpret, preach, propagate; admonish, advise, counsel, direct, guide, signify, show.

**teacher** n coach, educator, inculcator, informant, instructor, master, pedagogue, preceptor, schoolteacher, trainer, tutor; adviser, counsellor, guide, mentor; pastor, preacher.

**tear** vb burst, slit, rive, rend, rip; claw, lacerate, mangle, shatter, rend, wound; sever, sunder; fume, rage, rant, rave. * n fissure, laceration, rent, rip, wrench.

**tease** vb annoy, badger, beg, bother, chafe, chagrin, disturb, harass, harry, hector, importune, irritate, molest, pester, plague, provoke, tantalize, torment, trouble, vex, worry.

**tedious** adj dull, fatiguing, irksome, monotonous, tiresome, trying, uninteresting, wearisome; dilatory, slow, sluggish, tardy.

**teem** vb abound, bear, produce, swarm; discharge, empty, overflow.

**teeming** adj abounding, fraught, full, overflowing, pregnant, prolific, replete, swarming.

**tell** vb compute, count, enumerate, number, reckon; describe, narrate, recount, rehearse, relate, report; acknowledge, announce, betray, confess, declare, disclose, divulge, inform, own, reveal; acquaint, communicate, instruct, teach; discern, discover, distinguish; express, mention, publish, speak, state, utter.

**temper** vb modify, qualify; appease, assuage, calm, mitigate, mollify, moderate, pacify, restrain, soften, soothe; accommodate, adapt, adjust, fit, suit. * n character, constitution, nature, organization, quality, structure, temperament, type; disposition, frame, grain, humour, mood, spirits, tone, vein; calmness, composure, equanimity, moderation, tranquillity; anger, ill-temper, irritation, spleen, passion.

**temperament** n character, constitution, disposition, habit, idiosyncrasy, nature, organization, temper.

**temperate** adj abstemious, ascetic, austere, chaste, continent, frugal, moderate, self-controlled, self-denying, sparing; calm, cool, dispassionate, mild, sober, sedate.

**tempest** n cyclone, gale, hurricane, squall, storm, tornado; commotion, disturbance, excitement, perturbation, tumult, turmoil.

**temporal** adj civil, lay, mundane, political, profane, secular, terrestrial, worldly; brief, ephemeral, evanescent, fleeting, momentary, short-lived, temporal, transient, transitory.

**temporary** adj brief, ephemeral, evanescent, fleeting, impermanent, momentary, short-lived, transient, transitory.

**tempt** vb prove, test, try; allure, decoy, entice, induce, inveigle, persuade, seduce; dispose, incite, incline, instigate, lead, prompt, provoke.

**tempting** adj alluring, attractive, enticing, inviting, seductive.

**tenable** adj defensible, maintainable, rational, reasonable, sound.

**tenacious** adj retentive, unforgetful; adhesive, clinging, cohesive, firm, glutinous, gummy, resisting, retentive, sticky, strong, tough, unyielding, viscous; dogged, fast, obstinate, opinionated, opinionative, pertinacious, persistent, resolute, stubborn, unwavering.

**tenacity** n retentiveness, tenaciousness; adhesiveness, cohesiveness, glutinosity, glutinousness, gumminess, toughness, stickiness, strength, viscidity; doggedness, firmness, obstinacy, perseverance, persistency, pertinacity, resolution, stubbornness.

**tend**[1] vb accompany, attend, graze, guard, keep, protect, shepherd, watch.

**tend**[2] vb aim, exert, gravitate, head, incline, influence, lead, lean, point, trend, verge; conduce, contribute.

**tendency** n aim, aptitude, bearing, bent, bias, course, determination, disposition, direction, drift, gravitation, inclination, leaning, liability, predisposition, proclivity, proneness, propensity, scope, set, susceptibility, turn, twist, warp.

**tender**[1] vb bid, offer, present, proffer, propose, suggest, volunteer. * n bid, offer, proffer, proposal; currency, money.

**tender**[2] adj callow, delicate, effeminate, feeble, feminine, fragile, immature, infantile, soft, weak, young; affectionate, compassionate, gentle, humane, kind, lenient, loving, merciful, mild, pitiful, sensitive, sympathetic, tender-hearted; affecting, disagreeable, painful, pathetic, touching, unpleasant.

**tenebrous** adj cloudy, dark, darksome, dusky, gloomy, murky, obscure, shadowy, shady, sombre, tenebrious.

**tenement** n abode, apartment, domicile, dwelling, flat, house.

**tenet** n belief, creed, position, dogma, doctrine, notion, opinion, position, principle, view.

**tenor** n cast, character, cut, fashion, form, manner, mood, nature, stamp, tendency, trend, tone; drift, gist, import, intent, meaning, purport, sense, significance, spirit.

**tense** vb flex, strain, tauten, tighten. * adj rigid, stiff, strained, stretched, taut, tight; excited, highly strung, intent, nervous, rapt.

**tentative** adj essaying, experimental, provisional, testing, toying.

**tenure** n holding, occupancy, occupation, possession, tenancy, tenement, use.

**term** vb call, christen, denominate, designate, dub, entitle, name, phrase, style. * n bound, boundary, bourn, confine, limit, mete, terminus; duration, period, season, semester, span, spell, termination, time; denomination, expression, locution, name, phrase, word.

**termagant** n beldam, hag, scold, shrew, spitfire, virago, vixen.

**terminal** adj bounding, limiting; final, terminating, ultimate. * n end, extremity, termination; bound, limit; airport, depot, station, terminus.

**terminate** vb bound, limit; end, finish, close, complete, conclude; eventuate, issue, prove.

**termination** n ending, suffix; bound, extend, limit; end, completion, conclusion, consequence, effect, issue, outcome, result.

**terms** npl conditions, provisions, stipulations.

**terrestrial** adj earthly, mundane, subastral, subcelestial, sublunar, sublunary, tellurian, worldly. * n earthling, human.

**terrible** adj appalling, dire, dreadful, fearful, formidable, frightful, gruesome, hideous, horrible, horrid, shocking, terrific, tremendous; alarming, awe-inspiring, awful, dread; great, excessive, extreme, severe.

**terrific** adj marvellous, sensational, superb; immense, intense; alarming, dreadful, formidable, frightful, terrible, tremendous.

**terrify** vb affright, alarm, appal, daunt, dismay, fright, frighten, horrify, scare, shock, startle, terrorize.

**territory** n country, district, domain, dominion, division, land, place, province, quarter, region, section, tract.

**terror** n affright, alarm, anxiety, awe, consternation, dismay, dread, fear, fright, horror, intimidation, panic, terrorism.

**terse** adj brief, compact, concise, laconic, neat, pithy, polished, sententious, short, smooth, succinct.

**test** vb assay; examine, prove, try. * n attempt, essay, examination, experiment, ordeal, proof, trial; criterion, standard, touchstone; example, exhibition; discrimination, distinction, judgment.

**testify** vb affirm, assert, asseverate, attest, avow, certify, corroborate, declare, depose, evidence, state, swear.

**testimonial** n certificate, credential, recommendation, voucher; monument, record.

**testimony** n affirmation, attestation, confession, confirmation, corroboration, declaration, deposition, profession; evidence, proof, witness.

**testy** adj captious, choleric, cross, fretful, hasty, irascible, irritable, quick, peevish, peppery, pettish, petulant, snappish, splenetic, touchy, waspish.

**tetchy** adj crabbed, cross, fretful, irritable, peevish, sullen, touchy.

**tether** vb chain, fasten, picket, stake, tie. * n chain, fastening, rope.

**text** n copy, subject, theme, thesis, topic, treatise.

**texture** n fabric, web, weft; character, coarseness, composition, constitution, fibre, fineness, grain, make-up, nap, organization, structure, tissue.

**thankful** adj appreciative, beholden, grateful, indebted, obliged.

**thankfulness** n appreciation, gratefulness, gratitude.

**thankless** adj profitless, ungracious, ungrateful, unthankful.

**thaw** vb dissolve, liquefy, melt, soften, unbend.

**theatre** n opera house, playhouse; arena, scene, seat, stage.

**theatrical** adj dramatic, dramaturgic, dramaturgical, histrionic, scenic, spectacular; affected, ceremonious, meretricious, ostentatious, pompous, showy, stagy, stilted, unnatural.

**theft** n depredation, embezzlement, fraud, larceny, peculation, pilfering, purloining, robbery, spoliation, stealing, swindling, thieving.

**theme** n composition, essay, motif, subject, text, thesis, topic, treatise.

**theoretical** adj abstract; conjectural, doctrinaire, ideal, hypothetical, pure, speculative, unapplied.

**theory** n assumption, conjecture, hypothesis, idea, plan, postulation, principle, scheme, speculation, surmise, system; doctrine, philosophy, science; explanation, exposition, philosophy, rationale.

**therefore** adv accordingly, afterward, consequently, hence, so, subsequently, then, thence, whence.

**thesaurus** n dictionary, encyclopedia, repository, storehouse, treasure.

**thick** adj bulky, chunky, dumpy, plump, solid, squab, squat, stubby, thickset; clotted, coagulated, crass, dense, dull, gross, heavy, viscous; blurred, cloudy, dirty, foggy, hazy, indistinguishable, misty, obscure, vaporous; muddy, roiled, turbid; abundant, frequent, multitudinous, numerous; close, compact, crowded, set, thickset; confused, guttural, hoarse, inarticulate, indistinct; dim, dull, weak; familiar, friendly, intimate, neighbourly, well-acquainted. * adv fast, frequently, quick; closely, densely, thickly. * n centre, middle, midst.

**thicket** n clump, coppice, copse, covert, forest, grove, jungle, shrubbery, underbrush, undergrowth, wood, woodland.

**thief** n depredator, filcher, pilferer, lifter, marauder, purloiner, robber, shark, stealer; burglar, corsair, defaulter, defrauder, embezzler, footpad, highwayman, housebreaker, kidnapper, pickpocket, pirate, poacher, privateer, sharper, swindler, peculator.

**thieve** vb cheat, embezzle, peculate, pilfer, plunder, purloin, rob, steal, swindle.

**thin** vb attenuate, dilute, diminish, prune, reduce, refine, weaken. * adj attenuated, bony, emaciated, fine, fleshless, flimsy, gaunt, haggard, lank, lanky, lean, meagre, peaked, pinched, poor, scanty, scraggy, scrawny, slender, slight, slim, small, sparse, spindly.

**thing** n being, body, contrivance, creature, entity, object, something, substance; act, action, affair, arrangement, circumstance, concern, deed, event, matter, occurrence, transaction.

**think** vb cogitate, contemplate, dream, meditate, muse, ponder, reflect, ruminate, speculate; consider, deliberate, reason, undertake; apprehend, believe, conceive, conclude, deem, determine, fancy, hold, imagine, judge, opine, presume, reckon, suppose, surmise; design, intend, mean, purpose; account, count, deem, esteem, hold, regard; compass, design, plan, plot. * n assessment, contemplation, deliberation, meditation, opinion, reasoning, reflection.

**thirst** n appetite, craving, desire, hunger, longing, yearning; aridity, drought, dryness.

**thirsty** adj arid, dry, parched; eager, greedy, hungry, longing, yearning.

**thorn** n prickle, spine; annoyance, bane, care, evil, infliction, nettle, nuisance, plague, torment, trouble, scourge.

**thorny** adj briary, briery, prickly, spinose, spinous, spiny; acuminate, barbed, pointed, prickling, sharp, spiky; annoying, difficult, harassing, perplexing, rugged, troublesome, trying, vexatious.

**thorough, thoroughgoing** adj absolute, arrant, complete, downright, entire, exhaustive, finished, perfect, radical, sweeping, total unmitigated, utter; accurate, correct, reliable, trustworthy.

**though** conj admitting, allowing, although, granted, granting, if, notwithstanding, still. * adv however, nevertheless, still, yet.

**thought** n absorption, cogitation, engrossment, meditation, musing, reflection, reverie, rumination; contemplation, intellect, ratiocination, thinking, thoughtfulness; application, conception, consideration, deliberation, idea, pondering, speculation, study; consciousness, imagination, intellect, perception, understanding; conceit, fancy, notion; conclusion, judgment, motion, opinion, sentiment, supposition, view; anxiety, attention, care, concern, provision, regard, solicitude, thoughtfulness; design, expectation, intention, purpose.

**thoughtful** adj absorbed, contemplative, deliberative, dreamy, engrossed, introspective, pensive, philosophic, reflecting, reflective, sedate, speculative; attentive, careful, cautious, circumspect, considerate, discreet, heedful, friendly, kind-hearted, kindly, mindful, neighbourly, provident, prudent, regardful, watchful, wary; quiet, serious, sober, studious.

**thoughtless** adj careless, casual, flighty, heedless, improvident, inattentive, inconsiderate, neglectful, negligent, precipitate, rash, reckless, regardless, remiss, trifling, unmindful, unthinking; blank, blockish, dull, insensate, stupid, vacant, vacuous.

**thraldom** n bondage, enslavement, enthralment, serfdom, servitude, slavery, subjection, thrall, vassalage.

**thrash** vb beat, bruise, conquer, defeat, drub, flog, lash, maul, pommel, punish, thwack, trounce, wallop, whip.

**thread** vb course, direction, drift, tenor; reeve, trace. * n cord, fibre, filament, hair, line, twist; pile, staple.

**threadbare** adj napless, old, seedy, worn; common, commonplace, hackneyed, stale, trite, worn-out.

**threat** n commination, defiance, denunciation, fulmination, intimidation, menace, thunder, thunderbolt.

**threaten** vb denounce, endanger, fulminate, intimidate, menace, thunder; augur, forebode, foreshadow, indicate, portend, presage, prognosticate, warn.

**threshold** n doorsill, sill; door, entrance, gate; beginning, commencement, opening, outset, start.

**thrift** n economy, frugality, parsimony, saving, thriftiness; gain, luck, profit, prosperity, success.

**thriftless** adj extravagant, improvident, lavish, profuse, prodigal, shiftless, unthrifty, wasteful.

**thrifty** adj careful, economical, frugal, provident, saving, sparing; flourishing, prosperous, thriving, vigorous.

**thrill** vb affect, agitate, electrify, inspire, move, penetrate, pierce, rouse, stir, touch. * n excitement, sensation, shock, tingling, tremor.

**thrilling** adj affecting, exciting, gripping, moving, sensational, touching.

**thrive** vb advance, batten, bloom, boom, flourish, prosper, succeed.

**throng** vb congregate, crowd, fill, flock, pack, press, swarm. * n assemblage, concourse, congregation, crowd, horde, host, mob, multitude, swarm.

**throttle** vb choke, silence, strangle, suffocate.

**throw** vb cast, chuck, dart, fling, hurl, lance, launch, overturn, pitch, pitchfork, send, sling, toss, whirl.

* n cast, fling, hurl, launch, pitch, sling, toss, whirl; chance, gamble, try, venture.

**thrust** vb clap, dig, drive, force, impel, jam, plunge, poke, propel, push, ram, run, shove, stick. * n dig, jab, lunge, pass, plunge, poke, propulsion, push, shove, stab, tilt.

**thump** vb bang, batter, beat, belabour, knock, punch, strike, thrash, thwack, whack. * n blow, knock, punch, strike, stroke.

**thwart** vb baffle, balk, contravene, counteract, cross, defeat, disconcert, frustrate, hinder, impede, oppose, obstruct, oppugn; cross, intersect, traverse.

**tickle** vb amuse, delight, divert, enliven, gladden, gratify, please, rejoice, titillate.

**ticklish** adj dangerous, precarious, risky, tottering, uncertain, unstable, unsteady; critical, delicate, difficult, nice.

**tide** n course, current, ebb, flow, stream.

**tidings** npl advice, greetings, information, intelligence, news, report, word.

**tidy** vb clean, neaten, order, straighten. * adj clean, neat, orderly, shipshape, spruce, trig, trim.

**tie** vb bind, confine, fasten, knot, lock, manacle, secure, shackle, fetter, yoke; complicate, entangle, interlace, knit; connect, hold, join, link, unite; constrain, oblige, restrain, restrict. * n band, fastening, knot, ligament, ligature; allegiance, bond, obligation; bow, cravat, necktie.

**tier** n line, rank, row, series.

**tiff** n fit, fume, passion, pet, miff, rage.

**tight** adj close, compact, fast, firm; taut, tense, stretched; impassable, narrow, strait.

**till** vb cultivate, plough, harrow.

**tillage** n agriculture, cultivation, culture, farming, geoponics, husbandry.

**tilt** vb cant, incline, slant, slope, tip; forge, hammer; point, thrust; joust, rush. * n awning, canopy, tent; lunge, pass, thrust; cant, inclination, slant, slope, tip.

**time** vb clock, control, count, measure, regulate, schedule. * n duration, interim, interval, season, span, spell, tenure, term, while; aeon, age, date, epoch, eon, era; term; cycle, dynasty, reign; confinement, delivery, parturition; measure, rhythm.

**timely** adj acceptable, appropriate, apropos, early, opportune, prompt, punctual, seasonable, well-timed.

**timid** adj afraid, cowardly, faint-hearted, fearful, irresolute, meticulous, nervous, pusillanimous, skittish, timorous, unadventurous; bashful, coy, diffident, modest, shame-faced, shrinking.

**tincture** vb colour, dye, shade, stain, tinge, tint; flavour, season; imbue, impregnate, impress, infuse. * n grain, hue, shade, stain, tinge, tint, tone; flavour, smack, spice, taste; admixture, dash, infusion, seasoning, sprinkling, touch.

**tinge** vb colour, dye, stain, tincture, tint; imbue, impregnate, impress, infuse. * n cast, colour, dye, hue, shade, stain, tincture, tint; flavour, smack, spice, quality, taste.

**tint** n cast, colour, complexion, dye, hue, shade, tinge, tone.

**tiny** adj diminutive, dwarfish, Lilliputian, little, microscopic, miniature, minute, puny, pygmy, small, wee.

**tip**[1] n apex, cap, end, extremity, peak, pinnacle, point, top, vertex.

**tip**[2] vb incline, overturn, tilt; dispose of, dump. * n donation, fee, gift, gratuity, perquisite, reward; inclination, slant; hint, pointer, suggestion; strike, tap.

**tirade** n abuse, denunciation, diatribe, harangue, outburst.

**tire** vb exhaust, fag, fatigue, harass, jade, weary; bore, bother, irk.

**tiresome** adj annoying, arduous, boring, dull, exhausting, fatiguing, fagging, humdrum, irksome, laborious, monotonous, tedious, wearisome, vexatious.

**tissue** n cloth, fabric; membrane, network, structure, texture, web; accumulation, chain, collection, combination, conglomeration, mass, series, set.

**titanic** adj colossal, Cyclopean, enormous, gigantic, herculean, huge, immense, mighty, monstrous, prodigious, stupendous, vast.

**title** n call, designate, name, style, term. * n caption, legend, head, heading; appellation, application, cognomen, completion, denomination, designation, epithet, name; claim, due, ownership, part, possession, prerogative, privilege, right.

**tittle** n atom, bit, grain, iota, jot, mite, particle, scrap, speck, whit.

**tittle-tattle** vb, n babble, cackle, chatter, discourse, gabble, gossip, prattle.

**toast** vb brown, dry, heat; honour, pledge, propose, salute. * n compliment, drink, pledge, salutation, salute; favourite, pet.

**toil** vb drudge, labour, strive, work. * n drudgery, effort, exertion, exhaustion, grinding, labour, pains, travail, work; gin, net, noose, snare, spring, trap.

**toilsome** adj arduous, difficult, fatiguing, hard, laborious, onerous, painful, severe, tedious, wearisome.

**token** adj nominal, superficial, symbolic. * n badge, evidence, index, indication, manifestation, mark, note, sign, symbol, trace, trait; keepsake, memento, memorial, reminder, souvenir.

**tolerable** adj bearable, endurable, sufferable, supportable; fair, indifferent, middling, ordinary, passable, so-so.

**tolerance** n endurance, receptivity, sufferance, toleration.

**tolerate** vb admit, allow, indulge, let, permit, receive; abide, brook, endure, suffer.

**toll**[1] n assessment, charge, customs, demand, dues, duty, fee, impost, levy, rate, tax, tribute; cost, damage, loss.

**toll**[2] vb chime, knell, peal, ring, sound. * n chime, knell, peal, ring, ringing, tolling.

**tomb** n catacomb, charnel house, crypt, grave, mausoleum, sepulchre, vault.

**tone** vb blend, harmonize, match, suit. * n note, sound; accent, cadence, emphasis, inflection, intonation, modulation; key, mood, strain, temper; elasticity, energy, force, health, strength, tension, vigour; cast, colour, manner, hue, shade, style, tint; drift, tenor.

**tongue** n accent, dialect, language, utterance, vernacular; discourse, parlance, speech, talk; nation, race.

**too** adv additionally, also, further, likewise, moreover, overmuch.

**toothsome** adj agreeable, dainty, delicious, luscious, nice, palatable, savoury.

**top** vb cap, head, tip; ride, surmount; outgo, surpass. * adj apical, best, chief, culminating, finest, first, foremost, highest, leading, prime, principal, topmost, uppermost. * n acme, apex, crest, crown, head, meridian, pinnacle, summit, surface, vertex, zenith.

**topic** n business, question, subject, text, theme, thesis; division, head, subdivision; commonplace, dictum, maxim, precept, proposition, principle, rule; arrangement, scheme.

**topple** vb fall, overturn, tumble, upset.

**torment** vb annoy, agonize, distress, excruciate, pain, rack, torture; badger, fret, harass, harry, irritate, nettle, plague, provoke, tantalize, tease, trouble, vex, worry. * n agony, anguish, pang, rack, torture.

**tornado** n blizzard, cyclone, gale, hurricane, storm, tempest, typhoon, whirlwind.

**torpid** adj benumbed, lethargic, motionless, numb; apathetic, dormant, dull, inactive, indolent, inert, listless, sleepy, slothful, sluggish, stupid.

**torpor** n coma, insensibility, lethargy, numbness, torpidity; inaction, inactivity, inertness, sluggishness, stupidity.

**torrid** adj arid, burnt, dried, parched; burning, fiery, hot, parching, scorching, sultry, tropical, violent.

**tortuous** adj crooked, curved, curvilineal, curvilinear, serpentine, sinuate, sinuated, sinuous, twisted, winding; ambiguous, circuitous, crooked, deceitful, indirect, perverse, roundabout.

**torture** vb agonize, distress, excruciate, pain, rack, torment. * n agony, anguish, distress, pain, pang, rack, torment.

**toss** vb cast, fling, hurl, pitch, throw; agitate, rock, shake; disquiet, harass, try; roll, writhe. * n cast, fling, pitch, throw.

**total** vb add, amount to, reach, reckon. * adj complete, entire, full, whole; integral, undivided. * n aggregate, all, gross, lump, mass, sum, totality, whole.

**totter** vb falter, reel, stagger, vacillate; lean, oscillate, reel, rock, shake, sway, tremble, waver; fail, fall, flag.

**touch** vb feel, graze, handle, hit, pat, strike, tap; concern, interest, regard; affect, impress, move, stir; grasp, reach, stretch; melt, mollify, soften; afflict, distress, hurt, injure, molest, sting, wound. * n hint, smack, suggestion, suspicion, taste, trace; blow, contract, hit, pat, tap.

**touchiness** n fretfulness, irritability, irascibility, peevishness, pettishness, petulance, snappishness, spleen, testiness.

**touching** adj affecting, heart-rending, impressive, melting, moving, pathetic, pitiable, tender; abutting, adjacent, bordering, tangent.

**touchy** adj choleric, cross, fretful, hot-tempered, irascible, irritable, peevish, petulant, quick-tempered, snappish, splenetic, tetchy, testy, waspish.

**tough** adj adhesive, cohesive, flexible, tenacious; coriaceous, leathery; clammy, ropy, sticky, viscous; inflexible, intractable, rigid, stiff; callous, hard, obdurate, stubborn; difficult, formidable, hard, troublesome. * n brute, bully, hooligan, ruffian, thug.

**tour** vb journey, perambulate, travel, visit. * n circuit, course, excursion, expedition, journey, perambulation, pilgrimage, round.

**tow** vb drag, draw, haul, pull, tug. * n drag, lift, pull.

**tower** vb mount, rise, soar, transcend. * n belfry, bell tower, column, minaret, spire, steeple, turret; castle, citadel, fortress, stronghold; pillar, refuge, rock, support.

**towering** adj elevated, lofty; excessive, extreme, prodigious, violent.

**toy** vb dally, play, sport, trifle, wanton. * n bauble, doll, gewgaw, gimmick, knick-knack, plaything, puppet, trinket; bagatelle, bubble, trifle; play, sport.

**trace** vb follow, track, train; copy, deduce, delineate, derive, describe, draw, sketch. * n evidence, footmark, footprint, footstep, impression, mark, remains, sign, token, track, trail, vestige, wake; memorial, record; bit, dash, flavour, hint, suspicion, streak, tinge.

**track** vb chase, draw, follow, pursue, scent, track, trail. * n footmark, footprint, footstep, spoor, trace, vestige; course, pathway, rails, road, runway, trace, trail, wake, way.

**trackless** adj pathless, solitary, unfrequented, unused.

**tract**[1] n area, district, quarter, region, territory; parcel, patch, part, piece, plot, portion.

**tract**[2] n disquisition, dissertation, essay, homily, pamphlet, sermon, thesis, tractate, treatise.

**tractable** adj amenable, docile, governable, manageable, submissive, willing, yielding; adaptable, ductile, malleable, plastic, tractile.

**trade** vb bargain, barter, chaffer, deal, exchange, interchange, sell, traffic. * n bargaining, barter, business, commerce, dealing, traffic; avocation, calling, craft, employment, occupation, office, profession, pursuit, vocation.

**traditional** adj accustomed, apocryphal, customary, established, historic, legendary, old, oral, transmitted, uncertain, unverified, unwritten.

**traduce** vb abuse, asperse, blemish, brand, calumniate, decry, defame, depreciate, disparage, revile, malign, slander, vilify.

**traducer** n calumniator, defamer, detractor, slanderer, vilifier.

**traffic** vb bargain, barter, chaffer, deal, exchange, trade. * n barter, business, chaffer, commerce, exchange, intercourse, trade, transportation, truck.

**tragedy** n drama, play; adversity, calamity, catastrophe, disaster, misfortune.

**tragic** adj dramatic; calamitous, catastrophic, disastrous, dreadful, fatal, grievous, heart-breaking, mournful, sad, shocking, sorrowful.

**trail** vb follow, hunt, trace, track; drag, draw, float, flow, haul, pull. * n footmark, footprint, footstep, mark, trace, track.

**train** vb drag, draw, haul, trail, tug; allure, entice; discipline, drill, educate, exercise, instruct, school, teach; accustom, break in, familiarize, habituate, inure, prepare, rehearse, use. * n trail, wake; entourage, cortege, followers, retinue, staff, suite; chain, consecution, sequel, series, set, succession; course, method, order, process; allure, artifice, device, enticement, lure, persuasion, stratagem, trap.

**trait** n line, mark, stroke, touch; characteristic, feature, lineage, particularity, peculiarity, quality.

**traitor** n apostate, betrayer, deceiver, Judas, miscreant, quisling, renegade, turncoat; conspirator, deserter, insurgent, mutineer, rebel, revolutionary.

**traitorous** adj faithless, false, perfidious, recreant, treacherous; insidious, treasonable.

**trammel** vb clog, confine, cramp, cumber, hamper, hinder, fetter, restrain, restrict, shackle, tie. * n bond, chain, fetter, hindrance, impediment, net, restraint, shackle.

**tramp** vb hike, march, plod, trudge, walk. * n excursion, journey, march, walk; landloper, loafer, stroller, tramper, vagabond, vagrant.

**trample** vb crush, tread; scorn, spurn.

**trance** n dream, ecstasy, hypnosis, rapture; catalepsy, coma.

**tranquil** adj calm, hushed, peaceful, placid, quiet, serene, still, undisturbed, unmoved, unperturbed, unruffled, untroubled.

**tranquillity** n calmness, peace, peacefulness, placidity, placidness, quiet, quietness, serenity, stillness, tranquilness.

**tranquillize** vb allay, appease, assuage, calm, compose, hush, lay, lull, moderate, pacify, quell, quiet, silence, soothe, still.

**transact** vb conduct, dispatch, enact, execute, do, manage, negotiate, perform, treat.

**transaction** n act, action, conduct, doing, management, negotiation, performance; affair, business, deal, dealing, incident, event, job, matter, occurrence, procedure, proceeding.

**transcend** vb exceed, overlap, overstep, pass, transgress; excel, outstrip, outrival, outvie, overtop, surmount, surpass.

**transcendent** adj consummate, inimitable, peerless, pre-eminent, supereminent, surpassing, unequalled, unparalleled, unrivalled, unsurpassed; metempiric, metempirical, noumenal, super-sensible.

**transcript** n duplicate, engrossment, rescript.

**transfer** vb convey, dispatch, move, remove, send, translate, transmit, transplant, transport; abalienate, alienate, assign, cede, confer, convey, consign, deed, devise, displace, forward, grant, pass, relegate. * n abalienation, alienation, assignment, bequest, carriage, cession, change, conveyance, copy, demise, devisal, gift, grant, move, relegation, removal, shift, shipment, transference, transferring, transit, transmission, transportation.

**transfigure** vb change, convert, dignify, idealize, metamorphose, transform.

**transform** vb alter, change, metamorphose, transfigure; convert, resolve, translate, transmogrify, transmute.

**transgress** vb exceed, transcend, overpass, overstep; break, contravene, disobey, infringe, violate; err, intrude, offend, sin, slip, trespass.

**transgression** n breach, disobedience, encroachment, infraction, infringement, transgression, violation; crime, delinquency, error, fault, iniquity, misdeed, misdemeanour, misdoing, offence, sin, slip, trespass, wrongdoing.

**transient** adj diurnal, ephemeral, evanescent, fleeting, fugitive, impertinent, meteoric, mortal, passing, perishable, short-lived, temporary, transitory, volatile; hasty, imperfect, momentary, short.

**transitory** adj brief, ephemeral, evanescent, fleeting, flitting, fugacious, momentary, passing, short, temporary, transient.

**translate** vb remove, transfer, transport; construe, decipher, decode, interpret, render, turn.

**translucent** adj diaphanous, hyaline, pellucid, semiopaque, semi-transparent.

**transmit** vb forward, remit, send; communicate, conduct, radiate; bear, carry, convey.

**transparent** adj bright, clear, diaphanous, limpid, lucid; crystalline, hyaline, pellucid, serene, translucent, transpicuous, unclouded; open, porous, transpicuous; evident, obvious, manifest, patent.

**transpire** vb befall, chance, happen, occur; evaporate, exhale.

**transport** vb bear, carry, cart, conduct, convey, fetch, remove, ship, take, transfer, truck; banish, expel; beatify, delight, enrapture, enravish, entrance, ravish. * n carriage, conveyance, movement, transportation, transporting; beatification, beatitude, bliss, ecstasy, felicity, happiness, rapture, ravishment; frenzy, passion, vehemence, warmth.

**transude** vb exude, filter, ooze, percolate, strain.

**trap** vb catch, ensnare, entrap, noose, snare, springe; ambush, deceive, dupe, trick; enmesh, tangle, trepan. * n gin, snare, springe, toil; ambush, artifice, pitfall, stratagem, trepan.

**trappings** npl adornments, decorations, dress, embellishments, frippery, gear, livery, ornaments, paraphernalia, rigging; accoutrements, caparisons, equipment, gear.

**trash** n dregs, dross, garbage, refuse, rubbish, trumpery, waste; balderdash, nonsense, twaddle.

**travel** vb journey, peregrinate, ramble, roam, rove, tour, voyage, walk, wander; go, move, pass. * n excursion, expedition, journey, peregrination, ramble, tour, trip, voyage, walk.

**traveller** n excursionist, explorer, globe-trotter, itinerant, passenger, pilgrim, rover, sightseer, tourist, trekker, tripper, voyager, wanderer, wayfarer.

**traverse** vb contravene, counteract, defeat, frustrate, obstruct, oppose, thwart; ford, pass, play, range.

**travesty** vb imitate, parody, take off. * n burlesque, caricature, imitation, parody, take-off.

**treacherous** adj deceitful, disloyal, faithless, false, false-hearted, insidious, perfidious, recreant, sly, traitorous, treasonable, unfaithful, unreliable, unsafe, untrustworthy.

**treachery** n betrayal, deceitfulness, disloyalty, double-dealing, faithlessness, foul play, infidelity, insidiousness, perfidiousness, treason, perfidy.

**treason** n betrayal, disloyalty, lèse-majesté, lese-majesty, perfidy, sedition, traitorousness, treachery.

**treasonable** adj disloyal, traitorous, treacherous.

**treasure** vb accumulate, collect, garner, hoard, husband, save, store; cherish, idolize, prize, value, worship. * n cash, funds, jewels, money, riches, savings, valuables, wealth; abundance, reserve, stock, store.

**treasurer** n banker, bursar, purser, receiver, trustee.

**treat** vb entertain, feast, gratify, refresh; attend, doctor, dose, handle, manage, serve; bargain, covenant, negotiate, parley. * n banquet, entertainment, feast; delight, enjoyment, entertainment, gratification, luxury, pleasure, refreshment.

**treatise** n commentary, discourse, dissertation, disquisition, monograph, tractate.

**treatment** n usage, use; dealing, handling, management, manipulation; doctoring, therapy.

**treaty** n agreement, alliance, bargain, compact, concordat, convention, covenant, entente, league, pact.

**tremble** vb quake, quaver, quiver, shake, shiver, shudder, vibrate, wobble. * n quake, quiver, shake, shiver, shudder, tremor, vibration, wobble.

**tremendous** adj colossal, enormous, huge, immense; excellent, marvellous, wonderful; alarming, appalling, awful, dreadful, fearful, frightful, horrid, horrible, terrible.

**tremor** n agitation, quaking, quivering, shaking, trembling, trepidation, tremulousness, vibration.

**tremulous** adj afraid, fearful, quavering, quivering, shaking, shaky, shivering, timid, trembling, vibrating.

**trench** vb carve, cut; ditch, channel, entrench, furrow. * n channel, ditch, drain, furrow, gutter, moat, pit, sewer, trough; dugout, entrenchment, fortification.

**trenchant** adj cutting, keen, sharp; acute, biting, caustic, crisp, incisive, pointed, piquant, pungent, sarcastic, sententious, severe, unsparing, vigorous.

**trend** vb drift, gravitate, incline, lean, run, stretch, sweep, tend, turn. * n bent, course, direction, drift, inclination, set, leaning, tendency, trending.

**trepidation** n agitation, quaking, quivering, shaking, trembling, tremor; dismay, excitement, fear, perturbation, tremulousness.

**trespass** vb encroach, infringe, intrude, trench; offend, sin, transgress. * n encroachment, infringement, injury, intrusion, invasion; crime, delinquency, error, fault, sin, misdeed, misdemeanour, offence, transgression; trespasser.

**trial** adj experimental, exploratory, testing. * n examination, experiment, test; experience, knowledge; aim, attempt, effort, endeavour, essay, exertion, struggle; assay, criterion, ordeal, prohibition, proof, test, touchstone; affliction, burden, chagrin, dolour, distress, grief, hardship, heartache, inclination, mis-

ery, mortification, pain, sorrow, suffering, tribulation, trouble, unhappiness, vexation, woe, wretchedness; action, case, cause, hearing, suit.

**tribe** n clan, family, lineage, race, sept, stock; class, distinction, division, order.

**tribulation** n adversity, affliction, distress, grief, misery, pain, sorrow, suffering, trial, trouble, unhappiness, woe, wretchedness.

**tribunal** n bench, judgement seat; assizes, bar, court, judicature, session.

**tribute** n subsidy, tax; custom, duty, excise, impost, tax, toll; contribution, grant, offering.

**trice** n flash, instant, jiffy, moment, second, twinkling.

**trick** vb cheat, circumvent, cozen, deceive, defraud, delude, diddle, dupe, fob, gull, hoax, overreach. * n artifice, blind, deceit, deception, dodge, fake, feint, fraud, game, hoax, imposture, manoeuvre, shift, ruse, swindle, stratagem, wile; antic, caper, craft, deftness, gambol, sleight; habit, mannerism, peculiarity, practice.

**trickle** vb distil, dribble, drip, drop, ooze, percolate, seep. * n dribble, drip, percolation, seepage.

**tricky** adj artful, cunning, deceitful, deceptive, subtle, trickish.

**trifle** vb dally, dawdle, fool, fribble, palter, play, potter, toy. * n bagatelle, bauble, bean, fig, nothing, triviality; iota, jot, modicum, particle, trace.

**trifling** adj empty, frippery, frivolous, inconsiderable, insignificant, nugatory, petty, piddling, shallow, slight, small, trivial, unimportant, worthless.

**trill** vb shake, quaver, warble. * n quaver, shake, tremolo, warbling.

**trim** vb adjust, arrange, prepare; balance, equalize, fill; adorn, array, bedeck, decorate, dress, embellish, garnish, ornament; clip, curtail, cut, lop, mow, poll, prune, shave, shear; berate, chastise, chide, rebuke, reprimand, reprove, trounce; fluctuate, hedge, shift, shuffle, vacillate. * adj compact, neat, nice, shapely, snug, tidy, well-adjusted, well-ordered; chic, elegant, finical, smart, spruce. * n dress, embellishment, gear, ornaments, trappings, trimmings; case, condition, order, plight, state.

**trinket** n bagatelle, bauble, bijoux, gewgaw, gimcrack, knick-knack, toy, trifle.

**trinkets** npl bijouterie, jewellery, jewels, ornaments.

**trip** vb caper, dance, frisk, hop, skip; misstep, stumble; bungle, blunder, err, fail, mistake; overthrow, supplant, upset; catch, convict, detect. * n hop, skip; lurch, misstep, stumble; blunder, bungle, error, failure, fault, lapse, miss, mistake, oversight, slip; circuit, excursion, expedition, jaunt, journey, ramble, route, stroll, tour.

**trite** adj banal, beaten, common, commonplace, hackneyed, old, ordinary, stale, stereotyped, threadbare, usual, worn.

**triturate** vb beat, bray, bruise, grind, pound, rub, thrash; comminute, levigate, pulverize.

**triumph** vb exult, rejoice; prevail, succeed, win; flourish, prosper, thrive; boast, brag, crow, gloat, swagger, vaunt. * n celebration, exultation, joy, jubilation, jubilee, ovation; accomplishment, achievement, conquest, success, victory.

**triumphant** adj boastful, conquering, elated, exultant, exulting, jubilant, rejoicing, successful, victorious.

**trivial** adj frivolous, gimcrack, immaterial, inconsiderable, insignificant, light, little, nugatory, paltry, petty, small, slight, slim, trifling, trumpery, unimportant.

**trollop** n prostitute, slattern, slut, whore.

**troop** vb crowd, flock, muster, throng. * n company, crowd, flock, herd, multitude, number, throng; band, body, party, squad, troupe.

**trophy** n laurels, medal, palm, prize.

**troth** n candour, sincerity, truth, veracity, verity; allegiance, belief, faith, fidelity, word; betrothal.

**trouble** vb agitate, confuse, derange, disarrange, disorder, disturb; afflict, ail, annoy, badger, concern, disquiet, distress, fret, grieve, harass, molest, perplex, perturb, pester, plague, torment, vex, worry. * n adversity, affliction, calamity, distress, dolour, grief, hardship, misfortune, misery, pain, sorrow, suffering, tribulation, woe; ado, annoyance, anxiety, bother, care, discomfort, embarrassment, fuss, inconvenience, irritation, pains, perplexity, plague, torment, vexation, worry; commotion, disturbance, row; bewilderment, disquietude, embarrassment, perplexity, uneasiness.

**troublesome** adj annoying, distressing, disturbing, galling, grievous, harassing, painful, perplexing, vexatious, worrisome; burdensome, irksome, tiresome, wearisome; importunate, intrusive, teasing; arduous, difficult, hard, inconvenient, trying, unwieldy.

**troublous** adj agitated, disquieted, disturbed, perturbed, tumultuous, turbulent.

**trough** n hutch, manger; channel, depression, hollow, furrow.

**truant** vb be absent, desert, dodge, malinger, shirk, skive. * n absentee, deserter, idler, laggard, loiterer, lounger, malingerer, quitter, runaway, shirker, vagabond.

**truce** n armistice, breathing space, cessation, delay, intermission, lull, pause, recess, reprieve, respite, rest.

**truck** vb barter, deal, exchange, trade, traffic. * n lorry, van, wagon.

**truckle** vb roll, trundle; cringe, crouch, fawn, knuckle, stoop, submit, yield.

**truculent** adj barbarous, bloodthirsty, ferocious, fierce, savage; cruel, malevolent, relentless; destructive, deadly, fatal, ruthless.

**true** adj actual, unaffected, authentic, genuine, legitimate, pure, real, rightful, sincere, sound, truthful, veritable; substantial, veracious; constant, faithful, loyal, staunch, steady; equitable, honest, honourable, just, upright, trusty, trustworthy, virtuous; accurate, correct, even, exact, right, straight, undeviating. * adv good, well.

**truism** n axiom, commonplace, platitude.

**trumpery** adj pinchbeck, rubbishy, trashy, trifling, worthless. * n deceit, deception, falsehood, humbug, imposture; frippery, rubbish, stuff, trash, trifles.

**truncheon** n club, cudgel, nightstick, partisan, staff; baton, wand.

**trunk** n body, bole, butt, shaft, stalk, stem, stock, torso; box, chest, coffer.

**trundle** vb bowl, revolve, roll, spin, truckle, wheel.

**truss** vb bind, bundle, close, cram, hang, pack. * n bundle, package, packet; apparatus, bandage, support.

**trust** vb confide, depend, expect, hope, rely; believe, credit; commit, entrust. * n belief, confidence, credence, faith; credit, tick; charge, deposit; commission, duty, errand; assurance, conviction, expectation, hope, reliance, security.

**trustful** adj confiding, trusting, unquestioning, unsuspecting; faithful, trustworthy, trusty.

**trustworthy** adj confidential, constant, credible, dependable, faithful, firm, honest, incorrupt, upright, reliable, responsible, straightforward, staunch, true, trusty, uncorrupt, upright.

**truth** n fact, reality, veracity; actuality, authenticity, realism; canon, law, oracle, principle; right, truthfulness, veracity; candour, fidelity, frankness, honesty, honour, ingenuousness, integrity, probity, sincerity, virtue; constancy, devotion, faith, fealty, loyalty, steadfastness; accuracy, correctness, exactitude, exactness, nicety, precision, regularity, trueness.

**truthful** adj correct, reliable, true, trustworthy, veracious; artless, candid, frank, guileless, honest, ingenuous, open, sincere, straightforward, trusty.

**truthless** adj canting, disingenuous, dishonest, false, faithless, hollow, hypocritical, insincere, pharisaical, treacherous, unfair, untrustworthy.

**try** vb examine, prove, test; attempt, essay; adjudicate, adjudge, examine, hear; purify, refine; sample, sift, smell, taste; aim, attempt, endeavour, seek, strain, strive. * n attempt, effort, endeavour, experiment, trial.

**trying** adj difficult, fatiguing, hard, irksome, tiresome, wearisome; afflicting, afflictive, calamitous, deplorable, dire, distressing, grievous, hard, painful, sad, severe.

**tryst** n appointment, assignation, rendezvous.

**tube** n bore, bronchus, cylinder, duct, hollow, hose, pipe, pipette, worm.

**tuft** n brush, bunch, crest, feather, knot, plume, topknot, tussock; clump, cluster, group.

**tug** vb drag, draw, haul, pull, tow, wrench; labour, strive, struggle. * n drag, haul, pull, tow, wrench.

**tuition** n education, instruction, schooling, teaching, training.

**tumble** vb heave, pitch, roll, toss, wallow; fall, sprawl, stumble, topple, trip; derange, disarrange, dishevel, disorder, disturb, rumple, tousle. * n collapse, drop, fall, plunge, spill, stumble, trip.

**tumbler** n acrobat, juggler; glass.

**tumid** adj bloated, distended, enlarged, puffed-up, swelled, swollen, turgid; bombastic, declamatory, fustian, grandiloquent, grandiose, high-flown, inflated, pompous, puffy, rhetorical, stilted, swelling.

**tumour** n boil, carbuncle, swelling, tumefaction.

**tumult** n ado, affray, agitation, altercation, bluster, brawl, disturbance, ferment, flurry, feud, fracas, fray, fuss, hubbub, huddle, hurly-burly, melee, noise, perturbation, pother, quarrel, racket, riot, row, squabble, stir, turbulence, turmoil, uproar.

**tumultuous** adj blustery, breezy, bustling, confused, disorderly, disturbed, riotous, turbulent, unruly.

**tune** vb accord, attune, harmonize, modulate; adapt, adjust, attune. * n air, aria, melody, strain, tone; agreement, concord, harmony; accord, order.

**tuneful** adj dulcet, harmonious, melodious, musical.

**turbid** adj foul, impure, muddy, thick, unsettled.

**turbulence** n agitation, commotion, confusion, disorder, disturbance, excitement, tumult, tumultuousness, turmoil, unruliness, uproar; insubordination, insurrection, mutiny, rebellion, riot, sedition.

**turbulent** adj agitated, disturbed, restless, tumultuous, wild; blatant, blustering, boisterous, brawling, disorderly, obstreperous, tumultuous, uproarious, vociferous; factious, insubordinate, insurgent, mutinous, raging, rebellious, refractory, revolutionary, riotous, seditious, stormy, violent.

**turf** n grass, greensward, sod, sward; horse racing, racecourse, race-ground.

**turgid** adj bloated, distended, protuberant, puffed-up, swelled, swollen, tumid; bombastic, declamatory, diffuse, digressive, fustian, high-flown, inflated, grandiloquent, grandiose, ostentatious, pompous, puffy, rhetorical, stilted.

**turmoil** n activity, agitation, bustle, commotion, confusion, disorder, disturbance, ferment, flurry, huddle, hubbub, hurly-burly, noise, trouble, tumult, turbulence, uproar.

**turn** vb revolve, rotate; bend, cast, defect, inflict, round, spin, sway, swivel, twirl, twist, wheel; crank, grind, wind; deflect, divert, transfer, warp; form, mould, shape; adapt, fit, manoeuvre, suit; alter, change, conform, metamorphose, transform, transmute, vary; convert, persuade, prejudice; construe, render, translate; depend, hang, hinge, pivot; eventuate, issue, result, terminate; acidify, curdle, ferment. * n cycle, gyration, revolution, rotation, round; bending, deflection, deviation, diversion, doubling, flection, flexion, flexure, reel, retroversion, slew, spin, sweep, swing, swirl, swivel, turning, twist, twirl, whirl, winding; alteration, change, variation, vicissitude; bend, circuit, drive, ramble, run, round, stroll; bout, hand, innings, opportunity, shift, spell; act, action, deed, office; convenience, occasion, purpose; cast, fashion, form, guise, manner, mould, phase, shape; aptitude, bent, bias, disposition, faculty, genius, gift, inclination, leaning, proclivity, proneness, propensity, talent, tendency.

**turncoat** n apostate, backslider, deserter, recreant, renegade, traitor, wretch.

**turpitude** n baseness, degradation, depravity, vileness, wickedness.

**turret** n cupola, minaret, pinnacle.

**tussle** vb conflict, contend, contest, scuffle, struggle, wrestle. * n conflict, contest, fight, scuffle, struggle.

**tutelage** n care, charge, dependence, guardianship, protection, teaching, tutorage, tutorship, wardship.

**tutor** vb coach, educate, instruct, teach; discipline, train. * n coach, governess, governor, instructor, master, preceptor, schoolteacher, teacher.

**twaddle** vb chatter, gabble, maunder, prate, prattle. * n balderdash, chatter, flummery, gabble, gibberish, gobbledegook, gossip, jargon, moonshine, nonsense, platitude, prate, prattle, rigmarole, stuff, tattle.

**tweak** vb, n jerk, pinch, pull, twinge, twitch.

**twig**¹ n bough, branch, offshoot, shoot, slip, spray, sprig, stick, switch.

**twig**² vb catch on, comprehend, discover, grasp, realize, recognize, see, understand.

**twin** vb couple, link, match, pair. * adj double, doubled, duplicate, geminate, identical, matched, matching, second, twain. * n corollary, double, duplicate, fellow, likeness, match.

**twine** vb embrace, encircle, entwine, interlace, surround, wreathe; bend, meander, wind; coil, twist. * n convolution, coil, twist; embrace, twining, winding; cord, string.

**twinge** vb pinch, tweak, twitch. * n pinch, tweak, twitch; gripe, pang, spasm.

**twinkle** vb blink, twink, wink; flash, glimmer, scintillate, sparkle. * n blink, flash, gleam, glimmer, scintillation, sparkle; flash, instant, jiffy, moment, second, tick, trice, twinkling.

**twinkling** n flashing, sparkling, twinkle; flash, instant, jiffy, moment, second, tick, trice.

**twirl** vb revolve, rotate, spin, turn, twist, twirl. * n convolution, revolution, turn, twist, whirling.

**twist** vb purl, rotate, spin, twine; complicate, contort, convolute, distort, pervert, screw, wring; coil, writhe; encircle, wind, wreathe. * n coil, curl, spin, twine; braid, roll; change, complication, development, variation; bend, convolution, turn; defect, distortion, flaw, imperfection; jerk, pull, sprain, wrench; aberration, characteristic, eccentricity, oddity, peculiarity, quirk.

**twit**¹ vb banter, blame, censure, reproach, taunt, tease, upbraid.

**twit**² n blockhead, fool, idiot, nincompoop, nitwit.

**twitch** vb jerk, pluck, pull, snatch. * n jerk, pull; contraction, pull, quiver, spasm, twitching.

**type** n emblem, mark, stamp; adumbration, image, representation, representative, shadow, sign, symbol, token; archetype, exemplar, model, original, pattern, prototype, protoplast, standard; character, form, kind, nature, sort; figure, letter, text, typography.

**typical** adj emblematic, exemplary, figurative, ideal, indicative, model, representative, symbolic, true.

**typify** vb betoken, denote, embody, exemplify, figure, image, indicate, represent, signify.

**tyrannical** adj absolute, arbitrary, autocratic, cruel, despotic, dictatorial, domineering, high, imperious, irresponsible, severe, tyrannical, unjust; galling, grinding, inhuman, oppressive, overbearing, severe.

**tyranny** n absolutism, autocracy, despotism, dictatorship, harshness, oppression.

**tyrant** n autocrat, despot, dictator, oppressor.

**tyro** n beginner, learner, neophyte, novice; dabbler, smatterer.

# U

**ubiquitous** *adj* omnipresent, present, universal.

**udder** *n* nipple, pap, teat.

**ugly** *adj* crooked, homely, ill-favoured, plain, ordinary, unlovely, unprepossessing, unshapely, unsightly; forbidding, frightful, gruesome, hideous, horrible, horrid, loathsome, monstrous, shocking, terrible, repellent, repulsive; bad-tempered, cantankerous, churlish, cross, quarrelsome, spiteful, surly, spiteful, vicious.

**ulcer** *n* boil, fester, gathering, pustule, sore.

**ulterior** *adj* beyond, distant, farther; hidden, personal, secret, selfish, undisclosed.

**ultimate** *adj* conclusive, decisive, eventual, extreme, farthest, final, last. * *n* acme, consummation, culmination, height, peak, pink, quintessence, summit.

**ultra** *adj* advanced, beyond, extreme, radical.

**umbrage** *n* shadow, shade; anger, displeasure, dissatisfaction, dudgeon, injury, offence, pique, resentment.

**umpire** *vb* adjudicate, arbitrate, judge, referee. * *n* adjudicator, arbiter, arbitrator, judge, referee.

**unabashed** *adj* bold, brazen, confident, unblushing, undaunted, undismayed.

**unable** *adj* impotent, incapable, incompetent, powerless, weak.

**unacceptable** *adj* disagreeable, distasteful, offensive, unpleasant, unsatisfactory, unwelcome.

**unaccommodating** *adj* disobliging, noncompliant, uncivil, ungracious.

**unaccomplished** *adj* incomplete, unachieved, undone, unperformed, unexecuted, unfinished; ill-educated, uncultivated, unpolished.

**unaccountable** *adj* inexplicable, incomprehensible, inscrutable, mysterious, unintelligible; irresponsible, unanswerable.

**unaccustomed** *adj* uninitiated, unskilled, unused; foreign, new, strange, unfamiliar, unusual.

**unaffected** *adj* artless, honest, naive, natural, plain, simple, sincere, real, unfeigned; chaste, pure, unadorned; insensible, unchanged, unimpressed, unmoved, unstirred, untouched.

**unanimity** *n* accord, agreement, concert, concord, harmony, union, unity.

**unanimous** *adj* agreeing, concordant, harmonious, like-minded, solid, united.

**unassuming** *adj* humble, modest, reserved, unobtrusive, unpretending, unpretentious.

**unattainable** *adj* inaccessible, unobtainable.

**unavailing** *adj* abortive, fruitless, futile, ineffectual, ineffective, inept, nugatory, unsuccessful, useless, vain.

**unbalanced** *adj* unsound, unsteady; unadjusted, unsettled.

**unbearable** *adj* insufferable, insupportable, unendurable.

**unbecoming** *adj* inappropriate, indecent, indecorous, improper, unbefitting, unbeseeming, unseemly, unsuitable.

**unbelief** *n* disbelief, dissent, distrust, incredulity, incredulousness, miscreance, miscreancy, nonconformity; doubt, freethinking, infidelity, scepticism.

**unbeliever** *n* agnostic, deist, disbeliever, doubter, heathen, infidel, sceptic.

**unbending** *adj* inflexible, rigid, stiff, unpliant, unyielding; firm, obstinate, resolute, stubborn.

**unbiased** *adj* disinterested, impartial, indifferent, neutral, uninfluenced, unprejudiced, unwarped.

**unbind** *vb* loose, undo, unfasten, unloose, untie; free, unchain, unfetter.

**unblemished** *adj* faultless, guiltless, immaculate, impeccable, innocent, intact, perfect, pure, sinless, spotless, stainless, undefiled, unspotted, unsullied, untarnished.

**unblushing** *adj* boldfaced, impudent, shameless.

**unbounded** *adj* absolute, boundless, endless, immeasurable, immense, infinite, interminable, measureless, unlimited, vast; immoderate, uncontrolled, unrestrained, unrestricted.

**unbridled** *adj* dissolute, intractable, lax, licensed, licentious, loose, uncontrolled, ungovernable, unrestrained, violent, wanton.

**unbroken** *adj* complete, entire, even, full, intact, unimpaired; constant, continuous, fast, profound, sound, successive, undisturbed; inviolate, unbetrayed, unviolated.

**unbuckle** *vb* loose, unfasten, unloose.

**uncanny** *adj* inopportune, unsafe; eerie, eery, ghostly, unearthly, unnatural, weird.

**unceremonious** *adj* abrupt, bluff, blunt, brusque, course, curt, gruff, plain, rough, rude, ungracious; casual, familiar, informal, offhand, unconstrained.

**uncertain** *adj* ambiguous, doubtful, dubious, equivocal, indefinite, indeterminate, indistinct, questionable, unsettled; insecure, precarious, problematical; capricious, changeable, desultory, fitful, fluctuating, irregular, mutable, shaky, slippery, unreliable, variable.

**unchaste** *adj* dissolute, incontinent, indecent, immoral, lascivious, lecherous, libidinous, lewd, loose, obscene, wanton.

**unchecked** *adj* uncurbed, unhampered, unhindered, unobstructed, unrestrained, untrammelled.

**uncivil** *adj* bearish, blunt, boorish, brusque, discourteous, disobliging, disrespectful, gruff, ill-bred, ill-mannered, impolite, irreverent, rough, rude, uncomplaisant, uncourteous, uncouth, ungentle, ungracious, unmannered, unseemly.

**unclean** *adj* abominable, beastly, dirty, filthy, foul, grimy, grubby, miry, muddy, nasty, offensive, purulent, repulsive, soiled, sullied; improper, indecent, indecorous, obscene, polluted, risqué, sinful, smutty, unholy, uncleanly.

**uncomfortable** *adj* disagreeable, displeasing, disquieted, distressing, disturbed, uneasy, unpleasant, restless; cheerless, close, oppressive; dismal, miserable, unhappy.

**uncommon** *adj* choice, exceptional, extraordinary, infrequent, noteworthy, odd, original, queer, rare, remarkable, scarce, singular, strange, unexampled, unfamiliar, unusual, unwonted.

**uncommunicative** *adj* close, inconversable, reserved, reticent, taciturn, unsociable, unsocial.

**uncomplaining** *adj* long-suffering, meek, patient, resigned, tolerant.

**uncompromising** *adj* inflexible, narrow, obstinate, orthodox, rigid, stiff, strict, unyielding.

**unconcerned** *adj* apathetic, careless, indifferent.

**unconditional** *adj* absolute, categorical, complete, entire, free, full, positive, unlimited, unqualified, unreserved, unrestricted.

**uncongenial** *adj* antagonistic, discordant, displeasing, ill-assorted, incompatible, inharmonious, mismatched, unsuited, unsympathetic.

**uncouth** *adj* awkward, boorish, clownish, clumsy, gawky, inelegant, loutish, lubberly, rough, rude, rustic, uncourtly, ungainly, unpolished, unrefined, unseemly; odd, outlandish, strange, unfamiliar, unusual.

**uncover** *vb* denude, divest, lay bare, strip; disclose, discover, expose, reveal, unmask, unveil; bare, doff; open, unclose, unseal.

**unctuous** *adj* adipose, greasy, oily, fat, fatty, oleaginous, pinguid, sebaceous; bland, lubricious, smooth, slippery; bland, fawning, glib, obsequious, plausible, servile, suave, sycophantic; fervid, gushing.

**uncultivated** *adj* fallow, uncultured, unreclaimed, untilled; homely, ignorant, illiterate, rude, uncivilized, uncultured, uneducated, unfit, unlettered, unpolished, unread, unready, unrefined, untaught; rough, savage, sylvan, uncouth, wild.

**undaunted** *adj* bold, brave, courageous, dauntless, fearless, intrepid, plucky, resolute, undismayed.

**undefiled** *adj* clean, immaculate, pure, spotless, stainless, unblemished, unspotted, unsullied, untarnished; honest, innocent, inviolate, pure, uncorrupted, unpolluted, unstained.

**undemonstrative** *adj* calm, composed, demure, impassive, modest, placid, quiet, reserved, sedate, sober, staid, tranquil.

**undeniable** *adj* certain, conclusive, evident, incontestable, incontrovertible, indisputable, indubitable, obvious, unquestionable.

**under** *prep* below, beneath, inferior to, lower than, subordinate to, underneath. * *adv* below, beneath, down, lower.

**underestimate** *vb* belittle, underrate, undervalue.

**undergo** *vb* bear, endure, experience, suffer, sustain.

**underhand** *adj* clandestine, deceitful, disingenuous, fraudulent, hidden, secret, sly, stealthy, underhanded, unfair. * *adv* clandestinely, privately, secretly, slyly, stealthily, surreptitiously; fraudulently, unfairly.

**underling** *n* agent, inferior, servant, subordinate.

**undermine** *vb* excavate, mine, sap; demoralize, foil, frustrate, thwart, weaken.

**understand** *vb* apprehend, catch, comprehend, conceive, discern, grasp, know, penetrate, perceive, see, seize, twig; assume, interpret, take; imply, mean.

**understanding** *adj* compassionate, considerate, forgiving, kind, kindly, patient, sympathetic, tolerant. * *n* brains, comprehension, discernment, faculty, intellect, intelligence, judgement, knowledge, mind, reason, sense.

**undertake** vb assume, attempt, begin, embark on, engage in, enter upon, take in hand; agree, bargain, contract, covenant, engage, guarantee, promise, stipulate.

**undertaking** n adventure, affair, attempt, business, effort, endeavour, engagement, enterprise, essay, move, project, task, venture.

**undesigned** adj spontaneous, unintended, unintentional, unplanned, unpremeditated.

**undigested** adj crude, ill-advised, ill-considered, ill-judged; confused, disorderly, ill-arranged, unmethodical.

**undivided** adj complete, entire, whole; one, united.

**undo** vb annul, cancel, frustrate, invalidate, neutralize, nullify, offset, reverse; disengage, loose, unfasten, unmake, unravel, untie; crush, destroy, overturn, ruin.

**undoubted** adj incontrovertible, indisputable, indubitable, undisputed, unquestionable, unquestioned.

**undress** vb denude, dismantle, disrobe, unclothe, unrobe, peel, strip. * n disarray, nakedness, nudity; mufti, negligee.

**undue** adj illegal, illegitimate, improper, unlawful, excessive, disproportionate, disproportioned, immoderate, unsuitable; unfit.

**undulation** n billowing, fluctuation, pulsation, ripple, wave.

**undying** adj deathless, endless, immortal, imperishable.

**unearthly** adj preternatural, supernatural, uncanny, weird.

**uneasy** adj disquieted, disturbed, fidgety, impatient, perturbed, restless, restive, unquiet, worried; awkward, stiff, ungainly, ungraceful; constraining, cramping, disagreeable, uncomfortable.

**unending** adj endless, eternal, everlasting, interminable, never-ending, perpetual, unceasing.

**unequal** adj disproportionate, disproportioned, ill-matched, inferior, irregular, insufficient, not alike, uneven.

**unequalled** adj exceeding, incomparable, inimitable, matchless, new, nonpareil, novel, paramount, peerless, pre-eminent, superlative, surpassing, transcendent, unheard of, unique, unparalleled, unrivalled.

**unequivocal** adj absolute, certain, clear, evident,

incontestable, indubitable, positive; explicit, unambiguous, unmistakable.

**uneven** adj hilly, jagged, lumpy, ragged, rough, rugged, stony; motley, unequal, variable, variegated.

**uneventful** adj commonplace, dull, eventless, humdrum, quiet, monotonous, smooth, uninteresting.

**unexceptionable** adj excellent, faultless, good, irreproachable.

**unexpected** adj abrupt, sudden, unforeseen.

**unfair** adj dishonest, dishonourable, faithless, false, hypocritical, inequitable, insincere, oblique, one-sided, partial, unequal, unjust, wrongful.

**unfaithful** adj adulterous, derelict, deceitful, dishonest, disloyal, false, faithless, fickle, perfidious, treacherous, unreliable; negligent; changeable, inconstant, untrue.

**unfamiliar** adj bizarre, foreign, new, novel, outlandish, queer, singular, strange, uncommon, unusual.

**unfashionable** adj antiquated, destitute, disused, obsolete, old-fashioned, unconventional.

**unfavourable** adj adverse, contrary, disadvantageous, discouraging, ill, inauspicious, inimical, inopportune, indisposed, malign, sinister, unfriendly, unlucky, unpropitious, untimely; foul, inclement.

**unfeeling** adj apathetic, callous, heartless, insensible, numb, obdurate, torpid, unconscious, unimpressionable; adamantine, cold-blooded, cruel, hard, merciless, pitiless, stony, unkind, unsympathetic.

**unfit** vb disable, disqualify, incapacitate. * adj improper, inappropriate, incompetent, inconsistent, unsuitable; ill-equipped, inadequate, incapable, unqualified, useless; debilitated, feeble, flabby, unhealthy, unsound.

**unflagging** adj constant, indefatigable, never-ending, persevering, steady, unfaltering, unremitting, untiring, unwearied.

**unflinching** adj firm, resolute, steady, unshrinking.

**unfold** vb display, expand, open, separate, unfurl, unroll; declare, disclose, reveal, tell; decipher, develop, disentangle, evolve, explain, illustrate, interpret, resolve, unravel.

**unfortunate** adj hapless, ill-fated, ill-starred, infelicitous, luckless, unhappy, unlucky, unprosperous, unsuccessful, wretched; calamitous, deplorable, disastrous; inappropriate, inexpedient.

**unfrequented** adj abandoned, deserted, forsaken, lone, solitary, uninhabited, unoccupied.

**unfruitful** adj barren, fruitless, sterile; infecund, unprolific; unprofitable, unproductive.

**ungainly** adj awkward, boorish, clownish, clumsy, gawky, inelegant, loutish, lubberly, lumbering, slouching, stiff, uncourtly, uncouth, ungraceful.

**ungentlemanly** adj ill-bred, impolite, rude, uncivil, ungentle, ungracious, unmannerly.

**unhappy** adj afflicted, disastrous, dismal, distressed, drear, evil, inauspicious, miserable, painful, unfortunate, wretched.

**unhealthy** adj ailing, diseased, feeble, indisposed, infirm, poorly, sickly, toxic, unsanitary, unsound, toxic, venomous.

**uniform** adj alike, constant, even, equable, equal, smooth, steady, regular, unbroken, unchanged, undeviating, unvaried, unvarying. * n costume, dress, livery, outfit, regalia, suit.

**uniformity** n constancy, continuity, permanence, regularity, sameness, stability; accordance, agreement, conformity, consistency, unanimity.

**unimportant** adj immaterial, inappreciable, inconsequent, inconsequential, inconsiderable, indifferent, insignificant, mediocre, minor, paltry, petty, small, slight, trifling, trivial.

**unintentional** adj accidental, casual, fortuitous, inadvertent, involuntary, spontaneous, undesigned, unmeant, unplanned, unpremeditated, unthinking.

**uninterrupted** adj continuous, endless, incessant, perpetual, unceasing.

**union** n coalescence, coalition, combination, conjunction, coupling, fusion, incorporation, joining, junction, unification, uniting; agreement, concert, concord, concurrence, harmony, unanimity, unity; alliance, association, club, confederacy, federation, guild, league.

**unique** adj choice, exceptional, matchless, only, peculiar, rare, single, sole, singular, uncommon, unexampled, unmatched.

**unison** n accord, accordance, agreement, concord, harmony.

**unite** vb amalgamate, attach, blend, centralize, coalesce, confederate, consolidate, embody, fuse, incorporate, merge, weld; associate, conjoin, connect, couple, link, marry; combine, join; harmonize, reconcile; agree, concert, concur, cooperate, fraternize.

**universal** adj all-reaching, catholic, cosmic, encyclopedic, general, ubiquitous, unlimited; all, complete, entire, total, whole.

**unjust** adj inequitable, injurious, partial, unequal, unfair, unwarranted, wrong, wrongful; flagitious, heinous, influenced, iniquitous, nefarious, unrighteous, wicked; biased, prejudiced, uncandid.

**unjustifiable** adj indefensible, unjust, unreasonable, unwarrantable; inexcusable, unpardonable.

**unknown** adj unappreciated, unascertained; undiscovered, unexplored, uninvestigated; concealed, dark, enigmatic, hidden, mysterious, mystic; anonymous, incognito, inglorious, nameless, obscure, renownless, undistinguished, unheralded, unnoted.

**unladylike** adj ill-bred, impolite, rude, uncivil, ungentle, ungracious, unmannerly.

**unlamented** adj unmourned, unregretted.

**unlimited** adj boundless, infinite, interminable, limitless, measureless, unbounded; absolute, full, unconfined, unconstrained, unrestricted; indefinite, undefined.

**unlucky** adj baleful, disastrous, ill-fated, ill-starred, luckless, unfortunate, unprosperous, unsuccessful; ill-omened, inauspicious; miserable, unhappy.

**unmanageable** adj awkward, cumbersome, inconvenient, unwieldy; intractable, unruly, unworkable, vicious; difficult, impractical.

**unmatched** adj matchless, unequalled, unparalleled, unrivalled.

**unmitigated** adj absolute, complete, consummate, perfect, sheer, stark, thorough, unqualified, utter.

**unnatural** adj aberrant, abnormal, anomalous, foreign, irregular, prodigious, uncommon; brutal, cold, heartless, inhuman, unfeeling, unusual; affected, artificial, constrained, forced, insincere, self-conscious, stilted, strained; factitious.

**unpleasant** adj disagreeable, displeasing, distasteful, obnoxious, offensive, repulsive, unlovely, ungrateful, unacceptable, unpalatable, unwelcome.

**unpremeditated** adj extempore, impromptu, offhand, spontaneous, undesigned, unintentional, unstudied.

**unprincipled** adj bad, crooked, dishonest, fraudulent, immoral, iniquitous, knavish, lawless, profligate, rascally, roguish, thievish, trickish, tricky, unscrupulous, vicious, villainous, wicked.

**unqualified** adj disqualified, incompetent, ineligible, unadapted, unfit; absolute, certain, consummate, decided, direct, downright, full, outright, unconditional, unmeasured, unrestricted, unmitigated; exaggerated, sweeping.

**unreal** adj chimerical, dreamlike, fanciful, flimsy, ghostly, illusory, insubstantial, nebulous, shadowy, spectral, visionary, unsubstantial.

**unreasonable** adj absurd, excessive, exorbitant, foolish, ill-judged, illogical, immoderate, impractical, injudicious, irrational, nonsensical, preposterous, senseless, silly, stupid, unfair, unreasoning, unwarrantable, unwise.

**unreliable** adj fallible, fickle, irresponsible, treacherous, uncertain, undependable, unstable, unsure, untrustworthy.

**unremitting** adj assiduous, constant, continual, diligent, incessant, indefatigable, persevering, sedulous, unabating, unceasing.

**unrepentant** adj abandoned, callous, graceless, hardened, impenitent, incorrigible, irreclaimable, lost, obdurate, profligate, recreant, seared, shameless.

**unrequited** adj unanswered, unreturned, unrewarded.

**unreserved** adj absolute, entire, full, unlimited; above-board, artless, candid, communicative, fair, frank, guileless, honest, ingenuous, open, sincere, single-minded, undesigning, undissembling; demonstrative, emotional, open-hearted.

**unresisting** adj compliant, long-suffering, non-resistant, obedient, passive, patient, submissive, yielding.

**unresponsive** adj irresponsive, unsympathetic.

**unrestrained** adj unbridled, unchecked, uncurbed, unfettered, unhindered, unobstructed, unreserved; broad, dissolute, incontinent, inordinate, lax, lewd, licentious, loose, wanton; lawless, wild.

**unrestricted** adj free, unbridled, unconditional, unconfined, uncurbed, unfettered, unlimited, unqualified, unrestrained; clear, open, public, unobstructed.

**unrevealed** adj hidden, occult, secret, undiscovered, unknown.

**unrewarded** adj unpaid, unrecompensed.

**unriddle** vb explain, expound, solve, unfold, unravel.

**unrighteous** adj evil, sinful, ungodly, unholy, vicious, wicked, wrong; heinous, inequitable, iniquitous, nefarious, unfair, unjust.

**unripe** adj crude, green, hard, immature, premature, sour; incomplete, unfinished.

**unrivalled** adj incomparable, inimitable, matchless, peerless, unequalled, unexampled, unique, unparalleled.

**unrobe** vb disrobe, undress.

**unroll** vb develop, discover, evolve, open, unfold; display, lay open.

**unromantic** adj literal, matter-of-fact, prosaic.

**unroot** vb eradicate, extirpate, root out, uproot.

**unruffled** adj calm, peaceful, placid, quiet, serene, smooth, still, tranquil; collected, composed, cool, imperturbable, peaceful, philosophical, placid, tranquil, undisturbed, unexcited, unmoved.

**unruly** adj disobedient, disorderly, fractious, headstrong, insubordinate, intractable, mutinous, obstreperous, rebellious, refractory, riotous, seditious, turbulent, ungovernable, unmanageable, wanton, wild; lawless, obstinate, rebellious, stubborn, vicious.

**unsafe** adj dangerous, hazardous, insecure, perilous, precarious, risky, treacherous, uncertain, unprotected.

**unsaid** adj tacit, unmentioned, unspoken, unuttered.

**unsanctified** adj profane, unhallowed, unholy.

**unsatisfactory** adj insufficient; disappointing; faulty, feeble, imperfect, poor, weak.

**unsatisfied** adj insatiate, unsated, unsatiated, unstaunched; discontented, displeased, dissatisfied, malcontent; undischarged, unpaid, unperformed, unrendered.

**unsavoury** adj flat, insipid, mawkish, savourless, tasteless, unflavoured, unpalatable, vapid; disagreeable, disgusting, distasteful, nasty, nauseating, nauseous, offensive, rank, revolting, sickening, uninviting, unpleasing.

**unsay** vb recall, recant, retract, take back.

**unscathed** adj unharmed, uninjured.

**unschooled** adj ignorant, uneducated, uninstructed, undisciplined, untrained.

**unscrupulous** adj dishonest, reckless, ruthless, unconscientious, unprincipled, unrestrained.

**unsealed** adj open, unclosed.

**unsearchable** adj hidden, incomprehensible, inscrutable, mysterious.

**unseasonable** adj ill-timed, inappropriate, infelicitous, inopportune, untimely; late, too late; inexpedient, undesireable, unfit, ungrateful, unsuitable, unwelcome; premature, too early.

**unseasonably** adv malapropos, unsuitably, untimely.

**unseasoned** adj inexperienced, unaccustomed, unqualified, untrained; immoderate, inordinate, irregular; green; fresh, unsalted.

**unseeing** *adj* blind, sightless.

**unseemly** *adj* improper, indecent, inappropriate, indecorous, unbecoming, uncomely, unfit, unmeet, unsuitable.

**unseen** *adj* undiscerned, undiscovered, unobserved, unperceived; imperceptible, indiscoverable, invisible, latent.

**unselfish** *adj* altruistic, devoted, disinterested, generous, high-minded, impersonal, liberal, magnanimous, self-denying, self-forgetful, selfless, self-sacrificing.

**unserviceable** *adj* ill-conditioned, unsound, useless; profitless, unprofitable.

**unsettle** *vb* confuse, derange, disarrange, disconcert, disorder, disturb, trouble, unbalance, unfix, unhinge, upset.

**unsettled** *adj* changeable, fickle, inconstant, restless, transient, unstable, unsteady, vacillating, wavering; inequable, unequal; feculent, muddy, roiled, roily, turbid; adrift, afloat, homeless, unestablished, uninhabited; open, tentative, unadjusted, undecided, undetermined; due, outstanding, owing, unpaid; perturbed, troubled, unnerved.

**unshackle** *vb* emancipate, liberate, loose, release, set free, unbind, unchain, unfetter.

**unshaken** *adj* constant, firm, resolute, steadfast, steady, unmoved.

**unshapen** *adj* deformed, grotesque, ill-formed, ill-made, ill-shaped, misshapen, shapeless, ugly, uncouth.

**unsheltered** *adj* exposed, unprotected.

**unshrinking** *adj* firm, determined, persisting, resolute, unblenching, unflinching.

**unshroud** *vb* discover, expose, reveal, uncover.

**unsightly** *adj* deformed, disagreeable, hideous, repellent, repulsive, ugly.

**unskilful, unskillful** *adj* awkward, bungling, clumsy, inapt, inexpert, maladroit, rough, rude, unhandy, unskilled, unversed.

**unskilled** *adj* inexperienced, raw, undisciplined, undrilled, uneducated, unexercised, unpractised, unprepared, unschooled; unskilful.

**unslaked** *adj* unquenched, unslacked.

**unsleeping** *adj* unslumbering, vigilant, wakeful, watchful.

**unsmirched** *adj* undefiled, unpolluted, unspotted.

**unsociable** *adj* distant, reserved, retiring, segregative, shy, solitary, standoffish, taciturn, uncommunicative, uncompanionable, ungenial, unsocial; inhospitable, misanthropic, morose.

**unsoiled** *adj* clean, spotless, unspotted, unstained, unsullied, untarnished.

**unsophisticated** *adj* genuine, pure, unadulterated; good, guileless, innocent, undepraved, unpolluted, invitiated; artless, honest, ingenuous, naive, natural, simple, sincere, straightforward, unaffected, undesigning, unstudied.

**unsound** *adj* decayed, defective, impaired, imperfect, rotten, thin, wasted, weak; broken, disturbed, light, restless; diseased, feeble, infirm, morbid, poorly, sickly, unhealthy, weak; deceitful, erroneous, fallacious, false, faulty, hollow, illogical, incorrect, invalid, ill-advised, irrational, questionable, sophistical, unreasonable, unsubstantial, untenable, wrong; dishonest, false, insincere, unfaithful, untrustworthy, untrue; insubstantial, unreal; heretical, heterodox, unorthodox.

**unsparing** *adj* bountiful, generous, lavish, liberal, profuse, ungrudging; harsh, inexorable, relentless, rigorous, ruthless, severe, uncompromising, unforgiving.

**unspeakable** *adj* indescribable, ineffable, inexpressible, unutterable.

**unspiritual** *adj* bodily, carnal, fleshly, sensual.

**unspotted** *adj* clean, spotless, unsoiled, unstained, unsullied, untarnished; faultless, immaculate, innocent, pure, stainless, unblemished, uncorrupted, undefiled, untainted.

**unstable** *adj* infirm, insecure, precarious, top-heavy, tottering, unbalanced, unballasted, unreliable, unsafe, unsettled, unsteady; changeable, erratic, fickle, inconstant, irresolute, mercurial, mutable, vacillating, variable, wavering, weak, volatile.—*also* **instable**.

**unstained** *adj* colourless, uncoloured, undyed, untinged; clean, spotless, unspotted.

**unsteady** *adj* fluctuating, oscillating, unsettled; insecure, precarious, unstable; changeable, desultory, ever-changing, fickle, inconstant, irresolute, mutable, unreliable, variable, wavering; drunken, jumpy, tottering, vacillating, wobbly, tipsy.

**unstinted** *adj* abundant, ample, bountiful, full, large, lavish, plentiful, prodigal, profuse.

**unstrung** *adj* overcome, shaken, unnerved, weak.

**unstudied** adj extempore, extemporaneous, impromptu, offhand, spontaneous, unpremeditated; inexpert, unskilled, unversed.

**unsubdued** adj unbowed, unbroken, unconquered, untamed.

**unsubmissive** adj disobedient, contumacious, indocile, insubordinate, obstinate, perverse, refractory, uncomplying, ungovernable, unmanageable, unruly, unyielding.

**unsubstantial** adj airy, flimsy, gaseous, gossamery, light, slight, tenuous, thin, vaporous; apparitional, bodiless, chimerical, cloudbuilt, dreamlike, empty, fantastical, ideal, illusory, imaginary, imponderable, moonshiny, spectral, unreal, vague, visionary; erroneous, fallacious, flimsy, groundless, illogical, unfounded, ungrounded, unsolid, unsound, untenable, weak.

**unsuccessful** adj abortive, bootless, fruitless, futile, ineffectual, profitless, unavailing, vain; ill-fated, ill-starred, luckless, unfortunate, unhappy, unlucky, unprosperous.

**unsuitable** adj ill-adapted, inappropriate, malapropos, unfit, unsatisfactory, unsuited; improper, inapplicable, inapt, incongruous, inexpedient, infelicitous, unbecoming, unbeseeming, unfitting.

**unsuited** adj unadapted, unfitted, unqualified.

**unsullied** adj chaste, clean, spotless, unsoiled, unspotted, unstained, untarnished; immaculate, pure, stainless, unblemished, uncorrupted, undefiled, untainted, untouched, virginal.

**unsupplied** adj destitute, unfurnished, unprovided.

**unsupported** adj unaided, unassisted; unbacked, unseconded, unsustained, unupheld.

**unsurpassed** adj matchless, peerless, unequalled, unexampled, unexcelled, unmatched, unparagoned, unparalleled, unrivalled.

**unsusceptible** adj apathetic, cold, impassive, insusceptible, phlegmatic, stoical, unimpressible, unimpressionable.

**unsuspecting** adj confiding, credulous, trusting, unsuspicious.

**unsuspicious** adj confiding, credulous, gullible, simple, trustful, unsuspecting.

**unsustainable** adj insupportable, intolerable; controvertible, erroneous, unmaintainable, untenable.

**unswerving** adj direct, straight, undeviating; constant, determined, firm, resolute, staunch, steadfast, steady, stable, unwavering.

**unsymmetrical** adj amorphous, asymmetric, disproportionate, formless, irregular, unbalanced.

**unsystematic, unsystematical** adj casual, disorderly, haphazard, irregular, planless, unmethodical.

**untainted** adj chaste, clean, faultless, fresh, healthy, pure, sweet, wholesome; spotless, unsoiled, unstained, unsullied, untarnished; immaculate, stainless, unblemished, uncorrupted, undefiled, unspotted.

**untamable** adj unconquerable.

**untamed** adj fierce, unbroken, wild.

**untangle** vb disentangle, explain, explicate.

**untarnished** adj chaste, clean, spotless, unsoiled, unspotted, unstained, unsullied; immaculate, pure, spotless, stainless, unblemished, uncorrupted, undefiled, unspotted, unsullied, untainted, virginal, virtuous.

**untaught** adj illiterate, unenlightened, uninformed, unlettered; ignorant, inexperienced, undisciplined, undrilled, uneducated, uninitiated, uninstructed, untutored.

**untenable** adj indefensible, unmaintainable, unsound; fallacious, hollow, illogical, indefensible, insupportable, unjustifiable, weak.

**untenanted** adj deserted, empty, tenantless, uninhabited, unoccupied.

**unterrified** adj fearless, unappalled, unawed, undismayed, undaunted, unscared.

**unthankful** adj thankless, ungrateful.

**unthinking** adj careless, heedless, inconsiderate, thoughtless, unreasoning, unreflecting; automatic, mechanical.

**unthoughtful** adj careless, heedless, inconsiderable, thoughtless.

**unthrifty** adj extravagant, improvident, lavish, prodigal, profuse, thriftless, wasteful.

**untidy** adj careless, disorderly, dowdy, frumpy, mussy, slatternly, slovenly, unkempt, unneat.

**untie** vb free, loose, loosen, unbind, unfasten, unknot, unloose; clear, resolve, solve, unfold.

**until** adv, conj till, to the time when; to the place, point, state or degree that; * prep till, to.

**untimely** adj ill-timed, immature, inconvenient, inopportune, mistimed, premature, unseasonable, unsuitable; ill-considered, inauspicious, uncalled for, unfortunate. * adv unseasonably, unsuitably.

**untinged** adj achromatic, colourless, hueless, uncoloured, undyed, unstained.

**untiring** adj persevering, incessant, indefatigable, patient, tireless, unceasing, unfatiguable, unflagging, unremitting, unwearied, unwearying.

**untold** adj countless, incalculable, innumerable, uncounted, unnumbered; unrelated, unrevealed.

**untouched** adj intact, scatheless, unharmed, unhurt, uninjured, unscathed; insensible, unaffected, unmoved, unstirred.

**untoward** adj adverse, froward, intractable, perverse, refractory, stubborn, unfortunate; annoying, ill-timed, inconvenient, unmanageable, vexatious; awkward, uncouth, ungainly, ungraceful.

**untrained** adj green, ignorant, inexperienced, raw, unbroken, undisciplined, undrilled, uneducated, uninstructed, unpractised, unskilled, untaught, untutored.

**untrammelled** adj free, unhampered.

**untried** adj fresh, inexperienced, maiden, new, unassayed, unattempted, unattested, virgin; undecided.

**untrodden** adj pathless, trackless, unbeaten.

**untroubled** adj calm, careless, composed, peaceful, serene, smooth, tranquil, undisturbed, unvexed.

**untrue** adj contrary, false, inaccurate, wrong; disloyal, faithless, perfidious, recreant, treacherous, unfaithful.

**untrustworthy** adj deceitful, dishonest, inaccurate, rotten, slippery, treacherous, undependable, unreliable; disloyal, false; deceptive, fallible, illusive, questionable.

**untruth** n error, faithlessness, falsehood, falsity, incorrectness, inveracity, treachery; deceit, deception, fabrication, fib, fiction, forgery, imposture, invention, lie, misrepresentation, misstatement, story.

**untutored** adj ignorant, inexperienced, undisciplined, undrilled, uneducated, uninitiated, uninstructed, untaught; artless, natural, simple, unsophisticated.

**untwist** vb disentangle, disentwine, ravel, unravel, unwreathe.

**unused** adj idle, unemployed, untried; new, unaccustomed, unfamiliar.

**unusual** adj abnormal, curious, exceptional, extraordinary, odd, peculiar, queer, rare, recherché, remarkable, singular, strange, unaccustomed, uncommon, unwonted.

**unutterable** adj incommunicable, indescribable, ineffable, inexpressible, unspeakable.

**unvarnished** adj unpolished; candid, plain, simple, true, unadorned, unembellished.

**unvarying** adj constant, invariable, unchanging.

**unveil** vb disclose, expose, reveal, show, uncover, unmask.

**unveracious** adj false, lying, mendacious, untruthful.

**unversed** adj inexperienced, raw, undisciplined, undrilled, uneducated, unexercised, unpractised, unprepared, unschooled; unskilful.

**unviolated** adj inviolate, unbetrayed, unbroken.

**unwarlike** adj pacific, peaceful.

**unwarped** adj impartial, unbiased, undistorted, unprejudiced.

**unwarrantable** adj improper, indefensible, unjustifiable.

**unwary** adj careless, hasty, heedless, imprudent, incautious, indiscreet, precipitate, rash, reckless, remiss, uncircumspect, unguarded.

**unwavering** adj constant, determined, firm, fixed, resolute, settled, staunch, steadfast, steady, unhesitating.

**unwearied** adj unfatigued; constant, continual, incessant, indefatigable, persevering, persistent, unceasing, unremitting, untiring.

**unwelcome** adj disagreeable, unacceptable, ungrateful, unpleasant, unpleasing.

**unwell** adj ailing, delicate, diseased, ill, indisposed, sick.

**unwept** adj unlamented, unmourned, unregretted.

**unwholesome** adj baneful, deleterious, injurious, insalubrious, noisome, noxious, poisonous, unhealthful, unhealthy; injudicious, pernicious, unsound; corrupt, tainted.

**unwieldy** adj bulky, clumsy, cumbersome, cumbrous, elephantine, heavy, hulking, large, massy, ponderous, unmanageable, weighty.

**unwilling** adj averse, backward, disinclined, indisposed, laggard, loath, opposed, recalcitrant, reluctant; forced, grudging.

**unwind** vb unravel, unreel, untwine, wind off; disentangle.

**unwise** adj brainless, foolish, ill-advised, ill-judged, impolitic, imprudent, indiscreet, injudicious, inexpedient, senseless, silly, stupid, unwary, weak.

**unwitnessed** adj unknown, unseen, unspied.

**unwittingly** adv ignorantly, inadvertently, unconsciously, undesignedly, unintentionally, unknowingly.

**unwonted** adj infrequent, rare, uncommon, unusual; unaccustomed, unused.

**unworthy** adj undeserving; bad, base, blameworthy, worthless; shameful, unbecoming, vile; contemptible, derogatory, despicable, discreditable, mean, paltry, reprehensible, shabby.

**unwrap** vb open, unfold.

**unwrinkled** adj smooth, unforrowed.

**unwritten** adj oral, traditional, unrecorded; conventional, customary.

**unwrought** adj crude, rough, rude, unfashioned, unformed.

**unyielding** adj constant, determined, indomitable, inflexible, pertinacious, resolute, staunch, steadfast, steady, tenacious, uncompromising, unwavering; headstrong, intractable, obstinate, perverse, self-willed, stiff, stubborn, wayward, wilful; adamantine, firm, grim, hard, immovable, implastic, inexorable, relentless, rigid, unbending.

**unyoke** vb disconnect, disjoin, part, separate.

**unyoked** adj disconnected, separated; licentious, loose, unrestrained.

**upbraid** vb accuse, blame, chide, condemn, criticize, denounce, fault, reproach, reprove, revile, scold, taunt, twit.

**upheaval** n elevation, upthrow; cataclysm, convulsion, disorder, eruption, explosion, outburst, overthrow.

**uphill** adj ascending, upward; arduous, difficult, hard, laborious, strenuous, toilsome, wearisome.

**uphold** vb elevate, raise; bear up, hold up, support, sustain; advocate, aid, champion, countenance, defend, justify, maintain, vindicate.

**upland** n down, fell, ridge, plateau.

**uplift** vb raise, upraise; animate, elevate, inspire, lift, refine. * n ascent, climb, elevation, lift, rise, upthrust; exaltation, inspiration, uplifting; improvement, refinement.

**upon** prep on, on top of, over; about, concerning, on the subject of, relating to; immediately after, with.

**upper hand** n advantage, ascendancy, control, dominion, mastership, mastery, pre-eminence, rule, superiority, supremacy, whip hand.

**uppermost** adj foremost, highest, loftiest, supreme, topmost, upmost.

**uppish** adj arrogant, assuming, haughty, perky, proud, smart.

**upright** adj erect, perpendicular, vertical; conscientious, equitable, fair, faithful, good, honest, honourable, incorruptible, just, pure, righteous, straightforward, true, trustworthy, upstanding, virtuous.

**uprightness** n erectness, perpendicularity, verticality; equity, fairness, goodness, honesty, honour, incorruptibility, integrity, justice, probity, rectitude, righteousness, straightforwardness, trustiness, trustworthiness, virtue, worth.

**uproar** n clamour, commotion, confusion, din, disturbance, fracas, hubbub, hurly-burly, noise, pandemonium, racket, riot, tumult, turmoil, vociferation.

**uproarious** adj boisterous, clamorous, loud, noisy, obstreperous, riotous, tumultuous.

**uproot** vb eradicate, extirpate, root out.

**upset** vb capsize, invert, overthrow, overtumble, overturn, spill, tip over, topple, turn turtle; agitate, confound, confuse, discompose, disconcert, distress, disturb, embarrass, excite, fluster, muddle, overwhelm, perturb, shock, startle, trouble, unnerve, unsettle; checkmate, defeat, overthrow, revolutionize, subvert; foil, frustrate, nonplus, thwart. * adj disproved, exposed, overthrown; bothered, confused, disconcerted, flustered, mixed-up, perturbed; shocked, startled, unsettled; beaten, defeated, overcome, overpowered, overthrown; discomfited, distressed, discomposed, overexcited, overwrought, shaken, troubled, unnerved. * n confutation, refutation; foiling, frustration, overthrow, revolution, revulsion, ruin, subversdion, thwarting.

**upshot** n conclusion, consummation, effect, end, event, issue, outcome, result, termination.

**upside down** adj bottom side up, bottom up, confused, head over heels, inverted, topsy-turvy.

**upstart** n adventurer, arriviste, parvenu, snob, social cimber, yuppie.

**upturned** adj raised, uplifted; retroussé.

**upward** adj ascending, climbing, mounting, rising, uphill. * adv above, aloft, overhead, up; heavenwards, skywards.

**urbane** adj civil, complaisant, courteous, courtly, elegant, mannerly, polished, polite, refined, smooth, suave, well-mannered.

**urbanity** n amenity, civility, complaisance, courtesy, politeness, smoothness, suavity.

**urchin** n brat, child, kid, ragamuffin, rascal, scrap, squirt, tad.

**urge** vb crowd, drive, force on, impel, press, press on, push, push on; beg, beseech, conjure, entreat, exhort, implore, importune, ply, solicit, tease; animate, egg on, encourage, goad, hurry, incite, instigate, quicken, spur, stimulate. * n compulsion, desire, drive, impulse, longing, pressure, wish, yearning.

**urgency** n drive, emergency, exigency, haste, necessity, press, pressure, push, stress; clamorousness, entreaty, insistence, importunity, instance, solicitation; goad, incitement, spur, stimulus.

**urgent** adj cogent, critical, crucial, crying, exigent, immediate, imperative, important, importunate, insistent, instant, pertinacious, pressing, serious.

**urinal** n chamber, chamber pot, lavatory, pot, potty, jordan, toilet.

**urinate** vb make water, pee, pee-pee, piddle, piss, stale, wee.

**usage** n treatment; consuetude, custom, fashion, habit, method, mode, practice, prescription, tradition, use.

**use** vb administer, apply, avail oneself of, drive, employ, handle, improve, make use of, manipulate, occupy, operate, ply, put into action, take advantage of, turn to account, wield, work; exercise, exert, exploit, practice, profit by, utilize; absorb, consume, exhaust, expend, swallow up, waste, wear out; accustom, familiarize, habituate, harden, inure, train; act toward, behave toward, deal with, manage, treat; be accustomed, be wont. * n appliance, application, consumption, conversion, disposal, exercise, employ, employment, practice, utilization; adaptability, advantage, avail, benefit, convenience, profit, service, usefulness, utility, wear; exigency, necessity, indispensability, need, occasion, requisiteness; custom, habit, handling, method, treatment, usage, way.

**useful** adj active, advantageous, available, availing, beneficial, commodious, conducive, contributory, convenient, effective, good, helpful, instrumental, operative, practical, profitable, remunerative, salutary, suitable, serviceable, utilitarian; available, helpful, serviceable, valuable.

**usefulness** n advantage, profit, serviceableness, utility, value.

**useless** adj abortive, bootless, fruitless, futile, help-less, idle, incapable, incompetent, ineffective, ineffectual, inutile, nugatory, null, profitless, unavailing, unprofitable, unproductive, unserviceable, valueless, worthless; good for nothing, waste.

**usher** vb announce, forerun, herald, induct, introduce, precede; conduct, direct, escort, shepherd, show. * n attendant, conductor, escort, shepherd, squire.

**usual** adj accustomed, common, customary, everyday, familiar, frequent, general, habitual, normal, ordinary, prevailing, prevalent, regular, wonted.

**usurp** vb appropriate, arrogate, assume, seize.

**usurpation** n assumption, dispossession, infringement, seizure.

**usury** n interest; exploitation, extortion, profiteering.

**utensil** n device, implement, instrument, tool.

**utility** n advantageousness, avail, benefit, profit, service, use, usefulness; happiness, welfare.

**utilize** vb employ, exploit, make use of, put to use, turn to account, use.

**utmost** adj extreme, farthest, highest, last, main, most distant, remotest; greatest, uttermost. * n best, extreme, maximum, most.

**Utopian** adj air-built, air-drawn, chimerical, fanciful, ideal, imaginary, visionary, unreal.

**utricle** n bladder, cyst, sac, vesicle.

**utter**[1] adj complete, entire, perfect, total; absolute, blank, diametric, downright, final, peremptory, sheer, stark, thorough, thoroughgoing, unconditional, unqualified, total.

**utter**[2] vb articulate, breathe, deliver, disclose, divulge, emit, enunciate, express, give forth, pronounce, reveal, speak, talk, tell, voice; announce, circulate, declare, issue, publish.

**utterance** n articulation, delivery, disclosure, emission, expression, pronouncement, pronunciation, publication, speech.

**utterly** adv absolutely, altogether, completely, downright, entirely, quite, totally, unconditionally, wholly.

**uttermost** adj extreme, farthest; greatest, utmost.

# V

**vacant** adj blank, empty, unfilled, void; disengaged, free, unemployed, unoccupied, unencumbered; thoughtless, unmeaning, unthinking, unreflective; uninhabited, untenanted.

**vacate** vb abandon, evacuate, relinquish, surrender; abolish, abrogate, annul, cancel, disannul, invalidate, nullify, overrule, quash, rescind.

**vacillate** vb dither, fluctuate, hesitate, oscillate, rock, sway, waver.

**vacillation** n faltering, fluctuation, hesitation, inconstancy, indecision, irresolution, reeling, rocking, staggering, swaying, unsteadiness, wavering.

**vacuity** n emptiness, inanition, vacancy; emptiness, vacancy, vacuum, void; expressionlessness, inanity, nihility.

**vacuous** adj empty, empty-headed, unfilled, vacant, void; inane, unintelligent.

**vacuum** n emptiness, vacuity, void.

**vagabond** adj footloose, idle, meandering, rambling, roving, roaming, strolling, vagrant, wandering. * n beggar, castaway, landloper, loafer, lounger, nomad, outcast, tramp, vagrant, wanderer.

**vagary** n caprice, crotchet, fancy, freak, humour, whim.

**vagrant** adj erratic, itinerant, roaming, roving, nomadic, strolling, unsettled, wandering. * n beggar, castaway, landloper, loafer, lounger, nomad, outcast, tramp, vagabond, wanderer.

**vague** adj ambiguous, confused, dim, doubtful, indefinite, ill-defined, indistinct, lax, loose, obscure, uncertain, undetermined, unfixed, unsettled.

**vain** adj baseless, delusive, dreamy, empty, false, imaginary, shadowy, suppositional, unsubstantial, unreal, void; abortive, bootless, fruitless, futile, ineffectual, nugatory, profitless, unavailing, unprofitable; trivial, unessential, unimportant, unsatisfactory, unsatisfying, useless, vapid, worthless; arrogant, conceited, egotistical, flushed, high, inflated, opinionated, ostentatious, overweening, proud, self-confident, self-opinionated, vainglorious; gaudy, glittering, gorgeous, showy.

**valediction** n adieu, farewell, goodbye, leave-taking.

**valet** n attendant, flunky, groom, lackey, servant.

**valetudinarian** adj delicate, feeble, frail, infirm, sickly.

**valiant** adj bold, brave, chivalrous, courageous, daring, dauntless, doughty, fearless, gallant, heroic, intrepid, lion-hearted, redoubtable, Spartan, valorous, undaunted.

**valid** adj binding, cogent, conclusive, efficacious, efficient, good, grave, important, just, logical, powerful, solid, sound, strong, substantial, sufficient, weighty.

**valley** n basin, bottom, canyon, dale, dell, dingle, glen, hollow, ravine, strath, vale.

**valorous** adj bold, brave, courageous, dauntless, doughty, intrepid, stout.

**valour** n boldness, bravery, courage, daring, gallantry, heroism, prowess, spirit.

**valuable** adj advantageous, precious, profitable, useful; costly, expensive, rich; admirable, estimable, worthy. * n heirloom, treasure.

**value** vb account, appraise, assess, estimate, price, rate, reckon; appreciate, esteem, prize, regard, treasure. * n avail, importance, usefulness, utility, worth; cost, equivalent, price, rate; estimation, excellence, importance, merit, valuation.

**valueless** adj miserable, useless, worthless.

**vandal** n barbarian, destroyer, savage.

**vandalism** n barbarism, barbarity, savagery.

**vanish** vb disappear, dissolve, fade, melt.

**vanity** n emptiness, falsity, foolishness, futility, hollowness, insanity, triviality, unreality, worthlessness; arrogance, conceit, egotism, ostentation, self-conceit.

**vanquish** vb conquer, defeat, outwit, overcome, overpower, overthrow, subdue, subjugate; crush, discomfit, foil, master, quell, rout, worst.

**vapid** adj dead, flat, insipid, lifeless, savourless, spiritless, stale, tasteless; dull, feeble, jejune, languid, meagre, prosaic, prosy, tame.

**vapour** n cloud, exhalation, fog, fume, mist, rack, reek, smoke, steam; daydream, dream, fantasy, phantom, vagary, vision, whim, whimsy.

**variable** adj changeable, mutable, shifting; aberrant,

alterable, capricious, fickle, fitful, floating, fluctuating, inconstant, mobile, mutable, protean, restless, shifting, unsteady, vacillating, wavering.

**variance** n disagreement, difference, discord, dissension, incompatibility, jarring, strife.

**variation** n alteration, change, modification; departure, deviation, difference, discrepancy, innovation; contrariety, discordance.

**variegated** adj chequered, dappled, diversified, flecked, kaleidoscopic, mottled, multicoloured, pied, spotted, striped.

**variety** n difference, dissimilarity, diversity, diversification, medley, miscellany, mixture, multiplicity, variation; kind, sort.

**various** adj different, diverse, manifold, many, numerous, several, sundry.

**varnish** vb enamel, glaze, japan, lacquer; adorn, decorate, embellish, garnish, gild, polish; disguise, excuse, extenuate, gloss over, palliate. * n enamel, lacquer, stain; cover, extenuation, gloss.

**vary** vb alter, metamorphose, transform; alternate, exchange, rotate; diversify, modify, variegate; depart, deviate, swerve.

**vassal** n bondman, liegeman, retainer, serf, slave, subject, thrall.

**vassalage** n bondage, dependence, serfdom, servitude, slavery, subjection.

**vast** adj boundless, infinite, measureless, spacious, wide; colossal, enormous, gigantic, huge, immense, mighty, monstrous, prodigious, tremendous; extraordinary, remarkable.

**vaticination** n augury, divination, prediction, prognostication, prophecy.

**vault**[1] vb arch, bend, curve, span. * n cupola, curve, dome; catacomb, cell, cellar, crypt, dungeon, tomb; depository, strongroom.

**vault**[2] vb bound, jump, leap, spring; tumble, turn. * n bound, leap, jump, spring.

**vaunt** vb advertise, boast, brag, display, exult, flaunt, flourish, parade.

**veer** vb change, shift, turn.

**vegetate** vb blossom, develop, flourish, flower, germinate, grow, shoot, sprout, swell; bask, hibernate, idle, stagnate.

**vehemence** n impetuosity, violence; ardour, eagerness, earnestness, enthusiasm, fervency, fervour, heat, keenness, passion, warmth, zeal; force, intensity.

**vehement** adj furious, high, hot, impetuous, passionate, rampant, violent; ardent, burning, eager, earnest, enthusiastic, fervid, fiery, keen, passionate, sanguine, zealous; forcible, mighty, powerful, strong.

**veil** vb cloak, conceal, cover, curtain, envelop, hide, invest, mask, screen, shroud. * n cover, curtain, film, shade, screen; blind, cloak, disguise, mask, muffler, visor.

**vein** n course, current, lode, seam, streak, stripe, thread, wave; bent, character, faculty, humour, mood, talent, turn.

**velocity** n acceleration, celerity, expedition, fleetness, haste, quickness, rapidity, speed, swiftness.

**velvety** adj delicate, downy, smooth, soft.

**venal** adj corrupt, mean, purchasable, sordid.

**vend** vb dispose, flog, hawk, retail, sell.

**venerable** adj grave, respected, revered, sage, wise; awful, dread, dreadful; aged, old, patriarchal.

**venerate** vb adore, esteem, honour, respect, revere.

**veneration** n adoration, devotion, esteem, respect, reverence, worship.

**vengeance** n retaliation, retribution, revenge.

**venial** adj allowed, excusable, pardonable, permitted, trivial.

**venom** n poison, virus; acerbity, acrimony, bitterness, gall, hate, ill-will, malevolence, malice, maliciousness, malignity, rancour, spite, virulence.

**venomous** adj deadly, poisonous, septic, toxic, virulent; caustic, malicious, malignant, mischievous, noxious, spiteful.

**vent** vb emit, express, release, utter. * n air hole, hole, mouth, opening, orifice; air pipe, air tube, aperture, blowhole, bunghole, hydrant, plug, spiracle, spout, tap, orifice; effusion, emission, escape, outlet, passage; discharge, expression, utterance.

**ventilate** vb aerate, air, freshen, oxygenate, purify; fan, winnow; canvass, comment, discuss, examine, publish, review, scrutinize.

**venture** vb adventure, dare, hazard, imperil, jeopardize, presume, risk, speculate, test, try, undertake. * n adventure, chance, hazard, jeopardy, peril, risk, speculation, stake.

**venturesome** adj adventurous, bold, courageous, daring, doughty, enterprising, fearless, foolhardy, intrepid, presumptuous, rash, venturous.

**veracious** adj reliable, straightforward, true, trustworthy, truthful; credible, genuine, honest, unfeigned.

**veracity** n accuracy, candour, correctness, credibility, exactness, fidelity, frankness, honesty, ingenuousness, probity, sincerity, trueness, truth, truthfulness.

**verbal** adj nuncupative, oral, spoken, unwritten.

**verbose** adj diffusive, long-winded, loquacious, talkative, wordy.

**verdant** adj fresh, green, verdure, verdurous; green, inexperienced, raw, unsophisticated.

**verdict** n answer, decision, finding, judgement, opinion, sentence.

**verge** vb bear, incline, lean, slope, tend; approach, border, skirt. * n mace, rod, staff; border, boundary, brink, confine, edge, extreme, limit, margin; edge, eve, point.

**verification** n authentication, attestation, confirmation, corroboration.

**verify** vb attest, authenticate, confirm, corroborate, prove, substantiate.

**verily** adv absolutely, actually, confidently, indeed, positively, really, truly.

**verity** n certainty, reality, truth, truthfulness.

**vermicular** adj convoluted, flexuose, flexuous, meandering, serpentine, sinuous, tortuous, twisting, undulating, waving, winding, wormish, wormlike.

**vernacular** adj common, indigenous, local, mother, native, vulgar. * n cant, dialect, jargon, patois, speech.

**versatile** adj capricious, changeable, erratic, mobile, variable; fickle, inconstant, mercurial, unsteady; adaptable, protean, plastic, varied.

**versed** adj able, accomplished, acquainted, clever, conversant, practised, proficient, qualified, skilful, skilled, trained.

**version** n interpretation, reading, rendering, translation.

**vertex** n apex, crown, height, summit, top, zenith.

**vertical** adj erect, perpendicular, plumb, steep, upright.

**vertiginous** adj rotatory, rotary, whirling; dizzy, giddy.

**vertigo** n dizziness, giddiness.

**verve** n animation, ardour, energy, enthusiasm, force, rapture, spirit.

**very** adv absolutely, enormously, excessively, hugely, remarkably, surpassingly. * adj actual, exact, identical, precise, same; bare, mere, plain, pure, simple.

**vesicle** n bladder, blister, cell, cyst, follicle.

**vest** vb clothe, cover, dress, envelop; endow, furnish, invest. * n dress, garment, robe, vestment, vesture, waistcoat.

**vestibule** n anteroom, entrance hall, lobby, porch.

**vestige** n evidence, footprint, footstep, mark, record, relic, sign, token.

**veteran** adj adept, aged, experienced, disciplined, seasoned, old. * n campaigner, old soldier; master, past master, old-timer, old-stager.

**veto** vb ban, embargo, forbid, interdict, negate, prohibit. * n ban, embargo, interdict, prohibition, refusal.

**vex** vb annoy, badger, bother, chafe, cross, distress, gall, harass, harry, hector, molest, perplex, pester, plague, tease, torment, trouble, roil, spite, worry; affront, displease, fret, irk, irritate, nettle, offend, provoke; agitate, disquiet, disturb.

**vexation** n affliction, agitation, chagrin, discomfort, displeasure, disquiet, distress, grief, irritation, pique, sorrow, trouble; annoyance, curse, nuisance, plague, torment; damage, troubling, vexing.

**vexed** adj afflicted, agitated, annoyed, bothered, disquieted, harassed, irritated, perplexed, plagued, provoked, troubled, worried.

**vibrate** vb oscillate, sway, swing, undulate, wave; impinge, quiver, sound, thrill; fluctuate, hesitate, vacillate, waver.

**vibration** n nutation, oscillation, vibration.

**vicarious** adj commissioned, delegated, indirect, second-hand, substituted.

**vice** n blemish, defect, failing, fault, imperfection, infirmity; badness, corruption, depravation, depravity, error, evil, immorality, iniquity, laxity, obliquity, sin, viciousness, vileness, wickedness.

**vicinity** n nearness, proximity; locality, neighbourhood, vicinage.

**vicious** adj abandoned, atrocious, bad, corrupt, degenerate, demoralized, depraved, devilish, diabolical, evil, flagrant, hellish, immoral, iniquitous, mischievous, profligate, shameless, sinful, unprincipled, wicked; malicious, spiteful, venomous; foul, impure; debased, faulty; contrary, refractory.

**viciousness** n badness, corruption, depravity, immorality, profligacy.

**vicissitude** n alteration, interchange; change, fluctuation, mutation, revolution, variation.

**victim** n martyr, sacrifice, sufferer; prey; cat's-paw, cull, cully, dupe, gull, gudgeon, puppet.

**victimize** vb bamboozle, befool, beguile, cheat, circumvent, cozen, deceive, defraud, diddle, dupe, fool, gull, hoax, hoodwink, overreach, swindle, trick.

**victor** n champion, conqueror, vanquisher, winner.

**victorious** adj conquering, successful, triumphant, winning.

**victory** n achievement, conquest, mastery, triumph.

**victuals** npl comestibles, eatables, fare, food, meat, provisions, repast, sustenance, viands.

**vie** vb compete, contend, emulate, rival, strive.

**view** vb behold, contemplate, eye, inspect, scan, survey; consider, inspect, regard, study. * n inspection, observation, regard, sight; outlook, panorama, perspective, prospect, range, scene, survey, vista; aim, intent, intention, design, drift, object, purpose, scope; belief, conception, impression, idea, judgement, notion, opinion, sentiment, theory; appearance, aspect, show.

**vigilance** n alertness, attentiveness, carefulness, caution, circumspection, observance, watchfulness.

**vigilant** adj alert, attentive, careless, cautious, circumspect, unsleeping, wakeful, watchful.

**vigorous** adj lusty, powerful, strong; active, alert, cordial, energetic, forcible, strenuous, vehement, vivid, virile; brisk, hale, hardy, robust, sound, sturdy, healthy; fresh, flourishing; bold, emphatic, impassioned, lively, nervous, piquant, pointed, severe, sparkling, spirited, trenchant.

**vigour** n activity, efficacy, energy, force, might, potency, power, spirit, strength; bloom, elasticity, haleness, health, heartiness, pep, punch, robustness, soundness, thriftiness, tone, vim, vitality; enthusiasm, freshness, fire, intensity, liveliness, piquancy, strenuousness, vehemence, verve, raciness.

**vile** adj abject, base, beastly, beggarly, brutish, contemptible, despicable, disgusting, grovelling, ignoble, low, odious, paltry, pitiful, repulsive, scurvy, shabby, slavish, sorry, ugly; bad, evil, foul, gross, impure, iniquitous, lewd, obscene, sinful, vicious, wicked; cheap, mean, miserable, valueless, worthless.

**vilify** vb abuse, asperse, backbite, berate, blacken, blemish, brand, calumniate, decry, defame, disparage, lampoon, libel, malign, revile, scandalize, slander, slur, traduce, vituperate.

**villain** n blackguard, knave, miscreant, rascal, reprobate, rogue, ruffian, scamp, scapegrace, scoundrel.

**villainous** adj base, mean, vile; corrupt, depraved, knavish, unprincipled, wicked; atrocious, heinous, outrageous, sinful; mischievous, sorry.

**vindicate** vb defend, justify, uphold; advocate, avenge, assert, maintain, right, support.

**vindication** n apology, excuse, defence, justification.

**vindictive** adj avenging, grudgeful, implacable, malevolent, malicious, malignant, retaliative, revengeful, spiteful, unforgiving, unrelenting, vengeful.

**violate** vb hurt, injure; break, disobey, infringe, invade; desecrate, pollute, profane; abuse, debauch, defile, deflower, outrage, ravish, transgress.

**violent** adj boisterous, demented, forceful, forcible, frenzied, furious, high, hot, impetuous, insane, intense, stormy, tumultuous, turbulent, vehement, wild; fierce, fiery, fuming, heady, heavy, infuriate, passionate, obstreperous, strong, raging, rampant, rank, rapid, raving, refractory, roaring, rough, tearing, towering, ungovernable; accidental, unnatural; desperate, extreme, outrageous, unjust; acute, exquisite, poignant, sharp.

**virago** n amazon, brawler, fury, shrew, tartar, vixen.

**virgin** adj chaste, maidenly, modest, pure, undefiled, stainless, unpolluted, vestal, virginal; fresh, maiden, untouched, unused. * n celibate, damsel, girl, lass, maid, maiden.

**virile** adj forceful, manly, masculine, robust, vigorous.

**virtual** adj constructive, equivalent, essential, implicit, implied, indirect, practical, substantial.

**virtue** n chastity, goodness, grace, morality, purity; efficacy, excellence, honesty, integrity, justice, probity, quality, rectitude, worth.

**virtuous** adj blameless, equitable, exemplary, excellent, good, honest, moral, noble, righteous, upright, worthy; chaste, continent, immaculate, innocent, modest, pure, undefiled; efficacious, powerful.

**virulent** adj deadly, malignant, poisonous, toxic, venomous; acrid, acrimonious, bitter, caustic.

**visage** n aspect, countenance, face, guise, physiognomy, semblance.

**viscera** n bowels, entrails, guts, intestines.

**viscous** adj adhesive, clammy, glutinous, ropy, slimy, sticky, tenacious.

**visible** adj observable, perceivable, perceptible, seeable, visual; apparent, clear, conspicuous, discoverable, distinct, evident, manifest, noticeable, obvious, open, palpable, patent, plain, revealed, unhidden, unmistakable.

**vision** n eyesight, seeing, sight; eyeshot, ken; apparition, chimera, dream, ghost, hallucination, illusion, phantom, spectre.

**visionary** adj imaginative, impractical, quixotic, romantic; chimerical, dreamy, fancied, fanciful, fantastic, ideal, illusory, imaginary, romantic, shadowy, unsubstantial, utopian, wild. * n dreamer, enthusiast, fanatic, idealist, optimist, theorist, zealot.

**vital** adj basic, cardinal, essential, indispensable, necessary, needful; animate, alive, existing, life-giving, living; paramount.

**vitality** n animation, life, strength, vigour, virility.

**vitiate** vb adulterate, contaminate, corrupt, debase, defile, degrade, deprave, deteriorate, impair, infect, injure, invalidate, poison, pollute, spoil.

**vitiation** n adulteration, corruption, degeneracy, degeneration, degradation, depravation, deterioration, impairment, injury, invalidation, perversion, pollution, prostitution.

**vituperate** vb abuse, berate, blame, censure, denounce, overwhelm, rate, revile, scold, upbraid, vilify.

**vituperation** n abuse, blame, censure, invective, reproach, railing, reviling, scolding, upbraiding.

**vivacious** adj active, animated, breezy, brisk, buxom, cheerful, frolicsome, gay, jocund, light-hearted, lively, merry, mirthful, spirited, sportive, sprightly.

**vivacity** n animation, cheer, cheerfulness, gaiety, liveliness, sprightliness.

**vivid** adj active, animated, bright, brilliant, clear, intense, fresh, lively, living, lucid, quick, sprightly, strong; expressive, graphic, striking, telling.

**vivify** vb animate, arouse, awake, quicken, vitalize.

**vixen** n brawler, scold, shrew, spitfire, tartar, virago.

**vocabulary** n dictionary, glossary, lexicon, wordbook; language, terms, words.

**vocation** n call, citation, injunction, summons; business, calling, employment, occupation, profession, pursuit, trade.

**vociferate** vb bawl, bellow, clamour, cry, exclaim, rant, shout, yell.

**vociferous** adj blatant, clamorous, loud, noisy, obstreperous, ranting, stunning, uproarious.

**vogue** adj fashionable, modish, stylish, trendy. * n custom, fashion, favour, mode, practice, repute, style, usage, way.

**voice** vb declare, express, say, utter. * n speech, tongue, utterance; noise, notes, sound; opinion, option, preference, suffrage, vote; accent, articulation, enunciation, inflection, intonation, modulation, pronunciation, tone; expression, language, words.

**void** vb clear, eject, emit, empty, evacuate. * adj blank, empty, hollow, vacant; clear, destitute, devoid, free, lacking, wanting, without; inept, ineffectual, invalid, nugatory, null; imaginary, unreal, vain. * n abyss, blank, chasm, emptiness, hole, vacuum.

**volatile** adj gaseous, incoercible; airy, buoyant, frivolous, gay, jolly, lively, sprightly, vivacious; capricious, changeable, fickle, flighty, flyaway, giddy, harebrained, inconstant, light-headed, mercurial, reckless, unsteady, whimsical, wild.

**volition** n choice, determination, discretion, option, preference, will.

**volley** n fusillade, round, salvo; blast, burst, discharge, emission, explosion, outbreak, report, shower, storm.

**voluble** adj fluent, garrulous, glib, loquacious, talkative.

**volume** n book, tome; amplitude, body, bulk, compass, dimension, size, substance, vastness; fullness, power, quantity.

**voluminous** adj ample, big, bulky, full, great, large; copious, diffuse, discursive, flowing.

**voluntary** adj free, spontaneous, unasked, unbidden, unforced; deliberate, designed, intended, purposed; discretionary, optional, willing.

**volunteer** vb offer, present, proffer, propose, tender.

**voluptuary** n epicure, hedonist, sensualist.

**voluptuous** adj carnal, effeminate, epicurean, fleshy, licentious, luxurious, sensual, sybaritic.

**vomit** vb discharge, eject, emit, puke, regurgitate, spew, throw up.

**voracious** adj devouring, edacious, greedy, hungry, rapacious, ravenous.

**vortex** n eddy, maelstrom, whirl, whirlpool.

**votary** adj devoted, promised. * n adherent, devotee, enthusiast, follower, supporter, votarist, zealot.

**vote** vb ballot, elect, opt, return; judge, pronounce, propose, suggest. * n ballot, franchise, poll, referendum, suffrage, voice.

**vouch** vb affirm, asseverate, attest, aver, declare, guarantee, support, uphold, verify, warrant.

**vouchsafe** vb accord, cede, deign, grant, stoop, yield.

**vow** vb consecrate, dedicate, devote; asseverate. * n oath, pledge, promise.

**voyage** vb cruise, journey, navigate, ply, sail. * n crossing, cruise, excursion, journey, passage, sail, trip.

**vulgar** adj base-born, common, ignoble, lowly, plebeian; boorish, cheap, coarse, discourteous, flashy, homespun, garish, gaudy, ill-bred, inelegant, loud, rustic, showy, tawdry, uncultivated, unrefined; general, ordinary, popular, public; base, broad, loose, low, gross, mean, ribald, vile; inelegant, unauthorized.

**vulgarity** n baseness, coarseness, grossness, meanness, rudeness.

**vulnerable** adj accessible, assailable, defenceless, exposed, weak.

# W

**waddle** vb toddle, toggle, waggle, wiggle, wobble.

**waft** vb bear, carry, convey, float, transmit, transport.
* n breath, breeze, draught, puff.

**wag**[1] vb shake, sway, waggle; oscillate, vibrate, waver; advance, move, progress, stir. * n flutter, nod, oscillation, vibration.

**wag**[2] n humorist, jester, joker, wit.

**wage** vb bet, hazard, lay, stake, wager; conduct, undertake.

**wager** vb back, bet, gamble, lay, pledge, risk, stake.
* n bet, gamble, pledge, risk, stake.

**wages** npl allowance, compensation, earnings, emolument, hire, pay, payment, remuneration, salary, stipend.

**waggish** adj frolicsome, gamesome, mischievous, roguish, tricksy; comical, droll, facetious, funny, humorous, jocular, jocose, merry, sportive.

**wagon** n cart, lorry, truck, van, waggon, wain.

**wail** vb bemoan, deplore, lament, mourn; cry, howl, weep. * n complaint, cry, lamentation, moan, wailing.

**waist** n bodice, corsage, waistline.

**wait** vb delay, linger, pause, remain, rest, stay, tarry; attend, minister, serve; abide, await, expect, look for. * n delay, halt, holdup, pause, respite, rest, stay, stop.

**waiter, waitress** n attendant, lackey, servant, servitor, steward, valet.

**waive** vb defer, forgo, surrender, relinquish, remit, renounce; desert, reject.

**wake**[1] vb arise, awake, awaken; activate, animate, arouse, awaken, excite, kindle, provoke, stimulate.
* n vigil, watch, watching.

**wake**[2] n course, path, rear, track, trail, wash.

**wakeful** adj awake, sleepless, restless; alert, observant, vigilant, wary, watchful.

**wale** n ridge, streak, stripe, welt, whelk.

**walk** vb advance, depart, go, march, move, pace, saunter, step, stride, stroll, tramp. * n amble, carriage, gait, step; beat, career, course, department, field, province; conduct, procedure; alley, avenue, cloister, esplanade, footpath, path, pathway, pavement, promenade, range, sidewalk, way; constitutional, excursion, hike, ramble, saunter, stroll, tramp, turn.

**wall** n escarp, parapet, plane, upright.

**wallet** n bag, knapsack, pocketbook, purse, sack.

**wan** adj ashen, bloodless, cadaverous, colourless, haggard, pale, pallid.

**wand** n baton, mace, truncheon, sceptre.

**wander** vb forage, prowl, ramble, range, roam, rove, stroll; deviate, digress, straggle, stray; moon, rave.
* n amble, cruise, excursion, ramble, stroll.

**wane** vb abate, decrease, ebb, subside; decline, fail, sink. * n decrease, diminution, lessening; decay, declension, decline, failure.

**want** vb crave, desire, need, require, wish; fail, lack, neglect, omit. * n absence, defect, default, deficiency, lack; defectiveness, failure, inadequacy, insufficiency, meagreness, paucity, poverty, scantiness, scarcity, shortness; requirement; craving, desire, longing, wish; destitution, distress, indigence, necessity, need, penury, poverty, privation, straits.

**wanton** vb caper, disport, frisk, frolic, play, revel, romp, sport; dally, flirt, toy, trifle. * adj free, loose, unchecked, unrestrained, wandering; abounding, exuberant, luxuriant, overgrown, rampant; airy, capricious, coltish, frisky, playful, skittish, sportive; dissolute, irregular, licentious, loose; carnal, immoral, incontinent, lascivious, lecherous, lewd, libidinous, light, lustful, prurient, salacious, unchaste; careless, gratuitous, groundless, heedless, inconsiderate, needless, perverse, reckless, wayward, wilful. * n baggage, flirt, harlot, light-o'-love, prostitute, rake, roué, slut, whore.

**war** vb battle, campaign, combat, contend, crusade, engage, fight, strive. * n contention, enmity, hostility, strife, warfare.

**warble** vb sing, trill, yodel. * n carol, chant, hymn, hum.

**ward** vb guard, watch; defend, fend, parry, protect, repel. * n care, charge, guard, guardianship, watch; defender, guardian, keeper, protector, warden; custody; defence, garrison, protection; minor, pupil; district, division, precinct, quarter; apartment, cubicle.

**warehouse** n depot, magazine, repository, store, storehouse.

**wares** npl commodities, goods, merchandise, movables.

**warfare** n battle, conflict, contest, discord, engagement, fray, hostilities, strife, struggle, war.

**warily** adv carefully, cautiously, charily, circumspectly, heedfully, watchfully, vigilantly.

**wariness** n care, caution, circumspection, foresight, thought, vigilance.

**warlike** adj bellicose, belligerent, combative, hostile, inimical, martial, military, soldierly, watchful.

**warm** vb heat, roast, toast; animate, chafe, excite, rouse. * adj lukewarm, tepid; genial, mild, pleasant, sunny; close, muggy, oppressive; affectionate, ardent, cordial, eager, earnest, enthusiastic, fervent, fervid, glowing, hearty, hot, zealous; excited, fiery, flushed, furious, hasty, keen, lively, passionate, quick, vehement, violent.

**warmth** n glow, tepidity; ardour, fervency, fervour, zeal; animation, cordiality, eagerness, earnestness, enthusiasm, excitement, fervency, fever, fire, flush, heat, intensity, passion, spirit, vehemence.

**warn** vb caution, forewarn; admonish, advise; apprise, inform, notify; bid, call, summon.

**warning** adj admonitory, cautionary, cautioning, monitory. * n admonition, advice, caveat, caution, monition; information, notice; augury, indication, intimation, omen, portent, presage, prognostic, sign, symptom; call, summons; example, lesson, sample.

**warp** vb bend, bias, contort, deviate, distort, pervert, swerve, turn, twist. * n bent, bias, cast, crook, distortion, inclination, leaning, quirk, sheer, skew, slant, slew, swerve, twist, turn.

**warrant** vb answer for, certify, guarantee, secure; affirm, assure, attest, avouch, declare, justify, state; authorize, justify, license, maintain, sanction, support, sustain, uphold. * n guarantee, pledge, security, surety, warranty; authentication, authority, commission, verification; order, pass, permit, summons, subpoena, voucher, writ.

**warrantable** adj admissible, allowable, defensible, justifiable, lawful, permissible, proper, right, vindicable.

**warrior** n champion, captain, fighter, hero, soldier.

**wary** adj careful, cautious, chary, circumspect, discreet, guarded, heedful, prudent, scrupulous, vigilant, watchful.

**wash** vb purify, purge; moisten, wet; bathe, clean, flush, irrigate, lap, lave, rinse, sluice; colour, stain, tint. * n ablution, bathing, cleansing, lavation, washing; bog, fen, marsh, swamp, quagmire; bath, embrocation, lotion; laundry, washing.

**washy** adj damp, diluted, moist, oozy, sloppy, thin, watery, weak; feeble, jejune, pointless, poor, spiritless, trashy, trumpery, unmeaning, vapid, worthless.

**waspish** adj choleric, fretful, irascible, irritable, peevish, petulant, snappish, testy, touchy; slender, slim, small-waisted.

**waste** vb consume, corrode, decrease, diminish, emaciate, wear; absorb, deplete, devour, dissipate, drain, empty, exhaust, expend, lavish, lose, misspend, misuse, scatter, spend, squander; demolish, desolate, destroy, devastate, devour, dilapidate, harry, pillage, plunder, ravage, ruin, scour, strip; damage, impair, injure; decay, dwindle, perish, wither. * adj bare, desolated, destroyed, devastated, empty, ravaged, ruined, spoiled, stripped, void; dismal, dreary, forlorn; abandoned, bare, barren, uncultivated, unimproved, uninhabited, untilled, wild; useless, valueless, worthless; exuberant, superfluous. * n consumption, decrement, diminution, dissipation, exhaustion, expenditure, loss, wasting; destruction, dispersion, extravagance, loss, squandering, wanton; decay, desolation, destruction, devastation, havoc, pillage, ravage, ruin; chaff, debris, detritus, dross, excrement, husks, junk, matter, offal, refuse, rubbish, trash, wastrel, worthlessness; barrenness, desert, expanse, solitude, wild, wilderness.

**wasteful** adj destructive, ruinous; extravagant, improvident, lavish, prodigal, profuse, squandering, thriftless, unthrifty.

**watch** vb attend, guard, keep, oversee, protect, superintend, tend; eye, mark, observe. * n espial, guard, outlook, wakefulness, watchfulness, watching, vigil, ward; alertness, attention, inspection, observation, surveillance; guard, picket, sentinel, sentry, watchman; pocket watch, ticker, timepiece, wristwatch.

**watchful** adj alert, attentive, awake, careful, circumspect, guarded, heedful, observant, vigilant, wakeful, wary.

**watchword** n catchword, cry, motto, password, shibboleth, word.

**waterfall** n cascade, cataract, fall, linn.

**watery** adj diluted, thin, waterish, weak; insipid, spiritless, tasteful, vapid; moist, wet.

**wave** vb float, flutter, heave, shake, sway, undulate, wallow; brandish, flaunt, flourish, swing; beckon, signal. * n billow, bore, breaker, flood, flush, ripple, roll, surge, swell, tide, undulation; flourish, gesture, sway; convolution, curl, roll, unevenness.

**waver** vb flicker, float, undulate, wave; reel, totter; falter, fluctuate, flutter, hesitate, oscillate, quiver, vacillate.

**wax** vb become, grow, increase, mount, rise.

**way** n advance, journey, march, progression, transit, trend; access, alley, artery, avenue, beat, channel, course, highroad, highway, passage, path, road, route, street, track, trail; fashion, manner, means, method, mode, system; distance, interval, space, stretch; behaviour, custom, form, guise, habit, habitude, practice, process, style, usage; device, plan, scheme.

**wayfarer** n itinerant, nomad, passenger, pilgrim, rambler, traveller, walker, wanderer.

**wayward** adj capricious, captious, contrary, forward, headstrong, intractable, obstinate, perverse, refractory, stubborn, unruly, wilful.

**weak** adj debilitated, delicate, enfeebled, enervated, exhausted, faint, feeble, fragile, frail, infirm, invalid, languid, languishing, shaky, sickly, spent, strengthless, tender, unhealthy, unsound, wasted, weakly; accessible, defenceless, unprotected, vulnerable; light, soft, unstressed; boneless, cowardly, infirm; compliant, irresolute, pliable, pliant, undecided, undetermined, unsettled, unstable, unsteady, vacillating, wavering, yielding; childish, foolish, imbecile, senseless, shallow, silly, simple, stupid, weak-minded, witless; erring, foolish, indiscreet, injudicious, unwise; gentle, indistinct, low, small; adulterated, attenuated, diluted, insipid, tasteless, thin, watery; flimsy, frivolous, poor, sleazy, slight, trifling; futile, illogical, inconclusive, ineffective, ineffectual, inefficient, lame, unconvincing, unsatisfactory, unsupported, unsustained, vague, vain; unsafe, unsound, unsubstantial, untrustworthy; helpless, impotent, powerless; breakable, brittle, delicate, frangible; inconsiderable, puny, slender, slight, small.

**weaken** vb cramp, cripple, debilitate, devitalize, enervate, enfeeble, invalidate, relax, sap, shake, stagger, undermine, unman, unnerve, unstring; adulterate, attenuate, debase, depress, dilute, exhaust, impair, impoverish, lessen, lower, reduce.

**weakness** n debility, feebleness, fragility, frailty, infirmity, languor, softness; defect, failing, fault, flaw; fondness, inclination, liking.

**weal** n advantage, good, happiness, interest, profit, utility, prosperity, welfare; ridge, streak, stripe.

**wealth** n assets, capital, cash, fortune, funds, goods, money, possessions, property, riches, treasure; abundance, affluence, opulence, plenty, profusion.

**wean** vb alienate, detach, disengage, withdraw.

**wear** vb bear, carry, don; endure, last; consume, impair, rub, use, waste. * n corrosion, deterioration, disintegration, erosion, wear and tear; consumption, use; apparel, array, attire, clothes, clothing, dress, garb, gear.

**wearied** adj apathetic, bored, exhausted, fagged, fatigued, jaded, tired, weary, worn.

**weariness** n apathy, boredom, ennui, exhaustion, fatigue, languor, lassitude, monotony, prostration, sameness, tedium.

**wearisome** adj annoying, boring, dull, exhausting, fatiguing, humdrum, irksome, monotonous, prolix, prosaic, slow, tedious, tiresome, troublesome, trying, uninteresting, vexatious.

**weary** vb debilitate, exhaust, fag, fatigue, harass, jade, tire. * adj apathetic, bored, drowsy, exhausted, jaded, spent, tired, worn; irksome, tiresome, wearisome.

**weave** vb braid, entwine, interlace, lace, mat, plait, pleat, twine; compose, construct, fabricate, make.

**wed** vb contract, couple, espouse, marry, unite.

**wedding** n bridal, espousal, marriage, nuptials.

**wedlock** n marriage, matrimony.

**ween** vb fancy, imagine, suppose, think.

**weep** vb bemoan, bewail, complain, cry, lament, sob.

**weigh** vb balance, counterbalance, lift, raise; consider, deliberate, esteem, examine, study.

**weight** vb ballast, burden, fill, freight, load; weigh. * n gravity, heaviness, heft, tonnage; burden, load, pressure; consequence, efficacy, emphasis, importance, impressiveness, influence, moment, pith, power, significance, value.

**weighty** adj heavy, massive, onerous, ponderous,

unwieldy; considerable, efficacious, forcible, grave, important, influential, serious, significant.

**weird** adj eerie, ghostly, strange, supernatural, uncanny, unearthly, witching.

**welcome** vb embrace, greet, hail, receive. * adj acceptable, agreeable, grateful, gratifying, pleasant, pleasing, satisfying. * n greeting, reception, salutation.

**welfare** n advantage, affluence, benefit, happiness, profit, prosperity, success, thrift, weal, wellbeing.

**well**[1] vb flow, gush, issue, jet, pour, spring. * n fount, fountain, reservoir, spring, wellhead, wellspring; origin, source; hole, pit, shaft.

**well**[2] adj hale, healthy, hearty, sound; fortunate, good, happy, profitable, satisfactory, useful. * adv accurately, adequately, correctly, efficiently, properly, suitably; abundantly, considerably, fully, thoroughly; agreeably, commendably, favourably, worthily.

**wellbeing** n comfort, good, happiness, health, prosperity, welfare.

**welter** vb flounder, roll, toss, wallow. * n confusion, jumble, mess.

**wet** vb dabble, damp, dampen, dip, drench, moisten, saturate, soak, sprinkle, water. * adj clammy, damp, dank, dewy, dripping, humid, moist; rainy, showery, sprinkly. * n dampness, humidity, moisture, wetness.

**whack** vb, n bang, beat, rap, strike, thrash, thump, thwack.

**wharf** n dock, pier, quay.

**wheedle** vb cajole, coax, flatter, inveigle, lure.

**wheel** vb gyrate, revolve, roll, rotate, spin, swing, turn, twist, whirl, wind. * n circle, revolution, roll, rotation, spin, turn, twirl.

**whet** vb grind, sharpen; arouse, awaken, excite, provoke, rouse, stimulate; animate, inspire, kindle, quicken, warm.

**whiff** vb, n blast, gust, puff.

**whim** n caprice, crotchet, fancy, freak, frolic, humour, notion, quirk, sport, vagary, whimsy, wish.

**whimsical** adj capricious, crotchety, eccentric, erratic, fanciful, frolicsome, odd, peculiar, quaint, singular.

**whine** vb cry, grumble, mewl, moan, snivel, wail, whimper. * n complaint, cry, grumble, moan, sob, wail, whimper.

**whip** vb beat, lash, strike; flagellate, flog, goad, horsewhip, scourge, slash; hurt, sting, jerk, snap, snatch, whisk. * n bullwhip, cane, crop, horsewhip, knout, lash, scourge, switch, thong.

**whipping** n beating, castigation, dusting, flagellation, flogging, thrashing.

**whirl** vb gyrate, pirouette, roll, revolve, rotate, turn, twirl, twist, wheel. * n eddy, flurry, flutter, gyration, rotation, spin, swirl, twirl, vortex.

**whit** n atom, bit, grain, iota, jot, mite, particle, scrap, speck, tittle.

**white** adj argent, canescent, chalky, frosty, hoary, ivory, milky, silver, snowy; grey, pale, pallid, wan; candid, clean, chaste, immaculate, innocent, pure, spotless, unblemished.

**whole** adj all, complete, entire, intact, integral, total, undivided; faultless, firm, good, perfect, strong, unbroken, undivided, uninjured; healthy, sound, well. * adv entire, in one. * n aggregate, all, amount, ensemble, entirety, gross, sum, total, totality.

**wholesome** adj healthy, healthful, invigorating, nourishing, nutritious, salubrious, salutary; beneficial, good, helpful, improving, salutary; fresh, sound, sweet.

**wholly** adv altogether, completely, entirely, fully, totally, utterly.

**whoop** vb halloo, hoot, roar, shout, yell. * n bellow, hoot, roar, shout, yell.

**whore** n bawd, courtesan, drab, harlot, prostitute, streetwalker, strumpet.

**wicked** adj abandoned, abominable, depraved, devilish, godless, graceless, immoral, impious, infamous, irreligious, irreverent, profane, sinful, ungodly, unholy, unprincipled, unrighteous, vicious, vile, worthless; atrocious, bad, black, criminal, dark, evil, heinous, ill, iniquitous, monstrous, nefarious, unjust, villainous.

**wide** adj ample, broad, capacious, comprehensive, distended, expanded, large, spacious, vast; distant, remote; prevalent, rife, widespread. * adv completely, farthest, fully.

**wield** vb brandish, flourish, handle, manipulate, ply, work; control, manage, sway, use.

**wild** adj feral, undomesticated, untamed; desert, desolate, native, rough, rude, uncultivated; barbarous, ferocious, fierce, savage, uncivilized; dense, luxuriant, rank; disorderly, distracted, frantic, frenzied, furious, impetuous, irregular, mad, outrageous, raving, turbulent, ungoverned, uncontrolled, violent;

dissipated, fast, flighty, foolish, giddy, harebrained, heedless, ill-advised, inconsiderate, reckless, thoughtless, unwise; boisterous, rough, stormy; crazy, extravagant, fanciful, grotesque, imaginary, strange. * n desert, waste, wilderness.

**wilderness** n desert, waste, wild.

**wilful** adj cantankerous, contumacious, dogged, headstrong, heady, inflexible, intractable, mulish, obdurate, obstinate, perverse, pig-headed, refractory, self-willed, stubborn, unruly, unyielding; arbitrary, capricious; deliberate, intended, intentional, planned, premeditated.

**will** vb bid, command, decree, direct, enjoin, ordain; choose, desire, elect, wish; bequeath, convey, demise, devise, leave. * n decision, determination, resoluteness, resolution, self-reliance; desire, disposition, inclination, intent, pleasure, purpose, volition, wish; behest, command, decree, demand, direction, order, request, requirement.

**willing** adj adaptable, amenable, compliant, desirous, disposed, inclined, minded; deliberate, free, intentional, spontaneous, unasked, unbidden, voluntary; cordial, eager, forward, prompt, ready.

**willingly** adv cheerfully, gladly, readily, spontaneously, voluntarily.

**wily** adj arch, artful, crafty, crooked, cunning, deceitful, designing, diplomatic, foxy, insidious, intriguing, politic, sly, subtle, treacherous, tricky.

**win** vb accomplish, achieve, acquire, catch, earn, effect, gain, gather, get, make, obtain, procure, reach, realize, reclaim, recover; gain, succeed, surpass, triumph; arrive; allure, attract, convince, influence, persuade. * n conquest, success, triumph, victory.

**wind**[1] n air, blast, breeze, draught, gust, hurricane, whiff, zephyr; breath, breathing, expiration, inspiration, respiration; flatulence, gas, windiness.

**wind**[2] vb coil, crank, encircle, involve, reel, roll, turn, twine, twist; bend, curve, meander, zigzag. * n bend, curve, meander, twist, zigzag.

**winding** adj circuitous, devious, flexuose, flexuous, meandering, serpentine, tortuous, turning, twisting. * n bend, curve, meander, turn, twist.

**windy** adj breezy, blowy, blustering, boisterous, draughty, gusty, squally, stormy, tempestuous; airy, empty, hollow, inflated. **winning** adj alluring, attractive, bewitching, brilliant, captivating, charming, dazzling, delightful, enchanting, engaging, fascinat-

ing, lovely, persuasive, pleasing, prepossessing; conquering, triumphant, victorious.

**winnow** vb cull, glean, divide, fan, part, select, separate, sift.

**winsome** adj blithe, blithesome, bonny, buoyant, charming, cheerful, debonair, jocund, light-hearted, lively, lovable, merry, pleasant, sportive, winning.

**wintry** adj arctic, boreal, brumal, cold, frosty, icy, snowy.

**wipe** vb clean, dry, mop, rub. * n mop, rub, blow, hit, strike; gibe, jeer, sarcasm, sneer, taunt.

**wisdom** n depth, discernment, far-sightedness, foresight, insight, judgement, judiciousness, prescience, profundity, prudence, sagacity, sapience, sense, solidity, understanding, wiseness; attainment, edification, enlightenment, erudition, information, knowledge, learning, lore, scholarship; reason.

**wise** adj deep, discerning, enlightened, intelligent, judicious, penetrating, philosophical, profound, rational, seasonable, sensible, sage, sapient, solid, sound; erudite, informed, knowing, learned, scholarly; crafty, cunning, designing, foxy, politic, sly, subtle, wary, wily.

**wish** vb covet, desire, hanker, list, long; bid, command, desire, direct, intend, mean, order, want. * n behest, desire, intention, mind, pleasure, want, will; craving, desire, hankering, inclination, liking, longing, want, yearning.

**wistful** adj contemplative, engrossed, meditative, musing, pensive, reflective, thoughtful; desirous, eager, earnest, longing.

**wit** n genius, intellect, intelligence, reason, sense, understanding; brightness, banter, cleverness, drollery, facetiousness, fun, humour, jocularity, piquancy, point, raillery, satire, sparkle, whim; conceit, epigram, jest, joke, pleasantry, quip, quirk, repartee, sally, witticism; humorist, joker, wag.

**witch** n charmer, enchantress, fascinator, sorceress; crone, hag, sibyl.

**witchcraft** n conjuration, enchantment, magic, necromancy, sorcery, spell.

**withdraw** vb abstract, deduct, remove, retire, separate, sequester, sequestrate, subduct, subtract; disengage, wean; abjure, recall, recant, relinquish, resign, retract, revoke; abdicate, decamp, depart, dissociate, retire, shrink, vacate.

**wither** vb contract, droop, dry, sear, shrivel, wilt, wizen; decay, decline, languish, pine, waste.

**withhold** vb check, detain, hinder, repress, restrain, retain, suppress.

**withstand** vb confront, defy, face, oppose, resist.

**witless** adj daft, dull, foolish, halfwitted, obtuse, senseless, shallow, silly, stupid, unintelligent.

**witness** vb corroborate, mark, note, notice, observe, see. * n attestation, conformation, corroboration, evidence, proof, testimony; beholder, bystander, corroborator, deponent, eyewitness, onlooker, spectator, testifier.

**witty** adj bright, clever, droll, facetious, funny, humorous, jocose, jocular, pleasant, waggish; alert, penetrating, quick, sparkling, sprightly.

**wizard** n charmer, diviner, conjurer, enchanter, magician, necromancer, seer, soothsayer, sorcerer.

**woe** n affliction, agony, anguish, bitterness, depression, distress, dole, grief, heartache, melancholy, misery, sorrow, torture, tribulation, trouble, unhappiness, wretchedness.

**woeful** adj afflicted, agonized, anguished, burdened, disconsolate, distressed, melancholy, miserable, mournful, piteous, sad, sorrowful, troubled, unhappy, wretched; afflicting, afflictive, calamitous, deplorable, depressing, disastrous, distressing, dreadful, tragic, tragical, grievous, lamentable, pitiable, saddening.

**wonder** vb admire, gape, marvel; conjecture, ponder, query, question, speculate. * n amazement, astonishment, awe, bewilderment, curiosity, marvel, miracle, prodigy, surprise, stupefaction, wonderment.

**wonderful** adj amazing, astonishing, astounding, awe-inspiring, awesome, awful, extraordinary, marvellous, miraculous, portentous, prodigious, startling, stupendous, surprising.

**wont** adj accustomed, customary, familiar, habitual, ordinary, usual. * n custom, habit, practice, rule, usage.

**wonted** adj accustomed, common, conventional, customary, everyday, familiar, frequent, habitual, ordinary, regular, usual.

**wood** n coppice, copse, covert, forest, greenwood, grove, spinney, thicket, woodland.

**word** vb express, phrase, put, say, state, term, utter. * n expression, name, phrase, term, utterance; account, advice, information, intelligence, message, news, report, tidings; affirmation, assertion, averment, avowal, declaration, statement; conversation, speech; agreement, assurance, engagement, parole, pledge, plight, promise; behest, bidding, command, direction, order, precept; countersign, password, signal, watchword.

**wordy** adj circumlocutory, diffuse, garrulous, inflated, lengthened, long-winded, loquacious, periphrastic, rambling, talkative, tedious, verbose, windy.

**work** vb act, operate; drudge, fag, grind, grub, labour, slave, sweat, toil; move, perform, succeed; aim, attempt, strive, try; effervesce, ferment, leaven, rise; accomplish, beget, cause, effect, engender, manage, originate, produce; exert, strain; embroider, stitch. * n exertion, drudgery, grind, labour, pain, toil; business, employment, function, occupation, task; action, accomplishment, achievement, composition, deed, feat, fruit, handiwork, opus, performance, product, production; fabric, manufacture; ferment, leaven; management, treatment.

**workman** n journeyman, employee, labourer, operative, worker, wright; artisan, craftsman, mechanic.

**world** n cosmos, creation, earth, globe, nature, planet, sphere, universe.

**worldly** adj common, earthly, human, mundane, sublunary, terrestrial; carnal, fleshly, profane, secular, temporal; ambitious, grovelling, irreligious, selfish, proud, sordid, unsanctified, unspiritual; sophisticated, worldly-wise.

**worry** vb annoy, badger, bait, beset, bore, bother, chafe, disquiet, disturb, fret, gall, harass, harry, hector, infest, irritate, molest, persecute, pester, plague, tease, torment, trouble, vex. * n annoyance, anxiety, apprehensiveness, care, concern, disquiet, fear, misgiving, perplexity, solicitude, trouble, uneasiness, vexation.

**worship** vb adore, esteem, honour, revere, venerate; deify, idolize; aspire, pray. * n adoration, devotion, esteem, homage, idolatry, idolizing, respect, reverence; aspiration, exultation, invocation, laud, praise, prayer, supplication.

**worst** vb beat, choke, conquer, crush, defeat, discomfit, foil, master, overpower, overthrow, quell, rout, subdue, subjugate, vanquish.

**worth** n account, character, credit, desert, excellence, importance, integrity, merit, nobleness, worthiness, virtue; cost, estimation, price, value.

**worthless** adj futile, meritless, miserable, nugatory, paltry, poor, trifling, unproductive, unsalable, unserviceable, useless, valueless, wretched; abject, base, corrupt, degraded, ignoble, low, mean, vile.

**worthy** *adj* deserving, fit, suitable; estimable, excellent, exemplary, good, honest, honourable, reputable, righteous, upright, virtuous. * *n* celebrity, dignitary, luminary, notability, personage, somebody, VIP.

**wound** *vb* damage, harm, hurt, injure; cut, gall, harrow, irritate, lacerate, pain, prick, stab; annoy, mortify, offend. * *n* blow, hurt, injury; damage, detriment; anguish, grief, pain, pang, torture.

**wraith** *n* apparition, ghost, phantom, spectre, vision.

**wrangle** *vb* argue, bicker, brawl, cavil, dispute, jangle, jar, quarrel, squabble, spar, spat. * *n* altercation, argument, bickering, brawl, contest, controversy, jar, quarrel, squabble.

**wrap** *vb* cloak, cover, encase, envelop, muffle, swathe, wind. * *n* blanket, cape, cloak, cover, overcoat, shawl.

**wrath** *n* anger, choler, exasperation, fury, heat, resentment, indignation, ire, irritation, offence, passion, rage.

**wrathful** *adj* angry, enraged, exasperated, furious, hot, indignant, infuriated, irate, mad, passionate, provoked, rageful.

**wreak** *vb* execute, exercise, indulge, inflict, work.

**wreath** *n* chaplet, curl, festoon, garland, ring, twine.

**wreathe** *vb* encircle, festoon, garland, intertwine, surround, twine, twist.

**wreck** *vb* founder, shipwreck, strand; blast, blight, break, devastate, ruin, spoil. * *n* crash, desolation, destruction, perdition, prostration, ruin, shipwreck, smash, undoing.

**wrench** *vb* distort, pervert, twist, wrest, wring; sprain, strain; extort, extract. * *n* twist, wring; sprain, strain; monkey wrench, spanner.

**wrest** *vb* force, pull, strain, twist, wrench, wring.

**wrestle** *vb* contend, contest, grapple, strive, struggle.

**wretch** *n* outcast, pariah, pilgarlic, troglodyte, vagabond, victim, sufferer; beggar, criminal,

hound, knave, miscreant, rascal, ruffian, rogue, scoundrel, villain.

**wretched** *adj* afflicted, comfortless, distressed, forlorn, sad, unfortunate, unhappy, woebegone; afflicting, calamitous, deplorable, depressing, pitiable, sad, saddening, shocking, sorrowful; bad, beggarly, contemptible, mean, paltry, pitiful, poor, shabby, sorry, vile, worthless.

**wring** *vb* contort, twist, wrench; extort, force, wrest; anguish, distress, harass, pain, rack, torture.

**wrinkle**[1] *vb* cockle, corrugate, crease, gather, pucker, rumple. * *n* cockle, corrugation, crease, crimp, crinkle, crumple, fold, furrow, gather, plait, ridge, rumple.

**wrinkle**[2] *n* caprice, fancy, notion, quirk, whim; device, tip, trick.

**writ** *n* decree, order, subpoena, summons.

**write** *vb* compose, copy, indite, inscribe, pen, scrawl, scribble, transcribe.

**writer** *n* amanuensis, author, clerk, penman, scribe, secretary.

**writhe** *vb* contort, distort, squirm, twist, wriggle.

**written** *adj* composed, indited, inscribed, penned, transcribed.

**wrong** *vb* abuse, encroach, injure, maltreat, oppress. * *adj* inequitable, unfair, unjust, wrongful; bad, criminal, evil, guilty, immoral, improper, iniquitous, reprehensible, sinful, vicious, wicked; amiss, improper, inappropriate, unfit, unsuitable; erroneous, false, faulty, inaccurate, incorrect, mistaken, untrue. * *adv* amiss, erroneously, falsely, faultily, improperly, inaccurately, incorrectly, wrongly. * *n* foul, grievance, inequity, injury, injustice, trespass, unfairness; blame, crime, dishonesty, evil, guilt, immorality, iniquity, misdeed, misdoing, sin, transgression, unrighteousness, vice, wickedness, wrongdoing; error, falsity.

**wroth** *adj* angry, enraged, exasperated, furious, incensed, indignant, irate, passionate, provoked, resentful.

**wrought** *adj* done, effected, performed, worked.

**wry** *adj* askew, awry, contorted, crooked, distorted, twisted.

# XYZ

**xanthous** *adj* blonde, fair, light-complexioned, xanthic, yellow.

**xiphoid** *adj* ensiform, gladiate, sword-like, sword-shaped.

**Xmas** *n* Christmas, Christmastide, Noel, Yule, Yuletide.

**X-ray** *n* roentgen ray, röntgen ray.

**xylograph** *n* cut, woodcut, wood engraving.

**xylographer** *n* wood engraver.

**xylophagous** *adj* wood-eating, wood-nourished.

**yap** *vb* bark, cry, yelp. * *n* bark, cry, yelp.

**yard** *n* close, compound, court, courtyard, enclosure, garden.

**yarn** *n* anecdote, boasting, fabrication, narrative, story, tale, untruth.

**yawn** *vb* dehisce, gape, open wide. * *n* gap, gape, gulf.

**yearn** *vb* crave, desire, hanker after, long for.

**yell** *vb* bawl, bellow, cry out, howl, roar, scream, screech, shriek, squeal.* *n* cry, howl, roar, scream, screech, shriek.

**yellow** *adj* aureate, gilded, gilt, gold, golden, lemon, primrose, saffron, xanthic, xanthous.

**yelp** *vb* bark, howl, yap; complain, bitch, grouse. * *n* bark, sharp cry, howl.

**yet** *adv* at last, besides, further, however, over and above, so far, still, thus far, ultimately.* *conj* moreover, nevertheless, notwithstanding, now.

**yield** *vb* afford, bear, bestow, communicate, confer, fetch, furnish, impart, produce, render, supply; accede, accord, acknowledge, acquiesce, allow, assent, comply, concede, give, grant, permit; abandon, abdicate, cede, forgo, give up, let go, quit, relax, relinquish, resign, submit, succumb, surrender, waive. * *n* earnings, income, output, produce, profit, return, revenue.

**yielding** *adj* accommodating, acquiescent, affable, compliant, complaisant, easy, manageable, obedient, passive, submissive, unresisting; bending, flexible, flexile, plastic, pliant, soft, supple, tractable; fertile, productive.

**yoke** *vb* associate, bracket, connect, couple, harness, interlink, join, link, unite. * *n* bond, chain, ligature, link, tie, union; bondage, dependence, enslavement, service, servitude, subjection, vassalage; couple, pair.

**yokel** *n* boor, bumpkin, countryman, peasant, rustic.

**yore** *adj* ancient, antique, old, olden. * *n* long ago, long since, olden times.

**young** *adj* green, ignorant, inexperienced, juvenile, new, recent, youthful. * *n* young people, youth; babies, issue, brood, offspring, progeny, spawn.

**youngster** *n* adolescent, boy, girl, lad, lass, stripling, youth.

**youth** *n* adolescence, childhood, immaturity, juvenile, juvenility, minority, nonage, pupillage, wardship; boy, girl, lad, lass, schoolboy, schoolgirl, slip, sprig, stripling, youngster.

**youthful** *adj* boyish, childish, girlish, immature, juvenile, puerile, young.

**zany** *adj* comic, comical, crazy, droll, eccentric, funny, imaginative, scatterbrained; clownish, foolish, ludicrous, silly. * *n* buffoon, clown, droll, fool, harlequin, jester, punch.

**zeal** *n* alacrity, ardour, cordiality, devotedness, devotion, earnestness, eagerness, energy, enthusiasm, fervour, glow, heartiness, intensity, jealousness, passion, soul, spirit, warmth.

**zealot** *n* bigot, devotee, fanatic, freak, partisan.

**zealous** *adj* ardent, burning, devoted, eager, earnest, enthusiastic, fervent, fiery, forward, glowing, jealous, keen, passionate, prompt, ready, swift, warm.

**zenith** *n* acme, apex, climax, culmination, heyday, pinnacle, prime, summit, top, utmost, height.

**zero** *n* cipher, naught, nadir, nil, nothing, nought.

**zest** *n* appetite, enjoyment, exhilaration, gusto, liking, piquancy, relish, thrill; edge, flavour, salt, savour, tang, taste; appetizer, sauce.

**zone** *n* band, belt, cincture, girdle, girth; circuit, clime, region.

**zymotic** *adj* bacterial, fermentative, germinating.